Mierevelt pinxit.

PRINCE MAURICE OF ORANGE-NASSAU.

"Tandem fit surculus arbor."

HISTORY

OF THE

UNITED NETHERLANDS

FROM THE DEATH OF WILLIAM THE SILENT
TO THE TWELVE YEARS' TRUCE–1609

BY

JOHN LOTHROP MOTLEY, D.C.L., LL.D.
CORRESPONDING MEMBER OF THE INSTITUTE OF FRANCE, ETC.

IN FOUR VOLUMES—Vol. IV

1600–9

WITH PORTRAITS

NEW YORK

HARPER & BROTHERS, PUBLISHERS

FRANKLIN SQUARE

CONTENTS OF VOL. IV.

CHAPTER XLI.

CHAPTER XLII.

CHAPTER XLIII.

CHAPTER XLIV.

CHAPTER XLV.

CHAPTER XLVI.

CHAPTER XLVII.

CHAPTER XLVIII.

CHAPTER XLIX.

CHAPTER L.

CHAPTER LI.

CHAPTER LII.

CHAPTER LIII.

THE UNITED NETHERLANDS.

CHAPTER XXXVIII.

Military events — Aggressive movement of the Netherlanders — State of the Archduke's provinces — Mutiny of the Spanish forces — Proposed invasion of Flanders by the States-General — Disembarkation of the troops on the Spanish coasts — Capture of Oudenburg and other places — Surprise of Nieuport — Conduct of the Archduke — Oudenburg and the other forts re-taken — Dilemma of the States' army — Attack of the Archduke on Count Ernest's cavalry — Panic and total overthrow of the advance-guard of the States' army — Battle of Nieuport — Details of the action — Defeat of the Spanish army — Results of the whole expedition.

THE effect produced in the republic by the defensive and un-eventful campaigning of the year 1599 had naturally been depressing. There was murmuring at the vast amount of taxation, especially at the new imposition of one-half per cent. upon all property, and two-and-a-half per cent. on all sales, which seemed to produce so few results. The success-ful protection of the Isle of Bommel and the judicious pur-chase of the two forts of Crevecœur and St. Andrew, early in the following year, together with their garrisons, were not military events of the first magnitude, and were hardly enough to efface the mortification felt at the fact that the enemy had been able so lately to construct one of those strongholds within the territory of the commonwealth.

It was now secretly determined to attempt an aggressive movement on a considerable scale, and to carry the war once for all into the heart of the obedient provinces. It was from Flanders that the Spanish armies drew a great portion of their supplies. It was by the forts erected on the coast of

Flanders in the neighbourhood of Ostend that this important possession of the States was rendered nearly valueless. It was by privateers swarming from the ports of Flanders, especially from Nieuport and Dunkirk, that the foreign trade of the republic was crippled, and its intercommunications by river and estuary rendered unsafe. Dunkirk was simply a robbers' cave, a station from which an annual tax was levied upon the commerce of the Netherlands, almost sufficient, had it been paid to the national treasury instead of to the foreign freebooters, to support the expenses of a considerable army.

On the other hand the condition of the archdukes seemed deplorable. Never had mutiny existed before in so well-organised and definite a form even in the Spanish Netherlands.

Besides those branches of the "Italian republic," which had been established in the two fortresses of Crevecœur and St. Andrew, and which had already sold themselves to the States, other organisations quite as formidable existed in various other portions of the obedient provinces. Especially at Diest and Thionville the rebellious Spaniards and Italians were numbered by thousands, all veterans, well armed, fortified in strong cities, and supplying themselves with perfect regularity by contributions levied upon the peasantry, obeying their Eletto and other officers with exemplary promptness, and paying no more heed to the edicts or the solicitations of the archduke than if he had been the Duke of Muscovy.

The opportunity seemed tempting to strike a great blow. How could Albert and Isabella, with an empty exchequer and a mutinous army, hope either to defend their soil from attack or to aim a counter blow at the republic, even if the republic for a season should be deprived of a portion of its defenders?

The reasoning was plausible, the prize tempting. The States-General, who habitually discountenanced rashness, and were wont to impose superfluous restraints upon the valiant but discreet Lewis William, and upon the deeply pondering but energetic Maurice, were now grown as ardent as they had hitherto been hesitating. In the early days of June it was determined in secret session to organize a great force in Holland and Zeeland, and to embark suddenly for Nieuport, to carry that important position by surprise or assault, and from that basis to redeem Dunkirk. The possession of these two cities, besides that of Ostend, which had always been retained by the Republic, would ensure the complete subjugation of Flanders. The trifling force of two thousand men under Rivas—all that the archduke then had in that province—and the sconces and earthworks which had been constructed around Ostend to impede the movements and obstruct the supplies of the garrison, would be utterly powerless to prevent the consummation of the plan. Flanders once subjugated, it would not be long before the Spaniards were swept from the obedient Netherlands as thoroughly as they had been from the domains of the commonwealth, and all the seventeen provinces, trampling out every vestige of a hated foreign tyranny, would soon take their natural place as states of a free, prosperous, and powerful union.

But Maurice of Nassau did not share the convictions of the States-General. The unwonted ardour of Barneveld did not inflame his imagination. He urged that the enterprise was inexcusably rash ; that its execution would require the whole army of the States, except the slender garrisons absolutely necessary to protect important places from surprise ; that a defeat would not be simply disaster, but annihilation ; that retreat without absolute triumph would be impossible, and that amid such circumstances the archduke, in spite of his poverty and the rebellious condition of his troops, would doubtless assemble a sufficient force to dispute with reasonable prospects of victory, this invasion of his territory.

Sir Francis Vere, too, was most decidedly opposed to the plan. He pointed out with great clearness its dangerous and possibly fatal character ; assuring the States that, within a fortnight after the expedition had begun, the archduke would follow upon their heels with an army fully able to cope with

the best which they could put into the field.   But besides this
experienced and able campaigner, who so thoroughly shared
the opinions of Prince Maurice, every military man in the
provinces of any consideration was opposed to the scheme.
Especially Lewis William, than whom no more sagacious
military critic or accomplished strategist existed in Europe,
denounced it with energy and even with indignation.   It was,
in the opinion of the young stadholder of Friesland, to suspend
the existence of the whole commonwealth upon a silken
thread.   Even success, he prophesied, would bring no permanent fruits, while the consequences of an overthrow were
fearful to contemplate.   The immediate adherents and most
trusted counsellors of William Lewis were even more un-
measured in their denunciations than he was himself.   " 'Tis
all the work of Barneveld and the long-gowns," cried Everard
van Reyd.   " We are led into a sack from which there is no
extrication.   We are marching to the Caudine Forks.

Certainly it is no small indication of the vast influence and
the indomitable resolution of Barneveld that he never faltered
in this storm of indignation.   The Advocate had made up his
mind to invade Flanders and to capture Nieuport, and
the decree accordingly went forth, despite all opposition.
The States-General were sovereign, and the Advocate and
the States-General were one.

It was also entirely characteristic of Maurice that he should
submit his judgment on this great emergency to that of
Olden-Barneveld.   It was difficult for him to resist the
influence of the great intellect to which he had always
willingly deferred in affairs of state, and from which, even in
military matters, it was hardly possible for him to escape.
Yet in military matters Maurice was a consummate professor,
and the Advocate in comparison but a school-boy.

The ascendency of Barneveld was the less wholesome,
therefore, and it might have been better had the stadholder
manifested more resolution.   But Maurice had not a resolute
character.   Thorough soldier as he was, he was singularly
vacillating, at times almost infirm of purpose, but never before

in his career had this want of decision manifested itself in so striking a manner.[1]

Accordingly the States-General, or in other words John of Olden-Barneveld, proposed to invade Flanders, and lay siege to Nieuport.[2] The States-General were sovereign, and Maurice bowed to their authority. After the matter had been entirely decided upon the state-council was consulted, and the state-council attempted no opposition to the project. The preparations were made with matchless energy and extraordinary secrecy. Lewis William, who meanwhile was to defend the eastern frontier of the republic against any possible attack, sent all the troops that it was possible to spare, but he sent them with a heavy heart. His forebodings were dismal. It seemed to him that all was about to be staked upon a single cast of the dice. Moreover it was painful to him while the terrible game was playing to be merely a looker on and a prophet of evil from a distance, forbidden to contribute by his personal skill and experience to a fortunate result. Hohenlo too was appointed to protect the southern border, and was excluded from all participation in the great expedition.

As to the enemy, such rumors as might come to them from day to day of mysterious military preparations on the part of the rebels only served to excite suspicion in other directions. The archduke was uneasy in regard to the Rhine and the Gueldrian quarter, but never dreamt of a hostile descent upon the Flemish coast.

---

[1] "Un gleich wie seiner Exc. manheit und gute ordnung zu loben ist," says,with some bitterness,that devoted adherent of the Nassaus, Van Reid, "so können sie nit allerdings entschuldigt werden das sie sich lieber uf importunitet kriegsonerfarner leut in solche extremitet gestellet als mit Fabio dieselbe Verachten wollen und das er nit geantwort : *malo prudens hostis me metuat quam stulti cives laudent.*"—Groen v. Prinst., Archives II. Serie ii. 15.

[2] "Le Prince Maurjce n'a pas manqué de remontrer un plus asseuré chemin pour jetter la guerre dans le dit pays de Flandres et y prendre un pied qui les pourroit conduire peu a peu au but tant desiré. Mais ces Messieurs comme ennuyez de vivre en l'état incertain auquel ils se voyent reduits par les apprehensions et d'Angleterre et de notre France mesme ayment mieux hazarder ce coup de dé cependant ils se voyent de belles forces en main et celles de leur ennemi affoibliés," &c.—Buzanval to Villeroy, 18 June, 1600. (Royal Library of the Hague MS.)

Meantime, on the 19th June Maurice of Nassau made his appearance at Castle Rammekens, not far from Flushing, at the mouth of the Scheld, to superintend the great movement. So large a fleet as was there assembled had never before been seen or heard of in Christendom. Of war-ships, transports, and flat-bottomed barges there were at least thirteen hundred. Many eye-witnesses, who counted however with their imaginations, declared that there were in all at least three thousand vessels, and the statement has been reproduced by grave and trustworthy chroniclers. As the number of troops to be embarked upon the enterprise certainly did not exceed fourteen thousand, this would have been an allowance of one vessel to every five soldiers, besides the army munitions and provisions—a hardly reasonable arrangement.

Twelve thousand infantry and sixteen hundred cavalry, the consummate flower of the States' army, all well-paid, well-clad, well-armed, well-disciplined veterans, had been collected in this place of rendezvous and were ready to embark. It would be unjust to compare the dimensions of this force and the preparations for ensuring the success of the enterprise with the vast expeditions and gigantic armaments of later times, especially with the tremendous exhibitions of military and naval energy with which our own civil war has made us familiar. Maurice was an adept in all that science and art had as yet bequeathed to humanity for the purpose of human destruction, but the number of his troops was small compared to the mighty hosts which the world since those days has seen embattled. War, as a trade, was then less easily learned. It was a guild in which apprenticeship was difficult, and in which enrolment was usually for life. A little republic of scarce three million souls, which could keep always on foot a regular well-appointed army of twenty-five thousand men and a navy of one or two hundred heavily armed cruisers, was both a marvel and a formidable element in the general polity of the world. The lesson to be derived both in military and political philosophy from the famous campaign of Nieuport does not depend for its value on the

numbers of the ships or soldiers engaged in the undertaking.
Otherwise, and had it been merely a military expedition like
a thousand others which have been made and forgotten, it
would not now deserve more than a momentary attention.
But the circumstances were such as to make the issue of the
impending battle one of the most important in human history.
It was entirely possible that an overwhelming defeat of the
republican forces on this foreign expedition would bring with
it an absolute destruction of the republic, and place Spain
once more in possession of the heretic "islands," from which
basis she would menace the very existence of England more
seriously than she had ever done before.   Who could measure
the consequences to Christendom of such a catastrophe ?

The distance from the place where the fleet and army were
assembled to Nieuport—the objective point of the enterprise
—was but thirty-five miles as the crow flies.   And the crow
can scarcely fly in a straighter line than that described by
the coast along which the ships were to shape their course.
And here it is again impossible not to reflect upon the change
which physical science has brought over the conduct of
human affairs.   We have seen in a former chapter a most
important embassy sent forth from the States for the purpose
of preventing the consummation of a peace between their
ally and their enemy.   Celerity was a vital element in the
s_   ·‿s of such a mission ; for the secret negotiations which
it was intended to impede were supposed to be near their
termination.   Yet months were consumed in a journey
which in our day would have been accomplished in
twenty-four hours.   And now in this great military expedition the essential and immediate purpose was to surprise a small town almost within sight from the station at
which the army was ready to embark.   Such a midsummer
voyage in this epoch of steam-tugs and transports would
require but a few hours.   Yet two days long the fleet lay at
anchor while a gentle breeze blew persistently from the
south-west.   As there seemed but little hope that the wind
would become more favourable, and as the possibility of sur-

prise grew fainter with every day's delay, it was decided to
make a landing upon the nearest point of Flemish coast
placed by circumstances within their reach. Count Ernest
of Nassau, with the advance-guard, was accordingly despatched on the 21st June to the neighbourhood of the Sas of
Ghent, where he seized a weakly guarded fort, called Philippine, and made thorough preparations for the arrival of the
whole army. On the following day the rest of the
22 June. troops made their appearance, and in the course of
five hours were safely disembarked.

The army, which consisted of Zeelanders, Frisians, Hollanders, Walloons, Germans, English, and Scotch, was divided
into three corps. The advance was under the command of
Count Ernest, the battalia under that of Count George
Everard Solms, while the rear-guard during the march was
entrusted to that experienced soldier Sir Francis Vere.
Besides Prince Maurice, there were three other members of
the house of Nassau serving in the expedition—his half-
brother Frederic Henry, then a lad of sixteen, and the two
brothers of the Frisian stadholder, Ernest and Lewis Gunther,
whom Lewis William had been so faithfully educating in the
arts of peace and war both by precept and example. Lewis
Gunther, still a mere youth, but who had been the first to
scale the fort of Cadiz, and to plant on its height the orange
banner of the murdered rebel, and whose gallantry during
the whole expedition had called forth the special commendations of Queen Elizabeth—expressed in energetic and
affectionate terms to his father—now commanded all the
cavalry. Certainly if the doctrine of primordial selection
could ever be accepted among human creatures, the race of
Nassau at that day might have seemed destined to be chiefs
of the Netherland soil. Old John of Nassau, ardent and
energetic as ever in the cause of the religious reformation of
Germany and the liberation of Holland, still watched from
his retirement the progress of the momentous event. Four
of his brethren, including the great founder of the republic,
had already laid down their lives for the sacred cause. His

son Philip had already fallen under the banner in the fight of Bislich, and three other sons were serving the republic day and night, by sea and land, with sword, and pen, and purse, energetically, conscientiously, and honourably. Of the stout hearts and quick intellects on which the safety of the commonwealth then depended, none was more efficient or true than the accomplished soldier and statesman Lewis William. Thoroughly disapproving of the present invasion of Flanders, he was exerting himself, now that it had been decided upon by his sovereigns the States-Generals, with the same loyalty as that of Maurice, to bring it to a favourable issue, although not personally engaged in the adventure.

So soon as the troops had been landed the vessels were sent off as expeditiously as possible, that none might fall into the enemy's hands ; the transports under a strong convoy of war-ships having been directed to proceed as fast as the wind would permit in the direction of Nieuport. The march then began. On the 23rd they advanced a league and halted for the night at Assenede. The next day brought them three leagues further, to a place called Eckerloo. On the 25th they marched to Male, a distance of three leagues and a half, passing close to the walls of Bruges, in which they had indulged faint hopes of exciting an insurrection, but obtained nothing but a feeble cannonade from the fortifications which did no damage except the killing of one muleteer. The next night was passed at Jabbeke, four leagues from Male, and on the 27th, after marching another league, they came before the fort of Oudenburg.

This important post on the road which the army would necessarily traverse in coming from the interior to the coast was easily captured and then strongly garrisoned. Maurice with the main army spent the two following days at the fortress, completing his arrangements. Solms was sent forward to seize the sconces and redoubts of the enemy around Ostend, at Breedene, Snaaskerk, Plassendaal, and other points, and especially to occupy the important fort called St. Albert, which was in the downs at about a league from that city. All this work was thoroughly accomplished; little or no resistance having been made to the occupation of these various places. Meantime the States-General, who at the special request of Maurice were to accompany the expedition in order to observe the progress of events for which they were entirely responsible, and to aid the army when necessary by their advice and co-operation, had assembled to the number of thirteen in Ostend. Solms having strengthened the garrison of that place then took up his march along the beach to Nieuport. During the progress of the army through Holland and Zeeland towards its place of embarkation there had been nothing but dismal prognostics, with expressions of muttered indignation, wherever the soldiers passed. It seemed to the country people, and to the inhabitants of every town and village, that their defenders were going to certain destruction; that the existence of the commonwealth was hanging by a thread soon to be snapped asunder. As the forces subsequently marched from the Sas of Ghent towards the Flemish coast there was no rising of the people in their favour, and although Maurice had issued distinct orders that the peasantry were to be dealt with gently and justly, yet they found neither peasants nor villagers to deal with at all. The whole population on their line of march had betaken themselves to the woods, except the village sexton of Jabbeke and his wife, who were too old to run. Lurking in the thickets and marshes, the peasants fell upon all stragglers from the army and murdered them without mercy—so difficult is it in times of civil war to make human brains pervious to the light of reason. The stadholder and his soldiers came to liberate their brethren of the same race, and speaking the same language, from abject submission to a foreign despotism. The Flemings had but to speak a word, to lift a finger, and all the Netherlands, self-governed, would coalesce into one independent confederation of States, strong enough to defy all the despots of Europe. Alas! the benighted victims of superstition hugged their chains, and preferred the tyranny under which their kindred had been tortured, burned, and buried alive for half-a-century long, to the possibility of a single Calvinistic conventicle being opened in any village of obedient Flanders. So these excellent children of Philip and the pope, whose language was as unintelligible to them as it was to Peruvians or Iroquois, lay in wait for the men who spoke their own mother tongue, and whose veins were filled with their own blood, and murdered them, as a sacred act of duty. Retaliation followed as a matter of course, so that the invasion of Flanders, in this early stage of its progress, seemed not likely to call forth very fraternal feelings between the two families of Netherlanders.

The army was in the main admirably well supplied, but there was a deficiency of drink. The water as they advanced became brackish and intolerably bad, and there was great difficulty in procuring any substitute. At Male three cows were given for a pot of beer, and more of that refreshment might have been sold at the same price, had there been any sellers.

On the 30th June Maurice marched from Oudenburg, intending to strike a point called Niewendam—a fort in the neighbourhood of Nieuport—and so to march along the walls of that city and take up his position immediately in its front. He found the ground, however, so marshy and impracticable as he advanced, that he was obliged to countermarch, and to spend that night on the downs between forts Isabella and St. Albert.

On the 1st July he resumed his march, and passing a bridge over a small stream at a place called Leffin-gen, laying down a road as he went with sods and 1 July. sand, and throwing bridges over streams and swamps, he arrived in the forenoon before Nieuport. The fleet had reached the roadstead the same morning.

This was a strong, well-built, and well-fortified little city, situate half-a-league from the sea coast on low, plashy ground. At high water it was a seaport, for a stream or creek of very insignificant dimensions was then sufficiently filled by the tide to admit vessels of considerable burthen. This haven was immediately taken possession of by the stadholder, and two-thirds of his army were thrown across to the western side of the water, the troops remaining on the Ostend side being by a change of arrangement now under command of Count Ernest.

Thus the army which had come to surprise Nieuport had, after accomplishing a distance of nearly forty miles in thirteen days, at last arrived before that place. Yet there was no more expeditious or energetic commander in Christendom than Maurice, nor troops better trained in marching and fighting than his well-disciplined army.

It is now necessary to cast a glance towards the interior of Flanders, in order to observe how the archduke conducted himself in this emergency. So soon as the news of the landing of the States' army at the port of Ghent reached the sovereign's ears, he awoke from the delusion that danger was impending on his eastern border, and lost no time in assembling such troops as could be mustered from far and near to protect the western frontier. Especially he despatched messengers well charged with promises, to confer with the authorities of the "Italian Republic" at Diest and Thionville. He appealed to them in behalf of the holy Catholic religion, he sought to arouse their loyalty to himself and the Infanta Isabella—daughter of the great and good Philip II., once foremost of earthly potentates, and now eminent among the saints of heaven—by whose fiat he and his wife had now become legitimate sovereigns of all the Netherlands. And those mutineers responded with unexpected docility. Eight hundred foot soldiers and six hundred cavalry men came forth at the first summons, making but two conditions in addition to the stipulated payment when payment should be possible—that they should be commanded by their own chosen officers, and that they should be placed in the first rank in the impending conflict. The example spread. Other detachments of mutineers in various strongholds, scenting the battle from afar, came in with offers to serve in the campaign on similar terms. Before the last week of June the archduke had a considerable army on foot. On the 29th of that month, accompanied by the Infanta, 29 June, he reviewed a force of ten thousand foot and nearly 1600. two thousand cavalry in the immediate vicinity of Ghent. He addressed them in a few stirring words, reminding them of their duty to the Church and to himself, and assuring them—as commanders of every nation and every age are wont to assure their troops at the eve of every engagement— that the cause in which they were going forth to battle was the most sacred and inspiring for which human creatures could possibly lay down their lives. Isabella, magnificently attired, and mounted on a white palfrey, galloped along the lines, and likewise made an harangue. She spoke to the soldiers as "her lions," promised them boundless rewards in this world and the next, as the result of the great victory which they were now about to gain over the infidels ; while as to their wages, she vowed that, rather than they should remain unpaid, she would sacrifice all her personal effects, even to the plate from which she ate her daily bread, and to the jewels which she wore in her ears.

Thousands of hoarse voices greeted the eloquence of the archdukes with rude acclamations, while the discharge of arquebus and volleys of cannon testified to the martial ardour with which the troops were inspired ; none being more enthusiastic than the late mutineers. The army marched at once, under many experienced leaders—Villars, Zapena, and Avalos among the most conspicuous. The command of the artillery was entrusted to Velasco ; the marshal-general of the camp was Frederic van den Berg, in place of the super- annuated Peter Ernest ; while the Admiral of Arragon, Francisco de Mendoza, "terror of Germany and of Christen- dom," a little man with flowing locks, long hooked nose, and a sinister glance from his evil black eyes, was general of the cavalry. The admiral had not displayed very extra- ordinary genius in his recent campaigning in the Rhenish duchies, but his cruelty had certainly been conspicuous. Not even Alva could have accomplished more murders and

other outrages in the same space of time than had been per-
petrated by the Spanish troops during the infamous winter of
1598–9. The assassination of Count Broeck at his own castle
had made more stir than a thousand other homicides of nameless wretches at the same period had done, because the victim
had been a man of rank and large possessions, but it now
remained to be seen whether Mendoza was to gain fresh
laurels of any kind in the battle which was probably impending.

On the 1st of July the archduke came before Oudenburg.
Not a soul within that fortress nor in Ostend dreamed of an
enemy within twenty miles of them, nor had it been supposed
possible that a Spanish army could take the field for many
weeks to come. The States-General at Ostend were com-
placently waiting for the first bulletin from Maurice announc-
ing his capture of Nieuport and his advance upon Dunkirk,
according to the program so succinctly drawn up for him,
and meantime were holding meetings and drawing up comfortable protocols with great regularity. Colonel Piron, on
his part, who had been left with several companies of veterans
to hold Oudenburg and the other forts, and to protect the
rear of the invading army, was accomplishing that object by
permitting a large portion of his force to be absent on
foraging parties and general marauding. When the enemy
came before Oudenburg they met with no resistance. The
fort was surrendered at once, and with it fell the lesser sconces
of Breedene, Snaaskerk, and Plassendaal—all but the more
considerable fort St. Albert. The archduke, not thinking it
advisable to delay his march by the reduction of this position,
and having possession of all the other fortifications around
Ostend, determined to push forward next morning at daybreak. He had granted favourable terms of surrender to the
various garrisons, which, however, did not prevent them from
being dearly every man of them immediately butchered in
cold blood.

Thus were these strong and well-manned redoubts, by
which Prince Maurice had hoped to impede for many days the

march of a Spanish army—should a Spanish army indeed be able to take the field at all—already swept off in an hour. Great was the dismay in Ostend when Colonel Piron and a few stragglers brought the heavy news of discomfiture and massacre to the high and mighty States-General in solemn meeting assembled.

Meanwhile, the States' army before Nieuport, not dreaming of any pending interruption to their labours, proceeded in a steady but leisurely manner to invest the city. Maurice occupied himself in tracing the lines of encampment and entrenchment, and ordered a permanent bridge to be begun across the narrowest part of the creek, in order that the two parts of his army might not be so dangerously divided from each other as they now were, at high water, by the whole breadth and depth of the harbour. Evening came on before much had been accomplished on this first day of the siege. It was scarcely dusk when a messenger, much exhausted and terrified, made his appearance at Count Ernest's tent. He was a straggler who had made his escape from Oudenburg, and he brought the astounding intelligence that the archduke had already possession of that position and of all the other forts. Ernest instantly jumped into a boat and had himself rowed, together with the messenger, to the headquarters of Prince Maurice on the other side of the river. The news was as unexpected as it was alarming. Here was the enemy, who was supposed incapable of mischief for weeks to come, already in the field, and planted directly on their communications with Ostend. Retreat, if retreat were desired, was already impossible, and as to surprising the garrison of Nieuport and so obtaining that stronghold as a basis for further aggressive operations, it is very certain that if any man in Flanders was more surprised than another at that moment it was Prince Maurice himself. He was too good a soldier not to see at a glance that if the news brought by the straggler were true, the whole expedition was already a failure, and that, instead of a short siege and an easy victory, a great battle was to be fought upon the sands of Nieuport, in which defeat was destruction of the whole army of the republic, and very possibly of the republic itself.

The stadholder hesitated. He was prone in great emergencies to hesitate at first, but immovable when his resolution was taken. Vere, who was asleep in his tent, was sent for and consulted. Most of the generals were inclined to believe that the demonstrations at Oudenburg, which had been so successful, were merely a bravado of Rivas, the commander of the permanent troops in that district, which were comparatively insignificant in numbers. Vere thought otherwise. He maintained that the archduke was already in force within a few hours' march of them, as he had always supposed would be the case. His opinion was not shared by the rest, and he went back to his truckle-bed, feeling that a brief repose was necessary for the heavy work which would soon be upon him. At midnight the Englishman was again called from his slumbers. Another messenger, sent directly from the States-General at Ostend, had made his way to the stadholder. This time there was no possibility of error, for Colonel Piron had sent the accord with the garrison commanders of the forts which had been so shamefully violated, and which bore the signature of the archduke.

It was now perfectly obvious that a pitched battle was to be fought before another sunset, and most anxious were the deliberations in that brief midsummer's night. The dilemma was as grave a one as commander-in-chief had ever to solve in a few hours. A portentous change had come over the prospects of the commonwealth since the arrival of these despatches. But a few hours before, and never had its destiny seemed so secure, its attitude more imposing. The little republic, which Spain had been endeavouring forty years long to subjugate, had already swept every Spanish soldier out of its territory, had repeatedly carried fire and sword into Spain itself, and even into its distant dependencies, and at that moment—after effecting in a masterly manner the landing of a great army in the very face of the man who claimed to be sovereign of all the Netherlands, and after marching at ease through the heart of his territory—was preparing a movement, with every prospect of success, which should render the hold of that sovereign on any portion of Netherland soil as uncertain and shifting as the sands on which the States army was now encamped.

The son of the proscribed and murdered rebel stood at the head of as powerful and well-disciplined an army as had ever been drawn up in line of battle on that blood-stained soil. The daughter of the man who had so long oppressed the provinces might soon be a fugitive from the land over which she had so recently been endowed with perpetual sovereignty. And now in an instant these visions were fading like a mirage.

The archduke, whom poverty and mutiny were to render powerless against invasion, was following close up upon the heels of the triumphant army of the stadholder. A decision was immediately necessary. The siege of Nieuport was over before it had begun. Surprise had failed, assault for the moment was impossible, the manner how best to confront the advancing foe the only question.

Vere advised that the whole army should at once be concentrated and led without delay against the archduke before he should make further progress.[3] The advice involved an outrageous impossibility, and it seems incredible that it could have been given in good faith ; still more amazing that its rejection by Maurice should have been bitterly censured. Two-thirds of the army lay on the other side of the harbour, and it was high water at about three o'clock. While they were deliberating, the sea was rising, and, so soon as daybreak should make any evolutions possible, they would be utterly prohibited during several hours by the inexorable tide. More time would be consumed by the attempt to construct temporary bridges (for of course little progress had been made in the stone bridge hardly begun) or to make use of boats than in waiting for the falling of the water, and, should the enemy make his appearance while they were

[3] See the note on Sir Francis Vere at the end of this chapter.

engaged in such confusing efforts, the army would be hopelessly lost.

Maurice, against the express advice of Vere, decided to
send his cousin Ernest, with the main portion of the force
established on the right bank of the harbour, in search of the
archduke, for the purpose of holding him in check long enough
to enable the rest of the army to cross the water when the
tide should serve. The enemy, it was now clear, would
advance by precisely the path over which the States' army
had marched that morning. Ernest was accordingly instructed
to move with the greatest expedition in order to seize the
bridge at Leffingen before the archduke should reach the
deep, dangerous, and marshy river, over which it was the sole
passage to the downs. Two thousand infantry, being the
Scotch regiment of Edmonds and the Zeelanders of Van der
Noot, four squadrons of Dutch cavalry, and two pieces of
artillery composed the force with which Ernest set forth at a
little before dawn on his hazardous but heroic enterprise.

With a handful of troops he was to make head against an
army, and the youth accepted the task in the cheerful spirit
of self-sacrifice which characterized his house. Marching as
rapidly as the difficult ground would permit, he had the disappointment, on approaching the fatal point at about eight
o'clock, to see the bridge at Leffingen in the possession of the
enemy. Maurice had sent off a messenger early that morning with a letter marked post haste (*cito, cito*) to Ostend
ordering up some four hundred cavalry-men then stationed
in that city under Piron and Bruges, to move up to the support of Ernest, and to destroy the bridge and dams at
Leffingen before the enemy should arrive. That letter,
which might have been so effective, was delivered, as it
subsequently appeared, exactly ten days after it was written.[4]
The States, of their own authority, had endeavoured to send
out those riders towards the scene of action, but it was with
great difficulty that they could be got into the saddle at all,
and they positively refused to go further than St. Albert fort.

4 Duyck, ii. 662.

What course should he now pursue ? He had been sent to cut the archduke's road. He had failed. Had he remained in his original encampment his force would have been annihilated by the overwhelming numbers of the enemy so soon as they reached the right bank of Nieuport haven, while Maurice could have only looked hopelessly on from the opposite shore. At least nothing worse than absolute destruction could befal him now. Should he accept a combat of six or eight to one the struggle would be hopeless, but the longer it was protracted the better it would be for his main army, engaged at that very moment as he knew in crossing the haven with the ebbing tide. Should he retreat, it might be possible for him to escape into Fort Albert or even Ostend, but to do so would be to purchase his own safety and that of his command at the probable sacrifice of the chief army of the republic. Ernest hesitated but an instant. Coming within carbine-shot of the stream, where he met his cavalry which had been sent forward at full speed, in the vain hope of seizing or destroying the bridge before it should be too late, he took up a position behind a dyke, upon which he placed his two field-pieces, and formed his troops in line of battle exactly across the enemy's path. On the right he placed the regiment of Scots. On the left was Van der Noot's Zeeland infantry, garnished with four companies of riders under Risoir, which stood near St. Mary's church. The passage from the stream to the downs was not more than a hundred yards wide, being skirted on both sides by a swamp. Here Ernest with his two thousand men awaited the onset of the archduke's army. He was perfectly aware that it was a mere question of time, but he was sure that his preparations must interpose a delay to the advance of the Spaniards, should his troops, as he felt confident, behave themselves as they had always done, and that the delay would be of inestimable value to his friends at the haven of Nieuport.

The archduke paused ; for he, too, could not be certain, on observing the resolute front thus presented to him, that he was not about to engage the whole of the States' army. The

doubt was but of short duration, however, and the onset was
made. Ernest's artillery fired four volleys into the advancing
battalions with such effect as to stagger them for a moment,
but they soon afterwards poured over the dyke in overwhelming numbers, easily capturing the cannon. The attack
began upon Ernest's left, and Risoir's cavalry, thinking that
they should be cut off from all possibility of retreat into Fort
St. Albert, turned their backs in the most disgraceful manner,
without even waiting for the assault. Galloping around the
infantry on the left they infected the Zeelanders with their
own cowardice. Scarcely a moment passed before Van der
Noot's whole regiment was running away as fast as the
troopers, while the Scots on the right hesitated not for an
instant to follow their example. Even before the expected
battle had begun, one of those hideous and unaccountable
panics which sometimes break out like a moral pestilence to
destroy all the virtue of an army, and to sweep away the best-
considered schemes of a general, had spread through Ernest's
entire force. So soon as the demi-cannon had discharged
their fourth volley, Scots, Zeelanders, Walloons, pikemen,
musketeers, and troopers, possessed by the demon of cowardice,
were running like a herd of swine to throw themselves into
the sea. Had they even kept the line of the downs in the
direction of the fort many of them might have saved their
lives, although none could have escaped disgrace. But
the Scots, in an ecstasy of fear, throwing away their arms as
they fled, ran through the waters behind the dyke, skimmed
over the sands at full speed, and never paused till such as
survived the sabre and musket of their swift pursuers had
literally drowned themselves in the ocean. Almost every
man of them was slain or drowned. All the captains—Stuart,
Barclay, Murray, Kilpatrick, Michael, Nesbit—with the rest
of the company officers, doing their best to rally the fugitives,
were killed. The Zeelanders, more cautious in the midst of
their panic, or perhaps knowing better the nature of the
country, were more successful in saving their necks. Not
more than a hundred and fifty of Van der Noot's regi-

ment were killed, while such of the cavalry of Bruges and Piron as had come to the neighbourhood of Fort Albert, not caring to trust themselves to the shelter of that redoubt, now fled as fast as their horses' legs would carry them, and never pulled bridle till they found themselves in Ostend. And so beside themselves with panic were these fugitives, and so virulent was the contagion, that it was difficult to prevent the men who had remained in the fort from joining in the flight towards Ostend. Many of them indeed threw themselves over the walls and were sabred by the enemy when they might have been safe within the fortifications. Had these cavalry companies of Bruges and Piron been even tolerably self-possessed, had they concentrated themselves in the fort instead of yielding to the delirium which prompted them to participate in their comrades' flight, they would have had it entirely in their power, by making an attack, or even the semblance of an attack, by means of a sudden sally from the fort, to have saved, not the battle indeed, but a large number of lives. But the panic was hopeless and universal, and countless fugitives scrambling by the fort were shot in a leisurely manner by a comparative few of the enemy as easily as the rabbits which swarmed in those sands were often knocked down in multitudes by half-a-dozen sportsmen.

And thus a band of patriots, who were not cowards by nature, and who had often played the part of men, had horribly disgraced themselves, and were endangering the very existence of their country, already by mistaken councils brought within the jaws of death. The glory of Thermopylæ might have hung for ever over that bridge of Leffingen. It was now a pass of infamy, perhaps of fatal disaster. The sands were covered with weapons—sabre, pike, and arquebus —thrown away by almost every soldier as he fled to save the life which after all was sacrificed. The artillery, all the standards and colours, all the baggage and ammunition, every thing was lost. No viler panic, no more complete defeat was ever recorded. Such at half-past eight in the morning was that memorable Sunday of the 2nd July, 1600, big with the fate of the Dutch republic—the festival of the Visitation of the Virgin Mary, always thought of happy augury for Spanish arms.

Thus began the long expected battle of Nieuport. At least a thousand of the choicest troops of the stadholder were slain, while the Spanish had hardly lost a man.[5]

The archduke had annihilated his enemy,[6] had taken his artillery and thirty flags. In great exultation he despatched a messenger to the Infanta at Ghent, informing her that he had entirely defeated the advance-guard of the States' army, and that his next bulletin would announce his complete triumph and the utter overthrow of Maurice, who had now no means of escape. He stated also that he would very soon send the rebel stadholder himself to her as a prisoner. The Infanta, much pleased with the promise, observed to her attendants that she was curious to see how Nassau would conduct himself when he should be brought a captive into her presence. As to the Catholic troops, they were informed by the archduke that after the complete victory which they

---

[5] There can be no doubt whatever as to the rout of Leffingen. There was no fight at all. The journal of Antony Duyck and the accounts of Meteren, Bor, and other chroniclers entirely agree with the most boastful narratives of the Spaniards. Everard van Reyd to be sure stoutly maintains that the troops of Ernest fought to the uttermost ("zum euszersten gefochten"), and that hardly a whole spear was found in the hands of any of the dead on the field. Nor a broken one either, he might have added. It is a pity that the army had not been as stanch as the secretary and chronicler. But Reyd was not on the field nor near it, and there is not a word in Ernest's private letters to conflict with the minute and unvarnished statements of Duyck. See also the excellent note of Captain Mulder on pp. 668, 669, part ii. of his admirable edition of Duyck's journal.

The confessor of the archduke, Fray Inigo de Brizuelas, was as enthusiastic on his side as the privy counsellor of Lewis William. The troops of the archduke, he says, attacked Ernest and in one moment killed 1800 to 2000 men without losing a man themselves—" Elles mirent à mort en un moment 1800 à 2000 hommes s'emparirent de deux pieces d'artillerie et de plusieurs drapeaux sans avoir subi aucune perte . . . . . . On esperait généralement que ce jour mettrait fin aux guerres de Flandre." (! !)

Substance d'une lettre écrite de Bruges le 13 Juillet, 1600, par Fray J. de Brizuelas à unseigneur de la cour à Madrid et reposant en copie aux fol. 45–48 du vol. H. 49, (Varias Consultas en tiempo de los reyes Austriacos) appartenant à la Bibliothèque Nat[l] à Madrid. MS. kindly communicated to me by M. Gachard.

[6] "Qui fut si vivement chargée qu'elle y demeura toute" are the words of the archduke writing on the 4th July from Ghent to his council of state. (MS. Archives of Belgium.)

were that day to achieve, not a man should be left alive save
Maurice and his brother Frederic Henry. These should be
spared to grace the conqueror's triumph, but all else should
be put to the sword.[7]

Meantime artillery thundered, bonfires blazed, and bells
rang their merriest peals in Ghent, Bruges, and the other
obedient cities as the news of the great victory spread through
the land.

When the fight was done the archduke called a council of
war. It was a grave question whether the army should
at once advance in order to complete the destruction of the
enemy that day, or pause for an interval that the troops
fatigued with hard marching and with the victorious combat
in which they just had been engaged, should recover their full
strength. That the stadholder was completely in their
power was certain. The road to Ostend was barred, and
Nieuport would hold him at bay, now that the relieving army
was close upon his heels. All that was necessary in order to
annihilate his whole force, was that they should entrench
themselves for the night on the road which he must cross.
He would then be obliged to assault their works with troops
inferior in number to theirs and fatigued by the march.
Should he remain where he was he would soon be starved
into submission, and would be obliged to surrender his whole
army. On the other hand, by advancing now, in the intolerable heat of a July sun over the burning and glaring sands,
the troops already wearied would arrive on the field of battle
utterly exhausted, and would be obliged to attack an enemy
freshly and cheerfully awaiting them on ground of his own
selection.

Moreover it was absolutely certain that Fort Albert would
not hold an hour if resolutely assaulted in the midst of the
panic of Ernest's defeat, and, with its capture, the annihila-
lation of Maurice was certain.

Meantime the three thousand men under Velasco, who
had been detached to protect the rear, would arrive to rein-

---

[7] Le Petit on the authority of prisoners. De la Pise.

force the archduke's main army, should he pause until the next day.

These arguments, which had much logic in them, were strongly urged by Zapena, a veteran marshal of the camp who had seen much service, and whose counsels were usually received with deference. But on this occasion commanders and soldiers were hot for following up their victory. They cared nothing for the numbers of their enemy, they cried, " The more infidels the greater glory in destroying them." [8] Delay might after all cause the loss of the prize, it was eagerly shouted The archduke ought to pray that the sun might stand still for him that morning, as for Joshua in the vale of Ajalon. The foe seeing himself entrapped, with destruction awaiting him, was now skulking towards his ships, which still offered him the means of escape. Should they give him time he would profit by their negligence, and next morning when they reached Nieuport, the birds would be flown. Especially the leaders of the mutineers of Diest and Thionville were hoarse with indignation at the proposed delay. They had not left their brethren, they shouted, nor rallied to the archduke's banner in order to sit down and dig in the sand like ploughmen. There was triumph for the Holy Church, there was the utter overthrow of the heretic army, there was rich booty to be gathered, all these things were within their reach if they now advanced and smote the rebels while, confused and panic-stricken, they were endeavouring to embark in their ships.

While these vehement debates were at the hottest, sails were descried in the offing ; for the archduke's forces already stood upon the edge of the downs. First one ship, then another and another, moved steadily along the coast, returning from Nieuport in the direction of Ostend.

This was more than could be borne. It was obvious that the rebels were already making their escape, and it was urged upon the cardinal that probably Prince Maurice and the other chieftains were on board one of those very vessels, and were giving him the slip. With great expedition it

[8] " Quanto mas Moros tanto mas ganancias."—De la Pise.

would still be possible to overtake them before the main body could embark, and the attack might yet be made at the most favourable moment. Those white sails gleaming in the distance were more eloquent than Zapena or any other advocate of delay, and the order was given to advance. And it was exactly at this period that it still lay within the power of the States' cavalry at Ostend to partially redeem their character, and to render very effective service. Had four or five hundred resolute troopers hung upon the rear of the Spanish army now, as it moved toward Nieuport, they might, by judiciously skirmishing, advancing and retreating according to circumstances, have caused much confusion, and certainly have so harassed the archduke as to compel the detachment of a very considerable force of his own cavalry to protect himself against such assaults. But the terror was an enduring one. Those horsemen remained paralyzed and helpless, and it was impossible for the States, with all their commands or entreaties, to induce them to mount and ride even a half mile beyond the city gates.

While these events had been occurring in the neighbourhood of Ostend, Maurice had not been idle at Nieuport. No sooner had Ernest been despatched on his desperate errand than his brother Lewis Gunther was ordered by the stadholder to get on horseback and ride through the quarters of the army. On the previous afternoon there had been so little thought of an enemy that large foraging parties had gone out from camp in all directions, and had not returned. Lewis gave notice that a great battle was to be expected on the morrow, instead of the tranquil commencement of a leisurely siege, and that therefore no soul was henceforth to leave the camp, while a troop of horse was despatched at the first gleam of daylight to scour the country in search of all the stragglers. Maurice had no thought of retreating, and his first care was to bring his army across the haven. The arrangements were soon completed, but it was necessary to wait until nearly low water. Soon after eight o'clock Count Lewis began to cross with eight squadrons of cavalry, and partly swimming, partly wading, effected the passage in safety. The advanced guard of infantry, under Sir Francis Vere—consisting of two thousand six hundred Englishmen, and two thousand eight hundred Frisians, with some companies of horse, followed by the battalia under Solms, and the rearguard under Tempel—then slowly and with difficulty moved along the same dangerous path with the water as high as their armpits, and often rising nearly over their heads. Had the archduke not been detained near the bridge of Leffingen by Ernest's Scotchmen and Zeelanders during three or four precious hours that morning; had he arrived, as he otherwise might have done, just as the States' army—horse, foot, and artillery—was floundering through that treacherous tide, it would have fared ill for the stadholder and the republic. But the devotion of Ernest had at least prevented the attack of the archduke until Maurice and his men stood on dry land.

Dripping from head to foot, but safe and sound, the army had at last reached the beach at Nieuport. Vere had refused his soldiers permission to denude themselves in crossing of their shoes and lower garments. There was no time for that, he said, and they would either earn new clothes for themselves that day, or never need doublet and hose again any more in the world. Some hours had elapsed before the tedious and difficult crossing of infantry, cavalry, artillery, and munition trains had been accomplished.

Lewis Gunther, with eight squadrons of picked cavalry, including his own company, Maurice's own, Frederic Henry's own, with Batenburg's arquebus-men, and other veterans, was first to place himself in battle order on the beach. His squadrons in iron corslet and morion, and armed with lances, carbines, and sabres, stretched across from the water to the downs. He had not been long stationed there when he observed that far away in the direction of Ostend the beach was growing black with troops. He believed them at first to be his brother Ernest and his forces returning victorious from their hazardous expedition, but he was soon undeceived.

A couple of troopers from Ostend came spurring full gallop along the strand, and almost breathless with dismay, announced that it was the whole army of the archduke advancing in line of battle. They were instantly sent to the rear, without being allowed to speak further, in order that they might deliver their message in private to the commander-in-chief. And most terrible were the tidings to which Maurice now listened in very secret audience. Ernest was utterly defeated, his command cut to pieces, the triumphant foe advancing rapidly, and already in full sight. The stadholder heard the tale without flinching, and having quietly ordered the messengers upon their lives not to open their lips on the subject to living soul, sent them securely guarded in a boat on board one of the war-ships in the offing. With perfect cheerfulness he then continued his preparations, consulting with Vere, on whom he mainly relied for the marshalling of the army in the coming conflict. Undecided as he had sometimes shown himself, he was resolute now. He called no council of war, for he knew not how much might be known or suspected of the disaster already sustained, and he had fully made up his mind as to the course to be pursued. He had indeed taken a supreme resolution. Entirely out of his own breast, without advising with any man, he calmly gave directions that every war-ship, transport, barge, or wherry should put to sea at once. As the tide had now been long on the flood, the few vessels that had been aground within the harbour were got afloat, and the whole vast, almost innumerable armada, was soon standing out to sea. No more heroic decision was ever taken by fighting man.

Sir Francis gave advice that entrenchments should be thrown up on the north-east, and that instead of advancing towards the enemy they should await his coming, and refuse the battle that day if possible. The Englishman, not aware of the catastrophe at Leffingen, which Maurice had locked up in his own breast, was now informed by the stadholder that there were to be no entrenchments that day but those of pike and arquebus. It was not the fault of Maurice that the fate of the commonwealth had been suspended on a silken thread that morning, but he knew that but one of two issues was possible. They must fight their way through the enemy back to Ostend, or perish, every man of them. The possibility of surrender did not enter his mind, and he felt that it was better to hasten the action before the news of Ernest's disaster should arrive to chill the ardour of the troops.[9]

Meantime Lewis Gunther and his cavalry had been sitting motionless upon their horses on the beach. The enemy was already in full view, and the young general, most desirous to engage in a preliminary skirmish, sent repeated messages to the stadholder for permission to advance. Presently Sir Francis Vere rode to the front, to whom he eagerly urged his request that the infantry of the vanguard might be brought up at once to support him.[10] On the contrary the English general advised that the cavalry should fall back to the infantry, in order to avoid a premature movement. Lewis strongly objected to this arrangement, on the ground that the mere semblance of retreat, thus upon the eve of battle, would discourage all the troops. But he was over-ruled, for Maurice had expressly enjoined upon his cousin that morning to defer in all things to the orders of Vere. These eight squadrons of horse accordingly shifted their position, and were now placed close to the edge of the sea, on the left flank of the vanguard, which Vere had drawn up across the beach and in the downs. On the edge of the downs, on the narrow slip of hard sand above high-water mark, and on Vere's right, Maurice had placed a battery of six demi-cannon.

Behind the advance was the battalia, or centre, under command of that famous fighter, George Everard Solms, consisting of Germans, Swiss, French, and Walloons. The "New Beggars," as the Walloons were called, who had so recently surrendered the forts of Crevecœur and St. Andrew, and gone over from the archduke's service to the army of

---

[9] That Maurice concealed from Vere the news of the defeat at Leffingen is expressly stated by Antony Duyck.   [10] See note on Vere.

the States, were included in this division, and were as eager to do credit to their new chief as were the mutineers in the archduke's army to merit the approbation of their sovereign.

The rearguard under Tempel was made up, like the other divisions, of the blended nationalities of German, Briton, Hollander, and Walloon, and, like the others, was garnished at each flank with heavy cavalry.

The Spanish army, after coming nearly within cannon-shot of their adversary, paused. It was plain that the States' troops were not in so great a panic as the more sanguine advisers of the archduke had hoped. They were not cowering among the shipping, preparing to escape. Still less had any portion of them already effected their retreat in those vessels, a few of which had so excited the enemy's ardour when they came in sight. It was obvious that a great struggle, in which the forces were very evenly balanced, was now to be fought out upon those sands. It was a splendid tournament—a great duel for life and death between the champions of the Papacy and of Protestantism, of the Republic and of absolutism, that was to be fought out that midsummer's day. The lists were closed. The trumpet signal for the fray would soon be blown.

The archduke, in Milanese armour, on a wonderfully beautiful snow-white Spanish stallion, moved in the centre of his army. He wore no helmet, that his men might the more readily recognize him as he rode gallantly to and fro, marshalling, encouraging, exhorting the troops. Never before had he manifested such decided military talent, combined with unquestionable personal valour, as he had done since this campaign began. Friend and foe agreed that day that Albert fought like a lion. He was at first well seconded by Mendoza, who led the van, and by Villars, La Bourlotte, Avalos, Zapena, and many other officers of note. The mutinous Spanish and Italian cavalry, combined with a few choice squadrons of Walloon and German horse, were placed in front and on the flanks. They were under the special supervision of the admiral, who marshalled their squadrons and directed their charging, although mounted on a hackney himself, and not intending to participate in the action. Then came the battalia and rear, crowding very closely upon each other.

Face to face with them stood the republican host, drawn up in great solid squares of infantry, their standards waving above each closely planted clump of pikemen, with the musketeers fringing their skirts, while the iron-clad ponderous cavalry of Count Lewis and Marcellus Bax, in black casque and corslet, were in front, restlessly expecting the signal for the onset. The volunteers of high rank who were then serving on the staff of the stadholder—the Duke of Holstein, the Prince of Anhalt, two young Counts Solms, and others—had been invited and even urged to abandon the field while there was yet time for setting them on board the fleet. Especially it was thought desirable that young Frederic Henry, a mere boy, on whom the hopes of the Orange-Nassau house would rest if Maurice fell in the conflict, should be spared the fate which seemed hanging over the commonwealth and her defenders. But the son of William the Silent implored his brother with clasped hands not to send him from his side at that moment, so that Maurice granted his prayer, and caused him to be provided with a complete suit of armour. Thus in company with young Coligny—a lad of his own age, and like himself a grandson of the great admiral—the youth who was one day to play so noble a part on the stage of the world's affairs was now to be engaged in his first great passage of arms. No one left the field but Sir Robert Sidney, who had come over from Ostend, from irrepressible curiosity to witness the arrangements, but who would obviously have been guilty of unpardonable negligence had he been absent at such a crisis from the important post of which he was governor for the queen.[11]

[11] Duyck, however, with much injustice, as it would seem, accuses Sidney (whom he calls "Philip Sidney"!) of cowardice; stating that he paid a large sum to obtain a vessel in which to make his escape, and that he was obliged to hear many insulting observations on his flight.

The arena of the conflict seemed elaborately prepared by the hand of nature. The hard, level, sandy beach, swept clean and smooth by the ceaseless action of the tides, stretched out far as the eye could reach in one long, bold, monotonous line. Like the whole coast of Flanders and of Holland, it seemed drawn by a geometrical rule, not a cape, cove, or estuary breaking the perfect straightness of the design. On the right, just beyond high-water mark, the downs, fantastically heaped together like a mimic mountain chain, or like tempestuous ocean-waves suddenly changed to sand, rolled wild and confused, but still in a regularly parallel course with the line of the beach. They seemed a barrier thrown up to protect the land from being bitten quite away by the ever-restless and encroaching sea. Beyond the downs, which were seven hundred yards in width, extended a level tract of those green fertile meadows, artificially drained, which are so characteristic a feature of the Netherland landscapes, the stream which ran from Ostend towards the town of Nieuport flowing sluggishly through them. It was a bright warm midsummer day. The waves of the German Ocean came lazily rolling in upon the crisp yellow sand, the surf breaking with its monotonous music at the very feet of the armies. A gentle south-west breeze was blowing, just filling the sails of more than a thousand ships in the offing, which moved languidly along the sparkling sea. It was an atmosphere better befitting a tranquil holiday than the scene of carnage which seemed approaching.

Maurice of Nassau, in complete armour, rapier in hand, with the orange-plumes waving from his helmet and the orange-scarf across his breast, rode through the lines, briefly addressing his soldiers with martial energy. Pointing to the harbour of Nieuport behind them, now again impassable with the flood, to the ocean on the left where rode the fleet,

---

"De heere Philps (sic) Sidnei tsij uyt vrese ofte anders ont vont hem van daer ende geraeckte met groote moeite ende naer veel schampere woorden hem bij eenigen gegeven t'scheepe selfs met presentatie van geld ende voer doen wech, *niet dervende in den slach blijven*."—Journaal, ii. 667.

carrying with it all hope of escape by sea, and to the army of the archduke in front, almost within cannon-range, he simply observed that they had no possible choice between victory and death. They must either utterly overthrow the Spanish army, he said, or drink all the waters of the sea. Either drowning or butchery was their doom if they were conquered, for no quarter was to be expected from their unscrupulous and insolent foe. He was there to share their fate, to conquer or to perish with them, and from their tried valour and from the God of battles he hoped a more magnificent victory than had ever before been achieved in this almost perpetual war for independence. The troops, perfectly enthusiastic, replied with a shout that they were ready to live or die with their chieftain, and eagerly demanded to be led upon the foe. Whether from hope or from desperation they were confident and cheerful. Some doubt was felt as to the Walloons, who had so lately transferred themselves from the archduke's army, but their commander, Marquette, made them all lift up their hands, and swear solemnly to live or die that day at the feet of Prince Maurice.

Two hours long these two armies had stood looking each other in the face. It was near two o'clock when the archduke at last gave the signal to advance. The tide was again almost at the full. Maurice stood firm, awaiting the assault; the enemy slowly coming nearer, and the rising tide as steadily lapping away all that was left of the hard beach which fringed the rugged downs. Count Lewis chafed with impatience as it became each moment more evident that there would be no beach left for cavalry fighting, while in the downs the manœuvring of horse was entirely impossible. Meantime, by command of Vere, all those sandy hillocks and steeps had been thickly sown with musketeers and pikemen. Arquebus-men and carabineers were planted in every hollow, while on the highest and most advantageous elevation two pieces of cannon had been placed by the express direction of Maurice. It seemed obvious that the battle would, after all, be transferred to the downs. Not long before the action began, a private of the enemy's cavalry was taken, apparently with his own consent, in a very trifling preliminary skirmish. He bragged loudly of the immense force of the archduke, of the great victory already gained over Ernest, with the utter annihilation of his forces, and of the impending destruction of the whole States' army. Strange to say, this was the first intimation received by Count Lewis of that grave disaster,[12] although it had been for some hours known to Maurice. The prisoner was at once gagged, that he might spread his disheartening news no further, but as he persisted by signs and gestures in attempting to convey the information which he had evidently been sent forward to impart, he was shot by command of the stadholder, and so told no further tales.[13]

The enemy had now come very close, and it was the desire of Count Lewis that a couple of companies of horse, in accordance with the commands of Maurice, should charge the cavalry in front, and that after a brief skirmish they should retreat as if panic-stricken behind the advance column, thus decoying the Spanish vanguard in hot pursuit towards the battery upon the edge of the downs.[14] The cannon were then suddenly to open upon them, and during the confusion sure to be created in their ranks, the musketeers, ambushed among the hollows, were to attack them in flank, while the cavalry in one mass should then make a concentrated charge in front. It seemed certain that the effect of this movement would be to hurl the whole of the enemy's advance, horse and foot, back upon his battalia, and thus to break up his army in irretrievable rout. The plan was a sensible one, but it was not ingeniously executed. Before the handful of cavalry had time to make the proposed feint the cannonneers, being unduly excited, and by express command of Sir Francis Vere, fired a volley into the advancing columns of the archduke.[15] This precipitated the action; almost in an

---

[12] Letters of Lewis Gunther cited at end of the chapter.
[13] H. Wyts, in Bor, IV. Byvoeg, v. Auth. Stakken. Compare Van Wyn op Wagenaar, ix. 37–47. [14] See note on Vere. [15] Ibid.

instant changed its whole character, and defeated the original plan of the republican leader. The enemy's cavalry broke at the first discharge from the battery, and wheeled in considerable disorder, but without panic, quite into and across the downs. The whole army of the archduke, which had already been veering in the same direction, as it advanced, both because the tide was so steadily devouring the even surface of the sands, and because the position of a large portion of the States' forces among the hillocks exposed him to an attack in flank, was now rapidly transferred to the downs. It was necessary for that portion of Maurice's army which still stood on what remained of the beach to follow this movement. A rapid change of front was then undertaken, and—thanks to the careful system of wheeling, marching, and counter-marching in which the army had been educated by William Lewis and Maurice—was executed with less confusion than might have been expected.

But very few companies of infantry now remained on the strip of beach still bare of the waves, and in the immediate vicinity of the artillery planted high and dry beyond their reach.

The scene was transformed as if by magic, and the battle was now to be fought out in those shifting, uneven hills and hollows, where every soldier stood mid-leg deep in the dry and burning sand. Fortunately for the States' army, the wind was in its back, blowing both sand and smoke into the faces of its antagonists, while the already westering sun glared fiercely in their eyes. Maurice had skilfully made use of the great advantage which accident had given him that day, and his very refusal to advance and to bring on a premature struggle thus stood him in stead in a variety of ways Lewis Gunther was now ordered, with Marcellus Bax and six squadrons of horse, to take position within the belt of pastureland on the right of the downs. When he arrived there the van of the archduke's infantry had already charged the States' advance under Vere, while just behind and on the side of the musketeers and pikemen a large portion of the enemy's cavalry was standing stock still on the green. Without waiting for instructions Lewis ordered a charge. It was brilliantly successful. Unheeding a warm salutation in flank from the musketeers as they rode by them, and notwithstanding that they were obliged to take several ditches as they charged, they routed the enemy's cavalry at the first onset, and drove them into panic-stricken flight. Some fled for protection quite to the rear of their infantry, others were hotly pursued across the meadows till they took refuge under the walls of Nieuport. The very success of the attack was nearly fatal however to Count Lewis ; for, unable to restrain the ardour of his troopers in the chase, he found himself cut off from the army with only ten horsemen to support him, and completely enveloped by the enemy. Fortunately Prince Maurice had foreseen the danger, and had ordered all the cavalry to the meadows so soon as the charge was made. Captain Kloet, with a fresh company of mounted carabineers, marked the little squad of States' cavalry careering about in the midst of the Catholics, recognized their leader by the orange-plumes on his casque, and dashed forward to the rescue. Lewis again found himself at the head of his cavalry, but was obliged to wait a long time for the return of the stragglers.

While this brilliant diversion had been enacting as it were on the fringe of the battle, its real bustle and business had been going on in the downs. Just as Lewis made his charge in the pastures, the infantry of the archduke and the advance-guard of the republicans met in deadly shock. More than an hour long they contended with varying success. Musketeers, pikemen, arquebusmen, swordmen, charged, sabred, or shot each other from the various hollows or heights of vantage, plunging knee-deep in the sand, torn and impeded by the prickly broom-plant which grew profusely over the whole surface, and fighting breast to breast and hand to hand in a vast series of individual encounters. Thrice were the Spaniards repulsed in what for a moment seemed absolute rout, thrice they rallied and drove their assailants at push of

pike far beyond their original position ; and again the conquered republicans recovered their energy and smote their
adversaries as if the contest were just begun. The tide of
battle ebbed and flowed like the waves of the sea, but it
would be mere pedantry to affect any technical explanation
of its various changes. It was a hot struggle of twenty thousand men, pent up in a narrow space, where the very nature
of the ground had made artistic evolutions nearly impracticable.[16] The advance, the battalia, even the rearguard on
both sides were mixed together pell-mell, and the downs were
soon covered at every step with the dead and dying—Briton,
Hollander, Spaniard, Italian, Frisian, Frenchman, Walloon,
fighting and falling together, and hotly contesting every inch
of those barren sands.

It seemed, said one who fought there, as if the last day of
the world had come.

Political and religious hatred, pride of race, remembrance
of a half-century of wrongs, hope, fury, and despair ; these
were the real elements contending with each other that summer's day. It was a mere trial of ferocity and endurance, not
more scientific than a fight between packs of wolves and
of bloodhounds.

No doubt the brunt of the conflict fell upon Vere, with
his Englishmen and Frisians, for this advance-guard made
up nearly one-half of the States' army actually engaged.
And most nobly, indefatigably, did the hardy veteran discharge his duty. Having personally superintended almost all
the arrangements in the morning, he fought all day in the
front, doing the work both of a field-marshal and a corporal.

---

[16] "Car à raison de la situation du
pays, la science et dexterité en laquelle
nous presumions d'exceder nostre ennemy (qui estoit la prompte et agile
motion de nos bataillons) nous fust
entierement rendue infructueuse."—
Vere, La Bataille de Nieuport.

* Aussi est il impossible d'observer
aucun ordre, sinon par trouppes, vu
que la bataille s'est donnée aux
dunes où il faict si inegal que
tous ont ete pel et mesle, l'arriere-
garde ast este aussitost aux mains
que l'advant-garde en la bataille."
—Ernest Casimir to William Lewis,
20 July, 1600. Groen v. Prinsterer,
Archives, II. 36.

" Car s'estant les deux armées fort
furieusement attaquées il y a esté combattu plus de deux heures main a
main et pesle-mesle doubteusement de
la victoire," &c. &c.—Letter of the
States-General to Queen Elizabeth,
3 July, 1600. (Hague Archives MS.)

He was twice wounded, shot each time through the same leg, yet still fought on as if it were some one else's blood and not his own that was flowing from " those four holes in his flesh." [17] He complained that he was not sufficiently seconded, and that the reserves were not brought up rapidly enough to his support. He was manifestly unjust, for although it could not be doubted that the English and the Frisians did their best, it was equally certain that every part of the army was as staunch as the vanguard. It may be safely asserted that it would not have benefited the cause of the States, had every man been thrown into the fight at one and the same moment.

During this "bloody bit," as Vere called it, between the infantry on both sides, the little battery of two field-pieces planted on the highest hillock of the downs had been very effective. Meantime, while the desperate and decisive struggle had been going on, Lewis Gunther, in the meadow, had again rallied all the cavalry, which, at the first stage of the action, had been dispersed in pursuit of the enemy's horse. Gathering them together in a mass, he besought Prince Maurice to order him to charge. The stadholder bade him pause yet a little longer. The aspect of the infantry fight was not yet, in his opinion, sufficiently favourable. Again and again Lewis sent fresh entreaties, and at last received the desired permission. Placing three picked squadrons in front, the young general made a furious assault upon the Catholic cavalry, which had again rallied and was drawn up very close to the musketeers. Fortune was not so kind to him as at the earlier stage of the combat. The charge was received with dauntless front by the Spanish and Italian horse, while at the same moment the infantry poured a severe fire into their assailants. The advancing squadrons faltered, wheeled back upon the companies following them, and the whole mass of the republican cavalry broke into wild and disorderly retreat. At the same moment the archduke, observing his advantage, threw in his last reserves of infantry, and again there was a desperate charge upon Vere's wearied troops, as

[17] His own expression.

decisive as the counter charge of Lewis's cavalry had been unsuccessful. The English and Frisians, sorely tried during those hours of fighting with superior numbers in the intolerable heat, broke at last and turned their backs upon the foe. Some of them fled panic-stricken quite across the downs and threw themselves into the sea, but the mass retreated in a comparatively orderly manner, being driven from one down to another, and seeking a last refuge behind the battery placed on the high-water line of the beach. In the confusion and panic Sir Francis Vere went down at last. His horse, killed by a stray shot fell with and upon him, and the heroic Englishman would then and there have finished his career— for he would hardly have found quarter from the Spaniards— had not Sir Robert Drury, riding by in the tumult, observed him as he lay almost exhausted in the sand. By his exertion and that of his servant Higham, Vere was rescued from his perilous situation, placed on the crupper of Sir Robert's horse, and so borne off the field.

The current of the retreating and pursuing hosts swept by the spot where Maurice sat on horseback, watching and directing the battle. His bravest and best general, the veteran Vere, had fallen ; his cousin Lewis was now as utterly over-thrown as his brother Ernest had been but a few hours before at the fatal bridge of Leffingen ; the whole army, the only army, of the States was defeated, broken, panic-struck ; the Spanish shouts of victory rang on every side. Plainly the day was lost, and with it the republic. In the blackest hour that the Netherland commonwealth had ever known, the fortitude of the stadholder did not desert him. Immoveable as a rock in the torrent he stemmed the flight of his troops. Three squadrons of reserved cavalry, Balen's own, Vere's own, and Cecil's, were all that was left him, and at the head of these he essayed an advance. He seemed the only man on the field not frightened ; and menacing, conjuring, persuading the fugitives for the love of fatherland, of himself and his house, of their own honour, not to disgrace and destroy themselves for ever ; urging that all was not yet lost, and beseeching them at least to take despair for their master, and rather to die like men on the field than to drown like dogs in the sea, he succeeded in rallying a portion of those nearest him.[18] The enemy paused in their mad pursuit, impressed even more than were the States' troops at the dauntless bearing of the prince. It was one of those supreme moments in battle and in history which are sometimes permitted to influence the course of events during a long future. The archduke and his generals committed a grave error in pausing for an instant in their career. Very soon it was too late to repair the fault, for the quick and correct eye of the stadholder saw the point to which the whole battle was tending, and he threw his handful of reserved cavalry, with such of the fugitives as had rallied, straight towards the battery on the beach.

It was arranged that Balen should charge on the strand, Horace Vere through the upper downs, and Cecil along the margin of the beach. Balen rode slowly through the heavy sand, keeping his horses well in wind, and at the moment he touched the beach, rushed with fury upon the enemy's foot near the battery. The moment was most opportune, for the last shot had been fired from the guns, and they had just been nearly abandoned in despair. The onset of Balen was successful : the Spanish infantry, thus suddenly attacked, were broken, and many were killed and taken. Cecil and Vere were equally fortunate, so that the retreating English and Frisians began to hold firm again. It was the very crisis of the battle, which up to that instant seemed wholly lost by the republic, so universal was the overthrow and the flight. Some hundred and fifty Frisian pikemen now rallied from their sullen retreat, and drove the enemy off one hillock or dune.

Foiled in their attempt to intercept the backward movement of the States' army and to seize this vital point and the artillery with it, the Spaniards hesitated and were some-

[18] " Je vous assure que la victoire courut alors grand hazard, car au meme instant toute nostre infanterie se resteroit aussi le grand pas . . . . nostre cavallerie fuioit jusqu'à son Ex^ce lequel, estoit lors la seule occasion de la victoire," &c.—Letters of Lewis Gunther.

what discouraged. Some Zeeland sailors, who had stuck like wax to those demi-cannon during the whole conflict, now promptly obeyed orders to open yet once more upon the victorious foe. At the first volley the Spaniards were staggered, and the sailors with a lively shout of " Ian—fall on," inspired the defeated army with a portion of their own cheerfulness.[19] Others vehemently shouted victory without any reason whatever. At that instant Maurice ordered a last charge by those few cavalry squadrons, while the enemy was faltering under the play of the artillery. It was a forlorn hope, yet such was the shifting fortune of that memorable day that the charge decided the battle. The whole line of the enemy broke, the conquered became the victors, the fugitives quickly rallying and shouting victory almost before they had turned their faces to the foe, became in their turn the pursuers.[20] The Catholic army could no longer be brought to a stand, but fled wildly in every direction, and were shot and stabbed by the republicans as they fled. The Admiral of Arragon fell with his hackney in this last charge. Unwounded, but struggling to extricate himself from his horse that had been killed, he was quickly surrounded by the enemy.

Two Spaniards, Mendo and Villalobos by name, who had recently deserted to the States, came up at the moment and recognised the fallen admiral. They had reason to recognise him, for both had been in his service, and one of them, who was once in immediate household attendance upon him, bore the mark of a wound which he had received from his insolent master. " Admiral, look at this," cried Villalobos, pointing to the scar on his face.[21] The admiral looked and knew his

[19] " Sonder fundament nochtans." —Duyck, ii. 676.

[20] " Et jà la victoire estait comme nostre et son canon en nostre pouvoir mais nostre cavillerie estant chargée de celle de dudit ennemy se vint sauver en notre arriere-garde, ce que voyant je le fis retourner et chargerent l'en-nemy assez prochement. De quoy s'apercevant retourna pour la seconde fois sur eulx quy derechef se vindrent saulver en notre arriere-garde et rom-pre la plus grande partie d'icelle qui casa que l'infanterie perdit courage de passer oultre et poursuive ce qu'elle avait gagné avec tant d'honneur et lors commenca la retraite," &c.— MS. Letter of Albert before cited.

[21] De la Pise. Meteren.

old servants, and gave his scarf to the one and the hanger of his sword-belt to the other, as tokens that he was their prisoner. Thus his life was saved for heavy ransom, of which those who had actually captured him would receive a very trifling portion. The great prisoner was carried to the rear, where he immediately asked for food and drink, and fell to with an appetite, while the pursuit and slaughter went on in all directions.[22]

The archduke, too, whose personal conduct throughout the day was admirable, had been slightly wounded by a halberd stroke on the ear. This was at an earlier stage of the action, and he had subsequently mounted another horse, exchanged his splendid armour for a plain black harness, over which he wore a shabby scarf. In the confusion of the rout he was hard beset. " Surrender, scoundrel !" cried a Walloon pikeman, seizing his horse by the bridle. But a certain Flemish Captain Kabbeljaw recognising his sovereign and rushing to his rescue, slew his assailant and four others with his own hand.[23] He was at last himself killed, but Albert escaped, and, accompanied by the Duke of Aumale, who was also slightly wounded, by Colonel La Bourlotte, and half a dozen troopers rode for their life in the direction of Bruges. When they reached the fatal bridge of Leffingen, over which the archduke had marched so triumphantly but a few hours before to annihilate Count Ernest's division, he was nearly taken prisoner. A few soldiers, collected from the scattered garrisons, had occupied the position, but knowing nothing of the result of the action in the downs, took to their heels and fled as the little party of cavaliers advanced. Had the commander at Ostend or the States-General promptly sent out a company or two so soon as the news of the victory reached them to seize this vital point, the doom of the archduke would have been sealed. Nothing then could have saved him from capture. Fortunately escaping this danger, he now pushed on, and never pulled bridle till he reached Bruges. Thence without pausing he was conveyed to Ghent, where

[22] Meteren. [23] Ibid.

he presented himself to the Infanta. He was not accompanied by the captive Maurice of Nassau, and the curiosity of the princess to know how that warrior would demean himself as a prisoner was not destined on this occasion to be gratified.

Isabella bore the disappointment and the bitter intelligence of the defeat with a stoicism worthy of her departed father. She had already had intimations that the day was going against her army, and had successively received tidings that her husband was killed, was dangerously wounded, was a prisoner ; and she was now almost relieved to receive him, utterly defeated, but still safe and sound.

Meantime the mad chase continued along the beach and through the downs. Never was a rout more absolute than that of Albert's army. Never had so brilliant a victory been achieved by Hollander or Spaniard upon that great battle-ground of Europe—the Netherlands.[24]

Maurice, to whom the chief credit of the victory was unquestionably due, had been firm and impassive during the various aspects of the battle, never losing his self-command when affairs seemed blackest. So soon, however, as the triumph, after wavering so long, was decided in his favour— the veteran legions of Spain and Italy, the picked troops of

---

[24] "Prometo a V. Sᵃ," wrote the archduke to the Duke of Lorraine, "que no creo me pudiera consolar jamas desta disgracia interesando tanta el servico de su Magistad en ella si no me huviera costado sangre pero asi como ha sido poca la derramara de muy buena gana toda como lo haré y la tengo ofrecido al servicio de su Magestad siempre que sea menester."—Letter to Duke of Lorraine, Bibl. Nat. Madrid, kindly communicated to me by Mons. Gachard.

"L'archiduc a montré ce jour-là une grand valeur, c'est avec beaucoup de peine qu'on l'a determiné à se retirer du champ de bataille."—Letter of Fray Inigo de Brizuelas before cited.

"S. A. en personne combattant comme ung lion."—Extraits des procès-verbaux des Etats-Generaux de 1600. (MS. Archives of Belgium.)

"A quoy respondant, le greffier declaira que les Estats estoyent marriz de ladite disgrace mais tres contens et joyeux de connaitre la vaillandise de leur prince mesmes qu'il n'avoit espargné sa personne propre et de mettre sa vie en hazard pour la deffence de son pays et peuple," &c.—Ibid.

The defeat was mainly attributed in the obedient provinces to the bad conduct of the lately mutinous cavalry. ("Causée principalement par les chevaucheurs amutinez." said Nicolas Dubois, deputy of Tournay, to his constituents in a letter from Brussels of 4th July. MS. Archives of Belgium.) Consolation was also sought in the ridiculous assumption that the loss of the States' army was greater than that of the archduke's forces.

Christendom, all flying at last before his troops—the stad-holder was fairly melted. Dismounting from his horse, he threw himself on his knees in the sand, and with streaming eyes and uplifted hands exclaimed, " O God, what are we human creatures to whom Thou hast brought such honour, and to whom Thou hast vouchsafed such a victory ! " [25]

The slaughter went on until nightfall, but the wearied conquerors were then obliged to desist from the pursuit. Three thousand Spaniards were slain and about six hundred prisoners were taken.[26] The loss of the States' army, includ-ing the affair in the morning at Leffingen, was about two thousand killed. Maurice was censured for not following up his victory more closely, but the criticism seems unjust. The night which followed the warm summer's day was singularly black and cloudy, the army was exhausted, the distance for the enemy to traverse before they found themselves safe within their own territory was not great. In such circum-stances the stadholder might well deem himself sufficiently triumphant to have plucked a splendid victory out of the very jaws of death. All the artillery of the archduke—seven pieces besides the two captured from Ernest in the morning —one hundred and twenty standards, and a long list of distinguished prisoners, including the Admiral Zapena and many other officers of note, were the trophies of the con-queror. Maurice passed the night on the battle-field ; the admiral supping with him in his tent. Next morning he went to Ostend, where a great thanksgiving was held, Uyten-bogart preaching an eloquent sermon on the 116th Psalm. Afterwards there was a dinner at the house of the States-General, in honour of the stadholder, to which the Admiral of Arragon was likewise bidden. That arrogant but discom-

---

[25] " O Godt, wie zijn wy menschen dien ghy sulcken eere ghedaen ende Over-winninghe ghegheven hebt."—Letter of Uytenbogaert, in P. Fleming, Belegeringe van Oostende. S' Graven-hage, 1621.

[26] Count Ernest puts the loss of the archduke at 4000 killed on the battle-field and 1000 on the retreat. Maurice estimates his enemy's loss at more than 5000. Groen v. Prinsterer, Ar-chives II. s. ii. 15, 18, 19. Duyck says 3000 were killed on the field—as ascertained by counting — besides those who were drowned and slain in the retreat. The archduke's confes-sor says that 1000 *Spaniards* were killed. (MS. letter before cited.)

fited personage was obliged to listen to many a rough martial joke at his disaster as they sat at table, but he bore the brunt of the encounter with much fortitude.

" Monsieur the Admiral of Arragon," said the stadholder in French, " is more fortunate than many of his army. He has been desiring these four years to see Holland. Now he will make his entrance there without striking a blow."[27] The gibe was perhaps deficient in delicacy towards a fallen foe, but a man who had passed a whole winter in murdering his prisoners in cold blood might be satisfied if he were stung only by a sharp sarcasm or two, when he had himself become a captive.

Others asked him demurely what he thought of these awkward apprentices of Holland and Zeeland, who were good enough at fighting behind dykes and ramparts of cities, but who never ventured to face a Spanish army in the open field. Mendoza sustained himself with equanimity however, and found plenty of answers. He discussed the battle with coolness, blamed the archduke for throwing the whole of his force prematurely into the contest, and applauded the prudence of Maurice in keeping his reserves in hand. He ascribed a great share of the result to the States' artillery, which had been well placed upon wooden platforms and well served, while the archduke's cannon, sinking in the sands, had been of comparatively little use. Especially he expressed a warm admiration for the heroism of Maurice in sending away his ships, and in thus leaving himself and his soldiers no alternative but death or triumph.

While they still sat at table many of the standards taken from the enemy were brought in and exhibited ; the stadholder and others amusing themselves with reading the inscriptions and devices emblazoned upon them.

And thus on the 2nd July, 1600, the army of the States-General, led by Maurice of Nassau, had utterly defeated

---

[27] "Monsieur l'Admirante d'Arragon a este plus heureux que pas un de son armee, car il a fort desiré plus de quatre années continuellement de voir la Hollande, maintenant il y entrera sans coup ferir."—Letter of Uytenbogart, who sat at the table and heard Maurice make the remark.

Albert of Austria.[28] Strange to say—on another 2nd July, three centuries and two years before, a former Albert of Austria had overthrown the emperor Adolphus of Nassau, who had then lost both crown and life in the memorable battle of Worms. The imperial shade of Maurice's ancestor had been signally appeased.

In Ostend, as may well be imagined, ineffable joy had succeeded to the horrible gloom in which the day had been passed, ever since the tidings had been received of Ernest's overthrow.

Those very cavalry men, who had remained all day cowering behind the walls of the city, seeing by the clouds of dust which marked the track of the fugitives that the battle had been won by the comrades whom they had so basely deserted in the morning, had been eager enough to join in the pursuit. It was with difficulty that the States, who had been unable to drive them out of the town while the fight was impending or going on, could keep enough of them within the walls to guard the city against possible accident, now that the work was done. Even had they taken the field a few hours earlier, without participating in the action, or risking their own lives, they might have secured the pass of Leffingen, and made the capture of the archduke or his destruction inevitable.

The city, which had seemed deserted, swarmed with the garrison and with the lately trembling burghers, for it seemed to all as if they had been born again. Even the soldiers on the battle-field had embraced each other like comrades who had met in another world. "Blessed be His holy name," said the stadholder's chaplain, "for His right hand has led us into hell and brought us forth again. I know not," he continued, "if I am awake or if I dream, when I think how God has in one moment raised us from the dead." [29]

---

[28] "Enfin l'affaire vint aulx mains et fut combattu bien furieusement de deux costés l'espace de deux heures. Enfin Dieu par sa grace voulut que la victoire demeura de mon costé." Such were the simple words in which Maurice announced to his cousin Lewis William his victory in the most important battle that had been fought for half a century. Not even General Ulysses Grant could be more modest in the hour of immense triumph.

[29] Letter of Uytenbogart.

Lewis Gunther, whose services had been so conspicuous, was well rewarded. "I hope," said that general, writing to his brother Lewis William, "that this day's work will not have been useless to me, both for what I have learned in it and for another thing. His Excellency has done me the honour to give me the admiral for my prisoner."[30] And equally characteristic was the reply of the religious and thrifty stadholder of Friesland.

"I thank God," he said, "for His singular grace in that He has been pleased to make use of your person as the instrument of so renowned and signal a victory, for which, as you have derived therefrom not mediocre praise, and acquired a great reputation, it should be now your duty to humble yourself before God, and to acknowledge that it is He alone who has thus honoured you . . . . You should reverence Him the more, that while others are admonished of their duty by misfortunes and miseries, the good God invites you to His love by benefits and honours . . . . . I am very glad, too, that his Excellency has given you the admiral for your prisoner, both because of the benefit to you, and because it is a mark of your merit on that day. Knowing the state of our affairs, you will now be able to free your patrimony from encumbrances, when otherwise you would have been in danger of remaining embarrassed and in the power of others. It will therefore be a perpetual honour to you that you, the youngest of us all, have been able by your merits to do more to raise up our house out of its difficulties than your predecessors or myself have been able to do."[31]

The beautiful white horse which the archduke had ridden during the battle fell into the hands of Lewis Gunther, and was presented by him to Prince Maurice, who had expressed great admiration of the charger. It was a Spanish horse, for which the archduke had lately paid eleven hundred crowns.[32]

[30] Lewis Gunther to Lewis William, 20 July, 1600. (Groen v. Prinsterer Archives, II. 23.)
[31] Lewis William to Lewis Gunther, July 1600. Ibid. 42, 43.
[32] Letters last cited.

A white hackney of the Infanta had also been taken, and became the property of Count Ernest.[33]

The news of the great battle spread with unexampled rapidity, not only through the Netherlands but to neighbouring countries. On the night of the 7th July (N.S.) five days after the event, Envoy Caron, in England, received intimations of the favourable news from the French ambassador, who had received a letter from the Governor of Calais. Next morning, very early, he waited on Sir Robert Cecil at Greenwich, and was admitted to his chamber, although the secretary was not yet out of bed. He, too, had heard of the battle, but Richardot had informed the English ambassador in Paris that the victory had been gained, not by the stadholder, but by the archduke. While they were talking, a despatch-bearer arrived with letters from Vere to Cecil, and from the States-General to Caron, dated on the 3rd July. There could no longer be any doubt on the subject, and the envoy of the republic had now full details of the glorious triumph which the Spanish agent in Paris had endeavoured for a time to distort into a defeat.

While the two were conversing, the queen, who had heard of Caron's presence in the palace, sent down for the latest intelligence. Cecil made notes of the most important points in the despatches to be forthwith conveyed to her Majesty. The queen, not satisfied however, sent for Caron himself. That diplomatist, who had just ridden down from London in foul weather, was accordingly obliged to present himself— booted and spurred and splashed with mud from head to foot —before her Majesty.[34] Elizabeth received him with such extraordinary manifestations of delight at the tidings that he was absolutely amazed, and she insisted upon his reading the whole of the letter just received from Olden-Barneveld, her Majesty listening very patiently as he translated it out of Dutch into French. She then expressed unbounded admira-

[33] Letters last cited.
[34] " Hoewel ick daertoe niet gereet was, want ick daer te peerde was gekomen gants vuil en beslyckt door 't quade weder," &c. &c.—Caron to the States-General, in Deventer, ii. 290–293.

tion of the States-General and of Prince Maurice. " The sagacious administration of the States' government is so full of good order and policy," she said, " as to far surpass in its wisdom the intelligence of all kings and potentates." " We kings," she said, " understand nothing of such affairs in comparison, but require, all of us, to go to school to the States-General." She continued to speak in terms of warm approbation of the secrecy and discretion with which the invasion of Flanders had been conducted, and protested that she thanked God on both knees for vouchsafing such a splendid victory to the United Provinces.[35]

Yet after all, her Majesty, as mankind in general, both wise and simple, are apt to do, had judged only according to the result, and the immediate result. No doubt John of Barneveld was second to no living statesman in breadth of view and adroitness of handling, yet the invasion of Flanders, which was purely his work, was unquestionably a grave mistake, and might easily have proved a fatal one. That the deadly peril was escaped was due, not to his prudence, but to the heroism of Maurice, the gallantry of Vere, Count Lewis Gunther, and the forces under them, and the noble self-devotion of Ernest. And even, despite the exertions of these brave men, it seems certain that victory would have been impossible had the archduke possessed that true appreciation of a situation which marks the consummate general.

[35] Caron to States-General, in Deventer, ii. 290–293.

The French king, too, was much pleased with the result of the battle. So soon as he received the news he sent for the States' envoy, and amused himself by reading him only the earlier despatches, which related the success of the archduke at the forts and at Leffingen. Having sufficiently teased him, he then showed him the whole account. The satisfaction manifested by Henry naturally much scandalized the high Catholic party, with whom the king was most desirous of being on good terms.—Aerssens to States-General, 13 July, 1600. (Archives of the Hague MS.)

And in his confidential letters to

Valck the envoy expressed himself in similar terms, saying that his own despatches having accidentally been delayed, the king almost gave him a fever by concealing the good news, and telling him of the reverses sustained by the States' troops at the beginning of the day, and adding that his Majesty, although making a great effort, had found it very difficult to dissemble his delight, " car tous ne prennent cette victoire de meme biais, aucuns l'estimant prejudiciable, en tant qu'elle peut ayder a fonder solidement la religion, les autres s'en rejouyssent comme d'un eschecq et affoiblissement a l'Espagne," &c.— MS. before cited, 20 July, 1600.

Surely the Lord seemed to have delivered the enemy into his hands that morning. Maurice was shut in between Nieuport on one side and the archduke's army on the other, planted as it was on the only road of retreat. Had Albert entrenched himself, Maurice must either have attacked at great disadvantage or attempted embarkation in the face of his enemy. To stay indefinitely where he was would have proved an impossibility, and amid the confusion necessary to the shipping of his army, how could he have protected himself by six demi-cannon placed on the sea-beach ?

That Maurice was able to extricate himself from the horrible dilemma in which he had been placed, through no fault of his own, and to convert imminent disaster into magnificent victory, will always redound to his reputation as a great military chief. And this was all the fruit of the expedition, planned, as Elizabeth thought, with so much secrecy and discretion. Three days after the battle the stadholder came again before Nieuport, only to find the garrison strengthened meantime by La Bourlotte to three thousand men. A rainy week succeeded, and Maurice then announced to the States-General the necessity of abandoning an enterprise, a successful issue to which was in his opinion impossible. The States-General, grown more modest in military matters, testified their willingness to be governed by his better judgment, and left Ostend for the Hague on the 18th July. Maurice, after a little skirmishing with some of the forts around that city, in one of which the archduke's general La Bourlotte was killed, decided to close the campaign, and he returned with his whole army on the last day of July into Holland.[36]

[35] The chief authorities used by me for the campaign of Nieuport are the following:—Bentivoglio, P. III. lib. vi. pp. 496–504; Carnero, lib. xiv. cap. vii. 472–481; Meteren, 437–442; Reyd, B. xvii. 427–433; Bor, IV. 603–700; De la Pise, 681–687; Sir Francis Vere, La Bataille de Nieupoort apud Bor, Byvoegsels van Authent. Stukken, iv.; Wagenaar, ix. 76–88; Van Wyn op Wagen, ix. 37–47; Grotius, Histor. ix. 552–573; Van der Kemp, ii. 62–82 and 251–286; Philippe Fleming; Belegeringe van Oostende ('s Gravenhage, 1621), pp. 27–52; Henry Haestens, La Nouvelle Troie, ou Memorable Histoire du Siege d'Ostende. Leyden, Elzevir, 1615, pp. 1–69; Groen v. Prinsterer, Archives, &c. II. 14–43 (2nd series); MS. Letters of States-General, of Queen Elizabeth, and of Envoy Noel de Caron, in the Royal Archives of the Hague; De Thou, t. xiii. lib. 124, pp. 467–481; Le Petit,

The expedition was an absolute failure, but the stadholder had gained a great victory. The effect produced at home and abroad by this triumphant measuring of the republican forces, horse, foot, and artillery, in a pitched battle and on so conspicuous an arena, with the picked veterans of Spain and Italy, was perhaps worth the cost, but no other benefit was derived from the invasion of Flanders.

The most healthy moral to be drawn from this brief but memorable campaign is that the wisest statesmen are prone to blunder in affairs of war, success in which seems to require a special education and a distinct genius. Alternation between hope and despair, between culpable audacity and exaggerated prudence, are but too apt to mark the warlike counsels of politicians who have not been bred soldiers. This, at least, had been eminently the case with Barneveld and his colleagues of the States-General.

'Grande Chronique,' vol. ii. pp. 762–766 ; Camden's 'Elizabeth,' 590–593 ; MS. Letters of Buzanval to Villeroy in the Royal Library of the Hague, especially 4 July, 20 July, 5 August, 17 August, 1600 ; Antony Duyck, Journaal, ii. 661–681.

No one censured more sharply the policy of the expedition, nor reduced its results more pitilessly, than did the French envoy : " Croyez que ces Messrs.," said he, " avoient bien joué leur etat a un coup de dé et que le P. Maurice avoit fait paroistre sa prudence avant de partir de ce lieu en remonstrant aux Etats les accidents de cette entreprise et sa suite infailli- ble et forcée d'une bataille. Il a bien montré sa resolution quand il a fallu boire la lie de ces indigestes conseils." And again : — " La suite de cette bataille a été plus desavantageuse aux victorieux qu'aux vaincus qui se sont relevez avec plus de vigueur que les autres n'ont poursuivi leur pointe." And once more :—" C'est un eclair qui a passé qui a plus donné de lustre aux vainqueurs que fait du mal aux vain- cus. On diroit qu'elle auroit tout epuisé la vertu et vigueur de l'un et fait surgir la force de l'autre. Mais à la verité les fondemens de cette entre- prise de Flandres etoient si mal jettés comme vous avez peu voir par celles que je vous ai escrits lorsqu'elle fait resolue qu'il se faut peu estonner si ils ont eu si peu d'issue et de suite. . . . . car on fait ici beaucoup plus de plaintes du peu de suite de cette victoire qu'il ne m'en escrit de Brux- elles," &c. &c. As to the numbers engaged in the battle, Duyck puts the archduke's force at 10,000 foot and 1600 horse, including the detachment of 2000 or 3000 under Velasco, which was not in the action. More than a third of those engaged were killed. Maurice had at first 198 companies of foot and 25 companies of horse, but, with deduction of the detachments to strengthen the forts, his force was not more than 10,000 foot and 1200 horse (including the troops of Ernest destroyed before nine o'clock).

NOTE ON VERE.

I HAVE endeavoured in the account of this campaign to reconcile discrepancies where it was possible to reconcile them. I have studied carefully the narratives given by the most prominent actors in the battle; but, in regard to Sir Francis Vere, I am bound to say that, after much consideration, I have rejected his statements wherever they conflict with those of Maurice, Lewis Gunther, and Ernest of Nassau.

The mutual contradictions are often so direct as to make it impossible for both parties to be partly right and partly incorrect, and, as all were prominently engaged in the transactions, and all men of courage and distinction, it is absolutely necessary at times to decide between them.

The narrative of Vere was a publication; a party pamphlet in an age of pamphleteering. It is marked throughout by spleen, inordinate personal and national self-esteem, undisguised hostility to the Nassaus and the Hollanders, and wounded pride of opinion. It shows occasional looseness or recklessness of assertion which would have been almost impossible, had Maurice or his cousins been likely to engage in a controversy concerning the Nieuport expedition.

It is not agreeable to come to this conclusion in regard to a man of unquestionable talent, high character, and experience, who fought on that memorable day with splendid valour. I shall therefore give a few extracts from his narrative, and place them here and there in juxtaposition with passages from the correspondence of the Nassaus, in order to justify my opinion.

It must be borne in mind that these latter documents have remained in the family archives of Orange-Nassau for two centuries and a half, never having seen the light till they were edited by the learned and accomplished Groen van Prinsterer. The controversy with Vere is therefore an all unconscious one on the part of those buried warriors, but the examination of such samples of conflicting testimony may give the general reader a conception of the difficulty besetting the path of modern historians wishing to be conscientious and disinterested.

Sir Francis says, *without giving any dates*, that the army reached and crossed the haven of Nieuport on a certain morning, that they encamped and occupied *two or three days* in arranging their quarters, and in entrenching themselves in the most advantageous places for their own safety, and for the siege of the city; *making a bridge of stone* at the narrowest part of the harbour, to enable their troops and trains to cross and recross whenever necessary.

Now if there be two dates perfectly established in history by the concurrent testimony of despatches, resolutions of Assembly, contemporary chronicles,—Dutch, Spanish, Italian, or French,—and private letters of the chief personages engaged in the transactions, it is that Maurice's army came before Nieuport on the morning of the 1st July, crossing the harbour in the course of the same day, and that the battle was fought on the 2nd July.[1]

---

[1] "Je partoy droit devers Nieuport et m'y campoys le *premier de ce mois de juillet* et devant bien estre encores campé je fus adverti la même nuit que l'ennemi s'estoit anproché d'Ostende," &c. &c., says Maurice of Nassau. Letter to Count Lewis William, written 2nd July, evening after the battle. Groen van Prinsterer. Archives, II. 16, 17. Compare Bor, Meteren, Fleming.

What could Vere mean then by talking of two or three days in the trenches and of a stone bridge?   Yet these are his words :—" Le matin de bonne heure nous marchames vers Nieuport et a la basse marée traversames la riviere du coste ou elle faist le Havre de la ville, et ainsy nous campasmes mettans deux ou trois jours à faire les quartiers, et à nous retrancher ès lieux les plus advantageux pour notre seureté, et le siege de ville, *faisans un pont de pierre* au plus estroict du Havre pour y faire passer et repasser en tout temps nostre chariage et nos troupes, quand besoin en seroit."

On the intelligence received in the night of the arrival of the enemy at Oudenburg, Vere advised instantly crossing the harbour and marching against him with the whole army.   Maurice decided, however, to send the detachment under Ernest, to the great dissatisfaction of Sir Francis.

Vere then states that the army was ordered to *cross the haven at dawn of day, at the first low tide.*

" Le reste de l'armee fut commandé de marcher vers la riviere afin de la passer à l'aube du jour à la premiere basse marée."

Now it is certain that on the 2nd of July it was exactly *high tide* at 3 A.M., or *about dawn of day.*

Count Lewis Gunther states expressly in his letter, often cited, that he was first to cross with the cavalry, when the tide was out, at about 8 A.M.   It is also manifest by every account given of the battle, that it was high tide again at or after 3 P.M., which compelled the transferring of the fight from the submerged beach to the downs and to the pastures beyond.

In these statements Vere is so manifestly contradicted, not only by the accounts given by all contemporaries and eye-witnesses, but by other passages in his own narrative, that one has in general a right to prefer the assertions of other actors in the battle to his, if there is no other way of arriving at a clear understanding of the affair.

Thus he says that at the beginning of the action he wished the advanced cavalry under Lewis Gunther to approach the enemy, and that " the young lord " refused.   The account of the young lord is the exact reverse of these assertions.   I shall here give in juxtaposition the text of Vere and of the private letter of Lewis, observing that this letter—not written for publication, and never published, so far as I know, till two hundred and fifty years after it was written for the private information of the writer's brother—gives by far the most intelligible and succinct account of the battle to be met with anywhere.

LEWIS GUNTHER.	VERE.
" J'en avoy envoié advertir son Ex^{ce} que je m'estoy mis là en ordre et que je n'en bouger oy sans son expres commandement, le supliant de haster le passage de l'infanterie . . . . Monsieur Veer vint aussitot me trouver et jugeoit que je m'estois trop avancé, trouvant necessaire qu'on se resteroit	" Le ennemy approchant de plus en plus, et la cavaillerie sortant a la teste de leurs troupes en une distance competente pour pouvoir estre attiree au combat, j'avoy grand envie de voir la cavaillerie de l'avantguarde approcher d'elle et avec quelques gens d'eslite et bien montes battre leurs carbins et

---

Haestens, De Thou, Bentivoglio, original documents in Van der Kemp, vol. ii.   Archives de la Maison d'Orange-Nassau, *passim, et mult. al.* " Et le | tems ne voulant permettre que le pont qui estoit commencé à faire outre le dit havre s'ascheva," &c.   Letter of Lewis Gunther to Lewis William.

LEWIS GUNTHER.

plus pres de l'infanterie dont l'avant-garde estoit presques passee. Je craignois fort que ceste retraicte ne nous eust causé de confusion, l'ennemy nous estant si proche, et qu'elle eut refroidi le courage de nos soldats. Ce que me fit le prier qu'il avançast plustot l'infanterie jusques derriere ma troupe : ce que pourroit apporter de confort aux nostres et de l'etonnement a l'ennemy duquel l'infanterie n'estoit encor arrivé ny mise en ordre. Je demeuray encor a la mesme place une heure, y aiant esté desja bien davantage jusques á ce que son Ex^{ce}. y vint en personne. Il fut conclu que je me retirerois et me planterois à l'aisle gauche des Anglois .... Il fust résolu alors que j'envoieroy deux companies seulement bien pres d'eux pour leur faire prendre l'envie de se resoudre a les venir charger et que les notres s'enfuians derriere ma troupe donnassent occasion aux ennemis de les poursuivre la furie desquels nostre cannon appaisant un peu et nos musquetiers qui estoient bien avancés dans les dunes, à demy en embuscade, les frottant de coste, et aprés nostre cavallerie les chargeant en face, indubitablement nous eut des lors este ouvert le chemin de la victoire, car on les eut facilement renversez dans leur infanterie, la confusion de laquelle n'eut sçeu estre que bien grande : mais la haste de nos canoniers nous fit perdre les effects de cette belle resolution, a cause que la voiant si belle donnerent feu devant qu'on y eut envoié ces compagnise et avec la premiere volée les mit-on en desordre qu'ils quittarent le strang et se cacharent aux dunes pour n'estre offensez du canon."

Thus Lewis says most distinctly that he approved of the "beautiful resolution" as he calls it, which he rejected, according to Vere, from jealousy, and that the cause why it was not carried out was the premature cannonade, which Vere says that he himself ordered!

VERE.

escarmoucheurs jusques à dessus leur gros, en intention que s'ils eussent este recharges de retirer en haste avec la dite avantguarde de chevaulx entre la mer et l'avantgarde d'infanterie, et apres les avoir tirez arriere de leur infanterie soubs la mercy de nostre canon, avoir engagé le reste de nos chevaux a charger et suivre resolument. *Mais le jeusne seigneur ne peut trouver bon cest advis n'ayant pas eu agreable le pouvoir que le comte Maurice m'avoit donné par dessus sa charge et partant ne l'executa pas choississant plustot comme l'ennemy advancoit tout bellement reculer de mesme vers l'infanterie.* Ce mien conseil ne parvenant a autre meilleur effect et desja la cavaillerie estant venue soubs la portee de nostre canon, *je proposai qu'il le falloit descharger,* qui fut trouvé bon et si bien effectué qu'il faisoit escarter leurs troupes et fuir en desordre pour se sauver dedans les dunes, chose qui sans doute, nous eust donné la victoire si notre cavaillerie eust ete preste et volontaire a se prevaloir de l'occasion offerte."

These extracts will be sufficient to show the impossibility of making both accounts agree in regard to many momentous points.

When did two accounts of the same battle ever resemble each other? It must be confessed that modesty was not a leading characteristic of Sir Francis Vere. According to the whole tenor of his narrative he was himself not only a great part, but the whole of the events he describes; the victory of Nieuport was entirely due to his arrangements, and to the personal valour of himself and of the 1600 English soldiers; Prince Maurice filling hardly a subordinate part in superintendence of the battle, Count Lewis Gunther being dismissed with a single sneer, and no other name but Vere's own and that of his brother Horace being even mentioned. He admits that he did not participate in the final and conclusive charge, being then disabled, but observes that having satisfied himself that his directions would be carried out, and that nothing else was left but to pursue the enemy, he thought it time to have his wounds dressed.

"There was no loss worth speaking of," he says, "except that of the English, 600 of whom were killed. I should not venture to attribute," he observes, "the whole honour of the victory to the poor English troop of 1600 men, but I leave the judgment thereof to those who can decide with less suspicion of partiality. I will merely affirm that the English left nothing to do for the rest of the army but to follow the chase, and that one has never before heard that with so small a number in an indifferent position, where the only advantage was the choice and the good use which could be made of it, without the use of spade or other instrument of fortification, an army so large and so victorious as that of the archduke could have been resisted in such a continued struggle and so thoroughly defeated."

Certainly the defeat of an army of 10,000 veterans in the open field by 1600 men is a phenomenon rarely witnessed, and one must be forgiven for not accepting as gospel truth the account of the leader of the 1600, when it is directly contradicted by every other statement on record.

In Vere's advanced guard—nearly half the whole army—there were 2600 Englishmen and 2800 Frisians, besides several squadrons of cavalry, according to his own statement in another part of his narrative.

How, therefore, the whole battle should have been fought by a mere portion of the English contingent it is difficult to comprehend.

Vere makes no allusion to the combat of Leffingen, which was an essential part of the battle; to the heroic self-sacrifice of Ernest and his division, by which alone the rest of the army were enabled to gain the victory; nor has he a word for the repeated charges of cavalry by which the infantry fight was protected.

Lewis Gunther on the contrary, whose account is as modest as it is clear, gives full credit to the splendid achievements of the infantry under Vere, but in describing the cavalry combats, he mentions the loss in the six cavalry companies under his immediate command as 171 killed and wounded, while Ernest's loss has never been placed at less than 1000.

CHAPTER XXXIX.

Effects of the Nieuport campaign — The general and the statesman — The Roman empire and the Turk — Disgraceful proceedings of the mutinous soldiers in Hungary — The Dunkirk pirates — Siege of Ostend by the Archduke — Attack on Rheinberg by Prince Maurice — Siege and capitulation of Meurs — Attempt on Bois-le-Duc — Concentration of the war at Ostend — Account of the belligerents — Details of the siege — Feigned offer of Sir Francis Vere to capitulate — Arrival of reinforcements from the States — Attack and overthrow of the besiegers.

THE Nieuport campaign had exhausted for the time both belligerents. The victor had saved the republic from impending annihilation, but was incapable of further efforts during the summer. The conquered cardinal-archduke, remaining essentially in the same position as before, consoled himself with the agreeable fiction that the States, notwithstanding their triumph, had in reality suffered the most in the great battle. Meantime both parties did their best to repair damages and to recruit their armies.

The States—or in other words Barneveld, who was the States—had learned a lesson. Time was to show whether it would be a profitable one, or whether Maurice, who was the preceptor of Europe in the art of war, would continue to be a docile pupil of the great Advocate even in military affairs. It is probable that the alienation between the statesman and the general, which was to widen as time advanced, may be dated from the day of Nieuport.

Fables have even been told which indicated the popular belief in an intensity of resentment on the part of the prince, which certainly did not exist till long afterwards.

"Ah, scoundrel!" the stadholder was said to have exclaimed, giving the Advocate a box on the ear as he came to wish him joy of his great victory, "you sold us, but God prevented your making the transfer." [1]

History would disdain even an allusion to such figments— quite as disgraceful, certainly to Maurice as to Barneveld— did they not point the moral and foreshadow some of the vast but distant results of events which had already taken place, and had they not been so generally repeated that it is a duty for the lover of truth to put his foot upon the calumny, even at the risk for a passing moment of reviving it.

The condition of the war in Flanders had established a temporary equilibrium among the western powers—France and England discussing, intriguing, and combining in secret with each other, against each other, and in spite of each other, in regard to the great conflict—while Spain and the cardinal-archduke on the one side, and the republic on the other, prepared themselves for another encounter in the blood-stained arena.

Meantime, on the opposite verge of what was called European civilization, the perpetual war between the Roman Empire and the Grand Turk had for the moment been brought into a nearly similar equation. Notwithstanding the vast amount of gunpowder exploded during so many wearisome years, the problem of the Crescent and the Cross was not much nearer a solution in the East than was that of mass and conventicle in the West. War was the normal and natural condition of mankind. This fact, at least, seemed to have been acquired and added to the mass of human knowledge.

From the prolific womb of Germany came forth, to swell impartially the Protestant and Catholic hosts, vast swarms of human creatures. Sold by their masters at as high prices as could be agreed upon beforehand, and receiving for themselves five stivers a day, irregularly paid, until the carrion-crow rendered them the last service, they found at times more demand for their labor in the great European market

---

[1] See Van der Kemp, ii. 88 and 298, 299. The learned historian of course denounces the tale as a falsehood.

than they could fully supply. There were not Germans enough every year for the consumption of the Turk, and the pope, and the emperor, and the republic, and the Catholic king, and the Christian king, with both ends of Europe ablaze at once. So it happened that the Duke of Mercœur and other heroes of the League, having effected their reconciliation with the Béarnese, and for a handsome price paid down on the nail having acknowledged him to be their legitimate and Catholic sovereign, now turned their temporary attention to the Turk. The sweepings of the League—Frenchmen, Walloons, Germans, Italians, Spaniards—were tossed into Hungary, because for a season the war had become languid in Flanders. And the warriors grown grey in the religious wars of France astonished the pagans on the Danube by a variety of crimes and cruelties such as Christians only could imagine. Thus, while the forces of the Sultan were besieging Buda, a detachment of these ancient Leaguers lay in Pappa, a fortified town not far from Raab, which Archduke Maximilian had taken by storm two years before. Finding their existence monotonous and payments unpunctual, they rose upon the governor, Michael Maroti, and then entered into a treaty with the Turkish commander outside the walls. Bringing all the principal citizens of the town, their wives and children, and all their moveable property into the market-place, they offered to sell the lot, including the governor, for a hundred thousand rix dollars. The bargain was struck, and the Turk, paying him all his cash on hand and giving hostages for the remainder, carried off six hundred of the men and women, promising soon to return and complete the transaction.[2] Meantime the imperial general, Schwartzenberg, came before the place, urging the mutineers with promises of speedy payment, and with appeals to their sense of shame, to abstain from the disgraceful work. He might as well have preached to the wild swine swarming in the adjacent forests. Siege thereupon was laid to the place. In a sortie the brave Schwartzenberg was killed, but Colonitz coming up in force

2 Meteren, fol. 447.

the mutineers were locked up in the town which they had seized, and the Turk never came to their relief. Famine drove them at last to choose between surrender and a desperate attempt to cut their way out. They took the bolder course, and were all either killed or captured. And now—the mutineers having given the Turk this lesson in Christian honour towards captives—their comrades and the rest of the imperial forces showed them the latest and most approved Christian method of treating mutineers. Several hundred of the prisoners were distributed among the different nationalities composing the army to be dealt with at pleasure. The honest Germans were the most straightforward of all towards their portion of the prisoners, for they shot them down at once, without an instant's hesitation. But the Lorrainers, the remainder of the French troops, the Walloons, and especially the Hungarians—whose countrymen and women had been sold into captivity—all vied with each other in the invention of cruelties at which the soul sickens, and which the pen almost refuses to depict.[2]

These operations and diversions had no sensible effect upon the progress of the war, which crept on with the same monotonous and sluggish cruelty as ever ; but the incidents narrated paint the course of civilization more vividly than the detailed accounts of siege and battle, mining and counter-mining, assaults and ambuscades can do, of which the history books are full. The leaguers of Buda and of other cities and fortresses in Hungary went their course, and it was destined to remain for a still longer season doubtful whether Cross or Crescent should ultimately wave over the whole territory of Eastern Europe, and whether the vigorous Moslem, believing in himself, his mission, his discipline, and his resources, should ultimately absorb what was left of the ancient Roman Empire.

Meantime, such of the Walloons, Lorrainers, Germans, and Frenchmen as had grown wearied of the fighting on the Danube and the Theiss might have recourse for variety to

---

[3] Meteren, *ubi sup.*

the perpetual carnage on the Meuse, the Rhine, and the
Scheld. If there was not bloodshed enough for all, it was
surely not the fault of Mahomet, nor Clement, nor Philip.

During the remainder of the year not much was done in
the field by the forces of the stadholder or the cardinal,
but there was immense damage done to the Dutch shipping
by the famous privateersman, Van der Waecken, with his
squadron of twelve or fourteen armed cruisers. In vain had
the States exerted themselves to destroy that robber's cave,
Dunkirk. Shiploads of granite had been brought from Norway, and stone fleets had been sunk in the channel, but the
insatiable quicksands had swallowed them as fast as they
could be deposited, the tide rolled as freely as before, and
the bold pirates sailed forth as gaily as ever to prey upon
the defenceless trading vessels and herring-smacks of the
States. For it was only upon non-combatants that Admiral
Van der Waecken made war, and the fishermen especially,
who mainly belonged to the Memnonite religion, with its
doctrines of non-resistance[4]—not a very comfortable practice
in that sanguinary age—were his constant victims. And his
cruelties might have almost served as a model to the
Christian warriors on the Turkish frontier. After each vessel
had been rifled of everything worth possessing, and then
scuttled, the admiral would order the crews to be thrown
overboard at once, or, if he chanced to be in a merry mood,
would cause them to be fastened to the cabin floor, or nailed
crosswise to the deck, and would then sail away, leaving ship
and sailors to sink at leisure.[5] The States gave chase as well
as they could to the miscreant—a Dutchman born, and with
a crew mainly composed of renegade Netherlanders and other
outcasts, preying for base lucre on their defenceless countrymen—and their cruisers were occasionally fortunate enough
to capture and bring in one of the pirate ships. In such
cases, short shrift was granted, and the buccaneers were

---

[4] " Ergo imbelle hominum genus et
est plerisque piscatorum ea religio
quae nefas ducit vim armis propellere,"
&c. &c.—Grotii Hist. ix. 575. Compare Meteren, fol. 445.
[5] Meteren, Grotius, *ubi sup.*

hanged without mercy, thirty-eight having been executed in one morning at Rotterdam. The admiral with most of his vessels escaped, however, to the coast of Spain, where his crews during the autumn mainly contrived to desert, and where he himself died in the winter, whether from malady, remorse, or disappointment at not being rewarded by a high position in the Spanish navy, has not been satisfactorily decided.[6]

The war was in its old age. The leaf of a new century had been turned, and men in middle life had never known what the word Peace meant. Perhaps they could hardly imagine such a condition. This is easily said, but it is difficult really to picture to ourselves the moral constitution of a race of mankind which had been born and had grown up, marrying and giving in marriage, dying and burying their dead, and so passing on from the cradle towards the grave, accepting the eternal clang of arms, and the constant participation by themselves and those nearest to them in the dangers, privations, and horrors of siege and battle-field as the commonplaces of life. At least, those Netherlanders knew what fighting for independence of a foreign tyrant meant. They must have hated Spain very thoroughly, and believed in the right of man to worship God according to the dictates of his conscience, and to govern himself upon his own soil, however meagre, very earnestly, or they would hardly have spent their blood and treasure, year after year, with such mercantile regularity when it was always in their power to make peace by giving up the object for which they had been fighting.

Yet the war, although in its old age, was not fallen into decrepitude. The most considerable and most sanguinary pitched battle of what then were modern times had just been fought, and the combatants were preparing themselves for a fresh wrestle, as if the conflict had only begun. And now— although the great leaguers of Harlem, Leyden, and Antwerp, as well as the more recent masterpieces of Prince Maurice in Gelderland and Friesland were still fresh in men's memory— there was to be a siege, which for endurance, pertinacity,

---

[6] "Interiit morbo an quia Hispanis fastiditus," says Grotius, *ubi sup.*

valour, and bloodshed on both sides, had not yet been fore-shadowed, far less equalled, upon the fatal Netherland soil.

That place of fashionable resort, where the fine folk of Europe now bathe, and flirt, and prattle politics or scandal so cheerfully during the summer solstice—cool and comfortable Ostend—was throughout the sixteenth century as obscure a fishing village as could be found in Christendom. Nothing had ever happened there, nobody had ever lived there, and it was not until a much later period that the famous oyster, now identified with its name, had been brought to its bay to be educated. It was known for nothing except for claiming to have invented the pickling of herrings, which was not at all the fact.[7] Towards the latter part of the century, however, the poor little open village had been fortified to such purpose as to enable it to beat off the great Alexander Farnese, when he had made an impromptu effort to seize it in the year 1583, after his successful enterprise against Dunkirk and Nieuport, and subsequent preparation had fortunately been made against any further attempt. For in the opening period of the new century thousands and tens of thousands were to come to those yellow sands, not for a midsummer holiday, but to join hands in one of the most enduring struggles that history had yet recorded, and on which the attention of Europe was for a long time to be steadily fixed.

Ostend—East-end—was the only possession of the republic in Flanders. Having been at last thoroughly fortified ac-cording to the principles of the age, it was a place whence much damage was inflicted upon the enemy, and whence forays upon the obedient Flemings could very successfully be conducted. Being in the hands of so enterprising a naval power, it controlled the coast, while the cardinal-archduke on the other side fondly hoped that its possession would give him supremacy on the sea. The States of Flanders declared it to be a thorn in the Belgic lion's foot, and called urgently upon their soveregn to remove the annoyance.

[7] La Nouvelle Troie, ou Memorable Histoire du Siege d'Ostende, par Henry Haestens. Leyde, 1615, pp. 79, 80.

They offered Albert 300,000 florins a month so long as the
siege should last, besides an extraordinary sum of 300,000, of
which one third was to be paid when the place should be invested, one-third when the breach had been made, and one-third
after the town had been taken.[8] It was obvious that, although
they thought the extraction of the thorn might prove troublesome, the process would be accomplished within a reasonable
time. The cardinal-archduke, on his part, was as anxious as
the "members" of Flanders. Asking how long the Duke of
Parma had been in taking Antwerp, and being told " eighteen
months," he replied that, if necessary, he was willing to
employ eighteen years in reducing Ostend.[9]

The town thus about to assume so much importance in the
world's eye had about three thousand inhabitants within its
lowly, thatch-roofed houses. It fronted directly upon the sea-
coast and stretched backward in a southerly direction, having
the sandy downs on the right and left, and a swampy, spongy
soil on the inner verge, where it communicated with the land.
Its northern part, small and scarcely inhabited, was lashed
by the ocean, and exposed to perpetual danger from its storms
and flood-tides, but was partially protected from these encroachments by a dyke stretching along the coast on the west.
Here had hitherto been the harbour formed by the mouth of
the river Iperleda as it mingled with the sea, but this entrance
had become so choked with sand as to be almost useless at
low water. This circumstance would have rendered the
labours of the archduke comparatively easy, and much discouraged the States, had there not fortunately been a new
harbour which had formed itself on the eastern side exactly
at the period of threatened danger. The dwarf mountain
range of dunes which encircled the town on the eastern side
had been purposely levelled, lest the higher summits should
offer positions of vantage to a besieging foe. In consequence
of this operation, the sea had burst over the land and swept

[8] Haestens, 99. Philip Fleming.
Oostende. Vermaerde gheweldige,
lanckduyrighe ende Bloedighe Bele-
geringhe, etc. beschreven door Philippe Fleming. 's Gravenhage, 1621,
p. 62.
[9] Angeli Galluccii de Bello Belgico,
Romæ, 1671. Pars Altera, p. 184.

completely around the place, almost converting it into an island, while at high water there opened a wide and profound gulf which with the ebb left an excellent channel quite deep enough for even the ships of war of those days. The next care of the States authorities was to pierce their fortifications on this side at a convenient point, thus creating a safe and snug haven within the walls for the fleets of transports which were soon to arrive by open sea, laden with soldiers and munitions.

The whole place was about half an hour's walk in circumference. It was surrounded with a regular counterscarp, bastions, and casemates, while the proximity of the ocean and the humid nature of the soil ensured it a network of foss and canal on every side. On the left or western side, where the old harbour had once been, and which was the most vulnerable by nature, was a series of strong ravelins, the most conspicuous of which were called the Sand Hill, the Porcupine, and Hell's Mouth. Beyond these, towards the southwest, were some detached fortifications, resting for support, however, upon the place itself, called the Polder, the Square, and the South Square. On the east side, which was almost inaccessible, as it would seem, by such siege machinery as then existed, was a work called the Spanish half-moon, situate on the new harbour called the Guele or Gullet.

Towards the west and southwest, externally, upon the territory of Flanders—not an inch of which belonged to the republic, save the sea-beaten corner in which nestled the little town — eighteen fortresses had been constructed by the archduke as a protection against hostile incursions from the place. Of these, the most considerable were St. Albert, often mentioned during the Nieuport campaign, St. Isabella-St. Clara, and Great-Thirst.[10]

On the 5th July, 1601, the archduke came before the town, and formally began the siege. He established his 5 July, headquarters in the fort which bore the name of 1601.

---

[10] Fleming, Haestens, Guicciardini *in voce*. Bentivoglio, P. III. lib. vi. 505, 506. Meteren, 454, 455.

his patron saint. Frederic van den Berg meanwhile occupied fort Bredené on the eastern side, with the intention, if possible, of getting possession of the Gullet, or at least of rendering the entrance to that harbour impossible by means of his hostile demonstrations. Uuder Van den Berg was Count Bucquoy-Longueval, a Walloon officer of much energy and experience, now general-in-chief of artillery in the archduke's army.

The numbers with which Albert took the field at first have not been accurately stated, but it is probable that his object was to keep as many as twenty thousand constantly engaged in the siege, and that in this regard he was generally successful.

Within the town were fifty-nine companies of infantry, to which were soon added twenty-three more under command of young Chatillon, grandson of the great Coligny. It was "an *olla podrida* of nationalities," according to the diarist of the siege. English, Scotch, Dutch, Flemings, Frenchmen, Germans, mixed in about equal proportions.[11] Commander-in-chief at the outset was Sir Francis Vere, who established himself by the middle of July in the place, sent thither by order of the States-General. It had been the desire of that assembly that the stadholder should make another foray in Flanders for the purpose of driving off the archduke before he should have time to complete his preliminary operations. But for that year at least Maurice was resolved not to renounce his own schemes in deference to those so much more ignorant than himself of the art of war, even if Barneveld and his subordinates on their part had not learned a requisite lesson of modesty.

So the prince, instead of risking another Nieuport campaign, took the field with a small but well-appointed force, about ten thousand men in all, marched to the Rhine, and early in 10 June, June, laid siege to Rheinberg.[12] It was his purpose 1601. to leave the archduke for the time to break his

[11] Meteren, Bentivoglio, *ubi sup.* Fleming, 74, *seqq.*
[12] Meteren, 454. Grotius, x, 580-582. Van der Kemp, ii. 94, 95, and notes.

teeth against the walls of Ostend, while he would himself protect the eastern frontier, over which came regular reinforcements and supplies for the Catholic armies. His works were laid out with his customary precision and neatness. But, standing as usual, like a professor at his blackboard, demonstrating his proposition to the town, he was disturbed in his calculations by the abstraction from his little army of two thousand English troops ordered by the States-General to march to the defence of Ostend. The most mathematical but most obedient of princes, annoyed but not disconcerted, sent off the troops but continued his demonstration.

"By this specimen," cried the French envoy, with enthusiasm, "judge of the energy of this little commonwealth. They are besieging Berg with an army of twelve thousand men, a place beyond the frontier, and five days' march from the Hague. They are defending another important place, besieged by the principal forces of the archdukes, and there is good chance of success at both points. They are doing all this too with such a train of equipages of artillery, of munitions, of barks, of ships of war, that I hardly know of a monarch in the world who would not be troubled to furnish such a force of warlike machinery." [13]

By the middle of July he sprang a mine under the fortifications, doing much damage and sending into the air a considerable portion of the garrison. Two of the 11 July. soldiers were blown into his own camp, and one of them, strangely enough, was but slightly injured. Coming as he did through the air at cannon-ball speed, he was of course able to bring the freshest intelligence from the interior of the town His news as to the condition of the siege confirmed the theory of the stadholder. He persisted in his operations 30 July, for three weeks longer, and the place was then sur- 1601. rendered.[14] The same terms—moderate and honourable— were given to the garrison and the burghers as in all Maurice's victories. Those who liked to stay were at liberty to do so,

[13] Buzanval to Villeroy, 24 July, 1601, cited by Van Deventer, ii. 294.
[14] Meteren, Grotius, Van der Kemp, *ubi sup*.

accepting the prohibition of public worship according to the Roman ritual, but guaranteed against inquisition into household or conscience. The garrison went out with the honours of war, and thus the place, whose military value caused it to change hands almost as frequently as a counter in a game, was once more in possession of the republic. In the course of the following week Maurice laid siege to the city 6 August, 1601. of Meurs, a little farther up the Rhine, which immediately capitulated.[15] Thus the keys to the debatable land of Cleves and Juliers, the scene of the Admiral of Arragon's recent barbarities, were now held by the stadholder.

These achievements were followed by an unsuccessful attempt upon Bois-le-Duc in the course of November. The place would have fallen notwithstanding the slenderness of the besieging army had not a sudden and severe frost caused the prudent prince to raise the siege. Feeling that his cousin Frederic van den Berg, who had been despatched from before Ostend to command the relieving force near Bois-le-Duc, might take advantage of the prematurely frozen canals and rivers to make an incursion into Holland, he left his city just as his November, 1601. works had been sufficiently advanced to ensure possession of the prize, and hastened to protect the heart of the republic from possible danger.[16]

Nothing further was accomplished by Maurice that year, but meantime something had been doing within and around Ostend.

For now the siege of Ostend became the war, and was likely to continue to be the war for a long time to come; all other military operations being to a certain degree suspended, as if by general consent of both belligerants, or rendered subsidiary to the main design. So long as this little place should be beleaguered it was the purpose of the States, and of Maurice, acting in harmony with those authorities, to concentrate their resources so as to strengthen the grip with which the only scrap of Flanders was held by the republic.

---

[15] Meteren, Grotius, Van der Kemp, *ubi sup.*
[16] Meteren, 457 ; Van der Kemp, 96, 97, and notes.

And as time wore on, the supposed necessities of the wealthy province, which, in political importance, made up a full half of the archduke's dominions, together with self-esteem and an exaggerated idea of military honour, made that prelate more and more determined to effect his purpose.

So upon those barren sands was opened a great academy in which the science and the art of war were to be taught by the most skilful practitioners to all Europe ; for no general, corporal, artillerist, barber-surgeon, or engineer, would be deemed to know his trade if he had not fought at Ostend ; and thither resorted month after month warriors of every rank, from men of royal or of noblest blood to adventurers of lowlier degree, whose only fortune was buckled at their sides. From every land, of every religion, of every race, they poured into the town or into the besiegers' trenches. Habsburg and Holstein; Northumberland, Vere, and Westmoreland; Fairfax and Stuart ; Bourbon, Chatillon, and Lorraine , Bentivoglio, Farnese, Spinola, Grimaldi, Arragon, Toledo, Avila, Berlaymont, Bucquoy, Nassau, Orange, Solms — such were the historic names of a few only of the pupils or professors in that sanguinary high school, mingled with the plainer but well-known patronymics of the Baxes, Meetkerkes, Van Loons, Marquettes, Van der Meers, and Barendrechts, whose bearers were fighting, as they long had fought, for all that men most dearly prize on earth, and not to win honour or to take doctors' degrees in blood. Papist, Calvinist, Lutheran, Turk, Jew and Moor, European, Asiatic, African, all came to dance in that long carnival of death ; and every incident, every detail throughout the weary siege could if necessary be reproduced ; for so profound and general was the attention excited throughout Christendom by these extensive operations, and so new and astonishing were many of the inventions and machines employed—most of them now as familiar as gunpowder or as antiquated as a catapult—that contemporaries have been most bountiful in their records for the benefit of posterity, feeling sure of a gratitude which perhaps has not been rendered to their shades.

Especially the indefatigable Philip Fleming—auditor and secretary of Ostend before and during the siege, bravest, most conscientious, and most ingenious of clerks — has chronicled faithfully in his diary almost every cannon-shot that was fired, house that was set on fire, officer that was killed, and has pourtrayed each new machine that was invented or imagined by native or foreign genius. For the adepts or pretenders who swarmed to town or camp from every corner of the earth, bringing in their hands or brains to be disposed of by either belligerents infallible recipes for terminating the siege at a single blow, if only their theories could be understood and their pockets be filled, were as prolific and as sanguine as in every age.[17] But it would be as wearisome, and in regard to the history of human culture as superfluous, to dilate upon the technics of Targone and Giustianini, and the other engineers, Italian and Flemish, who amazed mankind at this period by their successes, still more by their failures, or to describe every assault, sortie, and repulse, every excavation, explosion, and cannonade, as to disinter the details of the siege of Nineveh or of Troy. But there is one kind of enginry which never loses its value or its interest, and which remains the same in every age—the machinery by which stout hearts act directly upon willing hands—and vast were the results now depending on its employment around Ostend.

On the outside and at a distance the war was superintended of course by the stadholder and commander-in-chief, while his cousin William Lewis, certainly inferior to no living man in the science of war, and whose studies in military literature, both ancient and modern, during the brief intervals of his active campaigning, were probably more profound than those of any contemporary, was always alert and anxious to assist with his counsels or to mount and ride to the fray.

In the town Sir Francis Vere commanded. Few shapes are more familiar to the student of those times than this

---

[17] Bentivoglio, Meteren, Fleming, Haestens, Gallucci, Grotius, *loc. cit. et passim, et mult. al.*

veteran campaigner, the offshoot of a time-honoured race. A man of handsome, weather-beaten, battle-bronzed visage, with massive forehead, broad intelligent eyes, a high straight nose, close-clipped hair, and a great brown beard like a spade ; captious, irascible, but most resolute, he seemed, in his gold inlaid Milan corslet and ruff of point-lace, the very image of a partizan chieftain ; one of the noblest relics of a race of fighters slowly passing off the world's stage.

An efficient colonel, he was not a general to be relied upon in great affairs either in council or the field. He hated the Nassaus, and the Nassaus certainly did not admire him, while his inordinate self-esteem, both personal and national, and his want of true sympathy for the cause in which, he fought, were the frequent source of trouble and danger to the republic.

Of the seven or eight thousand soldiers in the town when the siege began, at least two thousand were English. The queen, too intelligent, despite her shrewishness to the States, not to be faithful to the cause in which her own interests were quite as much involved as theirs, had promised Envoy Caron that although she was obliged to maintain twenty thousand men in Ireland to keep down the rebels, directly leagued as they were with Spain and the archdukes, the republic might depend upon five thousand soldiers from England.[18] Detachment after detachment, the soldiers came as fast as the London prisons could be swept and the queen's press-gang perform its office. It may be imagined that the native land of those warriors was not inconsiderably benefited by the grant to the republic of the right to make and pay for these levies. But they had all red uniforms, and were as fit as other men to dig trenches, to defend them, and to fill them afterwards, and none could fight more manfully or plunder friend and foe with greater cheerfulness or impartiality than did those islanders.[19]

[18] Wagenaar, ix. 111.
[19] Fleming, *passim*, especially 53, 58, 101. *E. g.* " Arriveerden dien dach duysent niewe Engelsche soldaten die in Engellandt gheprest waren ende uyt alle de ghevanghenisse ghe-

The problem which the archduke had set himself to solve was not an easy one. He was to reduce a town, which he could invest and had already succeeded very thoroughly in investing on the land side, but which was open to the whole world by sea ; while the besieged on their part could not only rely upon their own Government and people, who were more at home on the ocean than was any nation in the world, but upon their alliance with England, a State hardly inferior in maritime resources to the republic itself.

On the western side, which was the weakest, his progress was from the beginning the more encouraging, and his batteries were soon able to make some impression upon the outer works, and even to do considerable damage to the interior of the town. In the course of a few months he had fifty siege-guns in position, and had constructed a practicable road all around the place, connecting his own fortifications on the west and south with those of Bucquoy on the east.[20]

Albert's leading thought however was to cut off the supplies. The freaks of nature, as already observed, combined with his own exertions, had effectually disposed of the western harbour as a means of ingress. The tide ebbed and flowed through the narrow channel, but it was clogged with sand and nearly dry at low water. Moreover, by an invention then considered very remarkable, a foundation was laid for the besiegers' forts and batteries by sinking large and deep baskets of wicker-work, twenty feet in length, and filled with bricks and sand, within this abandoned harbour. These clumsy machines were called sausages,[21] and were the delight of the camp and of all Europe. The works thus established on the dry side crept slowly on towards the walls, and some demi-cannon were soon placed upon them, but the besieged, not liking these encroachments, took the resolution to cut the sea-dyke along the coast which had originally protected

licht, ghecleet met roode casacken," &c &c. p. 58.
  [20] Bentivoglio. P. III. 505-509.

Meteren, 455, 460. Grotii Hist. lib. x. Fleming, *passim*, for year 1601.
  [21] Ibid.

the old harbour. Thus the sea, when the tides were high and winds boisterous, was free to break in upon the archduke's works, and would often swallow sausages, men, and cannon far more rapidly than it was possible to place them there. Yet still those human ants toiled on, patiently restoring what the elements so easily destroyed; and still, despite the sea, the cannonade, and the occasional sorties of the garrison, the danger came nearer and nearer. Bucquoy on the other side was pursuing the same system, but his task was immeasurably more difficult. The Gullet, or new eastern entrance, was a whirlpool at high tide, deep, broad, and swift as a mill-race. Yet along its outer verge he too laid his sausages, protecting his men at their work as well as he could with gabions, and essayed to build a dyke of wicker-work upon which he might place a platform for artillery to prevent the ingress of the republican ships.

And his soldiers were kept steadily at work, exposed all the time to the guns of the Spanish half-moon from which the besieged never ceased to cannonade those industrious pioneers. It was a bloody business. Night and day the men were knee-deep in the trenches delving in mud and sand, falling every instant into the graves which they were thus digging for themselves, while ever and anon the sea would rise in its wrath and sweep them with their works away. Yet the victims were soon replaced by others, for had not the cardinal-archduke sworn to extract the thorn from the Belgic lion's paw even if he should be eighteen years about it, and would military honour permit him to break his vow? It was a piteous sight, even for the besieged, to see human life so profusely squandered. It is a terrible reflection, too, that those Spaniards, Walloons, Italians, confronted death so eagerly, not from motives of honour, religion, discipline, not inspired by any kind of faith or fanaticism, but because the men who were employed in this horrible sausage-making and dyke-building were promised five stivers a day instead of two.[22]

[22] Bentivoglio, *ubi sup.*

And there was always an ample supply of volunteers for the service so long as the five stivers were paid.

But despite all Bucquoy's exertions the east harbour remained as free as ever. The cool, wary Dutch skippers brought in their cargoes as regularly as if there had been no siege at all. Ostend was rapidly acquiring greater commercial importance, and was more full of bustle and business than had ever been dreamed of in that quiet nook since the days of Robert the Frisian, who had built the old church of Ostend, as one of the thirty which he erected in honour of St. Peter, five hundred years before.[23]

For the States did not neglect their favourite little city. Fleets of transports arrived day after day, week after week, laden with every necessary and even luxury for the use of the garrison. It was perhaps the cheapest place in all the Netherlands, so great was the abundance. Capons, hares, partridges, and butcher's meat were plentiful as blackberries, and good French claret was but two stivers the quart.[24] Certainly the prospect was not promising of starving the town into a surrender.

But besides all this digging and draining there was an almost daily cannonade. Her Royal Higness the Infanta was perpetually in camp by the side of her well-beloved Albert, making her appearance there in great state, with eighteen coaches full of ladies of honour, and always manifesting much impatience if she did not hear the guns.[25]

She would frequently touch off a forty-pounder with her own serene fingers in order to encourage the artillerymen, and great was the enthusiasm which such condescension excited.[26]

Assaults, sorties, repulses, ambuscades were also of daily occurrence, and often with very sanguinary results; but it would be almost as idle now to give the details of every encounter that occurred, as to describe the besieging of a snow-fort by schoolboys.

[23] Haestens, 81.
[25] Meteren, 496.
[24] Fleming.
[26] Ibid. 455ᵛᵒ, 460.

It is impossible not to reflect that a couple of Parrots and a *Monitor* or two would have terminated the siege in half an hour in favor of either party, and levelled the town or the besiegers' works as if they had been of pasteboard.

Bucquoy's dyke was within a thousand yards of the harbour's entrance, yet the guns on his platform never sank a ship nor killed a man on board,[27] while the archduke's batteries were even nearer their mark. Yet it was the most prodigious siege of modern days. Fifty great guns were in position around the place, and their balls weighed from ten to forty pounds apiece. It was generally agreed that no such artillery practice had ever occurred before in the world.[28]

For the first six months, and generally throughout the siege, there was fired on an average a thousand of such shots *a day*.[29] In the sieges of the American civil war there were sometimes three thousand shots *an hour*, and from guns compared to which in calibre and power those cannon and demi-cannon were but children's toys.[30]

Certainly the human arm was of the same length then as now, a pike-thrust was as effective as the stab of the most improved bayonet, and when it came, as it was always the purpose to do, to the close embrace of foemen, the work was done as thoroughly as it could be in this second half of the nineteenth century. Nevertheless it is impossible not to hope that such progress in science must at last render long wars impossible. The Dutch war of independence had already lasted nearly forty years. Had the civil war in America upon the territory of half a continent been waged with the Ostend machinery it might have lasted two centuries. Something then may have been gained for humanity by giving war such preter-human attributes as to make its demands of gold and blood too exhaustive to become chronic.

Yet the loss of human life during that summer and winter

[27] Fleming.
[28] Meteren, 455vo.
[29] Ibid.
[30] I have been informed that at the siege of Fort Fisher two hundred and forty shots were counted in three consecutive minutes—at the rate therefore of forty-eight hundred shots an hour —while at Ostend there was an average of eight shots per hour.

was sufficiently wholesale as compared with the meagre results. Blood flowed in torrents, for no man could be more free of his soldiers' lives than was the cardinal-archduke, hurling them as he did on the enemy's works before the pretence of a practical breach had been effected, and before a reasonable chance existed of purchasing an advantage at such a price. Five hundred were killed outright in half-an-hour's assault on an impregnable position one autumn evening, and lay piled in heaps beneath the Sand Hill fort—many youthful gallants from Spain and Italy among them, noble volunteers recognised by their perfumed gloves and golden chains, and whose pockets were worth rifling.[31] The Dutch surgeons, too, sallied forth in strength after such an encounter, and brought in great bags filled with human fat,[32] esteemed the sovereignst remedy in the world for wounds and disease.

August, 1601.

Leaders were killed on both sides. Catrici, chief of the Italian artillery, and Braccamonte, commander of a famous Sicilian legion, with many less-known captains, lost their lives before the town. The noble young Chatillon, grandson of Coligny, who had distinguished himself at Nieuport, fell in the Porcupine fort, his head carried off by a cannon-ball, which destroyed another officer at his side, and just grazed the ear of the distinguished Colonel Uchtenbroek. Sir Francis Vere, too, was wounded in the head by a fragment of iron, and was obliged to leave the town for six weeks till his wound should heal.

The unfortunate inhabitants—men, women, and children— were of course exposed to perpetual danger, and very many were killed. Their houses were often burned to the ground, in which cases the English auxiliaries were indefatigable, not in rendering assistance, but in taking possession of such household goods as the flames had spared. Nor did they always wait for such opportunities, but were apt, at the death of an eminent burgher, to constitute themselves at once universal legatees. Thus, while honest Bartholomew

[31] Haestens, 147   [32] Ibid.

Tysen, a worthy citizen grocer, was standing one autumn morning at his own door, a stray cannon-ball took off his head, and scarcely had he been put in a coffin before his house was sacked from garret to cellar and all the costly spices, drugs, and other valuable merchandize of his warehouse—the chief magazine in the town—together with all his household furniture, appropriated by those London warriors. Bartholomew's friends and relatives appealed to Sir Francis Vere for justice, but were calmly informed by that general that Ostend was like a stranded ship, on its beam-ends on a beach, and that it was impossible not to consider it at the mercy of the wreckers.[33] So with this highly figurative view of the situation from the lips of the governor of the place and the commander-in-chief of the English as well as the Dutch garrison, they were fain to go home and bury their dead, finding when they returned that another cannon-ball had carried away poor Bartholomew's coffin-lid.[34] Thus was never non-combatant and grocer, alive or dead, more out of suits with fortune than this citizen of Ostend ; and such were the laws of war, as understood by one of the most eminent of English practitioners in the beginning of the seventeenth century. It is true, however, that Vere subsequently hanged a soldier for stealing fifty pounds of powder and another for uttering counterfeit money, but robberies upon the citizens were unavenged.

Nor did the deaths by shot or sword-stroke make up the chief sum of mortality. As usual, the murrain-like pestilence, which swept off its daily victims both within and without the town, was more effective than any direct agency of man. By the month of December the number of the garrison had been reduced to less than three thousand, while it is probable that the archduke had not eight thousand effective men left in his whole army.

It was a black and desolate scene. The wild waves of the German ocean, lashed by the wintry gales, would often sweep over the painfully constructed works of besieger and besieged

[33] Fleming, 53.   [34] Ibid.

and destroy in an hour the labour of many weeks. The Por-cupine—a small but vitally-important ravelin lying out in the counterscarp between the old town and the new, guard-ing the sluices by which the water for the town moats and canals was controlled, and preventing the pioneers of the enemy from undermining the western wall—was so damaged by the sea as to be growing almost untenable. Indefatigably had the besieged attempted with wicker-work and timber and palisades to strengthen this precious little fort, but they had found, even as Bucquoy and the archduke on their part had learned, that the North Sea in winter was not to be dammed by bulrushes. Moreover, in a bold and successful assault the besiegers had succeeded in setting fire to the inflammable materials heaped about the ravelin to such effect that the fire burned for days, notwithstanding the flooding of the works at each high tide.[35] The men, working day and night, scorching in the flames, yet freezing knee-deep in the icy slush of the trenches and perpetually under fire of the hostile batteries, became daily more and more exhausted, notwithstanding their determination to hold the place. Christmas drew nigh, and a most gloomy festival it was like to be ; for it seemed as if the beleaguered garrison had been forgotten by the States. Weeks had passed away without a single company being sent to repair the hideous gaps made daily in the ranks of those defenders of a forlorn hope. It was no longer possible to hold the external works ; the Square, the Polder, and the other forts on the south-west which Vere had constructed with so much care and where he 23 Dec. had thus far kept his headquarters. On Sunday 1601. morning, 23rd December, he reluctantly gave orders that they should be abandoned on the following day and the whole garrison concentrated within the town.[36]

The clouds were gathering darkly over the head of the gallant Vere ; for no sooner had he arrived at this determi-nation than he learned from a deserter that the archduke

[35] Meteren, Bentivoglio, Grotius, *ubi sup.* Fleming, 172
[36] Fleming, 171-188. Meteren, 460.

had fixed upon that very Sunday evening for a general assault upon the place. It was hopeless for the garrison to attempt to hold these outer forts, for they required a far larger number of soldiers than could be spared from the attenuated little army. Yet with those forts in the hands of the enemy there would be nothing left but to make the best and speediest terms that might be obtained. The situation was desperate. Sir Francis called his principal officers together, announced his resolve not to submit to the humiliation of a surrender after all their efforts, if there was a possibility of escape from their dilemma, reminded them that reinforcements might be expected to arrive at any moment, and that with even a few hundred additional soldiers the outer works might still be manned and the city saved. The officers English, Dutch, and French, listened respectfully to his remarks, but, without any suggestions on their own part, called on him as their Alexander to untie the Gordian knot.[37] Alexander solved it, not with the sword, but with a trick which he hoped might prove sharper than a sword. He announced his intention of proposing at once to treat, and to protract the negotiations as long as possible, until the wished-for sails should be discerned in the offing, when he would at once break faith with them, resume hostilities, and so make fools of the besiegers.

This was a device worthy of a modern Alexander whose surname was Farnese. Even in that loose age such cynical trifling with the sacredness of trumpets of truce and offers of capitulation were deemed far from creditable among soldiers and statesmen, yet the council of war highly applauded[38] the scheme, and importuned the general to carry it at once into effect.

[37] Fleming, *ubi sup.* It is expressly stated by Fleming that there was a regular council of war on this subject, so that Meteren, Grotius, and, after them, Wagenaar and others, are mistaken in saying that Vere was alone responsible for the stratagem. Bentivoglio does not seem aware that it was a trick. See Meteren, 455–460. Bentivoglio, P. III. 505–509. Grot. Hist. lib. x.

[38] Fleming, 178. "Die van de vergaderinge sijne intentie ghehoort hebbende wert by haer lieder hoochlich ghelaudeert," &c.

When it came, however, to selecting the hostages necessary for the proposed negotiations, they became less ardent and were all disposed to recede. At last, after much discussion, the matter was settled, and before nightfall a drummer was set upon the external parapet of the Porcupine, who forthwith began to beat vigorously for a parley. The rattle was a welcome sound in the ears of the weary besiegers, just drawn up in column for a desperate assault, and the tidings were at once communicated to the archduke in Fort St. Albert. The prince manifested at first some unwillingness to forego the glory of the attack, from which he confidently expected a crowning victory, but yielding to the representations of his chief generals that it was better to have his town without further bloodshed, he consented to treat. Hostages were expeditiously appointed on both sides, and Captains Ogle and Fairfax were sent that same evening to the headquarters of the besieging army. It was at once agreed as a preliminary that the empty outer works of the place should remain unmolested. The English officers were received with much courtesy. The archduke lifted his hat as they were presented, asked them of what nation they were, and then inquired whether they were authorized to agree upon terms of capitulation. They answered in the negative ; adding, that the whole business would be in the hands of commissioners to be·immediately sent by his Highness, as it was supposed, into the town. Albert then expressed the hope that there was no fraudulent intention in the proposition just made to negotiate. The officers professed themselves entirely ignorant of any contemplated deception ; although Captain Ogle had been one of the council, had heard every syllable of Vere's stratagem, and had heartily approved of the whole plot. The Englishmen were then committed to the care of a Spanish nobleman of the duke's staff, and were treated with perfect politeness and hospitality.[39]

*Sunday,
23 Dec.
1601.*

---

[39] Meteren, Bentivoglio, Grotius, *ubi sup ;* but Fleming, 170–188, is by far the best authority, his diary recording every minute incident.

Meantime no time was lost in despatching hostages, who should be at the same time commissioners, to Ostend. The quartermaster-general of the army, Don Matteo Antonio, and Matteo Serrano, governor of Sluys, but serving among the besiegers, were selected for this important business as personages of ability, discretion, and distinction.[40]

They reached the town, coming in of course from the western side, as expeditiously as possible, but after nightfall. Before they arrived at headquarters there suddenly arose, from some unknown cause, a great alarm and beating to arms on the opposite or eastern side of the city. They were entirely innocent of any participation in this uproar and ignorant of its cause, but when they reached the presence of Sir Francis Vere they found that warrior in a towering passion. There was cheating going on, he exclaimed. The Spaniards, he cried, were taking advantage, by dishonourable stratagem, of these negotiations, and were about to assault the town.

Astounded, indignant, but utterly embarrassed, the grave Spaniards knew nōt how to reply. They were still more amazed when the general, rising to a still higher degree of exasperation, absolutely declined to exchange another word with them, but ordered Captains Carpentier and St. Hilaire, by whom they had been escorted to his quarters, to conduct them out of the town again by the same road which had brought them there. There was nothing for it but to comply, and to smother their resentment at such extraordinary treatment as best they could.[41] When they got to the old harbour on the western side the tide had risen so high that it was impossible to cross. Nobody knew better than Vere, when he gave the order, that this would be the case; so that when the escorting officers returned to state the fact, he simply ordered them to take the Spaniards back by the Gullet or eastern side. The strangers were not very young men, and being much fatigued with wandering to and fro in the darkness over the muddy roads, they begged permission to remain

[40] Fleming.   [41] Ibid.

all night in Ostend, if it were only in a guardhouse. But Vere was inexorable, after the duplicity which he affected to have discovered on the part of the enemy. So the quarter-master-general and the governor of Sluys, much to the detriment of their dignity, were forced once more to tramp through the muddy streets. And obeying their secret instructions, the escort led them round and round through the most miry and forlorn parts of the town, so that, sinking knee-deep at every step into sloughs and quicksands, and plunging about through the mist and sleet of a dreary December's night, they at last reached the precincts of the Spanish half-moon on the Gullet, be-draggled from head to foot and in a most dismal and exhausted condition.

" Ah, the villainous town of Ostend !" exclaimed Serrano,[4] ruefully contemplating his muddy boots and imploring at least a pipe of tobacco. He was informed, however, that no such medical drugs were kept in the fort,[43] but that a draught of good English ale was much at their service.[44] The beer was brought in four foaming flagons, and, a little refreshed by this hospitality, the Spaniards were put in a boat and rowed under the guns of the fort across the Gullet and delivered to their own sentries on the outposts of Bucquoy's entrench-ments. By this time it was midnight, so that it was necessary for them to remain for the night in the eastern encampment before reporting themselves at Fort St. Albert.

Thus far Vere's comedy had been eminently successful, and by taking advantage of the accidental alarm and so adroitly lashing himself into a fictitious frenzy, the general had gained nearly twenty-four additional hours of precious time on which he had not reckoned.

Next morning, after Serrano and Antonio had reported to the archduke, it was decided, notwithstanding the very inhos-pitable treatment which they had received, that those com-

---

[42] Fleming, 181. " Ah la mechante ville d'Oostende," &c.
[43] Ibid, Gelijck t'selfe quartier beter met bier dan met medicinale droo-ghen." It is interesting to know that two centuries and a half ago a pipe of tobacco was considered as medicine by Dutchmen.
[44] Ibid.

missioners should return to their labours. Ogle and Fairfax
still remained as hostages in camp, and of course professed
entire ignorance of these extraordinary proceedings, attribut-
ing them to some inexplicable misunderstanding.
So on Monday, 24th December, the quartermaster Monday,
24 Dec.
1601.
and the governor again repaired to Ostend with
orders to bring about the capitulation of the place as soon
as possible. The same sergeant-major was again appointed
by Vere to escort the strangers, and on asking by what
way he should bring them in, was informed by Sir Francis
that it would never do to allow those gentlemen, whose feet
were accustomed to the soft sand of the sea-beach and
downs, to bruise themselves upon the hard paving-stones of
Ostend, but that the softest and muddiest road must be carefully selected for them.[45] These reasons accordingly were
stated with perfect gravity to the two Spaniards, who, in
spite of their solemn remonstrances, were made to repeat a
portion of their experiences and to accept it as an act of
special courtesy from the English general.[46] Thus so much
time had been spent in preliminaries and so much more
upon the road that the short winter's day was drawing to a
close before they were again introduced to the presence of
Vere.

They found that fiery personage on this occasion all smiles
and blandishments. The Spaniards were received with most
dignified courtesy, to which they gravely responded ; and the
general then proceeded to make excuses for the misunderstanding of the preceding day with its uncomfortable consequences. Thereupon arose much animated discussion as to
the causes and the nature of the alarm on the east side
which had created such excitement. Much time was ingeniously consumed in this utterly superfluous discussion ; but at
last the commissioners of the archduke insisted on making
allusion to the business which had brought them to the town.
" What terms of negotiation do you propose ?" they asked Sir

[45] Fleming, 182.   [46] Ibid.

Francis. " His Highness has only to withdraw from before
Ostend," coolly replied the general, "and leave us, his poor
neighbours, in peace and quietness. This would be the
most satisfactory negotiation possible and the one most easily
made."

Serrano and Antonio found it difficult to see the matter in
that cheerful light, and assured Sir Francis that they had
not been commissioned by the archduke to treat for his own
withdrawal but for the surrender of the town. Hereupon
high words and fierce discussion very naturally arose, and at
last, when a good deal of time had been spent in the sharp
encounter of wits, Vere proposed an adjournment of the discussion until after supper ; politely expressing the hope that
the Spanish gentlemen would be his guests.

The conversation had been from the beginning in French,
as Vere, although a master of the Spanish language, was
desirous that the rest of the company present should understand everything said at the interview.[47]

The invitation to table was graciously accepted, and the
Christmas eve passed off more merrily than the preceding
night had done, so far as Vere's two guests were concerned.
Several distinguished officers were present at the festive
board : Captain Montesquieu de Roquette, Sir Horace Vere,
Captains St. Hilaire, Meetkerke, De Ryck, and others
among them.[48] As it was strict fast for the Catholics that
evening—while on the other hand the English, still reckon-
ing according to the old style, would not keep Christmas
until ten days later—the banquet consisted mainly of eggs
and fish, and the like meagre articles, in compliment to the
guests. It was, however, as well furnished as could be expected in a beleaguered town, out of whose harbour a winter
gale had been for many weeks blowing and preventing all
ingress. There was at least no lack of excellent Bordeaux
wine, while the servants waiting upon the table did not fail
to observe that Governor Serrano was not in all respects a

[47] Fleming, 170–188.   [48] Ibid.

model of the temperance usually characteristic of his race. They carefully counted and afterwards related with admiration, not unmingled with horror, that the veteran Spaniard drank fifty-two goblets of claret, and was emptying his glass as fast as filled, although by no means neglecting the beer, the quality of which he had tested the night before at the Half-moon.[49] Yet there seemed to be no perceptible effect produced upon him, save perhaps that he grew a shade more grave and dignified with each succeeding daught.[50] For while the banquet proceeded in this very genial manner business was by no means neglected ; the negotiations for the surrender of the city[51] being conducted on both sides with a fuddled solemnity very edifying for the attendants to contemplate.

Vere complained that the archduke was unreasonable, for he claimed nothing less from his antagonists than their all. The commissioners replied that all was no more than his own property. It certainly could not be thought unjust of him to demand his own, and all Flanders was his by legal donation from his Majesty of Spain. Vere replied that he had never studied jurisprudence, and was not versed at all in that science, but he had always heard in England that possession was nine points of the law. Now it so happened that they, and not his Highness, were in possession of Ostend, and it would be unreasonable to expect them to make a present of it to any one. The besiegers, he urged, had gained much honour by their steady persistence amid so many dangers, difficulties, and losses ; but winter had come, the weather was very bad, not a step of progress had been made, and he was bold enough to express his opinion that it would be far more sensible on the part of his Highness, after such deeds of valour, to withdraw his diminished forces out of the freezing and pestilential swamps before Ostend and go into comfortable winter-quarters at Ghent or Bruges. Enough had been done for glory, and it must certainly now be manifest that he had no chance of taking the city.

[49] Fleming, 183.   [50] Ibid.   [51] Ibid.

Serrano retorted that it was no secret to the besiegers that the garrison had dwindled to a handful; that it was quite impossible for them to defend their outer works any longer; that with the loss of the external boulevard the defence of the place would be impossible, and that, on the contrary, it was for the republicans to resign themselves to their fate. They, too, had done enough for glory, and had nothing for it but to retire into the centre of their ruined little nest, where they must burrow until the enemy should have leisure to entirely unearth them, which would be a piece of work very easily and rapidly accomplished.[52]

This was called negotiation; and thus the winter's evening wore away, until the Spaniards, heavy with fatigue and wine, were without much difficulty persuaded to seek the couches prepared for them.[53]

Next day the concourse of people around the city was Christmas, wonderful to behold. The rumour had spread 1601. through the provinces, and was on the wing to all foreign countries, that Ostend had capitulated, and that the commissioners were at that moment arranging the details. The cardinal-archduke, in complete Milanese armour, with a splendid feather-bush waving from his casque and surrounded by his brilliant body-guard, galloped to and fro outside the entrenchments, expecting every moment a deputation to come forth, bearing the keys of the town. The Infanta too, magnificent in ruff and farthingale and brocaded petticoat, and attended by a cavalcade of ladies of honour in gorgeous attire, pranced impatiently about, awaiting the dramatic termination of a leaguer which was becoming wearisome to besieger and besieged.[54] Not even on the famous second of July of the previous year, when that princess was pleasing herself with imaginations as to the deportment of Maurice of Nassau as a captive, had her soul been so full of anticipated triumph as on this Christmas morning.

[52] Fleming, 181, *seqq.*   [53] Ibid.
[54] Ibid, *ubi sup.* Compare Bentivoglio, Meteren, Grotius, *ubi sup.*

Such a festive scene as was now presented in the neighbourhood of Ostend had not been exhibited for many a long year in Flanders. From the whole country side came the peasants and burghers, men, women, and children, in holiday attire. It was like a kermiss or provincial fair.[55] Three thousand people at least were roaming about in all directions, gaping with wonder at the fortifications of the besieging army, so soon to be superfluous, sliding, skating, waltzing on the ice, admiring jugglers, dancing bears, puppet shows and merry-go-rounds, singing, and carousing upon herrings, sausages, waffles, with mighty draughts of Flemish ale, manifesting their exuberant joy that the thorn was nearly extracted from the lion's paw, and awaiting with delight a blessed relief from that operation.[56] Never was a merrier Christmas morning in Flanders. There should be an end now to the forays through the country of those red-coated English pikemen, those hard-riding, hard-drinking troopers of Germany and Holland, with the French and Scotch arquebus men, and terrible Zeeland sailors who had for years swept out of Ostend, at any convenient opportunity, to harry the whole province. And great was the joy in Flanders.

Meantime within the city a different scene was enacting. Those dignified Spaniards—governor Serrano and Don Matteo Antonio—having slept off their carouse, were prepared after breakfast next morning to resume the interrupted negotiations. But affairs were now to take an unexpected turn. In the night the wind had changed, and in the course of the forenoon three Dutch vessels of war were descried in the offing, and soon calmly sailed into the mouth of the Gullet. The news was at once brought to Vere's headquarters. That general's plans had been crowned with success even sooner than he expected. There was no further object in continuing the comedy of negotiation, for the ships now arriving seemed crowded with troops. Sir Francis accordingly threw off the mask, and assuring his guests with extreme politeness that it

[55] Fleming.   [56] Ibid.

had given him great pleasure to make the acquaintance of such distinguished personages, he thanked them cordially for their visit, but regretted that it would be no longer in his power to entertain any propositions of a pacific nature. The necessary reinforcements, which he had been so long expecting, had at last reached him, and it would not yet be necessary for him to retire into his ruined nest. Military honour therefore would not allow him to detain them any longer. Should he ever be so hard pressed again he felt sure that so magnanimous a prince as his Highness would extend to him all due clemency and consideration.[57]

The Spaniards, digesting as they best could the sauce of contumely with which the gross treachery of the transaction was now seasoned, solemnly withdrew, disdaining to express their spleen in words of idle menace.

They were escorted back through the lines, and at once made their report at headquarters. The festival had been dismally interrupted before it was well begun. The vessels were soon observed by friend and foe making their way triumphantly up to the town where they soon dropped anchor at the wharf of the inner Gullet, having only a couple of sailors wounded, despite all the furious discharges of Bucquoy's batteries. The holiday makers dispersed, much discomfited, the English hostages returned to the town, and the archduke shut himself up, growling and furious. His generals and counsellors, who had recommended the abandonment of his carefully prepared assault, and acceptance of the perfidious propositions to negotiate, by which so much golden time had been squandered, were for several days excluded from his presence.[58]

Meantime the army, disappointed, discontented, half-starved, unpaid, passed their days and nights as before, in the sloppy trenches, while deep and earnest were the complaints and the curses which succeeded to the momentary exultation of Christmas eve. The soldiers were more than ever

---

[57] Fleming.
[58] Ibid. Compare Bentivoglio, Meteren, Grotius, *ubi sup*, *et mult. al.*

embittered against their august commander-in-chief, for they had just enjoyed a signal opportunity of comparing the luxury and comfortable magnificence of his Highness and the Infanta, and of contrasting it with their own misery. Moreover, it had long been exciting much indignation in the ranks that veteran generals and colonels, in whom all men had confidence, had been in great numbers superseded in order to make place for court favourites, utterly without experience or talent.[59] Thus the veterans ; murmuring in the wet trenches. The archduke meanwhile, in his sullen retirement, brooded over a tragedy to follow the very successful comedy of his antagonist.

It was not long delayed. The assault which had been postponed in the latter days of December was to be renewed before the end of the first week of the new year. Vere, through scouts and deserters, was aware of the impending storm, and had made his arrangements in accordance with the very minute information which he had thus received. The reinforcements, so opportunely sent by the States, were not numerous—only six hundred in all—but they were an earnest of fresh comrades to follow. Meantime they sufficed to fill the gaps in the ranks, and to enable Vere to keep possession of the external line of fortifications, including the all-important Porcupine. Moreover, during the fictitious negotiations, while the general had thus been holding—as he expressed it—the wolf by both ears, the labor of repairing damages in dyke, moat, and wall had not been for an instant neglected.

The morning of the 7th January, 1602, opened with a vigorous cannonade from all the archduke's bat- 7 January, teries, east, west, and south. Auditor Fleming, 1602. counsellor and secretary of the city, aide-de-camp and right hand of the commander-in-chief, a grim, grizzled, leathern-faced man of fifty, steady under fire as a veteran arquebuseer,

[59] Fleming gives more than one scurrilous letter found in the pockets of dead Spanish soldiers, in which very opprobrious epithets are applied to the sovereign of the obedient Netherlands. See in particular p. 164.

ready with his pen as a counting-house clerk, and as fertile
in resource as the most experienced campaigner, was ever at
the general's side. At his suggestion several houses had
been demolished, to furnish materials in wood and iron to
stop the gaps as soon as made. Especially about the Sand
Hill fort and the Porcupine a plentiful supply was collected,
no time having been lost in throwing up stockades, palisades,
and every other possible obstruction to the expected assailants. Knowing perfectly well where the brunt of the battle
was to be, Vere had placed his brother Sir Horace at the
head of twelve picked companies of diverse nations in the
Sand Hill. Four of the very best companies of the garrison
were stationed in the Porcupine, and ten more of the choicest
in Fort Hell's Mouth, under Colonel Meetkerke. It must be
recollected that the first of these three works was the key to
the fortifications of the old or outer town. The other two
were very near it, and were the principal redoubts which
defended the most exposed and vulnerable portion of the
new town on the western side. The Sand Hill, as its name
imported, was the only existing relic within the city's verge
of the chain of downs once encircling the whole place. It
had however been cannonaded so steadily during the six
months' siege as to have become almost ironclad—a mass ot
metal gradually accumulating from the enemy's guns. With
the curtain extending from it towards east and west it protected the old town quite up to the little ancient brick
church, one of the only two in Ostend.[60]

All day long the cannon thundered—a bombardment
such as had never before been dreamed of in those days, two
thousand shots having been distinctly counted by the
burghers. There was but languid response from the besieged, who were reserving their strength. At last, to the
brief winter's day succeeded a pitch-dark evening. It was
dead low tide at seven. At that hour the drums suddenly

[60] Fleming's Diary, pp. 187–199, is
by far the best authority for this assault. He gives many plans, diagrams,
and pictures.   compare Grot. Hist.
lib. xi. 595–597. Meteren, 460vo
Bentivoglio, 510. Wagenaar, ix. 114,
115.

beat alarm along the whole line of fortifications from the Gullet on the east to the old harbour on the west, while through the mirky atmosphere sounded the trumpets of the assault, the shouts of the Spanish and Italian commanders, and the fierce responsive yells of their troops. Sir Francis, having visited every portion of the works, and satisfied himself that every man in the garrison was under arms, and that all his arrangements had been fulfilled, now sat on horseback, motionless as a statue, within the Sand Hill. Among the many serious and fictitious attacks now making he waited calmly for the one great assault, even allowing some of the enemy to scale the distant counterscarp of the external works towards the south, which he had by design left insufficiently guarded. It was but a brief suspense, for in a few moments two thousand men had rushed through the bed of the old harbour, out of which the tide had ebbed, and were vigorously assailing the Sand Hill and the whole length of its curtain. The impenetrable darkness made it impossible to count, but the noise and the surging fury of the advance rendered it obvious that the critical moment had arrived. Suddenly a vivid illumination burst forth. Great pine torches, piles of tar-barrels, and heaps of other inflammable material, which had been carefully arranged in Fort Porcupine, were now all at once lighted by Vere's command.[61] As the lurid blaze flashed far and wide there started out of the gloom not only the long lines of yellow-jerkined pikemen and arquebuseers, with their storm-hoods and scaling ladders, rushing swiftly towards the forts, but beyond the broken sea-dyke the reserved masses supporting the attack, drawn up in solid clumps of spears, with their gay standards waving above them, and with a strong force of cavalry in iron corslet and morion stationed in the rear to urge on the infantry and prevent their faltering in the night's work, became visible— phantom-like but perfectly distinct.

At least four thousand men were engaged in this chief attack, and the light now permitted the besieged to direct

[61] Fleming, *ubi sup.*

their fire from cannon, demi-cannon, culverin, and snaphance, with fatal effect. The assailants, thinned, straggling, but undismayed, closed up their ranks, and still came fiercely on. Never had Spaniards, Walloons, or Italians, manifested greater contempt of death than on this occasion. They knew that the archduke and the infanta were waiting breathlessly in Fort St. Albert for the news of that victory of which the feigned negotiations had defrauded them at Christmas, and they felt perfectly confident of ending both the siege and the forty years' war this January night. But they had reckoned without their wily English host. As they came nearer—van, and at last reserve—they dropped in great heaps under the steady fire of the musketry—as Philip Fleming, looking on, exclaimed—like apples when the autumn wind blows through the orchard. And as the foremost still pressed nearer and nearer, striving to clamber up the shattered counterscarp and through every practicable breach, the English, Hollanders, and Zeelanders, met them in the gap, not only at push of pike, but with their long daggers and with flaming pitch-hoops, and hurled them down to instant death.

And thus around the Sand Hill, the Porcupine, and Hell's Mouth, the battle raged nearly two hours long, without an inch of ground being gained by the assailants. The dead and dying were piled beneath the walls, while still the reserves, goaded up to the mark by the cavalry, mounted upon the bodies of their fallen comrades and strove to plant their ladders.[62] But now the tide was on the flood, the harbour was filling, and cool Auditor Fleming, whom nothing escaped, quietly asked the general's permission to open the western sluice. It was obvious, he observed, that the fury of the attack was over, and that the enemy would soon be effecting a retreat before the water should have risen too high. He even pointed out many stragglers attempting to escape through the already deepening shallows. Vere's consent was at once given, the flood-gate was opened, and the assailants —such as still survived—panic-struck in a moment, rushed

[62] Fleming, *ubi sup.*

wildly back through the old harbour towards their camp. It was too late. The waters were out, and the contending currents whirled the fugitives up and down through the submerged land, and beyond the broken dyke, until great numbers of them were miserably drowned in the haven, while others were washed out to sea. Horses and riders were borne off towards the Zeeland coast, and several of their corpses were picked up days afterwards in the neighbourhood of Flushing.[63]

Meantime those who had effected a lodgment in the Polder, the Square, and the other southern forts, found, after the chief assault had failed, that they had gained nothing by their temporary triumph but the certainty of being butchered. Retreat was impossible, and no quarter was given. Count Imbec, a noble of great wealth, offered his weight in gold for his ransom,[64] but was killed by a private soldier, who preferred his blood, or doubted his solvency. Durango, marshal of the camp, Don Alvarez de Suarez, and Don Matteo Antonio, sergeant-major and quarter-master-general, whose adventures as a hostage within the town on Christmas eve have so recently been related, were also slain.

On the eastern side Bucquoy's attack was an entire failure. His arrangements were too slowly made, and before he could bring his men to the assault the water was so high in the Gullet that they refused to lay their pontoons and march to certain death. Only at lowest ebb, and with most exquisite skill in fording, would it have been possible to effect anything like an earnest demonstration or a surprise. Moreover some of the garrison, giving themselves out as

Jan. 7.

---

[63] The historians Bentivoglio, Grotius, and many others give Vere, as a matter of course, the credit of this feat. But these are the words of Auditor Fleming himself, a man whom I should judge incapable of falsehood:—"Hebbe my vervordert den Generael te bidden dat hy my gheliefde te autoriseren ende West Sluyse te doen openen hem remonstrerende gelijck den Vyand sijn voornemen tot ghenen goeden effecte conde gebrenghen als oock dat sijn volck van den furieusen aenval begosten den moet te verliesen, haer lieder retraicte wederom door die onde West haven soude moeten nemen ende dat alsdan die spoelinghe vant water haer lieder inde Zee soude drijven waer over den voornoemden Generael my gheauthoriseert heeft die sluysen te doen openen."—pp. 195, 196

[64] Haestens, 199.

deserters, stole out of the Spanish Half-moon, which had
been purposely almost denuded of its defenders, towards the
enemy's entrenchments, and offered to lead a body of
Spaniards into that ravelin. Bucquoy fell into the trap, so
that the detachment, after a victory as easily effected as that
in the southern forts, found themselves when the fight was over
not the captors but the caught. A few attempted to escape
and were driven into the sea ; the rest were massacred.

Fifteen hundred of the enemy's dead were counted and
registered by Auditor Fleming.[65] The whole number of the
slain and drowned was reckoned as high as two thousand,
which was at least a quarter of the whole besieging army.
And so ended this winter night's assault, by which the
archduke had fondly hoped to avenge himself for Vere's
perfidy, and to terminate the war at a blow. Only sixty
of the garrison were killed, and Sir Horace Vere was
wounded.[66]

The winter now set in with severe sleet, and snow, and
rain, and furious tempests lashing the sea over the works of
besieger and besieged, and for weeks together paralyzing all
efforts of either army. Eight weary months the siege had
lasted ; the men in town and hostile camp, exposed to the
inclemency of the wintry trenches, sinking faster before the
pestilence which now swept impartially through all ranks
than the soldiers of the archduke had fallen at Nieuport, or
in the recent assault on the Sand Hill. Of seven thousand
hardly three thousand now remained in the garrison.[67]

Yet still the weary sausage making and wooden castle
building went on along the Gullet and around the old town.
The Bredené dyke crept on inch by inch, but the steady
ships of the republic came and went unharmed by the
batteries with which Bucquoy hoped to shut up the New
Harbour. The archduke's works were pushed up nearer on
the west, but, as yet, not one practical advantage had been
gained, and the siege had scarcely advanced a hair's breadth

---

[65] Fleming, 197.   voglio, Grotius, Meteren, Wagenaar.
[66] Ibid. 187–199. Compare Benti-   *ubi sup.*   [67] Grotius, xi. 590.

since the 5th of July of the preceding year, when the armies had first sat down before the place.

The stormy month of March had come, and Vere, being called to service in the field for the coming season, transferred the command at Ostend to Frederic van Dorp, a rugged, hard-headed, ill-favoured, stout-hearted Zeeland colonel, with the face of a bull-dog, and with the tenacious grip of one.[68]

[68] Fleming, 212, 215.

CHAPTER XL.

Protraction of the siege of Ostend — Spanish invasion of Ireland — Prince Maurice again on the march — Siege of Grave — State of the archduke's army — Formidable mutiny — State of Europe — Portuguese expedition to Java — Foundation there of the first Batavian trading settlement — Exploits of Jacob Heemskerk — Capture of a Lisbon carrack — Progress of Dutch commerce—Oriental and Germanic republics—Commercial embassy from the King of Atsgen in Sumatra to the Netherlands — Surrender of Grave — Privateer work of Frederic Spinola — Destruction of Spinola's fleet by English and Dutch cruisers — Continuation of the siege of Ostend — Fearful hurricane and its effects — The attack — Capture of external forts — Encounter between Spinola and a Dutch squadron — Execution of prisoners by the archduke — Philip Fleming and his diary — Continuation of operations before Ostend — Spanish veterans still mutinous — Their capital besieged by Van den Berg — Maurice marches to their relief — Convention between the prince and the mutineers — Great commercial progress of the Dutch — Opposition to international commerce—Organization of the Universal East India Company.

It would be desirable to concentrate the chief events of the siege of Ostend so that they might be presented to the reader's view in a single mass. But this is impossible. The siege was essentially the war—as already observed—and it was bidding fair to protract itself to such an extent that a respect for chronology requires the attention to be directed for a moment to other topics.

The invasion of Ireland under Aquila, so pompously heralded as almost to suggest another grand armada, had sailed in the beginning of the winter, and an army of six thousand men had been landed at Kinsale. Rarely had there been a better opportunity for the Celt to strike for his independence. Shane Mac Neil had an army on foot with which he felt confident of exterminating the Saxon oppressor, even without the assistance of his peninsular allies, while the queen's army, severely drawn upon as it had been for the exigencies of Vere and the States, might be supposed unable to cope with so formidable a combination. Yet Montjoy made short work of Aquila and Tyrone. The invaders, shut up in their meagre conquest, became the besieged instead of the assailants. Tyrone made a feeble attempt to relieve his Spanish allies, but was soon driven into his swamps, the peasants would not rise, in spite of proclamations and golden mountains of promise, and Aquila was soon glad enough to sign a capitulation by which he saved a portion of his army. He then returned, in transports provided by the January, English general, a much discomfited man, to Spain, 1602. instead of converting Ireland into a province of the universal empire.[1] He had not rescued Hibernia, as he stoutly proclaimed at the outset his intention of doing, from the jaws of the evil demon.[2]

The States, not much wiser after the experience of Nieuport, were again desirous that Maurice should march into Flanders, relieve Ostend, and sweep the archduke into the sea. As for Vere, he proposed that a great army of cavalry and infantry should be sent into Ostend, while another force equally powerful should take the field as soon as the season permitted. Where the men were to be levied, and whence the funds for putting such formidable hosts in motion were to be derived, it was not easy to say. "'Tis astonishing," said Lewis William, "that the evils already suffered cannot open his eyes ; but after all, 'tis no marvel. An old and good colonel, as I hold him to be, must go to school before he can become a general, and we must beware of committing any second folly, govern ourselves according to our means and the art of war, and leave the rest to God."[3]

Prince Maurice, however, yielding as usual to the persuasions or importunities of those less sagacious than himself, and being also much influenced by the advice of the English queen and the French king, after reviewing the most splendid army that even he had ever euqipped and set in 22 June, the field, crossed the Waal at Nymegen, and the 1602.

---

[1] Meteren, 458, *seqq.* Grot. x. 593.   [2] Grotius, *ubi sup.*
[3] Groen v. Prinsterer. Archives, 2nd Series, ii. 111

Meuse at Mook, and then moving leisurely along Meuse-side
by way of Sambeck, Blitterswyck, and Maasyk, came past St.
Truyden to the neighbourhood of Thienen, in Brabant.[4]   Here
he stood, in the heart of the enemy's country, and within a
day's march of Brussels.   The sanguine portion of his countrymen and the more easily alarmed of the enemy already
thought it would be an easy military promenade for the stadholder to march through Brabant and Flanders to the coast,
defeat the Catholic forces before Ostend, raise the weary siege
of that place, dictate peace to the archduke, and return in
triumph to the Hague, before the end of the summer.

But the experienced Maurice too well knew the emptiness
of such dreams.   He had a splendid army—eighteen thousand
foot and five thousand horse—of which Lewis William commanded the battalia, Vere the right, and Count Ernest the
left, with a train of two thousand baggage wagons, and a considerable force of sutlers and camp-followers.   He moved so
deliberately, and with such excellent discipline, that his two
wings could with ease be expanded for black-mail or forage
over a considerable extent of country, and again folded together in case of sudden military necessity.   But he had no
intention of marching through Brussels, Ghent, and Bruges,
to the Flemish coast.   His old antagonist, the Admiral of
Arragon, lay near Thienen in an entrenched camp, with a
force of at least fifteen thousand men, while the archduke,
leaving Rivas in command before Ostend, hovered in the
neighbourhood of Brussels, with as many troops as could be
spared from the various Flemish garrisons, ready to support
the admiral.[5]

But Maurice tempted the admiral in vain with the chances
of a general action.   That warrior, remembering perhaps too
distinctly his disasters at Nieuport, or feeling conscious that
his military genius was more fitly displayed in burning
towns and villages in neutral territory, robbing the peasantry, plundering gentlemen's castles and murdering the

---

[4] Meteren, 469, *seqq.* Van der Kemp, ii. 98, 99, and notes. Bentivoglio, P.
III. 517. Wagenaar, ix. 119, *seqq.*   [5] Same authorities.

proprietors, than it was like to be in a pitched battle with the first general of the age, remained sullenly within his entrenchments. His position was too strong and his force far too numerous to warrant an attack by the stadholder upon his works. After satisfying himself, therefore, that there was no chance of an encounter in Brabant except at immense disadvantage, Maurice rapidly counter- 18 July, marched towards the lower Meuse, and on the 18th 1602. July laid siege to Grave. The position and importance of this city have been thoroughly set before the reader in a former volume.[6] It is only necessary, therefore, to recal the fact that, besides being a vital possession for the republic, the place was in law the private property of the Orange family, having been a portion of the estate of Count de Buren, afterwards redeemed on payment of a considerable sum of money by his son-in-law, William the Silent, confirmed to him at the pacification of Ghent, and only lost to his children by the disgraceful conduct of Captain Hamart, which had cost that officer his head. Maurice was determined at least that the place should not now slip through his fingers, and that the present siege should be a masterpiece. His forts, of which he had nearly fifty, were each regularly furnished with moat, drawbridge, and bulwark. His counterscarp and parapet, his galleries, covered ways and mines, were as elaborate, massive, and artistically finished as if he were building a city instead of besieging one. Buzanval, the French envoy, amazed at the spectacle, protested that his works "were rather worthy of the grand Emperor of the Turks than of a little commonwealth, which only existed through the disorder of its enemies and the assistance of its friends;" but he admitted the utility of the stadholder's proceedings to be very obvious.[7]

While the prince calmly sat before Grave, awaiting the inexorable hour for burghers and garrison to surrender, the great Francis Mendoza, Admiral of Arragon, had been completing the arrangements for his exchange. A prisoner

[6] See vol. II. of this work, chap. ix.   [7] Groen v. Prinsterer. Archives, ii. 153.

after the Nieuport battle, he had been assigned by Maurice, as will be recollected, to his cousin, young Lewis Gunther, whose brilliant services as commander of the cavalry had so much contributed to the victory. The amount of ransom for so eminent a captive could not fail to be large, and accordingly the thrifty Lewis William had congratulated his brother on being able, although so young, thus to repair the fortunes of the family by his military industry to a greater extent than had yet been accomplished by any of the race. Subsequently, the admiral had been released on parole, the sum of his ransom having been fixed at nearly one hundred thousand Flemish crowns. By an agreement now made by the States, with consent of the Nassau family, the prisoner was definitely released, on condition of effecting the exchange of all prisoners of the republic, now held in durance by Spain in any part of the world.[8] This was in lieu of the hundred thousand crowns which were to be put into the impoverished coffers of Lewis Gunther. It may be imagined, as the hapless prisoners afterwards poured in—not only from the peninsula, but from more distant regions, whither they had been sent by their cruel taskmasters, some to relate their sufferings in the horrible dungeons of Spain, where they had long been expiating the crime of defending their fatherland, others to relate their experiences as chained galley-slaves in the naval service of their bitterest enemies, many with shorn heads and long beards like Turks, many with crippled limbs, worn out with chains and blows, and the squalor of disease and filth[9]—that the hatred for Spain and Rome did not glow any less fiercely within the republic, nor the hereditary love for the Nassaus, to whose generosity these poor victims were indebted for their deliverance, become fainter, in consequence of these revelations. It was at first vehemently disputed by many that the admiral could be exchanged as a prisoner of war, in respect to the manifold murders and other crimes which would seem to authorize his trial and chastisement by the tribunals of the republic. But it was decided by the States

[8] Meteren, 449ᵛᵒ, 470. Grotius, xi. 528, 599.   [9] Grotius, *ubi sup.*

that the sacred ægis of military law must be held to protect even so bloodstained a criminal as he, and his release was accordingly effected.[10] Not long afterwards he took his departure for Spain, where his reception was not enthusiastic.

From this epoch is to be dated a considerable reform in the laws regulating the exchange of prisoners of war.[11]

While Maurice was occupied with the siege of Grave, and thus not only menacing an important position, but spreading danger and dismay over all Brabant and Flanders, it was necessary for the archduke to detach so large a portion of his armies to observe his indefatigable and scientific enemy, as to much weaken the vigour of the operations before Ostend. Moreover, the execrable administration of his finances, and the dismal delays and sufferings of that siege, had brought about another mutiny—on the whole, the most extensive, formidable, and methodical of all that had hitherto occurred in the Spanish armies.[2]

By midsummer, at least three thousand five hundred veterans, including a thousand of excellent cavalry, the very best soldiers in the service, had seized the city of Hoogstraaten. Here they established themselves securely, and strengthened the fortifications ; levying contributions in corn, cattle, and every other necessary, besides wine, beer, and pocket-money, from the whole country round with exemplary regularity. As usual, disorder assumed the forms of absolute order. Anarchy became the best organized of governments, and it would have been difficult to find in the world—outside the Dutch commonwealth—a single community where justice appeared to be so promptly administered as in this temporary republic, founded upon rebellion and theft.

For, although a brotherhood of thieves, it rigorously punished such of its citizens as robbed for their own, not for the public good. The immense booty swept daily from the granges, castles, and villages of Flanders was divided with

[10] " Non visum Ordinibus in captivum belli jure munitum judicia exercere." —Grotius, *ubi sup.*   [11] Ibid.
[12] Bentivoglio, iii. 517.   Meteren, 470–472.   Grotius, xi. 604–606.

the simplicity of early Christians, while the success and steadiness of the operations paralyzed their sovereign, and was of considerable advantage to the States.

Albert endeavoured in vain to negotiate with the rebels. Nuncius Frangipani went to them in person, but was received with calm derision. Pious exhortations might turn the keys of Paradise, but gold alone, he was informed, would unlock the gates of Hoogstraaten. In an evil hour the cardinal-archduke was tempted to try the effect of sacerdotal thunder. The ex-archbishop of Toledo could not doubt that the terrors of the Church would make those brown veterans tremble who could confront so tranquilly the spring-tides of the North Sea, and the batteries of Vere and Nassau. So he launched a manifesto, as highly spiced as a pamphlet of Marnix, and as severe as a sentence of Torquemada. Entirely against the advice of the States-General of the obedient provinces, he denounced the mutineers as outlaws and accursed. He called on persons of every degree to kill any of them in any way, at any time, or in any place, promising that the slayer of a private soldier should receive a reward of ten crowns for each head brought in, while for a subaltern officer's head one hundred crowns were offered, for that of a superior officer two hundred, and for that of the Eletto or chief magistrate, five hundred crowns. Should the slayer be himself a member of the mutiny, his crime of rebellion was to be forgiven, and the price of murder duly paid. All judges, magistrates, and provost-marshals were ordered to make inventories of the goods, moveable and immoveable, of the mutineers, and of the clothing and other articles belonging to their wives and children, all which property was to be brought in and deposited in the hands of the proper functionaries of the archduke's camp, in order that it might be duly incorporated into the domains of his Highness.[13]

The mutineers were not frightened. The ban was an anachronism. If those Spaniards and Italians had learned nothing by their much campaigning in the land of Cal-

[13] "Om alle de selve te doen incorporeren aen onse Domeynen."—Met. 471.

vinism, they had at least unlearned their faith in bell, book,
and candle. It happened, too, that among their numbers
were to be found pamphleteers as ready and as unscrupulous
as the scribes of the archduke.

So there soon came forth and was published to the world,
in the name of the Eletto and council of Hoogstraaten, a
formal answer to the ban.[14]

"If scolding and cursing be payment," said the magistrates of
the mutiny, "then we might give a receipt in full for our wages.
The ban is sufficient in this respect; but as these curses give
no food for our bellies nor clothes for our backs, not preventing us, therefore, who have been fighting so long for the
honour and welfare of the archdukes from starving with cold
and hunger, we think a reply necessary in order to make
manifest how much reason these archdukes have for thunder-
ing forth all this choler and fury, by which women and
children may be frightened, but at which no soldier will feel
alarm.

"When it is stated," continued the mutineers, "that we have
deserted our banners just as an attempt was making by the
archduke to relieve Grave, we can only reply that the assertion proves how impossible it is to practise arithmetic with
disturbed brains. Passion is a bad schoolmistress for the
memory, but, as good friends, we will recal to the recollection
of your Highness that it was not your Highness, but the
Admiral of Arragon, that commanded the relieving force before
that city.

"'Tis very true that we summon your Highnesses, and levy
upon your provinces, in order to obtain means of living; for in
what other quarter should we make application. Your Highnesses give us nothing except promises; but soldiers are not
chameleons, to live on such air. According to every principle
of law, creditors have a lien on the property of their debtors.

"As to condemning to death as traitors and scoundrels those
who don't desire to be killed, and who have the means of
killing such as attempt to execute the sentence, this is hardly

[14] Meteren (470–472) gives the text.

in accordance with the extraordinary wisdom which has always characterized your Highnesses.

"As to the confiscation of our goods, both moveable and immoveable, we would simply make this observation :—

"Our moveable goods are our swords alone, and they can only be moved by ourselves. They are our immoveable goods as well ; for should any one but ourselves undertake to move them, we assure your Highnesses that they will prove too heavy to be handled.

"As to the official register and deposit ordained of the money, clothing, and other property belonging to ourselves, our wives and children, the work may be done without clerks of inventory. Certainly, if the domains of your Highnesses have no other sources of revenue than the proceeds of this confiscation, wherewith to feed the ostrich-like digestions of those about you, 'tis to be feared that ere long they will be in the same condition as were ours, when we were obliged to come together in Hoogstraaten to devise means to keep ourselves, our wives, and children alive. And at that time we were an unbreeched people, like the Indians—saving your Highnesses' reverence—and the climate here is too cold for such costume. Your Highnesses, and your relatives the Emperor and King of Spain, will hardly make your royal heads greasy with the fat of such property as we possess. 'Twill also be a remarkable spectacle after you have stripped our wives and children stark naked for the benefit of your treasury, to see them sent in that condition, within three days afterwards, out of the country, as the ban ordains.

"You order the ban to be executed against our children and our children's children, but your Highness never learned this in the Bible, when you were an archbishop, and when you expounded, or ought to have expounded, the Holy Scriptures to your flock. What theology teaches your Highness to vent your wrath upon the innocent ?

"Whenever the cause of discontent is taken away, the soldiers will become obedient and cheerful. All kings and princes may mirror themselves in the bad government of your Highness, and may see how they fare who try to carry on a war, while with their own hands they cut the sinews of war. The great leaders of old—Cyrus, Alexander, Scipio, Cæsar— were accustomed, not to starve, but to enrich their soldiers. What did Alexander, when in an arid desert they brought him a helmet full of water? He threw it on the sand, saying that there was only enough for him, but not enough for his army.

" Your Highnesses have set ten crowns, and one hundred, and five hundred crowns upon our heads, but never could find five hundred mites nor ten mites to keep our souls and bodies together.

" Yet you have found means to live yourselves with pomp and luxury, far exceeding that of the great Emperor Charles, and much surpassing the magnificence of your Highnesses' brothers, the emperor and the king." [15]

Thus, and much more, the magistrates of the "Italian republic"—answering their master's denunciations of vengeance, both in this world and the next, with a humorous scorn very refreshing in that age of the world to contemplate. The expanding influence of the Dutch commonwealth was already making itself felt even in the ranks of its most determined foes.

The mutineers had also made an agreement with the States-General, by which they had secured permission, in case of need, to retire within the territory of the republic. Maurice had written to them from his camp before Grave, and at first they were disposed to treat him with as little courtesy as they had shown the Nuncius; for they put the prince's letter on a staff, and fired at it as a mark, assuring the trumpeter who brought it that they would serve him in the same manner should he venture thither again.[16] Very soon afterwards, however, the Eletto and council, reproving the folly of their subordinates, opened negotiations with the stadholder, who, with the consent of the States, gave them preli-

[15] Meteren, *ubi sup.*   [16] Van der Kemp, ii. 386.

minary permission to take refuge under the guns of Bergen-op-Zoom, should they by chance be hard pressed.[17]

Thus throughout Europe a singular equilibrium of contending forces seemed established. Before Ostend, where the chief struggle between imperialism and republicanism had been proceeding for more than a year with equal vigour, there seemed no possibility of a result. The sands drank up the blood of the combatants on both sides, month after month, in summer; the pestilence in town and camp mowed down Catholic and Protestant with perfect impartiality during the winter, while the remorseless ocean swept over all in its wrath, obliterating in an hour the patient toil of months.

In Spain, in England, and Ireland; in Hungary, Germany, Sweden, and Poland, men wrought industriously day by day and year by year, to destroy each other, and to efface the products of human industry, and yet no progress could fairly be registered. The Turk was in Buda, on the right bank of the Danube, and the Christian in Pest, on the left, while the crescent, but lately supplanted by the cross, again waved in triumph over Stuhlweissenberg, capital city of the Magyars. The great Marshal Biron, foiled in his stupendous treachery,[18]

---

[17] Meteren, Grotius, Bentivoglio, _ubi sup_ Van der Kemp. Wagenaar, ix. 120-122.

[18] Henry knew quite as well as did the most Catholic king the share of Spain in this vile intrigue. Villeroy avowed to the States' envoy that the king would be quite justified in resorting to arms to punish the treason of the Spanish governor, who having employed such a servant as Biron to cut his master's throat, and stir up his subjects to mutiny, had more grievously violated the peace than if he had simply seized the best province of his kingdom. Nevertheless, Aerssens felt sure, even as he had done the year before, that the king's rage against Spain and his caresses of the republic were mere grimace. Henry was always horribly anxious lest the States should stop fighting, and, at this moment of emotion in France, he was especially suspicious of any appearance of treating between the archduke and the republic.

It was to be seen, at a little later period, how great or how trifling would be the indignation of the British king at a wholesale attempt at murder devised, as it was suspected, in Spain. It may at least be counted among the signs of human progress that assassination is no longer one of the commonplace means employed by anointed sovereigns against each other, and against individuals obnoxious to royal displeasure.

Certainly it may be doubted whether the practice, if now attempted, would be looked upon with such lenity by the civilized world as in the reigns of the Philips, Elizabeth, James, and Henry. Meantime the shallow artifices by which it was attempted at the French court to veil the share of Spain in Biron's plot were pitiable. Excuses for Spain were made by the French Government in order to conceal its own shame. "They don't consider," said

had laid down his head upon the block; the catastrophe following hard upon the madcap riot of Lord Essex in the Strand and his tragic end. The troublesome and restless favourites of Henry and of Elizabeth had closed their stormy career, but the designs of the great king and the great queen were growing wider and wilder, more false and more fantastic than ever, as the evening shadows of both were lengthening.

But it was not in Europe nor in Christendom alone during that twilight epoch of declining absolutism, regal and sacerdotal, and the coming glimmer of freedom, religious and commercial, that the contrast between the old and new civilizations was exhibiting itself.

The same fishermen and fighting men, whom we have but lately seen sailing forth from Zeeland and Friesland to confront the dangers of either pole, were now contending in the Indian seas with the Portuguese monopolists of the tropics.

A century long, the generosity of the Roman pontiff in bestowing upon others what was not his property had guaranteed to the nation of Vasco de Gama one half at least of the valuable possessions which maritime genius, unflinching valour, and boundless cruelty had won and kept.[19] But the spirit of change was abroad in the world. Potentates and merchants

Aerssens, " that the Spaniard will never change his designs, but will be ever seeking new opportunities. The sole result of the discovery of this conspiracy is that the king loses a good servant, and is obliged to show too clearly that he fears war, and therefore is seeking for peace. The pope pleads innocence, the king believes him, and Villeroy holds fast to his old maxim that the French crown can only prosper by keeping well with the pope.

" What fruit then shall we gather from the evil of this plot or the good of its discovery. The king says that the King of Spain is too good a brother, too devout, too inexperienced to hatch this perfidy. 'Tis all Fuentes and other ministers in combination with the Duke of Savoy. I have always observed that princes never avow mishaps, but are very forward about successes."—Van Deventer, ii. 294, 295,

324, 325.

[19] Borgia, Pope of Rome, had conscientiously divided something that was supposed to be a new world into two halves, for his two best children, the monarchs of Spain and Portugal ; Catholic majesty to take that portion lying west of a line drawn from north to south pole about 1000 miles beyond the Cape Verde Islands; Faithful majesty the other slice. Subsequently, when Catholic majesty, towards the end of the 16th century, swallowed Faithful majesty, with all his kingdoms, he legally absorbed the East Indian possessions, and became proprietor of the whole new world, under the Borgian grant.

This was public law, religion, high politics, and common sense in those days, but the unsophisticated Hollanders could not be made to understand the theory.

under the equator had been sedulously taught that there were
no other white men on the planet but the Portuguese and their
conquerors the Spaniards, and that the Dutch—of whom they
had recently heard, and the portrait of whose great military
chieftain they had seen after the news of the Nieuport battle
had made the circuit of the earth—were a mere mob of pirates
and savages inhabiting the obscurest of dens. They were
soon, however, to be enabled to judge for themselves as to the
power and the merits of the various competitors for their trade.

Early in this year Andreas Hurtado de Mendoza with a
stately fleet of galleons and smaller vessels, more than five-
and-twenty in all, was on his way towards the island of Java
to inflict summary vengeance upon those oriental rulers who
had dared to trade with men forbidden by his Catholic
Majesty and the Pope.

The city of Bantam was the first spot marked out for destruction, and it so happened that a Dutch skipper, Wolfert
Hermann by name, commanding five trading vessels, in
which were three hundred men, had just arrived in those seas
to continue the illicit commerce which had aroused the ire of
the Portuguese.[20] His whole force both of men and of guns
was far inferior to that of the flag-ship alone of Mendoza.
But he resolved to make manifest to the Indians that the
Batavians were not disposed to relinquish their promising
commercial relations with them, nor to turn their backs upon
their newly found friends in the hour of danger. To the
profound astonishment of the Portuguese admiral the Dutchman with his five little trading ships made an attack on the
pompous armada, intending to avert chastisement from the
king of Bantam. It was not possible for Wolfert to cope at
close quarters with his immensely superior adversary, but his
skill and nautical experience enabled him to play at what
was then considered long bowls with extraordinary effect.
The greater lightness and mobility of his vessels made them
more than a match, in this kind of encounter, for the clumsy,
top-heavy, and sluggish marine castles in which Spain and

[20] Grotius, ix. 688, *seqq.*

Portugal then went forth to battle on the ocean. It seems
almost like the irony of history, and yet it is the literal fact,
that the Duch galleot of that day—hardly changed in two
and a half centuries since—" the bull-browed galleot butting
through the stream,"[21]—was then the model clipper, conspicuous among all ships for its rapid sailing qualities and
ease of handling. So much has the world moved, on sea and
shore, since those simple but heroic days. And thus Wolfert's
swift-going galleots circled round and round the awkward,
ponderous, and much-puzzled Portuguese fleet, until by well-
directed shots and skilful manœuvring they had sunk several
ships, taken two, run others into the shallows, and, at last,
put the whole to confusion. After several days of such
fighting, Admiral Mendoza fairly turned his back upon his
insignificant opponent, and abandoned his projects upon Java.[22]
Bearing away for the Island of Amboyna with the remainder
of his fleet, he laid waste several of its villages and odoriferous
spice-fields, while Wolfert and his companions entered Bantam
in triumph, and were hailed as deliverers.[23] And thus on
the extreme western verge of this magnificent island was
founded the first trading settlement of the Batavian republic
in the archipelago of the equator—the foundation-stone of a
great commercial empire which was to encircle the earth.
Not many years later, at the distance of a dozen leagues from
Bantam, a congenial swamp was fortunately discovered in a
land whose volcanic peaks rose two miles into the air, and
here a town duly laid out with canals and bridges, and trim
gardens and stagnant pools, was baptized by the ancient and
well-beloved name of Good-Meadow or Batavia, which it bears
to this day.

Meantime Wolfert Hermann was not the only Hollander
cruising in those seas able to convince the Oriental mind that
all Europeans save the Portuguese were not pirates and
savages, and that friendly intercourse with other foreigners
might be as profitable as slavery to the Spanish crown.

Captain Nek made treaties of amity and commerce with the potentates of Ternate, Tydor, and other Molucca islands. The King of Candy on the Island of Ceylon, lord of the odoriferous fields of cassia which perfume those tropical seas, was glad to learn how to exchange the spices of the equator for the thousand fabrics and products of western civilization which found their great emporium in Holland.[24] Jacob Heemskerk, too, who had so lately astonished the world by his exploits and discoveries during his famous winter in Nova Zembla, was now seeking adventures and carrying the flag and fame of the republic along the Indian and Chinese coasts. The King of Johor on the Malayan peninsula entered into friendly relations with him, being well pleased, like so many of those petty rulers, to obtain protection against the Portuguese whom he had so long hated and feared. He informed Heemskerk of the arrival in the straits of Malacca of an immense Lisbon carrack, laden with pearls and spices, brocades and precious stones, on its way to Europe, and suggested an attack. It is true that the roving Hollander merely commanded a couple of the smallest galleots with about a hundred and thirty men in the two. But when was Jacob Heemskerk ever known to shrink from an encounter—whether from single-handed combat with a polar bear, or from leading a forlorn hope against a Spanish fort, or from assailing a Portuguese armada. The carrack, more than one thousand tons burthen, carried seventeen guns, and at least eight times as many men as he commanded.[25] Nevertheless, after a combat of but brief duration Heemskerk was master of the carrack. He spared the lives of his seven hundred prisoners, and set them on shore before they should have time to discover to what a handful of Dutchmen they had surrendered. Then dividing about a million florins' worth of booty among his men, who doubtless found such cruising among the spice-islands more attractive than wintering at the North Pole, he sailed in the carrack for Macao, where he found no difficulty in convincing the authorities of the celes-

[24] Grotius, xi. 608—613.   [25] Ibid.

tial empire that the friendship of the Dutch republic was worth cultivating.[26] There was soon to be work in other regions for the hardy Hollander—such as was to make the name of Heemskerk a word to conjure with down to the latest posterity. Meantime he returned to his own country to take part in the great industrial movements which were to make this year an epoch in commercial history.

The conquerors of Mendoza and deliverers of Bantam had however not paused in their work. From Java they sailed to Banda, and on those volcanic islands of nutmegs and cloves made, in the name of their commonwealth, a treaty with its republican antipodes. For there was no king to be found in that particular archipelago, and the two republics, the Oriental and the Germanic, dealt with each other with direct and becoming simplicity.[27] Their convention was in accordance with the commercial ideas of the day, which assumed monopoly as the true basis of national prosperity. It was agreed that none but Dutchmen should ever purchase the nutmegs of Banda, and that neither nation should harbour refugees from the other. Other articles, however, showed how much farther the practice of political and religious liberty had advanced than had any theory of commercial freedom. It was settled that each nation should judge its own citizens according to its own laws, that neither should interfere by force with the other in regard to religious matters, but that God should be judge over them all.[28] Here at least was progress beyond the system according to which the Holy Inquisition furnished the only enginry of civilization. The guardianship assumed by Holland over these children of the sun was at least an improvement on the tyranny which roasted them alive if they rejected religious dogmas which they could not comprehend, and which proclaimed with fire, sword, and gibbet that the Omnipotent especially forbade the nutmeg trade to all but the subjects of the most Catholic king.

[26] Grotius, Meteren, *ubi sup.*   [27] Grotius, xi. 609.
[28] Ibid. " Religionis ob causam molesti alii aliis ne essent sed Deo judici rem permitterent."

In Atsgen or Achim, chief city of Sumatra, a treaty was likewise made with the government of the place, and it was arranged that the king of Atsgen should send over an embassy to the distant but friendly republic. Thus he might judge whether the Hollanders were enemies of all the world, as had been represented to him, or only of Spain; whether their knowledge of the arts and sciences, and their position among the western nations entitled them to respect, and made their friendship desirable; or whether they were only worthy of the contempt which their royal and aristocratic enemies delighted to heap upon their heads.[29] The envoys sailed from Sumatra on board the same little fleet which, under the command of Wolfert Hermann, had already done such signal service, and on their way to Europe they had an opportunity of seeing how these republican sailors could deal with their enemies on the ocean.

Off St. Helena an immense Portuguese carrack richly laden and powerfully armed, was met, attacked, and overpowered by the little merchantmen with their usual audacity and skill. A magnificent booty was equitably divided among the captors, the vanquished crew were set safely on shore, and the Hollanders then pursued their home voyage without further adventures.[30]

The ambassadors, with an Arab interpreter, were duly presented to Prince Maurice in the lines before the city of Grave.[31] Certainly no more favourable opportunity could have been offered them for contrasting the reality of military power, science, national vigour, and wealth, which made the republic eminent among the nations, with the fiction of a horde of insignificant and bloodthirsty savages which her enemies had made so familiar at the antipodes. Not only were the intrenchments, bastions, galleries, batteries, the discipline and equipment of the troops, a miracle in the eyes of these newly arrived Oriental ambassadors, but they had awakened the astonishment of Europe, already accustomed to such spectacles. Evidently the amity of the stadholder

[29] Meteren, Grotius, Wagenaar, *ubi sup*.   [30] Ibid.   [31] Ibid.

and his commonwealth was a jewel of price, and the King of Achim would have been far more barbarous than he had ever deemed the Dutchmen to be, had he not well heeded the lesson which he had sent so far to learn.

The chief of the legation, Abdulzamar, died in Zeeland, and was buried with honourable obsequies at Middleburg, a monument being raised to his memory. The other envoys returned to Sumatra, fully determined to maintain close relations with the republic.[32]

There had been other visitors in Maurice's lines before Grave at about the same period. Among others, Gaston Spinola, recently created by the archduke Count of Bruay, had obtained permission to make a visit to a wounded relative, then a captive in the republican camp, and was hospitably entertained at the stadholder's table. Maurice, with soldierly bluntness, ridiculed the floating batteries, the castles on wheels, the sausages, and other newly-invented machines, employed before Ostend, and characterized them as rather fit to catch birds with than to capture a city, defended by mighty armies and fleets.

" If the archduke has set his heart upon it, he had far better try to buy Ostend," he observed.

" What is your price ?" asked the Italian ; " will you take 200,000 ducats?"

" Certainly not less than a million and a half," was the reply ; so highly did Maurice rate the position and advantages of the city. He would venture to prophesy, he added, that the siege of Ostend would last as long as the siege of Troy.

"Ostend is no Troy," said Spinola with a courtly flourish, " although there are certainly not wanting an Austrian Agamemnon, a Dutch Hector, and an Italian Achilles." [33] The last allusion was to the speaker's namesake and kinsman, the Marquis Ambrose Spinola, of whom much was to be heard in the world from that time forth.

Meantime, although so little progress had been made at

[32] Meteren, Grotius, Wagenaar, *ubi sup.*   [33] Gallucci, ii. 109.

Ostend, Maurice had thoroughly done his work before Grave. On the 18th September the place surrendered, after sixty days' siege, upon the terms usually granted by the stadholder. The garrison was to go out with the honours of war. Those of the inhabitants who wished to leave were to leave ; those who preferred staying were to stay ; rendering due allegiance to the republic, and abstaining in public from the rites of the Roman Church, without being exposed, however, to any inquiries as to their religious opinions, or any interference within their households.[34]

The work went slowly on before Ostend. Much effect had been produced, however, by the operations of the archduke's little naval force. The galley of that day, although a child's toy as compared with the wonders of naval architecture of our own time, was an effective machine enough to harass fishing and coasting vessels in creeks and estuaries, and along the shores of Holland and Zeeland during tranquil weather.

The locomotive force of these vessels consisted of galley-slaves, in which respect the Spaniards had an advantage over other nations ; for they had no scruples in putting prisoners of war into chains and upon the benches of the rowers. Humanity—" the law of Christian piety," in the words of the noble Grotius—forbade the Hollanders from reducing their captives to such horrible slavery,[35] and they were obliged to content themselves with condemned criminals, and with the few other wretches whom abject poverty and the impossibility of earning other wages could induce to accept the service. And as in the maritime warfare of our own day, the machinery—engines, wheels, and boilers—is the especial aim of the enemy's artillery, so the chain-gang who rowed in the waist of the galley, the living enginry, without which the vessel became a useless tub, was as surely marked out for destruction whenever a sea-fight took place.

The Hollanders did not very much favour this species of war-craft, both by reason of the difficulty of procuring the

[34] Meteren, 470. Grotius, xi. 604. Van der Kemp, ii. 99 and notes. Wage-naar, ix. 120.   [35] Hist. ix. 575.

gang, and because to a true lover of the ocean and of naval
warfare the galley was about as clumsy and amphibious a
production as could be hoped of human perverseness. High
where it should be low. Exposed, flat, and fragile, where elevation and strength were indispensable—encumbered and
top-heavy where it should be level and compact, weak in the
waist, broad at stem and stern, awkward in manœuvre, helpless in rough weather, sluggish under sail, although possessing
the single advantage of being able to crawl over a smooth
sea when better and faster ships were made stationary by
absolute calm, the galley was no match for the Dutch galleot,
either at close quarters or in a breeze.

Nevertheless for a long time there had been a certain awe
produced by the possibility of some prodigious but unknown
qualities in these outlandish vessels, and already the Hollanders had tried their hand at constructing them. On
a late occasion a galley of considerable size, built at Dort,
had rowed past the Spanish forts on the Scheld, gone up
to Antwerp, and coolly cut out from the very wharves of
the city a Spanish galley of the first class, besides seven war-
vessels of lesser dimensions, at first gaining advantage by surprise, and then breaking down all opposition in a brilliant
little fight. The noise of the encounter summoned the citizens and garrison to the walls, only to witness the triumph
achieved by Dutch audacity, and to see the victors dropping
rapidly down the river, laden with booty and followed by
their prizes. Nor was the mortification of these unwilling
spectators diminished when the clear notes of a bugle on
board the Dutch galley brought to their ears the well-known
melody of "Wilhelmus of Nassau," once so dear to every
patriotic heart in Antwerp, and perhaps causing many a renegade cheek on this occasion to tingle with shame.[36]

Frederic Spinola, a volunteer belonging to the great and
wealthy Genoese family of that name, had been performing a
good deal of privateer work with a small force of galleys
which he kept under his command at Sluys. He had suc-

[36] Hist. 576.

ceeded in inflicting so much damage upon the smaller merchantmen of the republic, and in maintaining so perpetual a
panic in calm weather among the seafaring multitudes of
those regions, that he was disposed to extend the scale of his
operations. On a visit to Spain he had obtained permission
from Government to employ in this service eight great galleys,
recently built on the Guadalquivir for the Royal Navy. He
was to man and equip them at his own expense, and was to
be allowed the whole of the booty that might result from his
enterprise. Early in the autumn he set forth with his eight
galleys on the voyage to Flanders, but, off Cezimbra, on
the Portuguese coast, unfortunately fell in with Sir Robert
Mansell, who, with a compact little squadron of English fri-
gates, was lying in wait for the homeward-bound India fleet
on their entrance to Lisbon. An engagement took place, in
which Spinola lost two of his galleys. His disaster might
have been still greater, had not an immense Indian carrack,
laden with the richest merchandize, just then hove in sight, to
attract his conquerors with a hope of better prize-money than
could be expected from the most complete victory over him
and his fleet.[37]

　　With the remainder of his vessels Spinola crept out of sight
while the English were ransacking the carrack. On
the 3rd of October he had entered the channel with
a force which, according to the ideas of that day, was still formidable. Each of his galleys was of two hundred and fifty
slave power, and carried, beside the chain-gang, four hundred
fighting men. His flag-ship was called the St. Lewis;
the names of the other vessels being the St. Philip, the
Morning Star, the St. John, the Hyacinth, and the Pa-
dilla. The Trinity and the Opportunity had been destroyed off Cezimbra. Now there happened to be cruising
just then in the channel, Captain Peter Mol, master of the
Dutch war-ship Tiger, and Captain Lubbertson, commanding
the Pelican. These two espied the Spanish squadron, pad-
dling at about dusk towards the English coast, and quickly

3 October, 1602.

　　　　　[37] Grotius, xi. 607, 608.

gave notice to Vice-Admiral John Kant, who in the States'
ship Half-moon, with three other war-galleots, was keeping
watch in that neighbourhood.   It was dead calm as the night
fell, and the galleys of Spinola, which had crept close up to
the Dover cliffs, were endeavouring to row their way across
in the darkness towards the Flemish coast, in the hope of
putting unobserved into the Gut of Sluys.[38] All went well
with Spinola till the moon rose; but, with the moon, sprang
up a steady breeze, so that the galleys lost all their advantage.   Nearly off Gravelines another States' ship, the Mackerel,
came in sight, which forthwith attacked the St. Philip, pouring a broadside into her by which fifty men were killed.
Drawing off from this assailant, the galley found herself close
to the Dutch admiral in the Half-moon, who, with all sail set,
bore straight down upon her, struck her amidships with a
mighty crash, carrying off her mainmast and her poop, and
then, extricating himself with difficulty from the wreck, sent
a tremendous volley of cannon-shot and lesser missiles
straight into the waist where sat the chain-gang.   A howl of
pain and terror rang through the air, while oars and benches,
arms, legs, and mutilated bodies, chained inexorably together,
floated on the moonlit waves.   An instant later, and another
galleot bore down to complete the work, striking with her
iron prow the doomed St. Philip so straightly and surely
that she went down like a stone, carrying with her galley-
slaves, sailors, and soldiers, besides all the treasure brought
by Spinola for the use of his fleet.

   The Morning Star was the next galley attacked, Captain
Sael, in a stout galleot, driving at her under full sail, with
the same accuracy and solidity of shock as had been displayed
in the encounter with the St. Philip and with the same result
The miserable, top-heavy monster galley was struck between
mainmast and stern, with a blow which carried away the
assailant's own bowsprit and fore-bulwarks, but which completely demolished the stern of the galley, and crushed out of

   [38] Fleming, 290-294.   Bentivoglio, iii. 516.   Grotius, *ubi sup.*   Haestens, 232
seqq.   Meteren, 474.

existence the greater portion of the live machinery sitting chained and rowing on the benches. And again, as the first enemy hauled off from its victim, Admiral Kant came up once more in the Half-moon, steered straight at the floundering galley, and sent her with one crash to the bottom. It was not very scientific practice perhaps. It was but simple butting, plain sailing, good steering, and the firing of cannon at short pistol-shot. But after all, the work of those unsophisticated Dutch skippers was done very thoroughly, without flinching, and, as usual, at great odds of men and guns. Two more of the Spanish galleys were chased into the shallows near Gravelines, where they went to pieces. Another was wrecked near Calais. The galley which bore Frederic Spinola himself and his fortunes succeeded in reaching Dunkirk, whence he made his way discomfited, to tell the tale of his disaster to the archduke at Brussels. During the fight the Dutch admiral's boats had been active in picking up such of the drowning crews, whether galley-slaves or soldiers, as it was possible to save. But not more than two hundred were thus rescued, while by far the greater proportion of those on board, probably three thousand in number, perished, and the whole fleet, by which so much injury was to have been inflicted on Dutch commerce, was, save one damaged galley, destroyed.[39] Yet scarcely any lives were lost by the Hollanders, and it is certain that the whole force in their fleet did not equal the crew of a single one of the enemy's ships. Neither Spinola nor the archduke seemed likely to make much out of the contract. Meantime, the Genoese volunteer kept quiet in Sluys, brooding over schemes to repair his losses and to renew his forays on the indomitable Zeelanders.

Another winter had now closed in upon Ostend, while still the siege had scarcely advanced an inch. During the ten months of Governor Dorp's administration, four thousand men had died of wounds or malady within the town, and certainly twice as many in the trenches of the besieging force. Still

[39] Authorities last cited.

the patient Bucquoy went on, day after day, night after night, month after month, planting his faggots and fascines, creeping forward almost imperceptibly with his dyke, paying five florins each to the soldiers who volunteered to bring the materials, and a double ducat to each man employed in laying them. So close were they under the fire of the town, that a life was almost laid down for every ducat, but the Gullet, which it was hoped to close, yawned as wide as ever, and the problem how to reduce a city, open by sea to the whole world, remained without solution. On the last day 31 Dec. of the year a splendid fleet of transports arrived in 1602. the town, laden with whole droves of beeves and flocks of sheep, besides wine and bread and beer enough to supply a considerable city ; so that market provisions in the beleaguered town were cheaper than in any part of Europe.[40] Thus skilfully did the States-General and Prince Maurice watch from the outside over Ostend, while the audacious but phlegmatic sea-captains brought their cargoes unscathed through the Gullet, although Bucquoy's batteries had now advanced to within seventy yards of the shore.

On the west side, the besiegers were slowly eating their way through the old harbour towards the heart of the place. Subterranean galleries, patiently drained of their water, were met by counter-galleries leading out from the town, and many were the desperate hand-to-hand encounters, by dim lanterns, or in total darkness, beneath the ocean and beneath the earth ; Hollander, Spaniard, German, Englishman, Walloon, digging and dying in the fatal trenches, as if there had been no graves at home. Those insatiable sand-banks seemed ready to absorb all the gold and all the life of Christendom. But the monotony of that misery it is useless to chronicle. Hardly an event of these dreary days has been left unrecorded by faithful diarists and industrious soldiers, but time has swept us far away from them, and the world has rolled on to fresher fields of carnage and ruin. All winter long those unwearied, intelligent, fierce, and cruel creatures

[40] Fleming, 321.

toiled and fought in the stagnant waters, and patiently burrowed in the earth. It seemed that if Ostend were ever lost it would be because at last entirely bitten away and consumed. When there was no Ostend left, it might be that the archduke would triumph.

As there was always danger that the movements on the east side might be at last successful, it was the command of Maurice that the labours to construct still another harbour should go on in case the Gullet should become useless, as the old haven had been since the beginning of the siege. And the working upon that newest harbour was as dangerous to the Hollanders as Bucquoy's dike-building to the Spaniards, for the pioneers and sappers were perpetually under fire from the batteries which the count had at last successfully established on the extremity of his work. It was a piteous sight to see those patient delvers lay down their spades and die, hour after hour, to be succeeded by their brethren only to share their fate. Yet still the harbour building progressed; for the republic was determined that the city should be open to the sea so long as the States had a stiver, or a ship, or a spade.

While this deadly industry went on, the more strictly military operations were not pretermitted day nor night. The Catholics were unwearied in watching for a chance of attack, and the Hollanders stood on the ramparts and in the trenches, straining eyes and ears through the perpetual icy mists of that black winter to catch the sight and sound of a coming foe. Especially the by-watches, as they were called, were enough to break down constitutions of iron; for, all day and night, men were stationed in the inundated regions, bound on pain of death to stand in the water and watch for a possible movement of the enemy, until the waves should rise so high as to make it necessary to swim. Then, until the tide fell again, there was brief repose.[41]

And so the dreary winter faded away at last into chill and blustering spring. On the 13th of April, 1603, a hurricane,

[41] Fleming, 350.

such as had not occurred since the siege began, raged across the ocean, deluging and shattering the devoted town.[42] The waters rose over dyke and parapet, and the wind swept from the streets and ramparts every living thing. Not a soldier or sailor could keep his feet, the chief tower of the church was blown into the square, chimneys and windows crashed on all sides, and the elements had their holiday, as if to prove how helpless a thing was man, however fierce and determined, when the powers of Nature arose in their strength. It was as if no siege existed, as if no hostile armies had been lying nearly two years long close to each other, and losing no opportunity to fly at each other's throats. The strife of wind and ocean gave a respite to human rage. It was but a brief respite. At nightfall there was a lull in the tempest, and the garrison crept again to the ramparts. Instantly the departing roar of the winds and waters were succeeded by fainter but still more threatening sounds, and the sentinels on duty had scarce time to give the alarm, and the drums and trumpets to rally the garrison, when the attack came. The sleepless Spaniards were already upon them. In the Porcupine fort, a blaze of wickerwork and building materials suddenly illuminated the gathering gloom of night, and the loud cries of the assailants, who had succeeded in kindling this fire by their missiles, proclaimed the fierceness of the attack. Governor Dorp was himself in the fort, straining every nerve to extinguish the flames, and to hold this most important position. He was successful. After a brief but bloody encounter the Spaniards were repulsed with heavy loss. All was quiet again, and the garrison in the Porcupine were congratulating themselves on their victory when suddenly the ubiquitous Philip Fleming plunged, with a face of horror, into the governor's quarters, informing him that the attack on the redoubt had been a feint, and that the Spaniards were at that very moment swarming all over the three external forts, called the South Square, the West Square, and the Polder.[43] These points, which have been already

13 April, 1603.

[42] Fleming, 351.　　　　[43] Ibid. 351-354.

described, were most essential to the protection of the place, as without them the whole counterscarp was in danger. It was to save those exposed but vital positions that Sir Francis Vere had resorted to the slippery device of the last Christmas Eve but one.

Dorp refused to believe the intelligence. The squares were well guarded, the garrison ever alert. Spaniards were not birds of prey to fly up those perpendicular heights, and for beings without wings the thing was impossible. He followed Fleming through the darkness, and was soon convinced that the impossible was true. The precious squares were in the hands of the enemy. Nimble as monkeys, those yellow-jerkined Italians, Walloons, and Spaniards—storm-hats on their heads and swords in their teeth—had planted rope-ladders, swung themselves up the walls by hundreds upon hundreds, while the fight had been going on at the Porcupine, and were now rushing through the forts grinning defiance, yelling and chattering with fierce triumph, and beating down all opposition. It was splendidly done. The discomfited Dorp met small bodies of his men, panic-struck, reeling out from their stronghold, wounded, bleeding, shrieking for help and for orders. It seemed as if the Spaniards had dropped from the clouds. The Dutch commandant did his best to rally the fugitives, and to encourage those who had remained. All night long the furious battle raged, every inch of ground being contested; for both Catholics and Hollanders knew full well that this triumph was worth more than all that had been gained for the archduke in eighteen months of siege. Pike to pike, breast to breast, they fought through the dark April night; the last sobs of the hurricane dying unheard, the red lanterns flitting to and fro, the fireworks hissing in every direction of earth and air, the great wicker piles, heaped up with pitch and rosin, flaming over a scene more like a dance of goblins than a commonplace Christian massacre. At least fifteen hundred were killed—besiegers and besieged—during the storming of the forts and the determined but unsuccessful attempt of the

Hollanders to retake them.   And when at last the day had
dawned, and the Spaniards could see the full extent of their
victory, they set themselves with unusual alacrity to killing
such of the wounded and prisoners as were in their hands,
while, at the same time, they turned the guns of their newly
'acquired works upon the main counterscarp of the town.[44]

Yet the besieged—discomfited but undismayed—lost not a
moment in strengthening their inner works, and in doing
their best, day after day, by sortie, cannonade, and every
possible device, to prevent the foe from obtaining full advantage of his success.   The triumph was merely a local one,
and the patient Hollanders soon proved to the enemy that
the town was not gained by carrying the three squares, but
that every inch of the place was to be contested as hotly as
those little redoubts had been.   Ostend, after standing nearly
two years of siege, was not to be carried by storm.   A goodly
slice of it had been pared off that April night, and was now
in possession of the archduke, but this was all.[45]   Meantime
the underground work was resumed on both sides.

Frederic Spinola, notwithstanding the stunning defeat sustained by him in the preceding October, had not lost heart
while losing all his ships.   On the contrary, he 25 May,
had been busy during the winter in building other   1603.
galleys.   Accordingly, one fine morning in May, Counsellor
Flooswyk, being on board a war vessel convoying some empty
transports from Ostend, observed signs of mischief brewing as
he sailed past the Gut of Sluys, and forthwith gave notice
of what he had seen to Admiral Joost de Moor, commanding the blockading squadron.   The counsellor was right.
Frederic Spinola meant mischief.   It was just before sun-
rise of a beautiful summer's day.   The waves were smooth—
not a breath of wind stirring—and De Moor, who had four
little war-ships of Holland, and was supported besides by a
famous vessel called the Black Galley of Zeeland, under Captain Jacob Michelzoon, soon observed a movement from Sluys.[46]

[44] Fleming, 351–354.   [45] Ibid. | counter are Groen van Prinsterer,
[46] The best authorities for this en- | Archives, II. 194 ; Fleming, 382–384 ;

Over the flat and glassy surface of the sea, eight galleys of
the largest size were seen crawling slowly, like vast reptiles,
towards his position. Four lesser vessels followed in the
wake of the great galleys. The sails of the admiral's little
fleet flapped idly against the mast. He could only placidly
await the onset. The Black Galley, however, moved forward
according to her kind, and was soon vigorously attacked by
two galleys of the enemy. With all the force that five
hundred rowers could impart, these two huge vessels ran
straight into the Zeeland ship, and buried their iron prows in
her sides. Yet the Black Galley was made of harder stuff
than were those which had gone down in the channel the
previous autumn under the blows of John Kant. Those on
board her, at least, were made of tougher material than
were galley-slaves and land-soldiers. The ramming was
certainly not like that of a thousand horse-power of steam,
and there was no very great display of science in the encounter;
yet Captain Jacob Michelzoon, with two enemy's ships thus
stuck to his sides, might well have given himself up for lost.
The disproportion of ships and men was monstrous. Beside
the chain-gang, each of Spinola's ships was manned by two
hundred soldiers,[47] while thirty-six musketeers[48] from the
Flushing garrison were the only men-at-arms in De Moor's
whole squadron. But those amphibious Zeelanders and Hollanders, perfectly at home in the water, expert in handling
vessels, and excellent cannoneers, were more than a match for
twenty times their number of landsmen. It was a very
simple-minded, unsophisticated contest. The attempt to
board the Black Galley was met with determined resistance,
but the Zeeland sailors clambered like cats upon the bowsprits
of the Spanish galleys, fighting with cutlass and handspike,
while a broadside or two was delivered with terrible effect
into the benches of the chained and wretched slaves. Captain
Michelzoon was killed,[49] but his successor, Lieutenant Hart,

Meteren, 485, 486; Gallucci, xv. 96–
98 ; Grotius, xii. 625, 626 ; Bentivoglio,
iii. 519.

[47] Fleming, 383.
[48] Grotius, 626.
[49] Gallucci, 97. Fleming, 383.

although severely wounded, swore that he would blow up his ship with his own hands rather than surrender. The decks of all the vessels ran with blood, but at last the Black Galley succeeded in beating off her assailants ; the Zeelanders, by main force, breaking off the enemy's bowsprits, so that the two ships of Spinola were glad to sheer off, leaving their stings buried in the enemy's body.[50]

Next, four galleys attacked the stout little galleot of Captain Logier, and with a very similar result. Their prows stuck fast in the bulwarks of the ship, but the boarders soon found themselves the boarded, and, after a brief contest, again the iron bowsprits snapped like pipe-stems, and again the floundering and inexperienced Spaniards shrank away from the terrible encounter which they had provoked. Soon afterwards, Joost de Moor was assailed by three galleys. He received them, however, with cannonade and musketry so warmly that they willingly obeyed a summons from Spinola, and united with the flag-ship in one more tremendous onset upon the Black Galley of Zeeland. And it might have gone hard with that devoted ship, already crippled in the previous encounter, had not Captain Logier fortunately drifted with the current near enough to give her assistance, while the other sailing ships lay becalmed and idle spectators. At last Spinola, conspicuous by his armour, and by magnificent recklessness of danger, fell upon the deck of his galley, torn to pieces with twenty-four wounds from a stone gun of the Black Galley, while at nearly the same moment a gentle breeze began in the distance to ruffle the surface of the waters. More than a thousand men had fallen in Spinola's fleet, inclusive of the miserable slaves, who were tossed overboard as often as wounds made them a cumbrous part of the machinery, and the galleys, damaged, discomfited, laden with corpses and dripping with blood, rowed off into Sluys as speedily as they could move, without waiting until the coming wind should bring all the sailing ships into the fight, together with such other vessels under Haultain as might be cruising in the

[50] Authorities cited.

distance. They succeeded in getting into the Gut of Sluys, and so up to their harbour of refuge.[51] Meantime, baldheaded, weather-beaten Joost de Moor—farther pursuit being impossible—piped all hands on deck, where officers and men fell on their knees, shouting in pious triumph the 34th Psalm :[52] "I will bless the Lord at all times, His praise shall continually be in my mouth. . . . . O magnify the Lord with me, and let us exalt His name together." So rang forth the notes of humble thanksgiving across the placid sea. And assuredly those hardy mariners, having gained a victory with their little vessels over twelve ships and three thousand men —a numerical force of at least ten times their number,—such as few but Dutchmen could have achieved, had a right to give thanks to Him from whom all blessings flow.

Thus ended the career of Frederic Spinola, a wealthy, gallant, high-born, brilliant youth, who might have earned distinction, and rendered infinitely better service to the cause of Spain and the archdukes, had he not persuaded himself that he had a talent for seamanship. Certainly, never was a more misplaced ambition, a more unlucky career. Not even in that age of rash adventure, when grandees became admirals and field-marshals because they were grandees, had such incapacity been shown by any restless patrician. Frederic Spinola, at the age of thirty-two, a landsman and a volunteer, thinking to measure himself on blue water with such veterans as John Kant, Joost de Moor, and the other Dutchmen and Zeelanders whom it was his fortune to meet, could hardly escape the doom which so rapidly befel him.

On board the Black Galley Captain Michelzoon, eleven of his officers, and fifteen of his men were killed ; Admiral de Moor was slightly wounded, and had five of his men killed and twenty wounded ; Captain Logier was wounded in the foot, and lost fifteen killed and twelve wounded.[52]

The number of those killed in Spinola's fleet has been placed as high as fourteen hundred, including two hundred

[51] Fleming, Meteren, Gallucci, Bentivoglio, Grotius, *ubi sup.*
[52] Meteren, 486.   [53] Ibid.

officers and gentlemen of quality, besides the crowds of galley-slaves thrown overboard.[54] This was perhaps an exaggeration. The losses were, however, sufficient to put a complete stop to the enterprise out of which the unfortunate Spinola had conceived such extravagant hopes of fame and fortune.

The herring-smacks and other coasters, besides the transports passing to and from Ostend, sailed thenceforth unmolested by any galleys from Sluys. One unfortunate sloop, however, in moving out from the beleaguered city, ran upon some shoals before getting out of the Gullet and thus fell a prize to the besiegers. She was laden with nothing more precious than twelve wounded soldiers on their way to the hospitals at Flushing. These prisoners were immediately hanged, at the express command of the archduke,[55] because they had been taken on the sea where, according to his Highness, there were no laws of war.[56]

The stadholder, against his will—for Maurice was never cruel—felt himself obliged to teach the cardinal better jurisprudence and better humanity for the future. In order to show him that there was but one belligerent law on sea and on land, he ordered two hundred Spanish prisoners within his lines to draw lots from an urn in which twelve of the tickets were inscribed with the fatal word gibbet. Eleven of the twelve thus marked by ill luck were at once executed. The twelfth, a comely youth, was pardoned at the intercession of a young girl.[57] It is not stated whether or not she became his wife. It is also a fact worth mentioning, as illustrating the recklessness engendered by a soldier's life, that the man who drew the first blank sold it to one of his comrades and plunged his hand again into the fatal urn.[58] Whether he succeeded in drawing the gibbet at his second trial has not been recorded. When these executions had taken place in full view of the enemy's camp, Maurice formally announced

[54] Letter of Ernest Casimir in Groen v. Prin., Arch. II. 194. Grotius says 300 killed and many wounded. Fleming, p. 384, says 1000 killed besides the wounded and slaves uncounted.

[55] Grotius, xii. 630.
[53] Ibid. " Sed aqua captos ubi nulla forent belli foedera."
[57] Ibid. Meteren, 487. Van der Kemp, 107.
[58] Grotius, ubi sup.

that for every prisoner thenceforth put to death by the arch-duke two captives from his own army should be hanged.[59] These stern reprisals, as usual, put an end to the foul system of martial murder.

Throughout the year the war continued to be exclusively the siege of Ostend. Yet the fierce operations, recently recorded, having been succeeded by a period of comparative languor, Governor Dorp at last obtained permission to depart to repair his broken health. He was succeeded in command of the forces within the town by Charles Van der Noot, colonel of the Zeeland regiment which had suffered so much in the first act of the battle of Nieuport. Previously to this exchange, however, a day of solemn thanksgiving and prayer was set apart on the anniversary of the beginning of the siege.[60] Since the 5th of July, 1601, two years had been spent by the whole power of the enemy in the attempt to reduce this miserable village, and the whole result thus far had been the capture of three little external forts. There seemed cause for thanksgiving.

Philip Fleming, too, obtained a four weeks' holiday—the first in eleven years—and went with his family outside the pestiferous and beleaguered town. He was soon to return to his multifarious duties as auditor, secretary, and chronicler of the city, and unattached aide-de-camp to the commander-in-chief, whoever that might be, and to perform his duty with the same patient courage and sagacity that had marked him from the beginning. "An unlucky cannon-ball of the enemy," as he observes, did some damage at this period to his diary, but it happened at a moment when comparatively little was doing, so that the chasm was of less consequence.[61]

"And so I, Philip Fleming, auditor to the Council of War," he says with homely pathos, "have been so continually employed as not to have obtained leave in all these years to refresh, for a few days outside this town, my troubled spirit after such perpetual work, intolerable cares, and slavery, having had no other pleasure allotted me than with daily

[59] Grotius, Meteren, *ubi sup.*   [60] Fleming, 397.   [61] Ibid. 399, *seqq.*

sadness, weeping eyes, and heavy yearnings to tread the ramparts, and, like a poor slave laden with fetters, to look at so many others sailing out of the harbour in order to feast their souls in other provinces with green fields and the goodly works of God. And thus it has been until it has nearly gone out of my memory how the fruits of the earth, growing trees, and dumb beasts appear to mortal eye."

He then, with whimsical indignation, alludes to a certain author who pleaded in excuse for the shortcomings of the history of the siege the damage done to his manuscripts by a cannon-ball. "Where the liar dreamt of or invented his cannon-ball," he says, "I cannot tell, inasmuch as he never saw the city of Ostend in his life ; but the said cannon-ball, to my great sorrow, did come one afternoon through my office, shot from the enemy's great battery, which very much damaged not his memoirs but mine ; taking off the legs and arms at the same time of three poor invalid soldiers seated in the sun before my door and killing them on the spot, and just missing my wife, then great with child, who stood by me with faithfulness through all the sufferings of the bloody siege and presented me twice during its continuance, by the help of Almighty God, with young Amazons or daughters of war." [62]

And so honest Philip Fleming went out for a little time to look at the green trees and the dumb creatures feeding in the Dutch pastures. Meantime the two armies—outside and within Ostend—went moiling on in their monotonous work ; steadily returning at intervals, as if by instinct, to repair the ruin which a superior power would often inflict in a half-hour on the results of laborious weeks.

In the open field the military operations were very trifling, the wager of battle being by common consent fought out on the sands of Ostend, and the necessities for attack and defence absorbing the resources of each combatant. France, England, and Spain were holding a perpetual diplomatic tournament to which our eyes must presently turn, and the Sublime

[62] Fleming, 399, *seqq.*

Realm of the Ottoman and the holy Roman Empire were in the customary equilibrium of their eternal strife.

The mutiny of the veterans continued ; the "Italian republic" giving the archduke almost as much trouble, despite his ban and edicts and outlawry, as the Dutch commonwealth itself. For more than a twelvemonth the best troops of the Spanish army had been thus established as a separate empire, levying black-mail on the obedient provinces, hanging such of their old officers as dared to re-monstrate, and obeying their elected chief magistrates with exemplary docility.

They had become a force of five thousand strong, cavalry and infantry together, all steady, experienced veterans—the best and bravest soldiers of Europe. The least of them demanded two thousand florins as owed to him by the King of Spain and the archduke. The burghers of Bois-le-Duc and other neighbouring towns in the obedient provinces kept watch and ward, not knowing how soon the Spaniards might be upon them to reward them for their obedience. Not a peasant with provisions was permitted by the mutineers to enter Bois-le-Duc, while the priests were summoned to pay one year's income of all their property on pain of being burned alive. "Very much amazed are the poor priests at these proceedings," said Ernest Nassau, "and there is a terrible quantity of the vile race within and around the city. I hope one day to have the plucking of some of their feathers myself." [63]

The mutiny governed itself as a strict military democracy, and had caused an official seal to be engraved, representing seven snakes entwined in one, each thrusting forth a danger-ous tongue, with the motto—

" tutto in ore
E sua Eccelenza in nostro favore." [64]

"His Excellency" meant Maurice of Nassau, with whom formal articles of compact had been arranged. It had become

[63] Groen van Prinsterer, Archives, II. 203.   [64] Meteren. 486.

necessary for the archduke, notwithstanding the steady drain of the siege of Ostend, to detach a considerable army against this republic and to besiege them in their capital of Hoogstraaten. With seven thousand foot and three thousand cavalry Frederic Van den Berg took the field against them in the latter part of July. Maurice, with nine thousand five hundred infantry and three thousand horse, lay near Gertruydenberg. When united with the rebel "squadron," two thousand five hundred strong, he would dispose of a force of fifteen thousand veterans, and he moved at once to relieve the besieged mutineers.[65] His cousin Frederic, however, had no desire to measure himself with the stadholder at such odds, and stole away from him in the dark without beat of drum.[66] Maurice entered Hoogstraaten, was received with rapture by the Spanish and Italian veterans,[67] and excited the astonishment of all by the coolness with which he entered into the cage of these dangerous serpents—as they called themselves—handling them, caressing them, and being fondled by them in return. But the veterans knew a soldier when they saw one, and their hearts warmed to the prince—heretic though he were—more than they had ever done to the unfrocked bishop who, after starving them for years, had doomed them to destruction in this world and the next.

The stadholder was feasted and honoured by the mutineers during his brief visit to Hoogstraaten, and concluded with them a convention, according to which that town was to be restored to him, while they were to take temporary possession of the city of Grave. They were likewise to assist, with all their strength, in his military operations until they should make peace on their own terms with the archduke. For two weeks after such treaty they were not to fight against the States, and meantime, though fighting on the republican side, they were to act as an independent corps and in no wise to be merged in the stadholder's forces.[68] So much and no more had resulted from the archduke's excommunication

---

[65] Meteren, 486–488. [66] Van der Kemp, ii. 104, and notes
[67] Van der Kemp. Meteren, *ubi sup.* [68] Ibid.

of the best part of his army. He had made a present of
those troops to the enemy. He had also been employing a
considerable portion of his remaining forces in campaigning
against their own comrades. While at Grave, the mutineers,
or the " squadron " as they were now called, were to be permitted to practise their own religious rites, without offering,
however, any interference with the regular Protestant worship of the place. When they should give up Grave, Hoogstraaten was to be restored to them if still in possession
of the States, and they were to enter into no negotiations with
the archduke except with full knowledge of the stadholder.

There were no further military operations of moment
during the rest of the year.

Much more important, however, than siege, battle, or
mutiny, to human civilization, were the steady movements
of the Dutch skippers and merchants at this period. The
ears of Europe were stunned with the clatter of destruction
going on all over Christendom, and seeming the only reasonable occupation of Christians ; but the little republic, while
fighting so heroically against the concentrated powers of despotism in the West, was most industriously building up a
great empire in the East. In the new era just dawning,
production was to become almost as honourable and potent
a principle as destruction.

The voyages among the spicy regions of the equator—so
recently wrested from their Catholic and Faithful Majesties
by Dutch citizens who did not believe in Borgia—and the
little treaties made with petty princes and commonwealths,
who for the first time were learning that there were other
white men in the world beside the Portuguese, had already led
to considerable results. Before the close of the previous year
that great commercial corporation had been founded—an
empire within an empire, a republic beneath a republic—
a counting-house company which was to organize armies,
conquer kingdoms, build forts and cities, make war and
peace, disseminate and exchange among the nations of the
earth the various products of civilization, more perfectly than

any agency hitherto known, and bring the farthest disjoined branches of the human family into closer connection than had ever existed before. That it was a monopoly, offensive to true commercial principles, illiberal, unjust, tyrannical, ignorant of the very rudiments of mercantile philosophy, is plain enough. For the sages of the world were but as clowns, at that period, in economic science.

Was not the great financier of the age, Maximilian de Bethune, at that very moment exhausting his intellect in devices for the prevention of *all* international commerce even in Europe? "The kingdom of France," he groaned, "is stuffed full of the manufactures of our neighbours, and it is incredible what a curse to us are these wares. The import of all foreign goods has now been forbidden under very great penalties." As a necessary corollary to this madhouse legislation an edict was issued, prohibiting the export of gold and silver from France, on pain, not only of confiscation of those precious metals, but of the whole fortune of such as engaged in or winked at the traffic. The king took a public oath never to exempt the culprits from the punishment thus imposed, and, as the thrifty Sully had obtained from the great king a private grant of all those confiscations, and as he judiciously promised twenty-five per cent. thereof to the informer, no doubt he filled his own purse while impoverishing the exchequer.[69]

The united States, not enjoying the blessings of a paternal government, against which they had been fighting almost half a century, could not be expected to rival the stupendous folly of such political economy, although certainly not emancipated from all the delusions of the age.

[69] Mémoires de Sully, iv. 8–10, ed. Londres, 1748. The great minister adds, with diverting simplicity :—"I found a remedy,shorter and less violent than chastisements and confiscations, to prevent the export of specie ; that was to raise the value of it." Accordingly the crown of sixty sous was declared to be worth sixty-five sous, and the crown of gold or pistolet of fifty-eight sous was put at sixty-two sous, and so with the other coins in proportion.—Ibid, p. 184.

Nothing was wanting but to declare that the three-hooped pot should have ten hoops, that seven halfpenny loaves should be sold for a penny, and to make it felony to drink small beer—according to the system of an earlier financial reformer.

Nor are we to forget how very recently, and even dimly, the idea of freedom in commerce has dawned upon nations, the freest of all in polity and religion. Certainly the vices and shortcomings of the commercial system now inaugurated by the republic may be justly charged in great part to the epoch, while her vast share in the expanding and upward movement which civilization, under the auspices of self-government, self-help, political freedom, free thought, and unshackled science, was then to undertake—never more perhaps to be permanently checked—must be justly ascribed to herself.

It was considered accordingly that the existence of so many private companies and copartnerships trading to the East was injurious to the interests of commerce. Merchants arriving at the different Indian ports would often find that their own countrymen had been too quick for them, and that other fleets had got the wind out of their sails, that the eastern markets had been stripped, and that prices had gone up to a ruinous height,[70] while on the other hand, in the Dutch cities, nutmegs and cinnamon, brocades and indigo, were as plentiful as red herrings. It was hardly to be expected at that day to find this very triumph of successful traffic considered otherwise than as a grave misfortune, demanding interference on the part of the only free Government then existing in the world. That already free competition and individual enterprise, had made such progress in enriching the Hollanders and the Javanese respectively with a superfluity of useful or agreeable things, brought from the farthest ends of the earth, seemed to the eyes of that day a condition of things likely to end in a general catastrophe. With a simplicity, amazing only to those who are inclined to be vain of a superior wisdom—not their own but that of their wisest contemporaries—one of the chief reasons for establishing the East India Company was stated to be the necessity of providing against low prices of Oriental productions in Europe.

[70] Wagenaar, ix. 147–150.

But national instinct is often wiser than what is supposed to be high national statesmanship, and there can be no doubt that the true foundation of the East India Company was the simple recognition of an iron necessity. Every merchant in Holland knew full well that the Portuguese and Spaniards could never be driven out of their commercial strongholds under the equator, except by a concentration of the private strength and wealth of the mercantile community. The Government had enough on its hands in disputing, inch by inch, at so prodigious an expenditure of blood and treasure, the meagre territory with which nature had endowed the little commonwealth. Private organization, self-help, union of individual purses and individual brains, were to conquer an empire at the antipodes if it were to be won at all. By so doing, the wealth of the nation and its power to maintain the great conflict with the spirit of the past might be indefinitely increased, and the resources of Spanish despotism proportionally diminished. It was not to be expected of Jacob Heemskerk, Wolfert Hermann, or Joris van Spilberg, indomitable skippers though they were, that each, acting on his own responsibility or on that of his supercargo, would succeed every day in conquering a whole Spanish fleet and dividing a million or two of prize-money among a few dozen sailors. Better things even than this might be done by wholesome and practical concentration on a more extended scale.

So the States-General granted a patent or charter to one great company with what, for the time, was an enormous paid-up capital, in order that the India trade might be made secure and the Spaniards steadily confronted in what they had considered their most impregnable possessions. All former trading companies were invited to merge themselves in the Universal East India Company, which, for twenty-one years, should alone have the right to trade to the east of the Cape of Good Hope and to sail through the Straits of Magellan.[71]

[71] Wagenaar, *ubi sup.* Meteren, 466 and ᵛᵒ. Grotius, xi. 612, 613.

The charter had been signed on 20th March, 1602, and was mainly to the following effect.

The company was to pay twenty-five thousand florins to March 20, 1602. the States-General for its privilege. The whole capital was to be six million six hundred thousand florins. The chamber of Amsterdam was to have one half of the whole interest, the chamber of Zeeland one fourth; the chambers of the Meuse, namely, Delft, Rotterdam, and the north quarter, that is to say, Hoorn and Enkhuizen, each a sixteenth. All the chambers were to be governed by the directors then serving, who however were to be allowed to die out, down to the number of twenty for Amsterdam, twelve for Zeeland, and seven for each of the other chambers. To fill a vacancy occurring among the directors, the remaining members of the board were to nominate three candidates, from whom the estates of the province should choose one. Each director was obliged to have an interest in the company amounting to at least six thousand florins, except the directors for Hoorn and Enkhuizen, of whom only three thousand should be required. The general assembly of these chambers should consist of seventeen directors, eight for Amsterdam, four for Zeeland, two for the Meuse, and two for the north quarter; the seventeenth being added by turns from the chambers of Zeeland, the Meuse, and the north quarter. This assembly was to be held six years at Amsterdam, and then two years in Zeeland. The ships were always to return to the port from which they had sailed. All the inhabitants of the provinces had the right, within a certain time, to take shares in the company. Any province or city subscribing for forty thousand florins or upwards might appoint an agent to look after its affairs.

The Company might make treaties with the Indian powers, in the name of the States-General of the United Netherlands or of the supreme authorities of the same, might build fortresses, appoint generals, and levy troops, provided such troops took oaths of fidelity to the States, or to the supreme authority, and to the Company. No ships, artillery, or other munitions of war belonging to the Company were to be used in service of the country without permission of the Company. The admiralty was to have a certain proportion of the prizes conquered from the enemy.

The directors should not be liable in property or person for the debts of the Company. The generals of fleets returning home were to make reports on the state of India to the States.[72]

Notification of the union of all India companies with this great corporation was duly sent to the fleets cruising in those regions, where it arrived in the course of the year 1603.[73]

Meantime the first fleet of the Company, consisting of fourteen vessels under command of Admiral Wybrand van Warwyk, sailed before the end of 1602, and was followed towards the close of 1603 by thirteen other ships, under Stephen van der Hagen.[74]

The equipment of these two fleets cost two million two hundred thousand florins.[75]

---

[72] Meteren, Grotius, Wagenaar, *ubi sup*.   [73] Ibid.   [74] Ibid.   [75] Ibid.

CHAPTER XLI.

Death of Queen Elizabeth — Condition of Spain — Legations to James I. —
Union of England and Scotland — Characteristics of the new monarch —
The English Court and Government — Piratical practices of the English —
Audience of the States' envoy with King James —Queen Elizabeth's scheme
for remodelling Europe — Ambassador extraordinary from Henry IV. to
James — De Rosny's strictures on the English people — Private interview
of De Rosny with the States' envoy — De Rosny's audience of the king —
Objects of his mission — Insinuations of the Duke of Northumberland —
Invitation of the embassy to Greenwich — Promise of James to protect the
Netherlands against Spain — Misgivings of Barneveld — Conference at
Arundel House — Its unsatisfactory termination — Contempt of De Rosny
for the English counsellors — Political aspect of Europe — De Rosny's dis-
closure to the king of the secret object of his mission — Agreement of James
to the proposals of De Rosny — Ratification of the treaty of alliance — Return of De Rosny and suite to France — Arrival of the Spanish ambassador.

On the 24th of March, 1603, Queen Elizabeth died at
Richmond, having nearly completed her seventieth year.[1]
The two halves of the little island of Britain were at last
politically adjoined to each other by the personal union of
the two crowns.

A foreigner, son of the woman executed by Elizabeth,
succeeded to Elizabeth's throne. It was most natural that
the Dutch republic and the French king, the archdukes and
his Catholic Majesty, should be filled with anxiety as to the
probable effect of this change of individuals upon the fortunes
of the war.

For this Dutch war of independence was the one absorbing
and controlling interest in Christendom. Upon that vast,
central, and, as men thought, baleful constellation the
fates of humanity were dependent. Around it lesser political

[1] Meteren, 484. Camden, 661.

events were forced to gravitate, and, in accordance to their relation to it, were bright or obscure. It was inevitable that those whose vocation it was to ponder the aspects of the political firmament, the sages and high-priests who assumed to direct human action and to foretell human destiny, should now be more than ever perplexed.

Spain, since the accession of Philip III. to his father's throne, although rapidly declining in vital energy, had not yet disclosed its decrepitude to the world. Its boundless ambition survived as a political tradition rather than a real passion, while contemporaries still trembled at the vision of universal monarchy in which the successor of Charlemagne and of Charles V. was supposed to indulge.

Meantime, no feebler nor more insignificant mortal existed on earth than this dreaded sovereign.

Scarcely a hairdresser or lemonade-dealer in all Spain was less cognizant of the political affairs of the kingdom than was its monarch, for Philip's first care upon assuming the crown was virtually to abdicate in favour of the man soon afterwards known as the Duke of Lerma.

It is therefore only by courtesy and for convenience that history recognizes his existence at all, as surely no human being in the reign of Philip III. requires less mention than Philip III. himself.

I reserve for a subsequent chapter such rapid glances at the interior condition of that kingdom with which it seemed the destiny of the Dutch republic to be perpetually at war, as may be necessary to illustrate the leading characteristics of the third Philip's reign.

Meantime, as the great queen was no more, who was always too sagacious to doubt that the Dutch cause was her own—however disposed she might be to browbeat the Dutchmen—it seemed possible to Spain that the republic might at last be deprived of its only remaining ally. Tassis was despatched as chief of a legation, precursory to a more stately embassy to be confided to the Duke of Frias. The archdukes sent the prince of Arenberg, while from the united States came

young Henry of Nassau, associated with John of Olden-
Barneveld, Falk, Brederode, and other prominent statesmen of the commonwealth.[2] Ministers from Denmark and
Sweden, from the palatinate and from numerous other powers,
small and great, were also collected to greet the rising sun
in united Britain, while the awkward Scotchman, who was
now called upon to play that prominent part in the world's
tragi-comedy which had been so long and so majestically
sustained by the "Virgin Queen," already began to tremble
at the plaudits and the bustle which announced how much
was expected of the new performer.

There was indeed a new sovereign upon the throne. That
most regal spirit which had well expressed so many of the
highest characteristics of the nation had fled. Mankind
has long been familiar with the dark, closing hours of the
illustrious reign. The great queen, moody, despairing,
dying, wrapt in profoundest thought, with eyes fixed upon
the ground or already gazing into infinity, was besought
by the counsellors around her to name the man to whom she
chose that the crown should devolve.

"Not to a Rough," said Elizabeth, sententiously and
grimly.[3]

When the King of France was named, she shook her head.
When Philip III. was suggested, she made a still more
significant sign of dissent. When the King of Scots was
mentioned, she nodded her approval, and again relapsed into
silent meditation.[4]

She died, and James was King of Great Britain and

---

[2] Meteren, *ubi sup.*

[3] "Poichè avvicinatisi all 'ultima
ora de' suoi giorni e ricercata da quei
signori del consiglio che quasi tutti la
assistevano quale fosse la volontà sua
ed a chi raccommandava il regno disse
ella queste sole parole : no ad un
Rough che in lingua inglese significa
persona bassa e vile, ma ad una, ed
accenando con la mano perchè perdè
la parola, che portass ecorona. Le fu
dimandato se al re di Francia ed ella
con la testa mostrò che no, fu diman-

data se a quel di Spagna e fece il
medesimo atto, nominatole poi quello
di Scozia diede segno questo essere il
desiderio suo e poche ore dopo passò
da questa vita con universal dis-
piacere."

[4] Ibid. The particulars of Elizabeth's death are narrated in Despatch
7 April, 1603, of Secretary Scaramelli.
Senato iii. Secreta, A. V. G. See N.
Barozzi, note, p. 45, of ser. iv. vol.
unico.

Ireland. Cecil had become his prime minister long before the queen's eyes were closed. The hard-featured, rickety, fidgety, shambling, learned, most preposterous Scotchman hastened to take possession of the throne. Never could there have been a more unfit place or unfit hour for such a man.

England, although so small in dimensions, so meagre in population, so deficient, compared to the leading nations of Europe, in material and financial strength, had already her great future swelling in her heart. Intellectually and morally she was taking the lead among the nations. Even at that day she had produced much which neither she herself nor any other nation seemed destined to surpass.

Yet this most redoubtable folk only numbered about three millions, one-tenth of them inhabiting London.[5] With the Scots and Irish added they amounted to less than five millions of souls,[6] hardly a third as many as the homogeneous and martial people of that dangerous neighbour France.

Ireland was always rebellious ; a mere conquered province, hating her tyrant England's laws, religion, and people; loving Spain, and believing herself closely allied by blood as well as sympathy to that most Catholic land.

Scotland, on the accession of James, hastened to take possession of England. Never in history had two races detested each other more fervently.[7] The leeches and locusts

[5] Niccolo Molin, ambassador from Venice to James I., puts the population of London in 1607 at more than 300,000. Relazione in Barozzi and Berchet, ser. iv. vol. unico.

[6] Antonio Foscarini, Venetian ambassador in England in 1618 (Relazione in Brozzi and Berchet, ser. iv. vol. unico), estimates the whole population of the empire at 5,200,000 souls, of which number 3,560,000 are assigned to England, a little more than 1,000,000 to Scotland, and 500,000 to Ireland.

The total revenue he states as three millions scudi = 750,000*l.* sterling, almost entirely derived from England:— "Perchè la Scozia con fatica dà ottanta mila (80,000*l.*) scudi l'anno," and Ire-

land, producing a less sum than that, to which money had to be added from England for current expenses.

[7] "Essendosi il regno della Scozia unito a quello dell' Inghilterra solamente nella persona del presente re, tuttavia per la divisione e contrarietà degli animi che passa fra Scozzesi ed Inglesi non solo viene giudicato che la potenza di quel regno non sia cresciuta ma diminuita piuttosto : poichè l'odio fra di loro è passato tant' oltre che s'insidiano la vita l'un l'altro con maniere molto stravaganti. Onde molti Scozzesi e de' più principali per salvezza delle loro vite pensano di ritirarsi alle proprie case ; e se non fosse la violenza per dire così che loro

of the north,[8] as they were universally designated in England, would soon have been swept forth from the country, or have left it of their own accord, had not the king employed all that he had of royal authority or of eloquent persuasion to retain them on the soil. Of union, save the personal union of the sceptre, there was no thought. As in Ireland there was hatred to England and adoration for Spain; so in Scotland, France was beloved quite as much as England was abhorred. Who could have foretold, or even hoped, that atoms so mutually repulsive would ever have coalesced into a sympathetic and indissoluble whole?

Even the virtues of James were his worst enemies. As generous as the day, he gave away with reckless profusion anything and everything that he could lay his hands upon. It was soon to appear that the great queen's most unlovely characteristic, her avarice, was a more blessed quality to the nation she ruled than the ridiculous prodigality of James.

Two thousand gowns, of the most expensive material, adorned with gold, pearls, and other bravery—for Elizabeth was very generous to herself—were found in the queen's wardrobe, after death. These magnificent and costly robes, not one of which had she vouchsafed to bestow upon or to bequeath to any of her ladies of honour, were now presented by her successor to a needy Scotch lord, who certainly did not intend to adorn his own person therewith.[9] "The hat was ever held out," said a splenetic observer, "and it was filled in overflowing measure by the new monarch."[10]

In a very short period he had given away—mainly to

fa il re per fermarli di già tutti ne se sariano andati." — N. Molin, Relazione.

[8] "Li (gli Scozzesi) chiamano locuste e sanguisughe d'Inghilterra, affermano che hanno trovato in quel regno le minere d'oro che dicono aver altre volte perduto in Scozia."—Marcantonio Correr, Relazione.

[9] "E per natura per educazione e per abito liberalissimo ed è tale la sua liberalità che quando fu assunto alla corona d'Inghilterra donò ad un Signor Scozzese tutte le vesti della regina Elizabetta ch'erano intorno due mille e d'un valor inestimabile essendo parte di esse fregiate d'oro, di perle e tutte richissime." — Francesco Contarini, Relazione.

[10] "Di una gran parte delle gioie della corona che valevano un tesoro fece mercede à diversi empiendosi di esse le mani senza alcun rigardo al valor loro e gettandole nel cappello di questo e di quello," &c. &c.—Ibid.

Scotchmen—at least two millions of crowns, in various articles of personal property.[11] Yet England was very poor.

The empire, if so it could be called, hardly boasted a regular revenue of more than two millions of dollars a-year ;[12] less than that of a fortunate individual or two, in our own epoch, both in Europe and America ; and not one-fifth part of the contemporary income of France. The hundred thousand dollars of Scotland's annual budget[13] did not suffice to pay its expenses, and Ireland was a constant charge upon the imperial exchequer.[14]

It is astounding, however, to reflect upon the pomp, extravagance, and inordinate pride which characterized the government and the court.

The expenses of James's household were at least five hundred thousand crowns,[15] or about one quarter of the whole revenue of the empire. Henry IV., with all his extravagance, did not spend more than one-tenth of the public income of France upon himself and his court.

Certainly if England were destined to grow great it would be in despite of its new monarch. Hating the People, most intolerant in religion, believing intensely in royal prerogative, thoroughly convinced of his regal as well as his personal infallibility, loathing that inductive method of thought which

[11] N. Molin, Relazione. " Essendo comune opinione che fra danari, gioie e beni stabili abbia donato il re più di due milioni la maggior parte a Scozzesi."

[12] N. Molin, Relazione. The ambassador puts the income of the crown domains at 125,000*l.* sterling, or about 500,000 dollars (scudi). Taxes and customs he reckons at 700,000 dollars, and income from miscellaneous sources at 100,000. To this total of 1,300,000 dollars he adds an annual parliamentary subsidy of 600,000 dollars (according to the average in Elizabeth's reign, although in 1607 James had not yet had one), and thus makes a general budget of 1,900,000 dols., or somewhat less than 500,000*l.* Marcantonio Correr, ambassador in 1611, gives nearly the same figures. The envoys of ten years later, Correr and F. Con-

tarini, make the total revenue 3,000,000 dollars.

[13] N. Molin.

[14] " Il regno poi d'Irlanda non solo non apporta beneficio ma spesa piuttosto."—N. Molin. " Gli altri due regni di Scozia e d'Irlanda apportano seco più spese che rendite."—M. A. Correr, Relazione.

[15] N. Molin, Relazione. " E prima nel viver della sua casa si consuma un anno per l'altro 500,000 scudi." " Ha un milione e mezzo d'entrata (ducats, four to the pound, subsidies not counted) . . . . la spesa della sua casa arriva a ducati 500,000 l'anno." Francesco Contarini, amb. app. Giacomo I. Relazioni in Barozzi and Berchet, ser. i. vol. unico. "Nelle spese della casa eccede senz' alcuna comparazione tutti gli altri re cristiani."—Ibid.

was already leading the English nation so proudly on the road of intellectual advancement, shrinking from the love of free inquiry, of free action, of daring adventure, which was to be the real informing spirit of the great British nation; abhorring the Puritans—that is to say, one-third of his subjects[16]—in whose harsh but lofty nature he felt instinctively that popular freedom was enfolded—even as the overshadowing tree in the rigid husk—and sending them forth into the far distant wilderness to wrestle with wild beasts and with savages more ferocious than beasts; fearing and hating the Catholics as the sworn enemies of his realm, his race, and himself, trampling on them as much as he dared, forcing them into hypocrisy to save themselves from persecution or at least pecuniary ruin if they would worship God according to their conscience;[17] at deadly feud, therefore, on religious grounds, with much more than half his subjects—Puritans or Papists—and yet himself a Puritan in dogma and a Papist in Church government, if only the king could be pope; not knowing, indeed, whether a Puritan, or a Jesuit whom he called a Papist-Puritan,[18] should be deemed the more dis-

[16] "Tre sono le religioni che universalmente sono abbracciate da quei popoli: la cattolica ed apostolica romana, la protestante e la puritana: questa oltre il danno e la rovina delle anime tende a quella di principati e di monarchie ancora poichè è dirizzata tutta alla libertà ed al governo popolare; e perchè questo nome di libertà è molto dolce e grato ad ognuno è però molto facilmente abbracciata; onde si crede che il terzo di quei popoli sieno puritani ancorchè il rè e li suoi usino ogni arte por distrugger'a."—M. A. Correr, Relazione.

"Sua Maestà odia questi puritani altre tanto quanto teme de' cattolici."—Ibid.

[17] "Dirò questo solo che un cattolico ricusante che s'intende quello che ricusa di andare alle loro chiese e prediche se ha il modo è obbligato a pagare 80 scudi al mese; se non ha da pagar tanto perde due terzi delli suoi beni; sicchè uno che averrà 600 ducati d'entrata ne perde 400; se è povero od

artifice che non abbia beni stabili ogni mese da' ministri gli viene visitata la casa e levato gli si può dir ogni cosa poichè gli portano via sino il letto; se uno sarà convinto di avere udito messe, di avere tenuto un prete o gesuita in casa, anzi di avergli solamente parlato s'intende incorso in delitto di lesa Maestà onde senz' altro perde la roba e la vita. Un cattolico s'intende privo della protezione delle leggi in tanto che se sarà egli creditore di alcuno non protrà esercitar la sua azione contro il debitore perchè dalla giustizia non sarà abbracciata; se il cattolico sara oltraggiato in parole o in fatti non ha ricorso alla giustizia: intanto che li poveri cattolici sono costituti in una condizione infelicissima, pretendendo con questa via il re e quelli che governano di andar a poco a poco costringendo e riducendo per dir così a niente la cattolica religione."—N. Molin, Relazione.

[18] "Aborrisce sopra tutti li padri Gesuiti . . . . e compara appunto la

gusting or dangerous animal; already preparing for his
unfortunate successor a path to the scaffold, by employing
all the pedantry, both theological and philosophical, at his
command to bring parliaments into contempt, and to place
the royal prerogative on a level with Divinity; at the head
of a most martial, dauntless, and practical nation, trembling,
with unfortunate physical timidity, at the sight of a drawn
sword; ever scribbling or haranguing in Latin, French, or
broad Scotch,[19] when the world was arming, it must always
be a special wonder that one who might have been a respectable, even a useful, pedagogue, should by the caprice
of destiny have been permitted, exactly at that epoch, to be
one of the most contemptible and mischievous of kings.[20]

But he had a most effective and energetic minister. Even
as in Spain and in France at the same period, the administration of government was essentially in one pair of hands.

Robert Cecil, Earl of Salisbury, ever since the termination
of the splendid duumvirate of his father and Walsingham, had
been in reality supreme.[21] The proud and terrible hunchback,
who never forgave, nor forgot to destroy, his enemies,[22] had
now triumphed over the last passion of the doting queen.
Essex had gone to perdition.

Son of the great minister who had brought the mother of
James to the scaffold, Salisbury had already extorted forgive-

loro dottrina di macchinar contro li
Stati e vite dei principi con quelle dei
puritani perciò li chiama puritani
papisti."—M. A. Correr, Ralazione.

[19] " È pieno di eloquenza non solo
nella propria sua lingua ma anco in
diverse altre e nella francese e latina
particolarmente." — Francesco Contarini. Relazione.

[20] " Ma molto più dispiace l'averSua
Maestà abbandonato in tutto e per
tutto il governo dei suoi regni, rimet-
tendo il tutto al suo consiglio, non
volendo egli nè trattar nè pensar ad
altro che alla caccia . . . . Così il
presente re resta piuttosto spregiato ed
odiato che altrimenti: essendo infine
la natura di S. M. piuttosto inclinata
a vivere retiramente con otto o dieci

dei suoi che viver alla libera, come è
il costume del paese ed il desiderio
del popolo."—Ibid.

[21] " L'autorità del quale è così asso-
luta che con verità si può dire esser
egli il re e governatore di quella
monarchia."—N. Molin, Ralazione.

[22] " È astuto e sagace e persecutore
acerrimo dei suoi nemici: il che si
vede dall' effetto perchè ne ha avuto
molti e tutti li ha fatti precipitare
ancorchè che fossero uomini eminen-
tissimi . . . . . è amico de' suoi
amici è fa volentieri servizio: ma
pero è più inclinato alla vendetta che
all' amore: è uomo superbo e terribile."
—Ibid. Compare M. A. Correr, Relazione.

ness for that execution from the feeble king. Before Elizabeth was in her grave, he was already as much the favourite of her successor as of herself, governing Scotland as well as England, and being Prime Minister of Great Britain before Great Britain existed.[23]

Lord High Treasurer and First Secretary of State, he was now all in all in the council. The other great lords, highborn and highly titled as they were and served at their banquets by hosts of lackeys on their knees—[24] Nottinghams, Northamptons, Suffolks—[25] were, after all, ciphers or at best, mere pensioners of Spain. For all the venality of Europe was not confined to the Continent.[26] Spain spent at least one hundred and fifty thousand crowns[27] annually among the leading courtiers of James while his wife, Anne of Denmark, a Papist at heart, whose private boudoir was filled with pictures and images of the Madonna and the saints, had already received one hundred thousand dollars in solid cash from the Spanish court, besides much jewelry, and other valuable

[23] "Perche s'insinuò nella grazia del presente re ajutandolo como 'S. M medesima mi ha detto e occultamente in vita della regina e scopertamente dopo la merte. Così non solo gli è riuscito di cancellar dalla sua memoria la morte della madre della quale fu principalmente autore il padre di esso conte ma ha condotto la propria fortuna a quella tanta eminenza nella quale si trova al presente."—M. A. Correr, Relazione.

[24] N. Molin, Ralazione.

[25] "Il co: di Northampton custode del privato sigillo . . . . . il gran ammiraglio conte di Nottingham ed il conte di Suffolk gran ciamberlano . . . . . tutti tre sono stati provisionati annualmente da Spagna con qualcheduno altro del consiglio regio."—M. A. Correr, Relazione.

[26] "Nè vi essendo alcuno che o tardi o per tempo non sia necessitato di ricorrer al consiglio di qui è che ognuno procura di acquistarsi la grazia e la protezione di alcuno dei consiglieri il che non si può fare in quel paese con altri mezzi nè con altre vie che con presenti e donativi ; li

quali sono così ordinarij in quei paesi che chi più riceve è più stimato ed onorato ricevendo non solo da sudditi ma da stranieri e da ministri di principi ancora siccome si è veduto in diverse occasioni."—N. Molin, Relazione D'Inghilterra.

"Rimettere il tutto si suoi ministri li quali sono si fattamente interessati che senza li modi che ordinariamente sogliono usar li Spagnoli non se ne può ricevere quel beneficio che si desidera." Ibid. "Avendo molti di essi (ministri) pensioni da Spagna, altri son ben affetti verso la Francia e forse il minor numero e quello che mira al solo ben e servizio del regno e di S. M." Francesco Contarini. Relazione. "La Spagna . . . . usando alcuna volta con la Maestà sua l'esca de' matrimonii con li ministri quella delle pensioni e donativi."—M. A. Correr, Relazione.

[27] "All' ambasciatore di Spagna residente alla corte d'Inghilterra sono mandati ogni anno 150,000 scudi, non per sua provizione ma per altri fini, e però impetra gran cose."—Fran. Contarini, Relazione.

things.[28] To negotiate with Government in England was to bribe, even as at Paris or Madrid. Gold was the only pass-key to justice, to preferment, or to power.

Yet the foreign subsidies to the English court were, after all, of but little avail at that epoch.[29] No man had influence but Cecil, and he was too proud, too rich, too powerful to be bribed.[30] Alone with clean fingers among courtiers and ministers, he had, however, accumulated a larger fortune than any. His annual income was estimated at two hundred thousand crowns, and he had a vast floating capital, always well employed. Among other investments, he had placed half a million on interest in Holland,[31] and it was to be expected, therefore, that he should favour the cause of the republic, rebellious and upstart though it were.

The pigmy, as the late queen had been fond of nicknaming him, was the only giant in the Government. Those crooked shoulders held up, without flinching, the whole burden of the State. Pale, handsome, anxious, suffering, and intellectual of visage, with his indomitable spirit, ready eloquence, and nervous energy, he easily asserted supremacy over all the intriguers, foreign and domestic, the stipendiaries, the generals, the admirals, the politicians, at court, as well as over the Scotch Solomon who sat on the throne.

But most certainly it was for the public good of Britain

[28] N. Molin, Relazione, &c. M. A. Correr, Relazione. "Vanno nutrendo le speranze di poter un giorno metter mano in quel regno (d'Inghilterra) e perciò col solito titolo di avantaggiare la fede cattolica mantengono diversi collegi d'Inglesi per spargere con loro beneficio i soggeti che escono da quelli e dopo la pace hanno dispensati fra quella nazione molti denari fra quali la regina ha avuto in contanti più di cento mille scudi oltre diverse gioie e altre cose di molto valsente."—F. Priuli, Relazione di Spagna, 1604–1608. N. Molin.

[29] "Pare che li Spagnuoli si sieno astenuti questi due ultimi anni per il poco frutto che ne cavano."—M. A. Correr, Relazione.

[30] "Nè ha mai voluto accettar pen-

sioni."—M. A. Correr, Relazione.
[31] "Della sua richezza non voglio parlare perocche è cosa che eccede il creder d'ognuno ; ma quasi tutto ha in contanti in diverse piazze di Europa, ma sotto diversi nomi ; e mi è stato affermato che in Olanda solamente abbia cinque cento mille scudi li quali gli rendono utili tali che se ne può contantare." Ibid. "Essendo opinione che degli uffici della corona abbi cavato meglio di 200,000 scudi all' anno. onde ha comprato molta quantità di terreni e gira denari in diverse piazze specialmente gran somma in Olanda che profittano più che mediocremente, cosa che lo tiene affezionato ed obbligato agli interessi di quelle provincie."—Ibid.

that Europe should be pacified. It is very true that the piratical interest would suffer, and this was a very considerable and influential branch of business. So long as war existed anywhere, the corsairs of England sailed with the utmost effrontery from English ports, to prey upon the commerce of friend and foe alike. After a career of successful plunder, it was not difficult for the rovers to return to their native land, and, with the proceeds of their industry, to buy themselves positions of importance, both social and political. It was not the custom to consider too curiously the source of the wealth. If it was sufficient to dazzle the eyes of the vulgar, it was pretty certain to prove the respectability of the owner.[32]

It was in vain that the envoys of the Dutch and Venetian republics sought redress for the enormous damage inflicted on their commerce by English pirates, and invoked the protection of public law. It was always easy for learned jurisconsuls to prove such depredations to be consistent with international usage and with sound morality. Even at that

[32] "Per assicurar questi mari dai bertoni inglesi che hanno apportato e tuttora apportano tanto danno alle navi e sudditi di Vostra Serenità che trafficano in levante : perchè non è dubbio per la informazione che ne ho avuto che molti vascelli partono d'Inghilterra sotto il nome di mercanti con qualche poco di carico per il viaggio di levante ma il loro fine è principalmente di far qualche preda se la occasione si presenta; onde partendo con questo nome di mercanti viene levata l'occasione ai rappresentanti di Vostra Serenità di opporsi alla loro uscita ; ma in effetto secondo l'occasione esercitano l'ufficio di corsari e quando loro riesce di far qualche preda si contentano di restare esuli e privi della patria per qualche spazio di tempo e con qualche donativo unico remedio in quel paese per superar tutte le difficoltà di poter ripatriare e godersi la guadagnata preda."—N. Molin, Relazione.

"Perchè con la pace viene loro levato il modo di andar in corso con che molti si sono arrichiti perchè sotto pretesto di andar contro i nemici de-predavano anco le navi degli amici come è pur troppo manifesto a V. S." —Ibid.

"Sono gli Inglesi sopra tutti gli uomini dediti al corseggiare, ne facevano particolar professione in tempo della regina Elizabetta la quale la permetteva contro gli Spagnuoli ed animava li suoi sudditi ad applicarvisi . . . . di quà sono procedute ricchezze grandi nelli particolari, accrescimenti delli dazii pubblici e sperienza e gloria nelli cittadini ed augumento di forze considerabilissime a tutto il regno. Ora queste depredazioni che vietate dalla pace contro Spagnuoli si sono indifferentemente voltate sopra tutti vengono più d'ogni tristizia odiate dal re . . . . . non di meno come non si trova officio di tanta santità e giustizia che l'avarizia degli uomini non la soglia guastar e corromper ; così è opinione che quelli medesimi che hanno principal carico di perseguitare questi scellerati li abbino spesse volte favoriti e protetti." —Marc Antonio Correr, Ambasc. appresso Giacomo I. 1611, in Barozzi and Berchet. S. iv. vol. unico.

period, although England was in population and in wealth so insignificant, it possessed a lofty, insular contempt for the opinions and the doctrines of other nations, and expected, with perfect calmness, that her own principles should be not only admitted, but spontaneously adored.[33]

Yet the piratical interest was no longer the controlling one. That city on the Thames, which already numbered more than three hundred thousand inhabitants,[34] had discovered that more wealth was to be accumulated by her bustling shopkeepers in the paths of legitimate industry than by a horde of rovers over the seas, however adventurous and however protected by Government.

As for France, she was already defending herself against piracy by what at the period seemed a masterpiece of internal improvement. The Seine, the Loire, and the Rhone were soon to be united in one chain of communication. Thus merchandise might be water-borne from the channel to the Mediterranean, without risking the five or six months' voyage by sea then required from Havre to Marseilles, and exposure along the whole coast to attack from the corsairs of England, Spain, and Barbary.[35]

The envoys of the States-General had a brief audience of the new sovereign, in which little more than phrases of compliment were pronounced.

"We are here," said Barneveld, "between grief and joy. We have lost her whose benefits to us we can never describe in

---

[33] "Essendo l'Inglese per natura superbo crede che ognuno per natura sia obbligato di accarezzarlo non solo ma di adorarlo." — Ibid. N. Molin, Relazione.

[34] Molin.

[35] Angelo Badoer, Ambasc. in Francia, Relazione in Barozzi and Berchet, ser. ii. vol. i. "Ma finito questo taglio che si lavora per far entrare la Loira nella Senna come ho detto s'è risolto di farne un altro per far entrare il Rodano che passa Lione nella Loira essendo già il disegno fatto con che s'andrebbe da un mare all' altro sempre per i fiumi senza aver

mai a smontare in terra e quando questo resti effettuato, come ponendovisi le mani egli resterebbe in non lunghi anni mentre continui la pace nella Francia con più brevità con più sicurezza e con grand' utile a quel regno si manderebbero le merci dal Mediterraneo sempre per acqua sino nell' Oceano senza averle a mandare per tanto mare come si fa ora che le navi hanno a circondare tutta la Spagna per arrivare in quelle parti con tanto rischio di venti e di corsari oltre il tempo di cinque o sei mesi che alle volte consumano nel viaggio."

words, but we have found a successor who is heir not only to her kingdom but to all her virtues."[35] And with this exordium the great Advocate plunged at once into the depths of his subject, so far as was possible in an address of ceremony. He besought the king not to permit Spain, standing on the neck of the provinces, to grasp from that elevation at other empires. He reminded James of his duty to save those of his own religion from the clutch of a sanguinary superstition, to drive away those lurking satellites of the Roman pontiff who considered Britain their lawful prey. He implored him to complete the work so worthily begun by Elizabeth. If all those bound by one interest should now, he urged, unite their efforts, the Spaniard, deprived not only of the Netherlands, but, if he were not wise in time, banished from the ocean and stripped of all his transmarine possessions, would be obliged to consent to a peace founded on the only secure basis, equality of strength. The envoy concluded by beseeching the king for assistance to Ostend, now besieged for two years long.[36]

But James manifested small disposition to melt in the fervour of the Advocate's eloquence. He answered with a few cold commonplaces. Benignant but extremely cautious, he professed goodwill enough to the States but quite as much for Spain, a power with which, he observed, he had never quarrelled, and from which he had received the most friendly offices. The archdukes, too, he asserted, had never been hostile to the realm, but only to the Queen of England. In brief, he was new to English affairs, required time to look about him, but would not disguise that his genius was literary, studious, and tranquil, and much more inclined to peace than to war.[37]

In truth, James had cause to look very sharply about him. It required an acute brain and steady nerves to understand and to control the whirl of parties and the conflict of interests and intrigues, the chameleon shiftings of character and colour, at this memorable epoch of transition in the realm which he

[35] Grotius. xii. 619. Meteren, *ubi sup.*   [36] Ibid.   [37] Ibid.

had just inherited. There was a Scotch party, favourable on the whole to France; there was a Spanish party, there was an English party, and, more busy than all, there was a party— not Scotch, nor French, nor English, nor Spanish—that un-dying party in all commonwealths or kingdoms which ever fights for itself and for the spoils.

France and Spain had made peace with each other at Vervins five years before, and had been at war ever since.

Nothing could be plainer nor more cynical than the language exchanged between the French monarch and the representative of Spain. That Philip III.—as the Spanish Government by a convenient fiction was always called—was the head and front of the great Savoy-Biron conspiracy to take Henry's life and dismember his kingdom, was hardly a stage secret. Yet diplomatic relations were still preserved between the two countries, and wonderful diplomatic inter-views had certainly been taking place in Paris.

Ambassador Tassis had walked with lofty port into Henry's cabinet, disdaining to salute any of the princes of the blood or high functionaries of state in the apartments through which he passed, and with insolent defiance had called Henry to account for his dealing with the Dutch rebels.

"Sire, the king my master finds it very strange," he said, "that you still continue to assist his rebels in Holland, and that you shoot at his troops on their way to the Netherlands. If you don't abstain from such infractions of his rights he prefers open war to being cheated by such a pretended peace. Hereupon I demand your reply."

"Mr. Ambassador," replied the king, "I find it still more strange that your master is so impudent as to dare to make such complaints—he who is daily making attempts upon my life and upon this State. Even if I do assist the Hollanders, what wrong is that to him? It is an organized common-wealth, powerful, neighbourly, acknowledging no subjection to him. But your master is stirring up rebellion in my own kingdom, addressing himself to the princes of my blood and my most notable officers, so that I have been obliged to cut off the head of one of the most beloved of them all. By these unchristian proceedings he has obliged me to take sides with the Hollanders, whom I know to be devoted to me ; nor have I done anything for them except to pay the debts I owed them. I know perfectly well that the king your master is the head of this conspiracy, and that the troops of Naples were meditating an attack upon my kingdom. I have two letters written by the hand of your master to Marshal Biron, telling him to trust Fuentes as if it were himself, and it is notorious that Fuentes has projected and managed all the attempts to assassinate me. Do you think you have a child to deal with ? The late King of Spain knew me pretty well. If this one thinks himself wiser I shall let him see who I am. Do you want peace or war ? I am ready for either."

The ambassador, whose head had thus been so vigorously washed—as Henry expressed it in recounting the interview afterwards to the Dutch envoy, Dr. Aerssens—stammered some unintelligible excuses, and humbly begged his Majesty not to be offended. He then retired quite crest-fallen, and took leave most politely of everybody as he went, down even to the very grooms of the chambers.

"You must show your teeth to the Spaniard," said Henry to Aerssens, "if you wish for a quiet life."

Here was unsophisticated diplomacy ; for the politic Henry, who could forgive assassins and conspirators, crowned or otherwise, when it suited his purpose to be lenient, knew that it was on this occasion very prudent to use the gift of language, not in order to conceal, but to express his thoughts.

"I left the king as red as a turkey-cock," said Tassis, as soon as he got home that morning, "and I was another turkey-cock. We have been talking a little bit of truth to each other."[38]

In truth, it was impossible, as the world was then con-

---

[38] "Ik weet doen Taxis t'huys quam | root als een callichoen gelaeten ende dat hy seÿde, ik hebbe den Coninck | ik ben een ander. Wy hebben malcan-

stituted, that France and Spain, in spite of many secret sympathies, should not be enemies ; that France, England, and the Dutch commonwealth, although cordially disliking each other, should not be allies.

Even before the death of Elizabeth a very remarkable interview had taken place at Dover, in which the queen had secretly disclosed the great thoughts with which that most imperial brain was filled just before its boundless activity was to cease for ever.

She had wished for a personal interview with the French king, whose wit and valour she had always heartily admired. Henry, on his part, while unmercifully ridiculing that preter-human vanity which he fed with fantastic adulation, never failed to do justice to her genius, and had been for a moment disposed to cross the channel, or even to hold council with her on board ship midway between the two countries.[9] It was however found impracticable to arrange any such meeting, and the gossips of the day hinted that the great Henry, whose delight was in battle, and who had never been known to shrink from danger on dry land, was appalled at the idea of sea-sickness, and even dreaded the chance of being kid-napped by the English pirates.[40]

The corsairs who drove so profitable a business at that period by plundering the merchantmen of their enemy, of their Dutch and French allies, and of their own nation, would assuredly have been pleased with such a prize.

The queen had confided to De Bethune that she had some-thing to say to the king which she could never reveal to other ears than his, but when the proposed visit of Henry was abandoned, it was decided that his confidential minister should slip across the channel before Elizabeth returned to her palace at Greenwich.

deren wat waerheyt geseyt," &c.— Aerssens to the States-General, 4 Oct. 1602. Hague Archives MS.

Henry recounted these conversations with his own lips to Dr. Aerssens, who communicated them to the States-General in his secret letters. I have read them in the Fransche Depê-chen, A°. 1602–1607, Royal Archives at the Hague MS. See especially Aerssens to the States-General, 4 and 18 October, 1602.

[39] Mémoires de Sully, iv. 34–46, anno 1601.   [40] Ibid.

De Bethune accordingly came incognito from Calais to Dover, in which port he had a long and most confidential interview with the queen. Then and there the woman, nearly seventy years of age, who governed despotically the half of a small island, while the other half was in the possession of a man whose mother she had slain, and of a people who hated the English more than they hated the Spaniards or the French—a queen with some three millions of loyal but most turbulent subjects in one island, and with about half-a-million ferocious rebels in another requiring usually an army of twenty thousand disciplined soldiers to keep them in a kind of subjugation, with a revenue fluctuating between eight hundred thousand pounds sterling, and the half of that sum, and with a navy of a hundred privateersmen—disclosed to the French envoy a vast plan for regulating the polity and the religion of the civilized world, and for remodelling the map of Europe.[41]

There should be three religions, said Elizabeth—not counting the dispensation from Mecca, about which Turk and Hun might be permitted to continue their struggle on the crepuscular limits of civilization. Everywhere else there should be toleration only for the churches of Peter, of Luther, and of Calvin. The house of Austria was to be humbled—the one branch driven back to Spain and kept there, the other branch to be deprived of the imperial crown, which was to be disposed of as in times past by the votes of the princely electors. There should be two republics—the Swiss and the Dutch—each of those commonwealths to be protected by France and England, and each to receive considerable parings out of the possessions of Spain and the empire.

Finally, all Christendom was to be divided off into a certain number of powers, almost exactly equal to each other; the weighing, measuring, and counting, necessary to obtain this international equilibrium, being of course the duty of the king and queen when they should sit some day together at table.

<hr>

[41] Mémoires de Sully, iv. 34–36, anno 1601.

Thus there were five points; sovereigns and politicians having always a fondness for a neat summary in five or six points. Number one, to remodel the electoral system of the holy Roman empire. Number two, to establish the republic of the United Provinces. Number three, to do as much for Switzerland. Number four, to partition Europe. Number five, to reduce all religions to three.[42] Nothing could be more majestic, no plan fuller fraught with tranquillity for the rulers of mankind and their subjects. Thrice happy the people, having thus a couple of heads with crowns upon them and brains within them to prescribe what was to be done in this world and believed as to the next!

The illustrious successor of that great queen now stretches her benignant sceptre over two hundred millions of subjects, and the political revenues of her empire are more than a hundredfold those of Elizabeth; yet it would hardly now be thought great statesmanship or sound imperial policy for a British sovereign even to imagine the possibility of the five points which filled the royal English mind at Dover.

But Henry was as much convinced as Elizabeth of the necessity and the possibility of establishing the five points, and De Bethune had been astonished at the exact similarity of the conclusion which those two sovereign intellects had reached, even before they had been placed in communion with each other. The death of the queen had not caused any change in the far-reaching designs of which the king now remained the sole executor, and his first thought, on the accession of James, was accordingly to despatch De Bethune, now created Marquis de Rosny, as ambassador extraordinary to England, in order that the new sovereign might be secretly but thoroughly instructed as to the scheme for remodelling Christendom.[43]

As Rosny was also charged with the duty of formally congratulating King James, he proceeded upon his journey with remarkable pomp. He was accompanied by two hundred gentlemen of quality, specially attached to his embassy—

---

[42] Mémoires de Sully, iv. 34–36, anno 1601.   [43] Ibid. 260, seqq.

young city fops, as he himself described them, who were out
of their element whenever they left the pavement of Paris
—and by an equal number of valets, grooms, and cooks.[44]
Such a retinue was indispensable to enable an ambassador
to transact the public business and to maintain the public
dignity in those days; unproductive consumption being accounted most sagacious and noble.

Before reaching the English shore the marquis was involved
in trouble. Accepting the offer of the English vice-admiral
lying off Calais, he embarked with his suite in two English
vessels, much to the dissatisfaction of De Vic, vice-admiral of
France, who was anxious to convey the French ambassador in
the war-ships of his country. There had been suspicion afloat
as to the good understanding between England and Spain,
caused by the great courtesy recently shown to the Count of
Arenberg, and there was intense irritation among all the seafaring people of France on account of the exploits of the
English corsairs upon their coast.[45] Rosny thought it best to
begin his embassy by an act of conciliation, but soon had cause
to repent his decision.

In mid-channel they were met by De Vic's vessels with the
French banner displayed, at which sight the English commander was so wroth that he forthwith ordered a broadside
to be poured into the audacious foreigner; swearing with
mighty oaths that none but the English flag should be shown
in those waters. And thus, while conveying a French ambassador and three hundred Frenchmen on a sacred mission
to the British sovereign, this redoubtable mariner of England
prepared to do battle with the ships of France. It was with
much difficulty and some prevarication that Rosny appeased
the strife, representing that the French flag had only been
raised in order that it might be dipped, in honour of the
French ambassador, as the ships passed each other. The full-
shotted broadside was fired from fifty guns, but the
English commander consented, at De Rosny's representations, that it should be discharged wide of the mark.[46]

15 June,
1603.

---

[44] Mémoires de Sully, iv. 268; v. 21.   [45] Ibid. iv. 272.   [46] Ibid. 273-6.

A few shots, however, struck the side of one of the French vessels, and at the same time, as Cardinal Richelieu afterwards remarked, pierced the heart of every patriotic Frenchman.[47]

The ambassador made a sign, which De Vic understood, to lower his flag and to refrain from answering the fire.[48] Thus a battle between allies, amid the most amazing circumstances, was avoided, but it may well be imagined how long and how deeply the poison of the insult festered.

Such an incident could hardly predispose the ambassador in favour of the nation he was about to visit, or strengthen his hope of laying, not only the foundation of a perpetual friendship between the two crowns, but of effecting the palingenesis of Europe. Yet no doubt Sully—as the world has so long learned to call him—was actuated by lofty sentiments in many respects in advance of his age. Although a brilliant and successful campaigner in his youth, he detested war, and looked down with contempt at political systems which had not yet invented anything better than gunpowder for the arbitrament of international disputes. Instead of war being an occasional method of obtaining peace, it pained him to think that peace seemed only a process for arriving at war. Surely it was no epigram in those days, but the simplest statement of commonplace fact, that war was the normal condition of Christians. Alas! will it be maintained that in the two and a half centuries which have since elapsed the world has made much progress in a higher direction? Is there yet any appeal among the most civilized nations except to the logic of the largest battalions and the eloquence of the biggest guns?

De Rosny came to be the harbinger of a political millennium, and he heartily despised war. The schemes, nevertheless, which were as much his own as his master's, and which he was instructed to lay before the English monarch as exclusively his own, would have required thirty years of

---

[47] Mémoires de Sully, iv. 273–6, and notes.   [48] Ibid.

successful and tremendous warfare before they could have a beginning of development.

It is not surprising that so philosophical a mind as his, while still inclining to pacific designs, should have been led by what met his eyes and ears to some rather severe generalizations.

" It is certain that the English hate us," he said, " and with a hatred so strong and so general that one is tempted to place it among the natural dispositions of this people. Yet it is rather the effect of their pride and their presumption ; since there is no nation in Europe more haughty, more disdainful, more besotted with the idea of its own excellence. If you were to take their word for it, mind and reason are only found with them ; they adore all their opinions and despise those of all other nations ; and it never occurs to them to listen to others, or to doubt themselves. . . . . Examine what are called with them maxims of state ; you will find nothing but the laws of pride itself, adopted through arrogance or through indolence." [49]

" Placed by nature amidst the tempestuous and variable ocean," he wrote to his sovereign, " they are as shifting, as impetuous, as changeable as its waves. So self-contradictory and so inconsistent are their actions almost in the same instant as to make it impossible that they should proceed from the same persons and the same mind. Agitated and urged by their pride and arrogance alone, they take all their imaginations and extravagances for truths and realities ; the objects of their desires and affections for inevitable events ; not balancing and measuring those desires with the actual condition of things, nor with the character of the people with whom they have to deal." [50]

When the ambassador arrived in London he was lodged at Arundel palace. He at once became the cynosure of all indigenous parties and of adventurous politicians from every

---

[49] Mémoires, iv. 291, 292. Compare the ambassador's letters in Vittorio Siri, vol. i.

[50] Rosny to the King, 13 June, 1603, in Vittorio Siri. Memorie Recondite, i. 226.

part of Europe ; few knowing how to shape their course since the great familiar lustre had disappeared from the English sky.

Rosny found the Scotch lords sufficiently favourable to France ; the English Catholic grandees, with all the Howards and the lord high admiral at their head, excessively inclined to Spain, and a great English party detesting both Spain and France with equal fervour and well enough disposed to the United Provinces, not as hating that commonwealth less but the two great powers more.

The ambassador had arrived with the five points, not in his portfolio but in his heart, and they might after all be concentrated in one phrase—Down with Austria, up with the Dutch republic. On his first interview with Cecil, who came to arrange for his audience with the king, he found the secretary much disposed to conciliate both Spain and the empire, and to leave the provinces to shift for themselves. He spoke of Ostend as of a town not worth the pains taken to preserve it, and of the India trade as an advantage of which a true policy required that the United Provinces should be deprived.[51] Already the fine commercial instinct of England had scented a most formidable rival on the ocean.

As for the king, he had as yet declared himself for no party, while all parties were disputing among each other for mastery over him. James found himself, in truth, as much astray in English politics as he was a foreigner upon English earth. Suspecting every one, afraid of every one, he was in mortal awe, most of all, of his wife, who being the daughter of one Protestant sovereign and wife of another, and queen of a united realm dependent for its very existence on antagonism to Spain and Rome, was naturally inclined to Spanish politics and the Catholic faith.

The turbulent and intriguing Anne of Denmark was not at the moment in London, but James was daily expecting and De Bethune dreading her arrival.

[51] Letter last cited, 307.

The ambassador knew very well that, although the king talked big in her absence about the forms which he intended to prescribe for her conduct, he would take orders from her as soon as she arrived, refuse her nothing, conceal nothing from her, and tremble before her as usual.[52]

The king was not specially prejudiced in favour of the French monarch or his ambassador, for he had been told that Henry had occasionally spoken of him as captain of arts and doctor of arms, and that both the Marquis de Rosny and his brother were known to have used highly disrespectful language concerning him.

Before his audience, De Rosny received a private visit from Barneveld and the deputies of the States-General, and was informed that since his arrival they had been treated with more civility by the king. Previously he had refused to see them after the first official reception, had not been willing to grant Count Henry of Nassau a private audience, and had spoken publicly of the States as seditious rebels.

On the 21st June Barneveld had a long private interview with the ambassador at Arundel palace, when he exerted all his eloquence to prove the absolute necessity of an offensive and defensive alliance between France and the United Provinces if the independence of the republic were ever to be achieved. Unless a French army took the field at once, Ostend would certainly fall, he urged, and resistance to the Spaniards would soon afterwards cease.[53]

21 June, 1603.

It is not probable that the Advocate felt in his heart so much despair as his words indicated, but he was most anxious that Henry should openly declare himself the protector of the young commonwealth, and not indisposed perhaps to exaggerate the dangers, grave as they were without doubt, by which its existence was menaced.

The ambassador however begged the Hollander to renounce any such hopes, assuring him that the king had no intention

---

[52] Despatches of Rosny, in Siri, i. 231.
[53] Ibid. 309, 310. Compare Rosny's letter to the King, in Groen v. Prinsterer, Archives, II. 206–210.

of publicly and singly taking upon his shoulders the whole
burden of war with Spain, the fruits of which would not be his
to gather.   Certainly before there had been time thoroughly to
study the character and inclinations of the British monarch it
would be impossible for De Rosny to hold out any encouragement in this regard.   He then asked Barneveld what he had
been able to discover during his residence in London as to the
personal sentiments of James.

The Advocate replied that at first the king, yielding to his
own natural tendencies, and to the advice of his counsellors,
had refused the Dutch deputies every hope, but that subsequently reflecting, as it would seem, that peace would cost
England very dear if English inaction should cause the
Hollanders to fall again under the dominion of the Catholic
king, or to find their only deliverance in the protection of
France, and beginning to feel more acutely how much
England had herself to fear from a power like Spain, he had
seemed to awake out of a profound sleep, and promised to
take these important affairs into consideration.

Subsequently he had fallen into a dreary abyss of indecision,
where he still remained.[54]   It was certain however that he
would form no resolution without the concurrence of the King
of France, whose ambassador he had been so impatiently
expecting, and whose proposition to him of a double marriage
between their respective children had given him much satisfaction.

De Rosny felt sure that the Dutch statesmen were far too
adroit to put entire confidence in anything said by James,
whether favourable or detrimental to their cause.   He con-
jured Barneveld therefore, by the welfare of his country, to
conceal nothing from him in regard to the most secret
resolutions that might have been taken by the States in the
event of their being abandoned by England, or in case of
their being embarrassed by a sudden demand on the part
of that power for the cautionary towns offered to Elizabeth.[55]

Barneveld, thus pressed, and considering the ambassador

[54] Letter of Rosny, *ubi sup.*   [55] Ibid, 313.

as the confidential counsellor of a sovereign who was the republic's only friend, no longer hesitated. Making a merit to himself of imparting an important secret, he said that the state-council of the commonwealth had resolved to elude at any cost the restoration of the cautionary towns.[56]

The interview was then abruptly terminated by the arrival of the Venetian envoy.

The 22nd of June arrived. The marquis had ordered mourning suits for his whole embassy and retinue, by particular command of his sovereign, who wished to pay this public tribute to the memory of the great queen.

22 June, 1603.

To his surprise and somewhat to his indignation, he was however informed that no one, stranger or native, Scotchman or Englishman, had been permitted to present himself to the king in black, that his appearance there in mourning would be considered almost an affront, and that it was a strictly enforced rule at court to abstain from any mention of Queen Elizabeth, and to affect an entire oblivion of her reign.[57]

At the last moment, and only because convinced that he might otherwise cause the impending negotiations utterly to fail, the ambassador consented to attire himself, the hundred and twenty gentlemen selected from his diplomatic family to accompany him on this occasion, and all his servants, in gala costume. The royal guards, with the Earl of Derby at their head, came early in the afternoon to Arundel House to escort him to the Thames, and were drawn up on the quay as the marquis and his followers embarked in the splendid royal barges provided to convey them to Greenwich.[58]

On arriving at their destination they were met at the landing by the Earl of Northumberland, and escorted with great pomp and through an infinite multitude of spectators to the palace. Such was the crowd, without and within, of courtiers and common people, that it was a long time before the marquis, preceded by his hundred and twenty gentlemen, reached the hall of audience.

[56] Letter of Rosny, *ubi sup.*   [57] Ibid, 320, 321.   [58] Ibid, 323, *seqq.*

At last he arrived at the foot of the throne, when James arose and descended eagerly two steps of the dais in order to greet the ambassador. He would have descended them all had not one of the counsellors plucked him by the sleeve, whispering that he had gone quite far enough.

" And if I honour this ambassador," cried James, in a loud voice, " more than is usual, I don't intend that it shall serve as a precedent for others. I esteem and love him particularly, because of the affection which I know he cherishes for me, of his firmness in our religion, and of his fidelity to his master." [59]

Much more that was personally flattering to the marquis was said thus emphatically by James. To all this the ambassador replied, not by a set discourse, but only by a few words of compliment, expressing his sovereign's regrets at the death of Queen Elizabeth, and his joy at the accession of the new sovereign. He then delivered his letters of credence, and the complimentary conversation continued ; the king declaring that he had not left behind him in Scotland his passion for the monarch of France, and that even had he found England at war with that country on his accession he would have instantly concluded a peace with a prince whom he so much venerated.

Thus talking, the king caused his guest to ascend with him to the uppermost steps of the dais, babbling on very rapidly and skipping abruptly from one subject to another. De Rosny took occasion to express his personal esteem and devotion, and was assured by the king in reply that the slanders in regard to him which had reached the royal ears had utterly failed of their effect. It was obvious that they were the invention of Spanish intriguers who wished to help that nation to universal monarchy. Then he launched forth into general and cordial abuse of Spain, much to the satisfaction of Count Henry of Nassau, who stood near enough to hear a good deal of the conversation, and of the other Dutch deputies who were moving about, quite unknown, in the crowd. He

[59] Letter of Rosny. Siri, vol. i. 324.

denounced very vigorously the malignity of the Spaniards in lighting fires everywhere in their neighbours' possessions, protested that he would always oppose their wicked designs, but spoke contemptuously of their present king as too feeble of mind and body ever to comprehend or to carry out the projects of his predecessors.

Among other gossip, James asked the envoy if he went to hear the Protestant preaching in London. Being answered in the affirmative, he expressed surprise, having been told, he said, that it was Rosny's intention to repudiate his religion as De Sancy had done, in order to secure his fortunes. The marquis protested that such a thought had never entered his head, but intimated that the reports might come from his familiar intercourse with the papal nuncius and many French ecclesiastics. The king asked if, when speaking with the nuncius, he called the pope his Holiness, as by so doing he would greatly offend God, in whom alone was holiness. Rosny replied that he commonly used the style prevalent at court, governing himself according to the rules adopted in regard to pretenders to crowns and kingdoms which they thought belonged to them, but the possession of which was in other hands, conceding to them, in order not to offend them, the titles which they claimed.[60]

James shook his head portentously, and changed the subject.

The general tone of the royal conversation was agreeable enough to the ambassador, who eagerly alluded to the perfidious conduct of a Government which, ever since concluding the peace of Vervins with Henry, had been doing its best to promote sedition and territorial dismemberment in his kingdom, and to assist all his open and his secret enemies.

James assented very emphatically, and the marquis felt convinced that a resentment against Spain, expressed so publicly and so violently by James, could hardly fail to be sincere. He began seriously to hope that his negotiations would be successful, and was for soaring at once into the

[60] Despatches of Rosny, in Vitt. Siri, i. 231.

regions of high politics, when the king suddenly began to talk of hunting.

"And so you sent half the stag I sent you to Count Arenberg," said James ; "but he is very angry about it, thinking that you did so to show how much more I make of you than I do of him. And so I do; for I know the difference between your king, my brother, and his masters who have sent me an ambassador who can neither walk nor talk, and who asked me to give him audience in a garden because he cannot go upstairs."[31]

The king then alluded to Tassis, chief courier of his Catholic Majesty and special envoy from Spain, asking whether the marquis had seen him on his passage through France.

"Spain sends me a postillion-ambassador," said he, "that he may travel the faster and attend to business by post."[62]

It was obvious that James took a sincere satisfaction in abusing everything relating to that country from its sovereign and the Duke of Lerma downwards;[63] but he knew very well that Velasco, constable of Castile, had been already designated as ambassador, and would soon be on his way to England.

De Rosny on the termination of his audience was escorted in great state by the Earl of Northumberland to the barges.

A few days later, the ambassador had another private audience, in which the king expressed himself with apparent candour concerning the balance of power.[64]   22 June.
Christendom, in his opinion, should belong in three equal shares to the families of Stuart, Bourbon, and Habsburg ; but personal ambition and the force of events had given to the house of Austria more than its fair third. Sound policy therefore required a combination between France and England, in order to reduce their copartner within proper limits. This was satisfactory as far as it went, and the ambassador complimented the king on his wide views of policy and his lofty sentiments in regard to human rights.

[61] Sully, Mémoires, iv. 331, seqq. Despatches of Rosny, in Vitt. Siri, i.
[62] Mémoires, ubi sup.
[63] See especially the despatches of the ambassador to the king in the month of July, in Vittorio Siri, Mem. Rec. i.
[64] Mémoires, 355, seqq.

Warming with the subject, James held language very similar to that which De Rosny and his master had used in their secret conferences, and took the ground unequivocally that the secret war levied by Spain against France and England, as exemplified in the Biron conspiracy, the assault on Geneva, the aid of the Duke of Savoy, and in the perpetual fostering of Jesuit intrigues, plots of assassination, and other conspiracies in the British islands, justified a secret war on the part of Henry and himself against Philip.

The ambassador would have been more deeply impressed with the royal language had he felt more confidence in the royal character.

Highly applauding the sentiments expressed, and desiring to excite still further the resentment of James against Spain, he painted a vivid picture of the progress of that aggressive power in the past century. She had devoured Flanders, Burgundy, Granada, Navarre, Portugal, the German Empire, Milan, Naples, and all the Indies. If she had not swallowed likewise both France and England those two crowns were indebted for their preservation, after the firmness of Elizabeth and Henry, to the *fortunate incident of the revolt of the Netherlands.*[65]

De Rosny then proceeded to expound the necessity under which James would soon find himself of carrying on open war with Spain, and of the expediency of making preparations for the great struggle without loss of time.

He therefore begged the king to concert with him some satisfactory measure for the preservation of the United Provinces.

" But," said James, " what better assistance could we give

[65] Mémoires, 359. And in thus speaking he expressed the firm conviction of the whole French court. " Provided the States remain at war," said Villeroy, " and the Spaniards have this bone to gnaw, it will always be in the power of the English to change their minds. If Spain could get this thorn out of her foot which God has put there, and thus far has kept there so miraculously, with what bridle could her insolence be checked? The kingdoms of France and England being filled with discords in regard to religion as they are, how can they resist Spanish power and Spanish corruption? Even now they can hardly do it, occupied, diverted, and wearied as are the Spaniards with their war against the Netherlands." Groen v. Prinsterer, Archives, II. 231, 232.

the Netherlanders than to divide their territory between the States and Spain; agreeing at the same time to drive the Spaniard out altogether, if he violates the conditions which we should guarantee."[66]

This conclusion was not very satisfactory to De Rosny, who saw in the bold language of the king—followed thus by the indication of a policy that might last to the Greek Kalends, and permit Ostend, Dutch Flanders, and even the republic to fall—nothing but that mixture of timidity, conceit, and procrastination which marked the royal character. He pointed out to him accordingly that Spanish statesmanship could beat the world in the art of delay, and of plucking the fruits of delay, and that when the United Provinces had been once subjugated, the turn of England would come. It would be then too late for him to hope to preserve himself by such measures as, taken now, would be most salutary.[67]

A few days later the king invited De Rosny and the two hundred members of his embassy to dine at Greenwich, and the excursion down the Thames took place with the usual pomp.

The two hundred dined with the gentlemen of the court; while at the king's table, on an elevated platform in the same hall, were no guests but De Rosny, and the special envoy of France, Count Beaumont.

29 June.

The furniture and decorations of the table were sumptuous, and the attendants, to the surprise of the Frenchmen, went on their knees whenever they offered wine or dishes to the king. The conversation at first was on general topics, such as the heat of the weather, which happened to be remarkable,

---

[66] Mémoires, iv. 404, *seqq.* Siri, *ubi sup.*

[67] Mémoires, *ubi sup.* 363. "In truth," wrote the ambassador to his sovereign, "Spain wishes to honey you both (the kings of France and England) in order to accomplish more easily the complete conquest of the Netherlands. When these are joined to her great and almost infinite power, she hopes to give the law to Christendom, to make herself formidable to all other princes, and to establish a universal monarchy. That is the bottom of their intentions. It is the regular covetousness and ambition of Spain, continued by the successors of Charles V. The two houses of Austria and of Spain being united, she has reached such an increase of power in less than one hundred years that the very imagination of it is terrific."—Sully to the King, in Groen v. Prinsterer, ii. 204, 205.

the pleasures of the chase, and the merits of the sermon which, as it was Sunday, De Rosny had been invited to hear before dinner in the royal chapel.

Soon afterwards, however, some allusion being made to the late queen, James spoke of her with contempt. He went so far as to say that, for a long time before her death, he had governed the councils of England; all her ministers obeying and serving him much better than they did herself.[68] He then called for wine, and, stretching out his glass towards his two guests, drank to the health of the king and queen and royal family of France.

De Rosny replied by proposing the health of his august host, not forgetting the queen and their children, upon which the king, putting his lips close to the ambassador's ear, re-marked that his next toast should be in honour of the matri-monial union which was proposed between the families of Britain and France.[69]

This was the first allusion made by James to the alliance, and the occasion did not strike the marquis as particularly appropriate to such a topic. He however replied in a whisper that he was rejoiced to hear this language from the king, having always believed that there would be no hesitation on his part between King Henry and the monarch of Spain, who, as he was aware, had made a similar proposition. James, expressing surprise that his guest was so well informed, avowed that he had in fact received the same offer of the Infanta for his son as had been made to his Christian Majesty for the Dauphin. What more convenient counters in the great game of state than an infant prince and princess in each of the three royal families to which Europe belonged! To how many grave political combinations were these unfortunate infants to give rise, and how distant the period when great nations might no longer be tied to the pinafores of children in the nursery!

After this little confidential interlude, James expressed in a loud voice, so that all might hear, his determination never

[68] Mémoires, iv. 378.   [69] Ibid.

to permit the subjugation of the Netherlands by Spain. Measures should be taken the very next day, he promised, in concert with the ambassador, as to the aid to be given to the States. Upon the faith of this declaration De Rosny took from his pocket the plan of a treaty, and forthwith, in the presence of all the ministers, placed it in the hands of the king, who meantime had risen from table. The ambassador also took this occasion to speak publicly of the English piracies upon French commerce while the two nations were at peace. The king, in reply, expressed his dissatisfaction at these depredations and at the English admiral who attempted to defend what had been done.

He then took leave of his guests, and went off to bed, where it was his custom to pass his afternoons.[70]

It was certain that the Constable of Castile was now to arrive very soon, and the marquis had, meantime, obtained information on which he relied, that this ambassador would come charged with very advantageous offers to the English court. Accounts had been got ready in council, of all the moneys due to England by France and by the States, and it was thought that these sums, payment of which was to be at once insisted upon, together with the Spanish dollars set afloat in London, would prove sufficient to buy up all resistance to the Spanish alliance.[71]

Such being the nature of the information furnished to De Rosny, he did not look forward with very high hopes to the issue of the conference indicated by King James at the Greenwich dinner. As, after all, he would have to deal once more with Cecil, the master-spirit of the Spanish party, it did not seem very probable that the king's whispered professions of affection for France, his very loud denunciations of Spanish ambition, and his promises of support to the struggling provinces, would be brought into any substantial form for human nourishment. Whispers and big words, touching of glasses at splendid banquets, and proposing of royal toasts, would not

[70] Mémoires, iv. 380.
[71] Ibid. 375, 376. Despatches of Rosny, in Siri.

go far to help those soldiers in Ostend, a few miles away, fighting two years long already for a square half-mile of barren sand, in which seemed centred the world's hopes of freedom.

Barneveld was inclined to take an even more gloomy view than that entertained by the French ambassador. He had, in truth, no reason to be sanguine. The honest republican envoys had brought no babies to offer in marriage. Their little commonwealth had only the merit of exchanging buffets forty years long with a power which, after subjugating the Netherlands, would have liked to annihilate France and England too, and which, during that period, had done its best to destroy and dismember both. It had only struggled as no nation in the world's history had ever done, for the great principle upon which the power and happiness of England were ever to depend. It was therefore not to be expected that its representatives should be received with the distinction conferred upon royal envoys. Barneveld and his colleagues accordingly were not invited, with two hundred noble hangers-on, to come down the Thames in gorgeous array, and dine at Greenwich palace; but they were permitted to mix in the gaping crowd of spectators, to see the fine folk, and to hear a few words at a distance which fell from august lips.[72] This was not very satisfactory, as Barneveld could rarely gain admittance to James or his ministers. De Rosny, however, was always glad to confer with him, and was certainly capable of rendering justice both to his genius and to the sacredness of his cause. The Advocate, in a long conference with the ambassador, thought it politic to paint the situation of the republic in even more sombre colours than seemed to De Rosny justifiable. He was, indeed, the more struck with Barneveld's present despondency, because, at a previous conference, a few days before, he had spoken almost with contempt of the Spaniards, expressing the opinion that the mutinous and disorganized condition of the archduke's army rendered the conquest of Ostend improbable, and hinted at a plan, of which the world as yet

[72] Mémoires, iv. 327.

knew nothing, which would save that place, or at any rate would secure such an advantage for the States as to more than counterbalance its possible loss.[73] This very sanguine demeanour had rather puzzled those who had conferred with the Advocate, although they were ere long destined to understand his allusions, and it was certainly a contrast to his present gloom. He assured De Rosny that the Hollanders were becoming desperate, and that they were capable of abandoning their country in mass, and seeking an asylum beyond the seas.[74] The menace was borrowed from the famous project conceived by William the Silent in darker days, and seemed to the ambassador a present anachronism. Obviously it was thought desirable to force the French policy to extreme lengths, and Barneveld accordingly proposed that Henry should take the burthen upon his shoulders of an open war with Spain, in the almost certain event that England would make peace with that power. De Rosny calmly intimated to the Advocate that this was asking something entirely beyond his power to grant, as the special object of his mission was to form a plan of concerted action with England.[75]

The cautionary towns being next mentioned, Barneveld stated that a demand had been made upon Envoy Caron by Cecil for the delivery of those places to the English Government, as England had resolved to make peace with Spain. The Advocate confided, however, to De Rosny that the States would interpose many difficulties, and that it would

[73] Mémoires, iv. 344, 345.

[74] Ibid. 381.

[75] The great object of Henry was to prevent a treaty between the kings of Spain and Britain, and above all to exclude the United Provinces from any such arrangement. "You know how much interest I have in this," he said to his ambassador; "it is the most important affair of my reign. You must never forget what my interest requires, that these two kings shall never come to an agreement. I don't wish the States to enter into the treaty or to lay down their arms on any pretext. Nevertheless, I ought not to appear to have any wish to prevent a peace between the two kingdoms, nor the reconciliation of the provinces, both on account of my reputation and because any demonstration that I might make would rather increase than diminish the desire of the two kings to come to an understanding."—(Groen v. Prinsterer, Archives, II. 224–226). These being the secret intentions of the monarch, candidly expressed, it was obviously a delicate matter for De Rosny, who knew that his master meant to remain at peace and yet reap the advantage of a successful war at the expense of his friends and enemies alike, to keep on good terms with all parties.

be long before the towns were delivered. This important information was given under the seal of strictest secrecy, and was coupled with an inference that a war between the republic and Britain would be the probable result, in which case the States relied upon the alliance with France. The ambassador replied that in this untoward event the republic would have the sympathy of his royal master, but that it would be out of the question for him to go to war with Spain and England at the same time.[76]

On the same afternoon there was a conference at Arundel House between the Dutch deputies, the English counsellors, and De Rosny, when Barneveld drew a most dismal picture of the situation ; taking the ground that now or never was the time for driving the Spaniards entirely out of the Netherlands. Cecil said in a general way that his Majesty felt a deep interest in the cause of the provinces, and the French ambassador summoned the Advocate, now that he was assured of the sympathy of two great kings, to furnish some plan by which that sympathy might be turned to account. Barneveld, thinking figures more eloquent than rhetoric, replied that the States, besides garrisons, had fifteen thousand infantry and three thousand cavalry in the field, and fifty war ships in commission, with artillery and munitions in proportion, and that it would be advisable for France and England to furnish an equal force, military and naval, to the common cause.[77]

De Rosny smiled at the extravagance of the proposition. Cecil, again taking refuge in commonplaces, observed that his master was disposed to keep the peace with all his neighbours, but that, having due regard to the circumstances, he was willing to draw a line between the wishes of the States and his own, and would grant them a certain amount of succour underhand.

Thereupon the Dutch deputies withdrew to confer. De Rosny, who had no faith in Cecil's sincerity—the suggestion being essentially the one which he had himself desired—went

[76] Mémoires, iv. 383   [77] Ibid. 383–395.

meantime a little deeper into the subject, and soon found that England, according to the Secretary of State, had no idea of ruining herself for the sake of the provinces, or of entering into any positive engagements in their behalf. In case Spain should make a direct attack upon the two kings who were to constitute themselves protectors of Dutch liberty, it might be necessary to take up arms. The admission was on the whole superfluous, it not being probable that Britain, even under a Stuart, would be converted to the doctrine of non-resistance. Yet in this case it was suggested by Cecil that the chief reliance of his Government would be on the debts owed by the Dutch and French respectively, which would then be forthwith collected.

De Rosny was now convinced that Cecil was trifling with him, and evidently intending to break off all practical negotiations. He concealed his annoyance, however, as well as he could, and simply intimated that the first business of importance was to arrange for the relief of Ostend ; that eventualities, such as the possible attack by Spain upon France and England, might for the moment be deferred, but that if England thought it a safe policy to ruin Henry by throwing on his shoulders the whole burthen of a war with the common enemy, she would discover and deeply regret her fatal mistake. The time was a very ill-chosen one to summon France to pay old debts, and his Christian Majesty had given his ambassador no instructions contemplating such a liquidation. It was the intention to discharge the sum annually, little by little, but if England desired to exhaust the king by these peremptory demands, it was an odious conduct, and very different from any that France had ever pursued.

The English counsellors were not abashed by this rebuke, but became, on the contrary, very indignant, avowing that if anything more was demanded of them, England would entirely abandon the United Provinces. "Cecil made himself known to me in this conference," said De Rosny, "for exactly what he was. He made use only of double meanings and vague propositions, feeling that reason was not on his side. He was forced to blush at his own self-contradictions, when, with a single word, I made him feel the absurdity of his language. Now, endeavouring to intimidate me, he exaggerated the strength of England, and again he enlarged upon the pretended offers made by Spain to that nation." [78]

The secretary, desirous to sow discord between the Dutch deputies and the ambassador, then observed that France ought to pay to England £50,000 upon the nail, which sum would be at once appropriated to the necessities of the States. "But what most enraged me," said De Rosny, "was to see these ministers, who had come to me to state the intentions of their king, thus impudently substitute their own; for I knew that he had commanded them to do the very contrary to that which they did." [79]

The conference ended with a suggestion by Cecil, that as France would only undertake a war in conjunction with England, and as England would only consent to this if paid by France and the States, the best thing for the two kings to do would be to do nothing, but to continue to live in friendship together, without troubling themselves about foreign complications.

This was the purpose towards which the English counsellors had been steadily tending, and these last words of Cecil seemed to the ambassador the only sincere ones spoken by him in the whole conference.

"If I kept silence," said the ambassador, "it was not because I acquiesced in their reasoning. On the contrary, the manner in which they had just revealed themselves, and avowed themselves in a certain sort liars and impostors, had given me the most profound contempt for them. I thought, however, that by heating myself and contending with them— so far from causing them to abandon a resolution which they had taken in concert—I might even bring about a total rupture. On the other hand, matters remaining as they were, and a friendship existing between the two kings, which might perhaps be cemented by a double marriage, a more

---

[78] Mémoires, iv. 391.   [79] Ibid. 392, 393.

favourable occasion might present itself for negotiation. I did not yet despair of the success of my mission, because I believed that the king had no part in the designs which his counsellors wished to carry out." [80]

That the counsellors, then struggling for dominion over the new king and his kingdom, understood the character of their sovereign better than did the ambassador, future events were likely enough to prove. That they preferred peace to war, and the friendship of Spain to an alliance, offensive and defensive, with France in favour of a republic which they detested, is certain. It is difficult, however, to understand why they were "liars and impostors" because, in a conference with the respresentative of France, they endeavoured to make their own opinions of public policy valid rather than content themselves simply with being the errand-bearers of the new king, whom they believed incapable of being stirred to an honourable action.

The whole political atmosphere of Europe was mephitic with falsehood, and certainly the gales which blew from the English court at the accession of James were not fragrant, but De Rosny had himself come over from France under false pretences. He had been charged by his master to represent Henry's childish scheme, which he thought so gigantic, for the regeneration of Europe, as a project of his own, which he was determined to bring to execution, even at the risk of infidelity to his sovereign, and the first element in that whole policy was to carry on war underhand against a power with which his master had just sworn to preserve peace. In that age at least it was not safe for politicians to call each other hard names.

The very next day De Rosny had a long private interview with James at Greenwich. Being urged to speak without reserve, the ambassador depicted the privy counsellors to the king as false to his instructions, traitors to the best interests of their country, the humble servants of Spain, and most desirous to make their royal master the slave of that power

[80] Mémoires, 394, 395.

under the name of its ally. He expressed the opinion, accordingly, that James would do better in obeying only the promptings of his own superior wisdom, rather than the suggestions of the intriguers about him. The adroit De Rosny thus softly insinuated to the flattered monarch that the designs of France were the fresh emanations of his own royal intellect. It was the whim of James to imagine himself extremely like Henry of Bourbon in character, and he affected to take the wittiest, bravest, most adventurous, and most adroit knight-errant that ever won and wore a crown as his perpetual model.

It was delightful, therefore, to find himself, in company with his royal brother, making and unmaking kings, destroying empires, altering the whole face of Christendom, and, better than all, settling then and for ever the theology of the whole world, without the trouble of moving from his easy chair, or of incurring any personal danger.

He entered at once, with the natural tendency to suspicion of a timid man, into the views presented by De Rosny as to the perfidy of his counsellors. He changed colour, and was visibly moved, as the ambassador gave his version of the recent conference with Cecil and the other ministers, and being thus artfully stimulated, he was prepared to receive with much eagerness the portentous communications now to be made.

The ambassador, however, caused him to season his admiration until he had taken a most solemn oath, by the sacrament of the Eucharist, never to reveal a syllable of what he was about to hear. This done, and the royal curiosity excited almost beyond endurance, De Rosny began to unfold the stupendous schemes which had been concerted between Elizabeth and Henry at Dover, and which formed the secret object of his present embassy. Feeling that the king was most malleable in the theological part of his structure, the wily envoy struck his first blows in that direction, telling him that his own interest in the religious condition of Europe, and especially in the firm establishment of the Protestant faith, far surpassed in his mind all considerations of fortune, country, or even of fidelity to his sovereign.[81] Thus far, political considerations had kept Henry from joining in the great Catholic League, but it was possible that a change might occur in his system, and the Protestant form of worship, abandoned by its ancient protector, might disappear entirely from France and from Europe. De Rosny had, therefore, felt the necessity of a new patron for the reformed religion in this great emergency, and had naturally fixed his eyes on the puissant and sagacious prince who now occupied the British throne. Now was the time, he urged, for James to immortalize his name by becoming the arbiter of the destiny of Europe. It would always seem his own design, although Henry was equally interested in it with himself. The plan was vast but simple, and perfectly easy of execution. There would be no difficulty in constructing an all-powerful league of sovereigns for the destruction of the house of Austria, the foundation-stones of which would of course be France, Great Britain, and the United Provinces. The double marriage between the Bourbon and Stuart families would indissolubly unite the two kingdoms, while interest and gratitude, a common hatred and a common love, would bind the republic as firmly to the union. Denmark and Sweden were certainly to be relied upon, as well as all other Protestant princes. The ambitious and restless Duke of Savoy would be gained by the offer of Lombardy and a kingly crown, notwithstanding his matrimonial connection with Spain. As for the German princes, they would come greedily into the arrangement, as the league, rich in the spoils of the Austrian house, would have Hungary, Bohemia, Silesia, Moravia, the archduchies, and other splendid provinces to divide among them.

The pope would be bought up by a present, in fee-simple, of Naples, and other comfortable bits of property, of which he was now only feudal lord. Sicily would be an excellent sop for the haughty republic of Venice. The Franche Comté, Alsace, Tirol, were naturally to be annexed to Switzerland;

[81] Mémoires, iv. 402.

Liège and the heritage of the Duke of Clèves and Juliers to the Dutch commonwealth.[82]

.The King of France, who, according to De Rosny's solemn assertions, was entirely ignorant of the whole scheme,[83] would, however, be sure to embrace it very heartily when James should propose it to him, and would be far too disinterested to wish to keep any of the booty for himself. A similar self-denial was, of course, expected of James, the two great kings satisfying themselves with the proud consciousness of having saved society, rescued the world from the sceptre of an Austrian universal monarchy, and regenerated European civilization for all future time.[84]

The monarch listened with ravished ears, interposed here and there a question or a doubt, but devoured every detail of the scheme, as the ambassador slowly placed it before him.

De Rosny showed that the Spanish faction was not in reality so powerful as the league which would be constructed for its overthrow. It was not so much a religious as a political frontier which separated the nations. He undertook to prove this, but, after all, was obliged to demonstrate that the defection of Henry from the Protestant cause had deprived him of his natural allies, and given him no true friends in exchange for the old ones.

Essentially the Catholics were ranged upon one side, and the Protestants on the other, but both religions were necessary to Henry the Huguenot. The bold free-thinker adroitly balanced himself upon each creed. In making use of a stern and conscientious Calvinist, like Maximilian de Béthune, in his first assault upon the theological professor who now stood in Elizabeth's place, he showed the exquisite tact which never failed him. Toleration for the two religions which had political power, perfect intolerance for all others ; despotic forms of polity, except for two little republics which were to be smothered with protection and never left out of leading strings, a thorough recasting of governments and races, a palingenesis of Europe, a nominal partition of its hegemony between

[82] Mémoires, iv. 204.   [83] Ibid.   [84] Ibid. 404, *seqq.*

France and England, which was to be in reality absorbed by France, and the annihilation of Austrian power east and west, these were the vast ideas with which that teeming Bourbon brain was filled. It is the instinct both of poetic and of servile minds to associate a sentiment of grandeur with such fantastic dreams, but usually on condition that the dreamer wears a crown. When the regenerator of society appears with a wisp of straw upon his head, unappreciative society is apt to send him back to his cell. There, at least, his capacity for mischief is limited.

If to do be as grand as to imagine what it were good to do, then the Dutchmen in Hell's Mouth and the Porcupine fighting Universal Monarchy inch by inch and pike to pike, or trying conclusions with the ice-bears of Nova Zembla, or capturing whole Portuguese fleets in the Moluccas, were effecting as great changes in the world, and doing perhaps as much for the advancement of civilization, as James of the two Britains and Henry of France and Navarre in those his less heroic days, were likely to accomplish. History has long known the results.

The ambassador did his work admirably. The king embraced him in a transport of enthusiasm, vowed by all that was most sacred to accept the project in all its details, and exacted from the ambassador in his turn an oath on the Eucharist never to reveal, except to his master, the mighty secrets of their conference.[85]

The interview had lasted four hours. When it was concluded, James summoned Cecil, and in presence of the ambassador and of some of the counsellors, lectured him soundly on his presumption in disobeying the royal commands in his recent negotiations with De Rosny. He then announced his decision to ally himself strictly with France against Spain in consequence of the revelations just made to him, and of course to espouse the cause of the United Provinces. Telling the crest-fallen Secretary of State to make the proper official communications on the subject to the ambassadors of my

[85] Mémoires, iv. 417, *et seqq.* Despatches in Siri, vol. 1.

lords the States-General,[86]—thus giving the envoys from the republic for the first time that pompous designation,—the king turned once more to the marquis with the exclamation,— " Well, Mr. Ambassador, this time I hope that you are satisfied with me ?"[87]

In the few days following De Rosny busied himself in drawing up a plan of a treaty embodying all that had been agreed upon between Henry and himself, and which he had just so faithfully rehearsed to James. He felt now some inconvenience from his own artfulness, and was in a measure caught in his own trap. Had he brought over a treaty in his pocket, James would have signed it on the spot, so eager was he for the regeneration of Europe. It was necessary, however, to continue the comedy a little longer, and the ambassador, having thought it necessary to express many doubts whether his master could be induced to join in the plot, and to approve what was really his own most cherished plan, could now do no more than promise to use all his powers of persuasion unto that end.

The project of a convention, which James swore most solemnly to sign, whether it were sent to him in six weeks or six months, was accordingly rapidly reduced to writing and approved. It embodied, of course, most of the provisions discussed in the last secret interview at Greenwich. The most practical portion of it undoubtedly related to the United Provinces, and to the nature of assistance to be at once afforded to that commonwealth, the only ally of the two kingdoms expressly mentioned in the treaty. England was to furnish troops, the number of which was not specified, and France was to pay for them, partly out of her own funds, partly out of the amount due by her to England. It was, however, understood, that this secret assistance should not be considered to infringe the treaty of peace which already existed between Henry and the Catholic king. Due and detailed arrangements were made as to the manner in which the allies were to assist each other, in case Spain, not re-

[86] Mémoires, iv, 420.　　　　[87] Ibid.

lishing this kind of neutrality, should think proper openly to attack either great Britain or France, or both.[88]

Unquestionably the Dutch republic was the only portion of Europe likely to be substantially affected by these secret arrangements ; for, after all, it had not been found very easy to embody the splendid visions of Henry, which had so dazzled the imagination of James in the dry clauses of a protocol.

It was also characteristic enough of the crowned conspirators, that the clause relating to the United Provinces provided that the allies would *either* assist them in the attainment of their independence, *or*[89]—if it should be considered expedient to restore them to the domination of Spain or the empire—would take such precautions and lay down such conditions as would procure perfect tranquillity for them, and remove from the two allied kings the fear of a too absolute government by the house of Austria in those provinces.

It would be difficult to imagine a more impotent conclusion. Those Dutch rebels had not been fighting for tranquillity. The tranquillity of the rock amid raging waves— according to the device of the father of the republic—they had indeed maintained ; but to exchange their turbulent and tragic existence, ever illumined by the great hope of freedom, for repose under one despot guaranteed to them by two others, was certainly not their aim. They lacked the breadth of vision enjoyed by the regenerators who sat upon mountain-tops.

They were fain to toil on in their own way. Perhaps, however, the future might show as large results from their work as from the schemes of those who were to begin the humiliation of the Austrian house by converting its ancient rebels into tranquil subjects.

The Marquis of Rosny, having distributed 60,000 crowns among the leading politicians and distinguished personages at the English court, with ample promises of future largess if they remained true to his master,[90] took an affec-

[88] Sully, Mémoires, v. 1–12.
[89] Ibid, 7, 8.
[90] Ibid, 20, 35, 40.   " L'objet du

roy en faisant tant de riches présens dont même une bonne partie fut continuée aux seigneurs Anglais en forme

tionate farewell of King James, and returned with his noble two hundred to recount his triumphs to the impatient Henry. The treaty was soon afterwards duly signed and ratified by the high contracting parties. It was, however, for future history to register its results on the fate of pope, emperor, kings, potentates, and commonwealths, and to show the changes it would work in the geography, religion, and polity of the world.[91]

The deputies from the States-General, satisfied with the practical assistance promised them, soon afterwards took their departure with comparative cheerfulness, having previously obtained the royal consent to raise recruits in Scotland. Meantime the great Constable of Castile, ambassador from his Catholic Majesty, had arrived in London, and was wroth at all that he saw and all that he suspected. He, too, began to scatter golden arguments with a lavish hand among the great lords and statesmen of Britain,[92] but found that the financier of France had, on the whole, got before him in the business, and was skilfully maintaining his precedence from the other side of the channel.

But the end of these great diplomatic manœuvres had not yet come.

de pension, étoit de les retenir et de les attacher de plus en plus à son parti. Je les fis sur ma propre connaissance et sur les recommandations de Beaumont, et ma principale attention fut de les distribuer de maniere qu'ils ne fissent naître aucune jalousie entre ces seigneurs Anglois et que le roy lui même n'en prît aucun soupçon," &c. &c.

[91] "Il multiplia le nombre de ses créatures parcequ'il fit des liberalités extraordinaires à tous ceux dont il crut avoir besoin, &c. &c. Ibid. 35

[92] Et pour user de toutes sortes de contre-batteries contre les Espagnols qui faisoient des présens à toutes mains, on en fit aussi et même des pensions à tout ce qu'il y avoit d'Anglois distingués à la cour du Roi Jacques . . . . c'est ainsi que l'Espagne se vit frustrée des brillantes esperances qu'elle avoit conçues contre nous de l'avènement du Roy d'Ecosse à la couronne d'Angleterre et qui etoit peut-etre le motif des armamens immenses qu'elle fit cette année." Ibid. 40.

CHAPTER XLII.

Siege of Ostend — The Marquis Spinola made commander-in-chief of the
besieging army—Discontent of the troops — General aspect of the operations — Gradual encroachment of the enemy.

THE scene again shifts to Ostend. The Spanish cabinet,
wearied of the slow progress of the siege, and not entirely
satisfied with the generals, now concluded almost without
consent of the archdukes, one of the most extraordinary jobs
ever made, even in those jobbing days. The Marquis Spinola,
elder brother of the ill-fated Frederic, and head of the illustrious Genoese family of that name, undertook to furnish a
large sum of money which the wealth of his house and its connection with the great money-lenders of Genoa enabled him
to raise, on condition that he should have supreme command
of the operations against Ostend and of the foreign armies in
the Netherlands.[1] He was not a soldier, but he entered into
a contract, by his own personal exertions both on the exchange
and in the field, to reduce the city which had now resisted all
the efforts of the archduke for more than two years. Certainly
this was an experiment not often hazarded in warfare. The
defence of Ostend was in the hands of the best and most
seasoned fighting-men in Europe. The operations were under
the constant supervision of the foremost captain of the age ;
for Maurice, in consultation with the States-General, received
almost daily reports from the garrison, and regularly furnished
advice and instructions as to their proceedings. He was moreover ever ready to take the field for a relieving campaign.
Nothing was known of Spinola save that he was a high-born
and very wealthy patrician who had reached his thirty-fourth

[1] Gallucci, II. lib. xvi. 109–137, 138. Bentivoglio, iii. 519. Grotius, xii.
633, 634. Wagenaar, ix. 162, 163.

year without achieving personal distinction of any kind, and who, during the previous summer, like so many other nobles from all parts of Europe, had thought it worth his while to drawl through a campaign or two in the Low Countries. It was the mode to do this, and it was rather a stigma upon any young man of family not to have been an occasional looker on at that perpetual military game. His brother Frederic, as already narrated, had tried his chance for fame and fortune in the naval service, and had lost his life in the adventure without achieving the one or the other. This was not a happy augury for the head of the family. Frederic had made an indifferent speculation. What could the brother hope by taking the field against Maurice of Nassau and Lewis William and the Baxes and Meetkerkes ? Nevertheless the archduke eagerly accepted his services, while the Infanta, fully confident of his success before he had ordered a gun to be fired, protested that if Spinola did not take Ostend nobody would ever take it.[2] There was also, strangely enough, a general feeling through the republican ranks that the long-expected man had come.

Thus a raw volunteer, a man who had never drilled a hundred men, who had never held an officer's commission in any army in the world, became, as by the waving of a wand, a field-marshal and commander-in-chief at a most critical moment in history, in the most conspicuous position in Christendom, and in a great war, now narrowed down to a single spot of earth, on which the eyes of the world were fixed, and the daily accounts from which were longed for with palpitating anxiety. What but failure and disaster could be expected from such astounding policy ? Every soldier in the Catholic forces—from grizzled veterans of half a century who had commanded armies and achieved victories when this dainty young Italian was in his cradle, down to the simple musketeer or rider who had been campaigning for his daily bread ever since he could carry a piece or mount a horse— was furious with discontent or outraged pride.

---

[2] Gallucci, *ubi sup.*

Very naturally too, it was said that the position of the archdukes had become preposterous. It was obvious, notwithstanding the pilgrimages of the Infanta to Our Lady of Hall,[3] to implore not only the fall of Ostend, but the birth of a successor to their sovereignty, that her marriage would for ever remain barren. Spain was already acting upon this theory, it was said, for the contract with Spinola was made, not at Brussels, but at Madrid, and a foreign army of Spaniards and Italians, under the supreme command of a Genoese adventurer, was now to occupy indefinitely that Flanders which had been proclaimed an independent nation, and duly bequeathed by its deceased proprietor to his daughter.

Ambrose Spinola, son of Philip, Marquis of Venafri, and his wife, Polyxena Grimaldi,[4] was not appalled by the murmurs of hardly suppressed anger or public criticism. A handsome, aristocratic personage, with an intellectual, sad, but sympathetic face, fair hair and beard, and imposing but attractive presence—the young volunteer, at the beginning of October, made his first visit of inspection in the lines before Ostend. After studying the situation of affairs very thoroughly, he decided that the operations on the Gullet or eastern side, including Bucquoy's dike, with Pompey Targone's perambulatory castles and floating batteries, were of secondary importance. He doubted the probability of closing up a harbour, now open to the whole world and protected by the fleets of the first naval power of Europe, with wickerwork, sausages, and bridges upon barrels. His attention was at once concentrated on the western side, and he was satisfied that only by hard fighting and steady delving could he hope to master the place. To gain Ostend he would be obliged to devour it piecemeal as he went on.

Whatever else might be said of the new commander-in-chief, it was soon apparent that, although a volunteer and a patrician, he was no milksop. If he had been accustomed all his life to beds of down, he was as ready now to lie in the trenches, with a cannon for his pillow, as the most ironclad

<hr />

[3] Meteren, 493vo.   [4] Gallucci, *ubi sup.*

veteran in the ranks. He seemed to require neither sleep nor food, and his reckless habit of exposing himself to unnecessary danger was the subject of frequent animadversion on the part both of the archdukes and of the Spanish Government.[5]

It was however in his case a wise temerity. The veterans whom he commanded needed no encouragement to daring deeds, but they required conviction as to the valour and zeal of their new commander, and this was afforded them in over-flowing measure.

It is difficult to decide, after such a lapse of years, as to how much of the long series of daily details out of which this famous siege was compounded deserves to be recorded. It is not probable that for military history many of the incidents have retained vital importance. The world rang, at the beginning of the operations, with the skill and inventive talent of Targone, Giustiniani, and other Italian engineers, artificers, and pyrotechnists, and there were great expectations conceived of the effects to be produced by their audacious and original devices. But time wore on. Pompey's famous floating battery would not float, his moving monster battery would not move. With the one, the subtle Italian had intended to close up the Gullet to the States' fleets. It was to rest on the bottom at low water at the harbour's mouth, to rise majestically with the flood, and to be ever ready with a formidable broad-side of fifty pounders against all comers. But the wild waves and tempests of the North Sea soon swept the ponderous toy into space, before it had fired a gun. The gigantic chariot, on which a moveable fort was constructed, was still more porten-tous upon paper than the battery. It was directed against that republican work, defending the Gullet, which was called in derision the Spanish Half-moon. It was to be drawn by forty horses, and armed with no man knew how many great guns, with a mast a hundred and fifty feet high in the centre of the fort, up and down which played pulleys raising and lowering a drawbridge long enough to span the Gullet.

It was further provided with anchors, which were to be

[5] Gallucci.

tossed over the parapet of the doomed redoubt, while the assailants, thus grappled to the enemy's work, were to dash over the bridge after having silenced the opposing fire by means of their own peripatetic battery.

Unfortunately for the fame of Pompey, one of his many wheels was crushed on the first attempt to drag the chariot to the scene of anticipated triumph, the whole structure remained embedded in the sand, very much askew ; nor did all the mules and horses that could be harnessed to it ever succeed in removing it an inch out of a position, which was anything but triumphant.[6]

It seemed probable enough therefore that, so far as depended on the operations from the eastern side, the siege of Ostend, which had now lasted two years and three months, might be protracted for two years and three months longer. Indeed, Spinola at once perceived that if the archduke was ever to be put in possession of the place for which he had professed himself ready to wait eighteen years, it would be well to leave Bucquoy and Targone to build dykes and chariots and bury them on the east at their leisure, while more energy was brought to bear upon the line of fortifications of the west than had hitherto been employed. There had been shooting enough, bloodshed enough, suffering enough, but it was amazing to see the slight progress made. The occupation of what were called the external Squares has been described. This constituted the whole result of the twenty-seven months' work.

The town itself—the small and very insignificant kernel which lay enclosed in such a complicated series of wrappings and layers of defences—seemed as far off as if it were suspended in the sky. The old haven or canal, no longer navigable for ships, still served as an admirable moat which the assailants had not yet succeeded in laying entirely dry. It protected the counterscarp, and was itself protected by an exterior series of works, while behind the counterscarp was

⁶ Meteren, 496, 497. Gallucci, lib. xvi. xvii. xviii. Bentivoglio, iii. 520–524. Fleming, 432, 433, *et passim.* Grotius, lib xii. xiii.

still another ditch, not so broad nor deep as the canal, but a formidable obstacle even after the counterscarp should be gained. There were nearly fifty forts and redoubts in these lines, of sufficient importance to have names which in those days became household words, not only in the Netherlands, but in Europe; the siege of Ostend being the one military event of Christendom, so long as it lasted. These names are of course as much forgotten now as those of the bastions before Nineveh. A very few of them will suffice to indicate the general aspect of the operations. On the extreme south-west of Ostend had been in peaceful times a polder—the general term to designate a pasture out of which the sea-water had been pumped—and the forts in that quarter were accordingly called by that name, as Polder Half-moon, Polder Ravelin, or great and little Polder Bulwark, as the case might be. Farther on towards the west, the north-west, and the north, and therefore towards the beach, were the West Ravelin, West Bulwark, Moses's Table, the Porcupine, the Hell's Mouth, the old church, and last and most important of all, the Sand Hill. The last-named work was protected by the Porcupine and Hell's Mouth, was the key to the whole series of fortifications, and was connected by a curtain with the old church, which was in the heart of the old town.[7]

Spinola had assumed command in October, but the winter was already closing in with its usual tempests and floods before there had been time for him to produce much effect. It seemed plain enough to the besieged that the object of the enemy would be to work his way through the Polder, and so gradually round to the Porcupine and the Sand Hill. Precisely in what directions his subterraneous passages might be tending, in what particular spot of the thin crust upon which they all stood an explosion might at any moment be expected, it was of course impossible to know. They were sure that the process of mining was steadily progressing, and Maurice sent orders to countermine under every bulwark, and to secretly isolate every bastion, so that it would be

---

[7] Fleming, Meteren, Bentivoglio, Grotius, *ubi sup.*

necessary for Spinola to make his way, fort by fort, and inch by inch.[8]

Thus they struggled drearily about under ground, friend and foe, often as much bewildered as wanderers in the catacombs. To a dismal winter succeeded a ferocious spring. Both in February and March were westerly storms, such as had not been recorded even on that tempest-swept coast for twenty years, and so much damage was inflicted on the precious Sand Hill and its curtain, that, had the enemy been aware of its plight, it is probable that one determined assault might have put him in possession of the place. But Ostend was in charge of a most watchful governor, Peter van Gieselles, who had succeeded Charles van der Noot at the close of the year 1603.[9] A plain, lantern-jawed, Dutch colonel, with close-cropped hair, a long peaked beard, and an eye that looked as if it had never been shut ; always dressed in a shabby old jerkin with tarnished flowers upon it, he took command with a stout but heavy heart, saying that the place should never be surrendered by him, but that he should never live to see the close of the siege.[10] He lost no time in repairing the damages of the tempest, being ready to fight the west wind, the North Sea, and Spinola at any moment, singly or conjoined. He rebuilt the curtain of the Sand Hill, added fresh batteries to the Porcupine and Hell's Mouth, and amused and distracted the enemy with almost daily sorties and feints. His soldiers passed their days and nights up to the knees in mud and sludge and sea-water, but they saw that their commander never spared himself, and having a superfluity of food and drink, owing to the watchful care of the States-General, who sent in fleets laden with provisions faster than they could be consumed, they were cheerful and content.

On the 12th March there was a determined effort to carry the lesser Polder Bulwark. After a fierce and bloody action, the place was taken by storm, and the first success in the game was registered for Spinola. The little fort was crammed full of dead, but such of the defenders

12 March. 1604.

---

[8] Fleming.   Ibid. 418.   [10] Ibid.

as survived were at last driven out of it, and forced to take
refuge in the next work.[11]   Day after day the same bloody
business was renewed, a mere monotony of assaults, repulses,
sallies, in which hardly an inch of ground was gained on either
side, except at the cost of a great pile of corpses.   " Men will
never know, nor can mortal pen ever describe," said one who
saw it all, " the ferocity and the pertinacity of both besiegers
and besieged."[12]   On the 15th of March, Colonel
Catrice, an accomplished Walloon officer of engineers, commanding the approaches against the Polder, was
killed.[13]   On the 21st March, as Peter Gieselles
was taking his scrambling dinner in company with
Philip Fleming, there was a report that the enemy was out
again in force.   A good deal of progress had been made during
the previous weeks on the south-west and west, and more was
suspected than was actually known.   It was felt that the
foe was steadily nibbling his way up to the counterscarp.
Moreover, such was the emulation among the Germans,
Walloons, Italians, and Spaniards for precedence in working
across the canal,[14] that a general assault and universal
explosion were considered at any instant possible.   The
governor sent Fleming to see if all was right in the Porcupine, while he himself went to see if a new battery, which
he had just established to check the approaches of the enemy
towards the Polder Half-moon and Ravelin in a point very near
the counterscarp, was doing its duty.   Being, as usual, anxious
to reconnoitre with his own eyes, he jumped upon the rampart.
But there were sharp-shooters in the enemy's trenches, and
they were familiar with the governor's rusty old doublet
and haggard old face.[15]   Hardly had he climbed upon the
breastwork when a ball pierced his heart, and he fell dead
without a groan.[16]   There was a shout of triumph from the
outside, while the tidings soon spread sadness through
the garrison, for all loved and venerated the man.[17]   Philip
Fleming, so soon as he learned the heavy news, lost no time

15 March.

21 March.

    [11] Fleming, 470, 471.   [12] Ibid.   [13] Ibid. 473.   [14] Bentivoglio, *ubi sup.*
          [15] Fleming, 479, 480.   [16] Ibid.   [17] Ibid.

in unavailing regrets, but instantly sent a courier to Prince Maurice ; meantime summoning a council of superior officers, by whom Colonel John van Loon was provisionally appointed commandant.[18]

A stately, handsome man, a good officer, but without extensive experience, he felt himself hardly equal to the immense responsibility of the post, but yielding to the persuasions of his comrades, proceeded to do his best. His first care was to secure the all-important Porcupine, towards which the enemy had been slowly crawling with his galleries and trenches. Four days after he had accepted the command he was anxiously surveying that fortification, 25 March, 1604. and endeavouring to obtain a view of the enemy's works, when a cannon-ball struck him on the right leg, so that he died the next day.[19] Plainly the post of commandant of Ostend was no sinecure. He was temporarily succeeded by Sergeant-Major Jacques de Bievry, but the tumults and confusion incident upon this perpetual change of head were becoming alarming. The enemy gave the garrison no rest night nor day, and it had long become evident that the young volunteer, whose name was so potent on the Genoa Exchange, was not a man of straw nor a dawdler, however the superseded veterans might grumble. At any rate the troops on either side were like to have their fill of work.

On the 2nd April the Polder Ravelin was carried by storm. It was a most bloody action. Never were a few square feet of earth more recklessly assailed, more 2 April. resolutely maintained. The garrison did not surrender the place, but they all laid down their lives in its defence. Scarcely an individual of them all escaped, and the foe, who paid dearly with heaps of dead and wounded for his prize, confessed that such serious work as this had scarce been known before in any part of that great slaughter-house, Flanders.[20]

A few days later, Colonel Bievry, provisional commandant, was desperately wounded in a sortie, and was carried off to

---

[18] Fleming, 479, 480.   [19] Ibid. 487, 492.   [20] Ibid. 501, 502.

Zeeland.[21]   The States-General now appointed Jacques van der
Meer, Baron of Berendrecht, to the post of honour and of
danger.[22]   A noble of Flanders, always devoted to the republican cause ; an experienced middle-aged officer, vigilant,
energetic, nervous ; a slight wiry man, with a wizened little
face, large bright eyes, a meagre yellow beard, and thin
sandy hair flowing down upon his well-starched ruff, the new
governor soon showed himself inferior to none of his predecessors in audacity and alertness.   It is difficult to imagine a
more irritating position in many respects than that of commander in such an extraordinary leaguer.   It was not a formal
siege.   Famine, which ever impends over an invested place,
and sickens the soul with its nameless horrors, was not the
great enemy to contend against here.   Nor was there the
hideous alternative between starving through obstinate resistance or massacre on submission, which had been the lot of
so many Dutch garrisons in the earlier stages of the war.
Retreat by sea was ever open to the Ostend garrison, and
there was always an ample supply of the best provisions
and of all munitions of war.   But they had been unceasingly
exposed to two tremendous enemies.   During each winter
and spring the ocean often smote their bastions and bulwarks
in an hour of wrath till they fell together like children's toys,
and it was always at work, night and day, steadily lapping at
the fragile foundations on which all their structures stood.
Nor was it easy to give the requisite attention to the devouring sea, because all the materials that could be accumulated
seemed necessary to repair the hourly damages inflicted by
their other restless foe.

Thus the day seemed to draw gradually but inexorably
nearer when the place would be, not captured, but consumed.
There was nothing for it, so long as the States were determined to hold the spot, but to meet the besieger at every point,
above or below the earth, and sell every inch of that little
morsel of space at the highest price that brave men could
impose.

[21] Fleming, 505.   [22] Ibid. 516.

So Berendrecht, as vigilant and devoted as even Peter Gieselles had ever been, now succeeded to the care of the Polders and the Porcupines, and the Hell's Mouths, and all the other forts, whose quaint designations had served, as usually is the case among soldiers, to amuse the honest patriots in the midst of their toils and danger. On the 18th April 18 April, the enemy assailed the great western Ravelin, and 1604. after a sanguinary hand-to-hand action, in which great numbers of officers and soldiers were lost on both sides, he carried the fort ; the Spaniards, Italians, Germans, and Walloons vieing with each other in deeds of extraordinary daring, and overcoming at last the resistance of the garrison.[23]

This was an important success. The foe had now worked his way with galleries and ditches along the whole length of the counterscarp till he was nearly up with the Porcupine, and it was obvious that in a few days he would be master of the counterscarp itself.

A less resolute commander, at the head of less devoted troops, might have felt that when that inevitable event should arrive all that honour demanded would have been done, and that Spinola was entitled to his city. Berendrecht simply decided that if the old counterscarp could no longer be held it was time to build a new counterscarp. This, too, had been for some time the intention of Prince Maurice. A plan for this work had already been sent into the place, and a distinguished English engineer, Ralph Dexter by name, arrived with some able assistants to carry it into execution.[24] It having been estimated that the labour would take three weeks of time, without more ado the inner line was carefully drawn, cutting off with great nicety and precision about one half the whole place. Within this narrowed circle the same obstinate resistance was to be offered as before, and the bastions and redoubts of the new entrenchment were to be baptized with the same uncouth names which two long years of terrible struggle had made so precious. The work was very laborious ; for the line was drawn straight through the

[23] Fleming, 515, 516.   [24] Ibid. 516-522.

town, and whole streets had to be demolished and the houses
to their very foundations shovelled away.   Moreover the men
were forced to toil with spade in one hand and matchlock in
the other, ever ready to ascend from the ancient dilapidated
cellars in order to mount the deadly breach at any point in
the whole circumference of the place.[25]

It became absolutely necessary therefore to send a sufficient
force of common workmen into the town to lighten the labours
of the soldiers.   Moreover the thought, although whistled to
the wind, would repeatedly recur, that, after all, there must
be a limit to these operations, and that at last there would
remain no longer any earth in which to find a refuge.

The work of the new entrenchment went slowly on, but it
was steadily done.   Meantime they were comforted by hearing that the stadholder had taken the field in Flanders, at the
head of a considerable force, and they lived in daily expectation of relief.   It will be necessary, at the proper moment, to
indicate the nature of Prince Maurice's operations.   For the
present, it is better that the reader should confine his attention within the walls of Ostend.

By the 11th May, the enemy had effected a lodgment in
11 May,   a corner of the Porcupine, and already from that
1604.   point might threaten the new counterscarp before it
should be completed.   At the same time he had gnawed
through to the West Bulwark, and was busily mining under the
Porcupine itself.   In this fort friend and foe now lay together,
packed like herrings, and profited by their proximity to each
other to vary the monotony of pike and snaphance with an
occasional encounter of epistolary wit.

Thus Spanish letters, tied to sticks, and tossed over into the
next entrenchment, were replied to by others, composed in four
languages by the literary man of Ostend, Auditor Fleming,
and shot into the enemy's trenches on cross-bow bolts.[26]

On the 29th May, a long prepared mine was sprung beneath
29 May.   the Porcupine.   It did its work effectively, and the
          assailants did theirs no less admirably, crowding into

[25] Fleming, 516–522.   [26] Ibid. 528, seqq.

the breach with headlong ferocity, and after a long and sanguinary struggle with immense loss on both sides, carrying
the precious and long-coveted work by storm.[27]   Inch by inch
the defenders were thus slowly forced back toward their new
entrenchment. On the same day, however, they inflicted
a most bloody defeat upon the enemy in an attempt to carry
the great Polder. He withdrew, leaving heaps of slain, so
that the account current for the day would have balanced
itself, but that the Porcupine, having changed hands, now
bristled most formidably against its ancient masters.[28]   The
daily slaughter had become sickening to behold. There were
three thousand effective men in the garrison. More could
have been sent in to supply the steady depletion in the ranks,
but there was no room for more. There was scarce space
enough for the living to stand to their work, or for the dead
to lie in their graves. And this was an advantage which
could not fail to tell. Of necessity the besiegers would
always very far outnumber the garrison, so that the final
success of their repeated assaults became daily more and
more possible.

Yet on the 2nd June the enemy met not only with another
signal defeat, but also with a most bitter surprise.
On that day the mine which he had been so long   2 June.
and so laboriously constructing beneath the great Polder
Bulwark was sprung with magnificent effect. A breach,
forty feet wide, was made in this last stronghold of the old
defences, and the soldiers leaped into the crater almost before
it had ceased to blaze, expecting by one decisive storm to
make themselves masters at last of all the fortifications, and
therefore of the town itself. But as, emerging from the
mine, they sprang exulting upon the shattered bulwark, a
transformation more like a sudden change in some holiday
pantomime than a new fact in this three years' most tragic
siege presented itself to their astonished eyes. They had
carried the last defence of the old counterscarp, and behold—
a new one, which they had never dreamed of, bristling before

---

[27] Fleming, 538.   [28] Ibid.

their eyes, with a flanking battery turned directly upon them.[29] The musketeers and pikemen, protected by their new works, now thronged towards the assailants ; giving them so hearty a welcome that they reeled back, discomfited, after a brief but severe struggle, from the spot of their anticipated triumph, leaving their dead and dying in the breach.[30]

Four days later, Berendrecht, with a picked party of English troops, stole out for a reconnaissance, not wishing to trust other eyes than his own in the imminent peril of the place.

6 June.

The expedition was successful. A few prisoners were taken, and valuable information was obtained, but these advantages were counterbalanced by a severe disaster. The vigilant and devoted little governor, before effecting his entrance into the sally port, was picked off by a sharpshooter, and died the next day.[31] This seemed the necessary fate of the commandants of Ostend, where the operations seemed more like a pitched battle lasting three years than an ordinary siege. Gieselles, Van Loon, Bievry, and now Berendrecht, had successively fallen at the post of duty since the beginning of the year. Not one of them was more sincerely deplored than Berendrecht. His place was supplied by Colonel Uytenhoove, a stalwart, hirsute, hard-fighting Dutchman, the descendant of an ancient race, and seasoned in many a hard campaign.

The enemy now being occupied in escarping and furnishing with batteries the positions he had gained, with the obvious intention of attacking the new counterscarp, it was resolved to prepare for the possible loss of this line of fortifications by establishing another and still narrower one within it.

Half the little place had been shorn away by the first change. Of the half which was still in possession of the besieged about one-third was now set off, and in this little corner of earth, close against the new harbour, was set up their last refuge. They called the new citadel Little Troy, and announced, with pardonable bombast, that they would hold

[29] Fleming, 543.   [30] Ibid.   [31] Ibid. 546.

out there as long as the ancient Trojans had defended Ilium.[32]
With perfect serenity the engineers set about their task with
line, rule, and level, measuring out the bulwarks and bastions,
the miniature salients, half-moons, and ditches, as neatly and
methodically as if there were no ceaseless cannonade in their
ears, and as if the workmen were not at every moment
summoned to repel assaults upon the outward wall. They
sent careful drawings of Little Troy to Maurice and the States,
and received every encouragement to persevere, together with
promises of ultimate relief.[33]

But there was one serious impediment to the contemplated
construction of the new earth-works. They had no earth.
Nearly everything solid had been already scooped away in
the perpetual delving. The sea-dykes had been robbed of
their material, so that the coming winter might find besiegers
and besieged all washed together into the German Ocean, and
it was hard digging and grubbing among the scanty cellarages
of the dilapidated houses. But there were plenty of graves,
filled with the results of three years' hard fighting. And
now, not only were all the cemeteries within the precincts
shovelled and carted in mass to the inner fortifications, but
rewards being offered of ten stivers for each dead body, great
heaps of disinterred soldiers were piled into the new
ramparts.[34] Thus these warriors, after laying down their
lives for the cause of freedom, were made to do duty after
death. Whether it were just or no thus to disturb the repose
—if repose it could be called—of the dead that they might
once more protect the living, it can scarcely be doubted that
they took ample revenge on the already sufficiently polluted
atmosphere.

On the 17th June the foe sprang a mine under the western
bulwark, close to a countermine exploded by the 17 June,
garrison the day before. The assailants thronged 1604.
as merrily as usual to the breach, and were met with
customary resolution by the besieged ; Governor Uytenhoove,

[32] Haestens, 272. Grotius, xiii. 645. [33] Fleming, 551, *seqq.*
[34] Haestens, 272.

clad in complete armour, leading his troops. The enemy, after an hour's combat, was repulsed with heavy loss, but the governor fell in the midst of the fight.[35] Instantly he was seized by the legs by a party of his own men, some English desperadoes among the number, who, shouting that the colonel was dead, were about to render him the last offices by plundering his body. The ubiquitous Fleming, observing the scene, flew to the rescue and, with the assistance of a few officers, drove off these energetic friends, and taking off the governor's casque, discovered that he still breathed.[36] That he would soon have ceased to do so, had he been dragged much farther in his harness over that jagged and precipitous pile of rubbish, was certain.[37] He was desperately wounded, and of course incapacitated for his post. Thus, in that year, before the summer solstice, a fifth commandant had fallen.

On the same day, simultaneously with this repulse in the West Bulwark, the enemy made himself at last completely master of the Polder. Here, too, was a savage hand-to-hand combat with broadswords and pikes, and when the pikes were broken, with great clubs and stakes pulled from the fascines;[38] but the besiegers were victorious, and the defenders sullenly withdrew with their wounded to the inner entrenchments.

On the 27th June, Daniel de Hartaing, Lord of Marquette, was sent by the States-General to take command
27 June.   in Ostend.[39] The colonel of the Walloon regiment which had rendered such good service on the famous field of Nieuport, the new governor, with his broad, brown, cheerful face, and his Milan armour, was a familiar figure enough to the campaigners on both sides in Flanders or Germany.

The stoutest heart might have sunk at the spectacle which the condition of the town presented at his first inspection. The States-General were resolved to hold the place, at all hazards, and Marquette had come to do their bidding, but it was difficult to find anything that could be called a town. The great heaps of rubbish, which had once been the outer walls, were almost entirely in the possession of the foe, who had

[35] Fleming, 555.   [36] Ibid.   [37] Ibid.   [38] Ibid. 556.   [39] Ibid. 560.

lodged himself in all that remained of the defiant Porcupine, the Hell's Mouth, and other redoubts, and now pointed from them at least fifty great guns against their inner walls. The old town, with its fortifications, was completely honeycombed, riddled, knocked to pieces, and, although the Sand Hill still held out, it was plain enough that its days were numbered unless help should soon arrive. In truth, it required a clear head and a practised eye to discover among those confused masses of prostrate masonry, piles of brick, upturned graves, and mounds of sand and rubbish, anything like order and regularity. Yet amid the chaos there was really form and meaning to those who could read aright, and Marquette saw, as well in the engineers' lines as in the indomitable spirit that looked out of the grim faces of the garrison, that Ostend, so long as anything of it existed in nature, could be held for the republic. Their brethren had not been firmer, when keeping their merry Christmas, seven years before, under the North Pole, upon a pudding made of the gunner's cartridge paste, or the Knights of the Invincible Lion in the horrid solitudes of Tierra del Fuego, than were the defenders of this sandbank.

Whether the place were worth the cost or not, it was for my lords the States-General to decide, not for Governor Marquette. And the decision of those "high and mighty" magistrates, to whom even Maurice of Nassau bowed without a murmur, although often against his judgment, had been plainly enough announced.

And so shiploads of deals and joists, bricks, nails, and fascines, with all other requisite building materials, were sent daily in from Zeeland,[40] in order that Little Troy might be completed; and, with God's help, said the garrison, the republic shall hold its own.

And now there were two months more of mining and countermining, of assaults and repulses, of cannonading and hand-to-hand fights with pikes and clubs. Nearer and nearer, day by day, and inch by inch, the foe had crawled up to

[40] Fleming.

the verge of their last refuge, and the walls of Little Troy, founded upon fresh earth and dead men's bones, and shifting sands, were beginning to quake under the guns of the inex-
27 August, orable volunteer from Genoa. Yet on the 27th
1604. August there was great rejoicing in the beleaguered town. Cannon thundered salutes, bonfires blazed, trumpets rang jubilant blasts, and, if the church-bells sounded no merry peals, it was because the only church in the place had been cut off in the last slicing away by the engineers. Hymns of thanksgiving ascended to heaven, and the whole garrison fell on their knees, praying fervently to Almighty God, with devout and grateful hearts.[41] It was not an ignoble spectacle to see those veterans kneeling where there was scarce room to kneel, amid ruin and desolation, to praise the Lord for his mercies. But to explain this general thanksgiving it is now necessary for a moment to go back.

[41] Fleming, 572.

CHAPTER XLIII.

Policy of the King of France — Operations of Prince Maurice — Plans for a
Flemish Campaign — Passage into Flanders — Fort St. Catharine — Flight
of its garrison, and occupation by Maurice — Surrender of Ysendyke and
Aardenburg — Skirmish at Stamper's Hook — Siege of Sluys by Prince
Maurice — Ineffectual attempt of Spinola to relieve the town — Its capitu-
lation and restoration to the States — Death of Lewis Gunther of Nassau —
Operations at Ostend — Surrender of the garrison — Desolation of the scene
after its evacuation.

THE States-General had begun to forget the severe lesson
taught them in the Nieuport campaign. Being determined to
hold Ostend, they became very impatient, in the early part of
the present year, that Maurice should once more invade
Flanders, at the head of a relieving army, and drive the archdukes from before the town.

They were much influenced in this policy by the persistent
advice of the French king. To the importunities of their
envoy at Paris, Henry had, during the past eighteen months,
replied by urging the States to invade Flanders and seize its
ports. When they had thus something to place as pledges in
his hands, he might accede to their clamour and declare war
against Spain. But he scarcely concealed his intention, in
such case, to annex both the obedient and the United Netherlands to his own dominions. Meantime, before getting into
the saddle, he chose to be guaranteed against loss. "Assure
my lords the States that I love them," he said, "and shall
always do my best for them."[1] His affection for the territory
of my lords was even warmer than the sentiments he entertained for themselves. Moreover, he grudged the preliminary
expenses which would be necessary even should he ultimately
make himself sovereign of the whole country. Rosny assured
the envoy that he was mistaken in expecting a declaration of

[1] Aerssens to Olden-Barneveld, in Van Deventer, ii. 333–335.

war against Spain. "Not that he does not think it useful
and necessary," said the minister, "but he wishes to have war
and peace both at once—peace because he wishes to make no
retrenchments in his pleasures of women, dogs, and buildings,
and so war would be very inopportune. In three months he
would be obliged to turn tail for want of means (to use his
own words), although I would furnish him funds enough, if he
would make the use of them that he ought."[2]

The Queen of England, who, with all her parsimony and
false pretences, never doubted in her heart that perpetual
hostility to Spain was the chief bulwark of her throne, and
that the republic was fighting her battles as well as its own,
had been ready to make such a lively war in conjunction with
France as would drive the Spaniard out of all the Netherlands. But Henry was not to be moved. "I know that if I
should take her at her word," said he, "she would at once
begin to screw me for money. She has one object, I another." Villeroy had said plainly to Aerssens, in regard to
the prevalent system of Englishmen, Spaniards, and Frenchmen being at war with each other, while the Governments
might be nominally at peace, "Let us take off our masks.
If the Spaniard has designs against our State, has he not
cause? He knows the aid we are giving you, and resents it.
If we should abstain, he would leave us in peace. If the
Queen of England expects to draw us into a league, she is
mistaken. Look to yourselves and be on your guard.
Richardot is intriguing with Cecil. You give the queen
securities, fortresses, seats in your council. The king asks
nothing but communication of your projects."[3]

In short, all the comfort that Aerssens had been able
to derive from his experiences at the French court in the
autumn of 1602, was that the republic could not be too suspicious both of England and France. Rosny especially he
considered the most dangerous of all the politicians in France.
His daughter was married to the Prince of Espinoy, whose
50,000 livres a year would be safer the more the archduke

[2] Aerssens to Olden-Barneveld, in Van Deventer, ii. 333–335.   [3] Ibid.

was strengthened. "But for this he would be stiffer," said
Aerssens.[4] Nevertheless there were strong motives at work,
pressing France towards the support of the States. There
were strong political reasons, therefore, why they should carry
the war into Flanders, in conformity with the wishes of the
king.

The stadholder, after much argument, yielded as usual to
the authority of the magistrates, without being convinced as
to the sagacity of their plans. It was arranged that an army
should make a descent upon the Flemish coast in the early
spring, and make a demonstration upon Sluys. The effect of
this movement, it was thought, would be to draw the enemy
out of his entrenchments, in which case it would be in the
power of Maurice to put an end at once to the siege. It is
unquestionable that the better alternative, in the judgment of
the prince, was to take possession, if possible, of Sluys itself.
His preparations were, however, made with a view to either
event, and by the middle of April he had collected at Wil-
lemstad a force of fifteen thousand foot and three thousand
horse. As on the former memorable expedition, he now again
insisted that a considerable deputation of the States and of
the States' council should accompany the army.[5] His brother
Henry, and his cousins Lewis William, Lewis Gunther, and
Ernest Casimir, were likewise with him, as well as the Prince
of Anhalt and other distinguished personages.

On the 25th April the army, having crossed the
mouth of the West Scheld, from Zeeland, in number- 25 April.
less vessels of all sizes and degrees, effected their debarkation
on the island of Cadzand.[6]

In the course of two days they had taken possession of the
little town, and all the forts of that island, having made their
entrance through what was called the Black Channel. Had
they steered boldly through the Swint or Sluys channel at
once, it is probable that they might have proceeded straight

[4] Aerssens to Olden-Barneveld, in
Van Deventer, ii. 333-335.
[5] V. d. Kemp, ii. 109, seqq., and notes.

[6] Bentivoglio, iii. 525-529. Meteren
494, 495. Grotius, xiii. 639-644. Fleming. Haestens.

up to Sluys, and taken the place by surprise. Maurice's habitual caution was, perhaps, on this occasion, a disadvantage to him, but he would have violated the rules of war, and what seemed the dictates of common sense, had he not secured a basis of operations, and a possibility of retreat, before plunging with his army into the heart of a hostile country. The republic still shuddered at the possible catastrophe of four years before, when circumstances had forced him to take the heroic but dangerous resolution of sending off his ships from Nieuport. Before he had completed his arrangements for supplies on the island of Cadzand, he learned from scouts and reconnoitring parties that Spinola had sent a thousand infantry, besides five hundred cavalry, under Trivulzio, to guard the passage across the Swint. Maurice was thus on the wrong side of the great channel by which Sluys communicated with the sea.[7]

The town of Sluys and its situation have been described in a former chapter.[8] As a port, it was in those days considered a commodious and important one, capable of holding five hundred ships. As a town, it was not so insignificant as geographical and historical changes have since made it, and was certainly far superior to Ostend, even if Ostend had not been almost battered out of existence. It had spacious streets and squares, and excellent fortifications in perfectly good condition. It was situate in a watery labyrinth, many slender streams from the interior and several saltwater creeks being complicated around it, and then flowing leisurely, in one deep sluggish channel, to the sea. The wrath of Leicester, when all his efforts to relieve the place had been baffled by the superior skill of Alexander Farnese, has been depicted, and during the seventeen years which had elapsed since its capture, the republic had not ceased to deplore that disaster. Obviously if the present expedition could end in the restoration of Sluys to its rightful owners, it would be a remarkable success, even if Ostend should fall. Sluys and its adjacent domains formed a natural portion of

<hr>

[7] Fleming, 584–587.   [8] Vol. II. chap. xvi.

the Zeeland archipelago, the geographical counterpart
of Flushing. With both branches of the stately Scheld in
its control, the republic would command the coast, and might
even dispense with Ostend, which, in the judgment of Maurice,
was an isolated and therefore not a desirable military possession. The States-General were of a different opinion. They
much desired to obtain Sluys, but they would not listen to the
abandonment of Ostend. It was expected of the stadholder,
therefore, that he should seize the one and protect the other.
The task was a difficult one. A less mathematical brain than
that of Maurice of Nassau would have reeled at the problem
to be solved. To master such a plexus of canals, estuaries,
and dykes, of passages through swamps, of fords at low water
which were obliterated by flood-tide ; to take possession of a
series of redoubts built on the only firm points of land, with
nothing but quaking morass over which to manœuvre troops
or plant batteries against them, would be a difficult study,
even upon paper. To accomplish it in the presence of a vigilant and anxious foe seemed bewildering enough.

At first it was the intention of the stadholder, disappointed
at learning the occupation of the Swint, to content himself
with fortifying Cadzand, in view of future operations at some
more favourable moment.[9] So meagre a result would certainly not have given great satisfaction to the States, nor
added much to the military reputation of Maurice. While
he hesitated between plunging without a clue into the watery
maze around him, and returning discomfited from the expedition on which such high hopes had been built, a Flemish
boor presented himself. He offered to guide the army around
the east and south of Sluys, and to point out passages where
it would be possible to cross the waters, which, through the
care of Spinola, now seemed to forbid access to the place.[10]
Maurice lingered no longer. On the 28th April, led
by the friendly boor, he advanced towards Oost-   28 April.
burg. Next morning a small force of the enemy's infantry
and cavalry was seen, showing that there must be foothold in

⁹ Fleming, 585.   ¹⁰ Ibid. Grotius, *ubi sup.*

that direction. He sent out a few companies to skirmish with those troops, who fled after a very brief action, and, in flying, showed their pursuers the road. Maurice marched in force, straight through the waters, on the track of the retreating foe. They endeavoured to rally at the fort of Coxie, which stood upon and commanded a dyke, but the republicans were too quick for them, and drove them out of the place.[11] The stadholder, thus obtaining an unexpected passage into Flanders, conceived strong hopes of success, despite the broken nature of the ground. Continuing to feel his way cautiously through the wilderness of quagmire, he soon came upon a very formidable obstacle. The well-built and well-equipped redoubt of St. Catharine rose frowning before him, overshadowing his path, and completely prohibiting all further progress. Plainly it would be necessary to reduce this work at once, unless he were willing to abandon his enterprise. He sent back to Cadzand for artillery, but it was flood-tide, the waters were out, and it was not till late in the afternoon that nine pieces arrived. The stadholder ordered a cannonade, less with the hope of producing an impression by such inadequate means on so strong a work, than with the intention of showing the enemy that he had brought field-guns with him, and was not merely on an accidental foray. At the same time, having learned that the garrison, which was commanded by Trivulzio, was composed of only a few regular troops, and a large force of guerillas, he gave notice that such combatants were not entitled to quarter, and that if captured they would be all put to the sword. The reply to this threat was not evacuation but defiance. Especially a volunteer ensign mounted upon a rampart, and danced about, waving his flag gaily in the face of the assailants. Maurice bitterly remarked to his staff that such a man alone was enough to hold the fort.[12] As it was obvious that the place would require a siege in form, and that it would be almost impossible to establish batteries upon that quaking soil, where there was no dry land

30 April.

1 May.

----

[11] Grotius, *ubi sup*.   [12] Fleming, 586.

for cavalry or artillery to move, Maurice ordered the nine guns to be carried back to Cadzand that night, betaking himself, much disappointed, in the same direction.[13] Yet it so happened that the cannoneers, floundering through the bogs, made such an outcry—especially when one of their guns became so bemired that it was difficult for them to escape the disgrace of losing it—that the garrison, hearing a great tumult, which they could not understand, fell into one of those panics to which raw and irregular troops are liable.[14] Nothing would convince them that fresh artillery had not arrived, that the terrible stadholder with an immense force was not creating invincible batteries, and that they should be all butchered in cold blood, according to proclamation, before the dawn of day. They therefore evacuated the place under cover of the night, so that this absurd accident absolutely placed Maurice in possession of the very fort—without striking a blow—which he was about to abandon in despair, and which formed the first great obstacle to his advance.[15]

3 May.

Having occupied St. Catharine's, he moved forward to Ysendyke, a strongly fortified place three leagues to the eastward of Sluys, and invested it in form. Meantime a great danger was impending over him. A force of well-disciplined troops, to the number of two thousand, dropped down in boats from Sluys to Cadzand, for the purpose of surprising the force left to guard that important place. The expedition was partially successful. Six hundred landed, beating down all opposition. But a few Scotch companies held firm, and by hard fighting were able at last to drive the invaders back to their sloops, many of which were sunk in the affray, with all on board. The rest ignominiously retreated.[16] Had the enterprise been as well executed as it was safely planned, it would have gone hard with the stadholder and his army. It is difficult to see in what way he could have extricated himself from such a dilemma, being thus cut off from his supplies and his fleet, and therefore from

6 May.

[13] Fleming, 587.   [14] Ibid.   [15] Ibid.   [16] Ibid. 588, Grotius, *ubi sup.*

all possibility of carrying out his design or effecting his escape to Zeeland. Certainly thus far, fortune had favoured his bold adventure.

He now sent his own trumpeter, Master Hans, to summon Ysendyke to a surrender. The answer was a bullet which went through the head of unfortunate Master Hans. Maurice, enraged at this barbarous violation of the laws of war, drew his lines closer. Next day the garrison, numbering six hundred, mostly Italians, capitulated, and gave up the musketeer who had murdered the trumpeter.[17]

10 May.

Two days later the army appeared before Aardenburg, a well-fortified town four miles south of Sluys. It surrendered disgracefully, without striking a blow. The place was a most important position for the investment of Sluys. Four or five miles further towards the west, two nearly parallel streams, both navigable, called the Sweet and the Salt, ran from Dam to Sluys. It was a necessary but most delicate operation, to tie up these two important arteries. An expedition despatched in this direction came upon Trivulzio with a strong force of cavalry, posted at a pass called Stamper's Hook, which controlled the first of these streams. The narrowness of the pathway gave the advantage to the Italian commander. A warm action took place, in which the republican cavalry were worsted, and Paul Bax severely wounded. Maurice coming up with the infantry at a moment when the prospect was very black, turned defeat into victory and completely routed the enemy, who fled from the precious position with a loss of five hundred killed and three hundred prisoners, eleven officers among them.[18] The Sweet was now in the stadholder's possession. Next day he marched against the Salt, at a pass where fourteen hundred Spaniards were stationed. Making very ostentatious preparations for an attack upon this position, he suddenly fell backwards down the stream to a point which he had discovered to be fordable at low water,

12 May.

16 May.

17 May.

[17] Grotius, *ubi sup.*
[18] Ibid. 591, 572.   Bentivoglio, iii. 527, 528.   Meteren, 494, 495.

and marched his whole army through the stream while the skirmishing was going on a few miles farther up. The Spaniards, discovering their error, and fearing to be cut off, scampered hastily away to Dam. Both streams were now in the control of the republican army, while the single fort of St. Joris was all that was now interposed between Maurice and the much-coveted Swint. This redoubt, armed with nine guns, and provided with a competent garrison, was surrendered on the 23rd May.[19]   23 May.

The Swint, or great sea-channel of Sluys, being now completely in the possession of the stadholder, he deliberately proceeded to lay out his lines, to make his entrenched camp, and to invest his city with the beautiful neatness which ever characterized his sieges. A groan came from the learned Lipsius, as he looked from the orthodox shades of Louvain upon the progress of the heretic prince.

"Would that I were happier," he cried, "but things are not going on in Flanders as I could wish. How easy it would have been to save Sluys, which we are now trying so hard to do, had we turned our attention thither in time! But now we have permitted the enemy to entrench and fortify himself, and we are the less excusable because we know to our cost how felicitously he fights with the spade, and that he builds works like an ancient Roman. . . . . Should we lose Sluys, which God forbid, how much strength and encouragement will be acquired by the foe, and by all who secretly or openly favour him! Our neighbours are all straining their eyes, as from a watch-tower, eager to see the result of all these doings. But what if they too should begin to move? Where should we be? I pray God to have mercy on the Netherlanders, whom He has been so many years chastising with heavy whips."[20]

It was very true. The man with the spade had been allowed to work too long at his felicitous vocation. There had been a successful effort made to introduce reinforcements

---

[19] Fleming, Bentivo., Met., *ubi sup*   Van der Kemp, ii. 110, 111, and notes.
[20] Letter to Heer de Vertering, in Haestens, 285. and Fleming, 289, 290.

to the garrison. Troops, to the number of fifteen hundred, had been added to those already shut up there, but the attempts to send in supplies were not so fortunate. Maurice had completely invested the town before the end of May, having undisputed possession of the harbour and of all the neighbouring country. He was himself encamped on the west side of the Swint; Charles van der Noot lying on the south. The submerged meadows, stretching all around in the vicinity of the haven, he had planted thickly with gunboats. Scarcely a bird or a fish could go into or out of the place. Thus the stadholder exhibited to the Spaniards who, fifteen miles off towards the west, had been pounding and burrowing three years long before Ostend without success, what he understood by a siege.

On the 22nd of May a day of solemn prayer and fasting was, by command of Maurice, celebrated through-out the besieging camp. In order that the day should be strictly kept in penance, mortification, and thanks-giving, it was ordered, on severe penalties, that neither the commissaries nor sutlers should dispense any food whatever, throughout the twenty-four hours.[21] Thus the commander-in-chief of the republic prepared his troops for the work before them.

22 May.

In the very last days of May the experiment was once more vigorously tried to send in supplies. A thou-sand galley-slaves, the remnant of Frederic Spinola's unlucky naval forces, whose services were not likely very soon to be required at sea, were sent out into the drowned land, accompanied by five hundred infantry. Simultaneously Count Berlaymont, at the head of four thousand men, con-veying a large supply of provisions and munitions, started from Dam. Maurice, apprised of the adventure, sallied forth with two thousand troops to meet them. Near Stamper's Hook he came upon a detachment of Berlaymont's force, routed them, and took a couple of hundred prisoners. Learn-ing from them that Berlaymont himself, with the principal

29, 30 May, 1604.

[21] Fleming, 593.

part of his force, had passed farther on, he started off in pursuit ; but, unfortunately taking a different path through the watery wilderness from the one selected by the flying foe, he was not able to prevent his retreat by a circuitous route to Dam. From the prisoners, especially from the galley-slaves, who had no reason for disguising the condition of the place, he now learned that there were plenty of troops in Sluys, but that there was already a great lack of provisions. They had lost rather than gained by their success in introducing reinforcements without supplies.[22] Upon this information Maurice now resolved to sit quietly down and starve out the garrison. If Spinola, in consequence, should raise the siege of Ostend, in order to relieve a better town, he was prepared to give him battle. If the marquis held fast to his special work, Sluys was sure to surrender. This being the position of affairs, the deputies of the States-General took their leave of the stadholder, and returned to the Hague.[23]

Two months passed. It was midsummer, and the famine in the beleaguered town had become horrible. The same hideous spectacle was exhibited as on all occasions where thousands of human beings are penned together without food. They ate dogs, cats, and rats, the weeds from the churchyards, old saddles, and old shoes, and, when all was gone, they began to eat each other. The small children diminished rapidly in numbers,[24] while beacons and signals of distress were fired day and night, that the obdurate Spinola, only a few miles off, might at last move to their relief.

The archdukes too were beginning to doubt whether the bargain were a good one. To give a strong, new, well-fortified city, with the best of harbours, in exchange for a heap of rubbish which had once been Ostend, seemed unthrifty enough. Moreover, they had not got Ostend, while sure to lose Sluys. At least the cardinal could no longer afford to dispense with the service of his best corps of veterans who had demanded

[22] Fleming, 592. Meteren, Bentivoglio, *ubi sup.*
[23] Fleming, 592.   [24] Gallucci, ii. 176.

their wages so insolently, and who had laughed at his offer of excommunication by way of payment so heartily. Flinging away his pride, he accordingly made a treaty with the mutinous " squadron" at Grave, granting an entire pardon for all their offences, and promising full payment of their arrears. Until funds should be collected sufficient for this purpose, they were to receive twelve stivers a day each foot-soldier, and twenty-four stivers each cavalryman, and were to have the city of Roermond in pledge. The treaty was negotiated by Guerrera, commandant of Ghent citadel, and by the Archbishop of Roermond, while three distinguished hostages were placed in the keeping of the mutineers until the contract should be faithfully executed : Guerrera himself, Count Fontenoy, son of Marquis d'Havré, and Avalos, commander of a Spanish legion.[25] Thus, after making a present of the services of these veterans for a twelvemonth to the stadholder, and after employing a very important portion of his remaining forces in a vain attempt to reduce their revolt, the archduke had now been fain to purchase their submission by conceding all their demands. It would have been better economy perhaps to come to this conclusion at an earlier day.

It would likewise have been more judicious, according to the lamentations of Justus Lipsius, had the necessity of saving Sluys been thought of in time. Now that it was thoroughly enclosed, so that a mouse could scarce creep through the lines, the archduke was feverish to send in a thousand wagon loads of provisions. Spinola, although in reality commander-in-chief of a Spanish army, and not strictly subject to the orders of the Flemish sovereigns, obeyed the appeal of the archduke, but he obeyed most reluctantly. Two-thirds of Ostend had been effaced, and it was hard to turn even for a moment from the spot until all should have been destroyed.

Leaving Rivas and Bucquoy to guard the entrenchments, and to keep steadily to the work, Spinola took the field with

[25] Meteren, 495, 496.

a large force of all arms, including the late mutineers and the troops of Count Trivulzio. On the 8th August he appeared in the neighbourhood of the Salt and Sweet streams, and exchanged a few cannon-shots with the republicans. Next day he made a desperate assault with three thousand men and some companies of cavalry, upon Lewis William's quarters, where he had reason to believe the lines were weakest. He received from that most vigilant commander a hearty welcome, however, and after a long skirmish was obliged to withdraw, carrying off his dead and wounded, together with a few cart-horses which had been found grazing outside the trenches. Not satisfied with these trophies or such results, he remained several days inactive, and then suddenly whirled around Aardenburg with his 16 Aug. whole army, directly southward of Sluys, seized the forts of St. Catharine and St. Philip, which had been left with very small garrisons, and then made a furious attempt to break the lines at Oostburg, hoping to cross the fords at that place, and thus push his way into the isle of Cadzand. The resistance to his progress was obstinate, the result for a time doubtful. After severe fighting however he crossed the waters of Oostburg in the face of the enemy.[26] Maurice meantime had collected all his strength at the vital position of Cadzand, hoping to deal, or at least to parry, a mortal blow.

On the 17th, on Cadzand dyke, between two redoubts, Spinola again met Lewis William, who had been transferred to that important position. A severe 17 May. struggle ensued. The Spaniards were in superior force, and Lewis William, commanding the advance only of the States troops, was hard pressed. Moving always in the thickest of the fight, he would probably have that day laid down his life, as so many of his race had done before in the cause of the republic, had not Colonel van Dorp come to his rescue, and so laid about him with a great broad sword, that the dyke was

---

[25] Fleming, 593, 594. Bentivoglio, *ubi sup.* Meteren, 495. Grotius, xii. 640, 641.

kept until Maurice arrived with Eytzinga's Frisian regiment and other reserves. Van Dorp then fell covered with wounds. Here was the decisive combat. The two commanders-in-chief met face to face for the first time, and could Spinola have gained the position of Cadzand the fate of Maurice must have been sealed. But all his efforts were vain. The stadholder, by coolness and promptness, saved the day, and inflicted a bloody repulse upon the Catholics. Spinola had displayed excellent generalship, but it is not surprising that the young volunteer should have failed upon his first great field day to defeat Maurice of Nassau and his cousin Lewis William. He withdrew discomfited at last, leaving several hundred dead upon the field, definitely renouncing all hope of relieving Sluys, and retiring by way of Dam to his camp before Ostend.[27]   Next day the town capitulated.[28]

18 Aug.

The garrison were allowed to depart with the honours of war, and the same terms were accorded to the inhabitants, both in secular and religious matters, as were usual when Maurice re-occupied any portion of the republic. Between three and four thousand creatures, looking rather like ghosts from the churchyards than living soldiers, marched out, with drums beating, colours displayed, matches lighted, and bullet in mouth. Sixty of them fell dead[29] before the dismal procession had passed out of the gates. Besides these troops were nearly fifteen hundred galley-slaves, even more like shadows than the rest, as they had been regularly sent forth during the latter days of the siege to browse upon soutenelle in the submerged meadows, or to drown or starve if unable to find a sufficient supply of that weed. These unfortunate victims of Mahometan and Christian tyranny were nearly all Turks, and by the care of the Dutch Government were sent back by sea to their homes.[30] A few of them entered the service of the States.

The evacuation of Sluys by Governor Serrano and his

---

[27] Fleming, 594, 595.   Bentivoglio, Meteren, Grotius, *ubi sup.*
[28] Ibid.   [29] Bentivoglio.   [30] Meteren, 495.

garrison was upon the 20th August. Next day the stadholder took possession, bestowing the nominal government
of the place upon his brother Frederic Henry. The atmosphere, naturally enough, was pestiferous, and young Count
Lewis Gunther of Nassau, who had so brilliantly led the
cavalry on the famous day of Nieuport, died of fever soon
after entering the town,[31] infinitely regretted by every one
who wished well to the republic.

Thus an important portion of Zeeland was restored to its
natural owners. A seaport which in those days was an excellent one, and more than a compensation for the isolated
fishing village already beleaguered for upwards of three
years, had been captured in three months. The States-
General congratulated their stadholder on such prompt
and efficient work, while the garrison of Ostend, first
learning the authentic news seven days afterwards, although
at a distance of only fourteen miles, had cause to 27 Aug.
go upon their knees and sing praises to the Most 1604.
High.

The question now arose as to the relief of Ostend. Maurice
was decidedly opposed to any such scheme.[32] He had got a
better Ostend in Sluys, and he saw no motive for spending
money and blood in any further attempt to gain possession of
a ruin, which, even if conquered, could only with extreme
difficulty be held. The States were of a diametrically
opposite opinion. They insisted that the stadholder, so soon
as he could complete his preparations, should march straight
upon Spinola's works and break up the siege, even at the
risk of a general action.[33] They were willing once more to
take the terrible chance of a defeat in Flanders. Maurice,
with a heavy heart, bowed to their decision, showing by
his conduct the very spirit of a republican soldier, obeying
the civil magistrate, even when that obedience was like to
bring disaster upon the commonwealth. But much was to be
done before he could undertake this new adventure.

[31] Meteren, 495. Fleming, 597.   [32] Van der Kemp, iii. and notes.   [33] Ibid

Meantime the garrison in Ostend were at their last gasp. On being asked by the States-General whether it was possible to hold out for twenty days longer, Marquette called a council of officers, who decided that they would do their best, but that it was impossible to fix a day or hour when resistance must cease. Obviously, however, the siege was in its extreme old age. The inevitable end was approaching.

Before the middle of September the enemy was thoroughly established in possession of the new Hell's Mouth, the new Porcupine, and all the other bastions of the new entrenchment. On the 13th of that month the last supreme effort was made, and the Sand Hill, that all-important redoubt, which during these three dismal years had triumphantly resisted every assault, was at last carried by storm.[34] The enemy had now gained possession of the whole town except Little Troy. The new harbour would be theirs in a few hours, and as for Troy itself, those hastily and flimsily constructed ramparts were not likely to justify the vaunts uttered when they were thrown up nor to hold out many minutes before the whole artillery of Spinola. Plainly on this last morsel of the fatal sandbank the word surrender must be spoken, unless the advancing trumpets of Maurice should now be heard. But there was no such welcome sound in the air. The weather was so persistently rainy and stormy that the roads became impassable, and Maurice, although ready and intending to march towards Spinola to offer him battle, was unable for some days to move.[35] Meantime a council, summoned by Marquette, of all the officers, decided that Ostend must be abandoned now that Ostend had ceased to exist.

13 Sept.

On the 20th September the Accord was signed with Spinola. The garrison were to march out with their arms. They were to carry off four cannon but no powder. All clerical persons were to leave the place, with their goods and chattels. All prisoners taken on both sides during the siege

[34] Fleming, 574. Bentivoglio, iii. 530. Meteren, 497vo, 498.
[35] Van der Kemp, ii. 461, note.

were to be released.   Burghers, sutlers, and others, to go
whither they would, undisturbed.[36]   And thus the
archdukes, after three years and seventy-seven days   20 Sept.
of siege, obtained their prize.   Three thousand men, in good
health, marched out of little Troy with the honours of war.
The officers were entertained by Spinola and his comrades
at a magnificent banquet, in recognition of the unexampled
heroism with which the town had been defended.[37]   Subsequently the whole force marched to the headquarters of the
States' army in and about Sluys.   They were received by
Prince Maurice, who stood bareheaded and surrounded by his
most distinguished officers, to greet them and to shake them
warmly by the hand.[38]   Surely no defeated garrison ever
deserved more respect from friend or foe.

The Archduke Albert and the Infanta Isabella entered the
place in triumph, if triumph it could be called.   It would be
difficult to imagine a more desolate scene.   The artillery of
the first years of the seventeenth century was not the terrible
enginry of destruction that it has become in the last third of
the nineteenth, but a cannonade, continued so steadily and so
long, had done its work.   There were no churches, no houses,
no redoubts, no bastions, no walls, nothing but a vague and
confused mass of ruin.   Spinola conducted his imperial guests
along the edge of extinct volcanoes, amid upturned cemeteries, through quagmires which once were moats, over huge
mounds of sand, and vast shapeless masses of bricks and
masonry, which had been forts.   He endeavoured to point out
places where mines had been exploded, where ravelins had
been stormed, where the assailants had been successful, and
where they had been bloodily repulsed.   But it was all
loathsome, hideous rubbish.   There were no human habita-
tions, no hovels, no casemates.   The inhabitants had burrowed
at last in the earth, like the dumb creatures of the swamps
and forests.   In every direction the dykes had burst, and the
sullen wash of the liberated waves, bearing hither and thither

[36] Accord, in Fleming, Haestens, Meteren, Bentivoglio, *ubi sup.*
[37] Van der Kemp, ii. 111.   Meteren, *ubi sup.*   [38] Meteren, *ubi sup.*

the floating wreck of fascines and machinery, of planks and building materials, sounded far and wide over what should have been dry land. The great ship channel, with the unconquered Half-moon upon one side and the incomplete batteries and platforms of Bucquoy on the other, still defiantly opened its passage to the sea, and the retiring fleets of the garrison were white in the offing. All around was the grey expanse of stormy ocean, without a cape or a headland to break its monotony, as the surges rolled mournfully in upon a desolation more dreary than their own. The atmosphere was mirky and surcharged with rain, for the wild equinoctial storm which had held Maurice spell-bound had been raging over land and sea for many days. At every step the unburied skulls of brave soldiers who had died in the cause of freedom grinned their welcome to the conquerors. Isabella wept at the sight.[39] She had cause to weep. Upon that miserable sandbank more than a hundred thousand men had laid down their lives[40] by her decree, in order that she and her husband might at last take possession of a most barren prize. This insignificant fragment of a sovereignty which her wicked old father had presented to her on his deathbed—a sovereignty which he had no more moral right or actual power to confer than if it had been in the planet Saturn—had at last been appropriated at the cost of all this misery. It was of no great value, although its acquisition had caused the expenditure of at least eight millions of florins, divided in nearly equal proportions between the two belligerents. It was in vain that great immunities were offered to those who would remain, or who would consent to

---

[39] Gallucci, ii. 485.

[40] The numbers of those who were killed or who died of disease in both armies during this memorable siege, have been placed as high as one hundred and forty thousand. (Gallucci. *ubi sup.*) Meteren, 498, says that on the body of a Spanish officer, who fell in one of the innumerable assaults, was found a list of all the officers and privates killed in the Catholic army up to that date (which he does not give), and the amount was 72,124. Another Spanish authority, Juan Ballono, puts the number of the besiegers who perished *in the last year* of the siege at sixty thousand—of course a ridiculous exaggeration. Such preposterous statistics show the impossibility of making anything like a correct estimate. Of the besieged the loss is supposed to have been as heavy as that of their antagonists, but no registers have been preserved.

settle in the foul Golgotha. The original population left the place in mass. No human creatures were left save the wife of a freebooter and her paramour, a journeyman blacksmith.[41] This unsavoury couple, to whom entrance into the purer atmosphere of Zeeland was denied, thenceforth shared with the carrion crows the amenities of Ostend.

[41] Fleming, 580.

CHAPTER XLIV.

Equation between the contending powers — Treaty of peace between King
James and the archdukes and the King of Spain — Position of the Provinces — States envoy in England to be styled ambassador — Protest of
the Spanish ambassador — Effect of James's peace-treaty on the people of
England — Public rejoicings for the victory at Sluys — Spinola appointed
commander-in-chief of the Spanish forces — Preparations for a campaign
against the States — Seizure of Dutch cruisers — International discord —
Destruction of Sarmiento's fleet by Admiral Haultain — Projected enterprise against Antwerp — Descent of Spinola on the Netherland frontier —
Oldenzaal and Lingen taken — Movements of Prince Maurice — Encounter of the two armies — Panic of the Netherlanders — Consequent loss
and disgrace — Wachtendonk and Cracow taken by Spinola — Spinola's
reception in Spain — Effect of his victories — Results of the struggle between Freedom and Absolutism — Affairs in the East — Amboyna taken
by Van der Hagen — Contest for possession of the Clove Islands —Commercial treaty between the States and the King of Ternate — Hostilities
between the Kings of Ternate and Tydor — Expulsion of the Portuguese
from the Moluccas — Du Terrail's attempted assault on Bergen-op-Zoom —
Attack on the Dunkirk pirate fleet — Practice of executing prisoners captured at sea.

I HAVE invited the reader's attention to the details of this
famous siege because it was not an episode, but almost the
sum total, of the great war during the period occupied by its
events. The equation between the contending forces indicated the necessity of peace. That equation seemed for
the time to have established itself over all Europe. France
had long since withdrawn from the actual strife, and kept its
idle thunders in a concealed although ever threatening hand.
In the East the Pacha of Buda had become Pacha of Pest.[1]
Even Gran was soon to fall before the Turk, whose advancing horse-tails might thus almost be descried from the
walls of Vienna.[2] Stephen Botschkay meantime had made
himself master of Transylvania, concluded peace with Ahmet,

[1] Meteren, 502vo.   [2] Ibid.

and laughed at the Emperor Rudolph for denouncing him as a rebel.[3]

Between Spain and England a far different result had been reached than the one foreshadowed in the portentous colloquies between King James and Maximilian de Bethune. Those conferences have been purposely described with some minuteness, in order that the difference often existing between vast projects and diametrically opposed and very insignificant conclusions might once more be exhibited.

In the summer of 1603 it had been firmly but mysteriously arranged between the monarchs of France and Great Britain that the House of Austria should be crushed, its territories parcelled out at the discretion of those two potentates, the imperial crown taken from the Habsburgs, the Spaniards driven out of the Netherlands, an alliance offensive and defensive made with the Dutch republic, while the East and West Indies were to be wrested by main force of the allies, from Spain, whose subjects were thenceforth to be for ever excluded from those lucrative regions. As for the Jesuits, who were to James as loathsome as were the Puritans to Elizabeth, the British sovereign had implored the ambassador of his royal brother, almost with tears, never to allow that pestilential brood to regain an entrance into his dominions.[4]

In the summer of 1604 King James made a treaty of peace and amity with the archdukes and with the monarch of Spain, thus extending his friendly relations with the doomed house of Austria. The republic of the Netherlands was left to fight her battles alone ; her imaginary allies looking down upon her struggle with benevolent indifference. As for the Indies, not a syllable of allusion in the treaty was permitted by Spain to that sacred subject ; the ambassador informing the British Government that he gave them access to twelve kingdoms and two seas, while Spain acquired by the treaty access only to two kingdoms and one sea.[5] The new world, however, east or west, from the Antilles to the Moluccas, was the pri-

[3] Meteren, 502vo.   [4] Sully, v. 18.   [4] Meteren, 500.

vate and indefeasible property of his Catholic Majesty. On religious matters, it was agreed that English residents in Spain should not be compelled to go to mass, but that they should kneel in the street to the Host unless they could get out of the way.[6] In regard to the Netherlands, it was agreed by the two contracting powers that one should never assist the rebels or enemies of the other. With regard to the cities and fortresses of Brill, Flushing, Rammekens, and other cautionary places, where English garrisons were maintained, and which King James was bound according to the contracts of Queen Elizabeth never to restore except to those who had pledged them to the English crown—the king would uphold those contracts. He would, however, endeavour to make an arrangement with the States by which they should agree within a certain period to make their peace with Spain. Should they refuse or fail, he would then consider himself liberated from these previous engagements and free to act concerning those cities in an honourable and reasonable manner, as became a friendly king.[7] Meantime the garrisons should not in any way assist the Hollanders in their hostilities with Spain.[8] English subjects were forbidden to carry into Spain or the obedient Netherlands any property or merchandize belonging to the Hollanders,[9] or to make use of Dutch vessels in their trade with Spain.[10] Both parties agreed to do their best to bring about a pacification in the Netherlands.

No irony certainly could be more exquisite that this last-named article. This was the end of that magnificent conception, the great Anglo-French League against the house of Austria. King James would combine his efforts with King Philip to pacify the Netherlands. The wolf and the watch-dog would unite to bring back the erring flock to the fold. Meantime James would keep the cautionary towns in his clutches, not permitting their garrisons or any of his subjects to assist the rebels on sea or shore. As for the Jesuits, their

---

[6] Treaty in Meteren, *ubi sup.* Compare Grotius, xiii. 647, 648.
[7] Article vii. of Treaty.   [8] Article viii.   [9] Article xii.   [10] Article xviii.

triumphant re-appearance in France, and the demolition of the pyramid raised to their dishonour on the site of the house where John Castel, who had stabbed Henry IV., had resided, were events about to mark the opening year.[11] Plainly enough Secretary Cecil had out-generalled the French party.

The secret treaty of Hampton Court, the result of the efforts of Rosny and Olden-Barneveld in July of the previous year, was not likely to be of much service in protecting the republic. James meant to let the dead treaties bury their dead, to live in peace with all the world, and to marry his sons and daughters to Spanish Infantes and Infantas. Meantime, although he had sheathed the sword which Elizabeth had drawn against the common enemy, and had no idea of fighting or spending money for the States, he was willing that their diplomatic agent should be called ambassador. The faithful and much experienced Noel de Caron coveted that distinction, and moved thereby the spleen of Henry's envoy at the Hague, Buzanval, who probably would not have objected to the title himself. "'Twill be a folly," he said, "for him to present himself on the pavement as a prancing steed, and then be treated like a poor hack. He has been too long employed to put himself in such a plight. But there are lunatics everywhere and of all ages."[12]

Never had the Advocate seemed so much discouraged. Ostend had fallen, and the defection of the British sovereign was an off-set for the conquest of Sluys. He was more urgent with the French Government for assistance than he had ever been before. "A million florins a year from France," he said "joined to two millions raised in the provinces, would enable them to carry on the war. The ship was in good condition," he added, "and fit for a long navigation without danger of shipwreck if there were only biscuit enough on board.[13] Otherwise she was lost. Before that time came he should quit the helm which he had been holding the more

[11] Meteren, 502.
[12] Buzanval to Villeroy, in Deventer, iii. 1-9. At the same epoch the French king asked Aerssens if he too was to have the rank of ambassador. That diplomatist replied that he hoped not, unless his salary was to be raised at the same time.—Ibid. p. 24.   [13] Ibid.

resolutely since the peace of Vervins because the king had told him, when concluding it, that if three years' respite should be given him he would enter into the game afresh, and take again upon his shoulders the burthen which inevitable necessity had made him throw down. But," added Olden-Barneveld, bitterly, "there is little hope of it now, after his neglect of the many admirable occasions during the siege of Ostend." [14]

So soon as the Spanish ambassador learned that Caron was to be accepted into the same diplomatic rank as his own, he made an infinite disturbance, protested most loudly and passionately to the king at the indignity done to his master by this concession to the representative of a crew of traitors and rebels, and demanded in the name of the treaty just concluded that Caron should be excluded in such capacity from all access to court. [15]

As James was nearly forty years of age, as the Hollanders had been rebels ever since he was born, and as the King of Spain had exercised no sovereignty over them within his memory, this was naturally asking too much of him in the name of his new-born alliance with Spain. So he assumed a position of great dignity, notwithstanding the Constable's clamour, and declared his purpose to give audience to the agents of the States by whatever title they presented themselves before him. In so doing he followed the example, he said, of others who (a strange admission on his part) were as wise as himself. It was not for him to censure the crimes and faults of the States, if such they had committed. He had not been the cause of their revolt from Spanish authority, and it was quite sufficient that he had stipulated to maintain neutrality between the two belligerents. [16] And with this the ambassador of his Catholic Majesty, having obtained the substance of a very advantageous treaty, was fain to abandon opposition to the shadowy title by which James sought to indemnify the republic for his perfidy. [17]

[14] Meteren, 502.
[15] Ibid. 501.　　[16] Ibid.

[17] At the same time the republican agent, although recognized as ambas-

The treaty of peace with Spain gave no pleasure to the English public. There was immense enthusiasm in London at the almost simultaneous fall of Sluys, but it was impossible for the court to bring about a popular demonstration of sympathy with the abandonment of the old ally and the new-born affection for the ancient enemy. "I can assure your mightinesses," wrote Caron, "that no promulgation was ever received in London with more coolness, yes—with more

sador, received but slender encouragement in his interviews with the British sovereign. "When I tell those on the other side," said James, "that you are not ready to treat with them, they will say that all wars must sooner or later come to an end. What reply shall I make to that?"

"Say that the king has long ago forfeited all right to these provinces," answered Caron; "that the sovereignty according to law has fallen into the bosom of my lords the States; that the Spaniard, having usurped so many other countries in the world, might leave us this little bit for the sake of living in peace."

James replied that kings never willingly gave up their provinces. "And the Netherlands are no longer the king's to give up," returned the ambassador. His majesty expressed his intention, however, to do nothing more in the matter. He should maintain strict neutrality. At the same time, with amusing inconsistency, he warmly recognised the identity of the Dutch cause with his own. "In your preservation lies my own interest. Your ruin would be my great loss. Rather than it should go so far I will venture my own person and all that God has given me in this world, but I trust that God will never let it come so far as this. As to the assistance you ask of me, God is my witness if it be not my wish that I were able to grant it, but I have told you many times that I was principally moved to make peace by my necessities."

This statement of the king's financial plight might be true enough. It is certain that in order to obtain the means to make decent provision for the household at his accession it had

been necessary to send jewelry and other valuable effects to Amsterdam as a pledge for a secret loan of 25,000*l.* But there were graver and far more dangerous causes at work in the English court to affect a pacification and even an alliance with Spain, than a temporary financial embarrassment.

It could also scarcely console the States' envoy to be told that in case of uttermost need the king meant to lay down his life for the republic. The spectacle of James leading a forlorn hope against Spain was not an inspiring one, especially as the martial sovereign of France had turned his face away from his old friends. "Had the Spaniard given me as much cause of quarrel as he has to the most Christian king," said James, "I should certainly have broken with him. Not only I should have done my best to help you, but I should have plunged into the fight at the risk of life and property."

These were brave words. The very near future was, however, to show whether the British king would feel the outrages of Spain against himself as deeply as he now resented the injuries of the same power to his brother Henry. It was soon obvious enough that the most to be hoped of England was that she would not interfere to prevent such assistance as France might be willing to grant to the republic, James becoming more and more besotted with the idea of an alliance with Spain. A few months later Rosny told Aerssens that the King of Spain found quite as much favour at the English court as he did with the Duke of Savoy. See De venter, iii. 10-14, 15, 40.

sadness. No mortal has shown the least satisfaction in words or deeds, but, on the contrary, people have cried out openly, 'God save our good neighbours the States of Holland and Zeeland, and grant them victory!' On Sunday, almost all the preachers gave thanks from their pulpits for the victory which their good neighbours had gained at Sluys, but would not say a word about the peace. The people were admonished to make bonfires, but you may be very sure not a bonfire was to be seen. But, in honour of the victory, all the vessels in St. Catharine's Docks fired salutes at which the Spaniards were like to burst with spite. The English clap their hands and throw their caps in the air when they hear anything published favourable to us, but, it must be confessed, they are now taking very dismal views of affairs. *Vox populi vox Dei.*"[18]

The rejoicing in Paris was scarcely less enthusiastic or apparently less sincere than in London. "The news of the surrender of Sluys," wrote Aerssens, "is received with so much joy by small and great that one would have said it was their own exploit. His Majesty has made such demonstrations in his actions and discourse that he has not only been advised by his council to dissemble in the matter, but has undergone reproaches from the pope's nuncius of having made a league with your Mightinesses to the prejudice of the King of Spain. His Majesty wishes your Mightinesses prosperity with all his heart, yea so that he would rather lose his right arm than see your Mightinesses in danger. Be assured that he means roundly, and we should pray God for his long life; for I don't see that we can expect anything from these regions after his death."[19]

It was ere long to be seen, however, roundly as the king meant it, that the republic was to come into grave peril without causing him to lose his right arm, or even to wag his finger, save in reproach of their Mightinesses.

The republic, being thus left to fight its battles alone, girded its loins anew for the conflict. During the remainder

18 Van der Kemp, ii. 457.   19 Ibid. 453.

of the year 1604, however, there were no military operations of consequence. Both belligerents needed a brief repose. The siege of Ostend had not been a siege. It was a long pitched battle between the new system and the old, between absolutism and the spirit of religious, political, and mercantile freedom. Absolutism had gained the lists on which the long duel had been fought, but the republic had meantime exchanged that war-blasted spot for a valuable and commodious position. It was certainly an advantage, as hostilities were necessarily to have continued somewhere during all that period, that all the bloodshed and desolation had been concentrated upon one insignificant locality, and one more contiguous to the enemy's possessions than to those of the united States. It was very doubtful, however, whether all that money and blood might not have been expended in some other manner more beneficial to the cause of the arch-dukes. At least it could hardly be maintained that they took anything by the capitulation of Ostend but the most barren and worthless of trophies. Eleven old guns, partly broken, and a small quantity of ammunition, were all the spoils of war found in the city after its surrender.

The Marquis Spinola went to Spain. On passing through Paris he was received with immense enthusiasm by Henry IV., whose friendship for the States, and whose desperate designs against the house of Austria, did not prevent him from warmly congratulating the great Spanish general on his victory. It was a victory, said Henry, which he could himself have never achieved, and, in recognition of so great a triumph, he presented Spinola with a beautiful Thracian horse, valued at twelve hundred ducats.[20] Arriving in Spain, the conqueror found himself at once the object of the open applause and the scarcely concealed hatred of the courtiers and politicians. He ardently desired to receive as his guerdon the rank of grandee of Spain. He met with a refusal.[21] To keep his hat on his head in presence of the sovereign was the highest possible reward. Should that be bestowed upon him now, urged

[20] Gallucci, ii. 194.   [21] Ibid. 200.

Lerma, what possible recompense could be imagined for the great services which all felt confident that he was about to render in the future ? He must continue to remove his hat in the monarch's company. Meantime, if he wished the title of prince, with considerable revenues attached to his principality, this was at his disposal.[22] It must be confessed that in a monarchy where the sentiment of honour was supposed to be the foundation of the whole structure there is something chivalrous and stimulating to the imagination in this preference by the great general of a shadowy but rare distinction to more substantial acquisitions. Nevertheless, as the grandeeship was refused, it is not recorded that he was displeased with the principality. Meantime there was a very busy intrigue to deprive him of the command-in-chief of the Catholic forces in Flanders, and one so nearly successful that Mexia, governor of Antwerp citadel, was actually appointed in Spinola's stead. It was only after long and anxious conferences at Valladolid with the king and the Duke of Lerma, and after repeated statements in letters from the archdukes that all their hopes of victory depended on retaining the Genoese commander-in-chief, that the matter was finally arranged. Mexia received an annual pension of eight thousand ducats, and to Spinola was assigned five hundred ducats monthly, as commander-in-chief under the archduke, with an equal salary as agent for the king's affairs in Flanders.[3]

Early in the spring he returned to Brussels, having made fresh preparations for the new campaign in which he was to measure himself before the world against Maurice of Nassau.

Spinola had removed the thorn from the Belgic lion's foot : " Ostendæ erasit fatalis Spinola spinam."[24] And although it may be doubted whether the relief was as thorough as had been hoped, yet a freedom of movement had unquestionably been gained. There was now at least what for a long time had not existed, a possibility for imagining some new and perhaps more effective course of campaigning. The

[22] Galucci, ii. 194-202.   [23] Ibid.   [24] Ibid. 182.

young Genoese commander-in-chief returned from Spain early in May, with the Golden Fleece around his neck, and with full powers from the Catholic king to lay out his work, subject only to the approbation of the archduke. It was not probable that Albert, who now thoroughly admired and leaned upon the man of whom he had for a time been disposed to be jealous, would interfere with his liberty of action. There had also been—thanks to Spinola's influence with the cabinet at Madrid and the merchants of Genoa—much more energy in recruiting and in providing the necessary sinews of war. Moreover it had been resolved to make the experiment of sending some of the new levies by sea, instead of subjecting them all to the long and painful overland march through Spain, Italy, and Germany.[25] A terzo of infantry was on its way from Naples, and two more were expected from Milan, but it was decided that the Spanish troops should be embarked on board a fleet of transports, mainly German and English, and thus carried to the shores of the obedient Netherlands.[26]

The States-General got wind of these intentions, and set Vice-Admiral Haultain upon the watch to defeat the scheme. That well-seasoned mariner accordingly, with a sufficient fleet of war-galleots, cruised thenceforth with great assiduity in the chops of the channel. Already the late treaty between Spain and England had borne fruits of bitterness to the republic. The Spanish policy had for the time completely triumphed in the council of James. It was not surprising therefore that the partisans of that policy should occasionally indulge in manifestations of malevolence towards the upstart little commonwealth which had presumed to enter into commercial rivalry with the British realm, and to assert a place among the nations of the earth. An order had just been issued by the English Government that none of its subjects should engage in the naval service of any foreign power. This decree was a kind of corollary to the Spanish treaty, was levelled directly against the

[25] Grotius, xiv. 658, 659.   Meteren, 519vo.   [26] Ibid.

Hollanders, and became the pretext of intolerable arrogance, both towards their merchantmen and their lesser war-vessels. Admiral Monson, an especial partisan of Spain, was indefatigable in exercising the right he claimed of visiting foreign vessels off the English coast, in search of English sailors violating the proclamation of neutrality. On repeated occasions prizes taken by Dutch cruisers from the Spaniards, and making their way with small prize crews to the ports of the republic, were overhauled, visited, and seized by the English admiral, who brought the vessels into the harbours of his own country, liberated the crews, and handed ships and cargoes over to the Spanish ambassador.[27] Thus prizes fairly gained by nautical skill and hard fighting, off Spain, Portugal, Brazil, or even more distant parts of the world, were confiscated almost in sight of port, in utter disregard of public law or international decency. The States-General remonstrated with bitterness. Their remonstrances were answered by copious arguments, proving, of course, to the entire satisfaction of the party who had done the wrong, that no practice could be more completely in harmony with reason and justice. Meantime the Spanish ambassador sold the prizes, and appropriated the proceeds towards carrying on the war against the republic ; the Dutch sailors, thus set ashore against their will and against law on the neutral coast of England, being left to get home as they could, or to starve if they could do no better. As for the States, they had the legal arguments of their late ally to console them for the loss of their ships.

Simultaneously with these events considerable levies of troops were made in England by the archduke, in spite of all the efforts of the Dutch ambassador to prevent this one-sided neutrality,[28] while at the other ends of the world mercantile jealousy in both the Indies was fast combining with other causes already rife to increase the international discord. Out of all this fuel it was fated that a blaze of hatred between the two leading powers of the new era, the United Kingdom and the United Republic, should one day burst forth, which was

---

[27] Grotius, xiv. 658, 659. Meteren, 518ᵛᵒ.   [28] Ibid. 518.

to be fanned by passion, prejudice, and a mistaken sentiment of patriotism and self-interest on both sides, and which not all the bloodshed of more than one fierce war could quench. The traces of this savage sentiment are burnt deeply into the literature, language, and traditions of both countries, and it is strange enough that the epoch at which chronic wrangling and international coolness changed into furious antipathy between the two great Protestant powers of Europe—for great they already both were, despite the paucity of their population and resources, as compared with nations which were less influenced by the spirit of the age or had less aptness in obeying its impulse—should be dated from the famous year of Guy Fawkes.

Meantime the Spanish troops, embarked in eight merchant ships and a few pinnaces, were slowly approaching their destination. They had been instructed, in case they found it impracticable to enter a Flemish port, to make for the hospitable shores of England, the Spanish ambassador and those whom he had bribed at the court of James having already provided for their protection.[29] Off Dover Admiral Haultain got sight of Sarmiento's little fleet. He made short work with it. Faithfully carrying out the strenuous orders of the States-General, he captured some of the ships, burned one, and ran others aground after a very brief resistance. Some of the soldiers and crews were picked up by English vessels cruising in the neighbourhood and narrowly watching the conflict. A few stragglers escaped by swimming, but by far the greater proportion of the newly-arrived troops were taken prisoners, tied together two and two, and then, at a given signal from the admiral's ship, tossed into the sea.[30]

Not Peter Titelmann, nor Julian Romero, nor the Duke of Alva himself, ever manifested greater alacrity in wholesale murder than was shown by this admiral of the young

---

[29] "Quorum omnium curam Petrus Cubiara acceperat hoc inter cætera mandato ut si Flandria negaretur vitato Galliæ litore Britanniæ oram adiret tutum ibi hospitium ope legati Hispanici et quos ille Britannorum donis emerat habiturus."—Grot. xiv. 658.

[30] Ibid. Meteren, *ubi sup.* Wagenaar, ix. 186.

republic in fulfilling the savage decrees of the States-General.[31]

Thus at least one-half of the legion perished. The pursuit of the ships was continued within English waters, when the guns of Dover Castle opened vigorously upon the recent allies of England, in order to protect her newly-found friends in their sore distress. Doubtless in the fervour of the work the Dutch admiral had violated the neutral coast of England, so that the cannonade from the castle was technically justified. It was however a biting satire upon the proposed Protestant league against Spain and universal monarchy in behalf of the Dutch republic, that England was already doing her best to save a Spanish legion and to sink a Dutch fleet. The infraction of English sovereignty was unquestionable if judged by the more scrupulous theory of modern days, but it was well remarked by the States-General, in answer to the remonstrances of James's Government, that the Dutch admiral, knowing that the pirates of Dunkirk roamed at will through English waters in search of their prey, might have hoped for some indulgence of a similar character to the ships of the republic.[32]

Thus nearly the whole of the Spanish legion perished. The soldiers who escaped to the English coast passed the winter miserably in huts, which they were allowed to construct on the sands, but nearly all, including the lieutenant-colonel commanding, Pedro Cubiera, died of famine or of wounds. A few small vessels of the expedition succeeded in reaching the Flemish coast, and landing a slight portion of the terzo.[33]

---

[31] Certainly it must be admitted that the world makes some little progress in civilization. To exterminate unorganized and irresponsible bands of brigands disgracing the name of soldiers, may still be inevitable in the interest of humanity, but that regular troops should be destroyed in cold blood, because embarked and captured not in war-vessels but in mercantile and neutral transports, was a barbarity which seems incredible to us, but which, in the beginning of the seventeenth century, was not rebuked by the most gentle and enlightened spirits of the age.

This whole story is minutely related by the illustrious Hugo Grotius, without a syllable of censure. Hist. xiv. 657, 658.   [32] Ibid. 659.

[33] Grotius, Meteren, *ubi sup.* Wagenaar, ix. 184–187. Winwood, ii. 82 ; who was informed by Lord Salisbury that more than one hundred men in the Dutch fleet were killed by the Dover cannon.

The campaign of 1605 opened but languidly. The strain upon the resources of the Netherlands, thus unaided, was becoming severe, although there is no doubt that, as the India traffic slowly developed itself, the productive force of the commonwealth visibly increased, while the thrifty habits of its citizens, and their comparative abstinence from unproductive consumption, still enabled it to bear the tremendous burthen of the war. A new branch of domestic industry had grown out of the India trade, great quantities of raw silk being now annually imported from the East into Holland, to be wrought into brocades, tapestries, damasks, velvets, satins, and other luxurious fabrics for European consumption.[34] It is a curious phenomenon in the history of industry that while at this epoch Holland was the chief seat of silk manufactures, the great financier of Henry IV. was congratulating his sovereign and himself that natural causes had for ever prevented the culture or manufacture of silk in France.[35] If such an industry were possible, he was sure that the decline of martial spirit in France and an eternal dearth of good French soldiers would be inevitable, and he even urged that the importation of such luxurious fabrics should be sternly prohibited, in order to preserve the moral health of the people.[36] The practical Hollanders were more inclined to leave silk farthingales and brocaded petticoats to be dealt with by thunderers from the pulpit or indignant fathers of families. Meantime the States-General felt instinctively that the little commonwealth grew richer, the more useful or agreeable things its burghers could call into existence out of nothingness, to be exchanged for the powder and bullets, timber and cordage, requisite for its eternal fight with universal monarchy, and that the richer the burghers grew the more capable they were of paying their taxes. It was not the fault of the States that the insane ambition of Spain and the archdukes compelled them to exhaust themselves annually by the most unproductive consumption that man is ever likely to devise, that of scientifically slaughtering his

[34] Meteren, 536.   [35] Sully, v. 77-79, *seqq.*   [36] Ibid.

brethren, because to practise economy in that regard would be to cease to exist, or to accept the most intolerable form of slavery.

The forces put into the field in the spring of 1605 were but meagre. There was also, as usual, much difference of opinion between Maurice and Barneveld as to the most judicious manner of employing them, and as usual the docile stadholder submitted his better judgment to the States.[37] It can hardly be too much insisted upon that the high-born Maurice always deported himself in fact, and as it were unconsciously, as the citizen soldier of a little republic, even while personally invested with many of the attributes of exalted rank, and even while regarded by many of his leading fellow-citizens as the legitimate and predestined sovereign of the newly-born state.

Early in the spring a great enterprise against Antwerp was projected. It failed utterly. Maurice, at Bergen-op-Zoom, despatched seven thousand troops up the Scheld, under command of Ernest Casimir. The flotilla was a long time getting under weigh, and instead of effecting a surprise, the army, on reaching the walls of Antwerp, found the burghers and garrison not in the least astonished, but on the contrary entirely prepared. Ernest returned after a few insignificant skirmishes, having accomplished nothing.[38]

Maurice next spent a few days in reducing the castle of Wouda, not far from Bergen, and then, transporting his army once more to the isle of Cadzand, he established his headquarters at Watervliet, near Yrendyke. Spinola followed him, having thrown a bridge across the Scheld. Maurice was disposed to reduce a fort, well called Patience,[39] lying over against the isle of Walcheren. Spinola took up a position by which he defended the place as with an impenetrable buckler. A game of skill now began between these two adepts in the art of war, for already the volunteer had taken rank among the highest professors of the new school. It was the object

[37] Van der Kemp, ii. 113.
[38] Ibid. 113, 114. Grotius, xiv. 656, 657. Meteren, 518.   [39] Grot. *ubi sup.*

of Maurice, who knew himself on the whole outnumbered, to divine his adversary's intentions. Spinola was supposed to be aiming at Sluys, at Grave, at Bergen-op-Zoom, possibly even at some more remote city, like Rheinberg, while rumours as to his designs, flying directly from his camp, were as thick as birds in the air. They were let loose on purpose by the artful Genoese, who all the time had a distinct and definite plan which was not yet suspected. The dilatoriness of the campaign was exasperating. It might be thought that the war was to last another half century, from the excessive inertness of both parties. The armies had all gone into winter quarters in the previous November, Spinola had spent nearly six months in Spain, midsummer had come and gone, and still Maurice was at Watervliet, guessing at his adversary's first move. On the whole, he had inclined to suspect a design upon Rheinberg, and had accordingly sent his brother Henry with a detachment to strengthen the garrison of that place. On the 1st of August however he learned that Spinola had crossed the Meuse and the Rhine, with ten thousand foot and three thousand horse, and that leaving Count Bucquoy with six thousand foot and one thousand five hundred horse in the neighbourhood of the Rhine, to guard a couple of redoubts which had been constructed for a basis at Kaiserswerth, he was marching with all possible despatch towards Friesland and Groningen.[40]

The Catholic general had concealed his design in a masterly manner. He had detained Maurice in the isle of Cadzand, the States still dreaming of a August. victorious invasion on their part of obedient Flanders, and the stadholder hesitating to quit his position of inactive observation, lest the moment his back was turned the rapid Spinola might whirl down upon Sluys, that most precious and skilfully acquired possession of the republic, when lo ! his formidable antagonist was marching in force upon what

[40] Bentivoglio, iii. 533, 534. Meteren, 521, 522. Grotius, xiv. 660, 661. Van der Kemp, ii. 114, 115, and notes.

the prince well knew to be her most important and least guarded frontier.

On the 8th August the Catholic general was before Oldenzaal, which he took in three days, and then advanced to Lingen. Should that place fall—and the
city was known to be most inadequately garrisoned and supplied—it would be easy for the foe to reduce Coeworden, and so seize the famous pass over the Bourtanger Morass, march straight to Embden—then in a state of municipal revolution on account of the chronic feuds between its counts and the population, and therefore an easy prey—after which all Friesland and Groningen would be at his mercy, and his road open to Holland and Utrecht; in short, into the very bowels of the republic.

On the 4th August Maurice broke up his camp in Flanders, and leaving five thousand men under Colonel Van der Noot, to guard the positions there, advanced rapidly to Deventer, with the intention of saving Lingen. It was too late. That very important place had been culpably neglected. The garrison consisted of but one cannoneer, and he had but one arm.[41] A burgher guard, numbering about three hundred, made such resistance as they could, and the one-armed warrior fired a shot or two from a rusty old demi-cannon. Such opposition to the accomplished Italian was naturally not very effective. On the 18th August the place capitulated.[42] Maurice, arriving at Deventer, and being now
strengthened by his cousin Lewis William with
such garrison troops as could be collected, learned the mortifying news with sentiments almost akin to despair. It was now to be a race for Coeworden, and the fleet-footed Spinola was a day's march at least in advance of his competitor. The key to the fatal morass would soon be in his hands. To the inexpressible joy of the stadholder, the Genoese seemed suddenly struck with blindness. The prize was almost in his hands and he threw away all his advan-

Aug. 8.

18 Aug.

---

[41] Meteren, *ubi sup.*
[42] Bentivoglio, Grotius, Meteren, Van der Kemp, *ubi sup.*

tages. Instead of darting at once upon Coeworden he paused
for nearly a month, during which period he seemed
intoxicated with a success so rapidly achieved, and   14 Sept.
especially with his adroitness in outwitting the great stadholder.[43]   On the 14th September he made a retrograde
movement towards the Rhine, leaving two thousand five
hundred men in Lingen. Maurice, giving profound thanks
to God for his enemy's infatuation, passed by Lingen, and
having now, with his cousin's reinforcements, a force of nine
thousand foot and three thousand horse, threw himself into
Coeworden, strengthened and garrisoned that vital fortress
which Spinola would perhaps have taken as easily as he had
done Lingen, made all the neighbouring positions
secure, and then fell back towards Wesel on the   24 Sept.
Rhine, in order to watch his antagonist.[44]   Spinola had
established his headquarters at Ruhrort, a place where the
river Ruhr empties into the Rhine. He had yielded to the
remonstrances of the Archbishop of Cologne, to whom
Kaiserwerth belonged, and had abandoned the forts which
Bucquoy, under his directions, had constructed at that
place.[45]

The two armies now gazed at each other, at a respectful
distance, for a fortnight longer, neither commander apparently
having any very definite purpose. At last, Maurice having
well reconnoitred his enemy, perceived a weak point in his
extended lines. A considerable force of Italian cavalry, with
some infantry, was stationed at the village of Mulheim, on
the Ruhr, and apparently out of convenient supporting
distance from Spinola's main army. The stadholder determined to deliver a sudden blow upon this tender spot, break
through the lines, and bring on a general action by surprise.
Assembling his well-seasoned and veteran troopers in force,
he divided them into two formidable bands, one under the
charge of his young brother Frederic Henry, the other under
that most brilliant of cavalry officers, Marcellus Bax, hero of
Turnhout and many another well-fought field.

[43] Meteren. Van der Kemp.   [44] Authorities cited.   [45] Bentivoglo, iii. 536.

The river Ruhr was a wide but desultory stream, easily fordable in many places. On the opposite bank to Mulheim was the Castle of Broek, and some hills of considerable elevation. Bax was ordered to cross the river and seize the castle and the heights, Count Henry to attack the enemy's camp in front, while Maurice himself, following rapidly with the advance of infantry and wagons, was to sustain the assault.

Marcellus Bax, rapid and dashing as usual, crossed the Ruhr, captured Broek Castle with ease, and stood ready to prevent the retreat of the Spaniards. Taken by surprise in front, they would naturally seek refuge on the other side of the river. That stream was not difficult for infantry, but as the banks were steep, cavalry could not easily extricate themselves from the water, except at certain prepared landings. Bax waited however for some time in vain for the flying Spaniards. It was not destined that the stadholder should effect many surprises that year. The troopers under Frederic Henry had made their approaches through an intricate path, often missing their way, and in far more leisurely fashion than was intended, so that outlying scouts had brought in information of the coming attack. As Count Henry approached the village, Trivulzio's cavalry was found drawn up in battle array, formidable in numbers, and most fully prepared for their visitors from Wesel. The party most astonished was that which came to surprise. In an instant one of those uncontrollable panics broke out to which even veterans are as subject as to dysentery or scurvy. The best cavalry of Maurice's army turned their backs at the very sight of the foe, and galloped off much faster than they had come.

Meantime, Marcellus Bax was assaulted, not only by his late handful of antagonists, who had now rallied, but by troops from Mulheim, who began to wade across the stream. At that moment he was cheered by the sight of Count Henry coming on with a very few of his troopers who had stood to their colours. A simultaneous charge from both banks at the enemy floundering in the river was attempted. It

8 Oct.

might have been brilliantly successful, but the panic had
crossed the river faster than the Spaniards could do, and
the whole splendid picked cavalry force of the republic,
commanded by the youngest son of William the Silent, and
by the favourite cavalry commander of her armies, was, after
a hot but brief action, in disgraceful and unreasonable flight.
The stadholder reached the bank of that fatal stream only to
witness this maddening spectacle, instead of the swift and
brilliant triumph which he was justified in expecting. He
did his best to stem the retreating tide. He called upon the
veterans, by the memory of Turnhout and Nieuport, and
so many other victories, to pause and redeem their name
before it was too late. He taunted them with their frequent
demands to be led to battle, and their expressed impatience
at enforced idleness. He denounced them as valiant only
for plundering defenceless peasants, and as cowards against
armed men ; as trusting more to their horses' heels than to
their own right hands. He invoked curses upon them for
deserting his young brother, who, conspicuous among them
by his gilded armour, the orange-plumes upon his casque, and
the bright orange-scarf across his shoulders, was now sorely
pressed in the struggling throng.[46]

It was all in vain. Could Maurice have thrown himself
into the field, he might, as in the crisis of the republic's fate
at Nieuport, have once more converted ruin into victory by
the magic of his presence. But the river was between him
and the battle, and he was an enforced spectator of his
country's disgrace.

For a few brief moments his demeanour, his taunts, and his
supplications had checked the flight of his troops.

A stand was made by a portion of the cavalry and a few
detached but fierce combats took place. Count
Frederic Henry was in imminent danger. Leading   8 Oct.
a mere handful of his immediate retainers, he threw himself
into the thickest of the fight, with the characteristic audacity
of his house. A Spanish trooper aimed his carbine full at his

[46] Grotius, xiv. 671.

face. It missed fire, and Henry, having emptied his own
pistol, was seized by the floating scarf upon his breast by more
than one enemy. There was a brief struggle, and death or
capture seemed certain; when an unknown hand laid his
nearest antagonist low, and enabled him to escape from over-
powering numbers.[47] The soldier, whose devotion thus saved
the career of the youngest Orange-Nassau destined to be so
long and so brilliant, from being cut off so prematurely, was
never again heard of,[43] and doubtless perished in the fray.

Meantime the brief sparkle of valour on the part of the
States' troops had already vanished. The adroit Spinola,
hurrying personally to the front, had caused such a clangor
from all the drums and trumpets in Broek and its neighbourhood to be made as to persuade the restive cavalry that the
whole force of the enemy was already upon them. The day
was obviously lost, and Maurice, with a heavy heart, now himself gave the signal to retreat. Drawing up the greater part
of his infantry in solid mass upon the banks to protect the
passage, he sent a force to the opposite side, Horace Vere
being the first to wade the stream. All that was then possible
to do was accomplished, and the panic flight converted into
orderly retreat, but it was a day of disaster and disgrace for
the republic.[49]

About five hundred of the best States' cavalry were left
dead on the field, but the stain upon his almost unsullied flag
was more cutting to the stadholder's heart than the death of
his veterans. The material results were in truth almost even.
The famous cavalry general, Count Trivulzio, with at least
three hundred Spaniards, fell in the combat,[50] but the glory of
having defeated the best cavalry of Europe in a stricken field
and under the very eyes of the stadholder would have been
sufficient compensation to Spinola for much greater losses.

Maurice withdrew towards Wesel, sullen but not despond-
ing. His forces were meagre, and although he had been out-

---

[47] Grotius, xiv. 671. Meteren, 523vo.   [48] Grotius, *ubi sup.*
[49] Ibid. xiv. 669–672. Meteren, 523 and vo. Bentivoglio, iii. 537. Van der
Kemp, ii. 116, 510, 511.   [50] Ibid.

generalled, out-marched, and defeated in the open field, at least the Genoese had not planted the blow which he had meditated in the very heart of the republic.

Autumn was now far advanced, and dripping with rain. The roads and fields were fast becoming impassable sloughs, and no further large operations could be expected in this campaign. Yet the stadholder's cup was not full, and he was destined to witness two more triumphs of his rival, now fast becoming famous, before this year of disasters should close. On the 27th October, Spinola took the city 27 Oct. of Wachtendonk, after ten days' siege, and on the 5 Nov. 5th of November the strong place of Cracow.[51]

Maurice was forced to see these positions captured almost under his eyes, being now quite powerless to afford relief. His troops had dwindled by sickness and necessary detachments for garrison-work to a comparatively insignificant force, and very soon afterwards both armies went into winter quarters.[52]

The States were excessively disappointed at the results of the year's work, and deep if not loud were the reproaches cast upon the stadholder. Certainly his military reputation had not been augmented by this campaign. He had lost many places, and had not gained an inch of ground anywhere. Already the lustre of Sluys, of Nieuport, and Turnhout were growing dim, for Maurice had so accustomed the republic to victories that his own past triumphs seemed now his greatest enemies. Moreover he had founded a school out of which apt pupils had already graduated, and it would seem that the Genoese volunteer had rapidly profited by his teachings as only a man endowed with exquisite military genius could have done.

Yet, after all, it seems certain that, with the stadholder's limited means, and with the awful consequences to the country of a total defeat in the open field, the Fabian tactics, which he had now deliberately adopted, were the most reasonable. The invader of foreign domains, the suppressor of great

[51] Meteren, 523[vo]. Bentivoglio, iii. 536. Grot. xiv. 673. Van der Kemp, ii. 117.   [52] Ibid.

revolts, can indulge in the expensive luxury of procrastination
only at imminent peril.   For the defence, it is always possible
to conquer by delay, and it was perfectly understood between
Spinola and his ablest advisers at the Spanish court [53] that
the blows must be struck thick and fast, and at the most
vulnerable places, or that the victory would be lost.

Time was the ally not of the Spanish invaders, who came
from afar, but of the Dutch burghers, who remained at home.
"Jam aut Nunquam," [54] was the motto upon the Italian's
banners.

In proportion to the depression in the republic at the results of this year's campaigning was the elation at the Spanish
court.   Bad news and false news had preceded the authentic
intelligence of Spinola's victories.   The English envoy had
received unquestionable information that the Catholic general
had sustained an overwhelming defeat at the close of the
campaign, with a loss of three thousand five hundred men. [55]
The tale was implicitly believed by king and cabinet, so that
when, very soon afterwards, the couriers arrived bringing
official accounts of the victory gained over the veteran cavalry
of the States in the very presence of the stadholder, followed
by the crowning triumph of Wachtendonk, the demonstrations
of joy were all the more vivacious in consequence of the previous gloom. [56]   Spinola himself followed hard upon the latest
messengers, and was received with ovations. [57]   Never, since
the days of Alexander Farnese, had a general at the Spanish
court been more cordially caressed or hated.   Had Philip the
Prudent been still upon the throne, he would have felt it his
duty to make immediate arrangements for poisoning him.
Certainly his plans and his popularity would have been undermined in the most artistic manner.

But Philip III., more dangerous to rabbits than to generals,
left the Genoese to settle the plans of his next campaign with
Lerma and his parasites.

The subtle Spinola, having, in his despatches, ascribed the
chief merit of the victories to Louis Velasco, a Spaniard, while

[53] Grot. xiv. 660.   [54] Ibid.   [55] Gallucci, ii. 253, seqq.   [56] Ibid.   [57] Ibid.

his own original conception of transferring the war to Friesland was attributed by him with magnificent effrontery to
Lerma and to the king[58]—who were probably quite ignorant
of the existence of that remote province—succeeded in maintaining his favourable position at court, and was allowed, by
what was called the war-council, to manage matters nearly
at his pleasure.

It is difficult however to understand how so much clamour
should have been made over such paltry triumphs. All
Europe rang with a cavalry fight in which less than a
thousand saddles on both sides had been emptied, leading to
no result, and with the capture of a couple of insignificant
towns, of which not one man in a thousand had ever heard.

Spinola had doubtless shown genius of a subtle and inventive
order, and his fortunate audacity in measuring himself, while
a mere apprentice, against the first military leader living had
been crowned with wonderful success. He had nailed the stadholder fast to the island of Cadzand, while he was perfecting
his arrangements and building boats on the Rhine; he had
propounded riddles which Maurice had spent three of the best
campaigning months in idle efforts to guess, and when he
at last moved, he had swept to his mark with the swiftness
and precision of a bird of prey. Yet the greatest of all
qualities in a military commander, that of deriving substantial
fruits from victory instead of barren trophies, he had not
manifested. If it had been a great stroke of art to seize
Lingen before Maurice could reach Deventer, it was an
enormous blunder, worthy of a journeyman soldier, to fail to
seize the Bourtange marshes, and drive his sword into the
very vitals of the republic, thus placed at his mercy.

Meantime, while there had been all these rejoicings and
tribulations at the great doings on the Rhine and the short-
coming in Friesland, the real operations of the war had been
at the antipodes.

It is not a very unusual phenomenon in history that the
events, upon whose daily development the contemporary

[58] Gallucci, ii. 253, seqq.

world hangs with most palpitating interest, are far inferior in permanent influence upon the general movement of humanity to a series of distant and apparently commonplace transactions.

Empires are built up or undermined by the ceaseless industry of obscure multitudes often slightly observed, or but dimly comprehended.

Battles and sieges, dreadful marches, eloquent debates, intricate diplomacy—from time to time but only perhaps at rare intervals—have decided or modified the destiny of nations, while very often the clash of arms, the din of rhetoric, the whiz of political spindles, produce nothing valuable for human consumption, and made the world no richer.

If the age of heroic and religious passion was rapidly fading away before the gradual uprising of a politico-mercantile civilization—as it certainly was—the most vital events, those in which the fate of coming generations was most deeply involved, were those inspired by the spirit of commercial enterprise.

Nor can it be denied that there is often a genial and poetic essence even among things practical or of almost vulgar exterior. In those early expeditions of the Hollanders to the flaming lands of the equator there is a rhythm and romance of historical movement not less significant than in their unexampled defence of fatherland and of the world's liberty against the great despotism of the age.

Universal monarchy was baffled by the little republic, not within its own populous cities only, or upon its own barren sands. The long combat between Freedom and Absolutism had now become as wide as the world. The greatest European states had been dragged by the iron chain of necessity into a conflict from which they often struggled to escape, and on every ocean, and on almost every foot of soil, where the footsteps of mankind had as yet been imprinted, the fierce encounters were every day renewed. In the east and the west, throughout that great vague new world, of which geographers had hardly yet made a sketch, which comprised

both the Americas and something called the East Indies, and
which Spain claimed as her private property, those humbly
born and energetic adventurers were rapidly creating a sym-
metrical system out of most dismal chaos.

The King of Spain warned all nations from trespassing
upon those outlying possessions.

His edicts had not however prevented the English in
moderate numbers, and the Hollanders in steadily increasing
swarms, from enlarging and making profitable use of these
new domains of the world's commerce.

The days were coming when the People was to have more
to say than the pope in regard to the disposition and arrangements of certain large districts of this planet. While the
world-empire, which still excited so much dismay, was yielding to constant corrosion, another empire, created by well-
directed toil and unflinching courage, was steadily rising out
of the depths. It has often been thought amazing that the
little republic should so long and so triumphantly withstand
the enormous forces brought forward for her destruction. It
was not, however, so very surprising. Foremost among nations, and in advance of the age, the republic had found the
strength which comes from the spirit of association. On a
wider scale than ever before known, large masses of men,
with their pecuniary means, had been intelligently banded
together to advance material interests. When it is remembered that, in addition to this force, the whole commonwealth
was inspired by the divine influence of liberty, her power will
no longer seem so wonderful.

A sinister event in the Isle of Ceylon had opened the series
of transactions in the East, and had cast a gloom over the
public sentiment at home. The enterprising voyager, Sebald
de Weerdt, one of the famous brotherhood of the Invincible
Lion which had wintered in the straits of Magellan,[59] had
been murdered through the treachery of the King of Candy.
His countrymen had not taken vengeance on his assassins.
They were perhaps too fearful of losing their growing trade

[59] Vol. iii. page 579 of this History.

in those lucrative regions to take a becoming stand in that emergency. They were also not as yet sufficiently powerful there.[60]

The East India Company had sent out in May of this year its third fleet of eleven large ships, besides some smaller vessels, under the general superintendence of Matelieff de Jonghe, one of the directors. The investments for the voyage amounted to more than nineteen hundred thousand florins.[61]

Meantime the preceding adventurers under Stephen van der Hagen, who had sailed at the end of 1603, had been doing much thorough work.[62] A firm league had been made with one of the chief potentates of Malabar, enabling them to build forts and establish colonies in perpetual menace of Goa, the great oriental capital of the Portuguese. The return of the ambassadors sent out from Astgen to Holland had filled not only the island of Sumatra but the Moluccas, and all the adjacent regions, with praises of the power, wealth, and high civilization of that distant republic so long depicted by rivals as a nest of uncouth and sanguinary savages.[63] The fleet now proceeded to Amboyna, a stronghold of the Spanish-Portuguese, and the seat of a most lucrative trade.

On the arrival of those foreign well-armed ships under the guns of the fortress, the governor sent to demand, with Castilian arrogance, who the intruders were, and by whose authority and with what intent they presumed to show themselves in those waters. The reply was that they came in the name and by the authority of their High Mightinesses the States-General, and their stadholder the Prince of Orange ; that they were sworn enemies of the King of Spain and all his subjects, and that as to their intent, this would soon be made apparent.[64] Whereupon, without much more ado, they began a bombardment of the fort, which mounted thirty-six guns. The governor, as often happened in those regions, being less valiant against determined European foes than towards the

[60] Wagenaar, ix. 197. Meteren, books xxvi. xxviii.
[61] Wagenaar, Meteren, *loc. cit.*
[62] Wagenaar, ix. 198
[63] Ibid. Grotius, xv. 700, *seqq.*
[64] Grotius, xv. 702.

feebler oriental races on which he had been accustomed to trample, succumbed with hardly an effort at resistance.[65] The castle and town and whole island were surrendered to the fleet, and thenceforth became virtually a colony of the republic with which, nominally, treaties of alliance and defence were negotiated. Thence the fleet, after due possession had been taken of these new domains, sailed partly to Banda and partly to two small but most important islands of the Moluccas.[66]

In that multitude of islands which make up the Eastern Archipelago there were but five at that period where grew the clove—Ternate, Tydor, Motiel, Makian, and Bacia.[67]

Pepper and ginger, even nutmegs, cassia, and mace, were but vulgar drugs, precious as they were already to the world and the world's commerce, compared with this most magnificent spice.

It is wonderful to reflect upon the strange composition of man. The world had lived in former ages very comfortably without cloves. But by the beginning of the seventeenth century that odoriferous pistil had been the cause of so many pitched battles and obstinate wars, of so much vituperation, negotiation, and intriguing, that the world's destiny seemed to have almost become dependent upon the growth of a particular gillyflower. Out of its sweetness had grown such bitterness among great nations as not torrents of blood could wash away. A commonplace condiment enough it seems to us now, easily to be dispensed with, and not worth purchasing at a thousand human lives or so the cargo, but it was once the great prize to be struggled for by civilized nations. From that fervid earth, warmed from within by volcanic heat, and basking ever beneath the equatorial sun, arose vapours as deadly to human life as the fruits were exciting and delicious to human senses. Yet the atmosphere of pestiferous fragrance had attracted rather than repelled. The poisonous delights of the climate, added to the perpetual and various warfare for

[65] Grotius, xv. 702. Wagenaar, ix. 197, 198.
[66] Ibid. Meteren, 537. [67] Grotius, *ubi sup.*

its productions, spread a strange fascination around those fatal isles.

Especially Ternate and Tydor were objects of unending strife. Chinese, Malays, Persians, Arabs, had struggled centuries long for their possession ; those races successively or simultaneously ruling these and adjacent portions of the Archipelago. The great geographical discoveries at the close of the fifteenth century had however changed the aspect of India and of the world. The Portuguese adventurers found two rival kings in the two precious islands, and by ingeniously protecting one of these potentates and poisoning the other, soon made themselves masters of the field. The clove trade was now entirely in the hands of the strangers from the antipodes. Goa became the great mart of the lucrative traffic, and thither came Chinese, Arabs, Moors, and other oriental traders to be supplied from the Portuguese monopoly. Two-thirds of the spices however found their way directly to Europe.

Naturally enough, the Spaniards soon penetrated into these seas, and claimed their portion of the spice trade. They insisted that the coveted islands were included in their portion of the great Borgian grant. As there had hardly yet been time to make a trigonometrical survey of an unknown world, so generously divided by the pope, there was no way of settling disputed boundary questions save by apostolic blows. These were exchanged with much earnestness, year after year, between Spaniards, Portuguese, and all who came in their way. Especially the unfortunate natives, and their kings most of all, came in for a full share. At last Charles V. sold out his share of the spice islands to his Portuguese rival and co-proprietor, for three hundred and fifty thousand ducats.[68] The emperor's very active pursuits caused him to require ready money more than cloves. Yet John III. had made an excellent bargain, and the monopoly thenceforth brought him in at least two hundred thousand ducats annually. Goa became more flourishing, the natives

[68] Grotius, xv. 704.

more wretched, the Portuguese more detested than ever. Occasionally one of the royal line of victims would consent to put a diadem upon his head, but the coronation was usually the prelude to a dungeon or death. The treaties of alliance, which these unlucky potentates had formed with their powerful invaders, were, as so often is the case, mere deeds to convey themselves and their subjects into slavery.

Spain and Portugal becoming one, the slender weapon of defence which these weak but subtle Orientals sometimes employed with success—the international and commercial jealousy between their two oppressors—was taken away. It was therefore with joy that Zaida, who sat on the throne of Ternate at the end of the sixteenth century, saw the sails of a Dutch fleet arriving in his harbours.[69] Very soon negotiations were opened, and the distant republic undertook to protect the Mahometan king against his Catholic master. The new friendship was founded upon trade monopoly, of course, but at that period at least the islanders were treated with justice and humanity by their republican allies. The Dutch undertook to liberate their friends from bondage, while the King of Ternate, panting under Portuguese oppression, swore to have no traffic, no dealings of any kind, with any other nation than Holland ; not even with the English. The Dutch, they declared, were the liberators of themselves, of their friends, and of the seas.[70]

The international hatred, already germinating between England and Holland, shot forth in these flaming regions like a tropical plant. It was carefully nurtured and tended by both peoples. Freedom of commerce, freedom of the seas, meant that none but the Dutch East India Company—so soon as the Portuguese and Spaniards were driven out—should trade in cloves and nutmegs. Decrees to that effect were soon issued, under very heavy penalties, by the States-General to the citizens of the republic and to the world at large.[71] It was natural therefore that the English traders should hail the appearance of the

[69] Grotius, xv. 706.
[70] " Batavos vere socios ac suos marisque liberatores vocans."—Ibid. [71] Ibid.

Dutch fleets with much less enthusiasm than was shown by the King of Ternate.

On the other hand, the King of Tydor, persisting in his oriental hatred towards the rival potentate in the other island, allowed the Portuguese to build additional citadels, and generally to strengthen their positions within his dominions. Thus when Cornelius Sebastian, with his division of Ver Hagen's fleet, arrived in the Moluccas in the summer of 1605, he found plenty of work prepared for him. The peace recently concluded by James with Philip and the archdukes placed England in a position of neutrality in the war now waging in the clove islands between Spain and the republic's East India Company. The English in those regions were not slow to avail themselves of the advantage. The Portuguese of Tydor received from neutral sympathy a copious supply of powder and of pamphlets. The one explosive material enabled them to make a more effective defence of their citadel against the Dutch fleet ; the other revealed to the Portuguese and their Mussulman allies that "the Netherlanders could not exist without English protection, that they were the scum of nations, and that if they should get possession of this clove monopoly, their insolence would become intolerable."[72] Samples of polite literature such as these, printed but not published, flew about in volleys. It was an age of pamphleteering, and neither the English nor the Dutch were behind their contemporaries in the science of attack and self-defence. Nevertheless Cornelius Sebastian was not deterred by paper pellets, nor by the guns of the citadel, from carrying out his purpose. It was arranged with King Zaida that the islanders of Ternate should make a demonstration against Tydor, being set across the strait in Dutch vessels. Sebastian, however, having little faith in oriental tenacity, entrusted the real work of storming the fortress to his own soldiers and sailors. On a fine morning in

---

[72] "Schrijvende seer verachtelijk ende schimpelijk vande Nederlanders als ofte sy sonder haer niet konden bestaen ende diergelijcke meer, die noemede het schuym van Natien die | welcke soodiesen handel alleen handel hadden haer vermetelheit souden onlydelijk wesen," &c. — Depositions made by the Netherlanders. Meteren, 535vo.

May the assault was delivered in magnificent style. The
resistance was obstinate ; many of the assailants fell, and
Captain Mol,[73] whom we have once before seen as master of
the Tiger, sinking the galleys of Frederic Spinola off the
Gat of Sluys, found himself at the head of only seven men
within the interior defences of the citadel. A Spanish soldier,
Torre by name, rushed upon him with a spear. Avoiding the
blow, Mol grappled with his antagonist, and both rolled to
the ground. A fortunate carbine-shot from one of the Dutch
captain's comrades went through the Spaniard's head.[74]
Meantime the little band, so insignificant in numbers, was
driven out of the citadel. Mol fell to the ground with a
shattered leg, and reproached his companions, who sought to
remove him, for neglecting their work in order to save his
life. Let them take the fort, he implored them, and when
that was done they might find leisure to pick him up if they
chose.[75] While he was speaking the principal tower of the
fortress blew up, and sixty of the garrison were launched into
the air.[76] A well-directed shot had set fire to the magazine.
The assault was renewed with fresh numbers, and the Dutch
were soon masters of the place. Never was a stronghold
more audaciously or more successfully stormed. The garrison
surrendered. The women and children, fearing to be at the
mercy of those who had been depicted to them as cannibals,
had already made their escape, and were scrambling like
squirrels among the volcanic cliffs. Famine soon compelled
them to come down, however, when they experienced sufficiently kind treatment, but were all deported in Dutch
vessels to the Philippine islands.[77] The conquerors not only
spared the life of the King of Tydor, but permitted him to
retain his crown. At his request the citadel was razed
to the ground. It would have been better perhaps to let it
stand, and it was possible that in the heart of the vanquished
potentate some vengeance was lurking which might bear evil

---

[73] I suppose at least this Captain
Mol to have been identical with the
gallant seaman who commanded the
Tiger in that action.
[74] Grotius, xv. 706, 707.   [75] Ibid.
[76] Ibid.   [77] Ibid.

fruit at a later day.   Meantime the Portuguese were driven entirely out of the Moluccas, save the island of Timos, where they still retained a not very important citadel.[78]

The East India Company was now in possession of the whole field.   The Moluccas and the clove trade were its own, and the Dutch republic had made manifest to the world that more potent instruments had now been devised for parcelling out the new world than papal decrees, although signed by the immaculate hand of a Borgia.

During the main operations already sketched in the Netherlands, and during those vastly more important oriental movements to which the reader's attention has just been called, a detached event or two deserves notice.

Twice during the summer campaign of this year Du Terrail, an enterprising French refugee in the service of the archdukes, had attempted to surprise the important city of Bergen-op-Zoom.   On the 21st August the intended assault had been discovered in time to prevent any very serious conflict on either side.   On the 20th September the experiment was renewed at an hour after midnight.   Du Terrail, having arranged the attack at three different points, had succeeded in forcing his way across the moat and through one of the gates.   The trumpets of the foremost Spaniards already sounded in the streets.   It was pouring with rain ; the town was pitch dark.   But the energetic Paul Bax was governor of the place, a man who was awake at any hour of the twenty-four, and who could see in the darkest night.   He had already informed himself of the enemy's project, and had strengthened his garrison by a large intermixture of the most trustworthy burgher guards, so that the advance of Du Terrail at the southern gate was already confronted by a determined band.   A fierce battle began in the darkness.   Meantime Paul Bax, galloping through the city, had aroused the whole population for the defence.   At the Steinberg gate, where the chief assault had been pre-

21 Aug.

20 Sept.

[78] Grotius, xv. 700–708.   Compare Meteren, 535–537.   Wagenaar, ix. 196–198.   Van der Hagen Reise, 92, 94, 95.

pared, Bax had caused great fires of straw and pitch barrels
to be lighted, so that the invaders, instead of finding, as they
expected, a profound gloom through the streets, saw themselves approaching a brilliantly illuminated city, fully prepared to give their uninvited guests a warm reception. The
garrison, the townspeople, even the women, thronged to the
ramparts, saluting the Spaniards with a rain of bullets, paving-
stones, and pitch hoops, and with a storm of gibes and
taunts. They were asked why they allowed their cardinal
thus to send them to the cattle market, and whether Our
Lady of Hall, to whom Isabella was so fond of making
pilgrimages, did not live rather too far off to be of much use
just then to her or to them.[79] Catholics and Protestants all
stood shoulder to shoulder that night to defend their firesides
against the foreign foe, while mothers laid their sleeping
children on the ground that they might fill their cradles with
powder and ball, which they industriously brought to the
soldiers. The less energetic women fell upon their knees in
the street, and prayed aloud through the anxious night. The
attack was splendidly repulsed. As morning dawned the
enemy withdrew, leaving one hundred dead outside the walls
or in the town, and carrying off thirty-eight wagon loads of
wounded.[80] Du Terrail made no further attempts that
summer, although the list of his surprises was not yet full.
He was a good engineer, and a daring partisan officer. He
was also inspired by an especial animosity to the States-
General, who had refused the offer of his services before he
made application to the archdukes.[81]

At sea there was no very important movement in European
waters, save that Lambert Heinrichzoon, commonly called
Pretty Lambert,[82] a Rotterdam skipper, whom we have seen
doing good service in the sea-fights with Frederic Spinola,
captured the admiral of the Dunkirk pirate fleet, Adrian
Dirkzoon. It was a desperate fight. Pretty Lambert,
sustained at a distance by Rear-Admiral Gerbrantzon, laid

[79] Grotius, xv. 667, 669. Meteren, 522, 523. Wagenaar, ix. 191, 192.
[80] Ibid. [81] Grotius, *ubi sup.* [82] "Mooi Lambert."—Wagenaar, ix. 196.

himself yard-arm to yard-arm alongside the pirate vessel, boarded her, and after beating down all resistance made prisoners such of the crew as remained alive, and carried them into Rotterdam. Next day they were hanged, to the number of sixty. A small number were pardoned on account of their youth, and a few individuals who effected their escape when led to the gallows, were not pursued.[83] The fact that the townspeople almost connived at the escape of these desperadoes showed that there had been a surfeit of hangings in Rotterdam. It is moreover not easy to distinguish with exactness the lines which in those days separated regular sea belligerents, privateers, and pirates from each other. It had been laid down by the archdukes that there was no military law at sea, and that sick soldiers captured on the water should be hanged. Accordingly they were hanged.[84] Admiral Fazardo, of the Spanish royal navy, not only captured all the enemy's merchant vessels which came in his way, but hanged, drowned, and burned alive every man found on board.[85] Admiral Haultain, of the republican navy, had just been occupied in drowning a whole regiment of Spanish soldiers, captured in English and German transports. The complaints brought against the English cruisers by the Hollanders for capturing and confiscating their vessels, and hanging, maiming, and torturing their crews—not only when England was neutral, but even when she was the ally of the republic—had been a standing topic for diplomatic discussion, and almost a standing joke. Why, therefore, these Dunkirk sea-rovers should not on the same principle be allowed to rush forth from their very convenient den to plunder friend and foe, burn ships, and butcher the sailors at pleasure, seems difficult to understand. To expect from the inhabitants of this robbers' cave—this "church on the downs"—a code of maritime law so much purer and sterner than the system adopted by the English, the Spaniards, and the Dutch, was hardly reasonable. Certainly the Dunkirkers, who were mainly

---

[83] Wagenaar, *ubi sup.* Meteren, 524vo.   [84] Vide *supra*, p. 125.
[85] " Quarum nautæ mersi, suspensi, exusti."—Grotius, xv. 685.

Netherlanders—rebels to the republic and partisans of the Spanish crown—did their best to destroy the herring fishery and to cut the throats of the fishermen, but perhaps they received the halter more often than other mariners who had quite as thoroughly deserved it. And this at last appeared the prevailing opinion in Rotterdam.

CHAPTER XLV.

Preparations for the campaign of 1606—Diminution of Maurice's popularity—
Quarrel between the pope and the Venetian republic—Surprise of Sluys
by Du Terrail—Dilatoriness of the republic's operations—Movements of
Spinola—Influence of the weather on the military transactions of the
year—Endeavours of Spinola to obtain possession of the Waal and Yssel
—Surrender of Lochem to Spinola—Siege of Groll—Siege and loss of
Rheinberg—Mutiny in the Catholic army—Recovery of Lochem by
Maurice—Attempted recovery of Groll—Sudden appearance of the
enemy—Withdrawal of the besieging army—Close of the campaign—
End of the war of independence—Motives of the Prince in his actions
before Groll—Cruise of Admiral Haultain to the coast of Spain and
Portugal—His encounter with the war-ships of Fazardo—Courageous
conduct of the vice-admiral—Deaths of Justus Lipsius, Hohenlo, and
Count John of Nassau.

AFTER the close of the campaign of 1605 Spinola had gone
once more to Spain. On his passage through Paris he had
again been received with distinguished favour by that warm
ally of the Dutch republic, Henry IV., and on being questioned by that monarch as to his plans for the next campaign
had replied that he intended once more to cross the Rhine,
and invade Friesland. Henry, convinced that the Genoese
would of course not tell him the truth on such an occasion,
wrote accordingly to the States-General that they might
feel safe as to their eastern frontier. Whatever else might
happen, Friesland and the regions adjacent would be safe
next year from attack.[1] The immediate future was to show
whether the subtle Italian had not compassed as neat a
deception by telling the truth as coarser politicians could
do by falsehood.

Spinola found the royal finances in most dismal condition.
Three hundred thousand dollars a month[2] were the least
estimate of the necessary expenses for carrying on the

[1] Gallucci, 256, 257.   [2] Bentivoglio, 538. Grotius. xv. 714.

Netherland war, a sum which could not possibly be spared by Lerma, Uceda, the Marquis of the Seven Churches, and other financiers then industriously occupied in draining dry the exchequer for their own uses. Once more the general aided his sovereign with purse and credit, as well as with his sword. Once more the exchange at Genoa was glutted with the acceptances of Marquis Spinola.[3] Here at least was a man of a nature not quite so depraved as that of the parasites bred out of the corruption of a noble but dying commonwealth, and doubtless it was with gentle contempt that the great favourite and his friends looked at the military and financial enthusiasm of the volunteer. It was so much more sagacious to make a princely fortune than to sacrifice one already inherited, in the service of one's country.

Spinola being thus ready not only to fight but to help to pay for the fighting, found his plans of campaigns received with great benignity by the king and his ministers. Meantime there was much delay. The enormous labours thus devolved upon one pair of shoulders by the do-nothing king and a mayor of the palace whose soul was absorbed by his own private robberies, were almost too much for human strength. On his return to the Netherlands Spinola fell dangerously ill in Genoa.[4]

Meantime, during his absence and the enforced idleness of the Catholic armies, there was an opportunity for the republicans to act with promptness and vigour. They displayed neither quality. Never had there been so much sluggishness as in the preparations for the campaign of 1606. The States' exchequer was lower than it had been for years. The republic was without friends. Left to fight their battle for national existence alone, the Hollanders found themselves perpetually subjected to hostile censure from their late allies, and to friendly advice still more intolerable. There were many brave Englishmen and Frenchmen sharing in the fatigues of the Dutch war of independence, but the govern-

---

[3] Grot. xv. 680. Compare Gallucci, lib. xviii.-xx.   [4] Gallucci, ii. 257, seqq.

ments of Henry and of James were as protective, as severely virtuous, as offensive, and, in their secret intrigues with the other belligerent, as mischievous as it was possible for the best-intentioned neutrals to be.

The fame and the popularity of the stadholder had been diminished by the results of the past campaign. The States-General were disappointed, dissatisfied, and inclined to censure very unreasonably the public servant who had always obeyed their decrees with docility. While Henry IV. was rapidly transferring his admiration from Maurice to Spinola, the disagreements at home between the Advocate and the Stadholder were becoming portentous.

There was a want of means and of soldiers for the new campaign. Certain causes were operating in Europe to the disadvantage of both belligerents. In the south, Venice had almost drawn her sword against the pope in her settled resolution to put down the Jesuits and to clip the wings of the church party, before, with bequests and donations, votive churches and magnificent monasteries, four-fifths of the domains of the republic should fall into mortmain, as was already the case in Brabant.[5]

Naturally there was a contest between the ex-Huguenot, now eldest son of the Church, and the most Catholic king, as to who should soonest defend the pope. Henry offered thorough protection to his Holiness, but only under condition that he should have a monopoly of that protection.[6] He lifted his sword, but meantime it was doubtful whether the blow was to descend upon Venice or upon Spain. The Spanish levies, on their way to the Netherlands, were detained in Italy by this new exigency. The States-General offered the sister republic their maritime assistance, and notwithstanding their own immense difficulties, stood ready

---

[5] Meteren, 536.

[6] "Nec dissimulabat Hispanus Pontifici se auxilio futurum, quo Gallus comperto significavit Romam, ita meritos majores suos ut ecclesiæ pericula non alias magis quam Francicas manus respicere deberent: sin Pontifex Hispanum prolatandæ dominationis avidum sibi assumeret haud immerito suspectum id sibi vel coactum contrariis in partibus fore."—Grotius, xv. 713. Compare Meteren, 516vo.

to send a fleet to the Mediterranean. The offer was grate-
fully declined, and the quarrel with the pope arranged,
but the incident laid the foundation of a lasting friendship
between the only two important republics then existing.[7] The
issue of the Gunpowder Plot, at the close of the preceding
year, had confirmed James in his distaste for Jesuits, and had
effected that which all the eloquence of the States-General
and their ambassador had failed to accomplish, the prohibition of Spanish enlistments in his kingdom. Guido Fawkes
had served under the archduke in Flanders.

Here then were delays additional to that caused by
Spinola's[8] illness. On the other hand, the levies of the
republic were for a season paralysed by the altercation, soon
afterwards adjusted, between Henry IV. and the Duke of
Bouillon, brother-in-law of the stadholder and of the Palatine,
and by the petty war between the Duke and Hanseatic
city of Brunswick, in which Ernest of Nassau was for a time
employed.[9]

During this period of almost suspended animation the war
gave no signs of life, except in a few spasmodic efforts on the
part of the irrepressible Du Terrail. Early in the spring, not
satisfied with his double and disastrous repulse before Bergen-
op-Zoom, that partisan now determined to surprise Sluys.
That an attack was impending became known to the
governor of that city, the experienced Colonel Van der Noot.
Not dreaming, however, that any mortal—even the most
audacious of Frenchmen and adventurers—would ever think
of carrying a city like Sluys by surprise, defended as it was
by a splendid citadel and by a whole chain of forts and water-
batteries, and capable of withstanding three months long, as
it had so recently done, a siege in form by the acknowledged
master of the beleaguering science, the methodical governor
went calmly to bed one fine night in June. His slumbers
were disturbed before morning by the sound of trumpets
sounding Spanish melodies in the streets, and by a great

---

[7] Grotius, xv. 684. Wagenaar, ix. 206. Meteren, 536.
[8] Meteren, 526. [9] Wagenaar, ix. 199-203.

uproar and shouting. Springing out of bed, he rushed half-dressed to the rescue. Less vigilant than Paul Bax had been the year before in Bergen, he found that Du Terrail had really effected a surprise. At the head of twelve hundred Walloons and Irishmen, that enterprising officer had waded through the drowned land of Cadzand, with the promised support of a body of infantry under Frederic Van den Berg, from Damm, had stolen noiselessly by the forts of that island unchallenged and unseen, had effected with petards a small breach through the western gate of the city, and with a large number of his followers, creeping two and two through the gap, had found himself for a time master of Sluys.[10]

The profound silence of the place had however somewhat discouraged the intruders. The whole population were as sound asleep as was the excellent commandant, but the stillness in the deserted streets suggested an ambush, and they moved stealthily forward, feeling their way with caution towards the centre of the town.

It so happened, moreover, that the sacristan had forgotten to wind up the great town clock. The agreement with the party first entering and making their way to the opposite end of the city, had been that at the striking of a certain hour after midnight they should attack simultaneously and with a great outcry all the guardhouses, so that the garrison might be simultaneously butchered. The clock never struck, the signal was never given, and Du Terrail and his immediate comrades remained near the western gate, suspicious and much perplexed. The delay was fatal. The guard, the whole garrison, and the townspeople flew to arms, and half-naked, but equipped with pike and musket, and led on by Van der Noot in person, fell upon the intruders. A panic took the place of previous audacity in the breasts of Du Terrail's followers. Thinking only of escape, they found the gap by which they had crept into the town much less convenient as a means of egress in the face of an infuriated multitude. Five hundred of them were put to death in a

[10] Grotius, xv. 687, *seqq.* Wagenaar, ix. 207, *seqq.*

very few minutes. Almost as many were drowned or suffocated in the marshes, as they attempted to return by the road over which they had come. A few stragglers of the fifteen hundred were all that were left to tell the tale.[11]

June, 1606.

It would seem scarcely worth while to chronicle such trivial incidents in this great war—the all-absorbing drama of Christendom—were it not that they were for the moment the whole war. It might be thought that hostilities were approaching their natural termination, and that the war was dying of extreme old age, when the Quixotic pranks of a Du Terrail occupied so large a part of European attention. The winter had passed, another spring had come and gone, and Maurice had in vain attempted to obtain sufficient means from the States to take the field in force. Henry, looking on from the outside, was becoming more and more exasperated with the dilatoriness which prevented the republic from profiting by the golden moments of Spinola's enforced absence.[12] Yet the best that could be done seemed to be to take measures for defensive operations.

Spinola never reached Brussels until the beginning of June, yet, during all the good campaigning weather which had been fleeting away, not a blow had been struck, nor a wholesome counsel taken by the stadholder or the States. It was midsummer before the armies were in the field. The plans of the Catholic general however then rapidly developed themselves. Having assembled as large a force as had ever been under his command, he now divided it into two nearly equal portions. Bucquoy, with ten thousand foot, twelve hundred cavalry, and twelve guns, arrived on the 18th July at Mook, on the Meuse. Spinola, with eleven thousand infantry, two thousand horse, and eight guns, crossed the Rhine at the old redoubts of Ruhrort, and on the same 18th July took position at Goor, in Overyssel.[13] The first

[11] Wagenaar, ix. 207, *seqq.*
[12] Van der Kemp, ii. 117, 520.
[13] For the campaign of 1606 compare Grotius, xv. 689–699. Meteren, 537–543. Bentivoglio, 539–546. Van der Kemp, ii. 117–120, and notes. Wagenaar, ix 209–220.

plan of the commander-in-chief was to retrace exactly his campaign of the previous year, even as he had with so much frankness stated to Henry. But the republic, although deserted by her former friends, and looked upon askance by the monarch of Britain, and by the most Christian king, had this year a most efficient ally in the weather. Jupiter Pluvius had descended from on high to the rescue of the struggling commonwealth, and his decrees were omnipotent as to the course of the campaign. The seasons that year seemed all fused into one. It was difficult to tell on midsummer day whether it were midwinter, spring, or autumn.[14] The rain came down day after day, week after week, as if the contending armies and the very country which was to be invaded and defended were to be all washed out of existence together.[15] Friesland resolved itself into a vast quagmire; the roads became fluid, the rivers lakes. Spinola turned his face from the east, and proceeded to carry out a second plan which he had long meditated, and even a more effective one, in the west.

The Waal and the Yssel formed two sides of a great quadrilateral, and furnished for the natural fortress, thus enclosed, two vast and admirable moats. Within lay Good-meadow and Foul-meadow—Bet-uwe and Vel-uwe—one, the ancient Batavian island which from time immemorial had given its name to the commonwealth, the other, the once dismal swamp which toil and intelligence had in the course of centuries transformed into the wealthy and flowery land of Gueldres.

Beyond, but in immediate proximity, lay the ancient episcopal city and province of Utrecht, over which lay the road to the adjacent Holland and Zeeland. The very heart of the republic would be laid bare to the conqueror's sword if he could once force the passage, and obtain the control of these two protecting streams. With Utrecht as his base, and all Brabant and Flanders — obedient provinces—at his back. Spinola might accomplish more in one season than Alva

[14] Bentivoglio, *ubi sup.*   [15] Bentivoglio, Grotius, Meteren, *ubi sup*

Don John, and Alexander Farnese had compassed in forty years, and destroy at a blow what was still called the Netherland rebellion. The passage of the rivers once effected, the two enveloping wings would fold themselves together, and the conquest would be made.

Thus reasoned the brilliant young general, and his projects, although far-reaching, did not seem wild. The first steps were, however, the most important as well as the most difficult, and he had to reckon with a wary and experienced antagonist. Maurice had at last collected and reviewed at Arnhem an army of nearly fifteen thousand men, and was now watching closely from Doesburg and Deventer every movement of the foe.

Having been forced to a defensive campaign, in which he was not likely at best to gain many additional laurels, he was the more determined to lay down his own life, and sacrifice every man he could bring into the field, before Spinola should march into the cherished domains of Utrecht and Holland. Meantime the rain, which had already exerted so much influence on the military movements of the year, still maintained the supremacy over human plans. The Yssel and the Waal, always deep, broad, sluggish, but dangerous rivers—the Rhine in its old age—were swollen into enormous proportions, their currents flowing for the time with the vigour of their far away youth.

Maurice had confided the defence of the Waal to Warner Du Bois, under whose orders he placed a force of about seven thousand men, and whose business it was to prevent Bucquoy's passage. His own task was to baffle Spinola.[16]

Bucquoy's ambition was to cross the Waal at a point as near as possible to the fork of that stream with the true Rhine, seize the important city of Nymegen, and then give the hand to Spinola, so soon as he should be on the other side of the Yssel. At the village of Spardorp or Kekerdom, he employed Pompeio Giustiniani to make a desperate effort, having secured a large number of barges in which he em-

[16] Meteren, Bentivoglio, Grotius, Wagenaar, Van der Kemp, *ubi sup.*

barked his troops. As the boatmen neared the opposite bank, however, they perceived that Warner Du Bois had made effective preparations for their reception. They lost heart, and on pretence that the current of the river was too rapid to allow them to reach the point proposed for their landing, gradually dropped down the stream, and, in spite of the remonstrances of the commanders, pushed their way back to the shore which they had left. From that time forth, the States' troops, in efficient numbers, fringed the inner side of the Waal, along the whole length of the Batavian island, while armed vessels of the republic patrolled the stream itself. In vain Count Bucquoy watched an opportunity, either by surprise or by main strength, to effect a crossing. The Waal remained as impassable as if it were a dividing ocean.[17]

On the other side of the quadrilateral, Maurice's dispositions were as effective as those of his lieutenant on the Waal. The left shore of the Yssel, along its whole length, from Arnhem and Doesburg quite up to Zwoll and Campen, where the river empties itself into the Zuyder Zee, was now sprinkled thickly with forts, hastily thrown up, but strong enough to serve the temporary purpose of the stadholder. In vain the fleet-footed and audacious Spinola moved stealthily or fiercely to and fro, from one point to another, seeking an opening through which to creep, or a weak spot where he might dash himself against the chain. The whole line was securely guarded. The swollen river, the redoubts, and the musketeers of Maurice, protected the heart of the republic from the impending danger.

Wearied of this fruitless pacing up and down, Spinola, while apparently intending an assault upon Deventer, and thus attracting his adversary's attention to that important city, suddenly swerved to the right, and came down upon Lochem. The little town, with its very slender garrison, surrendered at once. It was not a great conquest, but it might possibly be of use in the campaign. It was taken before

23 July.

[17] Authorities last cited.

the stadholder could move a step to its assistance, even had he deemed it prudent to leave Yssel-side for an hour. The summer was passing away, the rain was still descending, and it was the 1st of August before Spinola left Lochem. He then made a rapid movement to the north, between Zwoll and Hasselt, endeavouring to cross the Blackwater, and seize Geelmuyden, on the Zuyder Zee. Had he succeeded, he might have turned Maurice's position. But the works in that direction had been entrusted to an experienced campaigner, Warmelo, sheriff of Zalant, who received the impetuous Spinola and his lieutenant, Count Solre, so warmly, that they reeled backwards at last, after repeated assaults and great loss of men, and never more attempted to cross the Yssel.[18]

2 August.

Obviously, the campaign had failed. Utrecht and Holland were as far out of the Catholic general's reach as the stars in the sky, but at least, with his large armies, he could earn a few trophies, barren or productive, as it might prove, before winter, uniting with the deluge, should drive him from the field.

On the 3rd August, he laid siege to Groll (or Groenlo), a fortified town of secondary importance in the country of Zutphen, and, squandering his men with much recklessness, in his determination not to be baffled, reduced the place in eleven days. Here he paused for a breathing spell, and then, renouncing all his schemes upon the inner defences of the republic, withdrew once more to the Rhine and laid siege to Rheinberg.[19]

3-14 Aug.

22 Aug.

This frontier place had been tossed to and fro so often between the contending parties in the perpetual warfare, tha$t$ its inhabitants must have learned to consider themselves rather as a convenient circulating medium for military operations than as burghers who had any part in the ordinary business of life. It had old-fashioned defences of stone, which, during the recent occupation by the States, had been much improved, and had been strengthened with earthworks.

[18] Ibid.   [19] Ibid.

Before it was besieged, Maurice sent his brother Frederic Henry, with some picked companies, into the place, so that the garrison amounted to three thousand effective men.

The Prince de Soubise, brother of the Duc de Rohan, and other French volunteers of quality, also threw themselves into the place, in order to take lessons in the latest methods of attack and defence.[20] It was now admitted that no more accomplished pupil of the stadholder in the beleaguering art had appeared in Europe than his present formidable adversary. On this occasion, however, there was no great display of science. Maurice obstinately refused to move to the relief of the place, despite all the efforts of a deputation of the States-General who visited his camp in September, 26 Sept. urging him strenuously to take the chances of a stricken field.[21]

Nothing could induce the stadholder, who held an observing position at Wesel, with his back against the precious watery quadrilateral, to risk the defence of those most vital lines of the Yssel and the Waal. While attempting to save Rheinberg, he felt it possible that he might lose Nymegen, or even Utrecht. The swift but wily Genoese was not to be trifled with or lost sight of an instant. The road to Holland might still be opened, and the destiny of the republic might hang on the consequences of a single false move. That destiny, under God, was in his hands alone, and no chance of winning laurels, even from his greatest rival's head, could induce him to shrink from the path of duty, however obscure it might seem. There were a few brilliant assaults and sorties, as in all sieges, the French volunteers especially distinguishing themselves ; but the place fell at the end of forty 2 Oct. days. The garrison marched out with the honours of war. In the modern practice, armies were rarely captured in strongholds, nor were the defenders, together with the population, butchered.

The loss, after a six weeks' siege, of Rheinberg, which six years before, with far inferior fortifications, had held out a

[20] Wagenaar, ix. 214, 215.   [21] Van der Kemp, ii. 120.

much longer time against the States, was felt as a bitter disappointment throughout the republic. Frederic Henry, on leaving the place, made a feeble and unsuccessful demonstration against Venlo, by which the general dissatisfaction was not diminished. Soon afterwards, the war became more languid than ever. News arrived of a great crisis on the Genoa exchange. A multitude of merchants, involved in pecuniary transactions with Spinola, fell with one tremendous crash. The funds of the Catholic commander-in-chief were already exhausted, his acceptances could no longer be negotiated.[22] His credit was becoming almost as bad as the king's own. The inevitable consequence of the want of cash and credit followed. Mutiny, for the first time in Spinola's administration, raised its head once more, and stalked about defiant. Six hundred veterans marched to Breda, and offered their services to Justinus of Nassau. The proposal was accepted.[23] Other bands established their quarters in different places, chose their Elettos and lesser officers, and enacted the scenes which have been so often depicted in these pages. The splendid army of Spinola melted like April snow. By the last week of October there hardly seemed a Catholic army in the field. The commander-in-chief had scattered such companies as could still be relied upon in the villages of the friendly archiepiscopate of Cologne, and had obtained, not by murders and blackmail—according to the recent practice of the Admiral of Arragon, at whose grim name the whole country-side still shuddered—but from the friendship of the leading inhabitants and by honest loans, a sufficient sum to put bread into the mouths of the troops still remaining faithful to him.[24]

The opportunity had at last arrived for the stadholder to strike a blow before the season closed. Bankruptcy and mutiny had reduced his enemy to impotence in the very season of his greatest probable success. On the 24th October Maurice came before Lochem, which he recaptured in five days. Next in the order of Spinola's victo-

24 Oct.

---

[22] Grotius, xv. 696, 697.
[23] Grotius, Bentivoglio, Meteren, Wagenaar, *ubi sup.*   [24] Ibid.

ries was Groll, which the stadholder at once besieged. He
had almost fifteen thousand infantry and three thousand
horse.[25] A career of brief triumph before winter should close
in upon those dripping fields, seemed now assured. But the
rain, which during nearly the whole campaign had been his
potent ally, had of late been playing him false. The swollen
Yssel, during a brief period of dry weather, had sunk so low
in certain shallows as not to be navigable for his transports,[26]
and after his trains of artillery and munitions had been
dragged wearily overland as far as Groll, the deluge had
returned in such force, that physical necessity as well as considerations of humanity compelled him to defer his entrenching operations until the weather should moderate. As there
seemed no further danger to be apprehended from the broken,
mutinous, and dispersed forces of the enemy, the siege operations were conducted in a leisurely manner. What was the
astonishment, therefore, among the soldiers, when a rumour
flew about the camp in the early days of November that the
indomitable Spinola was again advancing upon them ![27] It
was perfectly true. With extraordinary perseverance he had
gathered up six or seven thousand infantry and twelve companies of horse—all the remnants of the splendid armies with
which he had taken the field at midsummer—and was now
marching to the relief of Groll, besieged as it was by a force at
least doubly as numerous as his own. It was represented to
the stadholder, however, that an impassable morass lay between
him and the enemy,[28] and that there would therefore be time
enough to complete his entrenchments before Spinola could
put his foolhardy attempt into execution. But the Catholic
general, marching faster than rumour itself, had crossed the
impracticable swamp almost before a spadeful of earth had
been turned in the republican camp. His advance was in
sight even while the incredulous were sneering at the absurdity of his supposed project. Informed by scouts of the
weakest point in the stadholder's extended lines, Spinola was

---

[25] Grotius, xv. 698.   [26] Letter of Prince Maurice, in Van der Kemp, ii. 545.
[27] Authorities cited.   [28] Van der Kemp, ii. 21.

directing himself thither with beautiful precision.[29] Maurice hastily contracted both his wings, and concentrated himself in the village of Lebel. At last the moment had come for a decisive struggle. There could be little doubt of the result. All the advantage was with the republican army. The Catholics had arrived in front of the enemy fatigued by forced marches through quagmires, in horrible weather, over roads deemed impassable. The States' troops were fresh, posted on ground of their own choosing, and partially entrenched. To the astonishment, even to the horror of the most eager portion of the army, the stadholder deliberately, and despite the groans of his soldiers, refused the combat, and gave immediate orders for raising the siege and abandoning the field.[30]

On the 12th of November he broke up his camp and withdrew to a village called Zelem. On the same day the marquis, having relieved the city, without 12 Nov. paying the expected price, retired in another direction, and established what was left of his army in the province of Munster. The campaign was closed.[31] And thus the great war, which had run its stormy course for nearly forty years, dribbled out of existence, sinking away that rainy November in the dismal fens of Zutphen. The long struggle for independence had come, almost unperceived, to an end.

Peace had not arrived, but the work of the armies was over for many a long year. Freedom and independence were secured. A deed or two, never to be forgotten by Netherland hearts, was yet to be done on the ocean, before the long and intricate negotiations for peace should begin, and the weary people permit themselves to rejoice ; but the prize was already won.

Meantime, the conduct of Prince Maurice in these last days of the campaign was the subject of biting censure by friend and foe. The military fame of Spinola throughout Europe grew apace, and the fame of his great rival seemed to shrink in the same proportion.

[29] Grotius, xv. 699.   [30] Authorities cited.   [31] Ibid.

Henry of France was especially indignant at what he considered the shortcomings of the republic and of its chief. Already, before the close of the summer, the agent Aerssens had written from Paris that his Majesty was very much displeased with Spinola's prosperity, ascribing it to the want of good councils on the part of the States' Government that so fine an army should lie idle so long, without making an attempt to relieve the beleaguered places, so that Spinola felt assured of taking anything as soon as he made his appearance. "Your Mightinesses cannot believe," continued the agent, "what a trophy is made by the Spanish ministers out of these little exploits, and they have so much address at this court, that if such things continue they may produce still greater results."[32]

In December he wrote that the king was so malcontent concerning the siege of Groll as to make it impossible to answer him with arguments, that he openly expressed regret at not having employed the money lent to the States upon strengthening his own frontiers, so distrustful was he of their capacity for managing affairs, and that he mentioned with disgust statements received from his ambassador at Brussels and from the Duc de Rohan, to the effect that Spinola had between five and six thousand men only at the relief of Groll, against twelve thousand in the stadholder's army.[33]

5 Dec.

The motives of the deeds and the omissions of the prince at this supreme moment must be pondered with great caution. The States-General had doubtless been inclined for vigorous movements, and Olden-Barneveld, with some of his colleagues, had visited the camp late in September to urge the relief of Rheinberg. Maurice was in daily correspondence with the Government, and regularly demanded their advice, by which, on many former occasions, he had bound himself, even when it was in conflict with his own better judgment.

But throughout this campaign, the responsibility was entirely, almost ostentatiously, thrown by the States-General

[32] Van der Kemp, ii. 549.   [33] Ibid. 550.

upon their commander-in-chief, and, as already indicated, their preparations in the spring and early summer had been entirely inadequate. Should he lose the army with which he had so quietly but completely checked Spinola in all his really important moves during the summer and autumn, he might despair of putting another very soon into the field. That his force in that November week before Groll was numerically far superior to the enemy is certain, but he had lost confidence in his cavalry since their bad behaviour at Mulheim the previous year, and a very large proportion of his infantry was on the sick-list at the moment of Spinola's approach. "Lest the continual bad weather should entirely consume the army," he said, "we are resolved, within a day or two after we have removed the sick who are here in great numbers, to break up, unless the enemy should give us occasion to make some attempt upon him."[31]

Maurice was the servant of a small republic, contending single-handed against an empire still considered the most formidable power in the world. His cue was not necessarily to fight on all occasions ; for delay often fights better than an army against a foreign invader. When a battle and a victory were absolutely necessary we have seen the magnificent calmness which at Nieuport secured triumph under the shadow of death. Had he accepted Spinola's challenge in November, he would probably have defeated him and have taken Groll. He might not, however, have annihilated his adversary, who, even when worsted, would perhaps have effected his escape. The city was of small value to the republic. The principal advantage of a victory would have been increased military renown for himself. Viewed in this light, there is something almost sublime in the phlegmatic and perfectly republican composure with which he disdained laurels, easily enough, as it would seem, to have been acquired, and denied his soldiers the bloodshed and the suffering for which they were clamouring.

And yet, after thoroughly weighing and measuring all these circumstances, it is natural to regret that he did not on

that occasion rise upon Spinola and smite him to the earth.
The Lord had delivered him into his hands. The chances of
his own defeat were small, its probable consequences, should
it occur, insignificant. It is hardly conceivable that he could
have been so completely overthrown as to allow the Catholic
commander to do in November what he had tried all summer
in vain to accomplish, cross the Yssel and the Waal, with
the dregs of his army, and invade Holland and Zeeland in
midwinter, over the prostrate bodies of Maurice and all his
forces. On the other hand, that the stadholder would have
sent the enemy reeling back to his bogs, with hardly the
semblance of an army at his heels, was almost certain.
The effect of such a blow upon impending negotiations, and
especially upon the impressible imagination of Henry and the
pedantic shrewdness of James, would have been very valuable. It was not surprising that the successful soldier who
sat on the French throne, and who had been ever ready to ·
wager life and crown on the results of a stricken field, should
be loud in his expressions of disapprobation and disgust.
Yet no man knew better than the sagacious Gascon that
fighting to win a crown, and to save a republic, were two
essentially different things.

In the early summer of this year Admiral Haultain, whom
we lately saw occupied with tossing Sarmiento's Spanish legion
into the sea off the harbour of Dover, had been despatched to
the Spanish coast on a still more important errand. The outward bound Portuguese merchantmen and the home returning fleets from America, which had been absent nearly two
years, might be fallen in with at any moment, in the latitude
of 36°-38°. The admiral, having received orders, therefore, to cruise carefully in those regions, sailed for the shores
of Portugal with a squadron of twenty-four war-ships. His
expedition was not very successful. He picked up a prize or
two here and there, and his presence on the coast prevented
the merchant-fleet from sailing out of Lisbon for the East
Indies, the merchandise already on board being disembarked
and the voyage postponed to a more favourable opportunity.

He saw nothing, however, of the long-expected ships from the golden West Indies—as Mexico, Peru, and Brazil were then indiscriminately called—and after parting company with six of his own ships, which were dispersed and damaged in a gale, and himself suffering from a dearth of provisions, he was forced to return without much gain or glory.[35]

In the month of September he was once more despatched on the same service. He had nineteen war-galleots of the first class, and two yachts, well equipped and manned.[36] Vice-admiral of the fleet was Regnier Klaaszoon (or Nicholson), of Amsterdam, a name which should always be held fresh in remembrance, not only by mariners and Netherlanders, but by all men whose pulses can beat in sympathy with practical heroism.

The admiral coasted deliberately along the shores of Spain and Portugal. It seemed impossible that the golden fleets, which, as it was ascertained, had not yet arrived, could now escape the vigilance of the Dutch cruisers. An occasional merchant-ship or small war-galley was met from time to time and chased into the harbours. A landing was here and there effected and a few villages burned. But these were not the prizes nor the trophies sought. On the 19th September a storm off the Portuguese coast scattered the fleet ; six of the best and largest ships being permanently lost sight of and separated from the rest. With the other thirteen Haultain now cruised off Cape St. Vincent directly across the ordinary path of the homeward-bound treasure ships.

On the 6th October many sails were descried in the distance, and the longing eyes of the Hollanders were at last gratified with what was supposed to be the great West India commercial squadrons. The delusion was brief. Instead of innocent and richly-freighted merchantmen, the new comers soon proved to be the war-ships of Admiral Don Luis de Fazardo, eighteen great galleons and eight

19 Sept.

6 Oct.

---

[35] Grotius, xv. 685. Wagenaar, 221. *seqq.*
[36] Meteren, 541. Grotius, xv. 699, 700. Wagenaar, ix 220–224.

galleys strong, besides lesser vessels—the most formidable fleet that for years had floated in those waters. There had been time for Admiral Haultain to hold but a very brief consultation with his chief officers. As it was manifest that the Hollanders were enormously over-matched, it was decided to manœuvre as well as possible for the weather-gage, and then to fight or to effect an escape, as might seem most expedient after fairly testing the strength of the enemy. It was blowing a fresh gale, and the Netherland fleet had as much as they could stagger with under close-reefed topsails.[37] The war-galleys, fit only for fair weather, were soon forced to take refuge under the lee of the land, but the eighteen galleons, the most powerful vessels then known to naval architecture, were bearing directly down, full before the wind, upon the Dutch fleet.[38]

It must be admitted that Admiral Haultain hardly displayed as much energy now as he had done in the Straits of Dover against the unarmed transports the year before. His ships were soon scattered, right and left, and the manœuvres for the weather-gage resolved themselves into a general scramble for escape.[39] Vice-Admiral Klaaszoon alone held firm, and met the onset of the first comers of the Spanish fleet. A fierce combat, yard-arm to yard-arm, ensued. Klaaszoon's mainmast went by the board, but Haultain, with five ships, all that could be rallied, coming to the rescue, the assailants for a moment withdrew. Five Dutch vessels of moderate strength were now in action against the eighteen great galleons of Fazardo. Certainly it was not an even game, but it might have been played with more heart and better skill. There was but a half-hour of daylight left when Klaaszoon's crippled ship was again attacked.[40] This time there was no attempt to offer him assistance ; the rest of the Dutch fleet crowding all the sails their masts would bear, and using all the devices of their superior seamanship, not to harass the enemy, but to steal as swiftly as possible out of

[37] Meteren, *ubi sup.*
[38] Ibid. It is true that two or three carracks of a large size and mount-ing twenty-two guns, were scattered among the galleons.
[39] Ibid.   [40] Ibid.

his way. Honestly confessing that they dared not come into the fight, they bore away for dear life in every direction.[41] Night came on, and the last that the fugitives knew of the events off Cape St. Vincent was that stout Regnier Klaaszoon had been seen at sunset in the midst of the Spanish fleet ; the sound of his broadsides saluting their ears as they escaped.

Left to himself, alone in a dismasted ship, the vice-admiral never thought of yielding to the eighteen Spanish galleons. To the repeated summons of Don Luis Fazardo that he should surrender he remained obstinately deaf. Knowing that it was impossible for him to escape, and fearing that he might blow up his vessel rather than surrender, the enemy made no attempt to board. Spanish chivalry was hardly more conspicuous on this occasion than Dutch valour, as illustrated by Admiral Haultain. Two whole days and nights Klaaszoon drifted about in his crippled ship, exchanging broadsides with his antagonists, and with his colours flying on the stump of his mast. The fact would seem incredible, were it not attested by perfectly trustworthy contemporary accounts. At last his hour seemed to have come. His ship was sinking ; a final demand for surrender,[42] with promise of quarter, was made. Out of his whole crew but sixty remained alive ; many of them badly wounded.

He quietly announced to his officers and men his decision never to surrender, in which all concurred. They knelt together upon the deck, and the admiral made a prayer in which all fervently joined. With his own hand Klaaszoon then lighted the powder magazine, and the ship was blown into the air. Two sailors, all that were left alive, were picked out of the sea by the Spaniards and brought on board one of the vessels of the fleet. Desperately mutilated, those grim Dutchmen lived a few minutes to tell the tale, and then died defiant on the enemy's deck.[43]

[41] "Ende daernade bleef den vice-admirael van d'een ende van d'ander verlaten d'een hem excuseerende of d'ander maer meest datse de Spaensche schepen nict dorsten aendoen."—Meteren, 541.

[42] Meteren, *ubi sup.* Ibid. Grot. xv. 700. Wagenaar, ix. 223.

[43] " Duo semiusti paulum provixere ab Hispanio excepti cum miraculo

Yet it was thought that a republic, which could produce men like Regnier Klaaszoon and his comrades, could be subjected again to despotism, after a war for independence of forty years, and that such sailors could be forbidden to sail the eastern and western seas. No epigrammatic phrase has been preserved of this simple Regnier, the son of Nicholas. He only did what is sometimes talked about in phraseology more or less melo-dramatic, and did it in a very plain way.

Such extreme deeds may have become so much less necessary in the world, that to threaten them is apt to seem fantastic. Exactly at that crisis of history, however, and especially in view of the Dutch admiral commanding having refused a combat of one to three, the speechless self-devotion of the vice-admiral was better than three years of eloquent arguments and a ship-load of diplomatic correspondence, such as were already impending over the world.

Admiral Haultain returned with all his ships uninjured— the six missing vessels having found their way at last safely back to the squadron—but with a very great crack to his reputation. It was urged very justly, both by the States-General and the public, that if one ship under a determined commander could fight the whole Spanish fleet two days and nights, and sink unconquered at last, ten ships more might have put the enemy to flight, or at least have saved the vice-admiral from destruction.[44]

But very few days after the incidents just described, the merchant fleet which, instead of Don Luis Fazardo's war-galleons, Admiral Haultain had so longed to encounter, arrived safely at San Lucar. It was the most splendid treasure-fleet that had ever entered a Spanish port, and the Dutch admiral's heart might well have danced for joy, had he chanced to come a little later on the track. There were fifty ships, under charge of General Alonzo de Ochares Galindo

spectantibus horridos vultus vocesque | ubi sup. Meteren. Wagenaar.
in ipsa morte contumaciam."—Grot. | [44] Meteren, Wagenaar, ubi sup.

and General Ganevaye. They had on board, according to
the registers, 1,914,176 dollars worth of bullion for the king,
and 6,086,617 dollars for merchants, or 8,000,000 dollars
in all, besides rich cargoes of silk, cochineal, sarsaparilla,
indigo, Brazil wood, and hides ; the result of two years of
pressure upon Peruvians, Mexicans, and Brazilians. Never
had Spanish finances been at so low an ebb. Never was so
splendid an income more desirable. The king's share of the
cargo was enough to pay half the arrearages due to his
mutinous troops ; and for such housekeeping this was to be
in funds.[45]

There were no further exploits on land or sea that year.
There were, however, deaths of three personages often mentioned in this history. The learned Justus Lipsius died in
Louvain, a good editor and scholar, and as sincere a Catholic
at last as he had been alternately a bigoted Calvinist and an
earnest Lutheran. His reputation was thought to have suffered by his later publications,[46] but the world at large was
occupied with sterner stuff than those classic productions, and
left the final decision to posterity.

A man of a different mould, the turbulent, high-born, hard-
fighting, hard-drinking Hohenlo, died also this year, brother-
in-law and military guardian, subsequently rival and political
and personal antagonist, of Prince Maurice. His daring deeds
and his troublesome and mischievous adventures have been
recounted in these pages. His name will be always prominent
in the history of the republic, to which he often rendered
splendid service, but he died, as he had lived, a glutton and
a melancholy sot.[47]

The third remarkable personage who passed away was one
whose name will be remembered as long as the Netherlands
have a history, old Count John of Nassau, only surviving
brother of William the Silent.[48] He had been ever prominent
and deeply interested in the great religious and political

---

[45] Meteren, 541vo.   [46] Grotius, xv. 709.   [47] Ibid, 708.   [48] Ibid.

movements of upper and lower Germany, and his services in the foundation of the Dutch commonwealth were signal, and ever generously acknowledged. At one period, as will be recollected, he was stadholder of Gelderland, and he was ever ready with sword, purse, and counsel to aid in the great struggle for independence.

CHAPTER XLVI.

General desire for peace — Political aspect of Europe — Designs of the kings of England, France, and Spain concerning the United Provinces — Matrimonial schemes of Spain — Conference between the French ministers and the Dutch envoy — Confidential revelations — Henry's desire to annex the Netherlands to France — Discussion of the subject — Artifice of Barneveld — Impracticability of a compromise between the Provinces and Spain — Formation of a West India Company — Secret mission from the archdukes to the Hague — Reply of the States-General — Return of the archdukes' envoy — Arrangement of an eight months' armistice.

THE general tendency towards a pacification in Europe at the close of the year could hardly be mistaken. The languor of fatigue, rather than any sincere desire for peace seemed to make negotiations possible. It was not likely that great truths would yet be admitted, or that ruling individuals or classes would recognise the rise of a new system out of the rapidly dissolving elements of the one which had done its work. War was becoming more and more expensive, while commerce, as the world slowly expanded itself, and manifested its unsuspected resources, was becoming more and more lucrative. It was not, perhaps, that men hated each other less, but that they had for a time exhausted their power and their love for slaughter. Meanwhile new devices for injuring humanity and retarding its civilization were revealing themselves out of that very intellectual progress which ennobled the new era. Although war might still be regarded as the normal condition of the civilized world, it was possible for the chosen ones to whom the earth and its fulness belonged, to inflict general damage otherwise than by perpetual battles.

In the east, west, north, and south of Europe peace was thrusting itself as it were uncalled for and unexpected upon the general attention. Charles and his nephew Sigismund, and the false Demetrius, and the intrigues of the Jesuits, had provided too much work for Sweden, Poland, and Russia to leave those countries much leisure for mingling in the more important business of Europe at this epoch, nor have their affairs much direct connection with this history. Venice, in its quarrels with the Jesuits, had brought Spain, France, and all Italy into a dead lock, out of which a compromise had been made not more satisfactory to the various parties than compromises are apt to prove. The Dutch republic still maintained the position which it had assumed, a quarter of a century before, of actual and legal independence ; while Spain, on the other hand, still striving after universal monarchy, had not, of course, abated one jot of its pretensions to absolute dominion over its rebellious subjects in the Netherlands.

The holy Roman and the sublime Ottoman empires had also drifted into temporary peace ; the exploits of the Persians and other Asiatic movements having given Ahmed more work than was convenient on his eastern frontier, while Stephen Botshkay had so completely got the better of Rudolph in Transylvania as to make repose desirable. So there was a treaty between the great Turk and the great Christian on the basis of what each possessed ; Stephen Botshkay was recognized as prince of Transylvania with part of Hungary, and, when taken off soon afterwards by family poison, he recommended on his death-bed the closest union between Hungary and Transylvania, as well as peace with the emperor, so long as it might be compatible with the rights of the Magyars.[1]

France and England, while suspecting each other, dreading each other, and very sincerely hating each other, were drawn into intimate relations by their common detestation of Spain, with which power both had now formal treaties of alliance and friendship. This was the result of their mighty projects for humbling the house of Austria and annihilating its power. England hated the Netherlands because of the injuries she

[1] Grotius. xv. 712, 713. Meteren, 543.

had done them, the many benefits she had conferred upon them, and more than all on account of the daily increasing commercial rivalry between the two most progressive states in Christendom, the two powers which, comparatively weak as they were in territory, capital, and population, were most in harmony with the spirit of the age.

The Government of England was more hostile than its people to the United Provinces. James never spoke of the Netherlanders but as upstarts and rebels, whose success ought to be looked upon with horror by the Lord's anointed everywhere. He could not shut his eyes to the fact that, with the republic destroyed, and a Spanish sacerdotal despotism established in Holland and Zeeland, with Jesuit seminaries in full bloom in Amsterdam and the Hague, his own rebels in Ireland might prove more troublesome than ever, and gunpowder plots in London become common occurrences. The Earl of Tyrone at that very moment was receiving enthusiastic hospitality at the archduke's court, much to the disgust of the presbyterian sovereign of the United Kingdom, who nevertheless, despite his cherished theology, was possessed with an unconquerable craving for a close family alliance with the most Catholic king. His ministers were inclined to Spain, and the British Government was at heart favourable to some kind of arrangement by which the Netherlands might be reduced to the authority of their former master, in case no scheme could be carried into effect for acquiring a virtual sovereignty over those provinces by the British crown. Moreover, and most of all, the King of France being supposed to contemplate the annexation of the Netherlands to his own dominions, the jealousy excited by such ambition made it even possible for James's Government to tolerate the idea of Dutch independence. Thus the court and cabinet of England were as full of contradictory hopes and projects as a madman's brain.

The rivalry between the courts of England and France for the Spanish marriages, and by means of them to obtain ultimately the sovereignty of all the Netherlands, was the key to most of the diplomacy and interpalatial intrigue of the several first years of the century. The negotiations of Cornwallis at Madrid were almost simultaneous with the schemes of Villeroy and Rosny at Paris.

A portion of the English Government, so soon as its treaty with Spain had been signed, seemed secretly determined to do as much injury to the republic as might lie in its power. While at heart convinced that the preservation of the Netherlands was necessary for England's safety, it was difficult for James and the greater part of his advisers to overcome their repugnance to the republic, and their jealousy of the great commercial successes which the republic had achieved.[2]

It was perfectly plain that a continuance of the war by England and the Netherlands united would have very soon ended in the entire humiliation of Spain.[3] Now that peace

---

[2] "For my own particular," wrote Cornwallis, "though I hold the preservation of the Low Countries most wholesome and necessary for the kingdom of Great Britain, yet dare I not wish their strength and wealth much increased; it being better to endure an advantage in a monarchy than in a people of their condition."—Memorials of affairs of State. from the Papers of Sir Ralph Winwood. London, 1725. Vol. II. p. 76.

"Though we must respect the Hollanders," wrote the Earl of Northampton, "(for such reasons as need no dilatation to a man of your capacity), yet we resolve to mark our favours that they be without exception to Spain."—Ibid. pp. 92, 93.

[3] "The King" (of Spain) wrote Cornwallis, "being now freed from the distractions he was wont to find by the encounters of the English, proceeds against the Hollanders with more life and hope. If this peace had not been concluded, in mine own understanding I see not how it had been possible for him to have borne out the infinite weight of charges and business laid upon him." And again, "England never lost such an opportunity of winning honour and wealth as by relinquishing the war with Spain. The

king and kingdom were reduced to such estate as they could not in all likelihood have endured the space of two years more; his own treasury was exhausted, his rents and customs assigned for the most part for money borrowed, his nobility poor and much indebted, his merchants wasted, his people of the country in all extremity of necessity, his devices of gaining by the increase of the valuation of money and other such of that nature all played over; his credit in borrowing, by means of the incertainty of his estate during the war with England, much decayed; the subjects of his many distracted dominions held in obedience by force and fear, not by love and duty. Himself very young, and in that regard with this people in no great veneration, and the less for suffering himself to be wholly governed by a man (viz. Duke of Lerma) generally hated of his own country. If this state, standing on such feeble foundations, had made but one such stumble as his father did in the time of the late queen, hardly could he have recovered without a fall; his nearest and last-gained kingdoms more hurting this nation than any other, desiring nothing more than the ruin of it."—Ibid. 72, 75, 76.

had been made, however, it was thought possible that England might make a bargain with her late enemy for destroying the existence and dividing the territory of her late ally. Accordingly the Spanish cabinet lost no time in propounding, under seal of secrecy, and with even more mystery than was usually employed by the most Catholic court, a scheme for the marriage of the Prince of Wales with the Infanta, the bridal pair, when arrived at proper age, to be endowed with all the Netherlands, both obedient and republican, in full sovereignty One thing was necessary to the carrying out of this excellent plot,—the reduction of the republic into her ancient subjection to Spain before her territory could be transferred to the future Princess of Wales.[4]

It was proposed by the Spanish Government that England should undertake this part of the job, and that King James for such service should receive an annual pension of one million ducats a year. It was also stipulated that certain cities in the republican dominions should be pledged to him as security for the regular payment of that stipend.[5] Sir Charles Cornwallis, English ambassador in Spain, lent a most favourable ear to these proposals, and James eagerly sanctioned them so soon as they were secretly imparted to that monarch. "The king here," said Cornwallis, "hath need of the King of Great Britain's arm. Our king . . . . hath good occasion to use the help of the King of Spain's purse. The assistance of England to help this nation out of that quicksand of the Low Countries, where so long they have struggled to tread themselves out, and by proof find that they sink deeper in, will be a sovereign medicine to the malady of this estate. The addition of a million of ducats to the revenue of our sovereign will be a good help to his estate."[6]

The Spanish Government had even the effrontery to offer

---

[4] The important facts connected with this intrigue—except such as, being too delicate to be committed to paper, were entrusted to confidential agents— may be found in Winwood's Memo- rials, vol. ii. pp. 160-177. Compare Van Deventer, iii. 74.

[5] See in particular Winwood, ii. 160, 161.

[6] Ibid. 177.

the English envoy a reward of two hundred thousand crowns
if the negotiations should prove successful.[7]   Care was to be
taken however that Great Britain, by this accession of power,
both present and in prospect, should not grow too great.
Spain reserving to herself certain strongholds and maritime
positions in the Netherlands, for the proper security of her
European and Indian commerce.[8]

It was thought high time for the bloodshed to cease in the
provinces ; and as England, by making a treaty of peace with
Spain when Spain was at the last gasp, had come to the
rescue of that power, it was logical that she should complete
the friendly work by compelling the rebellious provinces to
awake from their dream of independence. If the statesmen
of Holland believed in the possibility of that independence,
the statesmen of England knew better. If the turbulent
little republic was not at last convinced that it had no right
to create so much turmoil and inconvenience for its neighbours and for Christendom in general in order to maintain its
existence, it should be taught its duty by the sovereigns of
Spain and Britain.[9]

It was observed, however, that the more greedily James
listened day after day to the marriage propositions, the colder
became the Spanish cabinet in regard to that point, the more
disposed to postpone those nuptials " to God's providence
and future event."[10]

The high hopes founded on these secret stratagems were
suddenly dashed to the earth before the end of the year ;
the explosion of the Gunpowder Plot blowing the castles in
Spain into the air.

Of course the Spanish politicians vied with each other in

[7] Winwood, ii. 215. Cornwallis repelled with indignation the attempts to
bribe him.   " Would they give me for
every crown a million, I would not think
upon so unfaithful a work," he said.

[8] Ibid. 160

[9] " Never can those other people
(viz. of the United Provinces) take a
better opportunity to compound so
great a difference, neither can they
require more, with any proportion of

reason and justice, than will be yielded
unto them. If their purpose be to
maintain a popular liberty with the
yearly effusion of so much blood, and
the infesting of all Christendom so as
a few particulars may continue the
means of their authority, and enrich
themselves, they will by his Majesty
be unmasked."—Sir Charles Cornwallis to Earl of Salisbury. Ibid. 174.

[10] Ibid. 166.

expressions of horror and indignation at the Plot, and the wicked contrivers thereof, and suggested to Cornwallis that the King of France was probably at the bottom of it.[11]

They declined to give up Owen and Baldwin, however, and meantime the negotiations for the marriage of the Prince of Wales and the Infanta, the million ducats of yearly pension for the needy James, and the reduction of the Dutch republic to its ancient slavery to Spain "under the eye and arm of Britain," faded indefinitely away. Salisbury indeed was always too wise to believe in the possibility of the schemes with which James and some of his other counsellors had been so much infatuated.

It was almost dramatic that these plottings between James and the Catholic king against the life of the republic should have been signally and almost simultaneously avenged by the conspiracy of Guido Fawkes.

On the other hand, Rosny had imparted to the Dutch envoy the schemes of Henry and his ministers in regard to the same object, early in 1605. " Spain is more tired of the war," said he to Aerssens, under seal of absolute secrecy, " than you are yourselves. She is now negotiating for a marriage between the Dauphin and the Infanta, and means to give her the United Provinces, as at present constituted, for a marriage portion. Villeroy and Sillery believe the plan feasible, but demand all the Netherlands together. As for me, I shall have faith in it if they send their Infanta hither at once, or make a regular cession of the territory. Do you believe that my lords the States will agree to the proposition ?"[12]

It would be certainly difficult to match in history the effrontery of such a question. The republican envoy was asked point blank whether his country would resign her dearly gained liberty and give herself as a dowry for Philip the Second's three-years-old grand daughter. Aerssens replied cautiously that he had never heard the matter discussed in the provinces. It had always been thought that the French

[11] Winwood, ii. 173.   [12] Deventer, 41.

king had no pretensions to their territory, but had ever advocated their independence. He hinted that such a proposition
was a mere apple of discord thrown between two good allies
by Spain. Rosny admitted the envoy's arguments, and said
that his Majesty would do nothing without the consent of the
Dutch Government, and that he should probably be himself
sent ere long to the Hague to see if he could not obtain some
little recognition from the States.[13]

Thus it was confidentially revealed to the agent of the
republic that her candid adviser and ally was hard at work,
in conjunction with her ancient enemy, to destroy her independence, annex her territory, and appropriate to himself all
the fruits of her great war, her commercial achievements, and
her vast sacrifices ; while, as we have just seen, English
politicians at the same moment were attempting to accomplish the same feat for England's supposed advantage. All
that was wished by Henry to begin with was a little, a very
little, recognition of his sovereignty. " You will do well to
reflect on this delicate matter in time," wrote Aerssens to
the Advocate ; "I know that the King of Spain is inclined
to make this offer, and that they are mad enough in this
place to believe the thing feasible. For me, I reject all
such talk until they have got the Infanta—that is to say,
until the Greek Kalends. I am ashamed that they should
believe it here, and fearful that there is still more evil concealed than I know of." [14]

Towards the close of the year 1606 the French Government became still more eager to carry out their plans of
alliance and absorption. Aerssens, who loved a political intrigue better than became a republican envoy, was perfectly
aware of Henry's schemes. He was disposed to humour them,
in order to make sure of his military assistance, but with the
secret intention of seeing them frustrated by the determined
opposition of the States.

The French ministers, by command of their sovereign, were
disposed to deal very plainly. They informed the Dutch

<hr>

[13] Deventer, 42.　　　　[14] Ibid. 43.

diplomatist, with very little circumlocution, that if the republic wished assistance from France she was to pay a heavy price for it. Not a pound of flesh only, but the whole body corporate, was to be surrendered if its destruction was to be averted by French arms.

"You know," said Sillery, "that princes in all their actions consider their interests, and his Majesty has not so much affection for your conservation as to induce him to resign his peaceful position. Tell me, I pray you, what would you do for his Majesty in case anything should be done for you? You were lately in Holland. Do you think that they would give themselves to the king if he assisted them? Do you not believe that Prince Maurice has designs on the sovereignty, and would prevent the fulfilment of the king's hopes? What will you do for us in return for our assistance?" [15]

Aerssens was somewhat perplexed, but he was cunning at fence. "We will do all we can," said he, "for any change is more supportable than the yoke of Spain."

"What can you do then?" persisted Sillery. "Give us your opinion in plain French, I beg of you, and lay aside all passion; for we have both the same object—your preservation. Besides interest, his Majesty has affection for you. Let him only see some advantage for himself to induce him to assist you more powerfully. Suppose you should give us what you have and what you may acquire in Flanders, with the promise to treat secretly with us when the time comes. Could you do that?" [16]

The envoy replied that this would be tearing the commonwealth in pieces. If places were given away, the jealousy of the English would be excited. Certainly it would be no light matter to surrender Sluys, the fruit of Maurice's skill and energy, the splendidly earned equivalent for the loss of Ostend. "As to Sluys and other places in Flanders," said Aerssens, "I don't know if towns comprised in our Union could be transferred or pledged without their own consent and that of the States. Should such a thing get wind we

---

[15] Aerssens to Olden-Barneveld, 7 Oct. 1606, in Deventer, iii. 87-93.   [16] Ibid.

might be ruined. Nevertheless I will write to learn what his Majesty may hope."

"The people," returned Sillery, "need know nothing of this transfer ; for it might be made secretly by Prince Maurice, who could put the French quietly into Sluys and other Flemish places. Meantime you had best make a journey to Holland to arrange matters so that the deputies, coming hither, may be amply instructed in regard to Sluys, and no time be lost. His Majesty is determined to help you if you know how to help yourselves." [17]

The two men then separated, Sillery enjoining it upon the envoy to see the king next morning, "in order to explain to his Majesty, as he had just been doing to himself, that this sovereignty could not be transferred, without the consent of the whole people, nor the people be consulted in secret."

"It is necessary therefore to be armed," continued Henry's minister very significantly, "before aspiring to the sovereignty." [18]

Thus there was a faint glimmer of appreciation at the French court of the meaning of popular sovereignty. It did not occur to the minister that the right of giving consent was to be respected. The little obstacle was to be overcome by stratagem and by force. Prince Maurice was to put French garrisons stealthily into Sluys and other towns conquered by the republic in Flanders. Then the magnanimous ally was to rise at the right moment and overcome all resistance by force of arms. The plot was a good one. It is passing strange, however, that the character of the Nassaus and of the Dutch nation should after the last fifty years have been still so misunderstood. It seemed in France possible that Maurice would thus defile his honour and the Netherlanders barter their liberty, by accepting a new tyrant in place of the one so long ago deposed.

"This is the marrow of our conference," said Aerssens to Barneveld, reporting the interview, "and you may thus perceive whither are tending the designs of his Majesty. It seems

---

[17] Aerssens to Olden-Barneveld, *ubi sup*.   [18] Ibid.

that they are aspiring here to the sovereignty, and all my letters have asserted the contrary. If you will examine a little more closely, however, you will find that there is no contradiction. This acquisition would be desirable for France if it could be made peacefully. As it can only be effected by war you may make sure that it will not be attempted ; for the great maxim and basis of this kingdom is to preserve repose, and at the same time give such occupation to the King of Spain that his means shall be consumed and his designs frustrated. All this will cease if we make peace.

"Thus in treating with the king we must observe two rules. The first is that we can maintain ourselves no longer unless powerfully assisted, and that, the people inclining to peace, we shall be obliged to obey the people. Secondly, we must let no difficulty appear as to the desire expressed by his Majesty to have the sovereignty of these provinces. We ought to let him hope for it, but to make him understand that by ordinary and legitimate means he cannot aspire to it. We will make him think that we have an equal desire with himself, and we shall thus take from those evil-disposed counsellors the power to injure us who are always persuading him that he is only making us great for ourselves, and thus giving us the power to injure him. In short, the king can hope nothing from us overtly, and certainly nothing covertly. By explaining to him that we require the authorization of the people, and by showing ourselves prompt to grant his request, he will be the very first to prevent us from taking any steps, in order that his repose may not be disturbed. I know that France does not wish to go to war with Spain. Let us then pretend that we wish to be under the dominion of France, and that we will lead our people to that point if the king desires it, but that it cannot be done secretly. Believe me, he will not wish it on such conditions, while we shall gain much by this course. Would to God that we could engage France in war with Spain. All the utility would be ours, and the accidents of arms would so press them to Spain, Italy, and other places, that they would have little leisure to think of us. Consider all this and conceal it from Buzanval."[19]

Buzanval, it is well known, was the French envoy at the Hague, and it must be confessed that these schemes and paltry falsehoods on the part of the Dutch agent were as contemptible as any of the plots contrived every day in Paris or Madrid. Such base coin as this was still circulating in diplomacy as if fresh from the Machiavellian mint ; but the republican agent ought to have known that his Government had long ago refused to pass it current.

Soon afterwards this grave matter was discussed at the Hague between Henry's envoy and Barneveld. It was a very delicate negotiation. The Advocate wished to secure the assistance of a powerful but most unscrupulous ally, and at the same time to conceal his real intention to frustrate the French design upon the independence of the republic.

Disingenuous and artful as his conduct unquestionably was, it may at least be questioned whether in that age of deceit any other great statesman would have been more frank. If the comparatively weak commonwealth, by openly and scornfully refusing all the insidious and selfish propositions of the French king, had incurred that monarch's wrath, it would have taken a noble position no doubt, but it would have perhaps been utterly destroyed. The Advocate considered himself justified in using the artifices of war against a subtle and dangerous enemy who wore the mask of a friend. When the price demanded for military protection was the voluntary abandonment of national independence in favour of the protector, the man who guided the affairs of the Netherlands did not hesitate to humour and to outwit the king who strove to subjugate the republic. At the same time—however one may be disposed to censure the dissimulation from the standing-ground of a lofty morality—it should not be forgotten that Barneveld never hinted at any possible connivance on his part with an infraction of the laws. Whatever might be the result of time, of persuasion, of policy, he never led

[19] Aerssens to Olden-Barneveld, *ubi sup.*

Henry or his ministers to believe that the people of the Netherlands could be deprived of their liberty by force or fraud. He was willing to play a political game, in which he felt himself inferior to no man, trusting to his own skill and coolness for success. If the tyrant were defeated, and at the same time made to serve the cause of the free commonwealth, the Advocate believed this to be fair play.

Knowing himself surrounded by gamblers and tricksters, he probably did not consider himself to be cheating because he did not play his cards upon the table.

So when Buzanval informed him early in October that the possession of Sluys and other Flemish towns would not be sufficient for the king, but that they must offer the sovereignty on even more favourable conditions than had once been proposed to Henry III., the Advocate told him roundly that my lords the States were not likely to give the provinces to any man, but meant to maintain their freedom and their rights.[20] The envoy replied that his Majesty would be able to gain more favour perhaps with the common people of the country.

When it is remembered that the States had offered the sovereignty of the provinces to Henry III., abjectly and as it were without any conditions at all,[21] the effrontery of Henry IV. may be measured, who claimed the same sovereignty, after twenty years of republican independence, upon even more favourable terms than those which his predecessor had rejected.

Barneveld, in order to mitigate the effect of his plump refusal of the royal overtures, explained to Buzanval, what Buzanval very well knew, that the times had now changed ; that in those days, immediately after the death of William the Silent, despair and disorder had reigned in the provinces, " while that dainty delicacy—liberty—had not so long been sweetly tickling the appetites of the people ; that the English

---

[20] Memorandum of an interview with Buzanval by Olden-Barneveld, Oct. 1606. Deventer, iii. 94, 95.   [21] Vol. I. of this work, chaps. ii. and iv.

had not then acquired their present footing in the country, nor the house of Nassau the age, the credit, and authority to which it had subsequently attained."[22]

He then intimated—and here began the deception, which certainly did not deceive Buzanval—that if things were handled in the right way, there was little doubt as to the king's reaching the end proposed, but that all depended on good management. It was an error, he said, to suppose that in one, two, or three months, eight provinces and their principal members, to wit, forty good cities all enjoying liberty and equality, could be induced to accept a foreign sovereign.

Such language was very like irony, and probably not too subtle to escape the fine perception of the French envoy.

The first thing to be done, continued the Advocate, is to persuade the provinces to aid the king with all their means to conquer the dis-united provinces—to dispose of the arch-dukes, in short, and to drive the Spaniards from the soil—and then, little by little, to make it clear that there could be no safety for the States except in reducing the whole body of the Netherlands under the authority of the king. Let his Majesty begin by conquering and annexing to his crown the provinces nearest him, and he would then be able to persuade the others to a reasonable arrangement.

Whether the Advocate's general reply was really considered by Buzanval as a grave sarcasm, politely veiled, may be a question. That envoy, however, spoke to his Government of the matter as surrounded with difficulties, but not wholly desperate. Barneveld was, he said, inclined to doubt whether the archdukes would be able, before any negotiations were begun, to comply with the demand which he had made upon them to have a declaration in writing that the United Provinces were to be regarded as a free people over whom they pretended to no authority. If so, the French king would at once be informed of the fact. Meantime the envoy expressed the safe opinion that, if Prince Maurice and the Advocate

[22] Buzanval, in Deventer, iii. 95, 96.

together should take the matter of Henry's sovereignty in
hand with zeal, they might conduct the bark to the desired
haven. Surely this was an 'if' with much virtue in it. And
notwithstanding that he chose to represent Barneveld as rich,
tired, at the end of his Latin, and willing enough to drop his
anchor in a snug harbour, in order to make his fortune secure,
it was obvious enough that Buzanval had small hope at heart
of seeing his master's purpose accomplished.[23]

As to Prince Maurice, the envoy did not even affect to
believe him capable of being made use of, strenuous as the
efforts of the French Government in that direction had been.
"He has no private designs that I can find out," said Buzanval, doing full justice to the straightforward and sincere
character of the prince. "He asks no change for himself or
for his country." The envoy added, as a matter of private
opinion however, that if an alteration were to be made in
the constitution of the provinces, Maurice would prefer that
it should be made in favour of France than of any other
Government.

He lost no opportunity, moreover, of impressing it upon
his Government that if the sovereignty were to be secured
for France at all, it could only be done by observing great
caution, and by concealing their desire to swallow the republic
of which they were professing themselves the friends. The
jealousy of England was sure to be awakened if France appeared too greedy at the beginning. On the other hand,
that power "might be the more easily rocked into a profound
sleep if France did not show its appetite at the very beginning of the banquet."[24] That the policy of France should be
steadily but stealthily directed towards getting possession of
as many strong places as possible in the Netherlands had long
been his opinion. "Since we don't mean to go to war," said

<hr>

[23] Buzanval, in Deventer, iii. 95,
96. See also the letter of Aerssens to
Olden Barneveld, 14 November, 1606,
in which he again urges the propriety
of pretending to bestow the sovereignty
on France in the certainty that she
will find it impossible to accept it.
Also the Memoir of Aerssens of 6
January, 1606. Ibid. 99–103. Groen
v. Prinsterer, Archives, ii. 370–374.
[24] Authorities last cited.

he a year before to Villeroy, "let us at least follow the example of the English, who have known how to draw a profit out of the necessities of this state. Why should we not demand, or help ourselves to, a few good cities. Sluys, for example, would be a security for us, and of great advantage." [25]

Suspicion was rife on this subject at the court of Spain. Certainly it would be less humiliating to the Catholic crown to permit the independence of its rebellious subjects than to see them incorporated into the realms of either France or England. It is not a very striking indication of the capacity of great rulers to look far into the future that both France and England should now be hankering after the sovereignty of those very provinces, the solemn offer of which by the provinces themselves both France and England had peremptorily and almost contemptuously refused.

In Spain itself the war was growing very wearisome. Three hundred thousand dollars a month could no longer be relied upon from the royal exchequer, or from the American voyages, or from the kite-flying operations of the merchant princes on the Genoa exchange.

A greet fleet, to be sure, had recently arrived, splendidly laden, from the West Indies, as already stated. Pagan slaves, scourged to their dreadful work, continued to supply to their Christian taskmasters the hidden treasures of the New World in exchange for the blessings of the Evangel as thus revealed; but these treasures could never fill the perpetual sieve of the Netherland war, rapidly and conscientiously as they were poured into it, year after year.

The want of funds in the royal exchequer left the soldiers in Flanders unpaid, and as an inevitable result mutiny admirably organized and calmly defiant was again established throughout the obedient provinces. This happened regularly once a year, so that it seemed almost as business-like a proceeding for an Eletto to proclaim mutiny as for a sovereign to declare martial law. Should the whole army mutiny at once, what might become of the kingdom of Spain?

[25] Deventer, III. xiv.

Moreover, a very uneasy feeling was prevalent that, as formerly, the Turks had crossed the Hellespont into Europe by means of a Genoese alliance and Genoese galleys, so now the Moors were contemplating the reconquest of Granada, and of their other ancient possessions in Spain, with the aid of the Dutch republic and her powerful fleets.[25]

The Dutch cruisers watched so carefully on the track of the homeward-bound argosies, that the traffic was becoming more dangerous than lucrative, particularly since the public law established by Admiral Fazardo, that it was competent for naval commanders to hang, drown, or burn the crews of the enemy's merchantmen.

The Portuguese were still more malcontent than the Spaniards. They had gained little by the absorption of their kingdom by Spain, save participation in the war against the republic, the result of which had been to strip them almost entirely of the conquests of Vasco de Gama and his successors, and to close to them the ports of the Old World and the New.

In the republic there was a party for peace, no doubt, but peace only with independence. As for a return to their original subjection to Spain they were unanimously ready to accept forty years more of warfare rather than to dream of such a proposition. There were many who deliberately preferred war to peace. Bitter experience had impressed very deeply on the Netherlanders the great precept that faith would never be kept with heretics.[27] The present generation had therefore been taught from their cradles to believe that the word peace in Spanish mouths simply meant the Holy Inquisition. It was not unnatural, too, perhaps, that a people who had never known what it was to be at peace might feel, in regard to that blessing, much as the blind or the deaf towards colour or music ; as something useful and agreeable, no doubt, but with which they might the more cheerfully

[26] Grotius, xv. 715.

[27] "The Spaniard—who hath been accustomed to serve himself of all the advantages without mercy and sometimes to fail of treaties and contracts, *the memory of which is engraved in the marble hearts of this people to all posterity.*"—Winwood to Lord Cranborne, 12 Sept. 1604. Memorials, ii. 30.

dispense, as peculiar circumstances had always kept them in positive ignorance of its nature.   The instinct of commercial greediness made the merchants of Holland and Zeeland, and especially those of Amsterdam, dread the revival of Antwerp in case of peace, to the imagined detriment of the great trading centres of the republic.   It was felt also to be certain that Spain, in case of negotiations, would lay down as an indispensable preliminary the abstinence on the part of the Netherlanders from all intercourse with the Indies, East or West ; and although such a prohibition would be received by those republicans with perfect contempt, yet the mere discussion of the subject moved their spleen.   They had already driven the Portuguese out of a large portion of the field in the east, and they were now preparing by means of the same machinery to dispute the monopoly of the Spaniards in the west.   To talk of excluding such a people as this from intercourse with any portion of the Old World or the New was the mumbling of dotage ; yet nothing could be more certain than that such would be the pretensions of Spain.

As for the stadholder, his vocation was war, his greatness had been derived from war, his genius had never turned itself to pacific pursuits.   Should a peace be negotiated, not only would his occupation be gone, but he might even find himself hampered for means.   It was probable that his large salaries, as captain and admiral-general of the forces of the republic, would be seriously curtailed, in case his services in the field were no longer demanded, while such secret hopes as he might entertain of acquiring that sovereign power which Barneveld had been inclined to favour, were more likely to be fulfilled if the war should be continued.   At the same time, if sovereignty were to be his at all, he was distinctly opposed to such limitations of his authority as were to have been proposed by the States to his father.   Rather than reign on those conditions, he avowed that he would throw himself head foremost from the great tower of Hague Castle.

Moreover, the prince was smarting under the consciousness of having lost military reputation, however undeservedly,

1606. THE QUESTION OF PEACE.

in the latter campaigns, and might reasonably hope to gain new glory in the immediate future. Thus, while his great rival, Marquis Spinola, whose fame had grown to so luxuriant a height in so brief a period, had many reasons to dread the results of future campaigning, Maurice seemed to have personally much to lose and nothing to hope for in peace. Spinola was over head and ears in debt. In the past two years he had spent millions of florins out of his own pocket.[23] His magnificent fortune and boundless credit were seriously compromised. He had found it an easier task to take Ostend and relieve Grol than to bolster up the finances of Spain. His acceptances were becoming as much a drug upon the exchanges of Antwerp, Genoa, or Augsburg, as those of the most Catholic king or their Highnesses the archdukes. Ruin stared him in the face, notwithstanding the deeds with which he had startled the world, and he was therefore sincerely desirous of peace, provided, of course, that all those advantages for which the war had been waged in vain could now be secured by negotiation.

There had been, since the arrival of the Duke of Alva in the Netherlands, just forty years of fighting. Maurice and the war had been born in the same year, and it would be difficult for him to comprehend that his whole life's work had been a superfluous task, to be rubbed away now with a sponge. Yet that Spain, on the entrance to negotiations, would demand of the provinces submission to her authority, re-establishment of the Cathrlic religion, abstinence from Oriental or American commerce, and the toleration of Spanish soldiers over all the Netherlands, seemed indubitable.

It was equally unquestionable that the seven provinces would demand recognition of their national independence by Spain, would refuse public practice of the Roman religion within their domains, and would laugh to scorn any proposed limitations to their participation in the world's traffic. As to

[23] Hoofds Brieven, N. 3, bl. 3, cited by Wagenaar, ix. 234. The preposterous statement is there made that he had spent *fourteen millions* of his own money.

the presence of Spanish troops on their soil, that was, of course, an inconceivable idea.

Where, then, could even a loophole be found through which the possibility of a compromise could be espied ? The ideas of the contending parties were as much opposed to each other as fire and snow. Nevertheless, the great forces of the world seemed to have gradually settled into such an equilibrium as to make the continuance of the war for the present impossible.

Accordingly, the peace-party in Brussels had cautiously put forth its tentacles late in 1606, and again in the early days of the new year. Walrave van Wittenhorst and Doctor Gevaerts had been allowed to come to the Hague, ostensibly on private business, but with secret commission from the archdukes to feel and report concerning the political atmosphere. They found that it was a penal offence in the republic to talk of peace or of truce. They nevertheless suspected that there might be a more sympathetic layer beneath the very chill surface which they everywhere encountered. Having intimated in the proper quarters that the archdukes would be ready to receive or to appoint commissioners for peace or armistice, if becoming propositions should be made, they 10 Jan were allowed on the 10th of January, 1607, to make 1607. a communication to the States-General.[29] They indulged in the usual cheap commonplaces on the effusion of blood, the calamities of war, and the blessings of peace, and assured the States of the very benignant disposition of their Highnesses at Brussels.

The States-General, in their reply, seventeen days afterwards, remarking that the archdukes persisted in 27 Jan their unfounded pretensions of authority over them, took occasion to assure their Highnesses that they had no chance to obtain such authority except by the sword.[30] Whether they were like to accomplish much in that way the history of the past might sufficiently indicate, while on

---

[29] Gallucci, xx. 313. Meteren, 545, and vo. Grotius, xv. 717.
[30] Meteren, *ubi sup.*

the other hand the States would always claim the right, and never renounce the hope, of recovering those provinces which had belonged to their free commonwealth since the union of Utrecht, and which force and fraud had torn away.

During twenty-five years that union had been confirmed as a free state by solemn decrees, and many public acts and dealings with the mightiest potentates of Europe, nor could any other answer now be made to the archdukes than the one always given to his holy, Roman Imperial Majesty, and other princes, to wit, that no negotiations could be had with powers making any pretensions in conflict with the solemn decrees and well-maintained rights of the United Netherlands.[31]

It was in this year that two words became more frequent in the mouths of men than they had ever been before ; two words which as the ages rolled on were destined to exercise a wider influence over the affairs of this planet than was yet dreamed of by any thinker in Christendom. Those words were America and Virginia. Certainly both words were known before, although India was the more general term for these auriferous regions of the west, which, more than a century long, had been open to European adventure, while the land, baptized in honour of the throned Vestal, had been already made familiar to European ears by the exploits of Raleigh. But it was not till 1607 that Jamestown was founded, that Captain John Smith's adventures with Powhattan, " emperor of Virginia," and his daughter the Princess Pocahontas, became fashionable topics in England, that the English attempts to sail up the Chickahominy to the Pacific Ocean —as abortive as those of the Netherlanders to sail across the North Pole to Cathay—were creating scientific discussion in Europe, and that the first cargo of imaginary gold dust was exported from the James River.[32]

With the adventurous minds of England all aflame with enthusiasm for those golden regions, with the thick-coming fancies for digging, washing, refining the precious sands of Virginia rivers, it was certain that a great rent was now to be

[31] Meteren, ubi sup.   [32] Hildreth's History of the United States, i. 105.

made in the Borgian grant. It was inevitable that the rivalry of the Netherlanders should be excited by the achievements and the marvellous tales of Englishmen beyond the Atlantic, and that they too should claim their share of traffic with that golden and magnificent Unknown which was called America. The rivalry between England and Holland, already so conspicuous in the spicy Archipelagos of the east, was now to be extended over the silvery regions of the west. The two leading commercial powers of the Old World were now to begin their great struggle for supremacy in the western hemisphere.

A charter for what was called a West India Company was accordingly granted by the States-General. West India was understood to extend from the French settlements in Newfoundland or Acadia, along the American coast to the Straits of Magellan, and so around to the South Sea, including the Atlantic and Pacific Oceans, besides all of Africa lying between the tropic of Cancer and the Cape of Good Hope. At least, within those limits the West India Company was to have monopoly of trade, all other Netherlanders being warned off the precincts. Nothing could be more magnificent, nor more vague.[33]

The charter was for thirty-six years. The company was to maintain armies and fleets, to build forts and cities, to carry on war, to make treaties of peace and of commerce. It was a small peripatetic republic of merchants and mariners, evolved out of the mother republic—which had at last established its position among the powers of Christendom—and it was to begin its career full grown and in full armour.

The States-General were to furnish the company at starting with one million of florins and with twenty ships of war. The company was to add twenty other ships. The Government was to consist of four chambers of directors. One-half the capital was to be contributed by the chamber of Amsterdam, one-quarter by that of Zeeland, one-eighth respectively by the chambers of the Meuse and of North Holland. The

[33] Grotius. xvi. 721–725. Meteren, 545, 546. Wagenaar, ix. 226–230.

chambers of Amsterdam, of Zeeland, of the Meuse, and of North Holland were to have respectively thirty, eighteen, fifteen, and fifteen directors. Of these seventy-eight, one-third were to be replaced every sixth year by others, while from the whole number seventeen persons were to be elected as a permanent board of managers. Dividends were to be made as soon as the earnings amounted to ten per cent. on the capital. Maritime judges were to decide upon prizes, the proceeds of which were not to be divided for six years, in order that war might be self-sustaining. Afterwards, the treasury of the United Provinces should receive one-tenth, Prince Maurice one-thirtieth, and the merchant stockholders the remainder. Governors and generals were to take the oath of fidelity to the States-General. The merchandize of the company was to be perpetually free of taxation, so far as regarded old duties, and exempt from war-taxes for the first twenty years.[34]

Very violent and conflicting were the opinions expressed throughout the republic in regard to this project. It was urged by those most in favour of it that the chief sources of the greatness of Spain would be thus transferred to the States-General ; for there could be no doubt that the Hollanders, unconquerable at sea, familiar with every ocean-path, and whose hardy constitutions defied danger and privation and the extremes of heat and cold, would easily supplant the more delicately organized adventurers from Southern Europe, already enervated by the exhausting climate of America. Moreover, it was idle for Spain to attempt the defence of so vast a portion of the world. Every tribe over which she had exercised sway would furnish as many allies for the Dutch company as it numbered men ; for to obey and to hate the tyrannical Spaniard were one. The republic would acquire, in reality, the grandeur which with Spain was but an empty boast, would have the glory of transferring the great war beyond the limits of home into those far distant possessions, where the enemy deemed himself most secure,

[34] Authorities last cited.

and would teach the true religion to savages sunk in their own superstitions, and still further depraved by the imported idolatries of Rome.   Commerce was now world-wide, and the time had come for the Netherlanders, to whom the ocean belonged, to tear out from the pompous list of the Catholic king's titles his appellation of Lord of the Seas.

There were others, however, whose language was not so sanguine. They spoke with a shiver of the inhabitants of America, who hated all men, simply because they were men, or who had never manifested any love for their species except as an article of food.   To convert such cannibals to Christianity and Calvinism would be a hopeless endeavour, and meanwhile the Spaniards were masters of the country. The attempt to blockade half the globe with forty galleots was insane ; for, although the enemy had not occupied the whole territory, he commanded every harbour and position of vantage.   Men, scarcely able to defend inch by inch the meagre little sandbanks of their fatherland, who should now go forth in hopes to conquer the world, were but walking in their sleep. They would awake to the consciousness of ruin.

Thus men in the United Provinces spake of America. Especially Barneveld had been supposed to be prominent among the opponents of the new Company, on the ground that the more violently commercial ambition excited itself towards wider and wilder fields of adventure, the fainter grew inclinations for peace. The Advocate, who was all but omnipotent in Holland and Zeeland, subsequently denied the imputation of hostility to the new corporation, but the establishment of the West India Company, although chartered, was postponed.[35]

The archdukes had not been discouraged by the result of their first attempts at negotiation, for Wittenhorst had reported a disposition towards peace as prevalent in the rebellious provinces, so far as he had contrived, during his brief mission, to feel the public pulse.

[35] Wagenaar, ix. 230.

On the 6th February, 1607, Werner Cruwel, an insolvent tradesman of Brussels, and a relative of Recorder Aerssens, father of the envoy at Paris, made his appearance very unexpectedly at the house of his kinsman at the Hague. Sitting at the dinner-table, but neither eating nor drinking, he was asked by his host what troubled him. He replied that he had a load on his breast. Aerssens begged him, if it was his recent bankruptcy that oppressed him, to use philosophy and patience. The merchant answered that he who confessed well was absolved well. He then took from his pocket-book a letter from President Richardot, and said he would reveal what he had to say after dinner. The cloth being removed, and the wife and children of Aerssens having left the room, Cruwel disclosed that he had been sent by Richardot and Father Neyen on a secret mission. The recorder, much amazed and troubled, refused to utter a word, save to ask if Cruwel would object to confer with the Advocate. The merchant expressing himself as ready for such an interview, the recorder, although it was late, immediately sent a message to the great statesman. Barneveld was in bed and asleep, but was aroused to receive the communication of Aerssens. "We live in such a calumnious time," said the recorder, " that many people believe that you and I know more of the recent mission of Wittenhorst than we admit. You had best interrogate Cruwel in the presence of witnesses. I know not the man's humour, but it seems to me since his failure, that, in spite of his shy and lumpish manner, he is false and cunning." [36]

The result was a secret interview, on the 8th February, between Prince Maurice, Barneveld, and the recorder, in which Cruwel was permitted to state the object of his mission. He then produced a short memorandum, signed by Spinola and by Father Neyen, to the effect that the archdukes were willing to treat for a truce of ten or twelve years, on the sole condition that the States would abstain from the India navigation. He exhibited also another paper, signed only by

[36] Original documents in Deventer, iii. 104–109.

Neyen, in which that friar proposed to come secretly to the Hague, no one in Brussels to know of the visit save the arch-dukes and Spinola; and all in the United Provinces to be equally ignorant except the prince, the Advocate, and the recorder. Cruwel was then informed that if Neyen expected to discuss such grave matters with the prince, he must first send in a written proposal that could go on all fours and deserve attention. A week afterwards Cruwel came back with a paper in which Neyen declared himself authorized by the archdukes to treat with the States on the basis of their liberty and independence, and to ask what they would give in return for so great a concession as this renunciation of all right to "the so-called United Provinces." [37]

This being a step in advance, it was decided to permit the visit of Neyen. It was, however, the recorded opinion of the distinguished personages to whom the proposal was made that it was a trick and a deception. The archdukes would, no doubt, it was said, nominally recognise the provinces as a free State, but without really meaning it. Meantime, they would do their best to corrupt the Government and to renew the war after the republic had by this means been separated from its friends. [38]

John Neyen, father commissary of the Franciscans, who had thus invited himself to the momentous conference, was a very smooth Flemish friar, who seemed admirably adapted, for various reasons, to glide into the rebel country and into the hearts of the rebels. He was a Netherlander, born at Antwerp, when Antwerp was a portion of the united common-wealth, of a father who had been in the confidential service of William the Silent. He was eloquent in the Dutch language, and knew the character of the Dutch people. He had lived much at court, both in Madrid and Brussels, and was familiar with the ways of kings and courtiers. He was a holy man, incapable of a thought of worldly advancement for himself, but he was a master of the logic often thought most conclusive in those days; no man insinuating golden arguments more

[37] Original documents in Deventer, iii. 104–109.　　[38] Ibid.

adroitly than he into half-reluctant palms. Blessed with a visage of more than Flemish frankness, he had in reality a most wily and unscrupulous disposition. Insensible to contumely, and incapable of accepting a rebuff, he could wind back to his purpose when less supple negotiators would have been crushed.[39]

He was described by his admirers as uniting the wisdom of the serpent with the guilelessness of the dove.[40] Who better than he then, in this double capacity, to coil himself around the rebellion, and to carry the olive-branch in his mouth ?

On the 25th February the monk, disguised in the dress of a burgher, arrived at Ryswick, a village a mile and a half from the Hague. He was accompa-   25 Feb. 1607. nied on the journey by Cruwel, and they gave themselves out as travelling tradesmen."[41] After nightfall, a carriage having been sent to the hostelry, according to secret agreement, by Recorder Aerssens, John Neyen was brought to the Hague. The friar, as he was driven on through these hostile regions, was somewhat startled, on looking out, to find himself accompanied by two mounted musketeers on each side of the carriage, but they proved to have been intended as a protective escort. He was brought to the recorder's house, whence, after some delay, he was conveyed to the palace. Here he was received by an unknown and silent attendant, who took him by the hand and led him through entirely deserted corridors and halls. Not a human being was seen nor a sound heard until his conductor at last reached the door of an inner apartment through which he ushered him, without speaking a syllable.[42] The monk then found himself in the presence of two personages, seated at a table covered with books and papers. One was in military undress, with an air about him of habitual command, a fair-complexioned man of middle age, inclining to baldness, rather stout, with a large blue eye, regular features, and a mouse-coloured beard. The other was in the velvet cloak and grave habiliments of a civil

[39] Grotius, xvi. 728.   [40] Gallucci, xx. 316, 317.
[41] Wagenaar, ix. 272.   [42] Gallucci, *ubi sup.*

functionary, apparently sixty years of age, with a massive forehead, heavy features, and a shaggy beard. The soldier was Maurice of Nassau, the statesman was John of Olden-Barneveld.

Both rose as the friar entered, and greeted him with cordiality.

" But," said the prince, " how did you dare to enter the Hague, relying only on the word of a Beggar ?"

" Who would not confide," replied Neyen, " in the word of so exalted, so respectable a Beggar as you, O most excellent prince ?" [43]

With these facetious words began the negotiations through which an earnest attempt was at last to be made for terminating a seemingly immortal war. The conversation, thus begun, rolled amicably and informally along. The monk produced letters from the archdukes, in which, as he stated, the truly royal soul of the writers shone conspicuously forth. Without a thought for their own advantage, he observed, and moved only by a contemplation of the tears shed by so many thousands of human beings reduced to extreme misery, their Highnesses, although they were such exalted princes, cared nothing for what would be said by the kings of Europe and all the potentates of the universe about their excessive indulgence.[44]

" What indulgence do you speak of ?" asked the stadholder.

" Does that seem a trifling indulgence," replied John Neyen, " that they are willing to abandon the right which they inherited from their ancestors over these provinces, to allow it so easily to slip from their fingers, to declare these people to be free, over whom, as their subjects refusing the yoke, they have carried on war so long ?"

"It is our right hands that have gained this liberty," said Maurice, " not the archdukes that have granted it. It has been acquired by our treasure, poured forth how freely ! by the price of our blood, by so many thousands of souls sent to

---

[43] Gallucci, 317.   [44] Ibid.

their account. Alas, how dear a price have we paid for it ! All the potentates of Christendom, save the King of Spain alone, with his relatives the archdukes, have assented to our independence. In treating for peace we ask no gift of freedom from the archdukes. We claim to be regarded by them as what we are—free men. If they are unwilling to consider us as such, let them subject us to their dominion if they can. And as we have hitherto done, we shall contend more fiercely for liberty than for life." [45]

With this, the tired monk was dismissed to sleep off the effects of his journey and of the protracted discussion, being warmly recommended to the captain of the citadel, by whom he was treated with every possible consideration.

Several days of private discussion ensued between Neyen and the leading personages of the republic. The emissary was looked upon with great distrust. All schemes of substantial negotiation were regarded by the public as visions, while the monk on his part felt the need of all his tact and temper to wind his way out of the labyrinth into which he felt that he had perhaps too heedlessly entered. A false movement on his part would involve himself and his masters in a hopeless maze of suspicion, and make a pacific result impossible.

At length, it having been agreed to refer the matter to the States-General, Recorder Aerssens waited upon Neyen to demand his credentials for negotiation. He replied that he had been forbidden to deliver his papers, but that he was willing to exhibit them to the States-General.

He came accordingly to that assembly, and was respectfully received. All the deputies rose, and he was placed in a seat near the presiding officer. Olden-Barneveld then in a few words told him why he had been summoned. The monk begged that a want of courtesy might not be imputed to him, as he had been sent to negotiate with three individuals, not with a great assembly.

[45] Gallucci, 317, *et seqq.*, who wrote from the original letters and journals of Neyen, Spinola, and many others.

Thus already the troublesome effect of publicity upon diplomacy was manifesting itself. The many-headed, many-tongued republic was a difficult creature to manage, adroit as the negotiator had proved himself to be in gliding through the cabinets and council-chambers of princes and dealing with the important personages found there.

The power was, however, produced, and handed around the assembly, the signature and seals being duly inspected by the members. Neyen was then asked if he had anything to say in public. He replied in the negative, adding only a few vague commonplaces about the effusion of blood and the desire of the archdukes for the good of mankind. He was then dismissed.

A few days afterwards a committee of five from the States-General, of which Barneveld was chairman, conferred with Neyen. He was informed that the paper exhibited by him was in many respects objectionable, and that they had there-fore drawn up a form which he was requested to lay before the archdukes for their guidance in making out a new power. He was asked also whether the king of Spain was a party to these proposals for negotiation. The monk answered that he was not informed of the fact, but that he considered it highly probable.[46]

John Neyen then departed for Brussels with the form pre-scribed by the States-General in his pocket. Nothing could exceed the indignation with which the royalists and Catholics at the court of the archdukes were inspired by the extreme arrogance and obstinacy thus manifested by the rebellious heretics. That the offer on the part of their master to negotiate should be received by them with cavils, and almost with con-tempt, was as great an offence as their original revolt. That the servant should dare to prescribe a form for the sovereign to copy seemed to prove that the world was coming to an end. But it was ever thus with the vulgar, said the cour-tiers and church dignitaries, debating these matters. The insanity of plebeians was always enormous, and never more so

[46] Gallucci, *ubi sup.*

than when fortune for a moment smiled.[47] Full of arrogance and temerity when affairs were prosperous, plunged in abject cowardice when dangers and reverses came—such was the People—such it must ever be.

Thus blustered the priests and the parasites surrounding the archduke, nor need their sentiments amaze us. Could those honest priests and parasites have ever dreamed, before the birth of this upstart republic, that merchants, manufacturers, and farmers, mechanics and advocates—the People, in short—should presume to meddle with affairs of state? Their vocation had been long ago prescribed—to dig and to draw, to brew and to bake, to bear burdens in peace and to fill bloody graves in war—what better lot could they desire? Meantime their superiors, especially endowed with wisdom by the Omnipotent, would direct trade and commerce, conduct war and diplomacy, make treaties, impose taxes, fill their own pockets, and govern the universe. Was not this reasonable and according to the elemental laws? If the beasts of the field had been suddenly gifted with speech, and had constituted themselves into a free commonwealth for the management of public affairs, they would hardly have caused more profound astonishment at Brussels and Madrid than had been excited by the proceedings of the rebellious Dutchmen.

Yet it surely might have been suggested, when the lament of the courtiers over the abjectness of the People in adversity was so emphatic, that Dorp and Van Loon, Berendrecht and Gieselles, with the men under their command, who had disputed every inch of Little Troy for three years and three months, and had covered those fatal sands with a hundred thousand corpses, had not been giving of late such evidence of the People's cowardice in reverses as theory required. The siege of Ostend had been finished only three years

---

[47] "Sempre son grandi le insanie del volgo ma più allora che gli arride l' aura festigiante della fortuna. Pieno d' arroganza e di temerità nelle cose proprie, tutto abjettione e vilta all' incontro poi nelle avverse."—Bentivoglio, P. iii. 554.

before, and it is strange that its lessons should so soon have been forgotten.

It was thought best, however, to dissemble. Diplomacy in those days—certainly the diplomacy of Spain and Rome—meant simply dissimulation. Moreover, that solid apothegm, *hœreticis non servanda fides*, the most serviceable anchor ever forged for true believers, was always ready to be thrown out, should storm or quicksand threaten, during the intricate voyage to be now undertaken.

John Neyen soon returned to the Hague, having persuaded his masters that it was best to affect compliance with the preliminary demand of the States. During the discussions in regard to peace, it would not be dangerous to treat with the rebel provinces as with free states, over which the archdukes pretended to no authority, because—so it was secretly argued—this was to be understood with a sense of similitude. "We will negotiate with them *as if they were free*," said the greyfriar to the archduke and his counsellors, "but not with the signification of true and legitimate liberty. They have laid down in their formula that we are to pretend to no authority over them. Very well. For the time being we will pretend that we do not pretend to any such authority. To negotiate with them as if they were free will not make them free. It is no recognition by us that they are free. Their liberty could never be acquired by their rebellion.[48] This is so manifest that neither the king nor the archdukes can lose any of their rights over the United Provinces, even should they make this declaration."[49]

Thus the hair-splitters at Brussels—spinning a web that should be stout enough to entrap the noisy, blundering republicans at the Hague, yet so delicate as to go through the finest dialectical needle. Time was to show whether subtilty or bluntness was the best diplomatic material.

The monk brought with him three separate instruments or

[48] " Ciò si sarebbe dovuto sempre intendere con senso di similitudine ciò e come se fossero libere e non con significazione di vera e legitima libertà." —Bentivoglio, III. 552.
[49] Ibid.

powers, to be used according to his discretion. Admitted to the assembly of the States-General, he produced number one. It was instantly rejected. He then offered number two, with the same result. He now declared himself offended, not on his own account, but for the sake of his masters, and asked leave to retire from the assembly, leaving with them the papers which had been so benignantly drawn up, and which deserved to be more carefully studied.[50]

The States, on their parts, were sincerely and vehemently indignant. What did all this mean, it was demanded, this producing one set of propositions after another ? Why did the archdukes not declare their intentions openly and at once ? Let the States depart each to the several provinces, and let John Neyen be instantly sent out of the country. Was it thought to bait a trap for the ingenuous Netherlanders, and catch them little by little, like so many wild animals ? This was not the way the States dealt with the archdukes. What they meant they put in front—first, last, and always. Now and in the future they said and they would say exactly what they wished, candidly and seriously. Those who pursued another course would never come into negotiation with them.[51]

The monk felt that he had excited a wrath which it would be difficult to assuage. He already perceived the difference between a real and an affected indignation, and tried to devise some soothing remedy. Early next morning he sent a petition in writing to the States for leave to make an explanation to the assembly. Barneveld and Recorder Aerssens, in consequence, came to him immediately, and heaped invectives upon his head for his duplicity.[52]

Evidently it was a different matter dealing with this many-headed roaring beast, calling itself a republic, from managing the supple politicians with whom he was more familiar. The noise and publicity of these transactions were already somewhat appalling to the smooth friar who was accustomed to negotiate in comfortable secrecy. He now vehemently protested that

[50] Gallucci, 318-325, from Neyen's Letters and Journals.
[51] Ibid.   [52] Ibid.

never man was more sincere than he, and implored for time
to send to Brussels for another power. It is true that number three was still in his portfolio, but he had seen so much
indignation on the production of number two as to feel sure
that the fury of the States would know no bounds should he
now confess that he had come provided with a third.

It was agreed accordingly to wait eight days, in which
period he might send for and receive the new power already
in his possession. These little tricks were considered masterly
diplomacy in those days, and by this kind of negotiators ;
and such was the way in which it was proposed to terminate
a half century of warfare.[53] The friar wrote to his masters,
not of course to ask for a new power, but to dilate on the
difficulties to be anticipated in procuring that which the losing
party is always most bent upon in circumstances like these,
and which was most ardently desired by the archdukes—an
armistice. He described Prince Maurice as sternly opposed
to such a measure, believing that temporary cessation of hostilities was apt to be attended with mischievous familiarity
between the opposing camps, with relaxation of discipline,
desertion, and various kinds of treachery, and that there was
no better path to peace than that which was trampled by contending hosts.

Seven days passed, and then Neyen informed the States that
he had at last received a power which he hoped would prove
satisfactory. Being admitted accordingly to the assembly, he
delivered an eloquent eulogy upon the sincerity of the archdukes, who, with perhaps too little regard for their own dignity
and authority, had thus, for the sake of the public good, so
benignantly conceded what the States had demanded.

Barneveld, on receiving the new power, handed to Neyen a
draught of an agreement which he was to study at his leisure,
and in which he might suggest alterations. At the same time
it was demanded that within three months the written consent
of the King of Spain to the proposed negotiations should be

---

[53] The narrative is the monk's own, as preserved by his admirer, the Jesuit
Gallucci. (*ubi sup.*)

produced. The Franciscan objected that it did not comport with the dignity of the archdukes to suppose the consent of any other sovereign needful to confirm their acts. Barneveld insisted with much vehemence on the necessity of this condition. It was perfectly notorious, he said, that the armies commanded by the archdukes were subject to the King of Spain, and were called royal armies. Prince Maurice observed that all prisoners taken by him had uniformly called themselves soldiers of the Crown, not of the archdukes, nor of Marquis Spinola.[54]

Barneveld added that the royal power over the armies in the Netherlands and over the obedient provinces was proved by the fact that all commanders of regiments, all governors of fortresses, especially of Antwerp, Ghent, Cambray, and the like, were appointed by the King of Spain. These were royal citadels, with royal garrisons. That without the knowledge and consent of the King of Spain it would be impossible to declare the people of the United Provinces free, was obvious ; for in the cession by Philip II. of all the Netherlands it was provided that, without the consent of the king, no part of that territory could be ceded, and this on pain of forfeiting all the sovereignty. To treat without the king was therefore impossible.

The Franciscan denied that because the sovereigns of Spain sent funds and auxiliary troops to Flanders, and appointed military commanders there of various degrees, the authority of the archdukes was any the less supreme. Philip II. had sent funds and troops to sustain the League, but he was not King of France.

Barneveld probably thought it not worth his while to reply that Philip, with those funds and those troops, had done his best to become King of France, and that his failure proved nothing for the argument either way.

Neyen then returned once more to Brussels, observing as he took leave that the decision of the archdukes as to the king's consent was very doubtful, although he was sure that

[54] Gallucci, *ubi sup.*

the best thing for all parties would be to agree to an armistice out of hand.

This, however, was far from being the opinion of the States or the stadholder.

After conferring with his masters, the monk came down by agreement from Antwerp to the Dutch ships which lay in the Scheld before Fort Lillo. On board one of these, Dirk van der Does had been stationed with a special commission from the States to compare documents. It was expressly ordered that in these preliminary negotiations neither party was to go on shore.[55] On a comparison of the agreement brought by Neyen from Brussels with the draught furnished by Barneveld, of which Van der Does had a copy, so many discrepancies appeared that the document of the archdukes was at once rejected. But of course the monk had a number two, and this, after some trouble, was made to agree with the prescribed form. Brother John then, acting upon what he considered the soundest of principles—that no job was so difficult as not to be accomplished with the help of the precious metals—offered his fellow negotiator a valuable gold chain as a present from the archdukes.[56] Dirk van der Does accepted the chain, but gave notice of the fact to his Government.

The monk now became urgent to accompany his friend to the Hague, but this had been expressly forbidden by the States. Neyen felt sure, he said, of being able by arguments, which he could present by word of mouth, to overcome the opposition to the armistice were he once more to be admitted to the assembly. Van der Does had already much overstaid his appointed time, bound to the spot, as it were, by the golden chain thrown around him by the excellent friar,[57] and he now, in violation of orders, wrote to the Hague for leave to comply with this request. Pending the answer, the persuasive Neyen convinced him, much against his will, that they might both go together as far as Delft. To Delft they accordingly went;

[55] Gallucci, 322.
[56] " Optime quippe norant negotium nullum esse tam arduum quod auri ope non conficiatur."—Ibid. Compare

Wagenaar, ix. 249.
[57] " Quasi valde tenaciter aurea illa catena Neyo devinctus." — Gallucci, 323.

but, within half a league of that place, met a courier with strict orders that the monk was at once to return to Brussels. Brother John was in great agitation. Should he go back, the whole negotiation might come to nought ; should he go on, he might be clapped into prison as a spy. Being conscious, however, that his services as a spy were intended to be the most valuable part of his mission, he resolved to proceed in that capacity. [8] So he persuaded his friend Dirk to hide him in the hold of a canal-boat. Van der Does was in great trepidation himself, but on reaching the Hague and giving up his gold chain to Barneveld, he made his peace, and obtained leave for the trembling but audacious friar to come out of his hiding-place.

Appearing once more before the States-General on the afternoon of 7th May,[59] Neyen urged with much eloquence the propriety of an immediate armistice both by sea and land, insisting that it would be a sanguinary farce to establish a cessation of hostilities upon one element while blood and treasure were profusely flowing on the ocean.[60] There were potent reasons for this earnestness on the part of the monk to procure a truce to maritime operations, as very soon was to be made evident to the world. Meantime, on this renewed visit, the negotiator expressed himself as no longer doubtful in regard to the propriety of requesting the Spanish king's consent to the proposed negotiations. That consent, however, would in his opinion depend upon the earnestness now to be manifested by the States in establishing the armistice by sea and land, and upon their promptness in recalling the fleets now infesting the coast of Spain. No immediate answer was given to these representations, but Neyen was requested to draw up his argument in writing, in order that it might be duly pondered by the States of the separate provinces.

The radical defect of the Dutch constitution—the independent sovereignty claimed by each one of the provinces

[58] " Op dat hy den staat der verein-
igden Landen van naby doorsnuffelen
zou en heimelyk arbeiden tot bevor-
dering van den handel."—Wagenaar.

ix. 249.   Cf. Van der Kemp, iii. 12.
[59] Van der Kemp, iii. 119.
[60] Gallucci, 324.   Van der Kemp,
iii. 118.   Grotius, xvi 745.

composing the confederation, each of those provinces on its part being composed of cities, each again claiming something very like sovereignty for itself—could not fail to be manifested whenever great negotiations with foreign powers were to be undertaken. To obtain the unanimous consent of seven independent little republics was a work of difficulty, requiring immense expenditure of time in comparatively unimportant contingencies. How intolerable might become the obstructions, the dissensions, and the delays, now that a series of momentous and world-wide transactions was beginning, on the issue of which the admission of a new commonwealth into the family of nations, the international connections of all the great powers of Christendom, the commerce of the world, and the peace of Europe depended.

Yet there was no help for it but to make the best present use of the institutions which time and great events had bestowed upon the young republic, leaving to a more convenient season the task of remodelling the law. Meanwhile, with men who knew their own minds, who meant to speak the truth, and who were resolved to gather in at last the harvest honestly and bravely gained by nearly a half-century of hard fighting, it would be hard for a legion of friars, with their heads full of quirks and their wallets full of bills of exchange, to carry the day for despotism.

Barneveld was sincerely desirous of peace. He was well aware that his province of Holland, where he was an intellectual autocrat, was staggering under the burden of one half the expenses of the whole republic. He knew that Holland in the course of the last nine years, notwithstanding the constantly heightened rate of impost on all objects of ordinary consumption, was twenty-six millions of florins behindhand, and that she had reason therefore to wish for peace.[61] The great Advocate, than whom no statesman in Europe could more accurately scan the world's horizon, was convinced that the propitious moment for honourable straightforward nego-

---

[61] Remonstr. van Olden-Barneveld in Leven van Olden-Barneveld, bl. 157. Wagenaar, ix. 241.

tiations to secure peace, independence, and free commerce, free religion and free government, had come, and he had succeeded in winning the reluctant Maurice into a partial adoption, at least, of his opinions.[62]

The Franciscan remained at Delft, waiting, by direction of the States, for an answer to his propositions, and doing his best according to the instructions of his own Government to espy the condition and sentiments of the enemy. Becoming anxious after the lapse of a fortnight, he wrote to Barneveld. In reply the Advocate twice sent a secret messenger, urging him to be patient, assuring him that the affair was working well; that the opposition to peace came chiefly from Zeeland and from certain parties in Amsterdam vehemently opposed to peace or truce ; but that the rest of Holland was decidedly in favour of the negotiations.[63]

A few days passed, and Neyen was again summoned before the assembly. Barneveld now informed him that the Dutch fleet would be recalled from the coast of Spain so soon as the consent of his Catholic Majesty to the negotiations arrived, but that it would be necessary to confine the cessation of naval warfare within certain local limits. Both these conditions were strenuously opposed by the Franciscan, who urged that the consent of the Spanish king was certain, but that this new proposition to localize the maritime armistice would prove to be fraught with endless difficulties and dangers. Barneveld and the States remaining firm, however, and giving him a formal communication of their decision in writing, Neyen had nothing for it but to wend his way back rather malcontent to Brussels.

It needed but a brief deliberation at the court of the arch-dukes to bring about the desired arrangement. The desire for an armistice, especially for a cessation of hostilities by sea, had been marvellously stimulated by an event to be narrated in the next chapter. Meantime, more than the first three months of the year had been passed in these secret preliminary transactions, and so softly had the stealthy friar sped to

---

[62] Wagenaar, ix. 241. Grotius, xviii.   [63] Gallucci, 326, 327.

and fro between Brussels and the Hague, that when at last the armistice was announced it broke forth like a sudden flash of fine weather in the midst of a raging storm. No one at the archduke's court knew of the mysterious negotiations save the monk himself, Spinola, Richardot, Verreycken, the chief auditor, and one or two others.[64] The great Belgian nobles, from whom everything had been concealed, were very wroth, but the Belgian public was as much delighted as amazed at the prospects of peace. In the United Provinces opinions were conflicting, but doubtless joy and confidence were the prevailing emotions.

Towards the middle of April the armistice was publicly announced. It was to last for eight months from the 4th of May. During this period no citadels were to be besieged, no camps brought near a city, no new fortifications built, and all troops were to be kept carefully within walls. Meantime commissioners were to be appointed by the archdukes to confer with an equal number of deputies of the United Provinces for peace or for a truce of ten, fifteen, or twenty years, on the express ground that the archdukes regarded the United Provinces as free countries, over which their Highnesses pretended to no authority.[65]

The armistice on land was absolute. On sea, hostilities were to cease in the German Ocean and in the channel between England and France, while it was also provided that the Netherland fleet should, within a certain period, be recalled from the Spanish coast.

A day of public fast, humiliation, thanksgiving, and prayer was ordered throughout the republic for the 9th of May, in order to propitiate the favour of Heaven on the great work to be undertaken ; and, as a further precaution, Prince Maurice ordered all garrisons in the strong places to be doubled, lest the slippery enemy should take advantage of too much confidence reposed in his good faith. The preachers throughout the commonwealth, each according to his individual bias,

---

[64] Meteren, 551 vo. Gallucci, 325.
[65] Meteren, 551. Gallucci, 326. Grotius, xvi. 738. Wagenaar, ix. 250, et seq.

improved the occasion by denouncing the Spaniard from their pulpits and inflaming the popular hatred against the ancient enemy, or by dilating on the blessings of peace and the horrors of war.[63] The peace party and the war party, the believers in Barneveld and the especial adherents of Prince Maurice, seemed to divide the land in nearly equal portions.

While the Netherlands, both rebellious and obedient, were filled with these various emotions, the other countries of Europe were profoundly amazed at the sudden revelation. It was on the whole regarded as a confession of impotence on the part of Spain that the archdukes should now prepare to send envoys to the revolted provinces as to a free and independent people. Universal monarchy, brought to such a pass as this, was hardly what had been expected after the tremendous designs and the grandiloquent language on which the world had so long been feeding as its daily bread. The spectacle of anointed monarchs thus far humbling themselves to the people—of rebellion dictating terms, instead of writhing in dust at the foot of the throne—was something new in history. The heavens and earth might soon be expected to pass away, now that such a catastrophe was occurring.

The King of France had also been kept in ignorance of these events. It was impossible, however, that the negotiations could go forward without his consent and formal participation. Accordingly on receiving the news he appointed an especial mission to the Hague—President Jeannin and De Russy, besides his regular resident ambassador Buzanval. Meantime startling news reached the republic in the early days of May.

[63] Wagenaar, ix. 251.

CHAPTER XLVII.

A Dutch fleet under Heemskerk sent to the coast of Spain and Portugal —
   Encounter with the Spanish war-fleet under D'Avila — Death of both
   commanders-in-chief — Victory of the Netherlanders — Massacre of the
   Spaniards.

THE States-General had not been inclined to be tranquil
under the check which Admiral Haultain had received upon
the coast of Spain in the autumn of 1606. The deed of terrible self-devotion by which Klaaszoon and his comrades had
in that crisis saved the reputation of the republic, had proved
that her fleets needed only skilful handling and determined
leaders to conquer their enemy in the Western seas as certainly
as they had done in the archipelagos of the East. And there
was one pre-eminent naval commander, still in the very prime
of life, but seasoned by an experience at the poles and in the
tropics such as few mariners in that early but expanding
maritime epoch could boast. Jacob van Heemskerk, unlike
many of the navigators and ocean warriors who had made and
were destined to make the Orange flag of the United Provinces illustrious over the world, was not of humble parentage.
Sprung of an ancient, knightly race, which had frequently
distinguished itself in his native province of Holland, he had
followed the seas almost from his cradle. By turns a commercial voyager, an explorer, a privateer's-man, or an admiral
of war-fleets, in days when sharp distinctions between the
merchant service and the public service, corsairs' work and
cruisers' work, did not exist, he had ever proved himself equal
to any emergency—a man incapable of fatigue, of perplexity,
or of fear. We have followed his career during that awful
winter in Nova Zembla, where, with such unflinching cheerful heroism, he sustained the courage of his comrades—the

first band of scientific martyrs that had ever braved the dangers and demanded the secrets of those arctic regions. His glorious name—as those of so many of his comrades and countrymen—has been rudely torn from cape, promontory, island, and continent, once illustrated by courage and suffering, but the noble record will ever remain.[1]

Subsequently he had much navigated the Indian ocean; his latest achievement having been, with two hundred men, in a couple of yachts, to capture an immense Portuguese carrack, mounting thirty guns, and manned with eight hundred sailors, and to bring back a prodigious booty for the exchequer of the republic. A man with delicate features, large brown eyes, a thin high nose, fair hair and beard, and a soft, gentle expression, he concealed, under a quiet exterior, and on ordinary occasions a very plain and pacific costume, a most daring nature, and an indomitable ambition for military and naval distinction.

He was the man of all others in the commonwealth to lead any new enterprise that audacity could conceive against the hereditary enemy.

The public and the States-General were anxious to retrace the track of Haultain, and to efface the memory of his inglorious return from the Spanish coast. The sailors of Holland and Zeeland were indignant that the richly freighted fleets of the two Indies had been allowed to slip so easily through their fingers. The great East India Corporation was importunate with Government that such blunders should not be repeated, and that the armaments known to be preparing in the Portuguese ports, the homeward-bound fleets that might be looked for at any moment off the peninsular coast, and the Spanish cruisers which were again preparing to molest the merchant fleets of the Company, should be dealt with effectively and in season.

Twenty-six vessels of small size but of good sailing qualities,

[1] For a full and learned dissertation on the causes of the oblivion into which the early Dutch voyages have fallen see in particular Bennet and Van Wyk, 111; Hoofdstuk, 156, *et seq.*

according to the idea of the epoch, were provided, together with four tenders. Of this fleet the command was offered to Jacob van Heemskerk. He accepted with alacrity, expressing with his usual quiet self-confidence the hope that, living or dead, his fatherland would have cause to thank him. Inspired only by the love of glory, he asked for no remuneration for his services save thirteen per cent. of the booty, after half a million florins should have been paid into the public treasury. It was hardly probable that this would prove a large share of prize money, while considerable victories alone could entitle him to receive a stiver.

The expedition sailed in the early days of April for the coast of Spain and Portugal, the admiral having full discretion to do anything that might in his judgment redound to the advantage of the republic. Next in command was the vice-admiral of Zeeland, Laurenz Alteras. Another famous seaman in the fleet was Captain Henry Janszoon of Amsterdam, commonly called Long Harry, while the weather-beaten and well-beloved Admiral Lambert, familiarly styled by his countrymen " Pretty Lambert," some of whose achievements have already been recorded in these pages, was the comrade of all others upon whom Heemskerk most depended.[2] After the 10th April the admiral, lying off and on near the mouth of the Tagus, sent a lugger in trading disguise to reconnoitre that river. He ascertained by his spies, sent in this and subsequently in other directions, as well as by occasional merchantmen spoken with at sea, that the Portuguese fleet for India would not be ready to sail for many weeks ; that no valuable argosies were yet to be looked for from America, but that a great war-fleet, comprising many galleons of the largest size, was at that very moment cruising in the Straits of Gibraltar. Such of the Netherland traders as were returning from the Levant, as well as those designing to enter the Mediterranean, were likely to fall prizes to this formidable enemy. The heart of Jacob Heemskerk danced for joy. He had come forth for glory, not for booty, and here was what he

---

[2] Wagenaar, ix. 252.

had scarcely dared to hope for—a powerful antagonist instead of peaceful, scarcely resisting, but richly-laden merchantmen. The accounts received were so accurate as to assure him that the Gibraltar fleet was far superior to his own in size of vessels, weight of metal, and number of combatants. The circumstances only increased his eagerness. The more he was over-matched, the greater would be the honour of victory, and he steered for the straits, tacking to and fro in the teeth of a strong head-wind.

On the morning of the 25th April he was in the narrowest part of the mountain-channel, and learned that the whole Spanish fleet was in the Bay of Gibraltar. The marble pillar of Hercules rose before him. Heemskerk was of a poetic temperament, and his imagination was inflamed by the spectacle which met his eyes. Geographical position, splendour of natural scenery, immortal fable, and romantic history, had combined to throw a spell over that region. It seemed marked out for perpetual illustration by human valour. The deeds by which, many generations later, those localities were to become identified with the fame of a splendid empire—then only the most energetic rival of the young republic, but destined under infinitely better geographical conditions to follow on her track of empire, and with far more prodigious results—were still in the womb of futurity. But St. Vincent, Trafalgar, Gibraltar—words which were one day to stir the English heart, and to conjure heroic English shapes from the depths so long as history endures—were capes and promontories already familiar to legend and romance.

Those Netherlanders had come forth from their slender little fatherland to offer battle at last within his own harbours and under his own fortresses to the despot who aspired to universal monarchy, and who claimed the lordship of the seas. The Hollanders and Zeelanders had gained victories on the German Ocean, in the Channel, throughout the Indies, but now they were to measure strength with the ancient enemy in this most conspicuous theatre, and before the eyes of

VOL. IV.—Y

Christendom. It was on this famous spot that the ancient demigod had torn asunder by main strength the continents of Europe and Africa. There stood the opposite fragments of the riven mountain-chain, Calpe and Abyla, gazing at each other, in eternal separation, across the gulf, emblems of those two antagonistic races which the terrible hand of Destiny has so ominously disjoined. Nine centuries before, the African king, Moses son of Nuzir, and his lieutenant, Tarik son of Abdallah, had crossed that strait and burned the ships which brought them. Black Africa had conquered a portion of whiter Europe, and laid the foundation of the deadly mutual repugnance which nine hundred years of bloodshed had heightened into insanity of hatred. Tarik had taken the town and mountain, Carteia and Calpe, and given to both his own name. Gib-al-Tarik, the cliff of Tarik, they are called to this day.

Within the two horns of that beautiful bay, and protected by the fortress on the precipitous rock, lay the Spanish fleet at anchor. There were ten galleons of the largest size, besides lesser war-vessels and carracks, in all twenty-one sail. The admiral commanding was Don Juan Alvarez d'Avila, a veteran who had fought at Lepanto under Don John of Austria. His son was captain of his flag-ship, the St. Augustine. The vice-admiral's galleon was called 'Our Lady of La Vega,' the rear-admiral's was the 'Mother of God,' and all the other ships were baptized by the holy names deemed most appropriate, in the Spanish service, to deeds of carnage.

On the other hand, the nomenclature of the Dutch ships suggested a menagerie. There was the Tiger, the Sea Dog, the Griffin, the Red Lion, the Golden Lion, the Black Bear, the White Bear ; these, with the Æolus and the Morning Star, were the leading vessels of the little fleet.

On first attaining a distant view of the enemy, Heemskerk summoned all the captains on board his flag-ship, the Æolus, and addressed them in a few stirring words.

"It is difficult," he said, "for Netherlanders not to conquer on

salt water.[3] Our fathers have gained many a victory in distant seas, but it is for us to tear from the enemy's list of titles
his arrogant appellation of Monarch of the Ocean. Here, on
the verge of two continents, Europe is watching our deeds,
while the Moors of Africa are to learn for the first time in
what estimation they are to hold the Batavian republic.
Remember that you have no choice between triumph and
destruction. I have led you into a position whence escape is
impossible—and I ask of none of you more than I am prepared
to do myself — whither I am sure that you will follow.
The enemy's ships are far superior to ours in bulk; but .
remember that their excessive size makes them difficult to
handle and easier to hit, while our own vessels are entirely
within control. Their decks are swarming with men, and
thus there will be more certainty that our shot will take
effect. Remember, too, that we are all sailors, accustomed
from our cradles to the ocean ; while yonder Spaniards are
mainly soldiers and landsmen, qualmish at the smell of bilge-
water, and sickening at the roll of the waves.[4] This day
begins a long list of naval victories, which will make our
fatherland for ever illustrious, or lay the foundation of an
honourable peace, by placing, through our triumph, in the
hands of the States-General, the power of dictating its terms."

His comrades long remembered the enthusiasm which
flashed from the man, usually so gentle and composed in
demeanour, so simple in attire. Clad in complete armour,
with the orange-plumes waving from his casque and the
orange-scarf across his breast, he stood there in front of the
mainmast of the Æolus, the very embodiment of an ancient
Viking.

He then briefly announced his plan of attack. It was of
antique simplicity. He would lay his own ship alongside

[3] Grotius, Meteren, and Wagenaar
all give essentially the same report of
this speech, and I am inclined to think
therefore that something very like it
was really spoken.

[4] "Illud vero vel præcipuum quod
apud nos nautæ pugnant, apud illos
milites quos ego mihi videre videor ut
sunt delicati sentinæ odore ac jacta-
tione fluctuum prope exanimes in ver-
tiginem dari."—Grotius, 734.

that of the Spanish admiral. Pretty Lambert in the Tiger was to grapple with her on the other side. Vice-admiral Alteras and Captain Bras were to attack the enemy's vice-admiral in the same way. Thus, two by two, the little Netherland ships were to come into closest quarters with each one of the great galleons. Heemskerk would himself lead the way, and all were to follow, as closely as possible, in his wake. The oath to stand by each other was then solemnly renewed, and a parting health was drunk. The captains then returned to their ships.

As the Lepanto warrior, Don Juan d'Avila, saw the little vessels slowly moving towards him, he summoned a Hollander whom he had on board, one Skipper Gevaerts of a captured Dutch trading bark, and asked him whether those ships in the distance were Netherlanders.

"Not a doubt of it," replied the skipper.

The admiral then asked him what their purpose could possibly be, in venturing so near Gibraltar.

"Either I am entirely mistaken in my countrymen," answered Gevaerts, "or they are coming for the express purpose of offering you battle." [5]

The Spaniard laughed loud and long. The idea that those puny vessels could be bent on such a purpose seemed to him irresistibly comic, and he promised his prisoner, with much condescension, that the St. Augustine alone should sink the whole fleet.

Gevaerts, having his own ideas on the subject, but not being called upon to express them, thanked the admiral for his urbanity, and respectfully withdrew.

At least four thousand soldiers were in D'Avila's ships, besides seamen. There were seven hundred in the St. Augustine, four hundred and fifty in Our Lady of Vega, and so on in proportion. There were also one or two hundred noble volunteers who came thronging on board, scenting the battle from afar, and desirous of having a hand in the destruction of the insolent Dutchmen.

[5] Meteren, 547.

It was about one in the afternoon. There was not much wind, but the Hollanders, slowly drifting on the eternal river that pours from the Atlantic into the Mediterranean, were now very near. All hands had been piped on board every one of the ships, all had gone down on their knees in humble prayer, and the loving cup had then been passed around.[6]

25 April.

Heemskerk, leading the way towards the Spanish admiral, ordered the gunners of the Æolus not to fire until the vessels struck each other. " Wait till you hear it crack,"[7] he said, adding a promise of a hundred florins to the man who should pull down the admiral's flag. Avila, notwithstanding his previous merriment, thought it best, for the moment, to avoid the coming collision. Leaving to other galleons, which he interposed between himself and the enemy, the task of summarily sinking the Dutch fleet, he cut the cable of the St. Augustine and drifted farther into the bay. Heemskerk, not allowing himself to be foiled in his purpose, steered past two or three galleons, and came crashing against the admiral. Almost simultaneously, Pretty Lambert laid himself along her quarter on the other side. The St. Augustine fired into the Æolus as she approached, but without doing much damage. The Dutch admiral, as he was coming in contact, discharged his forward guns, and poured an effective volley of musketry into his antagonist.

The St. Augustine fired again, straight across the centre of the Æolus, at a few yards' distance. A cannon-ball took off the head of a sailor, standing near Heemskerk, and carried away the admiral's leg, close to the body. He fell on deck, and, knowing himself to be mortally wounded, implored the next in command on board, Captain Verhoef, to fight his ship to the last, and to conceal his death from the rest of the fleet. Then prophesying a glorious victory for the republic, and piously commending his soul to his Maker, he soon breathed his last. A cloak was thrown over him,

---

[6] Meteren, Wagenaar, Grotius.
[7] " En dat sy het hoorden kraaken."—Meteren, 547[vo].

and the battle raged. The few who were aware that the noble Heemskerk was gone, burned to avenge his death, and to obey the dying commands of their beloved chief. The rest of the Hollanders believed themselves under his directing influence, and fought as if his eyes were upon them. Thus the spirit of the departed hero still watched over and guided the battle.

The Æolus now fired a broadside into her antagonist, making fearful havoc, and killing Admiral D'Avila. The commanders-in-chief of both contending fleets had thus fallen at the very beginning of the battle. While the St. Augustine was engaged in deadly encounter, yard-arm and yard-arm, with the Æolus and the Tiger, Vice-admiral Alteras had, however, not carried out his part of the plan. Before he could succeed in laying himself alongside of the Spanish vice-admiral, he had been attacked by two galleons. Three other Dutch ships, however, attacked the vice-admiral, and, after an obstinate combat, silenced all her batteries and set her on fire. Her conquerors were then obliged to draw off rather hastily, and to occupy themselves for a time in extinguishing their own burning sails, which had taken fire from the close contact with their enemy. Our Lady of Vega, all ablaze from top-gallant-mast to quarter-deck, floated helplessly about, a spectre of flame, her guns going off wildly, and her crew dashing themselves into the sea, in order to escape by drowning from a fiery death. She was consumed to the water's edge.

Meantime, Vice-admiral Alteras had successively defeated both his antagonists; drifting in with them until almost under the guns of the fortress, but never leaving them until, by his superior gunnery and seamanship, he had sunk one of them, and driven the other a helpless wreck on shore.

Long Harry, while Alteras had been thus employed, had engaged another great galleon, and set her on fire. She, too, was thoroughly burned to her hulk ; but Admiral Harry was killed.

By this time, although it was early of an April afternoon, and heavy clouds of smoke, enveloping the combatants pent together in so small a space, seemed to make an atmosphere of midnight, as the flames of the burning galleons died away. There was a difficulty, too, in bringing all the Netherland ships into action—several of the smaller ones having been purposely stationed by Heemskerk on the edge of the bay to prevent the possible escape of any of the Spaniards. While some of these distant ships were crowding sail, in order to come to closer quarters, now that the day seemed going against the Spaniards, a tremendous explosion suddenly shook the air. One of the largest galleons, engaged in combat with a couple of Dutch vessels, had received a hot shot full in her powder magazine, and blew up with all on board. The blazing fragments drifted about among the other ships, and two more were soon on fire, their guns going off and their magazines exploding. The rock of Gibraltar seemed to reel. To the murky darkness succeeded the intolerable glare of a new and vast conflagration. The scene in that narrow roadstead was now almost infernal. It seemed, said an eye-witness, as if heaven and earth were passing away. A hopeless panic seized the Spaniards. The battle was over. The St. Augustine still lay in the deadly embrace of her antagonists, but all the other galleons were sunk or burned. Several of the lesser war-ships had also been destroyed. It was nearly sunset. The St. Augustine at last ran up a white flag, but it was not observed in the fierceness of the last moments of combat; the men from the Æolus and the Tiger making a simultaneous rush on board the vanquished foe.

The fight was done, but the massacre was at its beginning. The trumpeter of Captain Kleinsorg clambered like a monkey up the mast of the St. Augustine, hauled down the admiral's flag, the last which was still waving, and gained the hundred florins. The ship was full of dead and dying; but a brutal, infamous butchery now took place. Some Netherland prisoners were found in the hold, who related that two messengers had been successively despatched to take their lives, as they lay there in chains, and that each had been shot, as he made his way towards the execution of the orders.

This information did not chill the ardour of their victorious countrymen. No quarter was given. Such of the victims as succeeded in throwing themselves overboard, out of the St. Augustine, or any of the burning or sinking ships, were pursued by the Netherlanders, who rowed about among them in boats, shooting, stabbing, and drowning their victims by hundreds. It was a sickening spectacle. The bay, said those who were there, seemed sown with corpses. Probably two or three thousand were thus put to death, or had met their fate before. Had the chivalrous Heemskerk lived, it is possible that he might have stopped the massacre. But the thought of the grief which would fill the commonwealth when the news should arrive of his death—thus turning the joy of the great triumph into lamentations—increased the animosity of his comrades. Moreover, in ransacking the Spanish admiral's ship, all his papers had been found, among them many secret instructions from Government signed "I, the King;" ordering most inhuman persecutions, not only of the Netherlanders, but of all who should in any way assist them, at sea or ashore. Recent examples of the thorough manner in which the royal admirals could carry out these bloody instructions had been furnished by the hangings, burnings, and drownings of Fazardo. But the barbarous ferocity of the Dutch on this occasion might have taught a lesson even to the comrades of Alva.

The fleet of Avila was entirely destroyed. The hulk of the St. Augustine drifted ashore, having been abandoned by the victors, and was set on fire by a few Spaniards who had concealed themselves on board, lest she might fall again into the enemy's hands.

The battle had lasted from half-past three until sunset. The Dutch vessels remained all the next day on the scene of their triumph. The townspeople were discerned, packing up their goods, and speeding panic-struck into the interior. Had Heemskerk survived he would doubtless have taken Gibraltar —fortress and town—and perhaps Cadiz, such was the consternation along the whole coast.

But his gallant spirit no longer directed the fleet. Bent rather upon plunder than glory, the ships now dispersed in search of prizes towards the Azores, the Canaries, or along the Portuguese coast; having first made a brief visit to Tetuan, where they were rapturously received by the Bey.

' The Hollanders lost no ships, and but one hundred seamen were killed. Two vessels were despatched homeward directly, one with sixty wounded sailors, the other with the embalmed body of the fallen Heemskerk. The hero was honoured with a magnificent funeral in Amsterdam at the public expense— the first instance in the history of the republic—and his name was enrolled on the most precious page of her records.[8]

[8] The chief authorities for this remarkable battle are Meteren, 547, 548. Grotius, xvi. 731–738. Wagenaar, ix. 251–258.

CHAPTER XLVIII.

Internal condition of Spain — Character of the people — Influence of the Inqui-
    sition — Population and Revenue — Incomes of Church and Government
    — Degradation of Labour — Expulsion of the Moors and its consequences
    — Venality the special characteristic of Spanish polity — Maxims of the
    foreign polity of Spain — The Spanish army and navy — Insolvent state of
    the Government — The Duke of Lerma — His position in the State —
    Origin of his power — System of bribery and trafficking — Philip III. —
    His character — Domestic life of the king and queen.

A GLANCE at the interior condition of Spain, now that there
had been more than nine years of a new reign, should no
longer be deferred.

Spain was still superstitiously regarded as the leading
power of the world, although foiled in all its fantastic and
gigantic schemes. It was still supposed, according to current
dogma, to share with the Ottoman empire the dominion of
the earth.[1] A series of fortunate marriages having united
many of the richest and fairest portions of Europe under a
single sceptre, it was popularly believed in a period when
men were not much given as yet to examine very deeply the
principles of human governments or the causes of national
greatness, that an aggregation of powers which had resulted
from preposterous laws of succession really constituted a
mighty empire, founded by genius and valour.

The Spanish people, endowed with an acute and exuberant
genius, which had exhibited itself in many paths of literature,
science, and art ; with a singular aptitude for military adventure, organization, and achievement ; with a great variety, in
short, of splendid and ennobling qualities; had been, for a long
succession of years, accursed with almost the very worst political institutions known to history. The depth of their misery

---

[1] Giro. Soranzo, Relazione.

and of their degradation was hardly yet known to themselves, and this was perhaps the most hideous proof of the tyranny of which they had been the victims. To the outward world, the hollow fabric, out of which the whole pith and strength had been slowly gnawed away, was imposing and majestic still. But the priest, the soldier, and the courtier had been busy too long, and had done their work too thoroughly, to leave much hope of arresting the universal decay.

Nor did there seem any probability that the attempt would be made.

It is always difficult to reform wide-spread abuses, even when they are acknowledged to exist, but when gigantic vices are proudly pointed to as the noblest of institutions and as the very foundations of the state, there seems nothing for the patriot to long for but the deluge.

It was acknowledged that the Spanish population—having a very large admixture of those races which, because not Catholic at heart, were stigmatized as miscreants, heretics, pagans, and, generally, as accursed—was by nature singularly prone to religious innovation.[2] Had it not been for the Holy Inquisition, it was the opinion of acute and thoughtful observers in the beginning of the seventeenth century, that the infamous heresies of Luther, Calvin, and the rest, would have long before taken possession of the land.[3] To that most blessed establishment it was owing that Spain had not polluted itself in the filth and ordure of the Reformation, and had been spared the horrible fate which had befallen large portions of Germany, France, Britain, and other barbarous northern

[2] " Li popoli per la gran mescolanza che hanno avuto coi Mori e Giudei sono molto facili a divertire dal diretto sentiero della fede."—Girº. Soranzo. Relazione. " Tremando gli Spagnuoli perchè incominciarono a colpirli l' eresia nei tempi di Filippo II. non solo nel volgo ma anche nella alta nobiltà."—S. Contarini, Relazione.

[3] " È rispettato l' inquisitore maggiore come se fosse un papa, ha il tribunal del suo officio per tutte le terre. In somma si può dire che il rigore di questo officio mantiene il rito della vera religione in Spagna che senza questo si può grandemente temere che per li tanti Moreschi e Marani che sono sparsi per il paese si vederiano per questo rispetto di religione dei movimenti e delle commozioni importanti."—Soranzo.

nations. It was conscientiously and thankfully believed in Spain, two centuries ago, that the state had been saved from political and moral ruin by that admirable machine which detected heretics with unerring accuracy, burned them when detected, and consigned their descendants to political incapacity and social infamy to the remotest generation.[4]

As the awful consequences of religious freedom, men pointed with a shudder to the condition of nations already speeding on the road to ruin, from which the two peninsulas at least had been saved. Yet the British empire, with the American republic still an embryo in its bosom, France, North Germany, and other great powers, had hardly then begun their headlong career. Whether the road of religious liberty was leading exactly to political ruin, the coming centuries were to judge.

Enough has been said in former chapters for the characterization of Philip II. and his polity. But there had now been nearly ten years of another reign. The system, inaugurated by Charles and perfected by his son, had reached its last expression under Philip III.

The evil done by father and son lived and bore plentiful fruit in the epoch of the grandson. And this is inevitable in history. No generation is long-lived enough to reap the harvest, whether of good or evil, which it sows.

Philip II. had been indefatigable in evil, a thorough believer in his supernatural mission as despot, not entirely without capacity for affairs, personally absorbed by the routine of his bureau.

He was a king, as he understood the meaning of the kingly office. His policy was continued after his death; but there was no longer a king. That important regulator to the

---

[4] " Con tanta vergogna ed ignominia che in eterno resta macchiata quella discendenza di infamia nè sono capaci i posteri di dignità nè di onore alcuno onde tutti procurano di vivere in maniera da non imbrattarsi in tanta lordura mantenere la Spagna libera dall' infezione dell' eresia, peste che ha infettato e rovinato gran parte del mondo," &c., &c.—Giro. Soranzo, Relazione.

governmental machinery was wanting. How its place was supplied will soon appear.

Meantime the organic functions were performed very much in the old way. There was, at least, no lack of priests or courtiers.

Spain at this epoch had probably less than twelve millions of inhabitants, although the statistics of those days cannot be relied upon with accuracy.[5] The whole revenue of the state was nominally sixteen or seventeen millions of dollars, but the greater portion of that income was pledged for many coming years to the merchants of Genoa.[6] All the little royal devices for increasing the budget by debasing the coin of the realm, by issuing millions of copper tokens, by lowering the promised rate of interest on Government loans, by formally repudiating both interest and principal, had been tried, both in this and the preceding reign, with the usual success. An inconvertible paper currency, stimulating industry and improving morals by converting beneficent commerce into baleful gambling—that fatal invention did not then exist. Meantime, the legitimate trader and innocent citizen were harassed, and the general public endangered, as much as the limited machinery of the epoch permitted.

The available, unpledged revenue of the kingdom hardly amounted to five millions of dollars a-year. The regular annual income of the church was at least six millions.[7] The whole personal property of the nation was estimated—in a very clumsy and unsatisfactory way, no doubt—at sixty millions of dollars.[8] Thus the income of the priesthood was ten per cent. of the whole funded estate of the country, and

---

[5] Priuli (1604–1608) puts the population of Spain, inclusive of foreign residents, at thirteen millions (F. Priuli, Relazione). But Agostino de Blas, in his work on the population of Spain from official records, cited by N. Barozzi (Notes, s. 1, vol. i. p. 353) allows but 9,680,191 inhabitants for the whole peninsula.

[6] " Sono l' entrate di S. M. come dicono da 16 milioni in circa quasi tutte impegnate e non solo impegnate ma si può dire annullate perchè sono obbligate a maggior prezzo che vagliano," &c. &c.—Otto. Bon. Relazione. Compare Giro. Soranzo, who puts the nominal whole at seventeen millions, but " impegnate ed annihilate affatto."

[7] F. Priuli, Relazione.

[8] " Eppure la Spagna è povera non trovandosene in essa più di sessanta milioni fra capitali e robe di servizio." —Fran. Priuli, Ambas. a Filippo III. 1604–1608.

at least a million a year more than the income of the Government. Could a more biting epigram be made up•n the condition to which the nation had been reduced ?

Labour was more degraded than ever. The industrious classes, if such could be said to exist, were esteemed every day more and more infamous. Merchants, shopkeepers, mechanics, were reptiles, as vilely esteemed as Jews, Moors, Protestants, or Pagans. Acquiring wealth by any kind of production was dishonourable. A grandee who should permit himself to sell the wool from his boundless sheep-walks disgraced his caste, and was accounted as low as a merchant.[9] To create was the business of slaves and miscreants : to destroy was the distinguishing attribute of Christians and nobles. To cheat, to pick, and to steal, on the most minute and the most gigantic scale—these were also among the dearest privileges of the exalted classes. No merchandize was polluting save the produce of honest industry. To sell places in church and state, the army, the navy, and the sacred tribunals of law ; to take bribes from rich and poor, high and low, in sums infinitesimal or enormous, to pillage the exchequer in every imaginable form, to dispose of titles of honour, orders of chivalry, posts in municipal council,[10] at auction ; to barter influence, audiences, official interviews against money cynically paid down in rascal counters—all this was esteemed consistent with patrician dignity.

The ministers, ecclesiastics, and those about court, obtaining a monopoly of such trade, left the business of production and circulation to their inferiors, while, as has already been sufficiently indicated, religious fanaticism and a pride of race, which nearly amounted to idiocy, had generated a scorn for labour even among the lowest orders. As a natural consequence, commerce and the mechanical arts fell almost

[9] Ibid. Compare notes of Barozzi (s. 1, vol. i. p. 351).
[10] " Quelli che governano nelle città sono chiamati Regidores e sono nelle città grandi in numero di 40 e forse più e nelle piccole in minor numero;   questi impieghi il re vende per denari e secondo i luoghi dove vanno sogliono esser venduti per 4 o 6 mille ducati ciò che porta al popolo gran danno," &c. &c.—S. Contarini.

exclusively into the hands of foreigners—Italians, English, and French—who resorted in yearly increasing numbers to Spain for the purpose of enriching themselves by the industry which the natives despised.[11]

The capital thus acquired was at regular intervals removed from the country to other lands, where wealth resulting from traffic or manufactures was not accounted infamous.

Moreover, as the soil of the country was held by a few great proprietors—an immense portion in the dead-hand of an insatiate and ever-grasping church, and much of the remainder in vast entailed estates—it was nearly impossible for the masses of the people to become owners of any portion of the land. To be an agricultural day-labourer at less than a beggar's wage could hardly be a tempting pursuit for a proud and indolent race. It was no wonder therefore that the business of the brigand, the smuggler, the professional mendicant became from year to year more attractive and more overdone ; while an ever-thickening swarm of priests, friars, and nuns of every order, engendered out of a corrupt and decaying society, increasing the general indolence, immorality, and unproductive consumption, and frightfully diminishing the productive force of the country, fed like locusts upon what was left in the unhappy land. " To shirk labour, infinite numbers become priests and friars," said a good Catholic, in the year 1608.[12]

Before the end of the reign of Philip III. the peninsula, which might have been the granary of the world, did not produce food enough for its own population. Corn became a regular article of import into Spain, and would have come in larger quantities than it did had the industry of the country furnished sufficient material to exchange for necessary food.

And as if it had been an object of ambition with the priests and courtiers who then ruled a noble country, to make at exactly this epoch the most startling manifestation of human fatuity that the world had ever seen, it was now resolved by

---

[11] Giro. Soranzo.
[12] "Per schivar il travaglio ed infiniti si fanno preti e frati."—Giro. Soranzo, Ambas. a Filippo III. 1608-1611.

government to expel by armed force nearly the whole stock of intelligent and experienced labour, agricultural and mechanical, from the country. It is unnecessary to dwell long upon an event which, if it were not so familiarly known to mankind, would seem almost incredible. But the expulsion of the Moors is, alas ! no exaggerated and imaginary satire, but a monument of wickedness and insanity such as is not often seen in human history.

Already, in the very first years of the century, John Ribera, archbishop of Valencia, had recommended and urged the scheme.

It was too gigantic a project to be carried into execution at once, but it was slowly matured by the aid of other ecclesiastics. At last there were indications, both human and divine, that the expulsion of these miscreants could no longer be deferred. It was rumoured and believed that a general conspiracy existed among the Moors to rise upon the Government, to institute a general massacre, and, with the assistance of their allies and relatives on the Barbary coast, to re-establish the empire of the infidels.[13]

A convoy of eighty ass-loads of oil on the way to Madrid had halted at a wayside inn. A few flasks were stolen, and those who consumed it were made sick. Some of the thieves even died, or were said to have died, in consequence.[14] Instantly the rumour flew from mouth to mouth, from town to town, that the royal family, the court, the whole capital, all Spain, were to be poisoned with that oil. If such were the scheme it was certainly a less ingenious one than the famous plot by which the Spanish Government was suspected but a few years before to have so nearly succeeded in blowing the king, peers, and commons of England into the air.

The proof of Moorish guilt was deemed all-sufficient, especially as it was supported by supernatural evidence of the most portentous and convincing kind. For several days together a dark cloud, tinged with blood-red, had been seen to hang over Valencia.[15]

---

[13] Giro. Soranzo.   [14] Ibid.   [15] Ibid., and notes of N. Barozzi.

In the neighbourhood of Daroca, a din of drums and trumpets and the clang of arms had been heard in the sky, just as a procession went out of a monastery.[16]

At Valencia the image of the Virgin had shed tears. In another place her statue had been discovered in a state of profuse perspiration.[17]

What more conclusive indications could be required as to the guilt of the Moors? What other means devised for saving crown, church, and kingdom from destruction but to expel the whole mass of unbelievers from the soil which they had too long profaned?

Archbishop Ribera was fully sustained by the Archbishop of Toledo, and the whole ecclesiastical body received energetic support from Government.

Ribera had solemnly announced that the Moors were so greedy of money, so determined to keep it, and so occupied with pursuits most apt for acquiring it, that they had come to be the sponge of Spanish wealth. The best proof of this, continued the reverend sage, was that, inhabiting in general poor little villages and sterile tracts of country, paying to the lords of the manor one third of the crops, and being overladen with special taxes imposed only upon them, they nevertheless became rich, while the Christians, cultivating the most fertile land, were in abject poverty.[18]

It seems almost incredible that this should not be satire. Certainly the most delicate irony could not portray the vicious institutions under which the magnificent territory and noble people of Spain were thus doomed to ruin more subtly and forcibly than was done by the honest brutality of this churchman. The careful tillage, the beautiful system of irrigation by aqueduct and canal, the scientific processes by which these "accursed" had caused the wilderness to bloom with cotton, sugar, and every kind of fruit and grain ; the untiring industry, exquisite ingenuity, and cultivated taste by

<hr>

[16] Giro. Soranzo, and notes of N. Barozzi.
[17] Ibid.

[18] Escriba, Vida de Don Juan de Ribera, papel segundo, quoted by Lafuente, xv. 370-390.

which the merchants, manufacturers, and mechanics, guilty of a darker complexion than that of the peninsular Goths, had enriched their native land with splendid fabrics in cloth, paper, leather, silk, tapestry, and by so doing had acquired fortunes for themselves, despite iniquitous taxation, religious persecution, and social contumely—all these were crimes against a race of idlers, steeped to the lips in sloth which imagined itself to be pride.

The industrious, the intelligent, the wealthy, were denounced as criminals, and hunted to death or into exile as vermin, while the Lermas, the Ucedas, and the rest of the brood of cormorants, settled more thickly than ever around their prey.

Meantime, Government declared that the piece of four maravedis should be worth eight maravedis ; the piece of two maravedis being fixed at four.[19] Thus the specie of the kingdom was to be doubled, and by means of this enlightened legislation, Spain, after destroying agriculture, commerce, and manufacture, was to maintain great armies and navies, and establish universal monarchy.

This measure, which a wiser churchman than Ribera, Cardinal Richelieu, afterwards declared the most audacious and barbarous ever recorded by history, was carried out with great regularity of organization.[20] It was ordained that the Moors should be collected at three indicated points, whence they were not to move on pain of death, until duly escorted by troops to the ports of embarkation. The children under the age of four years were retained, of course without their parents, from whom they were forever separated. With admirable forethought, too, the priests took measures, as they supposed, that the arts of refining sugar, irrigating the rice-fields, constructing canals and aqueducts, besides many other useful branches of agricultural and mechanical business, should not die out with the intellectual, accomplished, and industrious race, alone competent to practise them, which was now sent forth to die. A very small number, not

---

[19] Lafuente, Hist. Gen. de España, xv. 295.
[20] Mem. de Richelieu, x. 231, cited by Lafuente, ubi sup.

more than six in each hundred, were accordingly reserved to instruct other inhabitants of Spain in those useful arts which they were now more than ever encouraged to despise.

Five hundred thousand full-grown human beings, as energetic, ingenious, accomplished, as any then existing in the world, were thus thrust forth into the deserts beyond sea, as if Spain had been overstocked with skilled labour, and as if its native production had already outgrown the world's power of consumption.

Had an equal number of mendicant monks, with the two archbishops who had contrived this deed at their head, been exported instead of the Moors, the future of Spain might have been a more fortunate one than it was likely to prove. The event was in itself perhaps of temporary advantage to the Dutch republic, as the poverty and general misery, aggravated by this disastrous policy, rendered the acknowledgment of the States' independence by Spain almost a matter of necessity.[21]

It is superfluous to enter into any farther disquisiton as to the various branches of the royal revenue. They remained essentially the same as during the preceding reign, and have been elaborately set forth in a previous chapter. The gradual drying up of resources in all the wide-spread and heterogeneous territories subject to the Spanish sceptre is the striking phenomenon of the present epoch. The distribution of such wealth as was still created followed the same laws which had long prevailed, while the decay and national paralysis, of which the prognostics could hardly be mistaken, were a natural result of the system.

The six archbishops had now grown to eleven,[22] and still received gigantic revenues ; the income of the Archbishop of Toledo, including the fund of one hundred thousand destined for repairing the cathedral, being estimated at three hundred thousand dollars a year, that of the Archbishop of

---

[21] Girᵒ. Soranzo, Relazione. The ambassador expressly states it as a fact. Compare especially Lafuente's admirable history of Spain, vol. xv. 294, 295, *seqq.*, 370-394.
[22] Ibid.

Seville and the others varying from one hundred and fifty thousand dollars to fifty thousand.[23] The sixty-three bishops perhaps averaged fifty thousand a year each,[24] and there were eight more in Italy.[25]

The commanderies of chivalry, two hundred at least in number, were likewise enormously profitable. Some of them were worth thirty thousand a year; the aggregate annual value being from one-and-a-half to two millions, and all in Lerma's gift, upon his own terms.[26]

Chivalry, that noblest of ideals, without which, in some shape or another, the world would be a desert and a sty; which included within itself many of the noblest virtues which can adorn mankind—generosity, self-denial, chastity, frugality, patience, protection to the feeble, the down-trodden, and the oppressed; the love of daring adventure, devotion to a pure religion and a lofty purpose, most admirably pathetic, even when in the eyes of the vulgar most fantastic—had been the proudest and most poetical of Spanish characteristics, never to be entirely uprooted from the national heart.

Alas! what was there in the commanderies of Calatrava, Alcantara, Santiago, and all the rest of those knightly orders, as then existing, to respond to the noble sentiments on which all were supposed to be founded? Institutions for making money, for pillaging the poor of their hard-earned pittance, trafficked in by greedy ministers and needy courtiers with a shamelessness which had long ceased to blush at vices however gross, at venality however mean.

Venality was in truth the prominent characteristic of the Spanish polity at this epoch. Everything political or ecclesiastical, from highest to lowest, was matter of merchandize.

It was the autocrat, governing king and kingdom, who disposed of episcopal mitres, cardinals' hats, commanders' crosses, the offices of regidores or municipal magistrates in

[23] S. Contarini, Relazione. Fran. Priuli.   [24] Ibid.   [25] Ibid.
[26] Ibid. Giro. Soranzo. "Essendo capaci li maritati e ogni altra condizione di persone non eccettuate le donne."

all the cities, farmings of revenues, collectorships of taxes, at prices fixed by himself.

It was never known that the pope refused to confirm the ecclesiastical nominations which were made by the Spanish court.

The nuncius had the privilege of dispensing the small cures from thirty dollars a year downwards,[27] of which the number was enormous. Many of these were capable, in careful hands, of becoming ten times as valuable as their nominal estimate,[28] and the business in them became in consequence very extensive and lucrative. They were often disposed of for the benefit of servants and the hangers-on of noble families, to laymen, to women, children, to babes unborn.

When such was the most thriving industry in the land, was it wonderful that the poor of high and low degree were anxious in ever-increasing swarms to effect their entrance into convent, monastery, and church, and that trade, agriculture, and manufactures languished?

The foreign polity of the court remained as it had been established by Philip II.

Its maxims were very simple. To do unto your neighbour all possible harm, and to foster the greatness of Spain by sowing discord and maintaining civil war in all other nations, was the fundamental precept. To bribe and corrupt the servants of other potentates, to maintain a regular paid body of adherents in foreign lands, ever ready to engage in schemes of assassination, conspiracy, sedition, and rebellion against the legitimate authority, to make mankind miserable, so far as it was in the power of human force or craft to produce wretchedness, were objects still faithfully pursued.[29]

[27] F Soranzo.   [28] Ibid.

[29] " In Francia medesimamente procurava col tener le provincie disunite, divise le forze, separati gli animi, diffidenti i pensieri, ribellati i principi, sollevati i popoli e tirando per questa via le cose al lungo di stancare e si fosse potuto di ridurre in niente le forze di quella corona . . . . la prima giova alla Spagna per conservarsi, procurando di tener lontane le sedizioni nei proprii regni e di nutrire le discordie negli altri potentati . . . e vedendo che questo imperio non è appoggiato alle richezze de' grandi chi pochissimi sono che non siano in qualche via consumati, non alle speranze dei popoli perchè questi con le molte gravezze sono oppresse, non alle armi poiche propria milizia che

They had not yet led to the entire destruction of other realms and their submission to the single sceptre of Spain, nor had they developed the resources, material or moral, of a mighty empire so thoroughly as might have been done perhaps by a less insidious policy, but they had never been abandoned.

It was a steady object of policy to keep such potentates of Italy as were not already under the dominion of the Spanish crown in a state of internecine feud with each other and of virtual dependence on the powerful kingdom. The same policy pursued in France, of fomenting civil war by subsidy, force, and chicane, during a long succession of years in order to reduce that magnificent realm under the sceptre of Philip, has been described in detail. The chronic rebellion of Ireland against the English crown had been assisted and inflamed in every possible mode, the system being considered as entirely justified by the aid and comfort afforded by the queen to the Dutch rebels.

It was a natural result of the system according to which kingdoms and provinces with the populations dwelling therein were transferable like real estate by means of marriage-settlements, entails, and testaments, that the proprietorship of most of the great realms in Christendom was matter of fierce legal dispute. Lawsuits, which in chancery could last for centuries before a settlement of the various claims was made, might have infinitely enriched the gentlemen of the long robe and reduced all the parties to beggary, had there been any tribunal but the battle-field to decide among the august litigants. Thus the King of Great Britain claimed the legal proprietorship and sovereignty of Brittany, Normandy, Anjou, Gascony, Calais, and Boulogne in France, besides the whole kingdom by right of conquest.[30] The French king claimed to be rightful

sia disciplinata non tiene la Spagna . . . . si può affirmare che resti il principale fondamento di questo imperio collocato negli travagli nella debolezza e divisione degli altri potentati," &c. &c.—F. Soranzo.

[30] Niccolo Molin, Ambasc. appresso Giacomo I. 1607, in Barozzi and Berchet, Ser. IV. vol. i. Pietro Priuli, Ambasc. in Francia, 1608. Ibid.

heir of Castile, Biscay, Guipuscoa, Arragon, Navarre, nearly all the Spanish peninsula in short, including the whole of Portugal and the Balearic islands to boot.[31] The King of Spain claimed, as we have seen often enough, not only Brittany but all France as his lawful inheritance. Such was the virtue of the prevalent doctrine of proprietorship. Every potentate was defrauded of his rights, and every potentate was a criminal usurper. As for the people, it would have excited a smile of superior wisdom on regal, legal, or sacerdotal lips, had it been suggested that by any possibility the governed could have a voice or a thought in regard to the rulers whom God in His grace had raised up to be their proprietors and masters.

The army of Spain was sunk far below the standard at which it had been kept when it seemed fit to conquer and govern the world. Neither by Spain nor Italy could those audacious, disciplined, and obedient legions be furnished,[32] at which the enemies of the mighty despot trembled from one extremity of earth to the other. Peculation, bankruptcy, and mutiny had done their work at last. We have recently had occasion to observe the conduct of the veterans in Flanders at critical epochs. At this moment, seventy thousand soldiers were on the muster and pay roll of the army serving in those provinces, while not thirty thousand men existed in the flesh.

The navy was sunk to fifteen or twenty old galleys, battered, dismantled, unseaworthy, and a few armed ships for convoying the East and West Indiamen to and from their destinations.[33]

The general poverty was so great that it was often absolutely impossible to purchase food for the royal household.[34] "If you ask me," said a cool observer, "how this great show of empire is maintained, when the funds are so small, I answer that it is done by not paying at all."[35] The Govern-

[31] P. Priuli, *ubi sup.*
[32] S. Contarini, Relazione. "Perchè la Spagna si trova spopolata." [33] Ibid.
[34] Ibid. "Momenti nei quali le mense reali mancavano del necessario onde cibarsi." [35] Ibid.

ment was shamelessly, hopelessly bankrupt. The noble band of courtiers were growing enormously rich. The state was a carcase which unclean vultures were picking to the bones.

The foremost man in the land—the autocrat, the absolute master in State and Church—was the Duke of Lerma.[36]

Very rarely in human history has an individual attained to such unlimited power under a monarchy, without actually placing the crown upon his own head. Mayors of the palace, in the days of the do-nothing kings, wielded nothing like the imperial control which was firmly held by this great favourite. Yet he was a man of very moderate capacity and limited acquirements, neither soldier, lawyer, nor priest.

The duke was past sixty years of age, a tall, stately, handsome man, of noble presence and urbane manner. Born of the patrician house of Sandoval, he possessed, on the accession of Philip, an inherited income of ten or twelve thousand dollars. He had now, including what he had bestowed on his son, a funded revenue of seven hundred thousand a year.[37] He had besides, in cash, jewels, and furniture, an estimated capital of six millions.[38] All this he had accumulated in ten years of service, as prime minister, chief equerry, and first valet of the chamber to the king.

The tenure of his authority was the ascendancy of a firm character over a very weak one. At this moment he was doubtless the most absolute ruler in Christendom, and Philip III. the most submissive and uncomplaining of his subjects.[39]

[36] Francesco Soranzo, Relazione di Spagna Ambasciatore dall' anno 1597–1602, in Barozzi and Berchet, Serie I. vol. i. pp. 1–214. Otto. Bon, Ambasciatore strao. a Filippo III. nel 1602, Relazione. Ibid. Ser I. vol. i., pp. 215–275. S. Contarini, Ambasc. a Filippo III. 1602–1604 Ibid. Ser. I. vol. i. pp. 277–337. F. Priuli. Ambasc. a Filippo III. 1604–1608. Ibid. Ser. I. vol. i. pp. 339–402. Giro. Soranzo, Ambasc. a Filippo III. 1608–1611. Ibid. Ser. I. vol. i. pp. 431–492.

[37] Giro. Soranzo. [38] Ibid.
[39] Ed in questo Duca si può dire che sia ridotta la somma di tutto il governo, la dispensa delle grazie e tutto il bene ed il male di chi pretende alcuna cosa a quelle corte, perchè e veramente senza esempio l'autorità e la grazia che egli possiede appresso il re; anzi che per ottenere quello che si pretende importa più l'aver favorevole il Duca di Lerma che quasi il re medesimo," &c., &c.—F. Soranzo.
" E che finalmente tutte le cose si riducono alla volontà ed all' autorità

The origin of his power was well known. During the reign of Philip II., the prince, treated with great severity by his father, was looked upon with contempt by every one about court. He was allowed to take no part in affairs, and, having heard of the awful tragedy of his eldest half-brother, enacted ten years before his own birth, he had no inclination to confront the wrath of that terrible parent and sovereign before whom all Spain trembled. Nothing could have been more humble, more effaced, more obscure, than his existence as prince.[40] The Marquis of Denia, his chamberlain, alone was kind to him, furnished him with small sums of money, and accompanied him on the shooting excursions in which his father occasionally permitted him to indulge.[41] But even these little attentions were looked upon with jealousy by the king ; so that the marquis was sent into honourable exile from court as governor of Valencia.[42] It was hoped that absence would wean the prince of his affection for the kind chamberlain. The calculation was erroneous. No sooner were the eyes of Philip II. closed in death than the new king made haste to send for Denia, who was at once created Duke of Lerma, declared of the privy council, and appointed master

del duca e gli altri consiglieri attendono non meno al insinuarsi nelle grazie di S. E. che alli loro proprii interessi in modo che si può dire che questo re sia assolutamente governato e che la maggiore parte delli ministri più principali, per non dire tutti, attendino fuori dell' ordinario al proprio bene."—Otto. Bon. Relazione.

" Dal che nasce il potere che tiene sopra di lui il privato che lo governa. Sarà difficile d' ottenere la volontà di questo principe perchè il privato lo tiene in suo potere fino dai primi anni della sua gioventù. Il potere di lui si conserva intieramente nella persona del Duca di Lerma."—S. Contarini, Relazione.

" Questo re viene retto da un solo servitore. In questo regno il padrone non ha parte di niente."—F. Priuli.

" Il Duca di Lerma, erminentissimo ed assoluto signore di quel governo .... si ha impossessato della volontà

di S. M. che ne è oggidi talmente signore che domina e regge il tutto ai suoi cenni. Assoluto maestro e dispensatore delle grazie regie, egli assegna tutti i vescovati e commende, egli fa i cardinali che sono nominati dal rè di Spagna ed è libero signore e padrone di tutta la corona reale." Giro. Soranzo, Relazione.

" Essendo il Duca così accorto ed avendo così ben disposto a suo gusto il governo del palazzo e circondato il semplice re da suoi dependenti ch' oltre il non esser possibile che alcuno gli parli senza sua saputa quando anco gli fosse parlato da chi si voglia sa tutto quello che gli viene detto da che segue che non è persona per grande per importante che sia che avesse tant' animo di svegliare il rè che non temesse di pagare subito con la sua rovina la pena del suo ardire." Otto. Bon Relazione.

[40] F. Sorenzo.   [41] Ibid.   [42] Ibid.

of the horse and first gentleman of the bed-chamber. From that moment the favourite became supreme. He was entirely without education, possessed little experience in affairs of state, and had led the life of a commonplace idler and voluptuary until past the age of fifty. Nevertheless he had a shrewd mother-wit, tact in dealing with men, aptitude to take advantage of events. He had directness of purpose, firmness of will, and always knew his own mind. From the beginning of his political career unto its end, he conscientiously and without swerving pursued a single aim. This was to rob the exchequer by every possible mode and at every instant of his life. Never was a more masterly financier in this respect. With a single eye to his own interests, he preserved a magnificent unity in all his actions. The result had been to make him in ten years the richest subject in the world, as well as the most absolute ruler.

He enriched his family, as a matter of course. His son was already made Duke of Uceda, possessed enormous wealth, and was supposed by those who had vision in the affairs of court to be the only individual ever likely to endanger the power of the father. Others thought that the young duke's natural dulness would make it impossible for him to supplant the omnipotent favourite.[43] The end was not yet, and time was to show which class of speculators was in the right. Meantime the whole family was united and happy. The sons and daughters had intermarried with the Infantados, and other most powerful and wealthy families of grandees.[44] The uncle, Sandoval, had been created by Lerma a cardinal and archbishop of Toledo ;[45] the king's own schoolmaster being removed from that dignity, and disgraced and banished from court for having spoken disrespectfully of the favourite.[46] The duke had reserved for himself twenty thousand a year from the revenues of the archbishopric,[47] as a moderate price for thus conducting himself as became a dutiful nephew. He had ejected Rodrigo de

---

[43] " Ma l'ottusità sua non lo renderà mai atto a un tanto carico."— F. Priuli.

[44] Otto. Bon.

[45] F. Soranzo.

[46] S. Contarini. F. Soranzo.

[47] F. Priuli, Relazione.

Vasquez from his post as president of the council.[48] As a more conclusive proof of his unlimited sway than any other of his acts had been, he had actually unseated and banished the inquisitor-general, Don Pietro Porto Carrero,[49] and supplanted him in that dread office, before which even anointed sovereigns trembled, by one of his own creatures.

In the discharge of his various functions, the duke and all his family were domesticated in the royal palace, so that he was at no charges for housekeeping. His apartments there were more sumptuous than those of the king and queen.[50] He had removed from court the Dutchess of Candia,[51] sister of the great Constable of Castile, who had been for a time in attendance on the queen, and whose possible influence he chose to destroy in the bud. Her place as mistress of the robes was supplied by his sister, the Countess of Lemos ; while his wife, the terrible Duchess of Lerma, was constantly with the queen, who trembled at her frown. Thus the royal pair were completely beleaguered, surrounded, and isolated from all except the Lermas.[52] When the duke conferred with the king, the doors were always double locked.[53]

In his capacity as first valet[54] it was the duke's duty to bring the king's shirt in the morning, to see to his wardrobe and his bed, and to supply him with ideas for the day. The king depended upon him entirely and abjectly, was miserable when separated from him four-and-twenty hours, thought with the duke's thoughts and saw with the duke's eyes. He

[48] F. Soranzo.   [49] Ibid.
[50] Otto. Bon, Relazione. " Tanto suntuosi da abbagliare quelli del re stesso."—S. Contarini.
[51] F. Soranzo.
[52] Ibid. " Vi saria anco la regina che potria e sapria svegliarlo per la comodità ma è lei ancora *tenuta oppressa* dalla Duchessa e dal medesimo Duca suo marito che non *può nè parlare nè respirare* e poi conoscendo il re di tanta semplicità como è veramente e vedendolo esser così innamorato del Duca si crede che temi prima di non fare frutto e poi di esser scoperta da S. M. al medesimo Duca da che ne potesse seguire mala disposizione tra loro tanta è in particolare la Duchessa terribile e formidabile il favore del Duca. In tanto che il povero Re per esser di natura poco atto al governare è circondato, sta e starà sempre così dormendo se non è svegliato di qualche gran rovina che estraordinariamente lo punga e che insieme necessiti una buona mano de soggetti grandi a sollevarlo ed a liberare tutto il governo da così violenta oppressione," &c. &c.— Otto. Bon, Relazione.
[53] S. Contarini, Relazione.
[54] " Somiglier del corpo. L'Uffizio del somiglier del corpo consiste nell' aver cura dei vestiti del re e del suo letto."—S. Contarini.

was permitted to know nothing of state affairs, save such portions as were communicated to him by Lerma. The people thought their monarch bewitched, so much did he tremble before the favourite, and so unscrupulously did the duke appropriate for his own benefit and that of his creatures everything that he could lay his hands upon. It would have needed little to bring about a revolution, such was the universal hatred felt for the minister, and the contempt openly expressed for the king.[55]

The duke never went to the council. All papers and documents relating to business were sent to his apartments. Such matters as he chose to pass upon, such decrees as he thought proper to issue, were then taken by him to the king, who signed them with perfect docility.[56] As time went on, this amount of business grew too onerous for the royal hand, or this amount of participation by the king in affairs of state came to be esteemed superfluous and inconvenient by the duke, and his own signature was accordingly declared to be equivalent to that of the sovereign's sign-manual. It is doubtful whether such a degradation of the royal prerogative had ever been heard of before in a Christian monarch.[57]

It may be imagined that this system of government was not of a nature to expedite business, however swiftly it might fill the duke's coffers. High officers of state, foreign ambas-

---

[55] " Il volgo si esprime dicendo che il rè fu stregato, altri che trema del su favorito . . vi vorrebbe poco per far nascere una revoluzione . il duca di Lerma prende per se e per i suoi quello che più gli pare e piace, l' odio del popolo è tanto grande verso il duca per il mal uso del suo potere come verso il re a cagione della sua debolezza."—S. Contarini

"Hat diese wenige Jahre für ihn und die Seinigen das gras wol geschnitten und so vil dasz ich mirs nicht trauwe zu schreiben, denn es mehr ein Gedicht als der Wahrheit gleich sieht und doch in re ipsa ist."—Khevenhüller, Ann. Ferd vi. 3041.

"Parlano del re in guisa che non oso riferirlo perche lo tengono in assai poca considerazione e perche fa tutto quello che vuole il duca di Lerma."—Ibid

[56] Ottaviano Bon, Relazione. Giro. Soranzo. S. Contarini, relazione. F. Priuli. " Rimettendoli quasi tutti al duca senza vederli."

[57] " La segnatura del duca di Lerma fu dal re parificata alla propria, esempio unico nella storia delle monarchie," says N. Barozzi, citing Relatione della vita del re Filippo III. e delli suoi favoriti.—MS. della Biblioteca reale di Berlino. (Barozzi and Berchet, s. i. vi. p. 288.) See also Lafuente, xv 294, s. 99.

" Dasz er absolutus Dominus kann genannt werden." — Khevenhüller, Annal. Ferdin. vi. 3041.

sadors, all men in short charged with important affairs, were obliged to dance attendance for weeks and months on the one man whose hands grasped all the business of the kingdom, while many departed in despair without being able to secure a single audience. It was entirely a matter of trade. It was necessary to bribe in succession all the creatures of the duke before getting near enough to headquarters to bribe the duke himself.[58] Never were such itching palms. To do business at court required the purse of Fortunatus. There was no deception in the matter. Everything was frank and above board in that age of chivalry. Ambassadors wrote to their sovereigns that there was no hope of making treaties or of accomplishing any negotiation except by purchasing the favour of the autocrat ;[59] and Lerma's price was always high. At one period the republic of Venice wished to put a stop to the depredations by Spanish pirates upon Venetian commerce, but the subject could not even be approached by the envoy until he had expended far more than could be afforded out of his meagre salary in buying an interview.[60]

[58] "'E che per fargli capitar polizze o d' udienzia o di negozio bisogna durar fatica di settimane entiere ed andar a diverse mani con favori straordinarii e per aver la risposta poi bisogna alle volte star a quella discrezione che mai viene," &c. &c.—Ottᵒ. Bon, Relazione.

"In modo che per la suprema autorità che lui tiene appresso S. M. (la qual non vede ni ricerca nè fa mai di più di quello che le vien detto e portato da esso duca) in suo potere sta l' espedire quello che comporta il suo interesse."—Ibid.

"Ogni principe o cavaliere avendo qualsivoglia interesse colla corona concorre con richissimi presenti e doni .... e non vi è ministro o rappresentate regio che non profondi per mantenere lo ben affetto e per goder l'autorità della sua intercessione."—G. Soranzo.

"Ottiene dal re ciò che vuole; ha avuto finora beni, commende, entrate donativi per la casa e per la persona sua pel valore di più di due milioni d'oro e ne averà quanti vorrà, e quante ne porterà l'occasione ; perciocchè oltre quelle mercedi che le sono fatte dal re che sono grandissime, la libertà ch' ha di accettar presenti lo farà opulentissimo, perchè non è chi pretenda in corte cosa di momento che passando necessariamente per mano del duca non lo presenta largamente, come si fa anco con gran parte di questi ministri novelli, che tutti però si vanno facendo richissimi."—F. Soranzo.

[59] F. Soranzo. Ottᵒ. Bon, Relaz.

[60] Ottᵒ. Bon, Relazione. The small amount of salary paid by the Venetian republic to its envoys, who had the rank of ambassador at all the principal courts, and were expected to live in as splendid style as did the better paid ministers of other powers, was a perpetual subject of complaint. Some of the royal ambassadors had five hundred dollars a month, a few had a thousand dollars a month, while the diplomatic agent (who was not ambassador) of the Grand Duke of Florence in France had a larger salary than that of the Venetian ambassador at the same court. "We are equal to royal ambassadors in dignity," said

When it is remembered that with this foremost power in
the world affairs of greater or less importance were perpetually
to be transacted by the representatives of other nations as
well as by native subjects of every degree ; that all these
affairs were to pass through the hands of Lerma, and that
those hands had ever to be filled with coin, the stupendous
opulence of the one man can be easily understood. Whether
the foremost power of the world, thus governed, were likely to
continue the foremost power, could hardly seem doubtful to
those accustomed to use their reason in judging of the things
of this world.[61]

Meantime the duke continued to transact business ; to sell
his interviews and his interest ; to traffic in cardinals' hats,
bishops' mitres, judges' ermine, civic and magisterial votes in
all offices, high or humble, of church, army, or state.

He possessed the art of remembering, or appearing to
remember, the matters of business which had been communicated to him. When a negotiator, of whatever degree, had
the good fortune to reach the presence, he found the duke to
all appearance mindful of the particular affair which led to

Badoer ; "we are obliged to approxi-
mate to them in expense ; one of three
things must therefore happen : our
salary must be increased over the sum
fixed sixty years ago, which averages
only one hundred and seventy miserable dollars a month, or the richest
citizens of the republic must always be
selected to fill all the embassies, or
persons must be made use of for the
posts who will prejudice the esteem
and service of this most serene republic. The esteem, because they
must suffer the thousand indignities
which are caused by contempt; the
service, because they will not be able
to make their way towards matters of
business and information which now-a-
days can only be done all over the
world with money."—A. Badoer, Relazione di Francia in Barozzi and Berchet, Serie II. vol. i. p. 168.

[61] "Questi sono tutti quelli che
governano questa gran macchina, la
maggiore parte de quali si lascia vincere e dominare dall' avarizia e per
ciò sono applicati a ricever volontieri

presenti e come presidenti dei consigli
liberamente vendono la maggior parte
delle vacanze e le volontà loro istesse
e con l'esempio di questi, gl' inferiori
che sono ad essi subordinati s' acco-
modano all' istesso e in questo tutto
sono talmente domesticati ed accordati
che sapendolo il rè e non lo proibendo
anzi approvandolo con il dare licenza
a quello che glielo domandano di
poter ricever da qualche soggetto cos-
picuo gran somma nelli negozii non si
cammina d' altra maniera nè par altra
via s' ottiene oggidì giustizia e favori
a quella corte e non mancano li mezzi
a quest' affetto ordinati e conosciuti da
tutti."—Ottᵒ. Bon, Relazione. Compare S. Contarini, Relazione. "Non
e difficile regalare il duca di Lerma.
Egli fa, sciogle ed ordina tutto quello
che vuole," &c. "They toss causes
from one to another like tennis balls,"
wrote Cornwallis from Madrid. "A
man may lawfully say here, non est qui
facit bonum, non usque ad unum. God
Almighty deliver me from amongst
them."—Winwood, II. 312.

the interview, and fully absorbed by its importance.[62] There were men who, trusting to the affability shown by the great favourite, and to the handsome price paid down in cash for that urbanity, had been known to go away from their interview believing that their business was likely to be accomplished, until the lapse of time revealed to them the wildness of their dream.

The duke perhaps never manifested his omnipotence on a more striking scale than when by his own fiat he removed the court and the seat of government to Valladolid, and kept it there six years long.[63] This was declared by disinterested observers to be not only contrary to common sense, but even beyond the bounds of possibility.[64] At Madrid the king had splendid palaces, and in its neighbourhood beautiful country residences, a pure atmosphere, and the facility of changing the air at will. At Valladolid there were no conveniences of any kind, no sufficient palace, no summer villa, no park, nothing but an unwholesome climate.[65] But most of the duke's estates were in that vicinity, and it was desirable for him to overlook them in person.[63] Moreover, he wished to get rid of the possible influence over the king of the Empress Dowager Maria, widow of Maximilian II. and aunt and grandmother of Philip III.[67] The minister could hardly drive this exalted personage from court, so easily as he had banished the ex-Archbishop of Toledo, the Inquisitor-General, the Duchess of Candia, besides a multitude of lesser note. So he did the next best thing, and banished the court from the empress, who was not likely to put up with the

---

[62] F. Soranzo.

[63] F. Soranzo. F. Priuli. "Essendo asceso tanto il credito appresso S.M. che teme di contradirgli e perciò guidato da' suoi interessi si lasciò persuadere a condurre la corte in Valladolid tenendove la vicino a sei anni contra il senso commune e quasi contro al possibile per l' incapacità del luogo."

[64] F. Priuli.   [65] F. Soranzo.

[66] Ibid. "I fear some evil event to that duke," wrote Cornwallis, "whose immoderate desires of his own particu-

lar interests draw him to precipitate himself into the gulf of envy and malediction of the people, by leading a king in such an unfitting sort after him, with manifest neglect of the important affairs of his kingdom, and disregard of what belongs to his kingly office. The wisest say here, according to our English proverb, that hell is broken loose." Winwood, II. 395.

[67] Ibid. She was sister of Philip II. Her daughter Anna was Philip II.'s fourth wife, and mother of Philip III.

inconveniences of Valladolid for the sake of outrivalling the duke. This Babylonian captivity lasted until Madrid was nearly ruined, until the desolation of the capital, the moans of the tradespeople, the curses of the poor, and the grumblings of the courtiers, finally produced an effect even upon the arbitrary Lerma.[68] He then accordingly re-emigrated, with king and Government, to Madrid, and caused it to be published that he had at last overcome the sovereign's repugnance to the old capital, and had persuaded him to abandon Valladolid.[69]

There was but one man who might perhaps from his position have competed with the influence of Lerma. This was the king's father-confessor, whom Philip wished—although of course his wish was not gratified—to make a member of the council of state.[70] The monarch, while submitting in everything secular to the duke's decrees, had a feeble determination to consult and to be guided by his confessor in all matters of conscience. As it was easy to suggest that high affairs of state, the duties of government, the interests of a great people, were matters not entirely foreign to the conscience of anointed kings, an opening to power might have seemed easy to an astute and ambitious churchman. But the Dominican who kept Philip's conscience, Gasparo de Cordova by name,[71] was, fortunately for the favourite, of a very tender paste, easily moulded to the duke's purpose. Dull and ignorant enough, he was not so stupid as to doubt that, should he whisper any suggestions or criticisms in regard to the minister's proceedings, the king would betray him and he would lose his office.[72] The cautious friar accordingly held his peace and his place, and there was none to dispute the sway of the autocrat.

What need to dilate further upon such a minister and upon

---

[68] Priuli. F. Soranzo.
[69] Ibid. [70] F. Soranzo. [71] Ibid.
[72] "Ed il confessore, che è quello che parlando al re di secreto potria avvertirlo, è di pasta così tenera, di così poco intendimento, del tutto ignaro del governo di stato ed incapace di tutte le cose grandi che non sapria farlo e forse per il timore che il re stesso non lo palesasse a S. E. dal che non seguisse la sua total depressione."
—Otto Bon, Relazione.

such a system of government ?   To bribe and to be bribed, to maintain stipendiaries in every foreign Government, to place the greatness of the empire upon the weakness, distraction, and misery of other nations, to stimulate civil war, revolts of nobles and citizens against authority; separation of provinces, religious discontents in every land of Christendom—such were the simple rules ever faithfully enforced.

The other members of what was called the council were insignificant.

Philip III., on arriving at the throne, had been heard to observe that the day of simple esquires and persons of low condition was past, and that the turn of great nobles had come.[73] It had been his father's policy to hold the grandees in subjection, and to govern by means of ministers who were little more than clerks, generally of humble origin ; keeping the reins in his own hands. Such great personages as he did employ, like Alva, Don John of Austria, and Farnese, were sure at last to excite his jealousy and to incur his hatred. Forty-three years of this kind of work had brought Spain to the condition in which the third Philip found it. The new king thought to have found a remedy in discarding the clerks, and calling in the aid of dukes. Philip II. was at least a king. The very first act of Philip III. at his father's death was to abdicate.

It was, however, found necessary to retain some members of the former Government. Fuentes, the best soldier and accounted the most dangerous man in the empire, was indeed kept in retirement as governor of Milan, while Cristoval di Mora, who had enjoyed much of the late king's confidence, was removed to Portugal as viceroy. But Don John of Idiaquez, who had really been the most efficient of the old administration, still remained in the council. Without the subordinate aid of his experience in the routine of business, it would have been difficult for the favourite to manage the great machine with his single hand. But there was no disposition on the part of the ancient minister to oppose the new order of things.

[73] F. Soranzo, Relazione.   "Scudieri, certa bassa taglia d'uomini."

A cautious, caustic, dry old functionary, talking more with his shoulders than with his tongue,[74] determined never to commit himself, or to risk shipwreck by venturing again into deeper waters than those of the harbour in which he now hoped for repose, Idiaquez knew that his day of action was past. Content to be confidential clerk to the despot duke, as he had been faithful secretary to the despot king, he was the despair of courtiers and envoys who came to pump, after having endeavoured to fill an inexhaustible cistern. Thus he proved, on the whole, a useful and comfortable man, not to the country, but to its autocrat.

Of the Count of Chinchon, who at one time was supposed to have court influence because a dabbler in architecture, much consulted during the building of the Escorial by Philip II. until the auditing of his accounts brought him into temporary disgrace,[75] and the Marquises of Velada, Villalonga, and other ministers, it is not necessary to speak. There was one man in the council, however, who was of great importance, wielding a mighty authority in subordination to the duke. This was Don Pietro de Franqueza.[76] An emancipated slave, as his name indicated, and subsequently the body-servant of Lerma, he had been created by that minister secretary of the privy council. He possessed some of the virtues of the slave, such as docility and attachment to the hand that had fed and scourged him, and many vices of both slave and freedman. He did much of the work which it would have been difficult for the duke to accomplish in person, received his fees, sold and dispensed his interviews, distributed his bribes. In so doing, as might be supposed, he did not neglect his own interest. It was a matter of notoriety, no man knowing it better than the king, that no business, foreign or domestic, could be conducted or even begun at court without large preliminary fees to the secretary of the council,

---

[74] "In modo che è conosciuto da tutti per testa secca e che poco possa ad altri che al rè solo giovare . . . . l' ho provato tanto cauto avido e riservato che alle volte più mi rispondeva con le spalle che con la bocca."— Otto. Bon, Relazione.

[75] F. Soranzo, Relazione.

[76] Otto. Bon, Relazione.

his wife, and his children. He had, in consequence, already accumulated an enormous fortune. His annual income, when it was stated, excited amazement. He was insolent and over-bearing to all comers until his dues had been paid, when he became at once obliging, supple, and comparatively efficient. Through him alone lay the path to the duke's sanctuary.[77]

The nominal sovereign, Philip III., was thirty years of age. A very little man, with pink cheeks, flaxen hair, and yellow beard, with a melancholy expression of eye, and protruding under lip and jaw, he was now comparatively alert and vigorous in constitution, although for the first seven years of his life it had been doubtful whether he would live from week to week.[78] He had been afflicted during that period with a chronic itch or leprosy, which had undermined his strength, but which had almost entirely disappeared as he advanced in life.[79]

He was below mediocrity in mind,[80] and had received scarcely any education. He had been taught to utter a few phrases, more or less intelligible, in French, Italian, and Flemish, but was quite incapable of sustaining a conversation in either of those languages.[81] When a child, he had learned and subsequently forgotten the rudiments of the Latin grammar.[82]

These acquirements, together with the catechism and the offices of the Church, made up his whole stock of erudition. That he was devout as a monk of the middle ages, conforming daily and hourly to religious ceremonies, need scarcely be stated. It was not probable that the son of Philip II. would be a delinquent to church observances. He was not deficient in courage, rode well, was fond of hunting, kept

---

[77] Ott⁰. Bon, Relazione. " Di bassis-sima condizione, nato d' uno schiavo fatto libero che ha conservato e portato il nome di franqueza," &c. &c.

[78] " È il rè di buona complessione, agile della vita, piccolo della persona ma ben formato, di pelo rosso e biondo, di carnagione bianca e colorita, col labbro del mento sollevato all' Aus-triaca. Ha la guardatura un poco malinconica," &c. &c.—F. Soranzo.

[79] Ibid.

[80] S. Contarini. " La sua intelli-genza meno che mediocre." — F. Priuli.

[81] S. Contarini. " Parla alcune lingue ma corrottemente solo che basti per farsi intendere . . . . ed ha avuto qualche principio di lingua Latina quondo era giovinissimo."

[82] Ibid

close to the staghounds, and confronted, spear in hand, the wild-boar with coolness and success.[83] He was fond of tennis, but his especial passion and chief accomplishment was dancing. He liked to be praised for his proficiency in this art, and was never happier than when gravely leading out the queen or his daughter, then four or five years of age—for he never danced with any one else—to perform a stately bolero.[84]

He never drank wine, but, on the other hand, was an enormous eater; so that, like his father in youth, he was perpetually suffering from stomach-ache as the effect of his gluttony.[85] He was devotedly attached to his queen, and had never known, nor hardly looked at, any other woman.[86] He had no vice but gambling, in which he indulged to a great extent, very often sitting up all night at cards.[87] This passion of the king's was much encouraged by Lerma, for obvious reasons. Philip had been known to lose thirty thousand dollars at a sitting, and always to some one of the family or dependents of the duke, who of course divided with them the spoils. At one time the Count of Pelbes, nephew of Lerma, had won two hundred thousand dollars in a very few nights from his sovereign.[88]

[83] "Corre dietro ai cani velocissamente, affronta i porchi cinghiali con grande ardire, tira d' archibugio in eccelenza bene," &c.—F. Soranzo.

[84] "Non beve vino e mangia assai, si diletta della caccia e perciò esce spesso in campagna e fa volentieri viaggi impiegando il resto del tempo in giuocare alla pillotta ed in danzare; è soggetto di debole ingegno, nimicissimo del negozio e di governare non pensando nè a guerra nè a pace come sè non fosse rè nè avesse stati, non inclinando al governo nè per natura nè per educazione anzi per propria volontà si è allontanato del tutto; è per sua natura liberale sebbene alli negozii di grazia e di giustizia ancora non fa nè più nè meno di quello che vuole il D. di Lerma è in continuo bisogno di denaro, ha qualche notizia degli travagli che gli occorrono di Fiandra, d' Inghilterra e d' altri luoghi ma come quello che non ha gusto nè si può dire parte nel governo . . . . ma non vedendo nè considerando l' espedizioni e credo io non essendo capace di cose grandi con il sotto scrivere pare che dalla S. M. esca il tutto ma realmente sebbene vi sono li consigli il Duca fa e risolve tutte le cose a suo beneplacito." — Ottaviano Bon, Relazione.

"Balla molto bene ed è la cosa che gusta di più piacendogli d' esser lodato in queste divertimento . . . . quando balla balla sempre con sua figlia o con la regina," &c.—S. Contarini, Relazione.

[85] S. Contarini. "Sottoposto al dolor di stomaco per il soverchio mangiare. Nondimeno mangia carne del continuo e con essa si nutrisce quattro volte il giorno."—F. Priuli, Relazione.

[86] Otta.vo Bon. F. Soranzo.

[87] S. Contarini. F. Priuli.

[88] S. Contarini, Relazione. "Si intratiene la sera dopo la cena nel giuoco con il quale ha arrichito molti cavalieri che lo servono."—Girolamo Soranzo.

For the rest, Philip had few peculiarities or foibles. He was not revengeful, nor arrogant, nor malignant. He was kind and affectionate to his wife and children, and did his best to be obedient to the Duke of Lerma. Occasionally he liked to grant audiences, but there were few to request them. It was ridiculous and pathetic at the same time to see the poor king, as was very frequently the case, standing at a solemn green table till his little legs were tired, waiting to transact business with applicants who never came ; while ushers, chamberlains, and valets were rushing up and down the corridors, bawling for all persons so disposed to come and have an audience of their monarch. Meantime, the doors of the great duke's apartments in the same palace would be beleaguered by an army of courtiers, envoys, and contractors, who had paid solid gold for admission, and who were often sent away grumbling and despairing without entering the sacred precincts.[89]

As time wore on, the king, too much rebuked for attempting to meddle in state affairs, became solitary and almost morose, moping about in the woods by himself,[90] losing satisfaction in his little dancing and ball-playing diversions, but never forgetting his affection for the queen nor the hours for his four daily substantial repasts of meats and pastry. It would be unnecessary and almost cruel to dwell so long upon a picture of what was after all not much better than human imbecility, were it not that humanity is a more sacred thing than royalty. A satire upon such an embodiment of kingship is impossible, the simple and truthful characteristics being more effective than fiction or exaggeration. It would be

[89] " Ed è cosa ridicula il vedere che quando il rè vuole dar udienza il che segue più giorni alla settimana non si ritrova alcuno che la voglia e per non lasciarlo con questa indignità, li valletti di camera salgono sino nelli corridori del palazzo gridando ed invitando le persone a entrare all' udienza di sua Maestà ; neppure poi questo giova in modo che ben spesso le occorre levarsi dalla tavola dove appoggiato suole stare aspettando senza che alcuno o pochi le abbino parlato, ed all' incontro alle stanze del duca di Lerma è tanta frequenza d'ogni sorte di persone che vorrebbero udienza che è cosa non meno di stupore che di compassione il vederlo."—Ottaviano Bon, Relazioni.

[90] " E dopo di aversi entieramente dato al duca di Lerma il suo carattere è divenuto solitario ed amante di vagar nei boschi tanto che si dice che questi boschi ed il duca di Lerma siano il re."—S. Contarini.

unjust to exhume a private character after the lapse of two centuries merely to excite derision, but if history be not powerless to instruct, it certainly cannot be unprofitable to ponder the merits of a system which, after bestowing upon the world forty-three years of Philip the tyrant, had now followed them up with a decade of Philip the simpleton.

In one respect the reigning sovereign was in advance of his age. In his devotion to the Madonna he claimed the same miraculous origin for her mother as for herself. When the prayer *"O Sancta Maria sine labe originali concepta"* was chanted, he would exclaim with emotion that the words embodied his devoutest aspirations. He had frequent interviews with doctors of divinity on the subject, and instructed many bishops to urge upon the pope the necessity of proclaiming the virginity of the Virgin's mother. Could he secure this darling object of his ambition, he professed himself ready to make a pilgrimage on foot to Rome.[91] The pilgrimage was never made, for it may well be imagined that Lerma would forbid any such adventurous scheme. Meantime, the duke continued to govern the empire and to fill his coffers, and the king to shoot rabbits.

The queen was a few years younger than her husband, and far from beautiful. Indeed, the lower portion of her face was almost deformed. She was graceful, however, in her movements, and pleasing and gentle in manner.[92] She adored the king, looking up to him with reverence as the greatest and wisest of beings. To please him she had upon her marriage given up drinking wine, which, for a German, was considered a great sacrifice.[93] She recompensed herself, as the king did, by eating to an extent which, according to contemporary accounts, excited amazement.[94] Thus there was perfect

---

[91] S. Contarini, Relazione. Giro. Soranzo. Notes of N. Barozzi (p. 289 ser. I. vol. i.) Poreno, Dichos y Hechos de Felipe III. ch. xii., cited by Barozzi.

[92] "Non si può dire brutta ma non è manco bella per avere la faccia deformata assai dalla bocca a basso, tuttavia la vaghezza del colore e l' agilità del corpo la fa riuscire grata

ad ognuno e dal marito è grandemente amata."—F. Priuli, Relazione.

[93] F. Soranzo. Otto. Bon, Relazione.

[94] "Le hanno levato il vino per rispetto della conversazione col rè che gli riesce molesto ma si rifà col mangiare tanto che è cosa di maraviglia." —Otto. Bon, Relazione.

sympathy between the two in the important article of diet. She had also learned to play at cards, in order to take a hand with him at any moment, feebly hoping that an occasional game for love might rescue the king from that frantic passion by which his health was shattered and so many courtiers were enriched.[95]

Not being deficient in perception, the queen was quite aware of the greediness of all who surrounded the palace. She had spirit enough too to feel the galling tyranny to which the king was subjected. That the people hated the omnipotent favourite, and believed the king to be under the influence of sorcery, she was well aware. She had even a dim notion that the administration of the empire was not the wisest nor the noblest that could be devised for the first power in Christendom. But considerations of high politics scarcely troubled her mind. Of a People she had perhaps never heard, but she felt that the king was oppressed. She knew that he was helpless, and that she was herself his only friend. But of what avail were her timid little flutterings of indignation and resistance? So pure and fragile a creature could accomplish little good for king or people. Perpetually guarded and surrounded by the Countess of Lemos and the Duchess of Lerma, she lived in mortal awe of both.[95] As to the duke himself, she trembled at his very name. On her first attempts to speak with Philip on political matters—to hint at the unscrupulous character of his government, to arouse him to the necessity of striking for a little more liberty and for at least a trifling influence in the state—the poor little king instantly betrayed her to the favourite and she was severely punished. The duke took the monarch off at once on a long journey, leaving her alone for weeks long with the terrible duchess and countess. Never before had she been separated for a day from her husband, it having been the king's uniform custom to take her with him in all his expeditions. Her

[95] "Ne mostra di gustare d' altro trattenimento che del giuoco per conformarsi col re pretendendo per tal via di deviarlo dal giuocar con altri che lo fa cadere nelle sopradette perdite." —F. Priuli.

[96] F. Priuli. F. Soranzo.

ambition to interfere was thus effectually cured.[97] The duke
forbade her thenceforth ever to speak of politics to her husband in public or in private—not even in bed—and the king
was closely questioned whether these orders had been
obeyed.[98] She submitted without a struggle. She saw how
completely her happiness was at Lerma's mercy. She had
no one to consult with, having none but Spanish people
about her, except her German father-confessor, whom, as a
great favour, and after a severe struggle, she had been
allowed to retain, as otherwise her ignorance of the national
language would have made it impossible for her to confess
her little sins.[99] Moreover her brothers, the archdukes at
Gratz, were in receipt of considerable annual stipends from
the Spanish exchequer, and the duke threatened to stop those
pensions at once should the queen prove refractory.[100] It is
painful to dwell any longer on the abject servitude in which
the king and queen were kept.[101] The two were at least

[97] "Voleva alcuni anni sono estender-
si nel maneggio dei negozii ma il duca
di Lerma che lo sentiva malissimo per
levarla da questi pensieri la mortificò
conducendo alcune volto il re in campagna senza di lei e tenendo glielo
separato le settimane entiere. Sentì
tanto la regina quest' assenza regia e
conobbe l'origine di questo disgusto
che da se si astenne affatto d' inge-
rirsi più nei negozii ed in questa
maniera si pacificò col duca."—Giro.
Soranzo.

[98] F. Contarini   "Nemmeno tro-
vandosi a letto."—N. Barozzi (Ser. I.
vol. i. p. 325) citing Relazione della
Vita, &c. &c.   MS. of Berlin.
"Ihr seyen alle Händt gebunden.
Wasz man ihr zuwider thun kan, das
thue man, sie was heimlich redt
so hält man sie in Argwohn, es sey
wider die Hertzogen Lerma und Uzeda
oder die ihrigen angesehen. *Ihren
Gemahl examinierten sie was sie mit
ihm im Bedt redt und haben ihr ver-
boten bey dem König um kein Sachen
zuintercediren noch im Bedt oder allein
mit ihm Negocio zu tractiren.* Was sie
nach Deutschland schreibt will man
wissen," etc. etc.—Khevenhüller,
Annales Ferdinandei, tom. vi. 3038.
Surely never was a more dismal pic-

ture painted of tyranny exercised by
subject over his sovereigns. It was no
wonder that the unfortunate queen protested to Count Khevenhüller that she
'would rather go into a convent at
Gratz than be Queen of Spain."—Ibid.

[99] Otto. Bon, Relazione.   " Confessore della medesima nazione da
lei tenuto a viva forza.—F. Priuli.
Relazione.

[100] Giro. Soranzo, Relazione.   Five
thousand crowns a month to the Arch
duke Ferdinand, and much help besides to the others. "L' arciduca
Ferdinando al quale ha assegnato 5000
scudi di provisione al mese, e lui ed i
fratelli cavano del continuo grossi
ajuti di corte, e la regina non cessa
mai di procurar loro alcuna cosa ; e
questa è una delle cause principali che
tiene la regina in necessità di stare
unita e si può dire dependente dal
duca di Lerma ; poichè procurando lei
sempre alcun sussidio per i fratelli e
convenendo valersi dell' autorità del
duca, non può per questo importante
rispetto dargli alcun disgusto nè intro-
mettersi in quello che non è di sua
soldisfazione."

[101] "Nel resto vive in continua servitù
e con tanto rispetto che maggiore non
si può dire."—Otto. Bon, Relazione.

happy in each other's society, and were blessed with mutual affection, with pretty and engaging children, and with a similarity of tastes. It is impossible to imagine anything more stately, more devout, more regular, more innocent, more utterly dismal and insipid, than the lives of this 'wedded pair.

This interior view of the court and council of Spain will suffice to explain why, despite the languor and hesitations with which the transactions were managed, the inevitable tendency was towards a peace. The inevitable slowness, secrecy, and tergiversations were due to the dignity of the Spanish court, and in harmony with its most sacred traditions. But what profit could the Duke of Lerma expect by the continuance of the Dutch war, and who in Spain was to be consulted except the Duke of Lerma?

CHAPTER XLIX.

Peace deliberations in Spain — Unpopularity of the project — Disaffection of the courtiers — Complaints against Spinola — Conference of the Catholic party — Position of Henry IV. towards the republic — State of France — Further peace negotiations — Desire of King James of England for the restoration of the States to Spain — Arrival of the French commissioners — President Jeannin before the States-General — Dangers of a truce with Spain — Dutch legation to England — Arrival of Lewis Verreyken at the Hague with Philip's ratification — Rejection of the Spanish treaty — Withdrawal of the Dutch fleet from the Peninsula — The peace project denounced by the party of Prince Maurice — Opposition of Maurice to the plans of Barneveld — Amended ratification presented to the States-General — Discussion of the conditions — Determination to conclude a peace — Indian trade — Exploits of Admiral Matelieff in the Malay penin sula — He lays siege to Malacca — Victory over the Spanish fleet — Endeavour to open a trade with China — Return of Matelieff to Holland.

THE Marquis Spinola had informed the Spanish Government that if 300,000 dollars a month could be furnished, the war might be continued, but that otherwise it would be better to treat upon the basis of *uti possidetis*, and according to the terms proposed by the States-General. He had further intimated his opinion that, instead of waiting for the king's consent, it more comported with the king's dignity for the archdukes to enter into negotiations, to make a preliminary and brief armistice with the enemy, and then to solicit the royal approval of what had been done.

In reply, the king—that is to say the man who thought, wrote, and signed in behalf of the king—had plaintively observed that among evils the vulgar rule was to submit to the least.[1] Although, therefore, to grant to the Netherland rebels not only peace and liberty, but to concede to them whatever they had obtained by violence and the most abominable outrages, was the worst possible example to all princes ;

[1] The King to Spinola, 28 February, 1607, in Gallucci, 328.

yet as the enormous sum necessary for carrying on the war was not to be had, even by attempting to scrape it together from every corner of the earth, he agreed with the opinion of the archdukes that it was better to put an end to this eternal and exhausting war by peace or truce, even under severe conditions. That the business had thus far proceeded without consulting him, was publicly known, and he expressed approval of the present movements towards a peace or a long truce, assuring Spinola that such a result would be as grateful to him as if the war had been brought to a successful issue.

When the Marquis sent formal notice of the armistice to Spain there were many complaints at court. Men said that the measure was beneath the king's dignity, and contrary to his interests. It was a cessation of arms under iniquitous conditions, accorded to a people formerly subject and now rebellious. Such a truce was more fatal than any conflict, than any amount of slaughter. During this long and dreadful war, the king had suffered no disaster so terrible as this, and the courtiers now declared openly that the archduke was the cause of the royal and national humiliation. Having no children, nor hope of any, he desired only to live in tranquillity and selfish indulgence, like the indolent priest that he was, not caring what detriment or dishonour might accrue to the crown after his life was over.

Thus murmured the parasites and the plunderers within the dominions of the do-nothing Philip, denouncing the first serious effort to put an end to a war which the laws of nature had proved to be hopeless on the part of Spain.

Spinola too, who had spent millions of his own money, who had plunged himself into debt and discredit, while attempting to sustain the financial reputation of the king, who had by his brilliant services in the field revived the ancient glory of the Spanish arms, and who now saw himself exposed with empty coffers to a vast mutiny, which was likely to make his future movements as paralytic as those of his immediate predecessors—Spinola, already hated because he was an Italian, because he was of a mercantile family, and because he had been successful, was now as much the object of contumely with the courtiers as with the archduke himself.

The splendid victory of Heemskerk had struck the government with dismay and diffused a panic along the coast. The mercantile fleets, destined for either India, dared not venture forth so long as the terrible Dutch cruisers, which had just annihilated a splendid Spanish fleet, commanded by a veteran of Lepanto, and under the very guns of Gibraltar, were supposed to be hovering off the Peninsula.[2] Very naturally, therefore, there was discontent in Spain that the cessation of hostilities had not originally been arranged for sea as well as land, and men said openly at court that Spinola ought to have his head cut off for agreeing to such an armistice.[3] Quite as reasonably, however, it was now felt to be necessary to effect as soon as possible the recal of this very inconvenient Dutch fleet from the coast of Spain.

The complaints were so incessant against Spinola that it was determined to send Don Diego d'Ybarra to Brussels, charged with a general superintendence of the royal interests in the present confused condition of affairs. He was especially instructed to convey to Spinola the most vehement reproaches in regard to the terms of the armistice, and to insist upon the cessation of naval hostilities, and the withdrawal of the cruisers.

Spinola, on his part, was exceedingly irritated that the arrangements which he had so carefully made with the archduke at Brussels should be so contumaciously assailed, and even disavowed, at Madrid. He was especially irritated that Ybarra should now be sent as his censor and overseer, and that Fuentes should have received orders to levy seven thousand troops in the Milanese for Flanders, the arrival of which reinforcements would excite suspicion, and probably break off negotiations.[4]

He accordingly sent his private secretary Biraga, post-haste to Spain with two letters. In number one he implored

---

[2] Letter of Henry IV., 13 June, 1607, in Jeannin, i. 146.
[3] Letters of F. Aerssens, in Van der Kemp, iii. 123. [4] Gallucci, 329.

his Majesty that Ybarra might not be sent to Brussels. If this request were granted, number two was to be burned. Otherwise, number two was to be delivered, and it contained a request to be relieved from all further employment in the king's service. The marquis was already feeling the same effects of success as had been experienced by Alexander Farnese, Don John of Austria, and other strenuous maintainers of the royal authority in Flanders. He was railed against, suspected, spied upon, put under guardianship, according to the good old traditions of the Spanish court. Public disgrace or secret poison might well be expected by him, as the natural guerdons of his eminent deeds.

Biraga also took with him the draught of the form in which the king's consent to the armistice and pending negotiations was desired, and he was particularly directed to urge that not one letter or comma should be altered, in order that no pretext might be afforded to the suspicious Netherlanders for a rupture.

In private letters to his own superintendent Strata, to Don John of Idiaquez, to the Duke of Lerma, and to Stephen Ybarra, Spinola enlarged upon the indignity about to be offered him, remonstrated vehemently against the wrong and stupidity of the proposed policy, and expressed his reliance upon the efforts of these friends of his to prevent its consummation. He intimated to Idiaquez that a new deliberation would be necessary to effect the withdrawal of the Dutch fleet—a condition not inserted in the original armistice—but that within the three months allowed for the royal ratification there would be time enough to procure the consent of the States to that measure.[5] If the king really desired to continue the war, he had but to alter a single comma in the draught, and, out of that comma, the stadholder's party would be certain to manufacture for him as long a war as he could possibly wish.[6]

In a subsequent letter to the king, Spinola observed that he was well aware of the indignation created in Spain by the

----

[5] Gallucci, 329, 331.   [6] Ibid.

cessation of land hostilities without the recal of the fleet, but that nevertheless John Neyen had confidentially represented to the archdukes the royal assent as almost certain. As to the mission of Ybarra, the marquis reminded his master that the responsibility and general superintendence of the negotiations had been almost forced upon him. Certainly he had not solicited them. If another agent were now interposed, it was an advertisement to the world that the business had been badly managed. If the king wished a rupture, he had but to lift his finger or his pen ; but to appoint another commissioner was an unfit reward for his faithful service. He was in the king's hands. If his reputation were now to be destroyed, it was all over with him and his affairs. The man, whom mortals had once believed incapable, would be esteemed incapable until the end of his days.

It was too late to prevent the mission of Ybarra, who, immediately after his arrival in Brussels, began to urge in the king's name that the words in which the provinces had been declared free by the archdukes might be expunged. What could be more childish than such diplomacy ? What greater proof could be given of the incapacity of the Spanish court to learn the lesson which forty years had been teaching ? Spinola again wrote a most earnest remonstrance to the king, assuring him that this was simply to break off the negotiation. It was ridiculous to suppose, he said, that concessions already made by the archdukes, ratification of which on the part of the king had been guaranteed, could now be annulled. Those acquainted with Netherland obstinacy knew better. The very possibility of the king's refusal excited the scorn of the States-General.[7]

Ybarra went about, too, prating to the archdukes and to others of supplies to be sent from Spain sufficient to carry on the war for many years, and of fresh troops to be forwarded immediately by Fuentes. As four millions of crowns a year were known to be required for any tolerable campaigning, such empty vaunts as these were preposterous. The king

[7] Letter to the king, 25 June, 1607, in Gallucci, 332.

knew full well, said Spinola, and had admitted the fact in
his letters, that this enormous sum could not be furnished.[8]
Moreover, the war cost the Netherlanders far less in proportion.   They had river transportation, by which they effected
as much in two days as the Catholic army could do in a fortnight, so that every siege was managed with far greater
rapidity and less cost by the rebels than by their opponents.
As to sending troops from Milan, he had already stated that
their arrival would have a fatal effect.   The minds of the
people were full of suspicion.   Every passing rumour excited
a prodigious sensation, and the war party was already gaining
the upper hand.   Spinola warned the king, in the most
solemn manner, that if the golden opportunity were now
neglected the war would be eternal.   This, he said, was more
certain than certain.   For himself, he had strained every
nerve, and would continue to do his best in the interest of
peace.   If calamity must come, he at least would be held
blameless.[9]

Such vehement remonstrances from so eminent a source
produced the needful effect.   Royal letters were immediately
sent, placing full powers of treating in the hands of the
marquis, and sending him a ratification of the archduke's
agreement.   Government moreover expressed boundless confidence in Spinola, and deprecated the idea that Ybarra's
mission was in derogation of his authority.   He had been
sent, it was stated, only to procure that indispensable
preliminary to negotiations, the withdrawal of the Dutch
fleet, but as this had now been granted, Ybarra was already
recalled.

Spinola now determined to send the swift and sure-footed
friar, who had made himself so useful in opening the path to
discussion, on a secret mission to Spain.   Ybarra objected;
especially because it would be necessary for him to go through
France, where he would be closely questioned by the king.
It would be equally dangerous, he said, for the Franciscan

---

[8] Letter last cited.   [9] Ibid.

in that case to tell the truth or to conceal it. But Spinola replied that a poor monk like him could steal through France undiscovered. Moreover, he should be disguised as a footman, travelling in the service of Aurelio Spinola, a relative of the marquis, then proceeding to Madrid. Even should Henry hear of his presence and send for him, was it to be supposed that so practised a hand would not easily parry the strokes of the French king—accomplished fencer as he undoubtedly was? After stealing into and out of Holland as he had so recently done, there was nothing that might not be expected of him. So the wily friar put on the Spinola livery, and, without impediment, accompanied Don Aurelio to Madrid.[10]

Meantime, the French commissioners—Pierre Jeannin, Buzanval, regular resident at the Hague, and De Russy, who was destined to succeed that diplomatist—had arrived in Holland.

The great drama of negotiation, which was now to follow the forty years' tragedy, involved the interests and absorbed the attention of the great Christian powers. Although serious enough in its substance and its probable consequences, its aspect was that of a solemn comedy. There was a secret disposition on the part of each leading personage—with a few exceptions—to make dupes of all the rest. Perhaps this was a necessary result of statesmanship, as it had usually been taught at that epoch.

Paul V., who had succeeded Clement VIII. in 1605, with the brief interlude of the twenty-six days of Leo XI.'s pontificate, was zealous, as might be supposed, to check the dangerous growth of the pestilential little republic of the north. His diplomatic agents, Millino at Madrid, Barberini at Paris, and the accomplished Bentivoglio, who had just been appointed to the nunciatura at Brussels, were indefatigable in their efforts to suppress the heresy and the insolent liberty of which the upstart commonwealth was the embodiment.[11]

---

[10] Gallucci, 335.   [11] Bentivoglio, 548, 549.

Especially Barberini exerted all the powers at his command to bring about a good understanding between the kings of France and Spain. He pictured to Henry, in darkest colours, the blight that would come over religion and civilization if the progress of the rebellious Netherlands could not be arrested. The United Provinces were becoming dangerous, if they remained free, not only to the French kingdom, but to the very existence of monarchy throughout the world.[12]

No potentate was ever more interested, so it was urged, than Henry IV. to bring down the pride of the Dutch rebels. There was always sympathy of thought and action between the Huguenots of France and their co-religionists in Holland. They were all believers alike in Calvinism—a sect inimical not less to temporal monarchies than to the sovereign primacy of the Church[13]—and the tendency and purposes of the French rebels were already sufficiently manifest in their efforts, by means of the so-called cities of security, to erect a state within a state ; to introduce, in short, a Dutch republic into France.[14]

A sovereign remedy for the disease of liberty, now threatening to become epidemic in Europe, would be found in a marriage between the second son of the King of Spain and a daughter of France. As the archdukes were childless, it might be easily arranged that this youthful couple should succeed them—the result of which would of course be the reduction of all the Netherlands to their ancient obedience.

It has already been seen, and will become still farther apparent, that nostrums like this were to be recommended in other directions. Meantime, Jeannin and his colleagues made their appearance at the Hague.

If there were a living politician in Europe capable of dealing with Barneveld on even terms, it was no doubt President Jeannin. An ancient Leaguer, an especial adherent of the

[12] Bentivoglio, 548, 549.

[13] " Sette inimica non meno alle monarchie temporali che al sovrano

primato ecclesiastico."—Ibid.

[14] "E di voler introdurre un governo di Olanda in Francia."—Ibid.

Duke of Mayenne, he had been deep in all the various plots and counter-plots of the Guises, and often employed by the extinct confederacy in various important intrigues. Being secretly sent to Spain to solicit help for the League after the disasters of Ivry and Arques, he found Philip II. so sincerely imbued with the notion that France was a mere province of Spain, and so entirely bent upon securing the heritage of the Infanta to that large property, as to convince him that the maintenance of the Roman religion was with that monarch only a secondary condition. Aid and assistance for the confederacy were difficult of attainment, unless coupled with the guarantee of the Infanta's rights to reign in France.

The Guise faction being inspired solely by religious motives of the loftiest kind, were naturally dissatisfied with the luke-warmness of his most Catholic Majesty. When therefore the discomfited Mayenne subsequently concluded his bargain with the conqueror of Ivry, it was a matter of course that Jeannin should also make his peace with the successful Huguenot, now become eldest son of the Church. He was very soon taken into especial favour by Henry, who recognised his sagacity, and who knew his hands to be far cleaner than those of the more exalted Leaguers with whom he had dealt. The "good old fellow," as Henry familiarly called him, had not filled his pockets either in serving or when deserting the League. Placed in control of the exchequer at a later period, he was never accused of robbery or peculation. He was a hard-working, not overpaid, very intelligent public func-tionary. He was made president of the parliament, or supreme tribunal of Burgundy, and minister of state, and was recognised as one of the ablest jurists and most skilful politi-cians in the kingdom. An elderly man, with a tall, serene forehead, a large dark eye and a long grey beard, he pre-sented an image of vast wisdom and reverend probity. He possessed—an especial treasure for a statesman in that plotting age—a singularly honest visage. Never was that face more guileless, never was his heart more completely worn upon his sleeve, than when he was harbouring the deepest or most dangerous designs.[15]   Such was the "good fellow," whom that skilful reader of men, Henry of France, had sent to represent his interests and his opinions at the approaching conferences.

What were those opinions ?   Paul V. and his legates Barberini, Millino, and the rest, were well enough aware of the secret strings of the king's policy, and knew how to touch them with skill.   Of all things past, Henry perhaps most regretted that not he, but the last and most wretched of the Valois line, was sovereign of France when the States-General came to Paris with that offer of sovereignty which had been so contumaciously refused.

If the object were attainable, the ex-chief of the Huguenots still meant to be king of the Netherlands as sincerely as Philip II. had ever intended to be monarch of France.[16]   But Henry was too accurate a calculator of chances, and had bustled too much in the world of realities, to exhaust his strength in striving, year after year, for a manifest impossibility.   The enthusiast, who had passed away at last from the dreams of the Escorial into the land of shadows, had spent a lifetime, and melted the wealth of an empire ; but universal monarchy had never come forth from his crucible. The French king, although possessed likewise of an almost boundless faculty for ambitious visions, was capable of distinguishing cloud-land from substantial empire.   Jeannin, as his envoy, would at any rate not reveal his master's secret aspirations to those with whom he came to deal, as openly as Philip had once unveiled himself to Jeannin.

There could be no doubt that peace at this epoch was the real interest of France.   That kingdom was beginning to flourish again, owing to the very considerable administrative genius of Bethune, an accomplished financier according to the lights of the age, and still more by reason of the general impoverishment of the great feudal houses and of the clergy. The result of the almost interminable series of civil and

[15] Grotius, xvi. 740 " Vultus autem sermonisque adeo potens ut cum maxime abderet sensus apertissimus videretur."

[16] See especially Seconde Instruction pour le S[r]. Jeannin. Negotiations de M. le President Jeannin, ed. Petitot, 1659, i, 40–43, and 62, 63.

religious wars had been to cause a general redistribution of property. Capital was mainly in the hands of the middle and lower classes, and the consequence of this general circulation of wealth through all the channels of society was precisely what might have been expected, an increase of enterprise and of productive industry in various branches.[17] Although the financial wisdom of the age was doing its best to impede commerce, to prevent the influx of foreign wares, to prohibit the outflow of specie—in obedience to the universal superstition, which was destined to survive so many centuries, that gold and silver alone constituted wealth—while, at the same time, in deference to the idiotic principle of sumptuary legislation, it was vigorously opposing mulberry culture, silk manufactures, and other creations of luxury, which, in spite of the hostility of government sages, were destined from that time forward to become better mines of wealth for the kingdom than the Indies had been for Spain, yet on the whole the arts of peace were in the ascendant in France.

The king, although an unscrupulous, self-seeking despot and the coarsest of voluptuaries, was at least a man of genius. He had also too much shrewd mother-wit to pursue such schemes as experience had shown to possess no reality. The talisman "Espoir," emblazoned on his shield, had led him to so much that it was natural for him at times to think all things possible.

But he knew how to renounce as well as how to dare. He had abandoned his hope to be declared Prince of Wales and successor to the English crown, which he had cherished for a brief period, at the epoch of the Essex conspiracy ;[18] he had

<hr />

[17] "Anche per richezza avanza la città di Parigi tutte le altre perchè essendo la nobiltà rovinata per le guerre passate ed il clero medesimamente per l'istessa causa, cominciando questo da poco in qua a ristorarsi, *resta il solo popolo con denari* nel qual numero sono quelli li quali fanno la facoltà con le liti, con li giudizii e con l'amministrazione della entrate pubbliche perchè si vendono tutte queste cariche a denari contanti però si può imaginare ognuno quanto se le facciano fruttare per farsi padroni di centinaja di migliaja dì scudi e vi sono molti di questi tali in Francia ma nella città di Parigi più che in ogni altra."—A. Badoer, Relazione.

[18] "I quali sono che egli pretende di essere dichiarato principe di Galles e successore del regno e spera in questa congiuntura di poter ottenere quello che per il passato no gli è riuscito." —Despatch of Cavalli, Venetian am-

forgotten his magnificent dream of placing the crown of
the holy German empire upon his head,[19] and if he still
secretly resolved to annex the Netherlands to his realms,
and to destroy his excellent ally, the usurping, rebellious,
and heretic Dutch republic, he had craft enough to work
towards his aim in the dark, and the common sense to know
that by now throwing down the mask he would be for ever
baffled of his purpose.

The history of France, during the last three-quarters of a
century, had made almost every Frenchman, old enough to
bear arms, an accomplished soldier. Henry boasted that the
kingdom could put three hundred thousand veterans into
the field—a high figure, when it is recollected that its population certainly did not exceed fifteen millions.[20] No man however was better aware than he, that in spite of the apparent
pacification of parties, the three hundred thousand would not
be all on one side, even in case of a foreign war. There were
at least four thousand great feudal lords,[21] as faithful to the
Huguenot faith and cause as he had been false to both ; many
of them still wealthy, notwithstanding the general ruin which
had swept over the high nobility, and all of them with
vast influence and a splendid following, both among the lesser
gentry and the men of lower rank.

Although he kept a Jesuit priest ever at his elbow,[22] and
did his best to persuade the world and perhaps himself that

bassador in England, 16 April, 1601.
Barozzi, Ser. II. vol. i. p. 38.

[19] " Era stata sua Maestà già tempo
desiderosa di farsi eleggere re de'
Romani ed allora si tratteneva più
amorevolmente con quei principi ma
scuoprendo poi d'aver debole fondamento per tale pretensione se la è
levata del tutto dall' animo."—A.
Badoer, Relazione. Ibid.

" Ebbe anco opinione di procurarsi
la elezione a re dei Romani dubitando
che il re di Spagna avesse questo
medesimo pensiero ma avendo scoperto
d'altra inclinazione non se n' è molto
occupato "—P. Priuli, Relazione.

[20] Computandosi che in tutto il
regno vi possono essere quindici milioni d'anime."—Angelo Badoer, Relazione, 1603. Barozzi and Berchet,
Ser. II. vol. i.

The population of Paris was estimated by the same ambassador at
400,000. Pietro Priuli (Relazione
Francia, 1608) was often told by the
king that he had 300,000 veterans in
France.

[21] A. Badoer, Relazione. P. Priuli.

[22] " Non avendo li religiosi in
Francia maggior protettore di lui
tenendo sempre a canto a sì un gesuita
suo favoritissimo che mai lo abban-
dona."—Ibid.

he had become a devout Catholic, in consequence of those memorable five hours' instruction from the Bishop of Bourges, and that there was no hope for France save in its return to the bosom of the Church, he was yet too politic and too far-seeing to doubt that for him to oppress the Protestants would be not only suicidal, but, what was worse in his eyes, ridiculous.

He knew, too, that with thirty or forty thousand fighting-men [23] in the field, with seven hundred and forty churches in the various provinces [24] for their places of worship, with all the best fortresses in France in their possession, with leaders like Rohan, Lesdiguieres, Bouillon, and many others, and with the most virtuous, self-denying, Christian government,[25] established and maintained by themselves, it would be madness for him and his dynasty to deny the Protestants their political and religious liberty, or to attempt a crusade against their brethren in the Netherlands.

France was far more powerful than Spain, although the world had not yet recognised the fact. Yet it would have been difficult for both united to crush the new common-wealth, however paradoxical such a proposition seemed to contemporaries.

Sully was conscientiously in favour of peace, and Sully was the one great minister of France. Not a Lerma, certainly; for France was not Spain, nor was Henry IV. a Philip III. The Huguenot duke was an inferior financier to his Spanish contemporary, if it were the height of financial skill for a minister to exhaust the resources of a great kingdom in order to fill his own pocket. Sully certainly did not neglect his own interests, for he had accumulated a fortune of at least seventy thousand dollars a year, besides a cash capital

---

[23] Badoer estimates the force at only 25,000.   [24] P. Pruili, Relazione.

[25] "Il governo politico degli eretici," said one who cordially hated heretics, "è così diligente ed accurato quanto ogni altro che sia al mondo ed in questo avanzano veramente loro mede-simi perchè *trascurano affatto l'inter-* *esse particolare per attender al solo publico*, proprietà contraria alla natura Francese se non vogliano dire che l'interesse pubblico serva per conserva-zione del particolare."—A. Badoer.

"Le più importanti fortezze del regno sono da essi tenute," &c.— P. Priuli.

estimated at a million and a half.[26] But while enriching himself, he had wonderfully improved the condition of the royal treasury. He had reformed many abuses and opened many new sources of income. He had, of course, not accomplished the whole Augean task of purification. He was a vigorous Huguenot, but no Hercules, and demigods might have shrunk appalled at the filthy mass of corruption which great European kingdoms everywhere presented to the reformer's eye. Compared to the Spanish Government, that of France might almost have been considered virtuous, yet even there everything was venal.

To negotiate was to bribe right and left, and at every step. All the ministers and great functionaries received presents, as a matter of course, and it was necessary to pave the pathway even of their ante-chambers with gold.

The king was fully aware of the practice, but winked at it, because his servants, thus paid enormous sums by the public and by foreign Governments, were less importunate for rewards and salaries from himself.[27]

One man in the kingdom was said to have clean hands, the venerable and sagacious chancellor, Pomponne de Bellièvre. His wife, however, was less scrupulous, and readily disposed of influence and court-favour for a price, without the knowledge, so it was thought, of the great judge.[28]

Jeannin, too, was esteemed a man of personal integrity, ancient Leaguer and tricky politician though he were.

[26] P. Priuli Relazione.

[27] " Con tutti il ministri indifferen temente l'uomo si fa strada in Francia con quei mezzi che ormai mi pare che usino per tutto il mondo . . . . il re medesimo lo sa e lo permette forse perchè profittando li ministri lascino di molestare la S. M. per altre ricompense del servizio che prestano ed essi per questa via pretendono riportare le giuste mercedi delle loro fatiche mentre veggono poter difficilmente sperarne altre dal re."—Ibid.

[28] " Il signore cancelliere solo si mantiene in concetto di molto ingegno ma ha una moglie che supplisce ai suo mancamento, ben si crede senza sua saputa, poichè nè anco la moglie basta a fargli fare quello che non conviene."—Ibid. The ambassador adds, on the general subject of corruption and bribery at the French court, " Queste cose sono tanto pubbliche nella corte che non pretendo far torto ad alcuno a riferirle in questo sacrario dove sono nondimento sicuro che saranno custodite con le altre cose dette e da darsi sotto quel sigillo di segretezza che conviene al servizio ed alla riputacione di questo stimatissimo con siglio."

Highest offices of magistracy and judicature, Church and State, were objects of a traffic almost as shameless as in Spain.[29] The ermine was sold at auction, mitres were objects of public barter, Church preferments were bestowed upon female children in their cradles. Yet there was hope in France, notwithstanding that the Pragmatic Sanction of St. Louis, the foundation of the liberties of the Gallican Church, had been annulled by Francis, who had divided the seamless garment of Church patronage with Leo.

Those four thousand great Huguenot lords, those thirty thousand hard-fighting weavers, and blacksmiths, and other plebeians, those seven hundred and forty churches, those very substantial fortresses in every province of the kingdom, were better facts than the Holy Inquisition to preserve a great nation from sinking into the slough of political extinction.

Henry was most anxious that Sully should convert himself to the ancient Church, and the gossips of the day told each other that the duke had named his price for his conversion. To be made high constable of France, it was said would melt the resolve of the stiff Huguenot.[30] To any other inducement or blandishment he was adamant. Whatever truth may have been in such chatter, it is certain that the duke never gratified his master's darling desire.

Yet it was for no lack of attempts and intrigues on the part of the king, although it is not probable that he would have ever consented to bestow that august and coveted dignity upon a Bethune.

[29] " Di qua nasce che oltre alle altre invenzioni s' è introdutto vendere non solo tutti li uffizii e le cariche anco di giustizia ma di più gli stessi servizii della casa del re di maestri di casa dei gentiluomini della camera, dei valletti, ed in sino li capitanati delle guardie della propria persona dei re che non si può dire più ; il che rende molto mal sodisfatto la nobiltà alla quale erano in altri tempi riservati per premii de' loro servizii questi luoghi che ora vendendosi convengono cadere in mano a chi ha più denari senza alcuna distinzione de' meriti. E siccome il re non è sotto posto all' odio manco è soggetto all' affezione verso le persone che per esso patiscono nell' interesse come faceva il re passato che per troppa amorevolezza donava più che non aveva."—A Badoer, Relazione.

[30] P. Priuli, Relazione. " Procura (il re) che egli (Sully) si faccia cattolico . . . . seppure avesse a venire a tal risoluzione si è lasciato intendere con i suoi confidenti che non lo farebbe per altro che con essere dichiarato Contestabile di Francia dignità si sublime che tiensi fermo che il re non gliela conferirebbe."

The king did his best by intrigue, by calumny, by tale-bearing, by inventions, to set the Huguenots against each other, and to excite the mutual jealousy of all his most trusted adherents, whether Protestant or Catholic. The most good-humoured, the least vindictive, the most un-grateful, the falsest of mankind, he made it his policy, as well as his pastime, to repeat, with any amount of embroidery that his most florid fancy could devise, every idle story or calumny that could possibly create bitter feeling and make mischief among those who surrounded him. Being aware that this propensity was thoroughly understood, he only multiplied fictions, so cunningly mingled with truths, as to leave his hearers quite unable to know what to believe and what to doubt. By such arts, force being impossible, he hoped one day to sever the band which held the conventicles together, and to reduce Protestantism to insignificance. He would have cut off the head of D'Aubigné or Duplessis Mornay to gain an object, and have not only pardoned but caressed and rewarded Biron when reeking from the con-spiracy against his own life and crown, had he been willing to confess and ask pardon for his stupendous crime. He hated vindictive men almost as much as he despised those who were grateful.[31]

[31] "Non vi è delitto per grande che pensassero commettere del quale non sieno sicuri d'ottener il perdono dalla Maestà sua e di siffatta maniera che da quell' ora in poi userà il re con essi gli stessi termini di confidenza che usa con i più antichi e fedeli servitori che abbia, il che non si scuopre solo nel trattare apparente, accarezzando tutti ad uno modo ma nell' esistente ancora perchè quando il re ha bisogno dell' opera di qualcheduno conosciuto che possa valere in quel servizio non dis-tingue antica da nuova, sincera da interessata servitù nè in somma fedel-tà infideltà ma chiama S. M. quel tale gli comunica il tutto e l'incarica di negoziare come ad un più vecchio più sincero e più fedele servitore suo. In fine è proprio del re non solo perdonare indifferentemente ad ognuno qual si voglia colpa mentre la confessi e gli dimandi il perdono ma quando conosce un uomo che sia di natura vendicativa l'odia più che per qualsivoglia altro vizio. Usa S. M un altro termine con li suoi servitori credendo convenirgli viver geloso dell' azione di ciascheduno che quando stima che qualche unione di particolari persone possa apportare pregiudizio al servizio suo procura dis-unirle con porle al punto l'uno contra l'altra non lasciando di ridire tutto quello che gli fosse stato referito ranco con obbligo di segretezza mente ciò possa giovare al suo disegno ed orna la relazione con quei fregi d'invenzione che vengono felicemente composti dal suo florido ingegno, quando conosca potere con essi generare e nutrire gelo-sia fra quelli amici, per disunirli e farli anco venire alli mani come molte volte

He was therefore far from preferring Sully to Villeroy or Jeannin, but he was perfectly aware that, in financial matters at least, the duke was his best friend and an important pillar of the state.

The minister had succeeded in raising the annual revenue of France to nearly eleven millions of dollars, and in reducing the annual expenditures to a little more than ten millions.[32] To have a balance on the right side of the public ledger was a feat less easily accomplished in those days even than in our own. Could the duke have restrained his sovereign's reckless extravagance in buildings, parks, hunting establishments, and harems, he might have accomplished even greater miracles. He lectured the king roundly, as a parent might remonstrate with a prodigal son, but it was impossible even for a Sully to rescue that hoary-headed and most indomitable youth from wantonness and riotous living. The civil-list of the king amounted to more than one-tenth of the whole revenue.[33]

On the whole, however, it was clear, as France was then constituted and administered, that a general peace would be, for the time at least, most conducive to its interests, and Henry and his great minister were sincerely desirous of bringing about that result.

Preliminaries for a negotiation which should terminate this mighty war were now accordingly to be laid down at the Hague. Yet it would seem rather difficult to effect a compromise. Besides the powers less interested, but which nevertheless sent representatives to watch the proceedings— such as Sweden, Denmark, Brandenburg, the Elector Pala-

accade. Con questo arriva S. M al fine che desidera, di dissolver le con venticole delle quali vive gelosissimo ma ne conviene provare anco danno notabile, perchè conosciuto ormai la sua natura non vi è chi si fidi di dirgli molte cose che saria suo servizio il saperle. Conosce il re medesimo questa sua facilità di ridire ma essendogli impossibile il mutare natura per rimediarvi in quanto può fra le cose vere mischia con arte dell' invenzione per ridurre l'uomo a non saper che si credere."—A. Badoer, Relazione.

[32] Badoer says 12,000,000 of scudi, (four to the pound sterling), of which however 6,000,000 were pledged. P. Priuli puts the whole receipts of the exchequer at 10,727,907 dollars, and the expenses at 10,333,114.

[33] To 1,233,632 dollars, according to P. Priuli.

tine—there were Spain, France, England, the republic, and the archdukes.

Spain knew very well that she could not continue the war; but she hoped by some quibbling recognition of an impossible independence to recover that authority over her ancient vassals which the sword had for the time struck down. Distraction in councils, personal rivalries, the well-known incapacity of a people to govern itself, commercial greediness, provincial hatreds, envies and jealousies, would soon reduce that jumble of cities and villages, which aped the airs of sovereignty, into insignificance and confusion. Adroit management would easily re-assert afterwards the sovereignty of the Lord's anointed. That a republic of freemen, a federation of independent states, could take its place among the nations did not deserve a serious thought.

Spain in her heart preferred therefore to treat. It was however indispensable that the Netherlands should re-establish the Catholic religion throughout the land, should abstain then and for ever from all insolent pretences to trade with India or America, and should punish such of their citizens as attempted to make voyages to the one or the other. With these trifling exceptions, the court of Madrid would look with favour on propositions made in behalf of the rebels.

France, as we have seen, secretly aspired to the sovereignty of all the Netherlands, if it could be had. She was also extremely in favour of excluding the Hollanders from the Indies, East and West. The king, fired with the achievements of the republic at sea, and admiring their great schemes for founding empires at the antipodes by means of commercial corporations, was very desirous of appropriating to his own benefit the experience, the audacity, the perseverance, the skill and the capital of their merchants and mariners. He secretly instructed his commissioners, therefore, and repeatedly urged it upon them, to do their best to procure the renunciation, on the part of the republic, of the Indian trade, and to contrive the transplantation into France of the mighty trading companies, so successfully established in Holland and Zeeland.[34]

The plot thus to deprive the provinces of their India trade was supposed by the statesmen of the republic to have been formed in connivance with Spain. That power, finding itself half pushed from its seat of power in the East by the "grand and infallible society created by the United Provinces,"[35] would be but too happy to make use of this French intrigue in order to force the intruding Dutch navy from its conquests.

Olden-Barneveld, too politic to offend the powerful and treacherous ally by a flat refusal, said that the king's friendship was more precious than the India trade. At the same time he warned the French Government that, if they ruined the Dutch East India Company, "neither France nor any other nation would ever put its nose into India again."[36]

James of England, too, flattered himself that he could win for England that sovereignty of the Netherlands which England as well as France had so decidedly refused. The marriage of Prince Henry with the Spanish Infanta was the bait, steadily dangled before him by the politicians of the Spanish court, and he deluded himself with the thought that the Catholic king, on the death of the childless archdukes, would make his son and daughter-in-law a present of the obedient Netherlands. He already had some of the most important places in the United Netherlands—the famous cautionary towns—in his grasp, and it should go hard but he would twist that possession into a sovereignty over the whole land. As for recognising the rebel provinces as an independent sovereignty, that was most abhorrent to him. Such a tampering with the great principles of Government was an offence against all crowned heads, a crime in which he was unwilling to participate.

---

[34] Negotiations de Jeannin, i. 71, 153, 183 (especially 196, 219). Compare Gallucci, 345, 346, and see especially the memoir of F. Aerssens, in Deventer, iii. 26–31. Correspondence between Henry IV. and Olden-Barneveld, pp. 46–50. Ibid.

[35] Memoir of Aerssens, *ubi sup.*

[36] Deventer, iii. 50.

His instinct against rebellion seemed like second sight. The king might almost be imagined to have foreseen in the dim future those memorable months in which the proudest triumph of the Dutch commonwealth was to be registered before the forum of Christendom at the congress of West-phalia, and in which the solemn trial and execution of his own son and successor, with the transformation of the monarchy of the Tudors and Stuarts into a British republic, were simultaneously to startle the world. But it hardly needed the gift of prophecy to inspire James with a fear of revolutions.

He was secretly desirous therefore, sustained by Salisbury and his other advisers, of effecting the restoration of the provinces to the dominion of his most Catholic Majesty.[37] It was of course the interest of England that the Netherland rebels should renounce the India trade. So would James be spared the expense and trouble of war; so would the great doctrines of divine right be upheld; so would the way be paved towards the ultimate absorption of the Netherlands by England. Whether his theological expositions would find as attentive pupils when the pope's authority had been re-established over all his neighbours; whether the Catholic rebels in Ireland would become more tranquil by the sub-jugation of the Protestant rebels in Holland; whether the principles of Guy Fawkes might not find more effective application, with no bulwark beyond the seas against the incursion of such practitioners—all this he did not perhaps sufficiently ponder.

Thus far had the discursive mind of James wandered from the position which it occupied at the epoch of Maximilian de Bethune's memorable embassy to England.

The archdukes were disposed to quiet. On them fell the burthen of the war. Their little sovereignty, where—if they could only be allowed to expend the money squeezed from the obedient provinces in court diversions, stately architecture, splendid encouragement of the fine arts, and luxurious living,

[37] Negotiations de Jeannin, i 128, 129, 152, 184, 199, 217, 240, 524, *et passim*.

surrounded by a train of great nobles, fit to command regiments in the field or assist in the counsels of state, but chiefly occupied in putting dishes on the court table, handing ewers and napkins to their Highnesses, or in still more menial offices—so much enjoyment might be had, was reduced to a mere parade ground for Spanish soldiery.[38] It was ridiculous, said the politicians of Madrid, to suppose that a great empire like Spain would not be continually at war in one direction or another, and would not perpetually require the use of large armies. Where then could there be a better mustering place for their forces than those very provinces, so easy of access, so opulent, so conveniently situate in the neighbourhood of Spain's most insolent enemies ?[39] It was all very fine for the archduke, who knew nothing of war, they declared, who had no hope of children, who longed only for a life of inglorious ease, such as he could have had as archbishop, to prate of peace and thus to compromise the dignity of the realm. On the contrary, by making proper use of the Netherlands, the repose and grandeur of the monarchy would be secured, even should the war become eternal.[40]

This prospect, not agreeable certainly for the archdukes or their subjects, was but little admired outside the Spanish court.

Such then were the sentiments of the archdukes, and such the schemes and visions of Spain, France, and England. On two or three points, those great powers were mainly, if unconsciously, agreed. The Netherlands should not be sovereign ; they should renounce the India navigation ; they should consent to the re-establishment of the Catholic religion.

On the other hand, the States-General knew their own minds, and made not the slightest secret of their intentions.

---

[38] " Il se fait servir par les plus grands et même par ses confrères et compagnons d'ordre jusques aux choses indignes d'être nommées. . . .
" L'on voit chacun jour grand nombre de noblesse, qui pourroit bien s'employer à la tête d'une compagnie de cavalerie ou d'un regiment, ne s'ex- ercer qu'à porter des plats sur une table, et d'autres encore à d'autres choses moins nécessaires." — Letter from Brussels in P. de l'Estoile. Supplement au Journal du Règne de Henri IV., 1599–1606, tom. iii. pp. 460, 461. In Petitot, vol. xlvii.
[39] Bentivoglio, 564.   [40] Ibid.

They would be sovereign, they would not renounce the India trade, they would not agree to the re-establishment of the Catholic religion.

Could the issue of the proposed negotiations be thought hopeful, or was another half century of warfare impending?

On the 28th May the French commissioners came before the States-General.[41]

There had been many wild rumours flying through the provinces in regard to the king's secret designs upon the republic, especially since the visit made to the Hague a twelvemonth before by Francis Aerssens, States' resident at the French court.[48] That diplomatist, as we know, had been secretly commissioned by Henry to feel the public pulse in regard to the sovereignty, so far as that could be done by very private and delicate fingering. Although only two or three personages had been dealt with—the suggestions being made as the private views of the ambassadors only—there had been much gossip on the subject, not only in the Netherlands, but at the English and Spanish courts. Throughout the commonwealth there was a belief that Henry wished to make himself king of the country.

As this happened to be the fact, it was natural that the President, according to the statecraft of his school, should deny it at once, and with an air of gentle melancholy.

Wearing therefore his most ingenuous expression, Jeannin addressed the assembly.

He assured the States that the king had never forgotten how much assistance he had received from them when he was struggling to conquer the kingdom legally belonging to him, and at a time when they too were fighting in their own country for their very existence.[43]

The king thought that he had given so many proofs of his sincere friendship as to make doubt impossible; but he had found the contrary, for the States had accorded an armistice, and listened to overtures of peace, without deigning to con-

---

[41] Meteren, 551. Jeannin, i. 109.   [42] Wagenaar, ix. 261, *seqq.*
[43] Jeannin, i. 109.

sult him on the subject. They had proved, by beginning and concluding so important a transaction without his knowledge, that they regarded him with suspicion, and had no respect for his name. Whence came the causes of that suspicion it was difficult to imagine, unless from certain false rumours of propositions said to have been put forward in his behalf, although he had never authorised anyone to make them, by which men had been induced to believe that he aspired to the sovereignty of the provinces.

"This falsehood," continued the candid President, "has cut our king to the heart, wounding him more deeply than anything else could have done. To make the armistice without his knowledge showed merely your contempt for him, and your want of faith in him. But he blamed not the action in itself, since you deemed it for your good, and God grant that you may not have been deceived. But to pretend that his Majesty wished to grow great at your expense, this was to do a wrong to his reputation, to his good faith, and to the desire which he has always shown to secure the prosperity of your state."[44]

Much more spoke Jeannin, in this vein, assuring the assembly that those abominable falsehoods proceeded from the enemies of the king, and were designed expressly to sow discord and suspicion in the provinces. The reader, already aware of the minute and detailed arrangements made by Henry and his ministers for obtaining the sovereignty of the United Provinces and destroying their liberties, will know how to appreciate the eloquence of the ingenuous President.

After the usual commonplaces concerning the royal desire to protect his allies against wrong and oppression, and to advance their interests, the President suggested that the States should forthwith communicate the pending deliberations to all the kings and princes who had favoured their cause, and especially to the King of England, who had so thoroughly proved his desire to promote their welfare.[45]

[44] Jeannin, i. 110.   [45] Ibid. 113.

As Jeannin had been secretly directed to pave the way by
all possible means for the king's sovereignty over the
provinces ; as he was not long afterwards to receive explicit
instructions to expend as much money as might be necessary
in bribing Prince Maurice, Count Lewis William, Barneveld
and his son, together with such others as might seem worth
purchasing, in order to assist Henry in becoming monarch of
their country ; [46] and as the English king was at that moment
represented in Henry's private letters to the commissioners as
actually loathing the liberty, power, and prosperity of the provinces,[47] it must be conceded that the President had acquitted
himself very handsomely in his first oration.

Such was the virtue of his honest face.

Barneveld answered with generalities and commonplaces.
No man knew better than the Advocate the exact position of
affairs ; no man had more profoundly fathomed the present
purposes of the French king ; no man had more acutely
scanned his character. But he knew the critical position of
the commonwealth. He knew that, although the public
revenue might be raised by extraordinary and spasmodic
exertion to nearly[48] a million sterling, a larger income than
had ever been at the disposition of the great Queen of
England, the annual deficit might be six millions of florins
—more than half the revenue—if the war continued,[49] and
that there was necessity of peace, could the substantial
objects of the war be now obtained. He was well aware too
of the subtle and scheming brain which lay hid beneath that
reverend brow of the President, although he felt capable of
coping with him in debate or intrigue. Doubtless he was
inspired with as much ardour for the intellectual conflict as
Henry might have experienced on some great field-day with
Alexander Farnese.

On this occasion, however, Barneveld preferred to glide
gently over the rumours concerning Henry's schemes. Those
reports had doubtless emanated, he said, from the enemies of

[46] Jeannin, i. 43, 62, 63, 69, 70, 71. [47] Ibid. 157.
[48] Wagenaar, ix. 274, 275. [49] Ibid. 277.

Netherland prosperity. The private conclusion of the armistice he defended on the ground of necessity, and of temporary financial embarrassment, and he promised that deputies should at once be appointed to confer with the royal commissioners in regard to the whole subject.

In private, he assured Jeannin that the communications of Aerssens had only been discussed in secret, and had not been confided to more than three or four persons.[50]

The Advocate, although the leader of the peace party, was by no means over anxious for peace.

The object of much insane obloquy, because disposed to secure that blessing for his country on the basis of freedom and independence, he was not disposed to trust in the sincerity of the archdukes, or the Spanish court, or the French king. "*Timeo Danaos etiam dona ferentes,*" he had lately said to Aerssens.[51] Knowing that the resistance of the Netherlands had been forty years long the bulwark of Europe against the designs of the Spaniard for universal empire, he believed the republic justified in expecting the support of the leading powers in the negotiations now proposed. "Had it not been for the opposition of these provinces," he said, "he might, in the opinion of the wisest, have long ago been monarch of all Europe, with small expense of men, money, or credit."[52] He was far from believing therefore that Spain, which had sacrificed, according to his estimate, three hundred thousand soldiers and two hundred million ducats in vain endeavours to destroy the resistance of the United Provinces, was now ready to lay aside her vengeance and submit to a sincere peace. Rather he thought to see "the lambkins, now frisking so innocently about the commonwealth, suddenly transform themselves into lions and wolves."[53] It would be a fatal error, he said, to precipitate the dear fatherland into the net of a simulated negotiation, from unwise impatience for peace. The Netherlanders were a simple, truthful

[50] Resol. Holl. 146, 147. Wagenaar, ix. 270.
[51] Olden-Barneveld to Aerssens, 2 June, 1607, in Deventer, iii. 135.
[52] Memoire van Olden-Barnevelt, in Deventer, iii. cxcix. 137–147.   [53] Ibid.

people and could hope for no advantage in dealing with
Spanish friars, nor discover all the danger and deceit
lurking beneath their fair words. Thus the man, whom his
enemies perpetually accused of being bought by the enemy,
of wishing peace at any price, of wishing to bring back the
Catholic party and ecclesiastical influence to the Netherlands,
was vigorously denouncing a precipitate peace, and warning
his countrymen of the danger of premature negotiations.

"As one can hardly know the purity and value of gold,"
he said, "without testing it, so it is much more difficult to
distinguish a false peace from a genuine one ; for one can
never touch it nor taste it, and one learns the difference when
one is cheated and lost. Ignorant people think peace
negotiations as simple as a private lawsuit. Many sensible
persons even think that, the enemy once recognising us for
a free, sovereign state, we shall be in the same position as
England and France, which powers have lately made peace
with the archdukes and with Spain. But we shall find a
mighty difference. Moreover, in those kingdoms the Spanish
king has since the peace been ever busy corrupting their
officers of state and their subjects, and exciting rebellion and
murder within their realms, as all the world must confess.
And the English merchants complain that they have suffered
more injustice, violence, and wrong from the Spaniards since
the peace than they did during the war."[54]

The Advocate also reminded his countrymen that the archduke, being a vassal of Spain, could not bind that power by
his own signature, and that there was no proof that the king
would renounce his pretended rights to the provinces. If he
affected to do so, it would only be to put the republic to sleep.
He referred, with much significance, to the late proceedings
of the Admiral of Arragon at Emmerich, who refused to
release that city according to his plighted word, saying
roundly that whatever he might sign and seal one day he
would not hesitate absolutely to violate on the next if the
king's service was thereby to be benefited.[55] With such

[54] Memoire van Olden-Barnevelt, in Deventer, iii. cxcix. 137–147.   [55] Ibid.

people, who had always learned law-doctors and ghostly con-
fessors to strengthen and to absolve them, they could never
expect anything but broken faith and contempt for treaties
however solemnly ratified.

Should an armistice be agreed upon and negotiations begun,
the Advocate urged that the work of corruption and bribery
would not be a moment delayed, and although the Netherlanders were above all nations a true and faithful race, it
could hardly be hoped that no individuals would be gained
over by the enemy.[56]

"For the whole country," said Barneveld, "would swarm
with Jesuits, priests, and monks, with calumnies and corruptions—the machinery by which the enemy is wont to produce
discord, relying for success upon the well-known maxim of
Philip of Macedon, who considered no city impregnable into
which he could send an ass laden with gold." [57]

The Advocate was charged too with being unfriendly to the
India trade, especially to the West India Company.

He took the opportunity, however, to enlarge with emphasis
and eloquence upon that traffic as constituting the very life-
blood of the country.

"The commerce with the East Indies is going on so pros-
perously," he said, "that not only our own inhabitants but all
strangers are amazed. The West India Company is sufficiently
prepared, and will cost the commonwealth so little, that the
investment will be inconsiderable in comparison with the
profits. And all our dangers and difficulties have nearly
vanished since the magnificent victory of Gibraltar, by which
the enemy's ships, artillery, and sailors have been annihilated,
and proof afforded that the Spanish galleys are not so terrible
as they pretend to be. By means of this trade to both the
Indies, matters will soon be brought into such condition that
the Spaniards will be driven out of all those regions and
deprived of their traffic. Thus will the great wolf's teeth be
pulled out, and we need have no farther fear of his biting
again. Then we may hope for a firm and assured peace, and

[56] Memoire van Olden-Barnevelt, in Deventer, iii. cxcix. 137–147.   [57] Ibid.

may keep the Indies, with the whole navigation thereon depending, for ourselves, sharing it freely and in common with our allies." [58]

Certainly no statesman could more strongly depict the dangers of a pusillanimous treaty, and the splendid future of the republic, if she held fast to her resolve for political independence, free religion, and free trade, than did the great Advocate at this momentous epoch of European history.

Had he really dreamed of surrendering the republic to Spain, that republic whose resistance ever since the middle of the previous century had been all that had saved Europe, in the opinion of learned and experienced thinkers, from the universal empire of Spain — had the calumnies, or even a thousandth part of the calumnies, against him been true — how different might have been the history of human liberty !

Soon afterwards, in accordance with the suggestions of the French king and with their own previous intentions, a special legation was despatched by the States to England, in order to notify the approaching conferences to the sovereign of that country, and to invite his participation in the proceedings.

The States' envoys were graciously received by James, who soon appointed Richard Spencer and Ralph Winwood as commissioners to the Hague, duly instructed to assist at the deliberations, and especially to keep a sharp watch upon French intrigues. There were also missions and invitations to Denmark and to the Electors Palatine and of Branden-burg, the two latter potentates having, during the past three years, assisted the States with a hundred thousand florins annually.[59]

The news of the great victory at Gibraltar had reached the Netherlands almost simultaneously with the arrival of the French commissioners. It was thought probable that John Neyen had received the weighty intelligence some days earlier, and the intense eagerness of the archdukes and of the Spanish Government to procure the recal of the Dutch fleet

[58] Memoire van Olden-Barnevelt in Deventer, iii. cxcix. 137–147.
[59] Wagenaar, ix. 274.

was thus satisfactorily explained. Very naturally this magnificent success, clouded though it was by the death of the hero to whom it was due, increased the confidence of the States in the justice of their cause and the strength of their position.

Once more, it is not entirely idle to consider the effect of scientific progress on the march of human affairs, as so often exemplified in history. Whether that half-century of continuous war would have been possible with the artillery, means of locomotion, and other machinery of destruction and communication now so terribly familiar to the world, can hardly be a question. The preterhuman prolixity of negotiation which appals us in the days when steam and electricity had not yet annihilated time and space, ought also to be obsolete. At a period when the news of a great victory was thirty days on its travels from Gibraltar to Flushing, aged counsellors justified themselves in a solemn consumption of time such as might have exasperated Jared or Methuselah in his boyhood. Men fought as if war was the normal condition of humanity, and negotiated as if they were all immortal. But has the art political kept pace with the advancement of physical science ? If history be valuable for the examples it furnishes both for imitation and avoidance, then the process by which these peace conferences were initiated and conducted may be wholesome food for reflection.

John Neyen, who, since his secret transactions already described at the Hague and Fort Lillo, had been speeding back and forth between Brussels, London, and Madrid, had once more returned to the Netherlands, and had been permitted to reside privately at Delft until the king's ratification should arrive from Spain.[60]

While thus established, the industrious friar had occupied his leisure in studying the situation of affairs. Especially he had felt inclined to renew some of those little commercial speculations which had recently proved so comfortable in the case of Dirk van der Does. Recorder Cornelius Aerssens

[60] Meteren, 553.

came frequently to visit him, with the private consent of the Government, and it at once struck the friar that Cornelius would be a judicious investment. So he informed the recorder that the archdukes had been much touched with his adroitness and zeal in facilitating the entrance of their secret agent into the presence of the Prince and the Advocate. Cruwel, in whose company the disguised Neyen had made his first journey to the Hague, was a near relative of Aerssens. The honest monk accordingly, in recognition of past and expected services, begged one day the recorder's acceptance of a bill, drawn by Marquis Spinola on Henry Beckman, merchant of Amsterdam, for eighty thousand ducats. He also produced a diamond ring, valued at ten thousand florins, which he ventured to think worthy the acceptance of Madame Aerssens. Furthermore, he declared himself ready to pay fifteen thousand crowns in cash, on account of the bill, whenever it might be desired, and observed that the archdukes had ordered the house which the recorder had formerly occupied in Brussels to be reconveyed to him.[61] Other good things were in store, it was delicately hinted, as soon as they had been earned.

Aerssens expressed his thanks for the house, which, he said, legally belonged to him according to the terms of the surrender of Brussels. He hesitated in regard to the rest, but decided finally to accept the bill of exchange and the diamond, apprising Prince Maurice and Olden-Barneveld of the fact, however, on his return to the Hague.[62] Being subsequently summoned by Neyen to accept the fifteen thousand crowns, he felt embarrassed at the compromising position in which he had placed himself. He decided accordingly to make a public statement of the affair to the States-General. This was done, and the States placed the ring and the bill in the hands of their treasurer, Joris de Bie.

The recorder never got the eighty thousand ducats, nor his wife the diamond; but although there had been no duplicity on his part, he got plenty of slander. His evil genius had

[61] Wagenaar, ix. 271, *et seq.* Grotius, xvi. 741, 742.   [62] Ibid.

prompted him, not to listen seriously to the temptings of the monk, but to deal with him on his own terms. He was obliged to justify himself against public suspicion with explanations and pamphlets, but some taint of the calumny stuck by him to the last.

Meantime, the three months allotted for the reception of Philip's ratification had nearly expired. In March, the royal Government had expressly consented that the archdukes should treat with the rebels on the ground of their independence. In June that royal permission had been withdrawn, exactly because the independence could never be acknowledged. Albert, naturally enough indignant at such double-dealing, wrote to the king that his disapprobation was incomprehensible, as the concession of independence had been made by direct command of Philip. "I am much amazed," he said, "that, having treated with the islanders on condition of leaving them free, by express order of your Majesty (which you must doubtless very well remember), your Majesty now reproves my conduct, and declares your dissatisfaction." [63] At last, on the 23rd July, Spinola requested a safe conduct for Louis Verreyken, auditor of the council at Brussels, to come to the Hague. [64]

On the 23rd of July that functionary accordingly arrived. He came before Prince Maurice and fifty deputies of the States-General, and exhibited the document. At the same time he urged them, now that the long-desired ratification had been produced, to fulfil at once their promise, and to recal their fleet from the coast of Spain. [65]

Verreyken was requested to withdraw while the instrument was examined. When recalled, he was informed that the States had the most staightforward intention to negotiate, but that the royal document did not at all answer their expectation. As few of the delegates could read Spanish, it would first of all be necessary to cause it to be translated.

[63] Extract from MS. Letter cited by Deventer, iii. xxvi.
[64] Wagenaar, ix. 278.
[65] Meteren, 552, 553. Gallucci, 336. Wagenaar, 278, *seqq.*

Next day, however, just as his preparations for departure had been made, he was once more summoned before the Assembly to meet with a somewhat disagreeable surprise. Barneveld, speaking as usual in behalf of the States-General, publicly produced Spinola's bill of exchange for eighty thousand ducats, the diamond ring intended for Madame Aerssens, and the gold chain given to Dirk van der Does, and expressed the feelings of the republican Government in regard to those barefaced attempts of Friar John at bribery and corruption, in very scornful language.[72] Netherlanders were not to be bought—so the agent of Spain and of the archdukes was informed—and, even if the citizens were venal, it would be necessary in a popular Government to buy up the whole nation. "It is not in our commonwealth as in despotisms," said the Advocate, "where affairs of state are directed by the nod of two or three individuals, while the rest of the inhabitants are a mob of slaves. By turns, we all govern and are governed. This great council, this senate—should it seem not sufficiently fortified against your presents—could easily be enlarged. Here is your chain, your ring, your banker's draught. Take them all back to your masters. Such gifts are not necessary to ensure a just peace, while to accept them would be a crime against liberty, which we are incapable of committing."[73]

Verreyken, astonished and abashed, could answer little save to mutter a few words about the greediness of monks, who, judging everyone else by themselves, thought no one inaccessible to a bribe.[74] He protested the innocence of the archdukes in the matter, who had given no directions to bribe, and who were quite ignorant that the attempt had been made.

He did not explain by whose authority the chain, the ring, and the draught upon Beckman had been furnished to the friar.

Meantime that ecclesiastic was cheerfully wending his way

---

[72] Meteren, 553vo. Grotius, xvi. 745. Wagenaar, ix. 283.
[73] Ibid.

[74] "Nec mirum si monachi avarum imprimis hominum genus alios ex se æstimarent."—Grotius, ubi sup.

to Spain in search of the new ratification, leaving his colleague vicariously to bide the pelting of the republican storm, and to return somewhat weather-beaten to Brussels.

During the suspension, thus ridiculously and gratuitously caused, of preliminaries which had already lasted the better portion of a year, party-spirit was rising day by day higher, and spreading more widely throughout the provinces Opinions and sentiments were now sharply defined and loudly announced. The clergy, from a thousand pulpits, thundered against the peace, exposing the insidious practices, the faithless promises, the monkish corruptions, by which the attempt was making to reduce the free republic once more into vassalage to Spain. The people everywhere listened eagerly and applauded. Especially the mariners, cordwainers, smiths, ship-chandlers, boatmen, the tapestry weavers, lace manufacturers, shopkeepers, and, above all, the India merchants and stockholders in the great commercial companies for the East and West, lifted up their voices for war. This was the party of Prince Maurice, who made no secret of his sentiments, and opposed, publicly and privately, the resumption of negotiations. Doubtless his adherents were the most numerous portion of the population.

Barneveld, however, was omnipotent with the municipal governments, and although many individuals in those bodies were deeply interested in the India navigation and the great corporations, the Advocate turned them as usual around his finger.

Ever since the memorable day of Nieuport there had been no love lost between the stadholder and the Advocate. They had been nominally reconciled to each other, and had, until lately, acted with tolerable harmony, but each was thoroughly conscious of the divergence of their respective aims.

Exactly at this period the long-smothered resentment of Maurice against his old preceptor, counsellor, and, as he believed, betrayer, flamed forth anew. He was indignant that a man, so infinitely beneath him in degree, should thus dare to cross his plans, to hazard, as he believed, the best interests of the state, and to interfere with the course of his legitimate ambition.[75] There was more glory for a great soldier to earn in future battle-fields, a higher position before the world to be won. He had a right by birth, by personal and family service, to claim admittance among the monarchs of Europe. The pistol of Balthasar Gerard had alone prevented the elevation of his father to the sovereignty of the provinces. The patents, wanting only a few formalities, were still in possession of the son. As the war went on—and nothing but blind belief in Spanish treachery could cause the acceptance of a peace which would be found to mean slavery —there was no height to which he might not climb. With the return of peace and submission, his occupation would be gone, obscurity and poverty the sole recompense for his life-long services and the sacrifices of his family. The memory of the secret movements twice made but a few years before to elevate him to the sovereignty, and which he In 1602 believed to have been baffled by the Advocate, and 1603. doubtless rankled in his breast. He did not forget that when the subject had been discussed by the favourers of the scheme in Barneveld's own house, Barneveld himself had prophesied that one day or another " the rights would burst out which his Excellency had to become prince of the provinces, on strength of the signed and sealed documents addressed to the late Prince of Orange ; that he had further alluded to the efforts then on foot to make him Duke of Gelderland ; adding with a sneer, that Zeeland was all agog on the subject, while in that province there were individuals very desirous of becoming children of Zebedee."[76]

Barneveld, on his part, although accustomed to speak in public of his Excellency Prince Maurice in terms of profoundest respect, did not fail to communicate in influential quarters his fears that the prince was inspired by excessive ambition, and that he desired to protract the war, not for the

[75] Wagenaar, ix. 283–285.
[76] Van der Kemp, iii. 100–103, 396–400, *i. e.* zealous disciples of their master, as Van der Kemp explains.

good of the commonwealth, but for the attainment of greater
power in the state. The envoys of France, expressly instructed
on that subject by the king, whose purposes would be frustrated if the ill-blood between these eminent personages could
not be healed, did their best to bring about a better understanding, but with hardly more than an apparent success.

Once more there were stories flying about that the stad
holder had called the Advocate liar, and that he had struck
him or offered to strike him[77]—tales as void of truth, doubtless,
as those so rife after the battle of Nieuport, but which indicated
the exasperation which existed.

When the news of the rejection of the king's ratification
reached Madrid, the indignation of the royal conscience-
keepers was vehement.[78]

That the potentate of so large a portion of the universe
should be treated by those lately his subjects with less
respect than that due from equals to equals, seemed intolerable. So thoroughly inspired, however, was the king
by the love of religion and the public good—as he informed
Marquis Spinola by letter—and so intense was his desire for
the termination of that disastrous war, that he did not hesitate
indulgently to grant what had been so obstinately demanded.
Little was to be expected, he said, from the stubbornness
of the provinces, and from their extraordinary manner of
transacting business, but looking, nevertheless, only to divine
duty, and preferring its dictates to a selfish regard for his
own interests, he had resolved to concede that liberty to the
provinces which had been so importunately claimed. He
however imposed the condition that the States should permit
free and public exercise of the Catholic religion throughout
their territories, and that so long as such worship was
unobstructed, so long and no longer should the liberty now
conceded to the provinces endure.[79]

" Thus did this excellent prince," says an eloquent Jesuit,
" prefer obedience to the Church before subjection to himself,

[77] Wagenaar, ix. 285.   [78] Gallucci, 338.
[79] The King to Spinola, *apud* Gallucci, *ubi sup.*

and insist that those, whom he emancipated from his own dominions, should still be loyal to the sovereignty of the Pope."[80]

Friar John, who had brought the last intelligence from the Netherlands, might have found it difficult, if consulted, to inform the king how many bills of exchange would be necessary to force this wonderful condition on the Government of the provinces. That the republic should accept that liberty as a boon which she had won with the red right hand, and should establish within her domains as many agents for Spanish reaction as there were Roman priests, monks, and Jesuits to be found, was not very probable. It was not thus nor then that the great lesson of religious equality and liberty for all men—the inevitable result of the Dutch revolt—was to be expounded. The insertion of such a condition in the preamble to a treaty with a foreign power would have been a desertion on the part of the Netherlands of the very principle of religious or civil freedom.

The monk, however, had convinced the Spanish Government that in six months after peace had been made the States would gladly accept the dominion of Spain once more, or, at the very least, would annex themselves to the obedient Netherlands under the sceptre of the archdukes.

Secondly, he assured the duke that they would publicly and totally renounce all connection with France.

Thirdly, he pledged himself that the exercise of the Catholic religion would be as free as that of any other creed.[81]

And the duke of Lerma believed it all : such and no greater was his capacity for understanding the course of events which he imagined himself to be directing. Certainly Friar John did not believe what he said.

"Master Monk is not quite so sure of his stick as he pretends to be," said Secretary-of-State Villeroy.[82] Of course, no one knew better the absurdity of those assurances than Master Monk himself.

[80] Gallucci, *ubi sup.*   [81] Negotiations de Jeannin, i, 360.
[82] Ibid. Letter of 19th Sept. 1607.

"It may be that he has held such language," said Jeannin, "in order to accomplish his object in Spain. But 'tis all dreaming and moonshine, which one should laugh at rather than treat seriously. These people here mean to be sovereign for ever and will make no peace except on that condition. This grandeur and vanity have entered so deeply into their brains that they will be torn into little pieces rather than give it up."[83]

Spinola, as acute a politician as he was a brilliant commander, at once demonstrated to his Government the impotence of such senile attempts. No definite agreements could be made, he wrote, except by a general convention. Before a treaty of peace, no permission would be given by the States to the public exercise of the Catholic religion, for fear of giving offence to what were called the Protestant powers. Unless they saw the proper ratification they would enter into no negotiations at all. When the negotiations had produced a treaty, the Catholic worship might be demanded. Thus peace might be made, and the desired conditions secured, or all parties would remain as they had been.[84]

The Spanish Government replied by sending a double form of ratification.[85] It would not have been the Spanish Government, had one simple, straightforward document been sent. Plenty of letters came at the same time, triumphantly refuting the objections and arguments of the States-General. To sign " Yo el Rey" had been the custom of the king's ancestors in dealing with foreign powers. Thus had Philip II. signed the treaty of Vervins. Thus had the reigning king confirmed the treaty of Vervins. Thus had he signed the recent treaty with England as well as other conventions with other potentates. If the French envoys at the Hague said the contrary they erred from ignorance or from baser reasons. The provinces could not be declared free until Catholic worship was conceded. The donations must be mutual and simultaneous and the States would gain a much more stable and

[83] Negotiations de Jeannin, i. 394.   Letter of 6th Oct. 1607.
[84] Gallucci, 338.   [85] Ibid. 340.

diuturnal liberty, founded not upon a simple declaration, but lawfully granted them as a compensation for a just and pious work performed. To this end the king sent ratification number one in which his sentiments were fully expressed. If, however, the provinces were resolved not to defer the declaration so ardently desired and to refuse all negotiation until they had received it, then ratification number two, therewith sent and drawn up in the required form, might be used. It was, however, to be exhibited but not delivered. The provinces would then see the clemency with which they were treated by the king, and all the world might know that it was not his fault if peace were not made.[86]

Thus the politicians of Madrid ; speaking in the name of their august sovereign and signing *"Yo el Rey"* for him without troubling him even to look at the documents.

When these letters arrived, the time fixed by the States for accepting the ratification had run out, and their patience was well-nigh exhausted. The archduke held council with Spinola, Verreyken, Richardot, and others, and it was agreed that ratification number two, in which the Catholic worship was not mentioned, should be forthwith sent to the States. Certainly no other conclusion could have been reached, and it was fortunate that a lucid interval in the deliberations of the lunatic sat Madrid had furnished the archduke with an alternative. Had it been otherwise and had number one been presented, with all the accompanying illustrations, the same dismal comedy might have gone on indefinitely until the Dutchmen hissed it away and returned to their tragic business once more.

On the 25th October, Friar John and Verreyken came before the States-General, more than a hundred members being present, besides Prince Maurice and Count Lewis William.[87] 25 Oct. 1607.

The monk stated that he had faithfully represented to his Majesty at Madrid the sincere, straightforward, and undissembling proceedings of their lordships in these negotiations.[88]

[86] Gallucci, 340.   [87] Wagenaar, ix. 285.   [88] Jeannin, i. 423.

He had also explained the constitution of their Government and had succeeded in obtaining from his royal Majesty the desired ratification, after due deliberation with the council. This would now give the assurance of a firm and durable peace, continued Neyen, even if his Majesty should come one day to die—being mortal. Otherwise, there might be inconveniences to fear. Now, however, the document was complete in all its parts, so far as regarded what was principal and essential, and in conformity with the form transmitted by the States-General. "God the Omnipotent knows," proceeded the friar, "how sincere is my intention in this treaty of peace as a means of delivering the Netherlands from the miseries of war, as your lordships will perceive by the form of the agreement, explaining itself and making manifest its pure and undissembling intentions, promising nothing and engaging to nothing which will not be effectually performed. This would not be the case if his Majesty were proceeding by finesse or deception. The ratification might be nakedly produced as demanded, without any other explanation. But his Majesty, acting in good faith, has now declared his last determination in order to avoid anything that might be disputed at some future day, as your lordships will see more amply when the auditor has exhibited the document." [89]

When the friar had finished Verreyken spoke.

He reminded them of the proofs already given by the archdukes of their sincere desire to change the long and sanguinary war into a good and assured peace. Their lordships the States had seen how liberally, sincerely, and roundly their Highnesses had agreed to all demands and had procured the ratification of his Majesty, even although nothing had been proposed in that regard at the beginning of the negotiations.

He then produced the original document, together with two copies, one in French the other in Flemish, to be carefully collated by the States. [90]

"It is true," said the auditor, "that the original is not

[89] Jeannin, i. 422, 423.   [90] Ibid. 423, 424.

made out in Latin nor in French as your lordships demanded, but in Spanish, and in the same form and style as used by his Majesty in treating with all the kings, potentates, and republics of Christendom. To tell you the truth, it has seemed strange that there should be a wish to make so great and puissant a king change his style, such demand being contrary to all reason and equity, and more so as his Majesty is content with the style which your lordships have been pleased to adopt."

The ratification was then exhibited.

It set forth that Don Philip, by grace of God King of Castile, Leon, Arragon, the Two Sicilies, Portugal, Navarre, and of fourteen or fifteen other European realms duly enumerated ; King of the Eastern and Western Indies and of the continents on terra firma adjacent, King of Jerusalem, Archduke of Antioch, Duke of Burgundy, and King of the Ocean, having seen that the archdukes were content to treat with the States-General of the United Provinces in quality of, and as holding them for, countries, provinces, and free states over which they pretended to no authority ; either by way of a perpetual peace or for a truce or suspension of arms for twelve, fifteen, or twenty years, at the choice of the said States, and knowing that the said most serene archdukes had promised to deliver the king's ratification ; had, after ripe deliberation with his council, and out of his certain wisdom and absolute royal power, made the present declarations, similar to the one made by the archdukes, for the accomplishment of the said promise so far as it concerned him :

"And we principally declare," continued the King of Spain, Jerusalem, America, India, and the Ocean, "that we are content that in our name, and on our part, shall be treated with the said States in the quality of, and as held by us for, free countries, provinces, and states, over which we make no pretensions. Thus we approve and ratify every point of the said agreement, promising on faith and word of a king to guard and accomplish it as entirely as if we had consented to it from the beginning."

"But we declare," said the king, in conclusion, "that if the treaty for a peace or a truce of many years, by which the pretensions of both parties are to be arranged—as well in the matter of religion as all the surplus—shall not be concluded, then this ratification shall be of no effect and as if it never had been made and, in virtue of it, we are not to lose a single point of our right, nor the United Provinces to acquire one, but things are to remain, so far as regards the rights of the two parties, exactly as they are at present ; each to do what to each shall seem best."[91]

Such were the substantial parts of the document—with much superfluous verbiage lopped away—which had been signed "I the King" at Madrid on the 18th September, and the two copies of which were presented to the States-General on the 25th October, the commissioners retaining the original.

The papers were accepted, with a few general commonplaces by Barneveld meaning nothing, and an answer was promised after a brief delay.[92]

A committee of seven, headed by the Advocate as chairman and spokesman, held a conference with the ambassadors of France and England, at four o'clock in the afternoon of the same day and another at ten o'clock next morning.[93]

The States were not very well pleased with the ratification. What especially moved their discontent was the concluding clause, according to which it was intimated that if the pretensions of Spain in regard to religion were not fulfilled in the final treaty, the ratification was waste-paper and the king would continue to claim all his rights.

How much more loudly would they have vociferated, could they have looked into Friar John's wallet and have seen ratification number one ! Then they would have learned that, after nearly a year of what was called negotiation, the king had still meant to demand the restoration of the Catholic worship before he would even begin to entertain the little fiction that the provinces were free.

[91] Jeannin, i. 425–429.   [92] Ibid. 433.   [93] Ibid. 432–438.

As to the signature, the paper, and the Spanish language, those were minor matters. Indeed, it is difficult to say why the King of Spain should not issue a formal document in Spanish. It is doubtful whether, had he taken a fancy to read it, he could have understood it in any other tongue. Moreover, Spanish would seem the natural language for Spanish state-papers. Had he, as King of Jerusalem, America, or India, chosen the Hebrew, Aztec, or Sanscrit, in his negotiations with the United Provinces, there might have been more cause for dissatisfaction.

Jeannin, who was of course the leading spirit among the foreign members of the conference, advised the acceptance of the ratification. Notwithstanding the technical objections to its form, he urged that in substance it was in sufficient conformity to the draught furnished by the States. Nothing could be worse, in his opinion, for the provinces than to remain any longer suspended between peace and war. They would do well, therefore, to enter upon negotiations so soon as they had agreed among themselves upon three points.

They must fix the great indispensable terms which they meant to hold, and from which no arguments would ever induce them to recede. Thus they would save valuable time and be spared much frivolous discourse.

Next, they ought to establish a good interior government.

Thirdly, they should at once arrange their alliances and treaties with foreign powers, in order to render the peace to be negotiated a durable one.[94]

As to the first and second of these points, the Netherlanders needed no prompter. They had long ago settled the conditions without which they would make no treaty at all, and certainly it was not the States-General that had thus far been frivolously consuming time.

As to the form of government, defective though it was, the leaders of the republic knew very well in whose interests such sly allusions to their domestic affairs were repeatedly ventured by the French envoys. In regard to treaties with

[94] Jeannin, i. 432–437.

foreign powers it was, of course, most desirable for the republic to obtain the formal alliance of France and England. Jeannin and his colleagues were ready to sign such a treaty, offensive and defensive, at once, but they found it impossible to induce the English ambassadors, with whom there was a conference on the 26th October, to come into any written engagement on the subject. They expressed approbation of the plan individually and in words, but deemed it best to avoid any protocol, by which their sovereign could be implicated in a promise. Should the negotiations for peace be broken off, it would be time enough to make a treaty to protect the provinces. Meantime, they ought to content themselves with the general assurance, already given them, that in case of war the monarchs of France and England would not abandon them, but would provide for their safety, either by succour or in some other way, so that they would be placed out of danger.[95]

Such promises were vague without being magnificent, and, as James had never yet lifted his finger to assist the provinces, while indulging them frequently with oracular advice, it could hardly be expected that either the French envoys or the States-General would reckon very confidently on assistance from Great Britain, should war be renewed with Spain.

On the whole, it was agreed to draw up a paper briefly stating the opinion of the French and English plenipotentiaries that the provinces would do well to accept the ratification.[96]

The committee of the States, with Barneveld as chairman, expressed acquiescence, but urged that they could not approve the clause in that document concerning religion. It looked as if the King of Spain wished to force them to consent by treaty that the Catholic religion should be re-established in their country. As they were free and sovereign, however, and so recognised by himself, it was not for him to meddle with such matters. They foresaw that this

[95] Jeannin. i. 434.   [96] Ibid. 429.

clause would create difficulties when the whole matter should be referred to the separate provinces, and that it would, perhaps, cause the entire rejection of the ratification.

The envoys, through the voice of Jeannin, remonstrated against such a course. After all, the objectionable clause, it was urged, should be considered only as a demand which the king was competent to make and it was not reasonable, they said, for the States to shut his mouth and prevent him from proposing what he thought good to propose.

On the other hand, they were not obliged to acquiesce in the proposition. In truth, it would be more expedient that the States themselves should grant this grace to the Catholics, thus earning their gratitude, rather than that it should be inserted in the treaty.[97]

A day or two later there was an interview between the French envoys and Count Lewis William, for whose sage, dispassionate, and upright character they had all a great respect.[98] It was their object—in obedience to the repeated instructions of the French king—to make use of his great influence over Prince Maurice in favour of peace. It would be better, they urged, that the stadholder should act more in harmony with the States than he had done of late, and should reflect that, the ratification being good, there was really no means of preventing a peace, except in case the King of Spain should refuse the conditions necessary for securing it. The prince would have more power by joining with the States than in opposing them. Count Lewis expressed sympathy with these views, but feared that Maurice would prefer that the ratification should not be accepted until the states of the separate provinces had been heard ; feeling convinced that several of those bodies would reject that instrument on account of the clause relating to religion.

Jeannin replied that such a course would introduce great discord into the provinces, to the profit of the enemy, and that the King of France himself—so far from being likely to wish the ratification rejected because of the clause—would

[97] Jeannin, i. 435.   [98] Ibid. 437.

never favour the rupture of negotiations if it came on account of religion. He had always instructed them to use their efforts to prevent any division among the States, as sure to lead to their ruin. He would certainly desire the same stipulation as the one made by the King of Spain, and would support rather than oppose the demand thus made, in order to content the Catholics. To be sure, he would prefer that the States should wisely make this provision of their own accord rather than on the requisition of Spain, but a rupture of the pending negotiations from the cause suggested would be painful to him and very damaging to his character at Rome.[99]

On the 2nd November the States-General gave their formal answer to the commissioners, in regard to the ratification.

2nd Nov.

That instrument, they observed, not only did not agree with the form as promised by the archdukes in language and style, but also in regard to the seal, and to the insertion and omission of several words. On this account, and especially by reason of the concluding clause, there might be inferred the annulment of the solemn promise made in the body of the instrument. The said king and archdukes knew very well that these States-General of free countries and provinces, over which the king and archdukes pretended to no authority, were competent to maintain order in all things regarding the good constitution and government of their land and its inhabitants. On this subject, nothing could be pretented or proposed on the part of the king and archdukes without violation of formal and solemn promises.[100]

"Nevertheless," continued the States-General, "in order not to retard a good work, already begun, for the purpose of bringing the United Provinces out of a long and bloody war into a Christian and assured peace, the letters of ratification will be received in respect that they contain the declaration, on part of both the king and the archdukes, that they will treat for a peace or a truce of many years with the States-

[99] Jeannin, i. 432–437.　[100] Ibid. V. d. Kemp, iii. 30.　Wagenaar, ix. 287. 288.

General of the United Provinces, in quality of, and as holding them to be, free countries, provinces, and states, over which they make no pretensions." [101]

It was further intimated, however, that the ratification was only received for reference to the estates of each of the provinces, and it was promised that, within six weeks, the commissioners should be informed whether the provinces would consent or refuse to treat. It was moreover declared that, neither at that moment nor at any future time, could any point in the letters of ratification be accepted which, directly or indirectly, might be interpreted as against that essential declaration and promise in regard to the freedom of the provinces. In case the decision should be taken to enter into negotiation upon the basis of that ratification, or any other that might meantime arrive from Spain, then firm confidence was expressed by the States that, neither on the part of the king nor that of the archdukes would there be proposed or pretended, in contravention of that promise, any point touching the good constitution, welfare, state, or government of the United Provinces, and of the inhabitants. The hope was furthermore expressed that, within ten days after the reception of the consent of the States to treat, commissioners would be sent by the archdukes to the Hague, fully authorised and instructed to declare roundly their intentions, in order to make short work of the whole business. In that case, the States would duly authorize and instruct commissioners to act in their behalf.

Thus in the answer especial warning was given against any possible attempt to interfere with the religious question. The phraseology could not be mistaken.

At this stage of the proceedings, the States demanded that the original instrument of ratification should be deposited with them. The two commissioners declared that they were without power to consent to this. Hereupon the Assembly became violent, and many members denounced the refusal as equivalent to breaking off the negotiations. Everything

---

[101] Jeannin, i, 430.

indicated, so it was urged, a desire on the Spanish side to spin delays out of delays, and, meantime, to invent daily some new trap for deception. Such was the vehemence upon this point that the industrious Franciscan posted back to Brussels, and returned with the archduke's permission to deliver the document.[102] Three conditions, however, were laid down. The States must give a receipt for the ratification. They must say in that receipt that the archdukes, in obtaining the paper from Spain, had fulfilled their original promise. If peace should not be made, they were to return the document.

When these conditions were announced, the indignation of the republican Government at the trifling of their opponents was fiercer than ever. The discrepancies between the form prescribed and the ratification obtained had always been very difficult of digestion, but, although willing to pass them by, the States stoutly refused to accept the document on these conditions.

Tooth and nail[103] Verreyken and Neyen fought out the contest and were worsted. Once more the nimble friar sped back and forth between the Hague and his employer's palace, and at last, after tremendous discussions in cabinet council, the conditions were abandoned.

"Nobody can decide," says the Jesuit historian, "which was greater—the obstinacy of the federal Government in screwing out of the opposite party everything it deemed necessary, or the indulgence of the archdukes in making every possible concession."[104]

Had these solemn tricksters of an antiquated school perceived that, in dealing with men who meant what they said and said what they meant, all these little dilatory devices were superfluous, perhaps the wholesome result might have sooner been reached. In a contest of diplomacy against time it generally happens that time is the winner, and on this occasion, time and the republic were fighting on the same side.

[102] Gallucci, 342.   [103] "Mordicus." Ibid.   [104] Ibid.

On the 13th December the States-General re-assembled at the Hague, the separate provinces having in the interval given fresh instructions to their representatives. It was now decided that no treaty should be made, unless the freedom of the commonwealth was recognized in phraseology which, after consultation with the foreign ambassadors, should be deemed satisfactory. Farther it was agreed that, neither in ecclesiastical nor secular matters, should any conditions be accepted which could be detrimental to freedom. In case the enemy should strive for the contrary, the world would be convinced that he alone was responsible for the failure of the peace negotiations. Then, with the support of other powers friendly to the republic, hostilities could be resumed in such a manner as to ensure a favourable issue for an upright cause.

The armistice, begun on the 4th of May, was running to an end, and it was now renewed at the instance of the States. That Government, moreover, on the 23rd December formally notified to the archdukes that, trusting to their declarations, and to the statements of Neyen and Verreyken, it was willing to hold conferences for peace.[105] Their Highnesses were accordingly invited to appoint seven or eight commissioners at once, on the same terms as formally indicated.

The original understanding had been that no envoys but Netherlanders should come from Brussels for these negotiations.[106]

Barneveld and the peace party, however, were desirous that Spinola, who was known to be friendly to a pacific result, should be permitted to form part of the mission. Accordingly the letters, publicly drawn up in the Assembly, adhered to the original arrangement, but Barneveld, with the privity of other leading personages, although without the knowledge of Maurice, Lewis William, and the State-Council, secretly enclosed a little note in the principal despatch to Neyen and Verreyken.[107] In this billet it was intimated that, notwith-

---

[105] Resol. Holl. 4 Dec. 1607. Wagenaar, ix. 290, 291.

[106] Wagenaar, ix. 247, 293.

[107] Resol. Holl. 4 Dec. Wagenaar, ix. 293-295. Van der Kemp, iii. 31, 134, 135.

standing the prohibition in regard to foreigners, the States were willing—it having been proposed that one or two who were not Netherlanders should be sent—that a single Spaniard, provided he were not one of the principal military commanders, should make part of the embassy.[108]

The phraseology had a double meaning. Spinola was certainly the chief military commander, but he was not a Spaniard. This eminent personage might be supposed to have thus received permission to come to the Netherlands, despite all that had been urged by the war-party against the danger incurred, in case of a renewal of hostilities, by admitting so clear-sighted an enemy into the heart of the republic. Moreover, the terms of the secret note would authorize the appointment of another foreigner—even a Spaniard—while the crafty president Richardot might creep into the commission, on the ground that, being a Burgundian, he might fairly call himself a Netherlander.

And all this happened.

Thus, after a whole year of parley, in which the States-General had held firmly to their original position, while the Spanish Government had crept up inch by inch, and through countless windings and subterfuges, to the point on which they might have all stood together at first, and thus have saved a twelvemonth, it was finally settled that peace conferences should begin.

Barneveld had carried the day. Maurice and his cousin Lewis William had uniformly, deliberately, but not factiously, used all their influence against any negotiations. The prince had all along loudly expressed his conviction that neither the archdukes nor Spain would ever be brought to an honourable peace. The most to be expected of them was a truce of twelve or fifteen years, to which his consent at least should never be given, and during which cessation of hostilities, should it be accorded, every imaginable effort would be made to regain by intrigue what the king had lost by the sword.[109] As for the King of England and his counsellors, Maurice

---

[108] Authorities last cited.　　　[109] Van der Kemp, iii. 16.

always denounced them as more Spanish than Spaniards, as doing their best to put themselves on the most intimate terms with his Catholic Majesty, and as secretly desirous— insane policy as it seemed—of forcing the Netherlands back again under the sceptre of that monarch.

He had at first been supported in his position by the French ambassadors, who had felt or affected disinclination for peace, but who had subsequently thrown the whole of their own and their master's influence on the side of Barne- veld. They had done their best—and from time to time they had been successful—to effect at least a superficial reconcilia- tion between those two influential personages. They had employed all the arguments at their disposal to bring the prince over to the peace party. Especially they had made use of the *argumentum ad crumenam*, which that veteran broker in politics, Jeannin, had found so effective in times past with the great lords of the League. But Maurice showed himself so proof against the golden inducements suggested by the President that he and his king both arrived at the conclusion that there were secret motives at work, and that Maurice was not dazzled by the brilliant prospects held out to him by Henry, only because his eyes were stedfastly fixed upon some unknown but splendid advantage, to be gained through other combinations. It was naturally difficult for Henry to imagine the possibility of a man, playing a first part in the world's theatre, being influenced by so weak a motive as conviction.

Lewis William too—that " grave and wise young man," as Lord Leicester used to call him twenty years before—re- mained steadily on the side of the prince. Both in private conversation and in long speeches to the States-General, he maintained that the Spanish court was incapable of sincere negotiations with the commonwealth, that to break faith with heretics and rebels would always prove the foundation of its whole policy, and that to deceive them by pretences of a truce or a treaty, and to triumph afterwards over the results of its fraud, was to be expected as a matter of course.

Sooner would the face of nature be changed than the cardinal maxim of Catholic statesmanship be abandoned.[110]

But the influence of the Nassaus, of the province of Zeeland, of the clergy, and of the war-party in general, had been overbalanced by Barneveld and the city corporations, aided by the strenuous exertions of the French ambassadors. The decision of the States-General was received with sincere joy at Brussels. The archdukes had something to hope from peace, and little but disaster and ruin to themselves from a continuance of the war. Spinola too was unaffectedly in favour of negotiations. He took the ground that the foreign enemies of Spain, as well as her pretended friends, agreed in wishing her to go on with the war, and that this ought to open her eyes as to the expediency of peace. While there was a general satisfaction in Europe that the steady exhaustion of her strength in this eternal contest made her daily less and less formidable to other nations, there were on the other hand puerile complaints at court that the conditions prescribed by impious and insolent rebels to their sovereign were derogatory to the dignity of monarchy.[111] The spectacle of Spain sending ambassadors to the Hague to treat for peace, on the basis of Netherland independence, would be a humiliation such as had never been exhibited before. That the haughty confederation should be allowed thus to accomplish its ends, to trample down all resistance to its dictation, and to defy the whole world by its insults to the Church and to the sacred principle of monarchy, was most galling to Spanish pride. Spinola, as a son of Italy, and not inspired by the fervent hatred to Protestantism which was indigenous to the other peninsula, steadily resisted those arguments. None knew better than he the sternness of the stuff out of which that republic was made, and he felt that now or never was the time to treat, even as, five years before, *jam aut nunquam* had been inscribed on his banner outside Ostend. But he protested that his friends gave him even

---

[110] See especially Resol. Stat.-Gen. 30 Oct 1607, in Van der Kemp, iii. 126–130.
[111] Spinola's letters, *apud* Gallucci, 347, *seqq.* Bentivoglio.

harder work than his enemies had ever done, and he stoutly maintained that a peace against which all the rivals of Spain seemed to have conspired from fear of seeing her tranquil and disembarrassed, must be advantageous to Spain. The genial and quick-witted Genoese could not see and hear all the secret letters and private conversations of Henry and James and their ambassadors, and he may be pardoned for supposing that, notwithstanding all the crooked and incomprehensible politics of Greenwich and Paris, the serious object of both England and France was to prolong the war. In his most private correspondence he expressed great doubts as to a favourable issue to the pending conferences, but avowed his determination that if they should fail it would be from no want of earnest effort on his part to make them succeed. It should never be said that he preferred his own private advantage to the duty of serving the best interests of the crown.[112]

Meantime the India trade, which was to form the great bone of contention in the impending conferences, had not been practically neglected of late by the enterprising Hollanders. Peter Verhoeff, fresh from the victory of Gibraltar, towards which he had personally so much contributed by the splendid manner in which he had handled the Æolus after the death of Admiral Heemskerk, was placed in command of a fleet to the East Indies, which was to sail early in the spring.[113]

Admiral Matelieff, who had been cruising in those seas during the three years past, was now on his way home. His exploits had been worthy the growing fame of the republican navy. In the summer of 1606 he had laid siege to the town and fortress of Malacca, constructed by the Portuguese at the southmost extremity of the Malay peninsula. Andreas Hurtado de Mendoza commanded the position, with a force of three thousand men, among whom were many Indians. The King or Sultan of Johore, at the south-eastern extremity of the peninsula, remained faithful to his Dutch

1606.

[112] Gallucci, 349, 350.   [113] Wagenaar, ix. 801.

allies, and accepted the proposition of Matelieff to take part in the hostilities now begun.   The admiral's fleet consisted of eleven small ships, with fourteen hundred men.   It was not exactly a military expedition.   To the sailors of each ship were assigned certain shares of the general profits, and as it was obvious that more money was likely to be gained by trade with the natives, or by the capture of such stray carracks and other merchantmen of the enemy as were frequently to be met in these regions, the men were not particularly eager to take part in sieges of towns or battles with cruisers.   Matelieff, however, had sufficient influence over his comrades to inflame their zeal on this occasion for the fame of the republic, and to induce them to give the Indian princes and the native soldiery a lesson in Batavian warfare.

A landing was effected on the peninsula, the sailors and guns were disembarked, and an imposing auxiliary force, sent, according to promise, after much delay, by the Sultan of Johore, proceeded to invest Malacca.   The ground proved wet, swampy, and impracticable for trenches, galleries, covered ways, and all the other machinery of a regular siege. Matelieff was not a soldier nor a naval commander by profession, but a merchant-skipper, like so many other heroes whose achievements were to be the permanent glory of their fatherland.   He would not, however, have been a Netherlander had he not learned something of the science which Prince Maurice had so long been teaching, not only to his own countrymen but to the whole world.   So moveable turrets, constructed of the spice-trees which grew in rank luxuriance all around, were filled with earth and stones, and advanced towards the fort. Had the natives been as docile to learn as the Hollanders were eager to teach a few easy lessons in the military art, the doom of Andreas Hurtado de Mendoza would have been sealed. But the great truths which those youthful pedants, Maurice and Lewis William, had extracted twenty years before from the works of the Emperor Leo and earlier pagans, amid the jeers of veterans, were not easy to transplant to the Malayan peninsula.

It soon proved that those white-turbaned, loose-garmented, supple-jointed, highly-picturesque troops of the sultan were not likely to distinguish themselves for anything but wonderful rapidity in retreat. Not only did they shrink from any advance towards the distant forts, but they were incapable of abiding an attack within or behind their towers, and, at every random shot from the enemy's works, they threw down their arms and fled from their stations in dismay. It was obvious enough that the conquest and subjugation of such feeble warriors by the Portuguese and Spaniards were hardly to be considered brilliant national trophies. They had fallen an easy prey to the first European invader. They had no discipline, no obedience, no courage ; and Matelieff soon found that to attempt a scientific siege with such auxiliaries against a well-constructed stone fortress, garrisoned with three thousand troops, under an experienced Spanish soldier, was but midsummer madness.

Fevers and horrible malaria, bred by the blazing sun of the equator out of those pestilential jungles, poisoned the atmosphere. His handful of troops, amounting to not much more than a hundred men to each of his ships, might melt away before his eyes. Nevertheless, although it was impossible for him to carry the place by regular approach, he would not abandon the hope of reducing it by famine. During four months long, accordingly, he kept every avenue by land or sea securely invested. In August, however, the Spanish viceroy of India, Don Alphonso de Castro, made his appearance on the scene. Coming from Goa with a splendid fleet, numbering fourteen great galleons, four galleys, and sixteen smaller vessels, manned by three thousand seven hundred Portuguese and other Europeans, and an equal number of native troops, he had at first directed his course towards Atchen, on the north-west point of Sumatra. Here, with the magnificent arrogance which Spanish and Portuguese viceroys were accustomed to manifest towards the natives of either India, he summoned the king to surrender his strongholds, to assist in constructing a fortress for the use of his conquerors, to deliver

up all the Netherlanders within his domains, and to pay the
expenses of the expedition which had thus been sent to
chastise him. But the King of Atchen had not sent ambassadors into the camp of Prince Maurice before the city of
Grave in vain. He had learned that there were other white
skins besides the Spaniards at the antipodes, and that the
republic whose achievements in arts and arms were conspicuous trophies of Western civilization, was not, as it had been
represented to him, a mere nest of pirates. He had learned
to prefer an alliance with Holland to slavery under Spain.
Moreover, he had Dutch engineers and architects in his service, and a well-constructed system of Dutch fortifications
around his capital. To the summons to surrender himself
and his allies he returned a defiant answer. The viceroy
ordered an attack upon the city. One fort was taken. From
before the next he was repulsed with great loss. The
Sumatrans had derived more profit from intercourse with
Europeans than the inhabitants of Johore or the Moluccas
had done. De Castro abandoned the siege. He had received
intelligence of the dangerous situation of Malacca, and moved
down upon the place with his whole fleet. Admiral Matelieff,
apprised by scouts of his approach, behaved with the readiness and coolness of a veteran campaigner. Before De Castro
could arrive in the roadstead of Malacca, he had withdrawn
all his troops from their positions, got all his artillery re-
shipped, and was standing out in the straits, awaiting the
enemy.

On the 17th August, the two fleets, so vastly dispropor-
17 Aug. tionate in number, size, equipment, and military
1606.   force—eighteen galleons and galleys, with four
or five thousand fighting men, against eleven small vessels
and twelve or fourteen hundred sailors—met in that narrow
sea. The action lasted all day. It was neither spirited nor
sanguinary. It ought to have been within the power of the
Spaniard to crush his diminutive adversary. It might have
seemed a sufficient triumph for Matelieft to manœuvre himself out of harm's way. No vessel on either side was boarded,

not one surrendered, but two on each side were set on fire and destroyed. Eight of the Dutchmen were killed—not a very sanguinary result after a day's encounter with so imposing an armada. De Castro's losses were much greater, but still the battle was an insignificant one, and neither fleet gained a victory. Night put an end to the cannonading, and the Spaniards withdrew to Malacca, while Matelieff bore away to Johore. The siege of Malacca was relieved, and the Netherlanders now occupied themselves with the defence of the feeble sovereign at the other point of the peninsula.

Matelieff lay at Johore a month, repairing damages and laying in supplies. While still at the place, he received information that a large part of the Spanish armada had sailed from Malacca. Several of his own crew, who had lost their shares in the adventure by the burning of the ships to which they belonged in the action of 17th August, were reluctant and almost mutinous when their admiral now proposed to them a sudden assault on the portion of the Spanish fleet still remaining within reach. They had not come forth for barren glory, many protested, but in search of fortune ; they were not elated by the meagre result of the expedition. Matelieff succeeded, however, at last in inspiring all the men of his command with an enthusiasm superior to sordid appeals, and made a few malcontents. On the 21st September, he sailed to Malacca, and late in the afternoon again attacked the Spaniards. Their fleet consisted of seven great galleons and three galleys lying in a circle before the town. The outermost ship, called the St. Nicholas, was boarded by men from three of the Dutch galleots with sudden and irresistible fury. There was a brief but most terrible action, the Netherlanders seeming endowed with superhuman vigour. So great was the panic that there was hardly an effort at defence, and within less than an hour nearly every Spaniard on board the St. Nicholas had been put to the sword. The rest of the armada engaged the Dutch fleet with spirit, but one of the great galleons was soon set on fire and burned to the water's edge. Another, dismasted and crippled, struck her flag, and all that remained would probably have been surrendered or destroyed had not the sudden darkness of a tropical nightfall put an end to the combat at set of sun. Next morning another galleon, in a shattered and sinking condition, was taken possession of and found filled with dead and dying. The rest of the Spanish ships made their escape into the harbour of Malacca. Matelieff stood off and on in the straits for a day or two, hesitating for fear of shallows to follow into the roadstead. Before he could take a decision, he had the satisfaction of seeing the enemy, panic-struck, save him any further trouble. Not waiting for another attack, the Spaniards set fire to every one of their ships, and retired into their fortress, while Matelieff and his men enjoyed the great conflagration as idle spectators. Thus the enterprising Dutch admiral had destroyed ten great war-ships of the enemy, and, strange to relate, had scarcely lost one man of his whole squadron. Rarely had a more complete triumph been achieved on the water than in this battle in the straits of Malacca. Matelieff had gained much glory but very little booty. He was also encumbered with a great number of prisoners. These he sent to Don Alphonso, exchanging them for a very few Netherlanders then in Spanish hands, at the rate of two hundred Spaniards for ten Dutchmen —thus showing that he held either the enemy very cheap, or his own countrymen very dear. The captured ships he burned as useless to him, but retained twenty-four pieces of artillery.

It was known to Matelieff that the Spanish viceroy had received instructions to inflict chastisement on all the oriental potentates and their subjects who had presumed of late to trade and to form alliances with the Netherlanders. Johore, Achem, Paham, Patane, Amboyna, and Bantam, were the most probable points of attack. Johore had now been effectually defended, Achem had protected itself. The Dutch fleet proceeded at first to Bantam for refreshment, and from this point Matelieff sent three of his ships back to Holland. With the six remaining to him, he sailed for the Moluccas, having heard of various changes which had taken place in that important archipelago. Pausing at the great emporium of nutmegs and all-spice, Amboyna, he took measures for strengthening the fortifications of the place, which was well governed by Frederick Houtman, and then proceeded to Ternate and Tidor.

During the absence of the Netherlanders, after the events on those islands recorded in a previous chapter, the Spaniards had swept down upon them from the Philippines with a fleet of thirty-seven ships, and had taken captive the Sultan of Ternate ; while the potentate of Tidor, who had been left by Stephen van der Hagen in possession of his territories on condition of fidelity to the Dutch, was easily induced to throw aside the mask, and to renew his servitude to Spain. Thus both the coveted clove-islands had relapsed into the control of the enemy. Matelieff found it dangerous, on account of quicksands and shallows, to land on Tydore, but he took very energetic measures to recover possession of Ternate. On the southern side of the island, the Spaniards had built a fort and a town. The Dutch admiral disembarked upon the northern side, and, with assistance of the natives, succeeded in throwing up substantial fortifications at a village called Malaya. The son of the former sultan, who was a Spanish prisoner at the Philippines, was now formally inducted into his father's sovereignty, and Matelieff established at Malaya for his protection a garrison of forty-five Hollanders and a navy of four small yachts. Such were the slender means with which Oriental empires were founded in those days by the stout-hearted adventurers of the little Batavian republic.

With this miniature army and navy, and by means of his alliance with the distant commonwealth, of whose power this handful of men was a symbol, the King of Ternate was thenceforth to hold his own against the rival potentate on the other island, supported by the Spanish king. The same convention of commerce and amity was made with the Ternatians as the one which Stephen van der Hagen had formerly concluded with the Bandians, and it was agreed that

the potentate should be included in any treaty of peace
that might be made between the republic and Spain.

Matelieff, with three ships and a cutter, now sailed for
China, but lost his time in endeavouring to open trade with
the Celestial empire. The dilatory mandarins drove him at
last out of all patience, and, on turning his prows once more
southward, he had nearly brought his long expedition to a
disastrous termination. Six well-armed, well-equipped Portuguese galleons sailed out of Macao to assail him. It was
not Matelieff's instinct to turn his back on a foe, however
formidable, but on this occasion discretion conquered instinct.
His three ships were out of repair ; he had a deficiency of
powder ; he was in every respect unprepared for a combat ;
and he reflected upon the unfavourable impression which
would be made on the Chinese mind should the Hollanders,
upon their first appearance in the flowery regions, be vanquished by the Portuguese. He avoided an encounter, therefore, and, by skilful seamanship, eluded all attempts of the
foe at pursuit. Returning to Ternate, he had the satisfaction
to find that during his absence the doughty little garrison of
Malaya had triumphantly defeated the Spaniards in an assault
on the fortifications of the little town. On the other hand,
the King of Johore, panic-struck on the departure of his
Dutch protectors, had burned his own capital, and had
betaken himself with all his court into the jungle.

Commending the one and rebuking the other potentate,
the admiral provided assistance for both, some Dutch trading-
vessels having meantime arrived in the archipelago. Matelieff
now set sail for Holland, taking with him some ambassadors
from the King of Siam and five ships well laden with spice.
On his return he read a report of his adventures to the States-
General, and received the warm commendations of their
High Mightinesses.[114] Before his departure from the tropics,
Paul van Kaarden, with eight war-ships, had reached Ban-

---

[114] The authorities for Matelieff's voyages are Grotius, xvii. 792-800 ; Meteren, 562, 563 ; and especially the original journals and records in "Begin und
Vortgang."

tam. On his arrival in Holland the fleet of Peter ver Hoef was busily fitting out for another great expedition to the East.[115] This was the nation which Spanish courtiers thought to exclude for ever from commerce with India and America, because the Pope a century before had divided half the globe between Ferdinand the Catholic and Emmanuel the Fortunate.

It may be supposed that the results of Matelieff's voyage were likely to influence the pending negotiations for peace.

[115] Authorities last cited.

CHAPTER L.

Movements of the Emperor Rudolph — Marquis Spinola's reception at the
Hague — Meeting of Spinola and Prince Maurice — Treaty of the Republic
with the French Government — The Spanish commissioners before the
States-General — Beginning of negotiations — Stormy discussions — Real
object of Spain in the negotiations — Question of the India trade —
Abandonment of the peace project — Negotiations for a truce — Prolongation of the armistice — Further delays — Treaty of the States with
England — Proposals of the Spanish ambassadors to Henry of France and
to James of England — Friar Neyen at the court of Spain — Spanish procrastination — Decision of Philip on the conditions of peace — Further
conference at the Hague — Answer of the States-General to the proposals
of the Spanish Government — General rupture.

TOWARDS the close of the year 1607 a very feeble demonstration was made in the direction of the Dutch republic by
the very feeble Emperor of Germany. Rudolph, awaking as
it might be from a trance, or descending for a moment from
his star-gazing tower and his astrological pursuits to observe
the movements of political spheres, suddenly discovered that
the Netherlands were no longer revolving in their pre-
ordained orbit. Those provinces had been supposed to form
part of one great system, deriving light and heat from the
central imperial sun. It was time therefore to put an end
to these perturbations. The emperor accordingly, as if he
had not enough on his hands at that precise moment with
the Hungarians, Transylvanians, Bohemian protestants, his
brother Matthias and the Grand Turk, addressed a letter to
the States of Holland, Zeeland, and the provinces confederated with them.[1]

Reminding them of the care ever taken by himself and his
father to hear all their petitions, and to obtain for them a
good peace, he observed that he had just heard of their con-

[1] Meteren, 553, *et seq.* Wagenaar, ix. 295-299. Grotius, xvi. 751, 752.

templated negotiations with King Philip and Archduke Albert, and of their desire to be declared free states and peoples. He was amazed, he said, that they should not have given him notice of so important an affair, inasmuch as all the United Provinces belonged to and were fiefs of the holy Roman Empire. They were warned, therefore, to undertake nothing that might be opposed to the feudal law   9 Oct. except with his full knowledge. This letter was   1607. dated the 9th of October. The States took time to deliberate, and returned no answer until after the new year.[2]

On the 2nd of January, 1608, they informed the emperor that they could never have guessed of his requiring notification as to the approaching conferences. They had   1608. not imagined that the archduke would keep them a secret from his brother, or the king from his uncle-cousin. Otherwise, the States would have sent due notice to his Majesty. They well remembered, they said, the appeals made by the provinces to the emperor from time to time, at the imperial diets, for help against the tyranny of the Spaniards. They well remembered, too, that no help was ever given them in response to those appeals. They had not forgotten either the famous Cologne negotiations for peace in presence of the imperial envoys, in consequence of which the enemy had carried on war against them with greater ferocity than before. At that epoch they had made use of an extreme remedy for an intolerable evil, and had solemnly renounced allegiance to the king. Since that epoch a whole generation of mankind had passed away, and many kings and potentates had recognised their freedom, obtained for just cause and maintained by the armed hand. After a long and bloody war, Albert and Philip had at last been brought to acknowledge the provinces as free countries over which they pretended to no right, as might be seen by the letters of both, copies of which were forwarded to the emperor. Full confidence was now expressed, therefore, that the emperor and all Germany would look with favour on such a God-fearing trans-

[2] Authorities last cited.

action, by which an end would be put to so terrible a war.[3]
Thus the States-General ; replying with gentle scorn to the
antiquated claim of sovereignty on the part of imperial
majesty.   Duly authenticated by citations of investitures,
indulgences, and concordates, engrossed on yellowest parch-
ment, sealed with reddest sealing-wax, and reposing in a
thousand pigeon-holes in mustiest archives, no claim could be
more solemn or stately.   Unfortunately, however, rebel pikes
and matchlocks, during the past forty years, had made too
many rents in those sacred parchments to leave much hope
of their ever being pieced handsomely together again.   As
to the historical theory of imperial enfeoffment, the States
thought it more delicate to glide smoothly and silently over
the whole matter.   It would have been base to acknowledge
and impolite to refute the claim.[4]

It is as well to imitate this reserve.   It is enough simply
to remind the reader that although so late as the time
of Charles V., the provinces had been declared constituent
parts of the empire, liable to its burthens, and entitled to its
protection ; the Netherlanders being practical people, and
deeming burthens and protection correlative, had declined
the burthen because always deprived of the protection.

And now, after a year spent in clearing away the mountains of dust which impeded the pathway to peace, and
which one honest vigorous human breath might at once have
blown into space, the envoys of the archduke set forth
towards the Hague.

Marquis Spinola, Don Juan de Mancicidor, private secretary to the King of Spain, President Richardot, Auditor
Verreyken, and Brother John Neyen—a Genoese, a Spaniard,
a Burgundian, a Fleming, and a Franciscan friar—travelling
in great state, with a long train of carriages, horses, lackeys,
cooks, and secretaries, by way of Breda, Bergen-op-Zoom,
31 Jan.   Dort, Rotterdam, and Delft, and being received in
1608.   each town and village through which they passed

Meteren, Wagenaar, *ubi sup.*   lere odiosum et fateri inglorium.''—
[4] '' De feudo silebatur quia et refel-   Grotius, xvi. 752.

with great demonstrations of respect and cordial welcome, arrived at last within a mile of the Hague.[5]

It was the dead of winter, and of the severest winter that had occurred for many years. Every river, estuary, canal was frozen hard. All Holland was one broad level sheet of ice, over which the journey had been made in sledges. On the last day of January Prince Maurice, accompanied by Lewis William, and by eight state coaches filled with distinguished personages, left the Hague and halted at the Hoorn bridge, about midway between Ryswyk and the capital. The prince had replied to the first request of the States that he should go forward to meet Spinola, by saying that he would do so willingly if it were to give him battle; otherwise not. Olden-Barneveld urged upon him however that, as servant of the republic, he was bound to do what the States commanded, as a matter involving the dignity of the nation. In consequence of this remonstrance Maurice consented to go, but he went unwillingly.[6] The advancing procession of the Spanish ambassadors was already in sight. Far and wide in whatever direction the eye could sweep, the white surface of the landscape was blackened with human beings. It seemed as if the whole population of the Netherlands had assembled, in mass meeting, to witness the pacific interview between those two great chieftains who had never before stood face to face except upon the battle-field.

In carriages, in donkey carts, upon horseback, in sledges, on skates, upon foot—men, women, and children, gentle and simple, Protestants, Catholics, Gomarites, Arminians, anabaptists, country squires in buff and bandaleer, city magistrates and merchants in furs and velvet, artisans, boatmen, and peasants, with their wives and daughters in well-starched ruff and tremendous head-gear—they came thronging in countless multitudes, those honest Hollanders, cheering and throwing up their caps in honour of the chieftain whose military genius had caused so much disaster to their country. This uproarious demonstration of welcome on the part of the

---

[5] Meteren, 563.   [6] Letter of Aerssens, in Deventer, iii. 168.

multitude moved the spleen of many who were old enough to remember the horrors of Spanish warfare within their borders. "Thus unreflecting, gaping, boorish, are nearly all the common people of these provinces,"[7] said a contemporary, describing the scene, and forgetting that both high and low, according to his own account, made up the mass of spectators on that winter's day. Moreover it seems difficult to understand why the Hollanders should not have indulged a legitimate curiosity, and made a holiday on this memorable occasion. Spinola was not entering their capital in triumph, a Spanish army was not marching—as it might have done had the course of events been different—over the protective rivers and marshes of the fatherland, now changed by the exceptional cold into solid highways for invasion. On the contrary, the arrival of the great enemy within their gates, with the olive-branch instead of the sword in his hand, was a victory not for Spain but for the republic.   It was known throughout the land that he was commissioned by the king and the archdukes to treat for peace with the States-General of the United Provinces as with the representatives of a free and independent nation, utterly beyond any foreign control.

Was not this opening of a cheerful and pacific prospect, after a half century's fight for liberty, a fair cause for rejoicing ?

The Spanish commissioners arrived at the Hoorn bridge, Spinola alighted from his coach, Prince Maurice stepped forward into the road to greet him. Then the two eminent soldiers, whose names had of late been so familiar in the mouths of men, shook hands and embraced with heroic cordiality, while a mighty shout went up from the multitude around. It was a stately and dramatic spectacle, that peaceful meeting of the rival leaders in a war which had begun before either of them was born. The bystanders observed, or thought that they observed, signs of great emotion on the faces of both.   It has also been recorded that

[7] Meteren, 563.

each addressed the other in epigrammatic sentences of compliment. "God is my witness," Maurice was supposed to have said, "that the arrival of these honourable negotiators is most grateful to me. Time, whose daughter is truth, will show the faith to be given to my words."[8]

"This fortunate day," replied Spinola, "has filled full the measure of my hopes and wishes, and taken from me the faculty of ever wishing for anything again. I trust in divine clemency that an opportunity may be given to show my gratitude, and to make a fit return for the humanity thus shown me by the most excellent prince that the sun shines upon."[9]

With this both got into the stadholder's carriage, Spinola being placed on Maurice's right hand. Their conversation during their brief drive to the capital, followed by their long retinue, and by the enthusiastic and vociferating crowd, has not been chronicled. It is also highly probable that the second-rate theatrical dialogue which the Jesuit historian, writing from Spinola's private papers, has preserved for posterity, was rather what seemed to his imagination appropriate for the occasion than a faithful shorthand report of anything really uttered. A few commonplace phrases of welcome, with a remark or two perhaps on the unexampled severity of the frost, seem more likely to have formed the substance of that brief conversation.

A couple of trumpeters of Spinola went braying through the streets of the village capital, heralding their master's approach with superfluous noise, and exciting the disgust of the quieter portion of the burghers.[10] At last however the envoys and their train were all comfortably housed. The Marquis, President Richardot, and Secretary Mancicidor, were established at a new mansion on the Vyverberg, belonging to Goswyn Menskens. The rest of the legation were lodged at the house of Wassenaer.[11]

It soon became plain that the ways of life and the style of

[8] Gallucci, 352.   [9] Ibid.
[10] Meteren, *ubi sup.*   [11] Ibid.

housekeeping habitual to great officers of the Spanish crown were very different from the thrifty manners and customs of Dutch republicans. It was so long since anything like royal pomp and circumstance had been seen in their borders that the exhibition, now made, excited astonishment. It was a land where every child went to school, where almost every individual inhabitant could read and write, where even the middle classes were proficients in mathematics and the classics, and could speak two or more modern languages; where the whole nation, with but few exceptions, were producers of material or intellectual wealth, and where comparatively little of unproductive consumption prevailed. Those self-governing and self-sustaining municipalities had almost forgotten the existence of the magnificent nothings so dear to the hearts of kings.

Spinola's house was open day and night. The gorgeous plate, gigantic candelabra, mighty ewers, shields and lavers of silver and gold, which decorated his tables and sideboards, amazed the gaping crowd. He dined and supped in state every day, and the public were admitted to gaze upon his banquets as if he had been a monarch. It seemed, said those homely republicans, as if "a silver christening were going on every day in his house." [12]

There were even grave remonstrances made to the magistracy and to the States-General against the effect of such ostentatious and immoral proceedings upon the popular mind, and suggestions that at least the doors should be shut, so that the scandal might be confined to Spinola's own household. But the republican authorities deciding, not without wisdom, that the spectacle ought to serve rather as a wholesome warning than as a contaminating example, declined any inquisitorial interference with the housekeeping of the Spanish ambassadors. [13]

Before the negotiations began, a treaty had been made between the republic and the French Government, by which it was stipulated that every effort should be made by both

[12] Meteren, 564   [13] Ibid.

contracting parties to bring about an honourable and assured peace between the United Provinces, Spain, and the arch-dukes. In case of the continuance of the war, however, it was agreed that France should assist the States with ten thousand men, while in case at any time, during the continuance of the league, France should be attacked by a foreign enemy, she should receive from her ally five thousand auxiliary troops, or their equivalent in maritime assistance. This convention was thought by other powers to be so profit-able to the Netherlands as to excite general uneasiness and suspicion.

The States would have gladly signed a similar agreement with England, but nothing was to be done with that Govern-ment until an old-standing dispute in regard to the cloth trade had been arranged. Middelburg had the exclusive right of deposit for the cloths imported from England. This monopoly for Zeeland being naturally not very palatable to Amsterdam and other cities of Holland, the States-General had at last authorized the merchant-adventurers engaged in this traffic to deposit their goods in any city of the United Provinces.[14] The course of trade had been to import the raw cloth from England, to dress and dye it in the Netherlands, and then to re-export it to England. Latterly, however, some dyers and clothiers emigrating from the provinces to that country, had obtained a monopoly from James for practising their art in his dominions. In consequence of this arrangement the exportation of undyed cloths had been forbidden. This prohibition had caused irritation both in the kingdom and the republic, had necessarily deranged the natural course of trade and manufacture, and had now pre-vented for the time any conclusion of an alliance offensive and defensive between the countries, even if political senti-ment had made such a league possible. The States-General had recourse to the usual expedient by which bad legislation on one side was counterveiled by equally bad legislation on the other The exportation of undyed English cloths being

---

[14] Wagenaar, ix. 317, 318.

forbidden by England, the importation of dyed English cloths was now prohibited by the Netherlands. The international cloth trade stopped. This embargo became at last so detestable to all parties that concession was made by the crown for a limited export of raw cloths. The concession was soon widened by custom into a general exportation, the royal Government looking through its fingers at the open infraction of its own laws, while the natural laws of trade before long re-established the old equilibrium. Meantime the ill-feeling produced by this dissension delayed any cordial political arrangement between the countries.

On the 5th of February the Spanish commissioners came for the first time before the States-General, assembled to the number of a hundred and thirty, in their palace at the Hague.[15]

The first meeting was merely one of mutual compliment, President Richardot, on behalf of his colleagues, expressing gratitude for the cordial welcome which had been manifested to the envoys on their journey through so many towns of the United Provinces. They had been received, he said, not as enemies with whom an almost perpetual war had been waged, but as friends, confederates, and allies. A warmer reception they could never have hoped for nor desired.

Two special commissioners were now appointed by the States-General to negotiate with the envoys. These were Count Lewis William and Brederode. With these delegates at large were associated seven others, one from each province. Barneveld of course represented Holland ; Maldere, Zeeland ; Berk, Utrecht ; Hillama, Friesland ; Sloat, Overyssel ; Koender van Helpen, Groningen; Cornelius van Gend, Gelderland.[16]

The negotiations began at once. The archdukes had empowered the five envoys to deal in their name and in that of the King of Spain. Philip had authorized the archdukes to take this course by an instrument dated 10th January.

---

[15] Van der Kemp, iii. 137, *et seq.* Meteren, 564, 565.
[16] Wagenaar, 322, ix. 323. Gallucci, 352–355.

In this paper he called the archdukes hereditary sovereigns of the Netherlands.

It was agreed that the various points of negotiation should be taken up in regular order; but the first question of all that presented itself was whether the conferences should be for a truce or a peace.[17]

The secret object of Spain was for a truce of years. Thus she thought to save her dignity, to reserve her rights of re-conquest, to replenish her treasury, and to repair her military strength. Barneveld and his party, comprising a large majority of the States-General, were for peace. Prince Maurice, having done his utmost to oppose negotiations for peace, was, for still stronger reasons, determined to avoid falling into what he considered the ambush of a truce. The French ambassadors were also for peace. The Spanish envoys accordingly concealed their real designs, and all parties began discussions for the purpose of establishing a permanent peace.

This preliminary being settled, Barneveld asked the Spaniards if they had full powers to treat with the States as with a free nation, and if they recognised them as such.

"The most ample power," was the reply; "and we are content to treat with you even if you should choose to call yourself a kingdom."

"By what right then are the archdukes called by the king hereditary sovereigns of the Netherlands, and why do they append the seals of the seven United Provinces to this document?" asked the Advocate, taking up from the table the full power of Albert and Isabella and putting his finger on the seals.[18]

"By the same right," replied President Richardot, "that the King of France calls himself King of Navarre, that the

[17] Ibid. Meteren, 564, 565.

[18] Negotiations de Jeannin, i. 538, 539. Gallucci, Meteren, Wagenaar, *ubi sup.* Compare also, for the whole course of these ratifications, the Minutes of Olden-Barneveld during the conferences, now first published in the invaluable and admirably-edited collection of Van Deventer. "Verhaal der Onderhandelingen te 's Hage tusschen de Nederlandsche en Spaansche gevolmagtigden," &c., 1 Februarij, 1608-4 Maart, 1609.—Deventer, iii. No. ccviii. pp. 169–239, *passim.*

King of Great Britain calls himself King of France, that the King of Spain calls himself King of Jerusalem."

Nothing could be more logical, nothing more historically accurate. But those plain-spoken republicans saw no advantage in beginning a negotiation for peace on the basis of their independence by permitting the archduke to call himself their sovereign, and to seal solemn state papers with their signet. It might seem picturesque to genealogical minds, it might be soothing to royal vanity, that paste counterfeits should be substituted for vanished jewels. It would be cruelty to destroy the mock glitter without cause. But there was cause. On this occasion the sham was dangerous. James Stuart might call himself King of France. He was not more likely to take practical possession of that kingdom than of the mountains in the moon. Henry of Bourbon was not at present contemplating an invasion of the hereditary possessions of the house of Albret. It was a matter of indifference to the Netherlands whether Philip III. were crowned in Jerusalem that very day, or the week afterwards, or never. It was very important however that the United Provinces should have it thoroughly recognised that they were a free and independent republic, nor could that recognition be complete so long as any human being in the whole world called himself their master, and signed with their seals of state. " 'Tis absurd," said the Hollanders, " to use the names and arms of our provinces. We have as yet no precedent to prove that you consider the United Provinces as lost, and name and arms to be but wind." Barneveld reminded them that they had all expressed the most straightforward intention, and that the father commissary especially had pledged his very soul for the sincerity of the king and the archdukes. " We ourselves never wished and never could deceive any one," continued the Advocate, " and it is also very difficult for others to deceive us." [19]

This being the universal sentiment of the Netherlanders, it was thought proper to express it in respectful but vigorous

[19] Minutes of Olden-Barneveld.

language. This was done and the session was terminated. The Spanish envoys, knowing very well that neither the king nor the archduke regarded the retention of the titles and seals of all the seventeen Netherlands as an empty show, but that a secret and solid claim lurked beneath that usurpation, were very indignant. They however dissembled their wrath from the States' commissioners. They were unwilling that the negotiations should be broken up at the very first session, and they felt that neither Prince Maurice nor Barneveld was to be trifled with upon this point.[20] But they were loud and magnificent in their demonstrations when they came to talk the matter over with the ambassadors of France and England.[21] It was most portentous, they thought, to the cause of monarchy and good government all over the world, that these republicans, not content to deal with kings and princes on a footing of equality, should presume to dictate to them as to inferiors. Having passed through rebellion to liberty, they were now proceeding to trample upon the most hallowed customs and rites. What would become of royalty, if in the same breath it should not only renounce the substance, but even put away the symbols of authority. This insolence of the people was not more dangerous to the king and the archdukes than it was to every potentate in the universe. It was a sacred duty to resist such insults.[22] Sage Jeannin did his best to pacify the vehemence of the commissioners. He represented to them that foreign titles borne by anointed kings were only ensigns of historical possessions which they had for ever renounced ; but that it might become one day the pleasure of Spain, or lie in the power of Spain, to vindicate her ancient rights to the provinces.

Hence the anxiety of the States was but natural. The old Leaguer and political campaigner knew very well, moreover, that at least one half of Richardot's noble wrath was feigned.[23] The commissioners would probably renounce the title and

---

[20] Gallucci, 355, 356. Grotius, xvii 764, 765. Wagenaar, ix. 324–326 Meteren, 564vo. Bentivoglio, 564.

[21] Ibid.
[22] Gallucci, Bentivoglio, *ubi sup.*
[23] Gallucci, 356.

the seven seals, but in so doing would drive a hard bargain. For an empty phrase and a pennyworth of wax they would extort a heavy price. And this was what occurred. The commissioners agreed to write for fresh instructions to Brussels. A reply came in due time from the archdukes, in which they signified their willingness to abandon the title of sovereigns over all the Netherlands, and to abstain from using their signet. In exchange for this concession they merely demanded from the States-General a formal abandonment of the navigation to both the Indies. This was all. The archdukes granted liberty to the republic. The republic would renounce its commerce with more than half the world.

The scorn of the States' commissioners at this proposition can be imagined, and it became difficult indeed for them to speak on the subject in decorous language. Because the archdukes were willing to give up something which was not their property, the republic was voluntarily to open its veins and drain its very life-blood at the bidding of a foreign potentate. She was to fling away all the trophies of Heemskerk and Sebalt de Weerd, of Balthasar de Cordes, Van der Hagen, Matelieff, and Verhoeff; she was to abdicate the position which she had already acquired of mistress of the seas, and she was to deprive herself for ever of that daily increasing ocean commerce which was rapidly converting a cluster of puny, half-submerged provinces into a mighty empire. Of a certainty the Spanish court at this new epoch was an astounding anachronism. In its view Pope Alexander VI. still lived and reigned.

Liberty was not a boon conferred upon the Netherlanders by their defeated enemy. It had been gained by their own right hands; by the blood, and the gold, and the sweat of two generations. If it were the king's to give, let him try once more if he could take it away. Such were the opinions and emotions of the Dutchmen, expressed in as courteous language as they could find.

"It would be a political heresy," said Barneveld to the Spanish commissioners at this session, "if my lords the

States should by contract banish their citizens out of two-thirds of the world, both land and sea."

"'Tis strange," replied the Spaniards, "that you wish to have more than other powers—kings or republics—who never make any such pretensions. The Indies, East and West, are our house, privately possessed by us for more than a hundred years, and no one has a right to come into it without our permission. This is not banishment, but a custom to which all other nations submit. We give you your sovereignty before all the world, quitting all claims upon it. We know very well that you deny receiving it from us; but to give you a quit claim, and to permit free trade besides, would be a little more than you have a right to expect." [24]

Was it not well for the cause of liberty, commercial inter-course, and advancement of the human intellect, that there was this obstinate little republic in the world, refusing to tolerate that to which all other great powers of the earth submitted; that there was one nation determined not to acknowledge three-quarters of the world, including America and India, as the private mansion of the King of Spain, to be locked against the rest of the human race ?

The next session of the negotiators after the arrival of this communication from the archdukes was a stormy one. The India trade was the sole subject of discussion. As the States were firmly resolved never to relinquish that navigation which in truth was one of their most practical and valuable possessions, and as the royal commissioners were as solemnly determined that it should never be conceded, it may be imagined how much breath, how much foolscap paper, was wasted.

In truth, the negotiation for peace had been a vile mockery from the beginning. Spain had no real intention of abdicating her claim to the United Provinces.

---

[24] Minutes of Olden-Barneveld, *ubi sup.* " Dattet hunl. Huys was over hundert jaren privatim beseten en dat men daer jegens hun danck niet be- hoorde te komen. Datter geen ban-nissement was maer een gebruyck als de andere Coningen en Republiquen deden," &c.

At the very moment when the commissioners were categorically making that concession in Brussels, and claiming such a price for it, Hoboken, the archduke's diplomatic representative in London, was earnestly assuring King James that neither his master nor Philip had the remotest notion of renouncing their sovereignty over all the Netherlands. What had been said and written to that effect was merely a device, he asserted, to bring about a temporary truce. During the interval of imaginary freedom it was certain that the provinces would fall into such dire confusion that it would be easier for Spain to effect their re-conquest, after a brief delay for repairing her own strength, than it would be by continuing the present war without any cessation.[25]

The Spanish ambassador at Vienna too on his part assured the Emperor Rudolph that his master was resolved never to abdicate the sovereignty of the provinces. The negotiations then going on, he said, were simply intended to extort from the States a renunciation of the India trade and their consent to the re-introduction of the Catholic religion throughout their territories.

Something of all this was known and much more suspected at the Hague ; the conviction therefore that no faith would be kept with rebels and heretics, whatever might be said or written, gained strength every day. That these delusive negotiations with the Hollanders were not likely to be so successful as the comedy enacted twenty years before at Bourbourg, for the amusement of Queen Elizabeth and her diplomatists while the tragedy of the Armada was preparing, might be safely prophesied. Richardot was as effective as ever in the part which he had so often played, but Spinola laboured under the disadvantage of being a far honester man than Alexander Farnese. Far from equal to that famous chieftain in the management of a great military campaign, it is certain that he was infinitely inferior to him in genteel comedy. Whether Maurice and Lewis William, Barneveld and Brederode, were to do better in the parts formerly assigned to John Rogers, Valentine Dale, Comptroller Croft, and their colleagues, remained to be seen.

On the 15th of February, at the fifth conference of the commissioners, the first pitched battle on the India 15 Feb. trade was fought. Thereafter the combat was 1608. almost every day renewed. Exactly, as a year before, the news of Heemskerk's victory at Gibraltar had made the king and the archdukes eager to obtain an armistice with the rebels both by land and sea, so now the report of Matelieff's recent achievements in the Indian ocean was increasing their anxiety to exclude the Netherlanders from the regions which they were rapidly making their own.

As we look back upon the negotiations, after the lapse of two centuries and a half, it becomes difficult to suppress our amazement at those scenes of solemn trickery and superhuman pride. It is not necessary to follow, step by step, the proceedings at each daily conference, but it is impossible for me not to detain the reader for yet a season longer with those transactions, and especially to invite him to ponder the valuable lesson which in their entirety they convey.

No higher themes could possibly be laid before statesmen to discuss. Questions of political self-government, religious liberty, national independence, divine Right, rebellious Power, freedom of commerce, supremacy of the seas, omnipotence claimed by the old world over the destiny of what was called the new, were importunately demanding solution. All that most influenced human passion, or stirred human reason to its depths—at that memorable point of time when two great epochs seemed to be sweeping against each other in elemental conflict—was to be dealt with. The emancipated currents of human thought, the steady tide of ancient dogma, were mingling in wrath. There are times of paroxysm in which Nature seems to effect more in a moment, whether intellectually or materially, than at other periods during a lapse of years. The shock of forces, long preparing and long delayed, is apt at last to make itself sensible to those neglectful of gradual but vital changes. Yet there are always ears that remain deaf to the most portentous din.

Thus, after that half century of war, the policy of Spain was still serenely planting itself on the position occupied before the outbreak of the revolt. The commonwealth, solidly established by a free people, already one of the most energetic and thriving among governments, a recognised member of the great international family, was now gravely expected to purchase from its ancient tyrant the independence which it had long possessed, while the price demanded for the free papers was not only extravagant, but would be disgraceful to an emancipated slave. Holland was not likely at that turning point in her history, and in the world's history, to be false to herself and to the great principles of public law. It was good for the cause of humanity that the republic should reappear at that epoch. It was wholesome for Europe that there should be just then a plain self-governing people, able to speak homely and important truths. It was healthy for the moral and political atmosphere—in those days and in the time to come—that a fresh breeze from that little sea-born commonwealth should sweep away some of the ancient fog through which a few very feeble and very crooked mortals had so long loomed forth like giants and gods.

To vindicate the laws of nations and of nature ; to make a noble effort for reducing to a system—conforming, at least approximately, to divine reason—the chaotic elements of war and peace ; to recal the great facts that earth, sea, and sky ought to belong to mankind, and not to an accidental and very limited selection of the species, was not an unworthy task for a people which had made such unexampled sacrifices for liberty and right.

Accordingly, at the conference on the 15th February, the Spanish commissioners categorically summoned the States to desist entirely from the trade to either India, exactly as before the war. To enforce this prohibition, they said, was the principal reason why Philip desired peace. To obtain their freedom was surely well worth renunciation of this traffic ; the more so, because their trade with Spain, which was so much shorter and safer, was now to be re-opened. If they had been able to keep that commerce, it was suggested, they would have never talked about the Indies. The commissioners added, that this boon had not been conceded to France nor England, by the treaties of Vervins and London, and that the States therefore could not find it strange that it should be refused to them.[26]

The States' commissioners stoutly replied that commerce was open to all the world, that trade was free by the great law of nature, and that neither France, England, nor the United Provinces, were to receive edicts on this great subject from Spain and Portugal. It was absurd to circumscribe commercial intercourse at the very moment of exchanging war for peace. To recognise the liberty of the States upon paper, and to attempt the imposition of servitude in reality, was a manifest contradiction. The ocean was free to all nations. It had not been enclosed by Spain with a rail-fence.[27]

The debate grew more stormy every hour. Spinola expressed great indignation that the Netherlanders should be so obstinate upon this point. The tall, spare President arose in wrath from his seat at the council-board, loudly protesting that the King of Spain would never renounce his sovereignty over the provinces until they had forsworn the India trade ; and with this menace stalked out of the room.[28]

The States' commissioners were not frightened. Barneveld was at least a match for Richardot, and it was better, after all, that the cards should be played upon the table. Subsequent

[26] Wagenaar, ix. 327, *seqq.* Meteren, 565, 567-593. Grotius, xvii 763-781. Gallucci. 356-358.

[27] Oceanum quippe *nullis clausum cancellis* cunctis nationibus patere."—Gallucci. 357. It is impossible in this connection not to recal the quaint words of a great poet of our own country in a famous idyl written two and a half centuries later than these transactions :—

" We own the ocean, too, John,
  You mustn't think it hard
If we can't think with you, John,
  It's just your own back yard.

Old uncle S., says he, I guess
  If that's his game, says he,
The fencing stuff will cost enough
  To bust up friend J. B.
As well as you and me."
          J. R. Lowell.

[28] Meteren, Grotius, Gallucci, Wagenaar, *ubi sup.*

meetings were quite as violent as the first, the country was agitated far and wide, the prospects of pacification dwindled to a speck in the remote horizon. Arguments at the Board of Conference, debates in the States-General, pamphlets by merchants and advocates—especially several emanating from the East India Company—handled the great topic from every point of view, and it became more and more evident that Spain could not be more resolute to prohibit than the republic to claim the trade.[29]

It was an absolute necessity, so it was urged, for the Hollanders to resist the tyrannical dominion of the Spaniards. But this would be impossible for them, should they rely on the slender natural resources of their own land. Not a sixth part of the population could be nourished from the soil. The ocean was their inheritance, their birthright, their empire. It was necessary that Spain should understand this first, last, and always. She ought to comprehend, too, that her recognition of Dutch independence was not a gift, but the acknowledgment of a fact. Without that acknowledgment peace was impossible. If peace were to be established, it was not to be bought by either party. Each gave and each received, and certainly Spain was in no condition to dictate the terms of a sale. Peace, without freedom of commerce, would be merely war without killing, and therefore without result. The Netherlanders, who in the middle of the previous century had risen against unjust taxation and arbitrary laws, had not grown so vile as to accept from a vanquished foe what they had spurned from their prince. To be exiled from the ocean was an unimaginable position for the republic. Moreover, to retire from the Indies would be to abandon her Oriental allies, and would be a dishonour as well as a disaster. Her good faith, never yet contaminated, would be stained, were she now to desert the distant peoples and potentates with whom she had formed treaties of friendship and commerce, and hand them over to the vengeance of the Spaniards and Portuguese.[30]

[29] Authorities last cited.   [30] Ibid.

And what a trade it was which the United Provinces were thus called upon to renounce ! The foreign commerce of no other nation could be compared in magnitude to that of their commonwealth. Twenty ships traded regularly to Guinea, eighty to the Cape de Verd Islands, twenty to America, and forty to the East Indies. Ten thousand sailors, who gained their living in this traffic, would be thrown out of employment, if the States should now listen to the Spanish propositions.[31]

It was well known too that the profits of the East India Company had vastly increased of late, and were augmenting with every year. The trade with Cambay, Malabar, Ceylon, Koromandel, and Queda, had scarcely begun, yet was already most promising. Should the Hollanders only obtain a footing in China, they felt confident of making their way through the South Seas and across the pole to India. Thus the search for a great commercial highway between Cathay, Europe, and the New World, which had been baffled in the arctic regions, should be crowned with success at the antarctic, while it was deemed certain that there were many lands, lighted by the Southern Cross, awaiting the footsteps of the fortunate European discoverer. What was a coasting-trade with Spain compared with this boundless career of adventure ? Now that the world's commerce, since the discovery of America and the passage around the Cape of Good Hope, had become oceanic and universal, was the nation which took the lead on blue water to go back to the creeping land-locked navigation of the ancient Greeks and Phœnicians ? If the East India Company, in whose womb was empire, were now destroyed, it would perish with its offspring for ever. There would be no regeneration at a future day. The Company's ships too were a navy in themselves, as apt for war as for trade. This the Spaniards and Portuguese had already learned to their cost. The merchant-traders to Spain would be always in the power of Spain, and at any favourable moment might be seized by Spain. The Spanish monopoly in the East and West was the great source of Spanish power, the chief cause of the contempt

[31] Authorities last cited.

with which the Spanish monarchy looked down upon other nations. Let those widely expanded wings be clipped, and Spain would fall from her dizzy height. To know what the States ought to refuse the enemy, it was only necessary to observe what he strenuously demanded, to ponder the avowed reason why he desired peace. The enemy was doing his best to damage the commonwealth ; the States were merely anxious to prevent injury to themselves and to all the world ; to vindicate for themselves, and for all men, the common use of ocean, land, and sky.

A nation which strove to shut up the seas, and to acquire a monopoly of the world's trade, was a pirate, an enemy of mankind. She was as deserving of censure as those who created universal misery in time of famine, by buying up all the corn in order to enrich themselves. According to the principles of the ancients, it was legitimate to make war upon such States as closed their own ports to foreign intercourse. Still more just was it, therefore, to carry arms against a nation which closed the ports of other people.[32]

The dispute about the India navigation could be settled in a moment, if Spain would but keep her word. She had acknowledged the great fact of independence, which could not be gainsaid. Let each party to the negotiation, therefore, keep that which it already possessed. Let neither attempt to prescribe to the other—both being free and independent States—any regulations about interior or foreign trade.[33]

Thus reasoned the States-General, the East India directors, the great majority of the population of the provinces, upon one great topic of discussion. A small minority only attempted to defend the policy of renouncing the India trade as a branch of industry, in which a certain class, and that only in the maritime provinces, was interested. It is certainly no slight indication of the liberty of thought, of speech, and of the press, enjoyed at that epoch in the Netherlands— and nowhere else to anything like the same extent—that

[32] Authorities last cited.   [33] Ibid.

such opinions, on a subject deemed vital to the very existence
of the republic, were freely published and listened to with
toleration, if not with respect.   Even the enlightened mind
of Grotius was troubled with terrors as to the effect on the
public mind at this crisis of anonymous pamphlets concerning
political affairs.[34]   But in this regard it must be admitted that
Grotius was not in advance of his age, although fully conceding that press-laws were inconsistent with human liberty.

Maurice and Barneveld were equally strenuous in maintaining the India trade ; the prince, because he hoped that
resistance to Spain upon this point would cause the negotiations to be broken off, the Advocate in the belief that firmness
on the part of the States would induce the royal commissioners to yield.

The States-General were not likely to be deficient in firmness. They felt that the republic was exactly on the point
of wresting the control of the East from the hands of the
Portuguese, and they were not inclined to throw away the
harvest of their previous labours just as it was ripening.   Ten
thousand persons at least, besides the sailors employed, were
directly interested in the traffic, most of whom possessed
great influence in the commonwealth, and would cause great
domestic dissension should they now be sacrificed to Spain.
To keep the India trade was the best guarantee for the future
possession of the traffic to Spain ; for the Spanish Government
would never venture an embargo upon the direct intercourse
between the provinces and its own dominions, for fear of
vengeance in the East.   On the other hand, by denouncing
oceanic commerce, they would soon find themselves without
a navy at all, and their peaceful coasting ships would be at
the mercy of Spain or of any power possessing that maritime
energy which would have been killed in the republic.   By
abandoning the ocean, the young commonwealth would sink
into sloth, and become the just object of contempt to the

---

[34] " Non minimum ego istius rei-
publicæ malum arbitror tantam in
plebe libellis concitanda proterviam
vetitam sæpe et tunc novo edicto nec
repressam tamen, dum acris indago et
graves pœnæ repudiantur ut libertati
contraria."—Grotius, xvii. 776.

world. It would cease to be an independent power, and deserve to fall a prey to any enterprising neighbour.[35]

Even Villeroy admitted the common belief to be, that if the India trade were abandoned "the States would melt away like snow in the sun."[36] He would not, on that account, however, counsel to the States obstinacy upon the subject, if Spain refused peace or truce except on condition of their exclusion from the traffic.[37] Jeannin, Villeroy, and their master; Isaac le Maire and Peter Plancius, could have told the reason why if they had chosen.

Early in March a triple proposition was made by the States' commissioners. Spain might take her choice to make peace on the basis of free trade; to make peace, leaving everything beyond the Tropic of Cancer to the chance of war; or to make peace in regard to all other than the tropical regions, concluding for those only a truce during a definite number of years.[38]

The Spaniards rejected decidedly two of these suggestions. Of course they would not concede freedom of the sea. They considered the mixture of peace and war a monstrous conception. They were, however, willing to favour peace for Europe and truce in the tropics, provided the States bound themselves, on the expiration of the limited period, to abandon the Indian and American trade for ever. And to this proposition the States of course were deaf. And thus they went on spinning around, day after day, in the same vicious circle, without more hope of progress than squirrels in a cage.

Barneveld, always overbearing with friend or foe, and often violent, was not disposed to make preposterous concessions, notwithstanding his eager desire for peace. "The might of the States-General," said he, "is so great, thank God, that they need not yield so much to the King of Spain as seems to be expected, nor cover themselves with dishonour."

"And do you think yourselves more mighty than the

---

[35] Wagenaar, ix. 332, 334.   [36] Jeannin, i. 625.   [37] Ibid.
[38] Wagenaar, ix. 334. Gallucci, 358, 359. Bentivoglio, 565.

Kings of England and France ?" cried Richardot in a great rage, "for they never dared to make any attempt upon the Indies, East or West."[39]

"We are willing to leave the king in his own quarters," was the reply, "and we expect him to leave us in ours."

"You had better take a sheet of paper at once," said Richardot, "write down exactly what you wish, and order us to agree to it all without discussion."

"We demand nothing that is unreasonable in these negotiations," was the firm rejoinder, "and expect that nothing unjust will be required of us."[40]

It was now suggested by the States' commissioners that a peace, with free navigation, might be concluded for Europe, and a truce for other parts of the world, without any stipulations as to what should take place on its termination.

This was hardly anything new, but it served as a theme for more intellectual buffeting. Hard words were freely exchanged during several hours, and all parties lost their temper. At last the Spaniards left the conference-chamber in a rage. Just as they were going, Barneveld asked them whether he should make a protocol of the session for the States-General, and whether it was desirable in future to resume the discussion.

"Let every one do exactly as he likes," replied Spinola, wrathfully, as he moved to the door.

Friar John, always plausible, whispered a few soothing words in the ear of the marquis, adding aloud, so that the commissioners might hear, "Night brings counsel." These words he spoke in Latin.

"He who wishes to get everything is apt to lose everything," cried out Maldere, the Zeeland deputy, in Spanish, to the departing commissioners.

"Take that to yourselves," rejoined Richardot, very fiercely; "you may be sure that it will be your case."[41]

So ended that interview.

---

[39] Minutes of Olden-Barneveld, 191, and note from Memoire van Staet.
[40] Ibid.　　　　　　　　　　　[41] Jeannin, i. 595.

Directly afterwards there was a conference between the States' commissioners and the French envoys.

Jeannin employed all his powers of argument and persuasion to influence the Netherlanders against a rupture of the negotiations because of the India trade. It would be better to abandon that commerce, so he urged, than to give up the hope of peace. The commissioners failed to see the logic or to melt at the eloquence of his discourse. They would have been still less inclined, if that were possible, to move from their position, had they known of the secret conferences which Jeannin had just been holding with Isaac le Maire of Amsterdam, and other merchants practically familiar with the India trade. Carrying out the French king's plan to rob the republic of that lucrative traffic, and to transplant it, by means of experienced Hollanders, into France, the president, while openly siding with the States, as their most disinterested friend, was secretly doing all in his power to destroy the very foundation of their commonwealth.[42]

Isaac le Maire came over from Amsterdam in a mysterious manner, almost in disguise. Had his nocturnal dealings with the French minister been known, he would have been rudely dealt with by the East India Company. He was a native of Tournay, not a sincere republican therefore, was very strongly affected to France, and declared that all his former fellow-townsmen, and many more, had the *fleur-de-lys* stamped on their hearts. If peace should be made without stipulation in favour of the East India Company, he, with his three brothers, would do what they could to transfer that corporation to France. All the details of such a prospective arrangement were thoroughly discussed, and it was intimated that the king would be expected to take shares in the enterprise. Jeannin had also repeated conferences on the same subject with the great cosmographer Plancius. It may be well understood, therefore, that the minister of Henry IV. was not very ardent to encourage the States in their resolve to oppose peace or truce, except with concession of the India trade.[43]

[42] Jeannin, i. 603-606.　　　　[43] Ibid.

The States preferred that the negotiations should come to nought on the religious ground rather than on account of the India trade. The provinces were nearly unanimous as to the prohibition of the Catholic worship, not from bigotry for their own or hatred of other creeds, but from larger views of what was then called tolerance, and from practical regard for the necessities of the State. To permit the old worship, not from a sense of justice but as an article of bargain with a foreign power, was not only to abase the government of the States but to convert every sincere Catholic throughout the republic into a grateful adherent of Philip and the arch-dukes. It was deliberately to place a lever, to be used in all future time, for the overthrow of their political structure.

In this the whole population was interested, while the India navigation, although vital to the well-being of the nation, was not yet universally recognised as so supremely import-ant, and was declared by a narrow-minded minority to con-cern the provinces of Holland and Zeeland alone.

All were silently agreed, therefore, to defer the religious question to the last.

Especially, commercial greed induced the States to keep a firm clutch on the great river on which the once splendid city of Antwerp stood. Ever since that commercial metropolis had succumbed to Farnese, the republic had maintained the lower forts, by means of which, and of Flushing at the river's mouth, Antwerp was kept in a state of suspended animation. To open the navigation of the Scheld, to permit free approach to Antwerp, would, according to the narrow notions of the Amsterdam merchants, be destructive to their own flourishing trade.

In vain did Richardot, in one well-fought conference, do his best to obtain concessions on this important point. The States' commissioners were as deaf as the Spaniards had been on the India question. Richardot, no longer loud and furious, began to cry. With tears running down his cheeks,[44] he be-sought the Netherlanders not to insist so strenuously upon all

[44] Grotius, xvii. 769.

their points, and to remember that concessions were mutually
necessary, if an amicable arrangement were to be framed.
The chances for peace were promising. "Let not a blight be
thrown over all our hopes," he exclaimed, "by too great pertinacity on either side. Above all, let not the States dictate
terms as to a captive or conquered king, but propose such conditions as a benevolent but powerful sovereign could accept."

These adjurations might be considered admirable, if it had
been possible for the royal commissioners to point to a single
mustard-seed of concession ever vouchsafed by them to the
republic.

Meantime the month of March had passed. Nothing had
been accomplished, but it was agreed to prolong the armistice
through April and May.

The negotiations having feebly dribbled off into almost
absolute extinction, Friar John was once more set in motion,
and despatched to Madrid. He was sent to get fresh instructions from Philip, and he promised, on departing, to return
in forty days. He hoped as his reward, he said, to be made
bishop of Utrecht. "That will be a little above your calibre,"
replied Barneveld.[45] Forty days was easily said, and the
States consented to the additional delay.

During his absence there was much tedious discussion of
minor matters, such as staple rights of wine and cloths, regulations of boundaries, removal of restrictions on trade and navigation, passports, sequestered estates, and the like ; all of
which were subordinate to the all-important subjects of India
and Religion, those two most tender topics growing so much
more tender the more they were handled as to cause at last a
shiver whenever they were approached. Nevertheless both
were to be dealt with, or the negotiations would fall to the
ground.[46]

The States felt convinced that they would fall to the
ground, that they had fallen to the ground, and they at
least would not stoop to pick them up again.

[45] Minutes of Olden-Barneveld, 205. | seqq. Meteren, B. xxix. Van der Kemp,
[46] Grotius, xvii. Wagenaar, ix. 343, | 36, 37, 154–157.

The forty days passed away, but the friar never returned. April and May came and went, and again the armistice expired by its own limitation. The war party was disgusted with the solemn trifling, Maurice was exasperated beyond endurance, Barneveld and the peace men began to find immense difficulty in confronting the gathering storm.

The prince, with difficulty, consented to a prolongation of the armistice for two months longer ; resolute to resume hostilities should no accord be made before the end of July. The Advocate, with much earnestness, and with more violence than was habitual with him, insisted on protracting the temporary truce until the end of the year. The debates in the States-General and the state-council were vehement ; passion rose to fever-heat, but the stadholder, although often half beside himself with rage, ended by submitting once more to the will of Barneveld.

This was the easier, as the Advocate at last proposed an agreement which seemed to Maurice and Lewis William even better than their own original suggestion. It was arranged that the armistice should be prolonged until the end of the year, but it was at the same time stipulated that unless the negotiations had reached a definite result before the 1st of August, they should be forthwith broken off.

Thus a period of enforced calm—a kind of vacation, as if these great soldiers and grey-beards had been a troop of idle school-boys—was now established, without the slightest reason.

President Jeannin took occasion to make a journey to Paris, leaving the Hague on the 20th June.

During his absence a treaty of the States with England, similar in its terms to the one recently concluded between the republic and France, but only providing for half the number of auxiliary troops arranged for in the French convention, was signed at the Hague. The English 26 June. plenipotentiaries, Winwood and Spencer, wished 1608. to delay the exchange of signatures under the pending negotiations with Spain and the archdukes were brought to a close, as King James was most desirous at that epoch to keep on good terms with his Catholic Majesty. The States were so urgent, however, to bring at least this matter to a termination, and the English so anxious lest France should gain still greater influence than she now enjoyed in the provinces, that they at last gave way. It was further stipulated in the convention that the debt of the States to England, then amounting to 818,408*l.* sterling, should be settled by annual payments of 60,000*l.* ; to begin with the expected peace.[47]

Besides this debt to the English Government, the States-General owed nine millions of florins (900,000*l.*), and the separate provinces altogether eighteen millions (1,800,000*l.*). In short, there would be a deficiency of at least three hundred thousand florins [48] a month if the war went on, although every imaginable device had already been employed for increasing the revenue from taxation. It must be admitted therefore, that the Barneveld party were not to be severely censured for their desire to bring about an honourable peace.

That Jeannin was well aware of the disposition prevailing throughout a great part of the commonwealth is certain. It is equally certain that he represented to his sovereign, while at Paris, that the demand upon his exchequer by the States, in case of the resumption of hostilities, would be more considerable than ever. Immense was the pressure put upon Henry by the Spanish court, during the summer, to induce him to abandon his allies. Very complicated were the nets thrown out to entangle the wary old politician in "the grey jacket and with the heart of gold," as he was fond of designating himself, into an alliance with Philip and the archdukes.

Don Pedro de Toledo, at the head of a magnificent embassy, arrived in Paris with projects of arranging single, double, or triple marriages between the respective nurseries of France and Spain. The Infanta might marry with a French prince, and have all the Netherlands for her dower, so soon as the childless archdukes should have departed this

[47] Wagenaar, ix. 344. [48] Ibid, 377. Compare Grotius, xvii. 777.

life. Or an Infante might espouse a daughter of France with the same heritage assigned to the young couple.

Such proposals, duly set forth in sonorous Spanish by the Constable of Castile, failed to produce a very soothing effect on Henry's delicate ear. He had seen and heard enough of gaining thrones by Spanish marriages. Had not the very crown on his own head, which he had won with foot in stirrup and lance in rest, been hawked about for years, appended to the wedding ring of the Spanish Infanta? It might become convenient to him, at some later day, to form a family alliance with the house of Austria, although he would not excite suspicion in the United Provinces by openly accepting it then. But to wait for the shoes of Albert and Isabella, and until the Dutch republic had been absorbed into the obedient Netherlands by his assistance, was not a very flattering prospect for a son or daughter of France. The ex-Huguenot and indomitable campaigner in the field or in politics was for more drastic measures. Should the right moment come, he knew well enough how to strike, and could appropriate the provinces, obedient or disobedient, without assistance from the Spanish babies.[49]

Don Pedro took little by his propositions. The king stoutly declared that the Netherlands were very near to his heart, and that he would never abandon them on any consideration. So near, indeed, that he meant to bring them still nearer, but this was not then suspected by the Spanish court; Henry, the while, repelling as a personal insult to himself the request that he should secretly labour to reduce the United Provinces under subjection to the archdukes. It had even been proposed that he should sign a secret convention to that effect, and there were those about the court who were not ill-disposed for such a combination. The king was, however, far too adroit to be caught in any such trap. The marriage proposals in themselves he did not dislike, but Jeannin and he were both of a mind that they should be kept entirely secret.

[49] Wagenaar, ix. 350–357. Grotius, xvii. 774. Jeannin.

Don Pedro, on the contrary, for obvious reasons, was for making the transactions ostentatiously public, and, as a guarantee of his master's good faith in regard to the heritage of the Netherlands, he proposed that every portion of the republic, thenceforth to be conquered by the allies, should be confided to hands in which Henry and the archdukes would have equal confidence.

But these artifices were too trivial to produce much effect. Henry remained true, in his way, to the States-General, and Don Pedro was much laughed at in Paris, although the public scarcely knew wherefore.

These intrigues had not been conducted so mysteriously but that Barneveld was aware of what was going on. Both before Jeannin's departure from the Hague in June, and on his return in the middle of August, he catechised him very closely on the subject. The old Leaguer was too deep, however, to be thoroughly pumped, even by so practised a hand as the Advocate's, so that more was suspected than at the time was accurately known.

As, at the memorable epoch of the accession of the King of Scots to the throne of Elizabeth, Maximilian de Bethune had flattered the new monarch with the prospect of a double marriage, so now Don Fernando Girono had been sent on solemn mission to England, in order to offer the same infants to James which Don Pedro was placing at the disposition of Henry.

The British sovereign, as secretly fascinated by the idea of a Spanish family alliance as he had ever been by the proposals of the Marquis de Rosny for the French marriages, listened with eagerness. Money was scattered as profusely among the English courtiers by Don Fernando as had been done by De Bethune four years before.[50] The bribes were accepted, and often by the very personages who knew the colour of Bourbon money, but the ducats were scarcely earned. Girono, thus urging on the English Government the necessity of deserting the republic and cementing a

[50] Wagenaar, ix. 355, 356. Jeannin.

cordial, personal, and political understanding between James and Philip, effected but little. It soon became thoroughly understood in England that the same bargaining was going on simultaneously in France. As it was evident that the Spanish children could not be disposed of in both markets at the same time, it was plain to the dullest comprehension that either the brokerage of Toledo or of Girono was a sham, and that a policy erected upon such flimsy foundations would soon be washed away.

It is certain, however, that James, while affecting friendship for the States, and signing with them the league of mutual assistance, was secretly longing to nibble the bait dangled before him by Girono, and was especially determined to prevent, if possible, the plans of Toledo.

Meantime, brother John Neyen was dealing with Philip and the Duke of Lerma, in Spain.

The friar strenuously urged upon the favourite and the rest of the royal advisers the necessity of prompt action with the States. This needed not interfere with an unlimited amount of deception. It was necessary to bring the negotiations to a definite agreement. It would be by no means requisite, however, to hold to that agreement whenever a convenient opportunity for breaking it should present itself. The first object of Spanish policy, argued honest John, should be to get the weapons out of the rebels' hands. The Netherlanders ought to be encouraged to return to their usual pursuits of commerce and manufactures, whence they derived their support, and to disband their military and naval forces. Their sailors and traders should be treated kindly in Spain, instead of being indulged as heretofore with no hospitality save that of the Holy Inquisition and its dungeons. Let their minds be disarmed of all suspicion. Now the whole population of the provinces had been convinced that Spain, in affecting to treat, was secretly devising means to re-impose her ancient yoke upon their necks.[51]

Time went by in Aranjuez and Madrid. The forty

[51] Gallucci, 361, 363.

days, promised as the period of Neyen's absence, were soon gone; but what were forty days, or forty times forty, at the Spanish court? The friar, who, whatever his faults, was anything but an idler, chafed at a procrastination which seemed the more stupendous to him, coming fresh as he did from a busy people who knew the value of time. In the anguish of his soul he went to Rodrigo Calderon, of the privy council, and implored his influence with Government to procure leave for him to depart. Calderon, in urbane but decisive terms, assured him that this would be impossible before the king should return to Madrid. The monk then went to Idiaquez, who was in favour of his proceeding at once to the Netherlands, but who on being informed that Calderon was of a different opinion, gave up the point. More distressed than ever, Neyen impored Prada's assistance, but Prada plunged him into still deeper despair. His Majesty, said that counsellor, with matchless effrontery, was studying the propositions of the States-General, and all the papers in the negotiation, line by line, comma by comma. There were many animadversions to make, many counter suggestions to offer. The king was pondering the whole subject most diligently. When those lucubrations were finished, the royal decision, aided by the wisdom of the privy council, would be duly communicated to the archdukes.[52]

To wait for an answer to the propositions of the suspicious States-General until Philip III. had mastered the subject in detail, was a prospect too dreary even for the equable soul of Brother John. Dismayed at the position in which he found himself, he did his best to ferret out the reasons for the preposterous delay; not being willing to be paid off in allusions to the royal investigations. He was still further appalled at last by discovering that the delay was absolutely for the delay's sake. It was considered inconsistent with the dignity of the Government not to delay. The court and cabinet had quite made up their minds as to the answer to be made to the last propositions of the rebels, but to make

[52] Gallucci, 361, 363.

it known at once was entirely out of the question. In the previous year his Majesty's administration, so it was now confessed with shame, had acted with almost indecent haste. That everything had been conceded to the confederated provinces was the common talk of Europe. Let the time-honoured, inveterate custom of Spain in grave affairs to proceed slowly, and therefore surely, be in future observed. A proper self-respect required the king to keep the universe in suspense for a still longer period upon the royal will and the decision of the royal council.[53]

Were the affairs of the mighty Spanish empire so subordinate to the convenience of that portion of it called the Netherlands that no time was to be lost before settling their affairs?[54]

Such dismal frivolity, such palsied pride, seems scarcely credible; but more than all this has been carefully recorded in the letters of the friar.

If it were precipitation to spend the whole year 1607 in forming a single phrase; to wit, that the archdukes and the king would treat with the United Provinces as with countries to which they made no pretensions; and to spend the best part of another year in futile efforts to recal that phrase; if all this had been recklessness and haste, then, surely, the most sluggish canal in Holland was a raging cataract, and the march of a glacier electric speed.

Midsummer had arrived. The period in which peace was to be made or abandoned altogether had passed. Jeannin had returned from his visit to Paris; the Danish envoys, sent to watch the negotiations, had left the Hague, utterly disgusted with a puppet-show, all the strings of which, they protested, were pulled from the Louvre. Brother John, exasperated by the superhuman delays, fell sick of a fever at Burgos, and was sent, on his recovery, to the court at Valladolid to be

[53] "An existimationem quoque rei facere ut diutius in expectatione regiæ voluntatis regiique senatus-consulti suspensus esset orbis terrarum."—Gal-

lucci, *ubi sup.*

[54] Neyen's letters to Spinola, 23 May, 1608, in Gallucci, 362 363.

made ill again by the same cause, and still there came no
sound from the Government of Spain.[55]

At last the silence was broken. Something that was called
the voice of the king reached the ears of the archduke.
Long had he wrestled in prayer on this great subject, said
Philip III., fervently had he besought the Omnipotent for
light. He had now persuaded himself that he should not
fulfil his duty to God, nor satisfy his own strong desire for
maintaining the Catholic faith, nor preserve his self-respect,
if he now conceded his supreme right to the Confederated
Provinces at any other price than the uncontrolled exercise,
within their borders, of the Catholic religion. He wished,
therefore, as obedient son of the Church and Defender of the
Faith, to fulfil this primary duty, untrammelled by any
human consideration, by any profit that might induce him towards a contrary course. That which he had on other occasions
more than once signified he now confirmed. His mind was
fixed ; this was his last and immutable determination, that if
the confederates should permit the free and public exercise of
the Catholic, Roman, Apostolic religion to all such as wished
to live and die in it, for this cause so grateful to God, and for
no other reason, he also would permit to them that supreme
right over the provinces, and that authority which now
belonged to himself. Natives and residents of those countries should enjoy liberty, just so long as the exercise of the
Catholic religion flourished there, and not one day nor hour
longer.

Philip then proceeded flatly to refuse the India navigation,
giving reasons very satisfactory to himself why the provinces
ought cheerfully to abstain from that traffic. If the confederates, in consequence of the conditions thus definitely
announced, moved by their innate pride and obstinacy, and
relying on the assistance of their allies, should break off the
negotiations, then it would be desirable to adopt the plan
proposed by Jeannin to Richardot, and conclude a truce for
five or six years. The king expressed his own decided pre-

[55] Neyen to Spinola, 20 Aug. 1608, in Gallucci, 369.

ference for a truce rather than a peace, and his conviction
that Jeannin had made the suggestion by command of his
sovereign.[56]

The negotiators stood exactly where they did when Friar
John, disguised as a merchant, first made his bow to the
Prince and Barneveld in the palace at the Hague.

The archduke, on receiving at last this peremptory letter
from the king, had nothing for it but to issue instructions
accordingly to the plenipotentiaries at the Hague. 20 Aug.
A decisive conference between those diplomatists 1608.
and the States' commissioners took place immediately afterwards.

It was on the 20th August.

Although it had been agreed on the 1st May to break off
negotiations on the ensuing 1st of August, should no result be
reached, yet three weeks beyond that period had been suffered
to elapse, under a tacit agreement to wait a little longer for the
return of the friar. President Jeannin, too, had gone to Paris
on the 20th June, to receive new and important instructions,
verbal and written, from his sovereign, and during his absence it had not been thought expedient to transact much
business. Jeannin returned to the Hague on the 15th of
August, and, as definite instructions from king and archduke
had now arrived, there seemed no possibility of avoiding an
explanation.

The Spanish envoys accordingly, with much gravity, and
as if they had been propounding some cheerful novelty, announced to the assembled commissioners that all reports
hitherto flying about as to the Spanish king's intentions were
false.

His Majesty had no intention of refusing to give up the
sovereignty of the provinces. On the contrary, they were
instructed to concede that sovereignty freely and frankly to
my lords the States-General—a pearl and a precious jewel,
the like of which no prince had ever given away before. Yet
the king desired neither gold nor silver, neither cities nor

[56] King to the Archdukes, in Gallucci, 365, 367.

anything else of value in exchange. He asked only for that which was indispensable to the tranquillity of his conscience before God, to wit, the re-establishment in those countries of the Catholic Apostolic Roman religion.[57] This there could surely be no reasons for refusing. They owed it as a return for the generosity of the king, they owed it to their own relatives, they owed it to the memory of their ancestors, not to show greater animosity to the ancient religion than to the new and pernicious sect of Anabaptists, born into the world for the express purpose of destroying empires ; they owed it to their many fellow-citizens, who would otherwise be driven into exile, because deprived of that which is dearest to humanity.[58]

In regard to the East India navigation, inasmuch as the provinces had no right whatever to it, and as no other prince but the sovereign of Spain had any pretensions to it, his Majesty expected that the States would at once desist from it.[59]

This was the magnificent result of twenty months of diplomacy. As the king's father had long ago flung away the pearl and precious jewel which the son now made a merit of selling to its proprietors at the price of their life's blood—the world's commerce—it is difficult to imagine that Richardot, while communicating this preposterous ultimatum, could have kept his countenance. But there were case-hardened politicians on both sides. The proposition was made and received with becoming seriousness, and it was decided by the States' commissioners to make no answer at all on that occasion. They simply promised to render their report to the States-General, who doubtless would make short work with the matter.

They made their report and it occasioned a tumult. Every member present joined in a general chorus of wrathful denunciation. The Spanish commissioners were infamous swindlers, it was loudly asserted. There should be no more dealings with them at all. Spain was a power only to be

---

[57] Van der Kemp, iii. 156–160, from Sec. Res. Stat.-Gen. Grotius, xvii. 775. Wagenaar.   [58] Grotius, *ubi sup.*   [59] Van der Kemp, *ubi sup.*

treated with on the battle-field. In the tempest of general rage no one would listen to argument, no one asked which would be the weaker, which the stronger party, what resources for the renewed warfare could be found, or who would be the allies of the republic. Hatred, warlike fury and scorn at the duplicity with which they had been treated, washed every more politic sentiment away, and metamorphosed that body of burghers as in an instant. The negotiations should be broken off, not on one point, but on all points, and nothing was left but to prepare instantly for war.[60]

Three days later, after the French and English ambassadors, as well as Prince Maurice and Count Lewis   23 August, William, had been duly consulted, comparative calm   1608. was restored, and a decisive answer was unanimously voted by the States-General. The proposition of the commissioners was simply declared to be in direct violation of the sovereignty and freedom of the country, and it was announced that, if it should be persisted in, the whole negotiation might be considered as broken off. A formal answer to the royal propositions would be communicated likewise to the envoys of foreign powers, in order that the royal commissioners might be placed completely in the wrong.[61]

On the 25th August an elaborate response was accordingly delivered in writing by the States' commissioners to   25 August, those of the archdukes and king, it being at the   1608. same time declared by Barneveld and his colleagues that their functions were ended, and that this document, emanating from the States-General, was a sovereign resolution, not a diplomatic note.[62]

The contents of this paper may be inferred from all that has been previously narrated. The republic knew its own mind, and had always expressed itself with distinctness. The Spanish Government having at last been brought to disclose its intentions, there was an end to the negotiations for peace. The rupture was formally announced.

[60] Jeannin, i. 819.   [61] Van der Kemp, *ubi sup.* Wagenaar, ix. 357, 358.
        [62] See the paper in Meteren, 605, 606.

CHAPTER LI.

Designs of Henry IV. — New marriage project between France and Spain — Formal proposition of negotiating for a truce between the States and Spain — Exertions of Prince Maurice to counteract the designs of Barneveld — Strife between the two parties in the republic — Animosity of the people against Barneveld — Return of the Spanish commissioners — Further trifling — Dismissal of the commissioners — Close of the negotiations — Accidental discovery of the secret instructions of the archdukes to the commissioners — Opposing factions in the republic — Oration of President Jeannin before the States-General — Comparison between the Dutch and Swiss republics — Calumnies against the Advocate — Ambassador Lambert in France — Henry's letter to Prince Maurice — Reconciliation of Maurice and Barneveld — Agreement of the States to accept a truce.

PRESIDENT JEANNIN had long been prepared for this result. It was also by no means distasteful to him. A peace would not have accorded with the ulterior and secretly cherished schemes of his sovereign, and during his visit to Paris, he had succeeded in persuading Henry that a truce would be far the most advantageous solution of the question, so far as his interests were concerned.

For it had been precisely during that midsummer vacation of the President at Paris that Henry had completed his plot against the liberty of the republic, of which he professed himself the only friend. Another phase of Spanish marriage-making had excited his ever scheming and insidious brain. It had been proposed that the second son of the Spanish king should espouse one of Henry's daughters.

The papal Nuncius asked what benefit the King of Spain would receive for his share, in case of the marriage. The French king replied by plainly declaring to the Nuncius that the united States should abstain from and renounce all navigation to and commerce with the Indies, and should permit public exercise of the Catholic religion. If they refused, he would incontinently abandon them to their fate. More than this, he said, could not honestly be expected of him.[1]

Surely this was enough. Honestly or dishonestly, what more could Spain expect of the republic's best ally, than that he should use all his efforts to bring her back into Spanish subjection, should deprive her of commerce with three-quarters of the world, and compel her to re-establish the religion which she believed, at that period, to be incompatible with her constitutional liberties? It is difficult to imagine a more profligate or heartless course than the one pursued at this juncture by Henry. Secretly, he was intriguing, upon the very soil of the Netherlands, to filch from them that splendid commerce which was the wonder of the age, which had been invented and created by Dutch navigators and men of science, which was the very foundation of their State, and without which they could not exist, in order that he might appropriate it to himself, and transfer the East India Company to France; while at Paris he was solemnly engaging himself in a partnership with their ancient and deadly enemy to rob them of their precious and nobly gained liberty. Was better proof ever afforded that God alone can protect us against those whom we trust? Who was most dangerous to the United Provinces during those memorable peace negotiations, Spain the avowed enemy, or France the friend?

The little republic had but her own sword, her own brain, and her own purse to rely upon. Elizabeth was dead, and James loved Spain better than he did the Netherlands, and quiet better than Spain. "I have told you often," said Caron, "and I say it once more, the Spaniard is lucky that he has such a peaceable king as this to deal with in England."[2]

[1] " Le nonce avait demandé au roy quel benefice recevrait de sa part le Roy d'Espagne en respect des mariages, Et pour parler plus clair le roy déclara au nonce que les Etats se deporteront de toute navigation et commerce aux Indes, et permettront quelque exercise public de la foy Catholique ès Provinces Unies, ou à faute de ce il les delaissera et abandonnera incontinent, en quoy il dit estre compris tout ce que l'on peut honnêtement prétendre de luy pour le présent."—Extract of Letter of Peckius, cited in Deventer, iii. 250.

[2] Deventer, iii. 253.

The details of the new marriage project were arranged at Paris between the Nuncius, the Spanish ambassador, Don Pedro de Toledo, the diplomatic agent of the archdukes, and Henry's ministers, precisely as if there had been no negotiations going on between the States and Spain. Yet the French king was supposed to be the nearest friend of the States, and was consulted by them on every occasion, while his most intimate and trusted counsellor, the ingenuous Jeannin, whose open brow was stamped with sincerity, was privy to all their most secret deliberations.

But the statesman thus dealing with the Hollanders under such a mask of friendly candour, knew perfectly well the reason why his Government preferred a truce to a peace. During a prolonged truce, the two royal children would grow old enough for the consummation of marriage, and the States—so it was hoped—would be corrupted and cajoled into renouncing their liberty. All the Netherlands would be then formed into a secundogeniture for Spain, and the first sovereign would be the husband of a French princess.[3] Even as an object of ambition, the prize to be secured

---

[3] "Et le point auquel nous travaillons maintenant est de pénétrer à quoy le Roy de France se résouldra advenant faulte de paix ; et tachons de faire trouver bon à ses dits ministres qu'en ce cas il abandonne les dits Etats et empoigne le party du mariage du second fils d'Espaigne avecq l'une de ses filles aux conditions ja proposées ; pour à quoy les induire sert de beaucoup de les avoir mené jusques là qu'ils confessent y avoir de la raison, equité et justice es conditions concernans la religion et la navigation aux Indes, soubs lesquelles l'on est content de quitter la souveraineté des dites provinces ; ce qu'aussi le roy mesme advoua assez clérement en ma derniere audience. Et sur ce a resparti qu'estans les dites conditions telles, il auroit juste occasion de s'offenser et retirer des dits Estats s'il ne s'y accomodaient, il me dit qu'il s'entendoit comme cela . . . . Et se resolvant le roy à cest abandon et delaissement des dits Estats, le dit

Don Pedro m'a dit qu'il a pouvoir d'accorder en tel cas le dit mariage avecq l'investiture des Pais-Bas et aultres conditions plus fortes pour asseurer le roy qu'iceulx pays demeuront séparez de la couronne d'Espaigne Mais il semble à aulcuns des ministres qu'à faulte de paix le plus expédient sera de faire une longue trève avecq les dits Estats et cependant arrester le dit mariage et attendre le temps de consommation d'icelluy et de la lignée qui en pourra procéder Auquel cas le roy tres Chretien ne seroit seulement content d'abandonner les dits Etats, mais encore de tenir la main à les faire rejoindre aux aultres provinces de l'obeyssance de votre altesse."
—Peckius to the Archduke, 18 Aug 1608, in Deventer, iii 250-252.
Two months before Peckius had written that the Duc de Sully had been feeling his pulse in regard to a truce in the Netherlands with reference to these marriage projects.—Ibid.

by so much procrastination and so much treachery was paltry.

When the Spanish commissioners came to the French and English ambassadors accordingly, complaining of the abrupt and peremptory tone of the States' reply, the suggestion of conferences for truce, in place of fruitless peace negotiations, was made at once, and of course favourably received. It was soon afterwards laid before the States-General. To this end, in truth, Richardot and his colleagues had long been secretly tending. Moreover, the subject had been thoroughly but secretly discussed long before between Jeannin and Barneveld.

The French and English ambassadors, accordingly, on the 27th August, came before the States-General, and made a formal proposition for the opening of negotiations for a truce. They advised the adoption of this course in the strongest manner. "Let the truce be made with you," they said, "as with free States, over which the king and the archdukes have no pretensions, with the understanding that, *during the time of the truce* you are to have free commerce as well to the Indies as to Spain and the obedient Netherlands, and to every part of the Spanish dominions ; that you are to retain all that you possess at present, and that such other conditions are to be added as you may find it reasonable to impose. During this period of leisure you will have time to put your affairs in order, to pay your debts, and to reform your Government, and if you remain united, the truce will change into an absolute peace."[4]

Maurice was more indignant when the new scheme was brought to his notice than he had ever been before, and used more violent language in opposing a truce than he had been used to employ when striving against a peace. To be treated with, *as* with a free State, and to receive permission to trade with the outside world until the truce should expire, seemed to him a sorry result for the republic to accept.

[4] Jeannin, i. 827.

The state-council declared, by way of answer to the foreign ambassadors, that the principal points and conditions which had been solemnly fixed, before the States had consented to begin the negotiations, had been disputed with infinite effrontery and shamelessness by the enemy.[5] The pure and perfect sovereignty notoriously included religion and navigation to any part of the world; and the republic would never consent to any discussion of truce unless these points were confirmed beforehand with the Spanish king's signature and seal.

28 August.

This resolution of the council—a body which stood much under the influence of the Nassaus—was adopted next day by the States-General, and duly communicated to the friendly ambassadors.[6]

The foreign commissioners, when apprised of this decision, begged for six weeks' time, in order to be able to hear from Madrid.

Even the peace party was disgusted with this impertinence. Maurice boiled over with wrath. The ambassadors recommended compliance with the proposal. Their advice was discussed in the States-General, eighty members being present, besides Maurice and Lewis William. The stadholder made a violent and indignant speech.[7]

He was justified in his vehemence. Nothing could exceed the perfidy of their great ally.

"I know that the King of France calculates thus"—wrote Aerssens at that moment from Paris—"'If the truce lasts seven years, my son will be old enough to accomplish the proposed marriage, and they will be obliged to fulfil their present offers. Otherwise, I would break the truce in the Netherlands, and my own peace with them, in order to take from the Spaniard by force what he led me to hope from alliance.[7] Thus it is," continued the States' envoy, "that his Majesty condescends to propose to us a truce, which may have a double interpretation, according to the disposition of the strongest, and thus our commonwealth will be kept in perpe-

"Vermeetelyk en onbeschaemd." [6] Van der Kemp, iii. 160, 162. [7] Ibid. 40.

tual disquiet, without knowing whether it is sovereign or not. Nor will it be sovereign unless it shall so please our neighbour, who by this means will always keep his foot upon our throat." [8]

" To treat with the States as if they were free," said Henry to the Nuncius soon afterwards, " is not to make them free. This clause does no prejudice to the rights of the King of Spain, except for the time of the truce." Aerssens taxed the king with having said this. His Majesty flatly denied it. The republican envoy bluntly adduced the testimony of the ambassadors of Venice and of Wirtemberg. The king flew into a rage on seeing that his secrets had been divulged, and burst out with these words :—" What you demand is not reasonable. You wish the king of Spain to renounce his rights in order to arrive at a truce. You wish to dictate the law to him. If you had just gained four battles over him, you could not demand more. I have always held you for sovereigns, because I am your friend, but if you would judge by equity and justice, you are not sovereigns. It is not reasonable that the king of Spain should quit the sovereignty *for always*, and you ought to be satisfied with having it so long as the treaty shall last." [9]

Here was playing at sovereignty with a vengeance. Sovereignty was a rattle for the States to amuse themselves with, until the royal infants, French and Spanish, should be grown old enough to take the sovereignty for good. Truly this was indeed keeping the republic under the king's heel to be crushed at his pleasure, as Aerssens, with just bitterness, exclaimed.

Two days were passed at the Hague in vehement debate. The deputies of Zeeland withdrew. The deputies from Holland were divided, but, on the whole, it was agreed to listen to propositions of truce, provided the freedom of the United Provinces—not under conditions nor during a certain period, but simply and for all time—should be recognised beforehand. [10]

[8] Correspondence in Deventer, iii. 262-267.   [9] Ibid.   [10] Wagenaar, ix. 378-380.

It was further decided on the 14th September to wait

until the end of the month for the answer from Spain.

After the 1st of October it was distinctly intimated to the Spanish commissioners that they must at once leave the country unless the king had then acknowledged the absolute independence of the provinces.[11]

A suggestion which had been made by these diplomatists to prolong the actually existing armistice into a truce of seven years, a step which they professed themselves willing to take upon their own responsibility, had been scornfully rejected by the States. It was already carrying them far enough away, they said, to take them away from a peace to a truce, which was something far less secure than a peace, but the continuance of this floating, uncertain armistice would be the most dangerous insecurity of all. This would be going from firm land to slippery ice, and from slippery ice into the water. By such a process, they would have neither war nor peace—neither liberty of government nor freedom of commerce—and they unanimously refused to listen to any such schemes.[12]

During the fortnight which followed this provisional consent of the States, the prince redoubled his efforts to counteract the Barneveld party.

He was determined, so far as in him lay, that the United Netherlands should never fall back under the dominion of Spain. He had long maintained the impossibility of effecting their thorough independence except by continuing the war, and had only with reluctance acquiesced in the arguments of the French ambassadors in favour of peace negotiations. As to the truce, he vehemently assured those envoys that it was but a trap. How could the Netherlanders know who their friends might be when the truce should have expired, and under what unfavourable auspices they might not be compelled to resume hostilities?[13]

As if he had been actually present at the council boards

[11] Van der Kemp, iii. 41.   [12] Meteren, 606, 607.   [13] Jeannin, i. 889, *seqq*

in Madrid and Valladolid, or had been reading the secret letters of Friar John to Spinola, he affirmed that the only object of Spain was to recruit her strength and improve her finances, now entirely exhausted. He believed, on the other hand, that the people of the provinces, after they should have once become accustomed to repose, would shrink from exchanging their lucrative pursuits for war, and would prefer to fall back under the yoke of Spain. During the truce they would object to the furnishing of necessary contributions for garrison expenses, and the result would be that the most important cities and strongholds, especially those on the frontier, which were mainly inhabited by Catholics, would become insecure. Being hostile to a Government which only controlled them by force, they would with difficulty be kept in check by diminished garrisons, unless they should obtain liberty of Catholic worship.[14]

It is a dismal proof of the inability of a leading mind, after half a century's war, to comprehend the true lesson of the war—that toleration of the Roman religion seemed to Maurice an entirely inadmissible idea. The prince could not rise to the height on which his illustrious father had stood ; and those about him, who encouraged him in his hostility to Catholicism, denounced Barneveld and Arminius as no better than traitors and atheists. In the eyes of the extreme party, the mighty war had been waged, not to liberate human thought, but to enforce predestination ; and heretics to Calvinism were as offensive in their eyes as Jews and Saracens had ever been to Torquemada.

The reasons were unanswerable for the refusal of the States to bind themselves to a foreign sovereign in regard to the interior administration of their commonwealth ; but that diversity of religious worship should be considered incompatible with the health of the young republic—that the men who had so bravely fought the Spanish Inquisition should now claim their own right of inquisition into the human conscience—this was almost enough to create despair as to the

[14] Jeannin, i. 889, *seqq.*

possibility of the world's progress. The seed of intellectual
advancement is slow in ripening, and it is almost invariably
the case that the generation which plants—often but half
conscious of the mightiness of its work—is not the generation
which reaps the harvest. But all mankind at last inherits
what is sown in the blood and tears of a few. That Government, whether regal or democratic, should dare to thrust
itself between man and his Maker—that the State, not
satisfied with interfering in a thousand superfluous ways with
the freedom of individual human action in the business of
life, should combine with the Church to reduce human
thought to slavery in regard to the sacred interests of
eternity, was one day to be esteemed a blasphemous presumption in lands which deserved to call themselves free. But that
hour had not yet come.

"If the garrisons should be weakened," said the prince,
"nothing could be expected from the political fidelity of the
town populations in question, unless they should be allowed
the exercise of their own religion. But the States could
hardly be disposed to grant this voluntarily, for fear of
injuring the general insecurity and violating the laws of the
commonwealth, built as it is upon a foundation which cannot suffer this diversity in the public exercise of religion.
Already," continued Maurice, "there are the seeds of dissension in the provinces and in the cities, sure to ripen in the
idleness and repose of peace to an open division. This would
give the enemy a means of intriguing with and corrupting
those who are already wickedly inclined."[15]

Thus in the year 1608, the head of the Dutch republic,
the son of William the Silent, seemed to express himself
in favour of continuing a horrible war, not to maintain the
political independence of his country, but to prevent Catholics
from acquiring the right of publicly worshipping God according to the dictates of their conscience.

Yet it would be unjust to the prince, whose patriotism
was as pure and unsullied as his sword, to confound his

[15] Jeannin, i. 889, *seqq.*

motives with his end. He was firmly convinced that liberty of religious worship, to be acquired during the truce, would inevitably cause the United Provinces to fall once more under the Spanish yoke. The French ambassador, with whom he conferred every day, never doubted his sincerity. Gelderland, Friesland, Overyssel, Groningen, and Utrecht, five provinces out of the united seven, the prince declared to be chiefly inhabited by Catholics. They had only entered the union, he said, because compelled by force. They could only be kept in the union by force, unless allowed freedom of religion. His inference from such a lamentable state of affairs was, not that the experiment of religious worship should be tried, but that the garrisons throughout the five provinces ought to be redoubled, and the war with Spain indefinitely waged. The President was likewise of opinion that "a revolt of these five provinces against the union might be at any moment expected, ill disposed as they were to recognise a sovereignty which abolished their religion." Being himself a Catholic, however, it was not unnatural that he should make a different deduction from that of the prince, and warmly recommend, not more garrisons, but more liberty of worship.[16]

Thus the very men who were ready to dare all, and to sacrifice all in behalf of their country, really believed themselves providing for the imperishable security of the commonwealth by placing it on the narrow basis of religious intolerance.

Maurice, not satisfied with making these vehement arguments against the truce in his conferences with the envoys of the French and British sovereigns, employed the brief interval yet to elapse before definitely breaking off or resuming the conferences with the Spanish commissioners in making vigorous appeals to the country.

"The weal or woe of the United Provinces for all time,"

---

[16] Thus Jeannin (i. 891, 892) reported in his letters to Villeroy the prince's conversation, yet certainly the prince was erroneously or falsely quoted. — Compare Van der Kemp, iii. 43.

he said, " is depending on the present transactions.[17] Weigh well the reasons we urge, and make use of those which seem to you convincing. You know that the foe, according to his old deceitful manner, laid down very specious conditions at the beginning, in order to induce my lords the States-General to treat.

" If the king and the archdudes sincerely mean to relinquish absolutely their pretensions to these provinces, they can certainly have no difficulty in finding honest and convenient words to express their intention. As they are seeking other phrases than the usual and straightforward ones, they give certain proof that they mean to keep back from us the substance. They are trying to cheat us with dark, dubious, loosely-screwed terms,[18] which secure nothing and bind to nothing. If it be wise to trust the welfare of our State to ambiguous words, you can judge according to your own discretion.

" Recognition of our sovereignty is the foundation-stone of these negotiations.

" Let every man be assured that, with such mighty enemies, we can do nothing by halves. We cannot afford to retract, mutilate, or moderate our original determination. He who swerves from the straight road at the beginning is lost ; he who stumbles at the first step is apt to fall down the whole staircase. If, on account of imaginable necessity, we postpone that most vital point, the assurance of our freedom, we shall very easily allow less important points to pass muster,[19] and at last come tamely into the path of reconciliation. That was exactly the danger which our ancestors in similar negotiations always feared, and against which we too have always done our best to guard ourselves.

" Wherefore, if the preservation of our beloved fatherland is dear to you, I exhort you to maintain that great fundamental resolution, at all times and against all men, even if this should

---

[17] The letter, dated 21 Sept. 1608, is published in full by Van der Kemp, iii 166-174. It is less accurately given by Meteren, 606-608.

[18] " Op schroeven gestelde woorden en termen."

[19] " Geringere punkten ook wel door de monstering passeren."

cause the departure of the enemy's commissioners. What can you expect from them but evil fruit?"

He then advised all the estates and magistracies which he was addressing to instruct their deputies, at the approaching session of the States-General, to hold on to the first article of the often-cited preliminary resolution without allowing one syllable to be altered. Otherwise nothing could save the commonwealth from dire and notorious confusion. Above all, he entreated them to act in entire harmony and confidence with himself and his cousin, even as they had ever done with his illustrious father.

Certainly the prince fully deserved the confidence of the States, as well for his own signal services and chivalrous self-devotion, as for the unexampled sacrifices and achievements of William the Silent. His words had the true patriotic ring of his father's frequent and eloquent appeals; and I have not hesitated to give these extracts from his discourse, because comparatively few of such utterances of Maurice have been preserved, and because it gives a vivid impression of the condition of the republic and the state of parties at that momentous epoch. It was not merely the fate of the United Netherlands and the question of peace or war between the little republic and its hereditary enemy that were upon the issue. The peace of all Christendom, the most considerable material interests of civilization, and the highest political and moral principles that can influence human action, were involved in those negotiations.

There were not wanting many to impeach the purity of the stadholder's motives. As admiral or captain-general, he received high salaries, besides a tenth part of all prize-money gained at sea by the fleets, or of ransom and blackmail on land by the armies of the republic. His profession, his ambition, his delights, were those of a soldier. As a soldier in a great war, he was more necessary to his countrymen than he could expect to be as a statesman in time of peace. But nothing ever appeared in public or in private, which threw a reasonable suspicion upon his lofty patriotism. Peace he had always believed to be difficult of attainment. It had now been proved impossible. A truce he honestly considered a pitfall of destruction, and he denounced it, as we have seen, in the language of energetic conviction. He never alluded to his pecuniary losses in case peace should be made. His disinterested patriotism was the frequent subject of comment in the most secret letters of the French ambassadors to the king. He had repeatedly refused enormous offers if he would forsake the cause of the republic. The King of France was ever ready to tempt him with bribes, such as had proved most efficacious with men as highly born and as highly placed as a cadet of the house of Orange-Nassau. But there is no record that Jeannin assailed him at this crisis with such temptations, although it has not been pretended that the prince was obdurate to the influence of Mammon when that deity could be openly approached.

That Maurice loved power, pelf, and war, can hardly be denied. That he had a mounting ambition; that he thought a monarchy founded upon the historical institutions and charters of the provinces might be better than the burgher-aristocracy which, under the lead of Barneveld, was establishing itself in the country; that he knew no candidate so eligible for such a throne as his father's son; all this is highly probable and scarcely surprising. But that such sentiments or aspirations caused him to swerve the ninth part of a hair from what he considered the direct path of duty; that he determined to fight out the great fight with Spain and Rome until the States were free in form, in name, and in fact, only that he might then usurp a sovereignty which would otherwise revert to Philip of Spain or be snatched by Henry of Navarre—of all this there is no proof whatever.

The language of Lewis William to the provinces under his government was quite as vigorous as the appeals of Maurice.[20]

During the brief interval remaining before the commissioners should comply with the demands of the States or take their departure, the press throughout the Netherlands was

[20] His letter is published by Van der Kemp, iii. 174-176.

most active. Pamphlets fell thick as hail. The peace party
and the war party contended with each other, over all the
territory of the provinces, as vigorously as the troops of
Fuentes or Bucquoy had ever battled with the columns of
Bax and Meetkerke. The types of Blaauw and Plantin were as
effective during the brief armistice, as pike and arquebus in
the field, but unfortunately they were used by Netherlanders
against each other. As a matter of course, each party im-
peached the motives as well as the actions of its antagonist.
The adherents of the Advocate accused the stadholder of desiring the continuance of the war for personal aims. They
averred that six thousand men for guarding the rivers would
be necessary, in addition to the forty-five thousand men, now
kept constantly on foot. They placed the requisite monthly
expenses, if hostilities were resumed, at 800,000 florins, while
they pointed to the 27,000,000 of debt over and above the
8,000,000 due to the British crown, as a burthen under which
the republic could scarcely stagger much longer.[21] Such
figures seem modest enough, as the price of a war of independence.

Familiar with the gigantic budgets of our own day, we
listen with something like wonder, now that two centuries
and a half have passed, to the fierce denunciations by the
war party of these figures as wilful fictions. Science has
made in that interval such gigantic strides. The awful intellect of man may at last make war impossible for his
physical strength. He can forge but cannot wield the
hammer of Thor ; nor has Science yet discovered the philosopher's stone. Without it, what exchequer can accept
chronic warfare and escape bankruptcy ? After what has
been witnessed in these latest days, the sieges and battles of
that distant epoch seem like the fights of pigmies and cranes.
Already an eighty years' war, such as once was waged, has
become inconceivable. Let two more centuries pass away, and
perhaps a three weeks' campaign may exhaust an empire.[22]

Meantime the war of words continued. A proclamation

[21] Wagenaar, ix. 377.   [22] This was written in March, 1866.

with penalties was issued by the States against the epidemic
plague of pamphlets or "blue-books," as those publications
were called in Holland[23] but with little result.[24] It was not
deemed consistent with liberty by those republicans to put
chains on the press because its utterances might occasionally
be distasteful to magistrates.[25] The writers, printers, and
sellers of the "blue-books" remained unpunished and
snapped their fingers at the placard.

We have seen the strenuous exertions of the Nassaus and
their adherents by public appeals and private conversation to
defeat all schemes of truce. The people were stirred by the
eloquence of the two stadholders. They were stung to fury
against Spain and against Barneveld by the waspish effusions
of the daily press. The magistrates remained calm, and took
part by considerable majorities with Barneveld. That statesman, while exercising almost autocratic influence in the
estates, became more and more odious to the humbler classes,
to the Nassaus, and especially to the Calvinist clergy. He
was denounced as a papist, an atheist, a traitor, because
striving for an honourable peace with the foe, and because
admitting the possibility of more than one road to the
kingdom of Heaven. To doubt the infallibility of Calvin
was as heinous a crime, in the eyes of his accusers, as to
kneel to the host. Peter Titelmann, half a century earlier,
dripping with the blood of a thousand martyrs, seemed
hardly a more loathsome object to all Netherlanders than
the Advocate now appeared to his political enemies, thus
daring to preach religious toleration, and boasting of humble
ignorance as the safest creed.[26] Alas ! we must always have
something to persecute, and individual man is never so
convinced of his own wisdom as when dealing with subjects
beyond human comprehension.

[23] "Blaauw boekje." Was the phrase derived from the name of the great printer Blaauw ?

[24] Groot Plakaat Bock, i. D. kol. 437. Wagenaar, ix. 373.

[25] "Alzo het streng onderzocken naar schryvers en verspreiden voor strydig met de vryheid aangezien en daerom gemyd werdt."—Wagenaar, ix. 373.

[26] "Nil scire tutissima fides."—Device of the Olden-Barneveld family, vide vol. i. of this work, page 315.

Unfortunately, however, while the great Advocate was clear in his conscience he had scarcely clean hands. He had very recently accepted a present of twenty thousand florins from the King of France. That this was a bribe by which his services were to be purchased for a cause not in harmony with his own convictions it would be unjust to say. We of a later generation, who have had the advantage of looking through the portfolio of President Jeannin, and of learning the secret intentions of that diplomatist and of his master, can fully understand however that there was more than sufficient cause at the time for suspecting the purity of the great Advocate's conduct. We are perfectly aware that the secret instructions of Henry gave his plenipotentiaries almost unlimited power to buy up as many influential personages in the Netherlands as could be purchased. So they would assist in making the king master of the United Provinces at the proper moment there was scarcely any price that he was not willing to pay.

Especially Prince Maurice, his cousin, and the Advocate of Holland, were to be secured by life pensions, property, offices, and dignities, all which Jeannin might offer to an almost unlimited amount, if by such means those great personages could possibly be induced to perform the king's work.

There is no record that the president ever held out such baits at this epoch to the prince. There could never be a doubt however in any one's mind that if the political chief of the Orange-Nassau house ever wished to make himself the instrument by which France should supplant Spain in the tyranny of the Netherlands, he might always name his own price. Jeannin never insulted him with any such trading propositions. As for Barneveld, he avowed long years afterwards that he had accepted the twenty thousand florins, and that the king had expressly exacted secrecy in regard to the transaction. He declared however that the money was a reward for public services rendered by him to the French Government ten years before, in the course of his mission to

France at the time of the peace of Vervins. The reward had been promised in 1598, and the pledge was fulfilled in 1608. In accepting wages fairly earned, however, he protested that he had bound himself to no dishonourable service, and that he had never exchanged a word with Jeannin or with any man in regard to securing for Henry the sovereignty of the Netherlands.[27]

His friends moreover maintained in his defence that there were no laws in the Netherlands forbidding citizens to accept presents or pensions from foreign powers. Such an excuse was as bad as the accusation. Woe to the republic whose citizens require laws to prevent them from becoming stipendiaries of foreign potentates ! If public virtue, the only foundation of republican institutions, be so far washed away that laws in this regard are necessary to save it from complete destruction, then already the republic is impossible. Many who bore illustrious names, and occupied the highest social positions at that day in France, England, and the obedient provinces, were as venal as cattle at a fair. Philip and Henry had bought them over and over again, whenever either was rich enough to purchase and strong enough to enforce the terms of sale. Bribes were taken with both hands in overflowing measure ; the difficulty was only in obtaining the work for the wage.

But it would have been humiliating beyond expression had the new commonwealth, after passing through the fiery furnace of its great war, proved no purer than leading monarchies at a most corrupt epoch. It was no wonder therefore that men sought to wipe off the stain from the reputation of Barneveld, and it is at least a solace that there was no proof of his ever rendering, or ever having agreed to render, services inconsistent with his convictions as to the best interests of the commonwealth. It is sufficiently grave that he knew the colour of the king's money, and that

[27] See for this whole story of the twenty thousand florins paid to the Advocate, Van der Kemp, iii. 43, 165, 166. Brandt, Regtspleging, 87, 88. Wagenaar, ix. 367–370.

in a momentous crisis of history he accepted a reward for former professional services, and that the broker in the transaction, President Jeannin, seriously charged him by Henry's orders to keep the matter secret. It would be still more dismal if Jeannin, in his private letters, had ever intimated to Villeroy or his master that he considered it a mercantile transaction, or if any effort had ever been made by the Advocate to help Henry to the Batavian throne. This however is not the case.

In truth, neither Maurice nor Barneveld was likely to assist the French king in his intrigues against the independence of their fatherland. Both had higher objects of ambition than to become the humble and well-paid servants of a foreign potentate. The stadholder doubtless dreamed of a crown which might have been his father's, and which his own illustrious services might.be supposed to have earned for himself. If that tempting prize were more likely to be gained by a continuance of the war, it is none the less certain that he considered peace, and still more truce, as fatal to the independence of the provinces.

The Advocate, on the other hand, loved his country well. Perhaps he loved power even better. To govern the city magistracies of Holland, through them the provincial estates, and through them again the States-General of the whole commonwealth; as first citizen of a republic to wield the powers of a king; as statesman, diplomatist, and financier, to create a mighty empire out of those slender and but recently emancipated provinces of Spain, was a more flattering prospect for a man of large intellect, iron will, and infinite resources, than to sink into the contemptible position of stipendiary to a foreign master. He foresaw change, growth, transformation in the existing condition of things. Those great corporations the East and West India Companies were already producing a new organism out of the political and commercial chaos which had been so long brooding over civilization. Visions of an imperial zone extending from the little Batavian island around the earth, a chain of forts and factories dotting the

newly-discovered and yet undiscovered points of vantage, on
island or promontory, in every sea ; a watery, nebulous, yet
most substantial empire—not fantastic, but practical—not
picturesque and mediæval, but modern and lucrative—a
world-wide commonwealth with a half-submerged metropolis, which should rule the ocean with its own fleets and,
like Venice and Florence, job its land wars with mercenary
armies—all these dreams were not the cloudy pageant of a
poet but the practical schemes of a great creative mind.
They were destined to become reality. Had the geographical
conditions been originally more favourable than they were,
had Nature been less a stepmother to the metropolis of the
rising Batavian realm, the creation might have been more
durable. Barneveld, and the men who acted with him, comprehended their age, and with slender materials were prepared
to do great things. They did not look very far perhaps into
futurity, but they saw the vast changes already taking place,
and felt the throb of forces actually at work.

The days were gone when the iron-clad man on horseback
conquered a kingdom with his single hand. Doubtless there
is more of poetry and romance in his deeds than in the
achievements of the counting-house aristocracy, the hier-
archy of joint-stock corporations that was taking the lead in
the world's affairs. Enlarged views of the social compact
and of human liberty, as compared with those which later
generations ought to take, standing upon the graves, heaped
up mountains high, of their predecessors, could hardly be
expected of them. But they knew how to do the work before
them. They had been able to smite a foreign and sacerdotal
tyranny into the dust at the expense of more blood and more
treasure, and with sacrifices continued through a longer cycle
of years, than had ever been recorded by history.

Thus the Advocate believed that the chief fruits of the
war—political independence, religious liberty, commercial
expansion—could be now secured by diplomacy, and that
a truce could be so handled as to become equivalent to a
peace. He required no bribes therefore to labour for that

which he believed to be for his own interests and for those of the country.

First citizen of Holland, perpetual chairman of a board of ambitious shopkeepers who purposed to dictate laws to the world from their counting-house table, with an unerring eye for the interests of the commonwealth and his own, with much vision, extraordinary eloquence, and a magnificent will, he is as good a sample of a great burgher—an imposing not a heroic figure—as the times had seen.

A vast stride had been taken in the world's progress. Even monopoly was freedom compared to the sloth and ignorance of an earlier epoch and of other lands, and although the days were still far distant when the earth was to belong to mankind, yet the modern republic was leading, half unconsciously, to a period of wider liberty of government, commerce, and above all of thought.

Meantime, the period assigned for the departure of the Spanish commissioners, unless they brought a satisfactory communication from the king, was rapidly approaching.

On the 24th September Verreyken returned from Brussels, but it was soon known that he came empty handed. He informed the French and English ambassadors ^{24 Sept.} that the archdukes, on their own responsibility, now suggested the conclusion of a truce of seven years for Europe only. This was to be negotiated with the States-General as with free people, over whom no pretensions of authority were made, and the hope was expressed that the king would give his consent to this arrangement.

The ambassadors naturally refused to carry the message to the States. To make themselves the mouthpieces of such childish suggestions was to bring themselves and their masters into contempt. There had been trifling enough, and even Jeannin saw that the storm of indignation about to burst forth would be irresistible. There was no need of any attempt on the part of the commissioners to prolong their stay if this was the result of the fifteen days' grace which had so reluctantly been conceded to them. To express a hope that the king might perhaps give his future approval to a proceeding for which his signed and sealed consent had been exacted as an indispensable preliminary, was carrying effrontery further than had yet been attempted in these amazing negotiations.

Prince Maurice once more addressed the cities of Holland, giving vent to his wrath in language with which there was now more sympathy than there had been before. "Verreyken has come back," he said, "not with a signature, but with a hope. The longer the enemy remains in the country the more he goes back from what he had originally promised. He is seeking for nothing more than, in this cheating way and in this pretence of waiting for the king's consent—which we have been expecting now for more than eighteen months—to continue the ruinous armistice. Thus he keeps the country in a perpetual uncertainty, the only possible consequence of which is our complete destruction. We adjure you therefore to send a resolution in conformity with our late address, in order that through these tricks and snares the fatherland may not fall into the clutch of the enemy, and thus into eternal and intolerable slavery. God save us all from such a fate ! " [28]

26 Sept.

Neither Barneveld nor Jeannin attempted to struggle against the almost general indignation. The deputies of Zeeland withdrew from the assembly of the States-General, protesting that they would never appear there again so long as the Spanish commissioners remained in the country. The door was opened wide, and it was plain that those functionaries must take their departure. Pride would not allow them to ask permission of the States to remain, although they intimated to the ambassadors their intense desire to linger for ten or twelve days longer. This was obviously inadmissible, and on the 30th September they appeared before the Assembly to take leave.[29]

[28] Document given in Van der Kemp, iii. 177, 178.
[29] Meteren, 608. Grotius, xvii. 780, 781. Wagenaar, ix. 385–388. Van der Kemp, iii. 178–183.

There were but three of them, the Genoese, the Spaniard, and the Burgundian—Spinola, Mancicidor, and Richardot. Of the two Netherlanders, brother John was still in Spain, and Verreyken found it convenient that day to have a lame leg.

President Richardot, standing majestically before the States-General, with his robes wrapped around his tall, spare form, made a solemn farewell speech of 30 Sept. mingled sorrow, pity, and the resentment of injured innocence. They had come to the Hague, he said, sent by the King of Spain and the archdukes to treat for a good and substantial peace, according to the honest intention of his Majesty and their Highnesses. To this end they had sincerely and faithfully dealt with the gentlemen deputed for that purpose by their High Mightinesses the States, doing everything they could think of to further the cause of peace. They lamented that the issue had not been such as they had hoped, notwithstanding that the king and archdukes had so far derogated from their reputation as to send their commissioners into the United Netherlands, it having been easy enough to arrange for negotiations on other soil. It had been their wish thus to prove to the world how straightforward were their intentions by not requiring the States to send deputies to them. They had accorded the first point in the negotiations, touching the free state of the country. Their High Mightinesses had taken offence upon the second, regarding the restoration of religion in the United Provinces. Thereupon the father commissary had gone to Spain, and had remained longer than was agreeable. Nevertheless, they had meantime treated of other points. Coming back at last to the point of religion, the States-General had taken a resolution, and had given them their dismissal, without being willing to hear a word more, or to make a single proposition of moderation or accommodation.

He could not refrain from saying that the commissioners had been treated roughly. Their High Mightinesses had fixed the time for their dismissal more precisely than one would do with a servant who was discharged for misconduct; for the lackey, if he asked for it, would be allowed at least a day longer to pack his trunk for the journey. They protested before God and the assembly of the States that the king and princes had meant most sincerely, and had dealt with all roundness and sincerity. They at least remained innocent of all the disasters and calamities to come from the war.

"As for myself," said Richardot, "I am no prophet, nor the son of a prophet; yet I will venture the prediction to you, my lords the States-General, that you will bitterly rue it that you did not embrace the peace thus presented, and which you might have had. The blood which is destined to flow, now that you have scorned our plan of reconciliation, will be not on our heads but your own."[30]

Barneveld replied by temperately but firmly repelling the charges brought against the States in this artful oration of the president. They had proceeded in the most straightforward manner, never permitting themselves to enter into negotiations except on the preliminary condition that their freedom should be once for all conceded and recognised. "You and you only," he continued, "are to bear the blame that peace has not been concluded; you who have not been willing or not been able to keep your promises. One might, with better reason, hold you guilty of all the bloodshed; you whose edicts, bloodier and more savage than war itself, long ago forced these provinces into the inevitable necessity of waging war; you whose cruelty, but yesterday exercised on the crews of defenceless and innocent merchantmen and fishing-vessels, has been fully exibited to the world."

Spinola's countenance betrayed much emotion as he listened to the exchange of bitter recriminations which took place on this farewell colloquy. It was obvious that the brave and accomplished soldier honestly lamented the failure of the attempt to end the war.

But the rupture was absolute. The marquis and the president dined that day with Prince Maurice, by whom they

[30] Authorities last cited.

were afterwards courteously accompanied a part of the way on their journey to Brussels.[31]

Thus ended the comedy which had lasted nearly two years. The dismal leave-taking, as the curtain fell, was not as entertaining to the public outside as the dramatic meeting between Maurice and Spinola had been at the opening scene near Ryswyk. There was no populace to throw up their hats for the departing guests. From the winter's night in which the subtle Franciscan had first stolen into the prince's cabinet down to this autumn evening, not a step of real progress could be recorded as the result of the intolerable quantity of speech-making and quill-driving. There were boat-loads of documents, protocols, and notes, drowsy and stagnant as the canals on which they were floated off towards their tombs in the various archives. Peace to the dust which we have not wantonly disturbed, believing it to be wholesome for the cause of human progress that the art of ruling the world by doing nothing, as practised some centuries since, should once and again be exhibited.

Not in vain do we listen to those long-bearded, venerable, very tedious old presidents, advocates, and friars of orders gray, in their high ruffs, taffety robes or gowns of frieze, as they squeak and gibber, for a fleeting moment, to a world which knew them not. It is something to learn that grave statesmen, kings, generals, and presidents could negotiate for two years long, and that the only result should be the distinction between a conjunction, a preposition, and an adverb. That the provinces should be held *as* free States, not *for* free States—that they should be free in similitude, not in substance—thus much and no more had been accomplished.

And now to all appearance every chance of negotiation was gone. The half-century war, after this brief breathing space, was to be renewed for another century or so, and more furiously than ever. So thought the public. So meant Prince Maurice. Richardot and Jeannin knew better.

---

[31] Authorities last cited.

The departure of the commissioners was recorded upon the register of the resolutions of Holland, with the ominous note: "God grant that they may not have sown evil seed here; the effects of which will one day be visible in the ruin of this commonwealth."[32]

Hardly were the backs of the commissioners turned, before the indefatigable Jeannin was ready with his scheme for repatching the rupture. He was at first anxious that the deputies of Zeeland should be summoned again, now that the country was rid of the Spaniards. Prince Maurice, however, was wrathful when the president began to talk once more of truce. The proposition, he said, was simply the expression of a wish to destroy the State. Holland and Zeeland would never agree to any such measure, and they would find means to compel the other provinces to follow their example. If there were but three or four cities in the whole country to reject the truce, he would, with their assistance alone, defend the freedom of the republic, or at least die an honourable death in its defence. This at least would be better than after a few months to become slaves of Spain. Such a result was the object of those who began this work, but he would resist it at the peril of his life.[33]

A singular incident now seemed to justify the wrath of the stadholder, and to be likely to strengthen his party.

Young Count John of Nassau happened to take possession of the apartments in Goswyn Meursken's hostelry at the Hague, just vacated by Richardot. In the drawer of a writing-table was found a document, evidently left there by the president. This paper was handed by Count John to his cousin, Frederic Henry, who at once delivered it to his brother Maurice. The prince produced it in the assembly of the States-General, members from each province were furnished with a copy of it within two or three hours, and it was soon afterwards printed and published. The document, being nothing less than the original secret instructions of

[32] Resol. Holl. 30 Sept. 1608, bl. 223. Wagenaar, ix. 388.
[33] Wagenaar, ix. 389, 390. Jeannin.

the archdukes to their commissioners, was naturally read with intense interest by the States-General, by the foreign envoys, and by the general public.[34]

It appeared, from an inspection of the paper,[35] that the commissioners had been told that, if they should find the French, English, and Danish ambassadors desirous of being present at the negotiations for the treaty, they were to exclude them from all direct participation in the proceedings. They were to do this, however, so sweetly and courteously that it would be impossible for those diplomatists to take offence, or to imagine themselves distrusted. On the contrary, the States-General were to be informed that their communication in private on the general subject with the ambassadors was approved by the archdukes, because they believed the sovereigns of France, England, and Denmark, their sincere and affectionate friends. The commissioners were instructed to domesticate themselves as much as possible with President Jeannin and to manifest the utmost confidence in his good intentions. They were to take the same course with the English envoys, but in more general terms, and were very discreetly to communicate to them whatever they already knew, and, on the other hand, carefully to conceal from them all that was still a secret.

They were distinctly told to make the point of the Catholic religion first and foremost in the negotiations ; the arguments showing the indispensable necessity of securing its public exercise in the United Provinces being drawn up with considerable detail. They were to insist that the republic should absolutely renounce the trade with the East and West Indies, and should pledge itself to chastise such of its citizens as might dare to undertake those voyages, as disturbers of the peace and enemies of the public repose, whether they went to the Indies in person or associated themselves with men of other nations for that purpose, under any pretext whatever. When these points, together with many matters of detail less difficult of adjustment, had been satisfactorily

---

[34] Jeannin, i. 925, *et seq.*   [35] See the document itself in Jeannin, i. 51–58.

settled, the commissioners were to suggest measures of union for the common defence between the united and the obedient provinces.   This matter was to be broached very gently. " In the sweetest terms possible," it was to be hinted that the whole body of the Netherlanders could protect itself against every enemy, but if dismembered, as it was about to be, neither the one portion nor the other would be safe. The commissioners were therefore to request the offer of some proposition from the States-General for the common defence. In case they remained silent, however, then the commissioners were to declare that the archdukes had no wish to speak of sovereignty over the United Provinces, however limited. " Having once given them that morsel to swallow," said their Highnesses, " we have nothing of the kind in our thoughts. But if they reflect, it is possible that they may see fit to take us for protectors."

The scheme was to be managed with great discreetness and delicacy, and accomplished by hook or by crook, if the means could be found.   " You need not be scrupulous as to the form or law of protection, provided the name of protector can be obtained," continued the archdukes.

At least the greatest pains were to be taken that the two sections of the Netherlands might remain friends.   " We are in great danger unless we rely upon each other," it was urged. " But touch this chord very gently, lest the French and English hearing of it suspect some design to injure them. At least we may each mutually agree to chastise such of our respective subjects as may venture to make any alliance with the enemies of the other."

It was much disputed whether these instructions had been .eft purposely or by accident in the table-drawer. Jeannin could not make up his mind whether it was a trick or not, and the vociferous lamentations of Richardot upon his misfortunes made little impression upon his mind. He had small confidence in any austerity of principle on the part of his former fellow-leaguer that would prevent him from leaving the document by stealth, and then protesting that he had been foully wronged by its coming to light. On the whole, he was inclined to think, however, that the paper had been stolen from him.[36]

Barneveld, after much inquiry, was convinced that it had been left in the drawer by accident.[37]

Richardot himself manifested rage and dismay when he found that a paper, left by chance in his lodgings, had been published by the States. Such a proceeding was a violation, he exclaimed, of the laws of hospitality. With equal justice, he declared it to be an offence against the religious respect due to ambassadors, whose persons and property were sacred in foreign countries. "Decency required the States," he said, "to send the document back to him, instead of showing it as a trophy, and he was ready to die of shame and vexation at the unlucky incident."[33]

Few honourable men will disagree with him in these complaints, although many contemporaries obstinately refused to believe that the crafty and experienced diplomatist could have so carelessly left about his most important archives. He was generally thought by those who had most dealt with him, to prefer, on principle, a crooked path to a straight one. "'Tis a mischievous old monkey," said Villeroy on another occasion, "that likes always to turn its tail instead of going directly to the purpose."[39] The archduke, however, was very indulgent to his plenipotentiary. "My good master," said the president, "so soon as he learned the loss of that accursed paper, benignantly consoled, instead of chastising me ; and, after having looked over the draught, was glad that the accident had happened ; for thus his sincerity had been proved, and those who sought profit by the trick had been confounded."[40] On the other hand, what good could it do to the cause of peace, that these wonderful instructions should be published throughout the republic? They might almost seem a fiction, invented by the war party to inspire a general disgust for any further negotiation. Every loyal

---

[35] Jeannin, i 914, 919, 925.   [37] Ibid. 919.   [38] Ibid. 924.
          [39] Ibid. ii. 129.   [40] Ibid. 21.

Netherlander would necessarily be qualmish at the word peace, now that the whole design of the Spanish party was disclosed.

The public exercise of the Roman religion was now known to be the indispensable condition—first, last, and always —to any possible peace. Every citizen of the republic was to be whipped out of the East and West Indies, should he dare to show his face in those regions. The States-General, while swallowing the crumb of sovereignty vouchsafed by the archdukes, were to accept them as protectors, in order not to fall a prey to the enemies whom they imagined to be their friends.

What could be more hopeless than such negotiations? What more dreary than the perpetual efforts of two lines to approach each other which were mathematically incapable of meeting? That the young republic, conscious of her daily growing strength, should now seek refuge from her nobly won independence in the protectorate of Albert, who was himself the vassal of Philip, was an idea almost inconceivable to the Dutch mind. Yet so impossible was it for the arch-dukes to put themselves into human relations with this new and popular Government, that in the inmost recesses of their breasts they actually believed themselves, when making the offer, to be performing a noble act of Christian charity.

The efforts of Jeannin and of the English ambassador were now unremitting, and thoroughly seconded by Barneveld. Maurice was almost at daggers drawn, not only with the Advocate but with the foreign envoys. Sir Ralph Winwood, who had, in virtue of the old treaty arrangements with England, a seat in the state-council at the Hague, and who was a man of a somewhat rough and insolent deportment, took occasion at a session of that body, when the prince was present, to urge the necessity of at once resuming the rup-tured negotiations. The King of Great Britain, he said, only recommended a course which he was himself always ready to pursue. Hostilities which were necessary, and no others,

were just. Such, and such only, could be favoured by God
or by pious kings. But wars were not necessary which could
be honourably avoided. A truce was not to be despised, by
which religious liberty and commerce were secured, and it
was not the part of wisdom to plunge into all the horrors of
immediate war in order to escape distant and problematical
dangers, that might arise when the truce should come to an
end. If a truce were now made, the kings of both France
and England would be guarantees for its faithful observance.
They would take care that no wrong or affront was offered
to the States-General.[41]

Maurice replied, with a sneer, to these sententious commonplaces derived at second-hand from King James that great
kings were often very indifferent to injuries sustained by
their friends. Moreover, there was an eminent sovereign, he
continued, who was even very patient under affronts directly
offered to himself. It was not very long since a horrible
plot had been discovered to murder the King of England,
with his wife, his children, and all the great personages of
the realm. That this great crime had been attempted under
the immediate instigation of the King of Spain was notorious
to the whole world, and certainly no secret to King James.
Yet his Britannic Majesty had made haste to exonerate the
great criminal from all complicity in the crime ; and had
ever since been fawning upon the Catholic king, and hankering for a family alliance with him. Conduct like this the
prince denounced in plain terms as cringing and cowardly,
and expressed the opinion that guarantees of Dutch independence from such a monarch could hardly be thought very
valuable.

These were terrible words for the representative of James
to have hurled in his face in full council by the foremost
personage of the republic. Winwood fell into a furious
passion, and of course there was a violent scene, with much
subsequent protesting and protocolling.

[41] Wagenaar, ix. 408, 409. Grotius, xvii. 785. Van der Kemp, iii. 48.
Jeannin.

The British king insisted that the prince should make public amends for the insult, and Maurice firmly refused to do anything of the kind. The matter was subsequently arranged by some amicable concessions made by the prince in a private letter to James, but there remained for the time a state of alienation between England and the republic, at which the French sincerely rejoiced. The incident, however, sufficiently shows the point of exasperation which the prince had reached, for, although choleric, he was a reasonable man, and it was only because the whole course of the negotiations had offended his sense of honour and of right that he had at last been driven quite beyond the bounds of self-control.[42]

On the 13th of October, the envoys of France, England, Denmark, and of the Elector Palatine, the Elector of Brandeburg, and other German princes, came before the States-General.

13 Oct.

Jeannin, in the name of all these foreign ministers, made a speech warmly recommending the truce."[43]

He repelled the insinuation that the measure proposed had been brought about by the artifices of the enemy, and was therefore odious. On the contrary, it was originated by himself and the other good friends of the republic.

In his opinion, the terms of the suggested truce contained sufficient guarantees for the liberty of the provinces, not only during the truce, but for ever.

No stronger recognition of their independence could be expected than the one given. It was entirely without example, argued the president, that in similar changes brought about by force of arms, sovereigns after having been despoiled of their states have been compelled to abandon their rights shamefully by a public confession, unless they had absolutely fallen into the hands of their enemies and were completely at their mercy. " Yet the princes who made this great concession," continued Jeannin, "are not lying vanquished at

---

[42] Jeannin, ii. 303, 304, and authorities last cited. Winwood, ii. 353, 354.
[43] See the text in Jeannin, ii. 3–8.

your feet, nor reduced by dire necessity to yield what they have yielded."

He reminded the assembly that the Swiss enjoyed at that moment their liberty in virtue of a simple truce, without ever having obtained from their former sovereign a declaration such as was now offered to the United Provinces.

The president argued, moreover, with much force and acuteness that it was beneath the dignity of the States, and inconsistent with their consciousness of strength, to lay so much stress on the phraseology by which their liberty was recognised. That freedom had been won by the sword, and would be maintained against all the world by the sword.

"In truth," said the orator, "you do wrong to your liberty by calling it so often in doubt, and in claiming with so much contentious anxiety from your enemies a title-deed for your independence. You hold it by your own public decree. In virtue of that decree, confirmed by the success of your arms, you have enjoyed it long. Nor could anything obtained from your enemies be of use to you if those same arms with which you gained your liberty could not still preserve it for you."

Therefore, in the opinion of the president, this persistence in demanding a more explicit and unlimited recognition of independence was only a pretext for continuing the war, ingeniously used by those who hated peace.

Addressing himself more particularly to the celebrated circular letter of Prince Maurice against the truce, the president maintained that the liberty of the republic was as much acknowledged in the proposed articles as if the words "for ever" had been added. "To acknowledge liberty is an act which, by its very nature, admits of no conditions," he observed, with considerable force.[44]

The president proceeded to say that in the original negotiations the qualifications obtained had seemed to him enough. As there was an ardent desire, however, on the part of many for a more explicit phraseology, as something

[44] Ecrit fait par Monsieur Jeannin, 13 Oct. 1608.   Text in Jeannin, ii. 8–19.

necessary to the public safety, he had thought it worth attempting.

"We all rejoiced when you obtained it," continued Jeannin, " but not when they agreed to renounce the names, titles, and arms of the United Provinces ; for that seemed to us shameful for them beyond all example. That princes should make concessions so entirely unworthy of their grandeur, excited at once our suspicion, for we could not imagine the cause of an offer so specious. We have since found out the reason." [45]

The archdukes being unable, accordingly, to obtain for the truce those specious conditions which Spain had originally pretended to yield, it was the opinion of the old diplomatist that the king should be permitted to wear the paste substitutes about which so many idle words had been wasted.

It would be better, he thought, for the States to be contented with what was precious and substantial, and not to lose the occasion of making a good treaty of truce, which was sure to be converted with time into an absolute peace.

" It is certain," he said, " that the princes with whom you are treating will never go to law with you to get an exposition of the article in question. After the truce has expired, they will go to war with you if you like, but they will not trouble themselves to declare whether they are fighting you as rebels or as enemies, nor will it very much signify. If their arms are successful, they will give you no explanations. If you are the conquerors, they will receive none. The fortune of war will be the supreme judge to decide the dispute, not the words of a treaty. Those words are always interpreted to the disadvantage of the weak and the vanquished, although they may be so perfectly clear that no man could doubt them ; never to the prejudice of those who have proved the validity of their rights by the strength of their arms." [46]

This honest, straightforward cynicism, coming from the lips of one of the most experienced diplomatists of Europe, was difficult to gainsay. Speaking as one having authority,

[45] Jeannin, ii. 8–19.　　　[46] Ibid.

the president told the States-General in full assembly, that there was no law in Christendom, as between nations, but the good old fist-law, the code of brute force.

Two centuries and a half have rolled by since that oration was pronounced, and the world has made immense progress in science during that period. But there is still room for improvement in this regard in the law of nations. Certainly there is now a little more reluctance to come so nakedly before the world. But has the cause of modesty or humanity gained very much by the decorous fig-leaves of modern diplomacy?

The president alluded also to the ungrounded fears that bribery and corruption would be able to effect much, during the truce, towards the reduction of the provinces under their repudiated sovereign. After all, it was difficult to buy up a whole people. In a commonwealth, where the People was sovereign, and the persons of the magistrates ever changing, those little comfortable commercial operations could not be managed so easily as in civilized realms like France and England. The old Leaguer thought with pensive regret, no doubt, of the hard, but still profitable bargains by which the Guises and Mayennes and Mercœurs, and a few hundred of their noble adherents, had been brought over to the cause of the king. He sighed at the more recent memories of the Marquis de Rosny's embassy in England, and his largess scattered broadcast among the great English lords. It would be of little use he foresaw—although the instructions of Henry were in his portfolio, giving him almost unlimited powers to buy up everybody in the Netherlands that could be bought—to attempt that kind of traffic on a large scale in the Netherlands.

Those republicans were greedy enough about the navigation to the East and West Indies, and were very litigious about the claim of Spain to put up railings around the ocean as her private lake, but they were less keen than were their more polished contemporaries for the trade in human souls.

"When we consider," said Jeannin, "the constitution of

your State, and that to corrupt a few people among you does no good at all, because the frequent change of magistracies takes away the means of gaining over many of them at the same time, capable by a long duration of their power to conduct an intrigue against the commonwealth, this fear must appear wholly vain."[47]

And then the old Leaguer, who had always refused bribes himself, although he had negotiated much bribery of others, warmed into sincere eloquence as he spoke of the simple virtues on which the little republic, as should be the case with all republics, was founded. He did homage to the Dutch love of liberty.

"Remember," he said, "the love of liberty which is engraved in the hearts of all your inhabitants, and that there are few persons now living who were born in the days of the ancient subjection, or who have not been nourished and brought up for so long a time in liberty that they have a horror for the very name of servitude. You will then feel that there is not one man in your commonwealth who would wish or dare to open his mouth to bring you back to subjection, without being in danger of instant punishment as a traitor to his country."[48]

He again reminded his hearers that the Swiss had concluded a long and perilous war with their ancient masters by a simple truce, during which they had established so good a government that they were never more attacked. Honest republican principles, and readiness at any moment to defend dearly won liberties, had combined with geographical advantages to secure the national independence of Switzerland.[49]

Jeannin paid full tribute to the maritime supremacy of the republic.

"You may have as much good fortune," he said, "as the Swiss, if you are wise. You have the ocean at your side, great navigable rivers enclosing you in every direction, a multitude of ships, with sailors, pilots, and seafaring men of

[47] Jeannin, ii. 8-19.   [48] Ibid.   [49] Ibid.

every description, who are the very best soldiers in battles at sea to be found in Christendom. With these you will preserve your military vigour and your habits of navigation, the long voyages to which you are accustomed continuing as usual. And such is the kind of soldiers you require. As for auxiliaries, should you need them you know where to find them."[50]

The president implored the States-General accordingly to pay no attention to the writings which were circulated among the people to prejudice them against the truce.

This was aimed directly at the stadholder, who had been making so many direct personal appeals to the people, and who was now the more incensed, recognising the taunt of the president as an arrow taken from Barneveld's quiver. There had long ceased to be any communication between the Prince and the Advocate, and Maurice made no secret of his bitter animosity both to Barneveld and to Jeannin.

He hesitated on no occasion to denounce the Advocate as travelling straight on the road to Spain, and although he was not aware of the twenty thousand florins recently presented by the French king, he had accustomed himself, with the enormous exaggeration of party spirit, to look upon the first statesman of his country and of Europe as a traitor to the republic and a tool of the archdukes. As we look back upon those passionate days, we cannot but be appalled at the depths to which theological hatred could descend.

On the very morning after the session of the assembly in which Jeannin had been making his great speech, and denouncing the practice of secret and incendiary publication, three remarkable letters were found on the doorstep of a house in the Hague. One was addressed to the States-General, another to the States of Holland, and a third to the burgomaster of Amsterdam. In all these documents, the Advocate was denounced as an infamous traitor, who was secretly intriguing to bring about a truce for the purpose of handing over the commonwealth to the enemy. A shameful death, it was added, would be his fitting reward.[51]

14 Oct.

50 Jeannin, ii. 8-19. 51 Wagenaar, ix. 411, 412. Van der Kemp, iii. 51, 52.

Thse letters were read in the Assembly of the States-General, and created great wrath among the friends of Barneveld. Even Maurice expressed indignation, and favoured a search for the anonymous author, in order that he might be severely punished.

It seems strange enough that anonymous letters picked up in the street should have been deemed a worthy theme of discussion before their High Mightinesses the States-General. Moreover, it was raining pamphlets and libels against Barneveld and his supporters every day, and the stories which grave burghers and pious elders went about telling to each other, and to everybody who would listen to them, about the Advocate's depravity, were wonderful to hear.

At the end of September, just before the Spanish commissioners left the Hague, a sledge of the kind used in the Dutch cities as drays stopped before Barneveld's front-door one fine morning, and deposited several large baskets, filled with money, sent by the envoys for defraying certain expenses of forage, hire of servants, and the like, incurred by them during their sojourn at the Hague, and disbursed by the States. The sledge, with its contents, was at once sent by order of the Advocate, under guidance of Commissary John Spronsen, to the Receiver-General of the republic.[52]

Yet men wagged their beards dismally as they whispered this fresh proof of Barneveld's venality. As if Spinola and his colleagues were such blunderers in bribing as to send bushel baskets full of Spanish dollars on a sledge, in broad daylight, to the house of a great statesman whom they meant to purchase, expecting doubtless a receipt in full to be brought back by the drayman ! Well might the Advocate say at a later moment, in the bitterness of his spirit, that his enemies, not satisfied with piercing his heart with their false, injurious and honour-filching libels and stories, were determined to break it. "He begged God Almighty," he said, "to be merciful to him, and to judge righteously between him and them."[53]

---

[52] Van der Kemp, iii. 54, 229, 230. [53] Ibid. 229.

Party spirit has rarely run higher in any commonwealth than in Holland during these memorable debates concerning a truce. Yet the leaders both of the war party and the truce party were doubtless pure, determined patriots, seeking their country's good with all their souls and strength.

Maurice answered the discourse of Jeannin by a second and very elaborate letter. In this circular, addressed to the magistracies of Holland, he urged his country- men once more with arguments already employed by him, and in more strenuous language than ever, to beware of a truce even more than of a peace, and warned them not to swerve by a hair's breadth from the formula in regard to the sovereignty agreed upon at the very beginning of the nego- tiations.[54]   To this document was appended a paper of con- siderations, drawn up by Maurice and Lewis William, in refutation, point by point, of all the arguments of President Jeannin in his late discourse.

21 Oct.

It is not necessary to do more than allude to these docu- ments, which were marked by the close reasoning and fiery spirit which characterized all the appeals of the prince and his cousin at this period, because the time had now come which comes to all controversies when argument is exhausted and either action or compromise begins.

Meantime, Barneveld, stung almost to madness by the poisonous though ephemeral libels which buzzed so per- petually about him, had at last resolved to retire from the public service. He had been so steadily denounced as being burthensome to his superiors in birth by the power which he had acquired, and to have shot up so far above the heads of his equals, that he felt disposed to withdraw from a field where his presence was becoming odious.

His enemies, of course, considered this determination a trick by which he merely wished to prove to the country how indispensable he was, and to gain a fresh lease of his almost unlimited power by the alarm which his proposed abdication would produce. Certainly, however, if it were a

---

[54] Jeannin, ii. 25-33, gives the text.

trick, and he were not indispensable, it was easy enough to prove it and to punish him by taking him at his word.

On the morning after the anonymous letters had been found in the street he came into the House of Assembly and made a short speech. He spoke simply of his thirty-one years of service, during which he believed himself to have done his best for the good of the fatherland and for the welfare of the house of Nassau. He had been ready thus to go on to the end, but he saw himself environed by enemies, and felt that his usefulness had been destroyed. He wished, therefore, in the interest of the country, not from any fear for himself, to withdraw from the storm, and for a time at least to remain in retirement. The displeasure and hatred of the great were nothing new to him, he said. He had never shrunk from peril when he could serve his fatherland; for against all calumnies and all accidents he had worn the armour of a quiet conscience. But he now saw that the truce, in itself an unpleasant affair, was made still more odious by the hatred felt towards him. He begged the provinces, therefore, to select another servant less hated than himself to provide for the public welfare.[55]

Having said these few words with the dignity which was natural to him he calmly walked out of the Assembly House.[56]

The personal friends of Barneveld and the whole truce party were in consternation. Even the enemies of the Advocate shrank appalled at the prospect of losing the services of the foremost statesman of the commonwealth at this critical juncture. There was a brief and animated discussion as soon as his back was turned. Its result was the appointment of a committee of five to wait upon Barneveld and solemnly to request him to reconsider his decision. Their efforts were successful. After a satisfactory interview with the committee he resumed his functions with greater authority than ever.[57] Of course there were not wanting many to

[55] Wagenaar, ix. 411, 412. Van der Kemp, iii. 51, 52.　[56] Ibid.　[57] Ibid.

whisper that the whole proceeding had been a comedy, and
that Barneveld would have been more embarrassed than he
had ever been in his life had his resignation been seriously
accepted. But this is easy to say, and is always said,
whenever a statesman who feels himself aggrieved, yet
knows himself useful, lays down his office. The Advocate
had been the mark of unceasing and infamous calumnies.
He had incurred the deadly hatred of the highest placed, the
most powerful, and the most popular man in the commonwealth. He had more than once been obliged to listen to
opprobrious language from the prince, and it was even whispered that he had been threatened with personal violence.
That Maurice was perpetually denouncing him in public and
private, as a traitor, a papist, a Spanish partisan, was notorious. He had just been held up to the States of the union
and of his own province by unknown voices as a criminal
worthy of death. Was it to be wondered at that a man of
sixty, who had passed his youth, manhood, and old age in
the service of the republic, and was recognised by all as the
ablest, the most experienced, the most indefatigable of her
statesmen, should be seriously desirous of abandoning an
office which might well seem to him rather a pillory than a
post of honour ?

"As for neighbour Barneveld," said recorder Aerssens,[58]
little dreaming of the foul witness he was to bear against that
neighbour at a terrible moment to come, "I do what I can
and wish to help him with my blood. He is more courageous
than I. I should have sunk long ago, had I been obliged to
stand against such tempests. The Lord God will, I hope,
help him and direct his understanding for the good of all
Christendom, and for his own honour. If he can steer this
ship into a safe harbour we ought to raise a golden statue of
him. I should like to contribute my mite to it. He deserves
twice as much honour, despite all his enemies, of whom
he has many rather from envy than from reason. May

[58] Aerssens and the Advocate were next door neighbours in the Spui straat,
at the Hague. Deventer, iii. 271.

the Lord keep him in health, or it will go hardly with us all."[59]

Thus spoke some of his grateful countrymen when the Advocate was contending at a momentous crisis with storms threatening to overwhelm the republic. Alas! where is the golden statue?

He believed that the truce was the most advantageous measure that the country could adopt. He believed this with quite as much sincerity as Maurice held to his conviction that war was the only policy. In the secret letter of the French ambassador there is not a trace of suspicion as to his fidelity to the commonwealth, not the shadow of proof of the ridiculous accusation that he wished to reduce the provinces to the dominion of Spain. Jeannin, who had no motive for concealment in his confidential correspondence with his sovereign, always rendered unequivocal homage to the purity and patriotism of the Advocate and the Prince.

He returned to the States-General and to the discharge of his functions as Advocate-General of Holland. His policy for the time was destined to be triumphant, his influence more extensive than ever. But the end of these calumnies and anonymous charges was not yet.

Meantime the opposition to the truce was confined to the States of Zeeland and two cities of Holland.[60] Those cities were very important ones, Amsterdam and Delft, but they were already wavering in their opposition. Zeeland stoutly maintained that the treaty of Utrecht forbade a decision of the question of peace and war except by a unanimous vote of the whole confederacy. The other five provinces and the friends of the truce began with great vehemence to declare that the question at issue was now changed. It was no longer to be decided whether there should be truce or war with Spain, but whether a single member of the confederacy could dictate its law to the other six States. Zeeland, on her part, talked loudly of seceding from the union, and

[59] Aerssens to Van der Veecken, 7 Nov. 1608.   In Deventer, iii. 272.
[60] Wagenaar, ix. 414.

setting up for an independent, sovereign commonwealth.[61]
She would hardly have been a very powerful one, with her
half-dozen cities, one prelate, one nobleman, her hundred
thousand burghers at most, bustling and warlike as they
were, and her few thousand mariners, although the most
terrible fighting men that had ever sailed on blue water.
She was destined ere long to abandon her doughty resolution of leaving her sister provinces to their fate.

Maurice had not slackened in his opposition to the truce,
despite the renewed vigour with which Barneveld pressed the
measure since his return to the public councils. The prince
was firmly convinced that the kings of France and England
would assist the republic in the war with Spain so soon as it
should be renewed. His policy had been therefore to force
the hand of those sovereigns, especially that of Henry, and to
induce him to send more stringent instructions to Jeannin
than those with which he believed him to be furnished. He
had accordingly despatched a secret emissary to the French
king, supplied with confidential and explicit instructions.
This agent was a Captain Lambert. Whether it was "Pretty
Lambert," "Dandy Lambert" — the vice-admiral who had
so much distinguished himself at the great victory of Gibraltar—does not distinctly appear. If it were so, that hard-
hitting mariner would seem to have gone into action with
the French Government as energetically as he had done
eighteen months before, when, as master of the Tiger, he
laid himself aboard the Spanish admiral and helped send the
St. Augustine to the bottom. He seemed indisposed to mince
matters in diplomacy. He intimated to the king and his
ministers that Jeannin and his colleagues were pushing the
truce at the Hague much further and faster than his Majesty
could possibly approve, and that they were obviously exceeding their instructions. Jeannin, who was formerly so much
honoured and cherished throughout the republic, was now
looked upon askance because of his intimacy with Barneveld

---

[61] Wagenaar, ix 416 "Zo ver liep de twist dat de Zeeuwen spraaken van
zich te willen af zonderen van de overigen.

and his partisans.[62] He assured the king that nearly all the cities of Holland, and the whole of Zeeland, were entirely agreed with Maurice, who would rather die than consent to the proposed truce.[63] The other provinces, added Lambert, would be obliged, will ye nill ye, to receive the law from Holland and Zeeland. Maurice, without assistance from France or any other power, would give Spain and the arch-dukes as much exercise as they could take for the next fifty years before he would give up, and had declared that he would rather die sword in hand than basely betray his country by consenting to such a truce.[64] As for Barne-veld, he was already discovering the blunders which he had made, and was trying to curry favour with Maurice.[65] Barne-veld and both the Aerssens were traitors to the State, had become the objects of general hatred and contempt, and were in great danger of losing their lives, or at least of being expelled from office.[66]

Here was altogether too much zeal on the part of Pretty Lambert; a quality which, not for the first time, was thus proved to be less useful in diplomatic conferences than in a sea-fight. Maurice was obliged to disavow his envoy, and to declare that his secret instructions had never authorized him to hold such language. But the mischief was done. The combustion in the French cabinet was terrible. The Dutch admiral had thrown hot shot into the powder-magazine of his friends, and had done no more good by such tactics than might be supposed. Such diplomacy was denounced as a mere mixture of "indiscretion and impudence."[67] Henry was very wroth, and forthwith indited an imperious letter to his cousin Maurice.[68]

[62] Jeannin, i 932.
[63] Ibid. 932, 933, and ii. 49.
[64] Ibid.   [65] Ibid
[66] Ibid Compare for this mission of Lambert, Wagenaar, ix. 384, 385 ; Van der Kemp, iii. 57, 232
[67] Jeannin, i 932 Every one of these amazing assertions of "the gentle ambassador Lambert" were denounced by Jeannin in his letters to Villeroy as impudent falsehoods Especially in

regard to the pretended vaunt of Maurice, that he could carry on the war fifty years if France would only remain neutral, the president said that he had been expressly informed by the prince that without the assistance of France the republic was lost for ever.—Jeannin, ii. 45-51. .
[68] The letter is given in Jeannin, ii. 58-64

"Lambert's talk to me by your orders," said the king, "has not less astonished than scandalized me. I now learn the new resolution which you have taken, and I observe that you have begun to entertain suspicions as to my will and my counsels on account of the proposition of truce." 23 Oct

Henry's standing orders to Jeannin, as we know, were to offer Maurice a pension of almost unlimited amount, together with ample rewards to all such of his adherents as could be purchased, provided they would bring about the incorporation of the United Provinces into France.[69] He was therefore full of indignation that the purity of his intentions and the sincerity of his wish for the independence of the republic could be called in question.

"People have dared to maliciously invent," he continued, "that I am the enemy of the repose and the liberty of the United Provinces, and that I was afraid lest they should acquire the freedom which had been offered them by their enemies, because I derived a profit from their war, and intended in time to deprive them of their liberty. Yet these falsehoods and jealousies have not been contradicted by you nor by anyone else, although you know that the proofs of my sincerity and good faith have been entirely without reproach or example. You knew what was said, written, and published everywhere, and I confess that when I knew this malice, and that you had not taken offence at it, I was much amazed and very malcontent."

Queen Elizabeth, in her most waspish moods, had not often lectured the States-General more roundly than Henry now lectured his cousin Maurice.

The king once more alluded to the secret emissary's violent talk, which had so much excited his indignation.

"If by weakness and want of means," he said, "you are forced to abandon to your enemies one portion of your country in order to defend the other—as Lambert tells me you are resolved to do, rather than agree to the truce without recognition of your sovereignty for ever—I pray you to con-

[69] Jeannin, i. 43, 62, 63, 69, 70, 71.

sider how many accidents and reproaches may befal you. Do you suppose that any ally of the States, or of your family, would risk his reputation and his realms in such a game, which would seem to be rather begun in passion and despair than required by reason or necessity ? "

Here certainly was plain speaking enough, and Maurice could no longer expect the king for his partner, should he decide to risk once more the bloody hazard of the die.

But Henry was determined to leave no shade of doubt on the subject.

" Lambert tells me," he said, " that you would rather perish with arms in your hands than fall shamefully into inevitable ruin by accepting truce. I have been and am of a contrary opinion. Perhaps I am mistaken, not knowing as well as you do the constitution of your country and the wishes of your people. But I know the general affairs of Christendom better than you do, and I can therefore judge more soundly on the whole matter than you can, and I know that the truce, established and guaranteed as proposed, will bring you more happiness than you can derive from war."

Thus the king, in the sweeping, slashing way with which he could handle an argument as well as a sword, strode forward in conscious strength, cutting down right and left all opposition to his will. He was determined, once for all, to show the stadholder and his adherents that the friendship of a great king was not to be had by a little republic on easy terms, nor every day. Above all, the Prince of Nassau was not to send a loud-talking, free and easy Dutch sea-captain to dictate terms to the King of France and Navarre. " Lambert tells me "—and Maurice might well wish that Pretty Lambert had been sunk in the bay of Gibraltar, Tiger and all, before he had been sent on this diplomatic errand— " Lambert tells me," continued his Majesty, "that you and the States-General would rather that I should remain neutral, and let you make war in your own fashion, than that I should do anything more to push on this truce. My cousin, it would be very easy for me, and perhaps more advantageous for me and my kingdom than you think, if I could give you this satisfaction, whatever might be the result. If I chose to follow this counsel, I am, thanks be to God, in such condition, that I have no neighbour who is not as much in need of me as I can be of him, and who is not glad to seek for and to preserve my friendship. If they should all conspire against me moreover, I can by myself, and with no assistance but heaven's, which never failed me yet, wrestle with them altogether, and fling them all, as some of my royal predecessors have done. Know then, that I do not favour war nor truce for the United Provinces because of any need I may have of the one or the other for the defence of my own sceptre. The counsels and the succours, which you have so largely received from me, were given because of my consideration for the good of the States, and of yourself in particular, whom I have always favoured and cherished, as I have done others of your house on many occasions."

The king concluded his lecture by saying, that after his ambassadors had fulfilled their promise, and had spoken the last word of their master at the Hague, he should leave Maurice and the States to do as they liked.

"But I desire," he said, "that you and the States should not do that wrong to yourselves or to me as to doubt the integrity of my counsels nor the actions of my ambassadors. I am an honest man and a prince of my word, and not ignorant of the things of this world. Neither the States nor you, with your adherents, can permit my honour to be compromised without tarnishing your own, and without being branded for ingratitude. I say not this in order to reproach you for the past nor to make you despair of the future, but to defend the truth: I expect, therefore, that you will not fall into this fault, knowing you as I do. I pay more heed to what you said in your letter than in all Lambert's fine talk, and you will find out that nobody wishes your prosperity and that of the States more sincerely than I do, or can be more useful to you than I can." [70]

---

[70] I have abbreviated this remarkable letter, but of course the text of the passages cited is literally given.

There could be but little doubt in the mind of Prince Maurice, after this letter had been well pondered, that Barneveld had won the game, and that the peace party had triumphed.

To resume the war, with the French king not merely neutral but angry and covertly hostile, and with the sovereign of Great Britain an almost open enemy in the garb of an ally, might well seem a desperate course.

And Maurice, although strongly opposed to the truce, and confident in his opinions at this crisis, was not a desperado.

He saw at once the necessity of dismounting from the high horse upon which, it must be confessed, he had been inclined for more rough-riding of late than the situation warranted. Peace was unattainable, war was impossible, truce was inevitable ; Barneveld was master of the field.

The prince acquiesced in the result which the letter from the French king so plainly indicated. He was, however, more incensed than ever against Barneveld ; for he felt himself not only checkmated but humiliated by the Advocate, and believed him a traitor, who was selling the republic to Spain. It was long since the two had exchanged a word.

Maurice now declared, on more than one occasion, that it was useless for him any longer to attempt opposition to the policy of truce. The States must travel on the road which they had chosen, but it should not be under his guidance, and he renounced all responsibility for the issue.

Dreading disunion, however, more than ought else that could befal the republic, he now did his best to bring about the return of Zeeland to the federal councils. He was successful.[71] The deputies from that province reappeared in the States-General on the 11th November. They were still earnest, however, in their opposition to the truce, and warmly maintained, in obedience to instructions, that the Union of Utrecht forbade the conclusion of a treaty except by unanimous consent of the Seven Provinces. They were very fierce in their remonstrances, and again talked loudly of secession.

Van der Kemp, iii. 58.   Jeannin.

After consultation with Barneveld, the French envoys now thought it their duty to take the recalcitrant Zeelanders in hand ; Maurice having, as it were, withdrawn from the contest.

On the 18th November, accordingly, Jeannin once more came very solemnly before the States-General, ac- 18 Nov. companied by his diplomatic colleagues.[72]

He showed the impossibility of any arrangement, except by the submission of Zeeland to a vote of the majority. " It is certain," he said, " that six provinces will never be willing to be conquered by a single one, nor permit her to assert that, according to a fundamental law of the commonwealth, her dissent can prevent the others from forming a definite conclusion.

"It is not for us," continued the president, "who are strangers in your republic, to interpret your laws, but common sense teaches us that, if such a law exist, it could only have been made in order to forbid a surrender.

" If any one wishes to expound it otherwise, to him we would reply, in the words of an ancient Roman, who said of a law which seemed to him pernicious, that at least the tablet upon which it was inscribed, if it could not be destroyed, should be hidden out of sight. Thus at least the citizens might escape observing it, when it was plain that it would cause detriment to the republic, and they might then put in its place the most ancient of all laws, *salus populi suprema lex.*"

The president, having suggested this ingenious expedient of the antique Roman for getting rid of a constitutional provision by hiding the statute-book, proceeded to give very practical reasons for setting up the supreme law of the people's safety on this occasion. And, certainly, that magnificent common-place, which has saved and ruined so many States, the most effective weapon in the political arsenal, whether wielded by tyrants or champions of freedom, was

[72] The speech of the president is given in full in his "Negotiations."— Jeannin, ii. 106–112.

not unreasonably recommended at this crisis to the States in their contest with the refractory Zeelanders. It was easy to talk big, but after all it would be difficult for that doughty little sandbank, notwithstanding the indomitable energy which it had so often shown by land and sea, to do battle by itself with the whole Spanish empire. Nor was it quite consistent with republican principles that the other six provinces should be plunged once more into war, when they had agreed to accept peace and independence instead, only that Zeeland should have its way.

The orator went on to show the absurdity, in his opinion, of permitting one province to continue the war, when all seven united had not the means to do it without the assistance of their allies. He pointed out, too, the immense blunders that would be made, should it be thought that the Kings of France and England were so much interested in saving the provinces from perdition as to feel obliged in any event to render them assistance.

" Beware of committing an irreparable fault," he said, " on so insecure a foundation. You are deceiving yourselves. And, in order that there may be no doubt on the subject, we declare to you by express command that if your adversaries refuse the truce, according to the articles presented to you by us, it is the intention of our kings to assist you with armies and subsidies, not only as during the past, but more powerfully than before. If, on the contrary, the rupture comes from your side, and you despise the advice they are giving you, you have no succour to expect from them. The refusal of conditions so honourable and advantageous to your commonwealth will render the war a useless one, and they are determined to do nothing to bring the reproach upon themselves."

The president then intimated, not without adroitness, that the republic was placing herself in a proud position by accepting the truce, and that Spain was abasing herself by giving her consent to it. The world was surprised that the States should hesitate at all.[73]

Jeannin, ubi sup.

There was much more of scholastic dissertation in the president's address, but enough has been given to show its very peremptory character.

If the war was to go on it was to be waged mainly by Zeeland alone. This was now plain beyond all peradventure. The other provinces had resolved to accept the proposed treaty. The cities of Delft and Amsterdam, which had stood out so long among the estates of Holland, soon renounced their opposition. Prince Maurice, with praiseworthy patriotism, reconciled himself with the inevitable, and now that the great majority had spoken, began to use his influence with the factious minority.

On the day after Jeannin's speech he made a visit to the French ambassadors. After there had been some little discussion among them, Barneveld made his appearance. His visit seemed an accidental one, but it had been previously arranged with the envoys.[74]

The general conversation went on a little longer, when the Advocate, frankly turning to the Prince, spoke of the pain which he felt at the schism between them. He defended himself with honest warmth against the rumours circulated, in which he was accused of being a Spanish partisan. His whole life had been spent in fighting Spain, and he was now more determined than ever in his hostility to that monarchy. He sincerely believed that by the truce now proposed all the solid advantages of the war would be secured, and that such a result was a triumphant one for the republic. He was also most desirous of being restored to the friendship and good opinion of the house of Nassau; having proved during his whole life his sincere attachment to their interests—a sentiment never more lively in his breast than at that moment.[75]

This advance was graciously met by the stadholder, and the two distinguished personages were, for the time at least, reconciled.[76]

[74] Van der Kemp, iii. 59, 60.   Compare Wagenaar, ix. 422, 423.
[75] Van der Kemp.   Wagenaar, *ubi sup.*   [76] Ibid.

It was further debated as to the number of troops that it would be advisable for the States to maintain during the truce, and Barneveld expressed his decided opinion that thirty thousand men, at least, would be required. This opinion gave the prince at least as much pleasure as did the personal devotion expressed by the Advocate, and he now stated his intention of working with the peace party.

The great result was now certain. Delft and Amsterdam withdrew from their opposition to the treaty, so that Holland was unanimous before the year closed ; Zeeland, yielding to the influence of Maurice, likewise gave in her adhesion to the truce.

The details of the mode in which the final arrangement was made are not especially interesting. The discussion was fairly at an end. The subject had been picked to the bones. It was agreed that the French ambassadors should go over the frontier, and hold a preliminary interview with the Spanish commissioners at Antwerp.

The armistice was to be continued by brief and repeated renewals, until it should be superseded by the truce of years.

Meantime, Archduke Albert sent his father confessor, Inigo Brizuela, to Spain, in order to make the treaty proposed by Jeannin palatable to the king.[77]

The priest was to set forth to Philip, as only a ghostly confessor could do with full effect, that he need not trouble himself about the recognition by the proposed treaty of the independence of the United Provinces. Ambiguous words had been purposely made use of in this regard, he was to explain, so that not only the foreign ambassadors were of opinion that the rights of Spain were not curtailed, but the emptiness of the imaginary recognition of Dutch freedom had been proved by the sharp criticism of the States.

It is true that Richardot, in the name of the archduke, had three months before promised the consent of the king, as having already been obtained. But Richardot knew very

[77] Wagenaar, ix. 425, 426. Jeannin.

well when he made the statement that it was false. The archduke, in subsequent correspondence with the ambassadors in December, repeated the pledge. Yet, not only had the king not given that consent, but he had expressly refused it by a courier sent in November.[78]

Philip, now convinced by Brother Inigo that while agreeing to treat with the States-General as with a free commonwealth, over which he pretended to no authority, he really meant that he was dealing with vassals over whom his authority was to be resumed when it suited his convenience, at last gave his consent to the proposed treaty. The royal decision was, however, kept for a time concealed, in order that the States might become more malleable.[79]

<hr/>

[78] Documents in Deventer, iii. 273.
[79] Wagenaar, ix. 425, 426. Jeannin. The reasoning was quite in accordance with the views of the French court. "Maintenant la caption est tout claire," wrote Aerssens, "en ce qu'ils refusent d'ôter le mot comme. Et ajoutent nos amis, que cette clause a esté conçue ainsi douteusement par M. Janin, pour au bout des dix ans réserver au roy de nous déclarer libres ou non selon que le Roy d'Espagne luy tiendra parole sur les mariages."—Deventer, iii. 275. "If a peace it prove," wrote Cornwallis from Madrid, "such are the difficulties as for my own part I should think it like the peace of God which passeth all understanding."—Winwood, ii. 387.

CHAPTER LII.

Vote of the States-General on the groundwork of the treaty — Meeting of the
plenipotentiaries for arrangement of the truce — Signing of the twelve
years' truce — Its purport — The negotiations concluded — Ratification by
the States-General, the Archdukes, and the King of Spain — Question
of toleration —Appeal of President Jeannin on behalf of the Catholics —
Religious liberty the fruit of the war — Internal arrangements of the
States under the rule of peace — Deaths of John Duke of Cleves and Jacob
Arminius — Doctrines of Arminius and Gomarus — Theological warfare
— Twenty years' truce between the Turkish and Roman empires — Ferdinand of Styria — Religious peace — Prospects of the future.

ON the 11th January, 1609, the States-General decided by
unanimous vote that the first point in the treaty should be
not otherwise fixed than thus : —

" That the archdukes—to superfluity—declare, as well in
their own name as in that of the King of Spain, their willingness to treat with the lords States of the United Provinces
in the capacity of, and as holding them for, free countries,
provinces, and states, over which they have no claim, and
that they are making a treaty with them in those said names
and qualities."[1]

It was also resolved not to permit that any ecclesiastical
or secular matters, conflicting with the above-mentioned
freedom, should be proposed ; nor that any delay should be
sought for, by reason of the India navigation or any other
point.

In case anything to the contrary should be attempted by
the king or the archdukes, and the deliberations protracted
in consequence more than eight days, it was further decided
by unanimous vote that the negotiations should at once be
broken off, and the war forthwith renewed, with the help, if

---

[1] Wagenaar, ix. 429, 430.

possible, of the kings, princes, and states, friends of the good cause.[2]

This vigorous vote was entirely the work of Barneveld, the man whom his enemies dared to denounce as the partisan of Spain, and to hold up as a traitor deserving of death. It was entirely within his knowledge that a considerable party in the provinces had grown so weary of the war, and so much alarmed at the prospect of the negotiations for truce coming to nought, as to be ready to go into a treaty without a recognition of the independence of the States. This base faction was thought to be instigated by the English Government, intriguing secretly with President Richardot. The Advocate, acting in full sympathy with Jeannin, frustrated the effects of the manœuvre by obtaining all the votes of Holland and Zeeland for this supreme resolution. The other five provinces dared to make no further effort in that direction against the two controlling states of the republic.

It was now agreed that the French and English ambassadors should delay going to Antwerp until informed of the arrival in that city of Spinola and his colleagues ; and that they should then proceed thither, taking with them the main points of the treaty, as laid down by themselves, and accepted with slight alterations by the States.[3]

When the Spanish commissioners had signed these points the plenipotentiaries were to come to Antwerp in order to settle other matters of less vital import. Meantime, the States-General were to be summoned to assemble in Bergen-op-Zoom, that they might be ready to deal with difficulties, should any arise.[4]

The first meeting took place on the 10th February, 1609. The first objection to the draught was made by the Spaniards. It was about words and wind. They liked not the title of high and puissant lords[5] which was given to the States-General, and they proposed to turn

10 Feb.

---

[2] Wagenaar, ix. 429, 430.
[3] Ibid. 431. Jeannin.
[4] Ibid. Jeannin. Grotius, xviii.

[5] Wagenaar, ix. 132. "Hoogmogende herren," "Hauts et puissants seigneurs."

the difficulty by abstaining from giving any qualifications whatever, either to the archdukes or the republican authorities. The States refused to lower these ensigns of their new-born power. It was, however, at last agreed that, instead of high and mighty, they should be called illustrious and serene.[6]

This point being comfortably adjusted, the next and most important one was accepted by the Spaniards. The independence of the States was recognised according to the prescribed form. Then came the great bone of contention, over which there had been such persistent wrangling—the India trade.

The Spanish Government had almost registered a vow in heaven that the word India should not be mentioned in the treaty. It was no less certain that India was stamped upon the very heart of the republic, and could not be torn from it while life remained. The subtle diplomatists now invented a phrase in which the word should not appear, while the thing itself should be granted. The Spaniards, after much altercation, at last consented.[7]

By the end of February, most of the plenipotentiaries thought it safe to request the appearance of the States-General at Bergen-op-Zoom.[8]

Jeannin, not altogether satisfied, however, with the language of the Spaniards in regard to India, raised doubts as to the propriety of issuing the summons. Putting on his most reverend and artless expression of countenance, he assured Richardot that he had just received a despatch from the Hague, to the effect that the India point would, in all probability, cause the States at that very moment to break off the negotiations.[9] It was surely premature, therefore, to invite them to Bergen. The despatch from the Hague was a neat fiction on the part of the president, but it worked

---

[6] Wagenaar, ix. 432.

[7] "Huic additamento Hispanici valde reluctabantur tum quod Indiam non minus quam si nominaretur claris indiciis exprimeret," &c.—Grotius, xviii. 808, 809.

[8] Wagenaar, ix. 432, 433, 434. Jeannin, vol. ii. Resol. Holl. 4 March, 1609.

[9] Jeannin, ii. 383.

admirably. The other president, himself quite as ready at inventions as Jeannin could possibly be, was nevertheless taken in; the two ex-leaguers being, on the whole, fully a match for each other in the art of intrigue. Richardot, somewhat alarmed, insisted that the States should send their plenipotentiaries to Antwerp as soon as possible. He would answer for it that they would not go away again without settling upon the treaty.[10] The commissioners were forbidden, by express order from Spain, to name the Indies in writing, but they would solemnly declare, by word of mouth, that the States should have full liberty to trade to those countries; the King of Spain having no intention of interfering with such traffic during the period of the truce.[11]

The commissioners came to Antwerp. The States-General assembled at Bergen. On the 9th April, 1609, the truce for twelve years was signed. This was its purport :—

The preamble recited that the most serene princes and archdukes, Albert and Isabella Clara Eugenia, had made, on the 24th April, 1607, a truce and cessation of arms for eight months with the illustrious lords the States-General of the United Provinces of the Netherlands, in quality of, and as holding them for, states, provinces, and free countries, over which they pretended to nothing; which truce was ratified by his Catholic Majesty, as to that which concerned him, by letters patent of 18th September, 1607; and that, moreover, a special power had been given to the archdukes on the 10th January, 1608, to enable them in the king's name as well as their own to do everything that they might think proper to bring about a peace or a truce of many years.

It then briefly recited the rupture of the negotiations for peace, and the subsequent proposition, originated by the foreign ambassadors, to renew the conference for the purpose of concluding a truce. The articles of the treaty thus agreed upon were :—

That the archdukes declared, as well in their own name as that of the king, that they were content to treat with the

---

[10] Jeannin, ii. 383.   [11] Winwood, ii. 489.

lords the States-General of the United Provinces in quality of, and as holding them for, countries, provinces, and free states, over which they pretended to nothing, and to make with them a truce on certain following conditions—to wit :—

That the truce should be good, firm, loyal, inviolable, and for the term of twelve years, during which time there was to be cessation of all acts of hostility between the king, archdukes, and States-General, as well by sea and other waters as by land, in all their kingdoms, countries, lands, and lordships, and for all their subjects and inhabitants of whatever quality and condition, without exception of places or of persons ;

That each party should remain seized of their respective possessions, and be not troubled therein by the other party during the truce ;

That the subjects and inhabitants of the respective countries should preserve amity and good correspondence during the truce, without referring to past offences, and should freely and securely entertain communication and traffic with each other by land and sea. This provision, however, was to be expressly understood as limited by the king to the kingdoms and countries possessed by him in Europe, and in other places and seas where the subjects of other kings and princes, his friends and allies, have amicable traffic. In regard, however, to places, cities, ports, and harbours which he possessed outside of those limits, the States and their subjects were to exercise no traffic, without express permission of the king. They could, however, if they chose, trade with the countries of all other princes, potentates, and peoples who were willing to permit it, even outside those limits, without any hindrance by the king ;

That the truce should begin in regard to those distant countries after a year from date, unless actual notification could be sooner served there on those concerned ;

That the subjects of the United Provinces should have the same liberty and privilege within the States of the king and archdukes as had been accorded to the subjects of the

King of Great Britain, according to the last treaty made with that sovereign ;

That letters of marque and reprisal should not be granted during the truce, except for special cause, and in cases permitted by the laws and imperial constitutions, and according to the rules therein prescribed ;

That those who had retired into neutral territory during the war were also to enjoy the benefit of the truce, and could reside wherever they liked without being deprived of their property ;

That the treaty should be ratified by the archdukes and the States-General within four days. As to the ratification of the king, the archdukes were bound to deliver it in good and due form within three months, in order that the lords the States-General, their subjects and inhabitants, might enjoy effectively the fruits of the treaty ;

That the treaty should be published everywhere immediately after the ratification of the archdukes and States-General.

This document was signed by the ambassadors of the Kings of France and Great Britain, as mediators, and then by the deputies of the archdukes, and afterwards by those of the lords the States-General.[12]

There were thirty-eight articles in all, but the chief provisions have been indicated. The other clauses, relating to boundaries, confiscations, regulations of duties, frontier fortifications, the estates of the Nassau family, and other sequestrated property, have no abiding interest.

There was also a secret and special treaty which was demanded of the King of Spain by the States-General, and by him accorded.

This secret treaty consisted of a single clause. That clause was made up of a brief preamble and of a promise. The preamble recited textually article fourth of the public treaty relative to the India trade. The promise was to this effect.[13]

---

[12] See the treaty in full in Jeannin, ii. 446–457. Compare Meteren, 613.
[13] The text of the second treaty is given in Jeannin, ii. 457, 458.

For the period of the truce the Spanish commissioners pledged the faith of the king and of his successors that his Majesty would cause no impediment, whether by sea or land, to the States nor their subjects, in the traffic that thereafter might be made in the countries of all princes, potentates, and peoples who might permit the same, in whatever place it might be, even without the limits designated, and every-where else, nor similarly to those carrying on such traffic with them, and that the king and his successors would faith-fully carry into effect everything thus laid down, so that the said traffic should be free and secure, consenting even, in order that the clause might be the more authentic, that it should be considered as inserted in the principal treaty, and as making part thereof.[14]

It will be perceived that the first article of all, and the last or secret article, contained the whole marrow of the treaty. It may be well understood, therefore, with what wry faces the Spanish plenipotentiaries ultimately signed the document.

After two years and a quarter of dreary negotiation, the republic had carried all its points, without swerving a hair's breadth from the principles laid down in the beginning. The only concession made was that the treaty was for a truce of twelve years, and not for peace. But as after all, in those days, an interval of twelve years might be almost con-sidered an eternity of peace, and as calling a peace per-petual can never make it so, the difference was rather one of phraseology than of fact.

On the other hand, the States had extorted from their former sovereign a recognition of their independence.

They had secured the India trade.

They had not conceded Catholic worship.

Mankind were amazed at this result—an event hitherto unknown in history. When before had a sovereign acknow-ledged the independence of his rebellious subjects, and signed a treaty with them as with equals? When before had Spain,

[14] Jeannin, ii. 457, 458.

expressly or by implication, admitted that the East and West Indies were not her private property, and that navigators to those regions, from other countries than her own, were not to be chastised as trespassers and freebooters ?

Yet the liberty of the Netherlands was acknowledged in terms which convinced the world that it was thenceforth an established fact. And India was as plainly expressed by the omission of the word, as if it had been engrossed in large capitals in Article IV.[15]

The King's Government might seek solace in syntax. They might triumph in Cardinal Bentivoglio's subtleties, and persuade themselves that to treat with the republic *as* a free nation was not to hold it *for* a free nation then and for ever. But the whole world knew that the republic really was free, and that it had treated, face to face, with its former sovereign, exactly as the Kings of France or Great Britain, or the Grand Turk, might treat with him. The new commonwealth had taken its place among the nations of the earth. Other princes and potentates made not the slightest difficulty in recognising it for an independent power and entering into treaties and alliances with it as with any other realm.

To the republic the substantial blessing of liberty : to his Catholic Majesty the grammatical quirk. When the twelve years should expire, Spain might reconquer the United Provinces if she could ; relying upon the great truth that an adverb was not a preposition. And France or Great Britain might attempt the same thing if either felt strong enough for the purpose. Did as plausible a pretext as that ever fail to a state ambitious of absorbing its neighbours ?

Jeannin was right enough in urging that this famous

---

[15] The words too of the certificate signed by the ambassadors of France and England were very explicit :— "Certifion aussi les députés des archiducs avoir consenty et accordé tout, ainsi que les sieurs estats et leurs sujets ne pourront trafiquer aux ports, lieux et places que tiennent les dits sieurs estats ès dites Indes si ce n'est avec leur permission. Et outre ce que les députés des dits sieurs ont déclaré plusieurs fois en notre présence et des députés des archiducs, si on entreprend sur leurs amis et allies ès dits pays qu'ils entendent les secourir et assister sans qu'on puisse prétendre la trefve estre enfreinte et violée à cette occasion."—Anvers, 9 Avril, 1609. Négotiations de Jeannin, ii. 458, 459.

clause of recognition ought to satisfy both parties. If the United Provinces, he said, happened not to have the best muskets and cannons on their side when it should once more come to blows, small help would they derive from verbal bulwarks and advantages in the text of treaties.[16]

Richardot consoled himself with his quibbles ; for quibbles were his daily bread. "Thank God our truce is made," said he, "and we have only lost the sovereignty for twelve years, if after that we have the means or the will to resume the war—whatever Don Pedro de Toledo may say." [17]

Barneveld, on his part, was devoutly and soberly pleased with the result. "To-day we have concluded our negotiations for the truce," he wrote to Aerssens. "We must pray to the Lord God, and we must do our highest duty that our work may redound to his honour and glory, and to the nation's welfare. It is certain that men will make their criticisms upon it according to their humours. But those who love their country, and all honest people who know the condition of the land, will say that it is well done." [18]

Thus modestly, religiously, and sincerely spoke a statesman, who felt that he had accomplished a great work, and that he had indeed brought the commonwealth through the tempest at last.

The republic had secured the India trade. On this point the negotiators had taken refuge in that most useful figure of speech for hard-pressed diplomatists and law-makers—the ellipsis. They had left out the word India, and his Catholic Majesty might persuade himself that by such omission a hemisphere had actually been taken away from the Dutch merchants and navigators. But the whole world saw that Article IV. really contained both the East and West Indies. It hardly needed the secret clause to make assurance doubly sure.

President Richardot was facetiously wont to observe that this point in the treaty was so obscure that he did not understand it himself.[19] But he knew better. He under-

16 Bentivoglio, 576.   17 Deventer, iii. 308.   18 Ibid. 309.   19 Bentivoglio, 576.

stood it very well. The world understood it very well. The United Provinces had throughout the negotiations ridiculde the idea of being excluded from any part of the old world or the new by reason of the Borgian grant. All the commissioners knew that the war would be renewed if any attempt were to be seriously made to put up those famous railings around the ocean, of which the Dutch diplomatists spoke in such bitter scorn. The Spanish plenipotentiaries, therefore, had insisted that the word itself should be left out, and that the republic should be forbidden access to territories subject to the crown of Spain.

So the Hollanders were thenceforth to deal directly with the kings of Sumatra and the Moluccas, and the republics of Banda, and all the rich commonwealths and principalities of nutmegs, cloves, and indigo, unless, as grew every day more improbable, the Spaniards and Portuguese could exclude them from that traffic by main force. And the Orange flag of the republic was to float with equal facility over all America, from the Isle of Manhattan to the shores of Brazil and the Straits of Magellan, provided Philip had not ships and soldiers to vindicate with the sword that sovereignty which Spanish swords and Spanish genius had once acquired.

As for the Catholic worship, the future was to prove that liberty for the old religion and for all forms of religion was a blessing more surely to flow from the enlightened public sentiment of a free people emerging out of the most tremendous war for liberty ever waged, than from the stipulations of a treaty with a foreign power.

It was characteristic enough of the parties engaged in the great political drama that the republic now requested from France and Great Britain a written recognition of its independence, and that both France and England refused.[20]

It was strange that the new commonwealth, in the very moment of extorting her freedom from the ancient tyranny, should be so unconscious of her strength as to think free papers from neutral powers a boon. As if the sign-manual

[20] Wagenaar, ix. 445. Jeannin, vol. ii.

of James and Henry were a better guarantee than the trophies of the Nassaus, of Heemskerk, of Matelieff, and of Olden-Barneveld !

It was not strange that the two sovereigns should decline the proposition ; for we well know the secret aspirations of each, and it was natural that they should be unwilling to sign a formal quit-claim, however improbable it might be that those dreams should ever become a reality.

Both powers, however, united in a guarantee of the truce. 17 June, 1609. This was signed on the 17th June, and stipulated that, without their knowledge and consent, the States should make no treaty during the period of truce with the King of Spain or the archdukes. On the other hand, in case of an infraction of the truce by the enemy, the two kings agreed to lend assistance to the States in the manner provided by the treaties concluded with the republic previously to the negotiation of the truce.[21]

The treaty had been at once ratified by the States-General, assembled for the purpose with an extraordinary number of deputies at Bergen-op-Zoom. It was also ratified without delay by the archdukes. The delivery of the confirmation by his Catholic Majesty had been promised within three months after the signatures of the plenipotentiaries.

It would however have been altogether inconsistent with the dignity and the traditions of the Spanish court to fulfil this stipulation. It was not to be expected that "I the King" could be written either by the monarch himself, or by his *alter ego* the Duke of Lerma, in so short a time as a quarter of a year.

Several weeks accordingly went by after the expiration of the stated period. The ratification did not come, and the Netherlanders began to be once more indignant. Before the storm had risen very high, however, the despatches arrived. The king's signature was ante-dated 7th April, being thus brought within the term of three months, and was a thorough confirmation of what had been done by his plenipotentiaries.

[21] Jeannin, ii 536, 538. Wagenaar, ix. 446.

His Majesty, however, expressed a hope that during the truce the States would treat their Catholic subjects with kindness.[22]

Certainly no exception could be taken to so reasonable an intimation as this. President Jeannin, too, just before his departure, handed in to the States-General an eloquent appeal on behalf of the Catholics of the Netherlands ; a paper which was not immediately made public.[23]

"Consider the great number of Catholics," he said, "in your territory, both in the cities and the country. Remember that they have worked with you, spent their property, have been exposed to the same dangers, and have always kept their fidelity to the commonwealth inviolate as long as the war endured, never complaining that they did not enjoy liberty of religious worship, believing that you had thus ordained because the public safety required such guaranty. But they always promised themselves, should the end of the war be happy, and should you be placed in the enjoyment of entire freedom, that they too would have some part in this good fortune, even as they had been sharers in the inconveniences, the expenses, and the perils of the war.

" But those cannot be said to share in any enjoyment from whom has been taken the power of serving God according to the religion in which they were brought up. On the contrary, no slavery is more intolerable nor more exasperates the mind than such restraint. You know this well, my lords States ; you know too that it was the principal, the most puissant cause that made you fly to arms and scorn all dangers, in order to effect your deliverance from this servitude. You know that it has excited similar movements in various parts of Christendom, and even in the kingdom of France, with such fortunate success everywhere as to make it appear that God had so willed it, in order to prove that religion ought to be taught and inspired by the movements which come from the Holy Ghost, and not by the force of man. Thus kings

---

[22] Meteren, xxx. 579vo. Wagenaar, ix. 467.
[23] Jeannin, ii. 589–597, gives the whole text of his address on this occasion.

and princes should be induced by the evils and ruin which they and their subjects have suffered from this cause, as by a sentiment of their own interest, to take more care than has hitherto been taken to practise in good earnest those remedies which were wont to be used at a time when the church was in its greatest piety, in order to correct the abuses and errors which the corruption of mankind had tried to introduce as being the true and sole means of uniting all Christians in one and the same creed."

Surely the world had made progress in these forty years of war. Was it not something to gain for humanity, for intellectual advancement, for liberty of thought, for the true interests of religion, that a Roman Catholic, an ex-leaguer, a trusted representative of the immediate successor of Charles IX. and Henry III., could stand up on the blood-stained soil of the Netherlands and plead for liberty of conscience for all mankind ?

"Those cannot be said to share in any enjoyment from whom has been taken the power of serving God according to the religion in which they have been brought up. No slavery is more intolerable nor more exasperating to the mind than such restraint."

Most true, O excellent president ! No axiom in mathematics is more certain than this simple statement. To prove its truth William the Silent had lived and died. To prove it a falsehood, emperors, and kings, and priests, had issued bans, and curses, and damnable decrees. To root it out they had butchered, drowned, shot, strangled, poisoned, tortured, roasted alive, buried alive, starved, and driven mad, thousands and tens of thousands of their fellow creatures. And behold there had been almost a century of this work, and yet the great truth was not rooted out after all ; and the devil-worshippers, who had sought at the outset of the great war to establish the Holy Inquisition in the Netherlands upon the ruins of religious and political liberty, were overthrown at last and driven back into the pit. It was progress ; it was worth all the blood and treasure which had been spilled, that, instead of the Holy Inquisition, there was now holy liberty of thought.

That there should have been a party, that there should have been an individual here and there, after the great victory was won, to oppose the doctrine which the Catholic president now so nobly advocated, would be enough to cause every believer in progress to hide his face in the dust, did we not know that the march of events was destined to trample such opposition out of existence, and had not history proved to us that the great lesson of the war was not to be rendered nought by the efforts of a few fanatics. Religious liberty was the ripened and consummate fruit, and it could not but be gathered.

" Consider too," continued the president, " how much injury your refusal, if you give it, will cause to those of your religion in the places where they are the weakest, and where they are every day imploring with tears and lamentations the grace of those Catholic sovereigns to whom they are subject, to enable them to enjoy the same religious liberty which our king is now demanding in favour of the Catholics among you. Do not cause it to come again into the minds of those sovereigns and their peoples, whom an inconsiderate zeal has often driven into violence and ferocity against protestants, that a war to compel the weakest to follow the religion of the strongest is just and lawful."

Had not something been gained for the world when this language was held by a Catholic on the very spot where less than a half century before the whole population of the Netherlands, men, women, and children, had been condemned to death by a foreign tyrant, for the simple reason that it was just, legal, and a Christian duty to punish the weak for refusing to follow the religion of the strong ?

"As for the perils which some affect to fear," said Jeannin, further, " if this liberty of worship is accorded, experience teaches us every day that diversity of religion is not the cause of the ruin of states, and that a government does not cease to be good, nor its subjects to live in peace and friendship with one another, rendering due obedience to the laws and to their rulers as well as if they had all been of the same religion, without having another thought, save for the preservation of the dignity and grandeur of the state in which God had caused them to be born. The danger is not in the permission, but in the prohibition of religious liberty."

All this seems commonplace enough to us on the western side of the Atlantic, in the middle of the nineteenth century, but it would have been rank blasphemy in New England in the middle of the seventeenth, many years after Jeannin spoke. It was a horrible sound, too, in the ears of some of his audience.

To the pretence so often urged by the Catholic persecutors, and now set up by their Calvinistic imitators, that those who still clung to the old religion were at liberty to depart from the land, the president replied with dignified scorn.

"With what justice," he asked, "can you drive into exile people who have committed no offence, and who have helped to conquer the very country from which you would now banish them? If you do drive them away, you will make solitudes in your commonwealth, which will be the cause of evils such as I prefer that you should reflect upon without my declaring them now. Although these reasons," he continued, "would seem sufficient to induce you to accord the free and public exercise of the Catholic religion, the king, not hoping as much as that, because aware that you are not disposed to go so far, is content to request only this grace in behalf of the Catholics, that you will tolerate them, and suffer them to have some exercise of their religion within their own households, without interference or inquiry on that account, and without execution of the rigorous decrees heretofore enforced against them."

Certainly if such wholesome, moderate, and modest counsels as these had been rejected, it would have been sound doctrine to proclaim that the world did not move. And there were individuals enough, even an influential party, prepared to oppose them for both technical and practical reasons. And the cause of intolerance derived much warmth and comfort at this juncture from that great luminary of theology and political philosophy, the King of Great Britain. Direful and solemn were the warnings uttered by James to the republic against permitting the old religion, or any religion save his own religion, to obtain the slightest foothold within her borders.

"Let the religion be taught and preached in its purity throughout your provinces without the least mixture," said Sir Ralph Winwood, in the name of his sovereign.

"On this foundation the justice of your cause is built. There is but one verity. Those who are willing to tolerate any religion, whatever it may be, and try to make you believe that liberty for both is necessary in your commonwealth, are paving the way towards atheism." [24]

Such were the counsels of King James to the united States of the Netherlands against harbouring Catholics. A few years later he was casting forth Calvinists from his own dominions as if they had been lepers ; and they went forth on their weary pilgrimage to the howling wilderness of North America, those exiled Calvinists, to build a greater republic than had ever been dreamed of before on this planet ; and they went forth, not to preach, but in their turn to denounce toleration and to hang heretics. "He who would tolerate another religion that his own may be tolerated, would if need be, hang God's bible at the devil's girdle." So spoke an early Massachusetts pilgrim, in the very spirit, almost the very words of the royal persecutor, who had driven him into outer darkness beyond the seas. He had not learned the lesson of the mighty movement in which he was a pioneer, any more than Gomarus or Uytenbogaart had comprehended why the Dutch republic had risen.

Yet the founders of the two commonwealths, the United States of the seventeenth and of the nineteenth centuries, although many of them fiercely intolerant, through a natural instinct of resistance, not only to the oppressor but to the

<hr>

[24] Cited in Van der Kemp, iii. 264.

creed of the'oppressor, had been breaking out the way, not to atheism, as King James believed, but to the only garden in which Christianity can perennially flourish—religious liberty.

Those most ardent and zealous path-finders may be forgiven, in view of the inestimable benefits conferred by them upon humanity, that they did not travel on their own road. It should be sufficient for us, if we make due use of their great imperishable work ourselves ; and if we never cease rendering thanks to the Omnipotent, that there is at least one great nation on the globe where the words toleration and dissenter have no meaning whatever.

For the Dutch fanatics of the reformed church, at the moment of the truce, to attempt to reverse the course of events, and to shut off the mighty movement of the great revolt from its destined expanse, was as hopeless a dream as to drive back the Rhine, as it reached the ocean, into the narrow channel of the Rheinwald glacier whence it sprang.

The republic became the refuge for the oppressed of all nations, where Jews and Gentiles, Catholics, Calvinists, and Anabaptists prayed after their own manner to the same God and Father. It was too much, however, to hope that passions which had been so fiercely bubbling during fifty years would subside at once, and that the most intense religious hatreds that ever existed would exhale with the proclamation of truce. The march of humanity is rarely rapid enough to keep pace with the leaders in its most sublime movements, and it often happens that its chieftains are dwarfed in the estimation of the contemporaneous vulgar, by the very distance at which they precede their unconscious followers. But even if the progress of the human mind towards the truth is fated to be a spiral one, as if to remind us that mankind is of the earth, earthy—a worm in the dust while inhabiting this lower sphere—it is at least a consolation to reflect upon the gradual advancement of the intellect from age to age.

The spirit of Torquemada, of Charles, of Philip, of Titelmann, is even now not extinct on this globe, but there are counter forces at work, which must ultimately blast it into insignificance. At the moment of the great truce, that evil spirit was not exorcised from the human breast, but the number of its victims and the intensity of its influence had already miraculously diminished.

The truce was made and announced all over the Netherlands by the ringing of bells, the happy discharge of innocent artillery, by illuminations, by Te Deums in all the churches. Papist and Presbyterian fell on their knees in every grand cathedral or humblest village church, to thank God that what had seemed the eternal butchery was over. The inhabitants of the united and of the obedient Netherlands rushed across the frontiers into a fraternal embrace, like the meeting of many waters when the flood-gates are lifted. It was pity that the foreign sovereignty, established at Brussels, could not then and there have been for ever swept away, and self-government and beneficent union extended over all the seventeen Netherlands, Walloon and Flemish, Catholic and reformed. But it hardly needs a word to show that the course of events had created a deeper chasm between the two sections than the gravest physical catastrophe could have produced. The opposing cliffs which religious hatred had rent asunder, and between which it seemed destined to flow for ever, seemed very close, and yet eternally separated.

The great war had established the republic, and apparently doomed the obedient Netherlands to perpetual servitude.

There were many details of minor importance to be settled between the various governments involved in these great transactions; but this history draws to its predestined close, and it is necessary to glide rapidly over matters which rather belong to a later epoch than the one now under consideration.

The treaty between the republic and the government of Great Britain, according to which each was to assist the other in case of war with four thousand troops and twenty ships of war, was confirmed in the treaty of truce. The debt of the United Provinces to the Crown of England was definitely reckoned at 8,184,080 florins, and it was settled by the truce that 200,000 florins should be paid semi-annually, to begin with the year 1611, until the whole debt should be discharged.[25]

The army establishment of the republic was fixed during the truce at thirty thousand infantry and three thousand horse. This was a reduction from the war footing of fifteen thousand men. Of the force retained, four thousand were a French legion maintained by the king, two thousand other French at the expense of the States, and distributed among other troops, two thousand Scotch, three thousand English, three thousand Germans. The rest were native Netherlanders, among whom, however, were very few Hollanders and Zeelanders, from which races the navy, both public and mercantile, was almost wholly supplied.

The revenue of the United Provinces was estimated at between seven and eight millions of florins.

It is superfluous to call attention again to the wonderful smallness of the means, the minuteness of the physical enginry, as compared with more modern manifestations, especially in our own land and epoch, by which so stupendous a result had been reached. In the midst of an age in which regal and sacerdotal despotism had seemed as omnipotent and irreversible as the elemental laws of the universe, the republic had been reproduced. A commonwealth of sand-banks, lagoons, and meadows, less than fourteen thousand square miles in extent, had done battle, for nearly half a century, with the greatest of existing powers, a realm whose territory was nearly a third of the globe, and which claimed universal monarchy. And this had been done with an army averaging forty-six thousand men, half of them foreigners hired by the job, and by a sea-faring population, volunteering into ships of every class and denomination, from a fly-boat to a galleot of war.

And when the republic had won its independence, after this

Meteren. 614[vo].

almost eternal warfare, it owed four or five millions of dollars, and had sometimes an annual revenue of nearly that amount.

It was estimated by Barneveld, at the conclusion of the truce, that the interest on the public debt of Spain was about thrice the amount of the yearly income of the republic, and it was characteristic of the financial ideas of the period, that fears were entertained lest a total repudiation of that burthen by the Spanish Government would enable it to resume the war against the provinces with redoubled energy [26]

The annual salary of Prince Maurice, who was to see his chief occupation gone by the cessation of the war, was fixed by the States at 120,000 florins.[27] It was agreed, that in case of his marriage he should receive a further yearly sum of 25,000 florins, and this addition was soon afterwards voted to him outright,[28] it being obvious that the prince would remain all his days a bachelor.

Count Frederic Henry likewise received a military salary of 25,000 florins,[29] while the emoluments of Lewis William were placed at 36,000 florins a year.[30]

It must be admitted that the republic was grateful. 70,000 dollars a year, in the seventeenth century, not only for life, but to be inherited afterwards by his younger brother, Frederic Henry, was surely a munificent sum to be accorded from the puny exchequer of the States-General to the chief magistrate of the nation.

The mighty transatlantic republic, with its population of thirty or forty millions, and its revenue of five hundred millions of dollars, pays 25,000 dollars annually for its president during his four years of office, and this in the second half of the nineteenth century, when a dollar is worth scarcely one-fifth of its value two hundred and fifty years ago.

Surely here is improvement, both in the capacity to produce and in the power to save.

[26] Van der Kemp, iii. 223.

[27] Van der Kemp (from the Sec. Res. Stat.-Gen.) iii. 250, 251.

[28] Ibid. 251, 252. "No one thing hath been of greater trouble to us," wrote Spencer and Winwood, "than the craving humour of Count Maurice."—Winwood's Memorials, iii. 1, 2

[29] Ibid. 255.

[30] Ibid.

In the year 1609, died John, the last sovereign of Cleves and Juliers, and Jacob Arminius, Doctor of Divinity at Leyden. It would be difficult to imagine two more entirely dissimilar individuals of the human family than this lunatic duke and that theological professor. And yet, perhaps, the two names, more concisely than those of any other mortals, might serve as an index to the ghastly chronicle over which a coming generation was to shudder. The death of the duke was at first thought likely to break off the negotiations for truce. The States-General at once declared that they would permit no movements on the part of the Spanish party to seize the inheritance in behalf of the Catholic claimants. Prince Maurice, nothing loth to make use of so well-timed an event in order to cut for ever the tangled skein at the Hague, was for marching forthwith into the duchies.

But the archdukes gave such unequivocal assurances of abstaining from interference, and the desire for peace was so strong both in the obedient and in the United Provinces, that the question of the duchies was postponed. It was to serve as both torch and fuel for one of the longest and most hideous tragedies that had ever disgraced humanity. A thirty years' war of demons was, after a brief interval, to succeed the forty years' struggle between slaves and masters, which had just ended in the recognition of Dutch independence.

The gentle Arminius was in his grave, but a bloody harvest was fast ripening from the seeds which he had sown. That evil story must find its place in the melancholy chapter where the fortunes of the Dutch republic are blended with the grim chronicle of the thirty years' war. Until the time arrives for retracing the course of those united transactions to their final termination in the peace of Westphalia, it is premature to characterize an epoch which, at the moment with which we are now occupied, had not fairly begun.

The Gomarites accused the Arminians of being more lax than Papists, and of filling the soul of man with vilest arrogance and confidence in good works ; while the Arminians complained that the God of the Gomarites was an unjust God, himself the origin of sin.[1]

The disputes on these themes had been perpetual in the provinces ever since the early days of the Reformation. Of late, however, the acrimony of theological conflict had been growing day by day more intense. It was the eternal struggle of religious dogma to get possession of the State, and to make use of political forces in order to put fetters on the human soul ; to condemn it to slavery where most it requires freedom. The conflict between Gomarus and Arminius proceeded with such ferocity in Leyden, that, since the days of the memorable siege, to which the university owed its origin, men's minds had never been roused to such feverish anxiety. The theological cannonades, which thundered daily from the college buildings and caused all Holland to quake, seemed more appalling to the burghers than the enginry of Valdez and Boisot had ever seemed to their fathers.

The Gomarite doctrine gained most favour with the clergy, the Arminian creed with the municipal magistracies. The magistrates claimed that decisions concerning religious matters belonged to the supreme authority. The Gomarites contended that sacred matters should be referred to synods of the clergy.[32] Here was the germ of a conflict which might one day shake the republic to its foundations.

Barneveld, the great leader of the municipal party, who loved political power quite as well as he loved his country, was naturally a chieftain of the Arminians ; for church matters were no more separated from political matters in the commonwealth at that moment than they were in the cabinets of Henry, James, or Philip.

It was inevitable therefore that the war party should pour upon his head more than seven vials of theological wrath. The religious doctrines which he espoused were odious not only because they were deemed vile in themselves, but because he believed in them.

Arminianism was regarded as a new and horrible epidemic,

[31] Grotius, xvii. 790–792.   [32] Grotius, xvii. 791.

daily gaining ground, and threatening to destroy the whole population. Men deliberated concerning the best means to cut off communication with the infected regions, and to extirpate the plague even by desperate and heroic remedies, as men in later days take measures against the cholera or the rinderpest.

Theological hatred was surely not extinct in the Netherlands. It was a consolation, however, that its influence was rendered less noxious by the vastly increased strength of principles long dormant in the atmosphere. Anna van dei Hoven, buried alive in Brussels, simply because her Calvinistic creed was a crime in the eyes of the monks who murdered her, was the last victim to purely religious persecution. If there were one day to be still a tragedy or two in the Netherlands it was inevitable that theological hatred would be obliged to combine with political party spirit in its most condensed form before any deadly effect could be produced.

Thus the year 1609 is a memorable one in the world's history. It forms a great landmark in human progress. It witnessed the recognition of a republic, powerful in itself, and whose example was destined to be most influential upon the career of two mighty commonwealths of the future. The British empire, just expanding for wider flight than it had hitherto essayed, and about to pass through a series of vast revolutions, gathering strength of wing as it emerged from cloud after cloud ; and the American republic, whose frail and obscure beginnings at that very instant of time scarcely attracted a passing attention from the contemporaneous world—both these political organisms, to which so much of mankind's future liberties had been entrusted, were deeply indebted to the earlier self-governing commonwealth.

The Dutch republic was the first free nation to put a girdle of empire around the earth. It had courage, enterprise, intelligence, perseverance, faith in itself, the instinct of self-government and self-help, hatred of tyranny, the disposition to domineer, aggressiveness, greediness, inquisitiveness, insolence, the love of science, of liberty, and of money—all this in unlimited extent. It had one great defect,—it had no country. Upon that meagre standing ground its hand had moved the world with an impulse to be felt through all the ages, but there was not soil enough in those fourteen thousand square miles to form the metropolis of the magnificent empire which the genius of liberty had created beyond the seas.

That the political institutions bequeathed by the United States of the seventeenth century have been vastly improved, both in theory and practice, by the United States of the nineteenth, no American is likely to gainsay. That the elder Republic showed us also what to avoid, and was a living example of the perils besetting a Confederacy which dared not become a Union, is a lesson which we might take closely to heart.

But the year 1609 was not only memorable as marking an epoch in Dutch history. It was the beginning of a great and universal pause. The world had need of rest. Disintegration had been going on too rapidly, and it was absolutely necessary that there should be a new birth, if civilization were not to vanish.

A twenty years' truce between the Turkish and Holy Roman empires was nearly simultaneous with the twelve years' truce between Spain and the United Provinces. The Emperor Rudolph having refused to ratify the treaty which his brother Matthias had made, was in consequence partially discrowned. The same archduke who, thirty years before, had slipped away from Vienna in his nightgown, with his face blackened, to outwit and outgeneral William the Silent at Brussels, was now more successful in his manœuvres against his imperial brother. Standing at the head of his army in battle array, in the open fields before the walls of Prague, he received from the unfortunate Rudolph the crown and regalia of Hungary, and was by solemn treaty declared sovereign of that ancient and chivalrous kingdom.[33]

[33] Meteren, 600, 601.

His triumphal entrance into Vienna succeeded, where,
14 July, surrounded by great nobles and burghers, with his
1608. brother Maximilian at his side, with immense
pomp and with flowers strewn before his feet, he ratified that
truce with Ahmed which Rudolph had rejected. Three
19 Oct. months later he was crowned at Pressburg, having
1608. first accepted the conditions proposed by the estates
of Hungary. Foremost among these was the provision that
the exercise of the reformed religion should be free in all
the cities and villages beneath his sceptre, and that every
man in the kingdom was to worship God according to his
conscience.

In the following March, at the very moment accordingly
12 March, when the conclusive negotiations were fast ripening
1609. at Antwerp, Matthias granted religious peace for
Austria likewise. Great was the indignation of his nephew
Leopold, the nuncius, and the Spanish ambassador in consequence, by each and all of whom the revolutionary mischief-
maker, with his brother's crown on his head, was threatened
with excommunication.[34]

As for Ferdinand of Styria, his wrath may well be imagined.
He refused religious peace in his dominions with scorn ineffable. Not Gomarus in Leyden could have shrunk from
Arminianism with more intense horror than that with which
the archduke at Gratz recoiled from any form of Protestantism. He wrote to his brother-in-law the King of Spain
and to other potentates—as if the very soul of Philip II. were
alive within him—that he would rather have a country without
inhabitants than with a single protestant on its soil.[35] He
strongly urged upon his Catholic Majesty—as if such urging
were necessary at the Spanish court—the necessity of extir-
pating heresy, root and branch.

Here was one man at least who knew what he meant, and
on whom the dread lessons of fifty years of bloodshed had
been lost. Magnificent was the contempt which this pupil
of the Jesuits felt for any little progress made by the world

---

[34] Meteren, 600, 601.   [35] Ibid.

since the days of Torquemada. In Ferdinand's view Alva was a Christian hero, scarcely second to Godfrey of Bouillon, Philip II. a sainted martyr, while the Dutch republic had never been born.

And Ferdinand was one day to sit on the throne of the holy Roman Empire. Might not a shudder come over the souls of men as coming events vaguely shaped themselves to prophetic eyes ?

Meantime there was religious peace in Hungary, in Austria, in Bohemia, in France, in Great Britain, in the Netherlands. The hangman's hands were for a period at rest, so far as theology had need of them. Butchery in the name of Christ was suspended throughout Christendom. The Cross and the Crescent, Santiago and the Orange banner, were for a season in repose.

There was a vast lull between two mighty storms. The forty years' war was in the past, the thirty years' war in the not far distant future.

CHAPTER LIII.

CONCLUSION.

FORTY-THREE years had passed since the memorable April morning in which the great nobles of the Netherlands presented their "Request" to the Regent Margaret at Brussels.

They had requested that the holy Spanish Inquisition might not be established on their soil to the suppression of all their political and religious institutions.

The war which those high-born "beggars" had then kindled, little knowing what they were doing, had now come to a close, and the successor of Philip II., instead of planting the Inquisition in the provinces, had recognised them as an independent, sovereign, protestant republic.

In the ratification which he had just signed of the treaty of truce the most Catholic king had in his turn made a Request. He had asked the States-General to deal kindly with their Catholic subjects.

That request was not answered with the axe and faggot; with the avenging sword of mercenary legions. On the contrary, it was destined to be granted. The world had gained something in forty-three years. It had at least begun to learn that the hangman is not the most appropriate teacher of religion.

During the period of apparent chaos with which this history of the great revolt has been occupied, there had in truth been a great re-organization, a perfected new birth. The republic had once more appeared in the world.

Its main characteristics have been indicated in the course of the narrative, for it was a polity which gradually unfolded itself out of the decay and change of previous organisms.

It was, as it were, in their own despite and unwittingly that the United Provinces became a republic at all.

In vain, after originally declaring their independence of the ancient tyrant, had they attempted to annex themselves to France and to England. The sovereignty had been spurned. The magnificent prize which France for centuries since has so persistently coveted, and the attainment of which has been a cardinal point of her perpetual policy—the Low Countries and the banks of the Rhine—was deliberately laid at her feet, and as deliberately refused.

It was the secret hope of the present monarch to repair the loss which the kingdom had suffered through the imbecility of his two immediate predecessors. But a great nation cannot with impunity permit itself to be despotically governed for thirty years by lunatics. It was not for the Béarnese, with all his valour, his wit, and his duplicity, to obtain the prize which Charles IX. and Henry III. had thrown away. Yet to make himself sovereign of the Netherlands was his guiding but most secret thought during all the wearisome and tortuous negotiations which preceded the truce ; nor did he abandon the great hope with the signature of the treaty of 1609.

Maurice of Nassau too was a formidable rival to Henry. The stadholder-prince was no republican. He was a good patriot, a noble soldier, an honest man. But his father had been offered the sovereignty of Holland and Zeeland, and the pistol of Balthasar Gerard had alone, in all human probability, prevented the great prince from becoming constitutional monarch of all the Netherlands, Batavian and Belgic.

Maurice himself asserted that not only had he been offered a million of dollars, and large estates besides in Germany, if he would leave the provinces to their fate, but that the arch-dukes had offered, would he join his fortunes with theirs, to place him in a higher position over all the Netherlands than he had ever enjoyed in the United Provinces, and that they had even unequivocally offered him the sovereignty over the whole land.[1]

Maurice was a man of truth, and we have no right to

[1] Jeannin, i. 174, 175.

dispute the accuracy of the extraordinary statement. He must however have reflected upon the offer once made by the Prince of Darkness from the mountain top, and have asked himself by what machinery the archdukes proposed to place him in possession of such a kingdom.

There had, however, been serious question among leading Dutch statesmen of making him constitutional, hereditary monarch of the United Netherlands. As late as 1602 a secret conference was held at the house of Olden-Barneveld, in which the Advocate had himself urged the claims of the prince to the sovereignty, and reminded his guests that the signed and sealed documents—with the concurrence of the Amsterdam municipality alone lacking—by which William the Silent had been invited to assume the crown were still in the possession of his son.[2]

Nothing came of these deliberations. It was agreed that to stir in the matter at that moment would be premature, and that the pursuit by Maurice of the monarchy in the circumstances then existing would not only overburthen him with expense, but make him a more conspicuous mark than ever for the assassin. It is certain that the prince manifested no undue anxiety at any period in regard to those transactions.

Subsequently, as Olden-Barneveld's personal power increased, and as the negotiations for peace became more and more likely to prove successful, the Advocate lost all relish for placing his great rival on a throne. The whole project, with the documents and secret schemes therewith connected, became mere alms for oblivion. Barneveld himself, although of comparatively humble birth and station, was likely with time to exercise more real power in the State than either Henry or Maurice; and thus while there were three individuals who in different ways aspired to supreme power, the republic, notwithstanding, asserted and established itself.

    [2] Van der Kemp, ii. 100–102, and 390–395. Leven van Olden-Barneveld, 156. Wagenaar, ix. 454.

Freedom of government and freedom of religion were, on the whole, assisted by this triple antagonism. The prince, so soon as war was over, hated the Advocate and his daily increasing power more and more. He allied himself more closely than ever with the Gomarites and the clerical party in general, and did his best to inflame the persecuting spirit, already existing in the provinces, against the Catholics and the later sects of Protestants.

Jeannin warned him that "by thus howling with the priests" he would be suspected of more desperately ambitious designs than he perhaps really cherished.[3]

On the other hand, Barneveld was accused of a willingness to wink at the introduction, privately and quietly, of the Roman Catholic worship. That this was the deadliest of sins, there was no doubt whatever in the minds of his revilers. When it was added that he was suspected of the Arminian leprosy, and that he could tolerate the thought that a virtuous man or woman, not predestined from all time for salvation, could possibly find the way to heaven, language becomes powerless to stigmatize his depravity. Whatever the punishment impending over his head in this world or the next, it is certain that the cause of human freedom was not destined on the whole to lose ground through the life-work of Barneveld.

A champion of liberties rather than of liberty, he defended his fatherland with heart and soul against the stranger; yet the government of that fatherland was, in his judgment, to be transferred from the hand of the foreigner, not to the self-governing people, but to the provincial corporations. For the People he had no respect, and perhaps little affection. He often spoke of popular rights with contempt. Of popular sovereignty he had no conception. His patriotism, like his ambition, was provincial. Yet his perceptions as to eternal necessity in all healthy governments taught him that comprehensible relations between the state and the population were needful to the very existence of a free commonwealth. The

[3] Van der Kemp, iii. 72. Jeannin.

United Provinces, he maintained, were not a republic, but a league of seven provinces very loosely hung together, a mere provisional organization for which it was not then possible to substitute anything better. He expressed this opinion with deep regret, just as the war of independence was closing, and added his conviction that, without some well-ordered government, no republic could stand.

Yet, as time wore on, the Advocate was destined to acquiesce more and more in this defective constitution. A settled theory there was none, and it would have been difficult legally and historically to establish the central sovereignty of the States-General as matter of right.

Thus Barneveld, who was anything but a democrat, became, almost unwittingly, the champion of the least venerable or imposing of all forms of aristocracy—an oligarchy of traders who imagined themselves patricians. Corporate rights, not popular liberty, seemed, in his view, the precious gains made by such a prodigious expenditure of time, money, and blood. Although such acquisitions were practically a vast addition to the stock of human freedom then existing in the world, yet torrents of blood and millions of treasure were to be wasted in the coming centuries before mankind was to convince itself that a republic is only to be made powerful and perpetual by placing itself upon the basis of popular right rather than on that of municipal privilege.

The singular docility of the Dutch people, combined with the simplicity, honesty, and practical sagacity of the earlier burgher patricians, made the defects of the system tolerable 'for a longer period than might have been expected ; nor was it until theological dissensions had gathered to such intensity as to set the whole commonwealth aflame that the grave defects in the political structure could be fairly estimated.

It would be anticipating a dark chapter in the history of the United Provinces were the reader's attention now to be called to those fearful convulsions. The greatest reserve is therefore necessary at present in alluding to the subject.

It was not to be expected that an imperious, energetic

but somewhat limited nature like that of Barneveld should at that epoch thoroughly comprehend the meaning of religious freedom. William the Silent alone seems to have risen to that height. A conscientious Calvinist himself, the father of his country would have been glad to see Protestant and Papist, Lutheran, Presbyterian, and Anabaptist living together in harmony and political equality. This was not to be. The soul of the immortal prince could not inspire the hearts of his contemporaries. That Barneveld was disposed to a breadth of religious sympathy unusual in those days, seems certain. It was inevitable, too, that the mild doctrines of Arminius should be more in harmony with such a character than were the fierce dogmas of Calvin. But the struggle, either to force Arminianism upon the Church which considered itself the established one in the Netherlands, or to expel the Calvinists from it, had not yet begun; although the seeds of religious persecution of Protestants by Protestants had already been sown broadcast.

The day was not far distant when the very Calvinists, to whom, more than to any other class of men, the political liberties of Holland, England, and America are due, were to be hunted out of churches into farm-houses, suburban hovels, and canal-boats by the arm of provincial sovereignty and in the name of state-rights, as pitilessly as the early reformers had been driven out of cathedrals in the name of emperor and pope ; and when even those refuges for conscientious worship were to be denied by the dominant sect. And the day was to come, too, when the Calvinists, regaining ascendency in their turn, were to hunt the heterodox as they had themselves been hunted ; and this, at the very moment when their fellow Calvinists of England were driven by the Church of that kingdom into the American wilderness.

Toleration—that intolerable term of insult to all who love liberty—had not yet been discovered. It had scarcely occurred to Arminian or Presbyterian that civil authority and ecclesiastical doctrine could be divorced from each other. As the individual sovereignty of the seven states established itself more and more securely, the right of provincial power to dictate religious dogmas, and to superintend the popular conscience, was exercised with a placid arrogance which papal infallibility could scarcely exceed. The alternation was only between the sects, each in its turn becoming orthodox, and therefore persecuting. The lessened intensity of persecution however, which priesthood and authority were now allowed to exercise, marked the gains secured.

Yet while we censure—as we have a right to do from the point of view which we have gained after centuries—the crimes committed by bigotry against liberty, we should be false to our faith in human progress did we not acknowledge our debt of gratitude to the hot gospellers of Holland and England.

The doctrine of predestination, the consciousness of being chosen soldiers of Christ, inspired those puritans, who founded the commonwealths of England, of Holland, and of America, with a contempt of toil, danger, and death which enabled them to accomplish things almost supernatural.

No uncouthness of phraseology, no unlovely austerity of deportment, could, except to vulgar minds, make that sublime enthusiasm ridiculous, which on either side the ocean ever confronted tyranny with dauntless front, and welcomed death on battle-field, scaffold, or rack with perfect composure.

The early puritan at least believed. The very intensity of his belief made him—all unconsciously to himself, and narrowed as was his view of his position—the great instrument by which the widest human liberty was to be gained for all mankind.

The elected favourite of the King of kings feared the power of no earthly king. Accepting in rapture the decrees of a supernatural tyranny, he rose on mighty wings above the reach of human wrath. Prostrating himself before a God of vengeance, of jealousy, and of injustice, he naturally imitated the attributes which he believed to be divine. It was inevitable, therefore, that Barneveld, and those who thought with him, when they should attempt to force the children of Belial into the company of the elect and to drive the faithful out of their own churches, should be detested as bitterly as papists had ever been.

Had Barneveld's intellect been broad enough to imagine in a great republic the separation of Church and State, he would deserve a tenderer sympathy, but he would have been far in advance of his age. It is not cheerful to see so power-ful an intellect and so patriotic a character daring to entrust the relations between man and his Maker to the decree of a trading corporation. But alas! the world was to wait for centuries until it should learn that the State can best defend religion by letting it alone, and that the political arm is apt to wither with palsy when it attempts to control the human conscience.

It is not entirely the commonwealth of the United Nether-lands that is of importance in the epoch which I have endeavoured to illustrate. History can have neither value nor charm for those who are not impressed with a conviction of its continuity.

More than ever during the period which we call modern history has this idea of the continuousness of our race, and especially of the inhabitants of Europe and America, become almost oppressive to the imagination. There is a sense of immortality even upon earth when we see the succes-sion of heritages in the domains of science, of intellectual and material wealth by which mankind, generation after generation, is enriching itself.

If this progress be a dream, if mankind be describing a limited circle instead of advancing towards the infinite, then no study can be more contemptible than the study of history.

Few strides more gigantic have been taken in the march of humanity than those by which a parcel of outlying pro-vinces in the north of Europe exchanged slavery to a foreign despotism and to the Holy Inquisition for the posi-tion of a self-governing commonwealth, in the front rank of contemporary powers, and in many respects the foremost of the world. It is impossible to calculate the amount of

benefit rendered to civilization by the example of the Dutch
republic. It has been a model which has been imitated, in
many respects, by great nations. It has even been valuable
in its very defects ; indicating to the patient observer many
errors most important to avoid.

Therefore, had the little republic sunk for ever in the sea
so soon as the treaty of peace had been signed at Antwerp, its
career would have been prolific of good for all succeeding
time.

Exactly at the moment when a splendid but decaying
despotism, founded upon wrong—upon oppression of the
human body and the immortal soul, upon slavery, in short,
of the worst kind—was awaking from its insane dream of
universal empire to a consciousness of its own decay, the new
republic was recognised among the nations.

It would hardly be incorrect to describe the Holland of the
beginning of the seventeenth century as the exact reverse of
Spain. In the commonwealth labour was most honourable ;
in the kingdom it was vile. In the north to be idle was
accounted and punished as a crime. In the southern peninsula, to be contaminated with mechanical, mercantile, commercial, manufacturing pursuits, was to be accursed. Labour
was for slaves, and at last the mere spectacle of labour
became so offensive that even the slaves were expelled from
the land. To work was as degrading in the south as to beg
or to steal was esteemed unworthy of humanity in the north.
To think a man's thought upon high matters of religion and
government, and through a thousand errors to pursue the
truth, with the aid of the Most High and with the best use of
human reason, was a privilege secured by the commonwealth,
at the expense of two generations of continuous bloodshed.
To lie fettered, soul and body, at the feet of authority wielded
by a priesthood in its last stage of corruption, and monarchy
almost reduced to imbecility, was the lot of the chivalrous,
genial, but much oppressed Spaniard.

The pictures painted of the republic by shrewd and caustic
observers, not inclined by nature or craft to portray freedom

in too engaging colours, seem, when contrasted with those revealed of Spain, almost like enthusiastic fantasies of an ideal commonwealth.

During the last twenty years of the great war the material prosperity of the Netherlands had wonderfully increased. They had become the first commercial nation in the world. They had acquired the supremacy of the seas. The population of Amsterdam had in twenty years increased from seventy thousand to a hundred and thirty thousand, and was destined to be again more than doubled in the coming decade.[4] The population of Antwerp had sunk almost as rapidly as that of its rival had increased; having lessened by fifty thousand during the same period.[5] The commercial capital of the obedient provinces, having already lost much of its famous traffic by the great changes in the commercial current of the world, was unable to compete with the cities of the United Provinces in the vast trade which the geographical discoveries of the preceding century had opened to civilization. Freedom of thought and action were denied, and without such liberty it was impossible for oceanic commerce to thrive. Moreover, the possession by the Hollanders of the Scheld forts below Antwerp, and of Flushing at the river's mouth, suffocated the ancient city, and would of itself have been sufficient to paralyze all its efforts.

In Antwerp the exchange, where once thousands of the great merchants of the earth held their daily financial parliament, now echoed to the solitary footfall of the passing stranger. Ships lay rotting at the quays; brambles grew in the commercial streets. In Amsterdam the city had been enlarged by two-thirds, and those who swarmed thither to seek their fortunes could not wait for the streets to be laid out and houses to be built, but established themselves in the

---

[4] Tomaso Contarini ritornato Amb^re dalli Signori Stati di Fiandra (anno 1610).—(MS. Archives of·Venice.) Antonio Donato in 1618 puts the number of inhabitants at 300,000. and describes the city as "the very image of Venice in its prime." The streets and public places were so thronged and bustling that "the scene looked to him like a fair to end in one day."—Relazione, MS.

[5] Ibid. Antwerp had sunk from 150,000 to 80,000.

environs, building themselves hovels and temporary residences, although certain to find their encampments swept away with the steady expanse of the city.[6] As much land as could be covered by a man's foot was worth a ducat in gold.[7]

In every branch of human industry these republicans took the lead. On that scrap of solid ground, rescued by human energy from the ocean, were the most fertile pastures in the world. On those pastures grazed the most famous cattle in the world. An ox often weighed more than two thousand pounds.[8] The cows produced two and three calves at a time, the sheep four and five lambs.[9] In a single village four thousand kine were counted.[10] Butter and cheese were exported to the annual value of a million, salted provisions to an incredible extent. The farmers were industrious, thriving, and independent. It is an amusing illustration of the agricultural thrift and republican simplicity of this people that on one occasion a farmer proposed to Prince Maurice that he should marry his daughter, promising with her a dowry of a hundred thousand florins.[11]

The mechanical ingenuity of the Netherlanders, already celebrated by Julius Cæsar and by Tacitus, had lost nothing of its ancient fame. The contemporary world confessed that in many fabrics the Hollanders were at the head of mankind. Dutch linen, manufactured of the flax grown on their own fields or imported from the obedient provinces, was esteemed a fitting present for kings to make and to receive. The name of the country had passed into the literature of England as synonymous with the delicate fabric itself. The Venetians confessed themselves equalled, if not outdone, by the crystal

---

[6] Contarini, Relazione, MS.

[7] Ibid. "All' habitationi di questa città concorrono i popoli con tanto ardore che non ostante la proibitione di alloggiarsi per certo spatio all' incontro si fabbrice non di meno ogni anno con allegro animo ogni giorno case di legni ben che sia certo di vederse le distruggere in breve tanto stimano il poter cominciare a metter il loro nido almeno vicino se non dentro a quella città nelle quale per il semplice fondo si paga un ducato d'oro tanto terreno quanto può coprire un huomo con la pianta del piede."

[8] Contarini, Relazione, MS.

[9] Ibid.   [10] Ibid.   [11] Ibid.

workers and sugar refiners of the northern republic.[12] The tapestries of Arras—the name of which Walloon city had become a household word of luxury in all modern languages—were now transplanted to the soil of freedom, more congenial to the advancement of art. Brocades of the precious metals ; splendid satins and velvets ; serges and homely fustians ; laces of thread and silk ; the finer and coarser manufactures of clay and porcelain ; iron, steel, and all useful fabrics for the building and outfitting of ships ; substantial broadcloths manufactured of wool imported from Scotland—all this was but a portion of the industrial production of the provinces.

They supplied the deficiency of coal, not then an article readily obtained by commerce, with other remains of antediluvian forests long since buried in the sea, and now recovered from its depths and made useful and portable by untiring industry. Peat was not only the fuel for the fireside, but for the extensive fabrics of the country, and its advantages so much excited the admiration of the Venetian envoys that they sent home samples of it, in the hope that the lagunes of Venice might prove as prolific of this indispensable article as the polders of Holland.[13]

But the foundation of the national wealth, the source of the apparently fabulous power by which the republic had at last overthrown her gigantic antagonist, was the ocean. The republic was sea-born and sea-sustained.

She had nearly one hundred thousand sailors, and three thousand ships.[14] The sailors were the boldest, the best disciplined, and the most experienced in the world, whether for peaceable seafaring or ocean warfare. The ships were capable of furnishing from out of their number in time of need the most numerous and the best appointed navy then known to mankind.

[12] Contarini, Relazione, MS.
[13] Contarini, Relazione, MS. "E perchè pare quasi questa cosa incredibile ho fatto mettere qualche pezzi di queste turbe con le mie robbe che vengono per mare acciò si piacesse al Signore Dio che in questi contorni si trovasse terreno simile potesse il pubblico ricevere due gran benefitii ; uno di cavare il terreno che riempe le lagune ; l'altro di abondar la città di materia per abbrucciare." [14] Ibid.

The republic had the carrying trade for all nations. Feeling its very existence dependent upon commerce, it had strode centuries in advance of the contemporary world in the liberation of trade. But two or three per cent. *ad valorem* was levied upon imports ; foreign goods however being subject, as well as internal products, to heavy imposts in the way of both direct and indirect taxation.

Every article of necessity or luxury known was to be purchased in profusion and at reasonable prices in the warehouses of Holland.

A swarm of river vessels and fly-boats were coming daily through the rivers of Germany, France and the Netherlands, laden with the agricultural products and the choice manufactures of central and western Europe. Wine and oil, and delicate fabrics in thread and wool, came from France, but no silks, velvets, nor satins; for the great Sully had succeeded in persuading his master that the white mulberry would not grow in his kingdom, and that silk manufactures were an impossible dream for France. Nearly a thousand ships were constantly employed in the Baltic trade.[15] The forests of Holland were almost as extensive as those which grew on Norwegian hills, but they were submerged. The foundation of a single mansion required a grove, and wood was extensively used in the superstructure. The houses, built of a framework of substantial timber, and filled in with brick or rubble, were raised almost as rapidly as tents, during the prodigious expansion of industry towards the end of the war.[16] From the realms of the Osterlings, or shores of the Baltic, came daily fleets laden with wheat and other grains, so that even in time of famine the granaries of the republic were overflowing, and ready to dispense the material of life to the outer world.

Eight hundred vessels of lesser size but compact build were perpetually fishing for herrings on the northern coasts. These hardy mariners, the militia of the sea, who had learned in their life of hardship and daring the art of

[15] Contarini, Relazione, MS.   [16] Ibid.

destroying Spanish and Portuguese armadas, and confronting the dangers of either pole, passed a long season on the deep. Commercial voyagers as well as fishermen, they salted their fish as soon as taken from the sea, and transported them to the various ports of Europe, thus reducing their herrings into specie before their return, and proving that a fishery in such hands was worth more than the mines of Mexico and Peru.

It is customary to speak of the natural resources of a country as furnishing a guarantee of material prosperity. But here was a republic almost without natural resources, which had yet supplied by human intelligence and thrift what a niggard nature had denied. Spain was overflowing with unlimited treasure, and had possessed half the world in fee ; and Spain was bankrupt, decaying, sinking into universal pauperism. Holland, with freedom of thought, of commerce, of speech, of action, placed itself, by intellectual power alone, in the front rank of civilization.

From Cathay, from the tropical coasts of Africa, and from farthest Ind, came every drug, spice, or plant, every valuable jewel, every costly fabric, that human ingenuity had discovered or created. The Spaniards, maintaining a frail tenure upon a portion of those prolific regions, gathered their spice harvests at the point of the sword,[17] and were frequently unable to prevent their northern rivals from ravaging such fields as they had not yet been able to appropriate.[18]

Certainly this conduct of the Hollanders was barbarism and supreme selfishness, if judged by the sounder political economy of our time. Yet it should never be forgotten that the contest between Spain and Holland in those distant regions, as everywhere else, was war to the knife between superstition and freedom, between the spirits of progress and of dogma. Hard blows and foul blows were struck in such a fight, and humanity, although gaining at last immense

---

[17] "Tengono quâ Hollandesi la maggior parte di detta Isola (Ternat) rimanendo la minore a Spagnuoli che | raccolgono i loro pochi garôfani con la punta della spada," &c. &c. &c.— Contarini, MS. [18] Ibid.

results, had much to suffer and much to learn ere the day was won.

But Spain was nearly beaten out of those eastern regions, and the very fact that the naval supremacy of the republic placed her ancient tyrant at her mercy was the main reason for Spain to conclude the treaty of truce. Lest she should lose the India trade entirely, Spain consented to the treaty article by which, without mentioning the word, she conceded the thing. It was almost pathetic to witness, as we have witnessed, this despotism in its dotage, mumbling so long over the formal concession to her conqueror of a portion of that India trade which would have been entirely wrested from herself had the war continued. And of this Spain was at heart entirely convinced. Thus the Portuguese, once the lords and masters, as they had been the European discoverers, of those prolific regions and of the ocean highways which led to them, now came with docility to the republic which they had once affected to despise, and purchased the cloves and the allspice, the nutmegs and the cinnamon, of which they had held the monopoly ; or waited with patience until the untiring Hollanders should bring the precious wares to the peninsula ports.[19]

A Dutch Indiaman would make her voyage to the antipodes and her return in less time than was spent by a Portuguese or a Spaniard in the outward voyage.[20] To accomplish such an enterprise in two years was accounted a wonder of rapidity, and when it is remembered that inland navigation through France by canal and river from the North Sea to the Mediterranean was considered both speedier and safer, because the sea voyage between the same points might last four or five months, it must be admitted that two years occupied in passing from one end of the earth to the other and back again might well seem a miracle.

The republic was among the wealthiest and the most powerful of organized States. Her population might be estimated at three millions and a half, about equal to that of

[19] Contarini, Relazione, MS.   [20] Ibid.

England at the same period. But she was richer than England. Nowhere in the world was so large a production in proportion to the numbers of a people. Nowhere were so few unproductive consumers. Every one was at work. Vagabonds, idlers, and do-nothings, such as must be in every community, were caught up by the authorities and made to earn their bread.[21] The devil's pillow, idleness, was smoothed for no portion of the population.

There were no beggars, few paupers, no insolently luxurious and ostentatiously idle class. The modesty, thrift, and simple elegance of the housekeeping, even among the wealthy, was noted by travellers with surprise.[22] It will be remembered with how much amused wonder, followed by something like contempt, the magnificent household of Spinola, during his embassy at the Hague, was surveyed by the honest burghers of Holland. The authorities showed their wisdom in permitting the absurd exhibition, as an example of what should be shunned, in spite of grave remonstrances from many of the citizens. Drunken Helotism is not the only form of erring humanity capable of reading lessons to a republic.

There had been monasteries, convents, ecclesiastical establishments of all kinds in the country, before the great war

[21] Contarini.

[22] " In somma sono quei popoli così inchinati all' industria et al negotio che niuna cosa e tanto difficile che non ardiscono di superarla. . . . . Sopra tutte le cose invigliarano a questo di mantenere il negotio et favorirlo in modo libero da soverchie gravezze che cessi ogni occasione di divertirlo e secarlo. Abbondano di richezze e di commodi con tal misura che non si vede nei piu ricchi lusso o pompe estraordinarie servando tutti et in casa et fuori nell' habito e nel rimanente la vera mediocrità di una modesta fortuna senza che si vedano nè additamenti ne argenterie ne fornimenti ne cadreghe de sete come apunto non si vedevano ne anco in questa città (Venezia) nei tempi de Vostri Antecessori. *Nei poveri non si conosce mancamento di alcuna delle cose necessarie* anzi nelle loro piccioli ed humili abitationi non meno che nelle case de' grandi risplende una politia singolare onde riducono da tutte le parti et sono tutti *così inimici del mal governo et dell' otio* che si sono luoghi particolari nelle citta fabbricata di ordine pubblico ove quei del governo fanno serrar le genti vagabonde et otiosi o che non governano bene le cose loro bastando che o le moglie o altre dei lor congionti se ne querelino al magistrato et in quei luoghi sono costretti di lavorare et guadagnarsi le spese ancorchè non vogliano."—Contarini Relazione MS.

" Li popoli di questo paese sono nati al travaglio ed al stentare e tutti travagliano, chi per una via, chi per l'altra. . . . . Non s'usa servitori, non si veste di seta, non si tapezza le case, tutto è menaggio molto sottile e limitato."—Antº. Donat. Relazione, MS.

between Holland and the Inquisition. These had, as a matter of course, been confiscated as the strife went on. The buildings, farms, and funds, once the property of the Church, had not, however, been seized upon, as in other Protestant lands, by rapacious monarchs, and distributed among great nobles according to royal caprice. Monarchs might give the revenue of a suppressed convent to a cook, as reward for a successful pudding; the surface of Britain and the continent might be covered with abbeys and monasteries now converted into lordly palaces—passing thus from the dead hand of the Church into the idle and unproductive palm of the noble; but the ancient ecclesiastical establishments of the free Netherlands were changed into eleemosynary institutions, admirably organized and administered with wisdom and economy, where orphans of the poor, widows of those slain in the battles for freedom by land and sea, and the aged and the infirm, who had deserved well of the republic in the days of their strength, were educated or cherished at the expense of the public, thus endowed from the spoils of the Church.[23]

In Spain, monasteries upon monasteries were rising day by day, as if there were not yet receptacles enough for monks and priests, while thousands upon thousands of Spaniards were pressing into the ranks of the priesthood, and almost forcing themselves into monasteries, that they might be privileged to beg, because ashamed to work. In the United Netherlands the confiscated convents, with their revenues, were appropriated for the good of those who were too young or too old to labour, and too poor to maintain themselves

---

[23] "Si vedono in quelle città chiese antiche bellissime parte distrutte et parte senza imagini ridotti per i loro esercitii che non consistono in altro che all' ascoltar le domeniche e pochi altri giorni le prediche da' loro predicatori. Dell' entrate di queste chiese ch' erano gia dei prelati, dei monasteri, e dei sacerdoti mantengono un buon numero de hospitali nelle principale città del paese fabbrichati con molte spese, governati con bellissimi ordini et custoditi con gran politia ne quali nutriscono allevano et mantengono i vecchi impotenti, i figli orfani ed altri de' benemeriti dello Stato che hanno spesi i migliori anni o perso le vite nei loro servitii. Et a questi hospitali si applicheranno ancora l'entrate di quei pochi monasterii et collegi Teutonici che si rimangono, morti che siano quelli che le godono al presente."—Contarini, MS. Antonio Donato, too, speaks of these hospitals as model institutions.—Relazione, MS.

without work. Need men look further than to this simple fact to learn why Spain was decaying while the republic was rising ?

The ordinary budget of the United Provinces was about equal to that of England, varying not much from four millions of florins, or four hundred thousand pounds. But the extraordinary revenue was comparatively without limits, and there had been years, during the war, when the citizens had taxed themselves as highly as fifty per cent. on each individual income, and doubled the receipts of the exchequer.[24] The budget was proposed once a year, by the council of state, and voted by the States-General, who assigned the quota of each province ; that of Holland being always one-half of the whole, that of Zeeland sixteen per cent., and that of the other five of course in lesser proportions. The revenue was collected in the separate provinces, one-third of the whole being retained for provincial expenses, and the balance paid into the general treasury.[25] There was a public debt, the annual interest of which amounted to 200,000 florins. During the war, money had been borrowed at as high a rate as thirty-six per cent., but at the conclusion of hostilities the States could borrow at six per cent., and the whole debt was funded on that basis. Taxation was enormously heavy, but patriotism caused it to be borne with cheerfulness, and productive industry made it comparatively light. Rents were charged twenty-five per cent. A hundred per cent. was levied upon beer, wine, meat, salt, spirits. Other articles of necessity and luxury were almost as severely taxed.[26] It is not easy to enumerate the tax-list, scarcely anything foreign or domestic being exempted, while the grave error was often committed of taxing the same article, in different forms, four, five, and six times.

The people virtually taxed themselves, although the superstition concerning the State, as something distinct from and superior to the people, was to linger long and work infinite mischief among those seven republics which were never destined

[24] Contarini, MS.   [25] Ibid.   [6] Ibid.

to be welded theoretically and legally into a union. The sacredness of corporations had succeeded, in a measure, to the divinity which hedges kings. Nevertheless, those corporations were so numerous as to be effectively open to a far larger proportion of the population than, in those days, had ever dreamed before of participating in the Government. The magistracies were in general unpaid and little coveted, being regarded as a burthen and a responsibility rather than an object of ambition. The jurisconsults, called pensionaries, who assisted the municipal authorities, received, however, a modest salary, never exceeding 1500 florins a year.

These numerous bodies, provincial and municipal, elected themselves by supplying their own vacancies. The magistrates were appointed by the stadholder, on a double or triple nomination from the municipal board. This was not impartial suffrage nor manhood suffrage. The germ of a hateful burgher-oligarchy was in the system, but, as compared with Spain, where municipal magistracies were sold by the crown at public auction ; or with France, where every office in church, law, magistrature, or court was an object of merchandise disposed of in open market, the system was purity itself, and marked a great advance in the science of government.

It should never be forgotten, moreover, that while the presidents and judges of the highest courts of judicature in other civilized lands were at the mercy of an irresponsible sovereign, and held office—even although it had been paid for in solid specie—at his pleasure, the supreme justices of the high courts of appeal at the Hague were nominated by a senate, and confirmed by a stadholder, and that they exercised their functions for life,[27] or so long as they conducted themselves virtuously in their high office—*quamdiu se bene gesserint.*

If one of the great objects of a civilized community is to secure to all men their own—*ut sua tenerent*—surely it must be admitted that the republic was in advance of all contem-

[27] Contarini, MS.

porary States in the laying down of this vital principle, the independence of judges.

As to the army and navy of the United Provinces, enough has been said, in earlier chapters of these volumes, to indicate the improvements introduced by Prince Maurice, and now carried to the highest point of perfection ever attained in that period. There is no doubt whatever, that for discipline, experience, equipment, effectiveness of movement, and general organization, the army of the republic was the model army of Europe.[28] It amounted to but thirty thousand infantry and two thousand five hundred cavalry, but this number was a large one for a standing army at the beginning of the seventeenth century. It was composed of a variety of materials, Hollanders, Walloons, Flemings, Scotch, English, Irish, Germans, but all welded together into a machine of perfect regularity. The private foot-soldier received twelve florins for a so-called month of forty-two days, the drummer and corporal eighteen, the lieutenant fifty-two, and the captain one hundred and fifty florins.[29] Prompt payment was made every week.[30] Obedience was implicit ; mutiny, such as was of periodical recurrence in the archduke's army, entirely unknown. The slightest theft was punished with the gallows,[31] and there was therefore no thieving.

The most accurate and critical observers confessed, almost against their will, that no army in Europe could compare with the troops of the States. As to the famous regiments of Sicily, and the ancient legions of Naples and Milan, a distinguished Venetian envoy, who had seen all the camps and courts of Christendom, and was certainly not disposed to overrate the Hollanders at the expense of the Italians, if any rivalry between them had been possible, declared that every private soldier in the republic was fit to be a captain in any

[28] "Ma tutta gente esquisita per la propria conditione per l' habito gia fermo al patire et al combattere per tanti anni di guerra et per la singolare obbedienza accompagnata da tutti gli ordini della vera militare disciplina essendo tenuti in continua esercitatione de' capitani es oggetti di gran qualità." —Contarini, MS.

[29] Ibid.   [30] Ibid.

[31] Ibid. "Ogni minimo furto si castiga con la forca."

Italian army; while, on the other hand, there was scarcely an Italian captain who would be accepted as a private in any company of the States.[32] So low had the once-famous soldiery of Alva, Don John, and Alexander Farnese descended.

The cavalry of the republic was even more perfectly organized than was the infantry. "I want words to describe its perfection," said Contarini.[33] The pay was very high, and very prompt. A captain received four hundred florins a month (of forty-two days), a lieutenant one hundred and eighty florins, and other officers and privates in proportion.[34] These rates would be very high in our own day. When allowance is made for the difference in the value of money at the respective epochs, the salaries are prodigious; but the thrifty republic found its account in paying well and paying regularly the champions on whom so much depended, and by whom such splendid services had been rendered.[35]

While the soldiers in the pay of Queen Elizabeth were crawling to her palace gates to die of starvation before her eyes; while the veterans of Spain and of Italy had organized themselves into a permanent military, mutinous republic, on the soil of the so-called obedient Netherland, because they were left by their masters without clothing or food; the cavalry and infantry of the Dutch commonwealth, thanks to the organizing spirit and the wholesome thrift of the burgher authorities, were contented, obedient, well fed, well clothed, and well paid; devoted to their Government, and ever ready to die in its defence.

Nor was it only on the regular army that reliance was

---

[32] Posso affirmar a Vostra Serenità che qual si voglia fante privato fra quelle militie si stimarebbe qui buono per comandare una compagnia tanto è declinato in Italia e l'uso et l'antico splendore della militar disciplina che ci bisogna impararla dalle nationi stranierechepur l'appriessero daquelle di questa provincia. Et a tale sono arrivati i gradi della militia che molti presso di noi capitani difficilmente presso di loro sarebbono admessi per buoni soldati."—Contarini, MS.
"Le qualità delle militie terrestri

che servono in questi Stati sono senza dubbio le migliori di Europa e del Mondo," says Antonio Donato, adding that among them "the first place is held by the English infantry, best beloved by the natives, brave, patient veterans, whose habits and character are in conformity with the country."—Relazione, MS.

[33] Ibid. "Della Cavalleria debbo dire poco poiche poco si può dire che arrivi ad esprimere la sua perfezione."

[34] Ibid.   [35] Ibid.

placed. On the contrary, every able-bodied man in the country was liable to be called upon to serve, at any moment, in the militia. All were trained to arms, and provided with arms, and there had been years during this perpetual war in which one man out of three of the whole male population was ready to be mustered at any moment into the field.[36]

Even more could be said in praise of the navy than has been stated of the armies of the republic ; for the contemporary accounts of foreigners, and of foreigners who were apt to be satirical, rather than enthusiastic, when describing the institutions, leading personages, and customs of other countries, seemed ever to speak of the United Provinces in terms of eulogy. In commerce, as in war, the naval supremacy of the republic was indisputable. It was easy for the States to place two thousand vessels of war in commission, if necessary, of tonnage varying from four hundred to twelve hundred tons, to man them with the hardiest and boldest sailors in the world, and to despatch them with promptness to any quarter of the globe.[37]

It was recognised as nearly impossible to compel a warvessel of the republic to surrender.[38] Hardly an instance was

[36] " Si dimostrano tutti quei popoli così inchinati alla militia per la difesa commune che si piacesse a' Serenissimi Stati di ricercare il terzo uomo da tutto il paese offerirano essi che pochi si sarebbono i quali non desiderassero che a loro ne toccasse la sorte tanto si rende piacevole all' orecchie di quelle genti il nome della guerra."—Contarini, MS.

[37] Contarini, MS. "Le forze del mare dei Serenissimi Stati sono veramente estimate le maggiori che posse havere altro Principe per la copia dei vascelli et per il numero di marinari et per la qualità degli uomini di comando. Tenendosi per cosa certa che possan essere in quelle Provincie settanta mille marinari buoni et intelligenti non solo per l'uso delle navigationi ma insieme ancora per le battaglie navali nelle quali si adoperano per soldati et ognuno di essi per la singolare attitudine et ordinaria assuefattione è solito di far più che molti soldati insieme. Et ogni volta

che volessero fare un sforzo per qualunque occasione potrebbono metter insieme il numero di due mille vascelli sufficienti per ogni fattione senza far in essi spese di momento per la prontezza et delle genti e dei vascelli medesimi sempre apparrechiate in mano de particolari." Antonio Donato puts the number of Dutch vessels of all classes at nearly 6,000. Relazione, MS. "This fury for dominion upon the sea," he says, " increases every day, and is sustained by such assiduity, intelligence, and interest as to show that it is the business of all, and the whole business, strength, and security of the States."

[38] "Mentre sono certi che gli Hollandesi piu tosto che lasciarsi vincere darebbero fuoco al proprio vascello per abbruciare con se medesimi l'inimico insieme. Onde con questi due termini della clemenza (agli inimici) *e del sommo rigore sono fatti padroni del mar.*"—Contarini, MS.

on her naval record of submission, even to far superior force, while it was filled with the tragic but heroic histories of commanders who had blown their ships, with every man on board, into the air, rather than strike their flag. Such was the character, and such the capacity of the sea-born republic.

That republic had serious and radical defects, but the design remained to be imitated and improved upon, centuries afterwards. The history of the rise and progress of the Dutch republic is a leading chapter in the history of human liberty.

The great misfortune of the commonwealth of the United Provinces, next to the slenderness of its geographical proportions, was the fact that it was without a centre and without a head, and therefore not a nation capable of unlimited vitality. There were seven states. Each claimed to be sovereign. The pretension on the part of several of them was ridiculous. Overyssel, for example, contributed two and three-quarters per cent. of the general budget. It was a swamp of twelve hundred square miles in extent, with some heath-spots interspered, and it numbered perhaps a hundred thousand inhabitants. The doughty Count of Embden alone could have swallowed up such sovereignty, have annexed all the buckwheat patches and cranberry marshes of Overyssel to his own meagre territories, and nobody the wiser.

Zeeland, as we have seen, was disposed at a critical moment to set up its independent sovereignty. Zeeland, far more important than Overyssel, had a revenue of perhaps five hundred thousand dollars,—rather a slender budget for an independent republic, wedged in as it was by the most powerful empires of the earth, and half drowned by the ocean, from which it had scarcely emerged.

There was therefore no popular representation, and on the other hand no executive head. As sovereignty must be exercised in some way, however, in all living commonwealths, and as a low degree of vitality was certainly not the defect of those bustling provinces, the supreme functions had now fallen into the hands of Holland.

While William the Silent lived, the management of war, foreign affairs, and finance, for the revolted provinces, was in his control. He was aided by two council boards, but the circumstances of history and the character of the man had invested him with an inevitable dictatorship.

After his death, at least after Leicester's time, the powers of the state-council, the head of which, Prince Maurice, was almost always absent at the wars, fell into comparative disuse. The great functions of the confederacy passed into the possession of the States-General. That body now came to sit permanently at the Hague. The number of its members, deputies from the seven provinces—envoys from those seven immortal and soulless sovereigns—was not large. The extraordinary assembly held at Bergen-op-Zoom for confirmation of the truce was estimated by Bentivoglio at eight hundred. Bentivoglio, who was on the spot, being then nuncius at Brussels, ought to have been able to count them, yet it is very certain that the number was grossly exaggerated.

At any rate the usual assembly at the Hague rarely amounted to one hundred members. The presidency was changed once a week, the envoy of each province taking his turn as chairman.

Olden-Barneveld, as member for Holland, was always present in the diet. As Advocate-General of the leading province, and keeper of its great seal, more especially as possessor of the governing intellect of the whole commonwealth, he led the administration of Holland, and as the estates of Holland contributed more than half of the whole budget of the confederacy,[39] it was a natural consequence of the actual supremacy of that province, and of the vast legal and political experience of the Advocate, that Holland should

[39] Gelderland contributed 4½ per cent.
Utrecht   „   5¾   „
Friesland   „   11½   „
Overyssel   „   2¾   „
Groningen   „   6½   „
Zeeland   „   13½   „
Holland   „   55½   „

           100

govern the confederacy, and that Barneveld should govern Holland.

The States-General remained virtually supreme, receiving envoys from all the great powers, sending abroad their diplomatic representatives, to whom the title and rank of ambassador was freely accorded, and dealing in a decorous and dignified way with all European affairs. The ability of the republican statesmen was as fully recognised all over the earth, as was the genius of their generals and great naval commanders.

The People did not exist ; but this was merely because, in theory, the People had not been invented. It was exactly because there was a People—an energetic and intelligent People—that the republic was possible.

No scheme had yet been devised for laying down in primary assemblies a fundamental national law, for distributing the various functions of governmental power among selected servants, for appointing representatives according to population or property, and for holding all trustees responsible at reasonable intervals to the nation itself.

Thus government was involved, fold within fold, in successive and concentric municipal layers. The States-General were the outer husk, of which the separate town-council was the kernel or bulb. Yet the number of these executive and legislative boards was so large, and the whole population comparatively so slender, as to cause the original inconveniences from so incomplete a system to be rather theoretic than practical. In point of fact, almost as large a variety of individuals served the State as would perhaps have been the case under a more philosophically arranged democracy. The difficulty was rather in obtaining a candidate for the post than in distributing the posts among candidates.

Men were occupied with their own affairs. In proportion to their numbers they were more productive of wealth than any other nation then existing. An excellent reason why the people were so well governed, so productive, and so enterprising, was the simple fact that they were an educated people. There was hardly a Netherlander—man, woman, or child—that could not read and write. The school was the common property of the people, paid for among the municipal expenses. In the cities, as well as in the rural districts, there were not only common schools but classical schools. In the burgher families it was rare to find boys who had not been taught Latin, or girls unacquainted with French. Capacity to write and speak several modern languages was very common, and there were many individuals in every city, neither professors nor pedants, who had made remarkable progress in science and classical literature.[40] The position, too, of women in the commonwealth proved a high degree of civilization. They are described as virtuous, well-educated, energetic, sovereigns in their households, and accustomed to direct all the business at home. "It would be ridiculous," said Donato, "to see a man occupying himself with domestic house-keeping. The women do it all, and command absolutely." The Hollanders, so rebellious against Church and King, accepted with meekness the despotism of woman.

The great movement of emancipation from political and ecclesiastical tyranny had brought with it a general advancement of the human intellect. The foundation of the Leyden university in memory of the heroism displayed by the burghers during the siege was as noble a monument as had ever been raised by a free people jealous of its fame. And the scientific lustre of the university well sustained the nobility of its origin. The proudest nation on earth might be more proud of a seat of learning, founded thus amidst carnage and tears, whence so much of profound learning and brilliant literature had already been diffused. The classical labours of Joseph Scaliger, Heinsius — father and son — the elder Dousa, almost as famous with his pen in Latin poetry as his sword had made him in the vernacular chronicle; of Dousa the son, whom Grotius called "the crown and flower of all good learning, too soon snatched away by

---

[40] Antonio Donato, Relazione, MS. Grot. Paralell. Rer. publ. ed. Meerman, iii. 51. Van Kampen, i. 608, 609.

envious death, than whom no man more skilled in poetry, more consummate in acquaintance with ancient science and literature, had ever lived;"[41] of Hugo Grotius himself, who at the age of fifteen had taken his doctor's degree at Leyden, who as a member of Olden-Barneveldt's important legation to France and England very soon afterwards had excited the astonishment of Henry IV. and Elizabeth, who had already distinguished himself by editions of classic poets, and by original poems and dramas in Latin, and was already, although but twenty-six years of age, laying the foundation of that magnificent reputation as a jurist, a philosopher, a historian, and a statesman, which was to be one of the enduring glories of humanity,—all these were the precious possessions of the high school of Leyden.

The still more modern university of Franeker, founded amid the din of perpetual warfare in Friesland, could at least boast the name of Arminius, whose theological writings and whose expansive views were destined to exert such influence over his contemporaries and posterity.

The great history of Hoofd, in which the splendid pictures and the impassioned drama of the great war of independence were to be preserved for his countrymen through all time, was not yet written. It was soon afterwards, however, to form not only a chief source of accurate information as to the great events themselves, but a model of style never since surpassed by any prose writer in either branch of the German tongue.

Had Hoofd written for a wider audience, it would be difficult to name a contemporary author of any nation whose work would have been more profoundly studied or more generally admired.

But the great war had not waited to be chronicled by the classic and impassioned Hoofd. Already there were thorough and exhaustive narrators of what was instinctively felt to be one of the most pregnant episodes of human his-

---

[41] Van Kampen, i. 608.   Grot. Paralell. Rer. pub. iii. 49.

tory. Bor of Utrecht, a miracle of industry, of learning, of unwearied .perseverance, was already engaged in the production of those vast folios in which nearly all the great transactions of the forty years' war were conscientiously portrayed, with a comprehensiveness of material and an impartiality of statement, such as might seem almost impossible for a contemporary writer. Immersed in attentive study and profound contemplation, he seemed to lift his tranquil head from time to time over the wild ocean of those troublous times, and to survey with accuracy without being swayed or appalled by the tempest. There was something almost sublime in his steady, unimpassioned gaze.

Emanuel van Meteren, too, a plain Protestant merchant of Antwerp and Amsterdam, wrote an admirable history of the war and of his own times, full of precious details, especially rich in statistics—a branch of science which he almost invented—which still remains as one of the leading authorities, not only for scholars, but for the general reader.

Reyd and Burgundius, the one the Calvinist private secretary of Lewis William, the other a warm Catholic partisan, both made invaluable contemporaneous contributions to the history of the war.

The trophies already secured by the Netherlanders in every department of the fine arts, as well as the splendour which was to enrich the coming epoch, are too familiar to the world to need more than a passing allusion.

But it was especially in physical science that the republic was taking a leading part in the great intellectual march of the nations.

The very necessities of its geographical position had forced it to pre-eminence in hydraulics and hydrostatics. It had learned to transform water into dry land with a perfection attained by no nation before or since. The wonders of its submarine horticulture were the despair of all gardeners in the world.

And as in this gentlest of arts, so also in the dread science of war, the republic had been the instructor of mankind.

The youthful Maurice and his cousin Lewis William had so restored and improved the decayed intelligence of antique strategy, that the greybeards of Europe became docile pupils in their school. The mathematical teacher of Prince Maurice amazed the contemporary world with his combinations and mechanical inventions ; the flying chariots of Simon Stevinus seeming products of magical art.

Yet the character of the Dutch intellect was averse to sorcery. The small but mighty nation, which had emancipated itself from the tyranny of Philip and of the Holy Inquisition, was foremost to shake off the fetters of superstition. Out of Holland came the first voice to rebuke one of the hideous delusions of the age. While grave magistrates and sages of other lands were exorcising the devil by murdering his supposed victims, John Wier, a physician of Grave, boldly denounced the demon which had taken possession, not of the wizards, but of the judges.

The age was lunatic and sick, and it was fitting that the race which had done so much for the physical and intellectual emancipation of the world, should have been the first to apply a remedy for this monstrous madness. Englishmen and their descendants were drowning and hanging witches in New England, long after John Wier had rebuked and denounced the belief in witchcraft.

It was a Zeelander, too, who placed the instrument in the hand of Galileo by which that daring genius traced the movements of the universe, and who, by another wondrous invention, enabled future discoverers to study the infinite life which lies all around us, hidden not by its remoteness but its minuteness. Zacharias Jansens of Middelburg, in 1590, invented both the telescope and the microscope.

The wonder-man of Alkmaar, Cornelius Drebbel, who performed such astounding feats for the amusement of Rudolph of Germany and James of Britain, is also supposed to have invented the thermometer and the barometer. But this claim has been disputed. The inventions of Jansens are proved.

Willebrod Snellius, mathematical professor of Leyden, introduced the true method of measuring the degrees of longitude and latitude, and Huygens, who had seen his manuscripts, asserted that Snellius had invented, before Descartes, the doctrine of refraction.

But it was especially to that noble band of heroes and martyrs, the great navigators and geographical discoverers of the republic, that science is above all indebted.

Nothing is more sublime in human story than the endurance and audacity with which those pioneers of the sixteenth and seventeenth centuries confronted the nameless horrors of either pole, in the interests of commerce, and for the direct purpose of enlarging the bounds of the human intellect.

The achievements, the sufferings, and the triumphs of Barendz and Cordes, Heemskerk, Van der Hagen, and many others, have been slightly indicated in these pages. The contributions to botany, mineralogy, geometry, geography, and zoology, of Linschoten, Plancius, Wagenaar, and Houtmann, and so many other explorers of pole and tropic, can hardly be overrated.

The Netherlanders had wrung their original fatherland out of the grasp of the ocean. They had confronted for centuries the wrath of that ancient tyrant, ever ready to seize the prey of which he had been defrauded.

They had waged fiercer and more perpetual battle with a tyranny more cruel than the tempest, with an ancient superstition more hungry than the sea. It was inevitable that a race, thus invigorated by the ocean, cradled to freedom by their conflicts with its power, and hardened almost to invincibility by their struggle against human despotism, should be foremost among the nations in the development of political, religious, and commercial freedom.

The writer now takes an affectionate farewell of those who have followed him with an indulgent sympathy as he has attempted to trace the origin and the eventful course

of the Dutch commonwealth. If by his labours a generous
love has been fostered for that blessing, without which
everything that this earth can afford is worthless—freedom
of thought, of speech, and of life—his highest wish has been
fulfilled.

INDEX.

The *Roman numerals* indicate the *volumes*, the *Arabic numerals* the *pages*. Names having the prefix of De, or Van, are generally, but not invariably, placed under their prefix.

BAX, Paul and Marcellus, iii, 338, 339.
Narrow escape of Marcellus, 340. A
suggestion of his and its brilliant
results, 423—433. Marcellus at Nieu-
port, iv, 30. 34. Paul wounded at
Sluys, 206. At Mulheim, 235, 236.
His prompt action at Bergen-op-
Zoom, 250, 251.

BEALE, Mr, Leicester's curt eulogium
on, ii, 327.

BEAUFORT, Duchess of, *See* Gabrielle.

BELIN, Count, threats of Sega against,
iii, 125. Wounded and captured,
333. His surrender of Ardres, 393,
394.

BELLIEVRE, Pomponne de ; purport of
his "long oration" to the Dutch envoys, i, 290. Greed of his wife, iv,
375. *See* ii, 305. iii, 126. 234.

BENITES, his command at the Kowenstyn, i, 207.

BENTIVOGLIO, Cardinal, point whereon
he was in error, ii, 57 *note*. On taxation in the Netherlands, iii, 375. On
the Infanta's character, 588. *See* iv,
368. 395. 523. 565.

BENTIVOGLIO, nephew of the above, at
the rescue of the Kowenstyn, i, 220.
Wounded, iii, 148.

BERENDRECHT, Jacques van der Meer,
Baron of, commandant of Ostend, the
man for his post, iv, 190. Foiling
the enemy, 191. Killed, 194.

BERGEN-OP-ZOOM, Leicester's halt at,
ii, 35. Situation of the city, 537.
Result of Parma's attempt to carry
it by siege, 538. 541—544. Du Tor-
rail's double attack upon it, iv, 250.
Prompt course of Governor Bax and
heroism of the women, 251. Peace
conferences with Spain carried on
here, 517—519. 526. Extraordinary
assembly, 565.

BERLAYMONT, bishop of Cambray, iii,
335.

BERLAYMONT, Count, nickname given
to the patriots by, i, 176.—Hiring an
assassin to kill Maurice, iii, 297, 298.
299 *note*. Maurice in pursuit of
him, iv, 208.

BERLOT, Claude, command assigned
to, ii, 45.

BEVILACQUA, at the rescue of the Kowenstyn, i, 220.

BIEVRY, Captain Jacques de, hazardous
exploit shared by, iii, 262, 263. Appointed commandant at Ostend, iv,
189. Wounded and *hors de combat*,
ibid. Fellow sufferers, 194.

BILLY. *See* Robles.

BIRON, Armand, French marshal, at

the battle of Ivry, iii, 51. 54, 55.
Rescued by his king, 90. *See* 58. 66.

BIRON, Charles, Baron, son of the
above, iii, 121. Rescued by his king,
344. His stupendous treachery, and
its result, iv, 104, 105. His object,
104 *note*. 150. *See* iii, 139. 140. 143.
iv, 149. 164. 377.

BLAEUW, or Blaauw, William, the
Amsterdam printer, his geographical
publications, iii, 549. 558. Party use
made of his types, iv, 477. An etymological query, 478 *note*.

BLOUNT, Christopher, and his brother,
spying upon Leicester, i, 375, 376.

BLOUNT, Thomas, reporting result of
inquest on Amy Robsart, i, 369.

BOBADIL, Spanish officer, ii, 12.

BODLEY, Sir Thomas, iii, 32. Defects
in his character and their results,
33, 34. *See* 172. 181.

BODMAN, William, volunteer diplomatist between Parma and Elizabeth, i, 480. 491. Reporting progress, 493, 494. Condoling with
Grafigny, 511, 512. In secret con-
clave with English statesmen, 513—
517. *See* 500. 509. 510. 519. 520. 524.

BOIS-LE-DUC, Brabant, its importance
to the Spaniards, i, 174. Attacked
by the States troops : Their subsequent repulse, 175—177. A blow
from a dead man's hand, 177. Hair-
breadth escapes of some of the
leaders, 178. What success would
have produced, 178, 179. Effect of
a frost upon a renewed attempt to
besiege it, iv, 66. Embargo laid on
the town by the Spanish mutineers,
128. *See* iii, 103, 104.

BONE-FLOUR bread and its effects during Paris famine, iii, 65.

BONN captured by Schenk, ii, 348.
421. Retaken by the Spaniards, 549.

BOR of Utrecht : character of his history of his own times, iv, 569.

BORGIA, Pope of Rome, his paternal
allocation of the new world, iv, 1.5
note. Respect paid by the Dutch
thereto, 130.

BORY, Antwerp clockmaker, associated
with Gianibelli in his project against
Parma's bridge, i, 191.

BOTSCHKAY, Stephen, position achieved by, iv, 218. Poisoned : his death-
bed recommendation, 278.

BOUCHER, father, the one-eyed, iii, 63.

BOUILLON, Duke of, *See* Turenne.

BOURBON, Charles, cardinal, called also
Charles X, put forward by the Guises
as heir to the Crown : his character,

495, 496. Reporting the results of his intrigues 498—500. ii, 290. 293 note, 294, 295. Much depressed : in spirits again, ii, 296. Credulous himself, and inoculating English statesmen with his credulity, 297, 298. 301. See i, 516. 519. 521. 522.

DE MAISSE, Hurault, envoy from Henry IV to Elizabeth, iii, 467. His conference with her, 468—471. Difference between his report and hers, 481, 482.

DE MASIERES, governor of Gertruydenberg, killed, iii, 262.

DE MEXIA, Ardres besieged and captured by, iii, 393.

DEMOCRACY, tendency of mankind towards, iii, 513.

DE MORLANS, envoy from Henry IV, iii, 254. Results of his eloquence, 310—312.

DENDERMONDE, treachery of the governor of, i, 21. Capitulated, 139. See 136. 138.

DENMARK, sovereignty of Holland offered to the king of, ii, 81, 82. Surmised effect of Indian gold, 248. His offer of mediation to Philip, and advice of Parma thereon, 303, 304. Sending envoys to the States, iv, 389. 459. 489. 494. See ii, 447. 500. iv, 138.

DERBY, Henry Stanley, Earl of, taking farce for reality, ii, 299. One in an embassy to Parma, 358. No match for the latter and his agents, 360. His spirited reply to a threat of invasion, 395. See ii, 385. 393. 452. iv, 160.

DE RONSOY, Count, slain, iii, 334.

DE ROSNES, see Rosnes.

DE ROSNY, see Sully.

DE RUSSY, French envoy at the Hague, iv, 368.

DE SANCY, French minister, on the shilly-shallying of England, iii, 314, 315 note. His arrival in England, 372. 397. His interviews with Elizabeth and Burghley, and dignified rebuke to the latter, 398, 399.

DES PRUNEAUX, French envoy to the States-General, i, 56. His extravagant professions relative to the cavalier treatment of the Dutch agents, 57. His character, 58. Result of his eloquence upon the deliberations of the States-General, 60, 61. 63, 64. Complimentary gift to him, 64. Rebuking both his own court and the States-General for neglected promises, 94. 95. His pronunciation on the articles of annexation, 96. His emotions and pro-

verb utterances on parting with the Dutch envoys, 97.

DE VARENNE, sent by Henry IV to Spain: alleged object of his mission, iii, 304. His real name and degrading antecedents, 305, 306. 306 note. Opposite views as to his errand : Calvaert's report, 307, 308. Mendoza's reply to a request of his, 309. His own report of his Spanish mission, and subsequent mission to Elizabeth, 309 note.

DE VEER, Gerrit, diarist of the Arctic expedition, on the egg-tree tradition, iii, 562, 563. On the vicissitudes of the voyage, 564. 566. 569. 573, 574.

DE VEGA, Parma's life saved by, i, 195.

DEVENTER, Leicester's protégé, see Proninck.

DEVENTER, the historian, value of a work of, iii, 306 note.

DEVENTER, city of, its importance: seized by the English, ii, 153, 154. Consequences of Stanley's appointment to its governorship, 155—161. Treacherous surrender of the city to the Spaniards, 169—172. Conditions imposed on the citizens, 173. Fate of the chief traitors, 177, 178. Results of the treason, 181. 186. 206. 210. Invested by Maurice, and recaptured for the States, iii, 105—110. Again taken by the Spaniards, iv, 234. See iii, 73, 102. iv, 241. 261.

DE VICH, a good soldier, but only half a man, iii, 348, 349.

DE VIDOSAN, responsible post inherited by, iii, 367. Evidences of his incompetency, 367, 368. His fatal mistake, 373. Killed, 374.

DE VILLARS, admiral of France, boasting of his successes at Rouen, iii, 142, 143. Beseeching help, 145. Goes over to Henry IV, 331. Terms of the bargain, ibid note. His equipment and fate at the siege of Dourlens, 331, 332. Short-sightedness of his murderer : censure passed on him, 333. See 233.

DEXTER, Ralph, English engineer at Ostend, iv, 191.

D'HUMIERES, killed at Ham, iii, 325. Grief of the king, 326.

DIALYN, Paul, Polish envoy, his oration to and reception by the States-General, iii, 448, 449. Thence to England : how set down by Elizabeth, 450, 451.

DIEGO DE YEPES, Philip's confessor, announces his master's approaching end and receives his confession, iii, 504, 505. 509, 510.

DIEPPE, gallant victory of the English at, iii, 122 note. See 135. 147. 148. 478.

of its charter, iv, 132—135. Its third fleet, 244. English opposition to its monopolies, 247, 248. Result of its victory at Tydor, 249, 250. *See* iv, 380. 444, 445.

DUTCH, West India Company's charter, its conditions, &c. iv, 298—300. 388.

DU TERRAIL, his attack on and repulse at Bergen-op-Zoom, iv, 250, 251. Cause of his animosity to the States, 251. Result of his attempt upon Sluys, 257, 258.

EAST India Companies, iii, 577. *See* Dutch East India Company.

EDICTS: of Nemours, i, 131. Of Nantes, iii, 500.

EDMONDES, English envoy, iii, 242 *note*. On La Varenne's mission to Spain, 309 *note*. What the States thought and the queen said on his reception in the Netherlands, 595, 596.

EGMONT, Lamoral, Count, cruelty of his execution, i, 355. An ungrateful agent in the crime, ii, 68. *See* iii, 29. 71. 203. 318. 361, 362.

EGMONT, Count Philip, son of the above, sacrificing dignity for the sake of liberty, i, 232. A foremost man in the Spanish army, iii, 29. Boasting at Ivry, 53. His successful first and fatal second charge, 54, 55. *See* i. 258.

ELIZABETH, Queen: Frustration of her intended assassination, i, 2. Warnings sent to her from the continent, 3. Her advice to the provinces relative to Anjou, 11. 30. Her harsh treatment of sectaries, and comparative tolerance towards papists, 25, 26. Her alleged ground for putting papists to death, 27. Her refusal to recognize Mary Stuart as her successor, 28. How regarded by the prince of Orange: her conduct towards the Dutch provinces, 29, 30. French caricatures upon her, 42. Causes of timidity in her councils relative to Spain and the Netherlands: course favoured by her, 65. 66. Device to set France and Spain by the ears alleged against her, 70. Her position in the esteem of Dutch statesmen, 72, 73. Idea to which she still clung, 81. 86. Her tantalizing course towards the Provinces, 82. Deliberations and ultimate resolve of her council, 82—84. Her perplexities relative to the nature of the French king's offers to the provinces, 86. Real object contemplated by her government as between the Provinces and the French king, 87. Over-

subtlety of her lord-treasurer, 87, 88. Walsingham's comment on the impolicy of her proceedings, 89. Instructing Davison to encourage the Dutch people to rely upon her, 92. Their appeal through him to her, 93. Her true intentions towards the Netherlanders, 106. 107. Eloquence of a Spanish ambassador upon her "abominations," 124. Her persecution of her catholic subjects, its causes and its consequences, 127, 128. Compliment paid to her by Sixtus V, 133. Result of her intercession for Treslong, 150. Her encouraging assurances to the Antwerpers, 231. Mutual distrust between herself and Sainte Aldegonde, 264. 265. 266. 271. Anxiety of the latter to set himself right with her, 280, 281. Shape determined to be given by her to her alliance with the Hollanders: her diplomatic coquettings, 286—288. Conferences of her ministers and herself with the Dutch envoys, 290—295. 297. Ill effects of her holding her hand at a critical moment, 299. Chaffering attitude taken up both by herself and the Dutch States: the bone of contention, 299—301. Financial reasons for caution on the part of her advisers, 303. What she wanted from Holland, 304. Affection of the Pope and Philip of Spain towards her, 305. What in her apprehensions Mary Stuart embodied, 306. Her personal appearance, costume, and linguistic acquirements, 317, 318. Her conferences with and replies to a new Dutch deputation: ultimatum insisted on by her, 320, 321. 323. 325. 326—329. 329—331. Her attitude on learning of the fall of Antwerp, 332. Her encouraging letters to the States, 333. 334. Still in a chaffering humour, 335. Motive from which her parsimony sprang, 336. A truth thoroughly comprehended by her, 338. Becoming furious: upbraiding the Dutch envoys: terms at length agreed on, 339—341. Frank submission of Prince Maurice to the conditions required by her, 341—343. Perplexing effect of her caprices, 345. 352. Her conduct towards Leicester in money matters, 346—351. Her manifesto on espousing the Dutch cause, and charges against Spain therein, 354—357. Her animus towards Sir Philip Sidney, 358. 360. Appointment she ultimately gave him, 362. Her unwavering affection for Leicester, 370. Why she made common cause with

VOL. IV.—2 Q

against him, 265. 275. His foray into Brabant, 267. His report on the capture of Breda, iii, 15. Knuckling under to his old pupil, 261. His marriage and its accompaniments, 319. Hunting brigands, 337. Quarrelling with Maurice: King Philip's attempt upon his fidelity, 356. At the siege of Turnhout, 426. 429. Affair from which he was excluded, iv, 5. His death: summing up of his character, 275. See i, 200. 424. 520. ii. 39. 79. 86. 91. 137. 157. 158. 188. 215, 216. 243. 257. 325. 327. 350. 355. 413. iii, 7.

HOLLAND, its physical features, population, &c., i, 8. Medal emblematic of its forlorn condition, 18. Charge against it and Zeeland of indifference to the fate of Antwerp, 171. Their bearing in reference to a reconciliation with Spain, 267, 268. Influence on their prosperity of the subjugation of the Belgian cities, 269. England's stake in the safety of the Islands, 374—376. 381. Era inaugurated by England and Holland, 382. State of the Islands after twenty years' war: pictures drawn by Leicester and his suite, 383—386. Naval strength, and contempt for Philip's intended armada, 386—388. Its complaint as to its share in the State Council, iii, 34. Ever ready to bear its quota of taxation, 375, 376. Its dealing with the users of starch in a time of scarcity, 377. Its progress in silk manufacture, iv, 231. Omnipotence of Advocate Barneveldt, 300. Cities opposed to a truce, 504, 505. Their submission, 514. Its per centage of contribution to general fund, 559. 565 note. See Netherlands. Zeeland.

HOLY League, scheme contemplated by the, i, 5. 'Madam League,' 41. Its chief, 45. Conclusion of the treaty whereon it was based: its parties and objects, 113, 114. Its progress, 116, 117. Position of European rulers and peoples at its advent, 118, 119. Its manifesto issued: scope thereof, 119. 120. Henry of Valois its plaything ii, 341. Its intents with regard to England, 346. Its head, and its chief commander, 400. Pursuing its objects in Paris: Guise's triumphs: its first victims at the stake, 422—431. More papist than Pope Sixtus, iii, 45. 61. Bent on dismembering France, 46. Defeat of its forces at Ivry, 52—58. Its envoys in conference with Henry IV and his representatives, 66—68. 233—

237. Triumphant in Paris, 84, 85. 89. 125—127. Burnt in effigy, 242. Outgeneralled by Henry, 245. Departure of its garrison, 247. Costly and useless to Philip, 290. 305. 315. Dead and buried, 409. See. iii, 139—144. 147. iv, 57.

HOOFD's great history of the War of Independence, iv, 568.

HOOGSTRAATEN, seized and fortified by the Spanish mutineers, iv, 92, 100. 102. Their reception of Maurice there and delivery of the town to him, 129, 130.

HOUTMANN brothers, pioneer Dutch navigators, iii, 577.

HOUTMANN, Frederick, governor of Amboyna, iv, 423.

HOUWAERTS, John Baptist, description of his pageant, vision, &c. in honour of Archduke Ernest, iii, 285—289.

HOWARD of Effingham, Charles Lord, Lord Admiral, ii, 204. 407. 445. A trinity he trusted never to be saved by, 448. His defiant bearing and his complaints, 449—451. Complement of his fleet: his chief officers, 454, 455. His prayer to the queen, 457. His fleet at sea: the fight with the Armada, 474. 479—505. Neglect of, and ravages of sickness among his sailors afterwards: his griefs thereat, 524. Heading a new attack on Spain, iii, 384. Result of his over-cautiousness, 388.

HUGUENOTS, characteristic utterances of an old leader of the, i. 25. Hatred of Henry of Valois towards them, 38. Their conduct before battle: their royal chieftain, 50. Their views as to the results of an alliance between France and the States-General, 59, 60. Promulgation of the edict of Nemours against them, 131. Fighting at Ivry, iii, 55. Hanging their heads in despair, 245. 252. Their leaders denounced by Henry IV, 591, 592. Their numbers, strength, and influence in France, iv, 373, 374. 376. Efforts of Henry to set them against each other, 377.

HULST, iii, 100. Captured by Maurice, 115. Subsequent surrender to the Spaniards: alleged slaughter on the occasion, 394—396.

HUMAN fat, why esteemed by the Dutch surgeons, iv, 74.

HUNGARY, iv. 104.

HUNSDON, Henry Lord, ii, 204. His army a fiction, 451. 515. Grumbled at by Leicester, 520.

HUY, captured and recaptured, iii, 319.

IDIAQUEZ, Don Juan de, secretary of state

KOEWORDEN, iii, 5. *See* Coeworden.

KOWENSTYN and Blawgaren Dykes, how proposed to be dealt with by William the Silent, i, 141—143. Successful opposition of the Antwerpers to his plans, 152. Their too-late repentance, 161. The Kowenstyn taken by the Spaniards: forts erected by them upon it, 161, 162. Determination of the patriots to attempt to regain it; their tactics while preparing for the assault, 205. Its extent: labour expended by Parma in fortifying it, 206, 207. Incidents of the first attack, 208, 209. The like of the second attack, 209—213. Expulsion of the Spaniards and piercing of the Dyke, 213, 214. Folly of the patriot leaders in their hour of triumph, 215. Heroism and final victory of the Spaniards, 215—225. Blunder upon blunder, 299.

KOWENSTYN, Seigneur de, why he went over to the Spaniards, i, 161.

LA BOURLOTTE, (*not* Barlotte) Colonel, iii, 582. iv, 41, killed at Nieuport, 49.

LA FERE, town of, held in pledge by Farnese, iii, 138. 366. *see* 391. 393.

LA FERTÉ, iii, 319, besieged and relieved, 326.

LAGNY, iii, 78. 81. Captured by Parma and the garrison butchered, 81—83. Retaken by Henry IV, 90.

LAMBALLE, Brittany, fatal accident to La Noue at, iii, 124.

LAMBERT Heinrichzoon, "pretty Lambert," capturing a Dunkirk pirate vessel, iv, 251. Comrade with Heemskirk at the attack on the Spanish fleet, 324, 325. Playing the ambassador in a way to give offence, 505—508.

LA MOTTE, Valentin Pardieu de, Count of Everbeck, his attempt upon Ostend: success converted into failure, i. 186, 187. His fort on the Kowenstyn, 207. His cue in his conference with Elizabeth's representative, 495. His assurance to Parma: Fort captured by him, ii, 262. Outstripped by the Duchmen, 499. His command at the relief of Paris, iii, 75, 76. 81. In a mural caricature, 223. Implicated in a poison-plot, 300. Recaptures Huy, 319. Occasion of his death; his career, brutalities, &c. 327—329. *See* ii, 36.

LANFRANCHI, Antwerp merchant, on the effect of Spanish domination, ii, 370.

LA NOUE, " Iron-armed," French Huguenot officer, on the apathy of the German princes, 35, 36. Terms of his

release from captivity : his views on the chances of Antwerp, 232, 233. His estimate of Sainte Aldegonde, 283. His advice to Henry IV, iii, 58. His harangue to the starving Parisians, 68. Wounded, 85. His work while in captivity: occasion of his death, 123, 124. *See* Teligny.

LANUZA, John of, why put to death, iii, 534.

LANZAVECCHIA, Edward, governor of Breda and Gertruydenberg, iii, 6. On the wrong scent, 11. Cashiered, 15.

LARCHER, Paris magistrate, put to death : his crime, iii, 127.

LAVARDIN, French general, iii, 140. Wounded while rescuing his king, 141

LEAGUE. *See* Holy League.

LEFFINGEN, its position, &c, iv, 11: taken by Maurice, 12. Panic and rout of the Dutch, 18—22. Dutch and Spanish writers on the affair, 22 *note*. *See* 41.

LEICESTER, Robert Dudley Earl of, ("the gipsy ") his apprehensions concerning Sainte Aldegonde, and change of opinions thereon, i, 266. 275. 280. Fillip given to his ambition by the refusal of France to aid the Netherlands, 289. His encouraging assurances to the Dutch envoys, 293, 294. Characterising some of them, 311. 313. Desire of the States for his leadership, 335. Elizabeth's regard for him, 340. Tender of service to him from Prince Maurice, 342, 343. Nominated to the post he coveted, 345. His troubles at the outset; character of his courtship of the queen, 346. Financial squabbles between them : his complaints and her avarice, 347—351. Rendering thanks where thanks were due, 352. His entry into Flushing, 365. His immediate ancestors and their fate : lavish bounty of the queen towards him, 366. Romance of his character : his Jesuit accuser, 367. Monstrous crimes imputed to him, 368. His animus against the Queen of Scots, 369. His queen's firm affection: why called the "gipsy": his magnificent attire, 370. His progress through Holland, banquettings, pageants, &c, 371, 372. Indiscretions of speech : spies and libellers about him, 373, 374. Vehement in his advocacy of the alliance with Holland, 381 *note*. 384. On the naval strength of the Hollanders and their enthusiasm for Elizabeth, 386. 388, 389. On Drake's expedition and Philip's dread of it, 387. Nature of his authority in Holland : his queen's instructions· advice of the

THE END.

VALUABLE AND INTERESTING WORKS

FOR

PUBLIC & PRIVATE LIBRARIES,

PUBLISHED BY HARPER & BROTHERS, NEW YORK.

☞ *For a full List of Books suitable for Libraries published by* HARPER & BROTH-
ERS, *see* HARPER'S CATALOGUE, *which may be had gratuitously on application
to the publishers personally, or by letter enclosing Ten Cents in postage stamps.*

☞ HARPER & BROTHERS *will send their publications by mail, postage prepaid, on
receipt of the price.*

MACAULAY'S ENGLAND. The History of England from the Accession of James II. By THOMAS BABINGTON MACAULAY. New
Edition, from New Electrotype Plates. 5 vols., in a Box, 8vo, Cloth,
with Paper Labels, Uncut Edges and Gilt Tops, $10 00; Sheep,
$12 50; Half Calf, $21 25. Sold only in Sets. Cheap Edition,
5 vols., 12mo, Cloth, $2 50.

MACAULAY'S MISCELLANEOUS WORKS. The Miscellaneous
Works of Lord Macaulay. From New Electrotype Plates. 5 vols.,
in a Box, 8vo, Cloth, with Paper Labels, Uncut Edges and Gilt
Tops, $10 00; Sheep, $12 50; Half Calf, $21 25. Sold only in
Sets.

HUME'S ENGLAND. History of England, from the Invasion of
Julius Cæsar to the Abdication of James II., 1688. By DAVID
HUME. New and Elegant Library Edition, from New Electrotype
Plates. 6 vols., in a Box, 8vo, Cloth, with Paper Labels, Uncut
Edges and Gilt Tops, $12 00; Sheep, $15 00; Half Calf, $25 50.
Sold only in Sets. Popular Edition, 6 vols., in a Box, 12mo, Cloth,
$3 00.

GIBBON'S ROME. The History of the Decline and Fall of the Ro-
man Empire. By EDWARD GIBBON. With Notes by Dean MIL-
MAN, M. GUIZOT, and Dr. WILLIAM SMITH. New Edition, from
New Electrotype Plates. 6 vols., 8vo, Cloth, with Paper Labels,
Uncut Edges and Gilt Tops, $12 00; Sheep, $15 00; Half Calf,
$25 50. Sold only in Sets. Popular Edition, 6 vols., in a Box,
12mo, Cloth, $3 00; Sheep, $6 00.

GOLDSMITH'S WORKS. The Works of Oliver Goldsmith. Edited
by PETER CUNNINGHAM, F.S.A. From New Electrotype Plates.
4 vols., 8vo, Cloth, Paper Labels, Uncut Edges and Gilt Tops,
$8 00; Sheep, $10 00; Half Calf, $17 00.

MOTLEY'S LETTERS. The Correspondence of John Lothrop Motley, D.C.L., Author of " The United Netherlands," " John of Barneveld," " The Rise of the Dutch Republic," etc. Edited by GEORGE WILLIAM CURTIS. With Portrait. Two Volumes, 8vo, Cloth.

MOTLEY'S DUTCH REPUBLIC. The Rise of the Dutch Republic. A History. By JOHN LOTHROP MOTLEY, LL.D., D.C.L. With a Portrait of William of Orange. Cheap Edition, 3 vols., in a Box. 8vo, Cloth, with Paper Labels, Uncut Edges and Gilt Tops, $6 00; Sheep, $7 50; Half Calf, $12 75. Sold only in Sets. Original Library Edition, 3 vols., 8vo, Cloth, $10 50.

MOTLEY'S UNITED NETHERLANDS. History of the United Netherlands : From the Death of William the Silent to the Twelve Years' Truce—1584–1609. With a full View of the English-Dutch Struggle against Spain, and of the Origin and Destruction of the Spanish Armada. By JOHN LOTHROP MOTLEY, LL.D., D.C.L. Portraits. Cheap Edition, 4 vols., in a Box, 8vo, Cloth, with Paper Labels, Uncut Edges and Gilt Tops, $8 00; Sheep, $10 00; Half Calf, $17 00. Sold only in Sets. Original Library Edition, 4 vols., 8vo, Cloth, $14 00.

MOTLEY'S JOHN OF BARNEVELD. The Life and Death of John of Barneveld, Advocate of Holland. With a View of the Primary Causes and Movements of the " Thirty Years' War." By JOHN LOTHROP MOTLEY, LL.D., D.C.L. Illustrated. Cheap Edition, 2 vols., in a Box, 8vo, Cloth, with Paper Labels, Uncut Edges and Gilt Tops, $4 00; Sheep, $5 00; Half Calf, $8 50. Sold only in Sets. Original Library Edition, 2 vols., 8vo, Cloth, $7 00.

HILDRETH'S UNITED STATES. History of the United States. FIRST SERIES : From the Discovery of the Continent to the Organization of the Government under the Federal Constitution. SECOND SERIES : From the Adoption of the Federal Constitution to the End of the Sixteenth Congress. By RICHARD HILDRETH. Popular Edition, 6 vols., in a Box, 8vo, Cloth, with Paper Labels, Uncut Edges and Gilt Tops, $12 00; Sheep, $15 00; Half Calf, $25 50. Sold only in Sets.

TREVELYAN'S LIFE OF MACAULAY. The Life and Letters of Lord Macaulay. By his Nephew, G. OTTO TREVELYAN, M.P. With Portrait on Steel. 2 vols., 8vo, Cloth, Uncut Edges and Gilt Tops, $5 00; Sheep, $6 00; Half Calf, $9 50. Popular Edition, 2 vols. in one, 12mo, Cloth, $1 75.

TREVELYAN'S LIFE OF FOX. The Early History of Charles James Fox. By GEORGE OTTO TREVELYAN. 8vo, Cloth, Uncut Edges and Gilt Tops, $2 50; Half Calf, $4 75.

WRITINGS AND SPEECHES OF SAMUEL J. TILDEN. Edited by JOHN BIGELOW. 2 vols., 8vo, Cloth, Gilt Tops and Uncut Edges, $6 00 per set.

GENERAL DIX'S MEMOIRS. Memoirs of John Adams Dix. Compiled by his Son, MORGAN DIX. With Five Steel-plate Portraits. 2 vols., 8vo, Cloth, Gilt Tops and Uncut Edges, $5 00.

HUNT'S MEMOIR OF MRS. LIVINGSTON. A Memoir of Mrs. Edward Livingston. With Letters hitherto Unpublished. By LOUISE LIVINGSTON HUNT. 12mo, Cloth, $1 25.

GEORGE ELIOT'S LIFE. George Eliot's Life, Related in her Letters and Journals. Arranged and Edited by her Husband, J. W. CROSS. Portraits and Illustrations. In Three Volumes. 12mo, Cloth, $3 75. New Edition, with Fresh Matter. (Uniform with "Harper's Library Edition" of George Eliot's Works.)

PEARS'S FALL OF CONSTANTINOPLE. The Fall of Constantinople. Being the Story of the Fourth Crusade. By EDWIN PEARS, LL.B. 8vo, Cloth, $2 50.

RANKE'S UNIVERSAL HISTORY. The Oldest Historical Group of Nations and the Greeks. By LEOPOLD VON RANKE. Edited by G. W. PROTHERO, Fellow and Tutor of King's College, Cambridge. Vol. I. 8vo, Cloth, $2 50.

LIFE AND TIMES OF THE REV. SYDNEY SMITH. A Sketch of the Life and Times of the Rev. Sydney Smith. Based on Family Documents and the Recollections of Personal Friends. By STUART J. REID. With Steel-plate Portrait and Illustrations. 8vo, Cloth, $3 00.

STORMONTH'S ENGLISH DICTIONARY. A Dictionary of the English Language, Pronouncing, Etymological, and Explanatory: embracing Scientific and other Terms, Numerous Familiar Terms, and a Copious Selection of Old English Words. By the Rev. JAMES STORMONTH. The Pronunciation Revised by the Rev. P. H. PHELP, M.A. Imperial 8vo, Cloth, $6 00; Half Roan, $7 00; Full Sheep, $7 50. (New Edition.)

PARTON'S CARICATURE. Caricature and Other Comic Art, in All Times and Many Lands. By JAMES PARTON. 203 Illustrations. 8vo, Cloth, Uncut Edges and Gilt Tops, $5 00; Half Calf, $7 25.

DU CHAILLU'S LAND OF THE MIDNIGHT SUN. Summer and Winter Journeys in Sweden, Norway, Lapland, and Northern Finland. By PAUL B. DU CHAILLU. Illustrated. 2 vols., 8vo, Cloth, $7 50; Half Calf, $12 00.

LOSSING'S CYCLOPÆDIA OF UNITED STATES HISTORY. From the Aboriginal Period to 1876. By B. J. LOSSING, LL.D. Illustrated by 2 Steel Portraits and over 1000 Engravings. 2 vols., Royal 8vo, Cloth, $10 00; Sheep, $12 00; Half Morocco, $15 00. (*Sold by Subscription only.*)

LOSSING'S FIELD-BOOK OF THE REVOLUTION. Pictorial Field-Book of the Revolution; or, Illustrations by Pen and Pencil of the History, Biography, Scenery, Relics, and Traditions of the War for Independence. By BENSON J. LOSSING. 2 vols., 8vo, Cloth, $14 00; Sheep or Roan, $15 00; Half Calf, $18 00.

LOSSING'S FIELD-BOOK OF THE WAR OF 1812. Pictorial Field-Book of the War of 1812; or, Illustrations by Pen and Pencil of the History, Biography, Scenery, Relics, and Traditions of the last War for American Independence. By BENSON J. LOSSING. With several hundred Engravings. 1088 pages, 8vo, Cloth, $7 00; Sheep or Roan, $8 50; Half Calf, $10 00.

MÜLLER'S POLITICAL HISTORY OF RECENT TIMES (1816–1875). With Special Reference to Germany. By WILLIAM MÜLLER. Translated, with an Appendix covering the Period from 1876 to 1881, by the Rev. JOHN P. PETERS, Ph.D. 12mo, Cloth, $3 00.

STANLEY'S THROUGH THE DARK CONTINENT. Through the Dark Continent; or, The Sources of the Nile, Around the Great Lakes of Equatorial Africa, and Down the Livingstone River to the Atlantic Ocean. 149 Illustrations and 10 Maps. By H. M. STANLEY. 2 vols., 8vo, Cloth, $10 00; Sheep, $12 00; Half Morocco, $15 00.

STANLEY'S CONGO. The Congo and the Founding of its Free State, a Story of Work and Exploration. With over One Hundred Full-page and smaller Illustrations, Two Large Maps, and several smaller ones. By H. M. STANLEY. 2 vols., 8vo, Cloth, $10 00; Sheep, $12 00; Half Morocco, $15 00.

GREEN'S ENGLISH PEOPLE. History of the English People. By JOHN RICHARD GREEN, M.A. With Maps. 4 vols., 8vo, Cloth, $10 00; Sheep, $12 00; Half Calf, $19 00.

GREEN'S MAKING OF ENGLAND. The Making of England. By JOHN RICHARD GREEN. With Maps. 8vo, Cloth, $2 50; Sheep, $3 00; Half Calf, $3 75.

GREEN'S CONQUEST OF ENGLAND. The Conquest of England. By JOHN RICHARD GREEN. With Maps. 8vo, Cloth, $2 50; Sheep, $3 00; Half Calf, $3 75.

ENGLISH MEN OF LETTERS. Edited by JOHN MORLEY. The following volumes are now ready. Others will follow:

JOHNSON. By L. Stephen.—GIBBON. By J. C. Morison.—SCOTT. By R. H. Hutton.—SHELLEY. By J. A. Symonds.—GOLDSMITH. By W. Black.—HUME. By Professor Huxley.—DEFOE. By W. Minto.—BURNS. By Principal Shairp.—SPENSER. By R. W. Church.—THACKERAY. By A. Trollope.—BURKE. By J. Morley.—MILTON. By M. Pattison.—SOUTHEY. By E. Dowden.—CHAUCER. By A. W. Ward.—BUNYAN. By J. A. Froude.—COWPER. By G. Smith.—POPE. By L. Stephen.—BYRON. By J. Nichols.—LOCKE. By T. Fowler.—WORDSWORTH. By F. W. H. Myers.—HAWTHORNE. By Henry James, Jr.—DRYDEN. By G. Saintsbury.—LANDOR. By S. Colvin.—DE QUINCEY. By D. Masson.—LAMB. By A. Ainger.—BENTLEY. By R. C. Jebb.—DICKENS. By A. W. Ward.—GRAY. By E. W. Gosse.—SWIFT. By L. Stephen.—STERNE. By H. D. Traill.—MACAULAY. By J. C. Morison.—FIELDING. By A. Dobson.—SHERIDAN. By Mrs. Oliphant.—ADDISON. By W. J. Courthope.—BACON. By R. W. Church.—COLERIDGE. By H. D. Traill.—SIR PHILIP SIDNEY. By J. A. Symonds.—KEATS. By Sidney Colvin. 12mo, Cloth, 75 cents per volume. POPULAR EDITION, 36 volumes in 12, $12 00.

REBER'S HISTORY OF ANCIENT ART. History of Ancient Art. By Dr. FRANZ VON REBER. Revised by the Author. Translated and Augmented by Joseph Thacher Clarke. With 310 Illustrations and a Glossary of Technical Terms. 8vo, Cloth, $3 50.

REBER'S MEDIÆVAL ART. History of Mediæval Art. By Dr. FRANZ VON REBER. Translated and Augmented by Joseph Thacher Clarke. With 422 Illustrations, and a Glossary of Technical Terms. 8vo, Cloth, $5 00.

NEWCOMB'S ASTRONOMY. Popular Astronomy. By SIMON NEWCOMB, LL.D. With 112 Engravings, and 5 Maps of the Stars. 8vo, Cloth, $2 50; School Edition, 12mo, Cloth, $1 30.

DAVIS'S INTERNATIONAL LAW. Outlines of International Law, with an Account of its Origin and Sources, and of its Historical Development. By GEO. B. DAVIS, U.S.A., Assistant Professor of Law at the United States Military Academy. Crown 8vo, Cloth, $2 00.

CESNOLA'S CYPRUS. Cyprus: its Ancient Cities, Tombs, and Temples. A Narrative of Researches and Excavations during Ten Years' Residence in that Island. By L. P. DI CESNOLA. With Portrait, Maps, and 400 Illustrations. 8vo, Cloth, Extra, Uncut Edges and Gilt Tops, $7 50; Half Calf, $10 00.

TENNYSON'S COMPLETE POEMS. The Complete Poetical Works of Alfred, Lord Tennyson. With an Introductory Sketch by Anne Thackeray Ritchie. With Portraits and Illustrations. 8vo, Extra Cloth, Bevelled, Gilt Edges, $2 50.

LEA'S HISTORY OF THE INQUISITION. History of the Inquisition of the Middle Ages. By HENRY CHARLES LEA. Three Volumes. 8vo, Cloth, Uncut Edges and Gilt Tops, $3 00 per volume.

GROTE'S HISTORY OF GREECE. 12 vols., 12mo, Cloth, $18 00; Sheep, $22 80; Half Calf, $39 00.

FLAMMARION'S ATMOSPHERE. Translated from the French of CAMILLE FLAMMARION. With 10 Chromo-Lithographs and 86 Wood-cuts. 8vo, Cloth, $6 00; Half Calf, $8 25.

BAKER'S ISMAÏLIA: a Narrative of the Expedition to Central Africa for the Suppression of the Slave-trade, organized by Ismaïl, Khedive of Egypt. By Sir SAMUEL W. BAKER. With Maps, Portraits, and Illustrations. 8vo, Cloth, $5 00; Half Calf, $7 25.

LIVINGSTONE'S ZAMBESI. Narrative of an Expedition to the Zambesi and its Tributaries, and of the Discovery of the Lakes Shirwa and Nyassa, 1858 to 1864. By DAVID and CHARLES LIVINGSTONE. Ill'd. 8vo, Cloth, $5 00; Sheep, $5 50; Half Calf, $7 25.

LIVINGSTONE'S LAST JOURNALS. The Last Journals of David Livingstone, in Central Africa, from 1865 to his Death. Continued by a Narrative of his Last Moments, obtained from his Faithful Servants Chuma and Susi. By HORACE WALLER. With Portrait, Maps, and Illustrations. 8vo, Cloth, $5 00; Sheep, $6 00.

CHARNAY'S ANCIENT CITIES OF THE NEW WORLD. The Ancient Cities of the New World: Being Voyages and Explorations in Mexico and Central America, from 1857 to 1882. By DÉSIRÉ CHARNAY. Translated by J. GONINO and HELEN S. CONANT. Illustrations and Map. Royal 8vo, Ornamental Cloth, Uncut Edges, Gilt Tops, $6 00.

"THE FRIENDLY EDITION" of Shakespeare's Works. Edited by W. J. ROLFE. In 20 vols. Illustrated. 16mo, Gilt Tops and Uncut Edges, Sheets, $27 00; Cloth, $30 00; Half Calf, $60 00 per Set.

GIESELER'S ECCLESIASTICAL HISTORY. A Text-Book of Church History. By Dr. JOHN C. L. GIESELER. Translated from the Fourth Revised German Edition. Revised and Edited by Rev. HENRY B. SMITH, D.D. Vols. I., II., III., and IV., 8vo, Cloth, $2 25 each; Vol. V., 8vo, Cloth, $3 00. Complete Sets, 5 vols., Sheep, $14 50; Half Calf, $23 25.

CURTIS'S LIFE OF BUCHANAN. Life of James Buchanan, Fifteenth President of the United States. By GEORGE TICKNOR CURTIS. With Two Steel Plate Portraits. 2 vols., 8vo, Cloth, Uncut Edges and Gilt Tops, $6 00.

COLERIDGE'S WORKS. The Complete Works of Samuel Taylor Coleridge. With an Introductory Essay upon his Philosophical and Theological Opinions. Edited by Professor W. G. T. SHEDD. With Steel Portrait, and an Index. 7 vols., 12mo, Cloth, $2 00 per volume; $12 00 per set; Half Calf, $24 25.

GRIFFIS'S JAPAN. The Mikado's Empire: Book I. History of Japan, from 660 B.C. to 1872 A.D. Book II. Personal Experiences, Observations, and Studies in Japan, from 1870 to 1874. With Two Supplementary Chapters: Japan in 1883, and Japan in 1886. By W. E. GRIFFIS. Copiously Illustrated. 8vo, Cloth, $4 00; Half Calf, $6 25.

SMILES'S HISTORY OF THE HUGUENOTS. The Huguenots: their Settlements, Churches, and Industries in England and Ireland. By SAMUEL SMILES. With an Appendix relating to the Huguenots in America. Crown, 8vo, Cloth, $2 00.

SMILES'S HUGUENOTS AFTER THE REVOCATION. The Huguenots in France after the Revocation of the Edict of Nantes; with a Visit to the Country of the Vaudois. By SAMUEL SMILES. Crown 8vo, Cloth, $2 00.

SMILES'S LIFE OF THE STEPHENSONS. The Life of George Stephenson, and of his Son, Robert Stephenson; comprising, also, a History of the Invention and Introduction of the Railway Locomotive. By SAMUEL SMILES. Illustrated. 8vo, Cloth, $3 00.

THE POETS AND POETRY OF SCOTLAND: From the Earliest to the Present Time. Comprising Characteristic Selections from the Works of the more Noteworthy Scottish Poets, with Biographical and Critical Notices. By JAMES GRANT WILSON. With Portraits on Steel. 2 vols., 8vo, Cloth, $10 00; Gilt Edges, $11 00.

SCHLIEMANN'S ILIOS. Ilios, the City and Country of the Trojans. A Narrative of the Most Recent Discoveries and Researches made on the Plain of Troy. By Dr. HENRY SCHLIEMANN. Maps, Plans, and Illustrations. Imperial 8vo, Illuminated Cloth, $12 00; Half Morocco, $15 00.

SCHLIEMANN'S TROJA. Troja. Results of the Latest Researches and Discoveries on the Site of Homer's Troy, and in the Heroic Tumuli and other Sites, made in the Year 1882, and a Narrative of a Journey in the Troad in 1881. By Dr. HENRY SCHLIEMANN. Preface by Professor A. H. Sayce. With Wood-cuts, Maps, and Plans. 8vo, Cloth, $7 50; Half Morocco, $10 00.

SCHWEINFURTH'S HEART OF AFRICA. Three Years' Travels and Adventures in the Unexplored Regions of the Centre of Africa— from 1868 to 1871. By GEORG SCHWEINFURTH. Translated by ELLEN E. FREWER. Illustrated. 2 vols., 8vo, Cloth, $8 00.

NORTON'S STUDIES OF CHURCH-BUILDING. Historical Studies of Church-Building in the Middle Ages. Venice, Siena, Florence. By CHARLES ELIOT NORTON. 8vo, Cloth, $3 00.

THE VOYAGE OF THE "CHALLENGER." The Atlantic: an Account of the General Results of the Voyage during 1873, and the Early Part of 1876. By Sir WYVILLE THOMSON, K.C.B., F.R.S. Illustrated. 2 vols., 8vo, Cloth, $12 00.

THE STUDENT'S SERIES. Maps and Illustrations. 12mo, Cloth:
> FRANCE.—GIBBON.—GREECE.—ROME (by LIDDELL).—OLD TES-TAMENT HISTORY. — NEW TESTAMENT HISTORY. — STRICKLAND'S QUEENS OF ENGLAND.—ANCIENT HISTORY OF THE EAST.—HAL-LAM'S MIDDLE AGES. — HALLAM'S CONSTITUTIONAL HISTORY OF ENGLAND.— LYELL'S ELEMENTS OF GEOLOGY.— MERIVALE'S GEN-ERAL HISTORY OF ROME.—COX'S GENERAL HISTORY OF GREECE.—CLASSICAL DICTIONARY.—SKEAT'S ETYMOLOGICAL DICTIONARY.—RAWLINSON'S ANCIENT HISTORY. $1 25 per volume.
>
> LEWIS'S HISTORY OF GERMANY.—ECCLESIASTICAL HISTORY, TWO VOLS.—HUME'S ENGLAND.—MODERN EUROPE. $1 50 per volume.
> WESTCOTT AND HORT'S GREEK TESTAMENT, $1 00.

THOMSON'S SOUTHERN PALESTINE AND JERUSALEM. Southern Palestine and Jerusalem. Biblical Illustrations drawn from the Manners and Customs, the Scenes and Scenery, of the Holy Land. By W. M. THOMSON, D.D. 140 Illustrations and Maps. Square 8vo, Cloth, $6 00; Sheep, $7 00; Half Morocco, $8 50; Full Morocco, Gilt Edges, $10 00.

THOMSON'S CENTRAL PALESTINE AND PHŒNICIA. Cen-tral Palestine and Phœnicia. Biblical Illustrations drawn from the Manners and Customs, the Scenes and Scenery, of the Holy Land. By W. M. THOMSON, D.D. 130 Illustrations and Maps. Square 8vo, Cloth, $6 00; Sheep, $7 00; Half Morocco, $8 50; Full Morocco, $10 00.

THOMSON'S LEBANON, DAMASCUS, AND BEYOND JORDAN. Lebanon, Damascus, and beyond Jordan. Biblical Illustrations drawn from the Manners and Customs, the Scenes and Scenery, of the Holy Land. By W. M. THOMSON, D.D. 147 Illustrations and Maps. Square 8vo, Cloth, $6 00; Sheep, $7 00; Half Morocco, $8 50; Full Morocco, $10 00.
> Popular Edition of the above three volumes, 8vo, Ornamental Cloth. $9 00 per set.

CYCLOPÆDIA OF BRITISH AND AMERICAN POETRY. Ed-ited by EPES SARGENT. Royal 8vo, Illuminated Cloth, Colored Edges, $4 50; Half Leather, $5 00.

LODGE'S ENGLISH COLONIES IN AMERICA. A Short History of the English Colonies in America. By HENRY CABOT LODGE. With Colored Map. 8vo, Half Leather, $3 00.